THE MEN'S FASHION READER

THE
FASHION

MEN'S READER

EDITED BY PETER MCNEIL AND VICKI KARAMINAS

OXFORD · NEW YORK

First published in 2009 by

Berg

Editorial offices:
1st Floor, Angel Court, 81 St Clements Street, Oxford, OX4 1AW, UK
175 Fifth Avenue, New York, NY 10010, USA

Berg is the imprint of Oxford International Publishers Ltd.

Library of Congress Cataloguing-in-Publication Data

A catalog record for this book is available from the Library of Congress.

The men's fashion reader / edited by Peter McNeil and Vicki Karaminas.
p. cm.
Includes bibliographical references and index.
ISBN-13: 978-1-84520-787-8 (pbk.)
ISBN-10: 1-84520-787-4 (pbk.)
ISBN-13: 978-1-84520-786-1 (cloth)
ISBN-10: 1-84520-786-6 (cloth)
1. Men's clothing. 2. Fashion design. I. McNeil, Peter, 1966– II.
Karaminas, Vicki.
TT617.M43 2009
391'.1—dc22
2008047664

British Library Cataloguing-in-Publication Data

A catalog record for this book is available from the British Library.

ISBN 978 184520 786 1 (Cloth)
ISBN 978 184520 787 8 (Paper)

Typeset by Apex CoVantage, LLC, Madison, WI, USA

Printed by the MPG Books Group in the UK

www.bergpublishers.com

Peter McNeil dedicates this book to Anthony O'Brien,
and Vicki Karaminas dedicates it to Michelle and Dante Bakar.

CONTENTS

ACKNOWLEDGMENTS

Producing *The Men's Fashion Reader* was made possible by the encouragement and academic advice of numerous friends and colleagues. We wish to thank Hannah Shakespeare who supported us in the genesis of this project, and Bronwyn Clark-Coollee for her academic and practical support. We also thank Tristan Palmer, our editor at Berg, for his expertise; Paul Pavlou for his photography; and copyeditor Pat Skinner. We thank our contributors, including those who agreed to newly commissioned work and those who granted permission to republish material. We are grateful to Professor Desley Luscombe, dean of the Faculty of Design, Architecture and Building, University of Technology, Sydney; and Dr. Louise Wallenberg, director of the Centre for Fashion Studies, Stockholm University, Sweden. Both universities provided generous funding that enabled the type of academic and creative project that we envisaged. We also thank the following for their gracious assistance in obtaining permissions for image reproductions: Dr. George Boeck; Titi Halle and Leigh Wishner, Cora Ginsburg LLC, New York; Dr. Elisabeth Hackspiel; Elisabeth Höier and Dr. Martin Olin, Nationalmuseum/The Nationalmuseum of Fine Art, Stockholm; Dr. Toby Slade, University of Tokyo; Dr. Patrik Stoern, Centre for Fashion Studies, Stockholm University; Dr. William Scott, University of Delaware. Dr. Stoern kindly translated texts from the Swedish.

INTRODUCTION
The Field of Men's Fashion

SEX APPEAL

In the early summer of 1929 Sydney women could read about the lecture delivered by Professor J. C. Flügel at the International Congress of the World League for Sexual Reform, Wigmore Hall, London, the very conference at which Radclyffe Hall's *The Well of Loneliness* (1928) was defended. "Are men afraid of being too beautiful?"—"Women's Costumes Indicted by a Professor" the masthead ran. Citing the latest psychoanalytic thought, the Sydney lady's magazine *Herself in Australia's Affairs* went on to detail for the dominion reader a series of "scientific" findings on men and their clothes. What did such a story, inserted amid fairly banal reportage, mean to the Australian "new woman"?[1] How do ideas about men's fashion and male beauty circulate? What are its main narratives? Why is the discussion of men's dress so often predicated on an argument about women? How, in the space of sixty years, had Paul de Saint-Victor's "black prince of elegance" come to be framed as a psychological "problem"? How has the idea of men's fashion been put together within the history of dress and the history of costume? How do the body and gesture work together to create a fashionable male image?

This reader introduces students and researchers to both important episodes within and debates on the subject of men's fashion. It explores the complex relationship between male fashion, appearance, and subjectivity. Insufficient attention has been paid to men's dress within fashion history, as in the social imagination women have been more closely equated with the consumption of fashion in the West, certainly in twentieth-century life. Hence the title of Christopher Breward's *The Hidden Consumer* (1999), which revealed the careful iteration of fashionability, pleasure, and detail, a reversal of the stereotype of Victorian masculine dress as somber and uninteresting. Despite the recent interest in the "metrosexual" and the "new man," the convention that men have a radically different attitude toward their clothes is still present in much contemporary culture. The available information concerning men's fashion and ideas of fashionability is extensive but widely dispersed in the historical record. It can be retrieved from art, design, social, economic, and cultural history and also requires access to literary, film, and other social studies influenced by poststructuralist theory and theories of identity and sexuality. The readings presented in this anthology, written from a variety of scholarly disciplines, point instead to a complex range of responses by men about their fashions as well as changing cultural perceptions of the relationship of masculinity and fashion.

Nonacademic friends often accuse the scholarly community of "overreading." Why infer so much from men's choices, motives, behaviors, and actions, especially those of the past, that appear no different from ours? The study of fashion over long periods of time, including men's fashion, provides ample testimony that the clothes of historical subjects created appearances and cemented alliances. We cannot "overread" a medieval hunt or a 1980s rave, because the complexity of meanings, actors, and audiences must be both contextualized and understood within broader cultural patterns. As the historian Keith Thomas notes, "The human body, in short, is as much a historical document as a charter or a diary or a parish register (though unfortunately one which is a good deal harder to preserve) and it deserves to be studied accordingly."[2] Thomas goes on to note that two things can be concluded from the study of history: "Those who study the past usually find themselves arriving at two contradictory conclusions. The first is that the past was very different from the present. The second is that it was very much the same."[3] The evidence of this volume points to the former, that the meanings of men's dress are transformed in different cultural and historical contexts.

The writings assembled here rebut the view that men's fashion after the first years of the nineteenth century simply became "dull." The corollary to this view is that women's clothes became marks of distinction for the male household in which they dwelt, as well as functioning as tools of interfemale competition. Such a view was promoted by influential sociologists such as Thorstein Veblen writing in the 1890s, as well as within the burgeoning field of psychoanalysis. Flügel, it was reported in the 1929 Sydney feature, argued that "men's costume needs rescuing from the abject slavery to convention into which it has fallen" and that women's costume "needed above all things a severe purging from the elements of plutocratic snobbery ... [that] fostered extravagance and jealousy." Flügel, the woman reader was further informed, believed that men's clothes would improve only if "men would dare to commit themselves to make a slightly greater sex appeal to women," rendering them "less monstrously attired than was actually the case." This passage, appearing in a ladies' home journal, indicates that men's dress is always bound up with its "other," women's dress. One of the challenges in this reader has been to identify texts that focus to a sufficient degree on the dress of men rather than that of both men and women, while keeping in mind that the two are always related (color plate 1).

Flügel's argument revolved around his claim that men had repressed narcissism in the last hundred years or so, a topic he explicitly examined in *Men and Their Motives* (1934).[4] "Modern clothing, for instance, allows few outlets for personal vanity among men; to be dressed 'correctly' or 'in good taste' is the utmost that a modern man can hope for; all originality or beauty in clothing (to say nothing of the even more direct gratification of Narcissism in actual bodily exposure) being reserved for women." In a direct critique of the muscular Christian movement associated with sports and scouting, Flügel noted that "some of the male substitutes for female Narcissism (e.g. pride in muscular development) may lead to forms of rivalry which are as disrupting to social bonds as is the more passive love of the female for her own bodily beauty."[5]

Flügel also introduced into the rhetoric of men's fashion the notion of loss, that men had suddenly and finally relinquished something special in the eighteenth century:

> men may be said to have suffered a great defeat in the sudden reduction of male sartorial decorativeness which took place at the end of the eighteenth century ... Man abandoned his claim to be considered beautiful.[6]

Flügel argued that the renunciation worked to inhibit the narcissistic and exhibitionistic desires that were so flamboyantly expressed through aristocratic sumptuousness in preceding centuries. He stated that twentieth-century men seek alternate routes of gratification: sublimation into showing off (sport), or a reversal into scopophilia, that is, a male identification of woman as spectacle. According to Flügel, the latter results in the desire to be associated with a beautifully dressed woman or is expressed as a "deviance," such as adopting female mannerisms and dress.[7] Although he did not identify the moment of the shift, Flügel clearly associated it with the late 1780s and the French Revolution, claiming that "democracy had no use for the gorgeous and complicated trappings which had flourished in a preceding age of absolutism and of highly accentuated class distinctions."[8] John Harvey's study of the nineteenth-century cult of black, *Men in Black* (1995), argues that Flügel's notion of renunciation is distorting, that men's use of black should be viewed not as loss but as the "signature of what they have; of standing, goods, mastery."[9] A part of his influential text is reproduced in this volume.

"CONSPICUOUS WAIST"[10]

Is "fashion" female? The economic historian S.A.M. Adshead, in his *Material Culture in Europe and China, 1400–1800* (1997), has gone so far as to suggest that fashion is a type of female intelligence and practice in the west. Is the notion that fashion is "feminine" just a matter of rhetoric in post-Enlightenment culture? This introduction tests the idea that fashion is promulgated by and for women in Western culture. It does so by examining the significance of fashion to masculine identity within state, family, and personal networks. This section introduces readers to some of the main ideas that have structured understandings and expectations of men's fashion. These range from the emotional structure of emblematic fashion and melancholy (Elizabethan and Jacobean dress), richness, and display; to foppery (the French courtier type—*petit-maître,* the English macaroni, the *Incroyable*); to Romanticism (introspection, neo-classicism, "naturalness," the cult of the soldier) and eugenics and athleticism, aspects of which the Men's Dress Reform Party of the interwar years made use.

THE BODY OF MEN

There have been times in history when the most significant vestimentary changes were made in the wardrobes of men. The men of the Middle Ages probably made the first fashion youth quake. As Désirée Koslin and Janet Snyder argue, they could travel, go to war, and adopt foreign mores.[11] Twelfth-century knights required quilted clothing that was worn under their armor; the sleeve emerging from the customary T-shaped gown worn by men and women was not suitable for such heightened activity. In daily life as well as on the horse, men began to wear new garments of hose and a *pourpoint,* a padded doublet with a very tight-fitting sleeve with a rounded top. From about 1350 in Italy, France, England, Germany, and Bohemia, chroniclers noted that men were changing their appearance, increasingly differing from women in their dress. Although we associate a radically altered body with the nineteenth-century female corset, the superfashionable man in the Franco-Flemish court was the one who modified his body to a tiny waist and an inverted triangular shape. Moralists complained particularly of the young men wearing such body-hugging fashions, who frequently appear in medieval illuminated (handcolored) manuscripts. Most saw this as a source of weakness or decline; one, however, a cleric in Mainz in 1377, who was the author of the chronicle of Limbourg, interpreted it as a sign of joy after the specter of the Black Death.[12] The matter of pleasure and delight in male dressing is another theme that runs throughout this anthology.

Many historians see the shift between the Middle Ages and the Renaissance as involving the rediscovery of the physicality and the ideal dimensions of the body. The historian of medieval dress, Odile Blanc, disagrees, seeing in the late medieval dress of the Franco-Flemish male elites a rigid envelope that constructed the body and diminished the space between cloth and body, imposing a curious posture. These new garments involved major feats of cutting; the surviving *pourpoint* of Charles of Blois (ca. 1364, Lyon, Musée des Tissus) is constructed of thirty-two pieces of cloth. The new tight-fitting garments reduced the volume between the dress and body that often gives a body a particular type of spatial importance. As Blanc notes, at the end of the Middle Ages men's shoulders became more important, and the male body was exalted. Dress amplified the body in particular ways and was part of male power strategies.[13] Blanc does not go so far as to call the tightening of the upper part of the body "fashion," using instead the cautious term "vestimentary novelty."[14] The adoption of the *pourpoint,* a former military garment, was accompanied by a new emphasis on a refined mode of behavior. The French courtier demonstrated his presence not through arms but through a courtly presentation and demonstration. A sense of the physical body remained very present in seventeenth-century men's fashion, seen here in a rare surviving knitted garment (color plate 2). A knight was also someone "comely of gesture," gesture being the general set of the body.[15] Kinesics, the study of communicative body movements, whether it be the distance we keep from someone or the degree of touch, is central to understanding men's fashion. The emergence of the handshake between men, for example, was very much a matter of a shift to a more egalitarian society in Protestant Europe.

The significance of color for men's fashion in the late Middle Ages and the Renaissance cannot be underestimated. Twelfth-century heraldry reinforced the importance of colors. Gold stood for virtue and prestige, purple for majesty, green for hope, joy, and resurrection. Color was a type of magic, and dyers were sometimes associated with alchemy and deceit. Color was also about status and belonging, as, for example, the "livery" or issues of clothes presented to retainers and also aristocrats signaled allegiance. Color might also reflect deep philosophical ideas, from Ezekiel's vision of Eden to Neoplatonic ideas concerning the power of light. Some of the colors that appear in the pigments of medieval manuscripts could not actually have been obtained in dyed cloths of that period. The portrait miniature, a new form of painting that emerged in the court of François I (1494–1547), was a form that captured a new type of masculine fashion intensity. Whether the support was vellum or later ivory, or the miniature was executed in enamels, they captured the saturated colors popular in elite fashion, possibly expanding them. The form was particularly popular in the courtly life of England, where the paintings of Nicholas Hilliard (1547–1619) in the period from 1570 presented numerous images of the melancholy man, reclining among nature in a pensive mood emblematic of melancholy. Melancholy, meaning "black bile," one of the humors that controlled the health of the body, was a humor of great men and heroes. Within the humanist thinking of the Renaissance it became related to study and introspection, thus accordingly also to artists, but could also be expressed as a negative state related to failure or inadequacy.[16] John Harvey, in this *Reader,* notes that the melancholic vision carries the charge of the danger to love, as well as a sense of blankness or fear when looking at women.

PRINCELY SPLENDOR

Dress for monarchs and the superrich was once about rank marked by display and profusion. The dress of kings was a matter of sumptuousness and traditions but also concerned access to other regions' customs and fashions (color plate 3). The late fifteenth- and early sixteenth-century accounts in Latin or English kept by household officials in the reigns of Edward IV and Henry VIII indicate the importance of furred garments to the medieval and Renaissance European male wardrobe. Fashion was also connected to a wider arena of textile and equine culture. A series of keepers, tailors, mercers, pavilioners, saddlers, and arras makers provided the fitting context in which a king might be seen.[17] Smooth silk-satin surfaces showed off the details of slashing, trimming, lace, and incredible buttons. Both lavish expenditure and quantity were expected: from 1608 to 1613 King James bought a new cloak every month, a new waistcoat every three weeks, a new suit every ten days, a new pair of stockings, boots, and garters every four or five days, and a new pair of gloves every day (color plate 4). King Charles continued the pace, buying 513 items for his feet in the year 1626–1627.[18] A king influenced the clothes of all around him, bringing ruin to some courtiers who tried to compete. Seventeenth-century and eighteenth-century patricians and wealthy citizens tended to replicate the fashionable forms of aristocratic clothes but had them made in less expensive textiles and with less trimming.[19]

CONDUCT BOOKS AND THE GENTLEMAN

A shift occurred between the Middle Ages and the sixteenth century regarding the management of dress and the body. Replacing the world of chivalry, in which battle was central, a new court nobility defined itself through the idea of civility, which had a major impact on clothes and deportment. Ideas of a well-proportioned posture related to the Renaissance interest in geometry and interrelationships between cultural types such as the body and architecture. The training of men's bodies, through fencing, equitation, and dance, was designed to make the body appear graceful with no sign of affectation.

Conduct books are also a repository of attitudes toward models of appropriate masculinity as well as regional differences between the European courts, which were not all equally lavish. Most are based on Baldesar Castiglione's *The Courtier* (1528), which advocated a restraint that appears to be absent from the eighteenth-century French court. Castiglione explains that grace is "very agreeable and pleasant to all" but argues against excess and feminine modifications:

> I don't want him to appear soft and feminine as so many try to do, when they not only curl their hair and pluck their eyebrows but also preen themselves like the most wanton and dissolute creatures imaginable. Indeed, they appear so effeminate and languid in the way they walk, or stand, or do anything at all, that their limbs look as if they are about to fall apart; and they pronounce their words in such a drawling way that it seems as if they are about to expire on the spot. And the more they find themselves in the company of men of rank, the more they carry on like that. Since Nature has not in fact made them the ladies they want to seem and be, they should be treated not as honest women but as common whores, and be driven out from all gentlemanly society, let alone the Courts of great lords.[20]

The early modern period was as much interested in the difference between men and boys as women and men; their mindset often used a triangulated gender system. This system had a major impact on fashion, as, in some Italian towns and cities, men under the age of thirty could not wear civic clothes until they reached that transition. Thus they had to wear clothing types in which a strong temptation existed to engage with fashion, and there was also more innuendo about same-sex attraction and effeminacy. Effeminacy frequently stood in for ideas of deception and corruption and was not necessarily linked to same-sex behavior. Nor were elaborate clothes simply a marker of vanity or corruption. If we consider the extraordinarily colored and patterned gentleman's garments dating from the seventeenth to the mid-nineteenth century—wallets, waistcoats, slippers, banyans, or dressing gowns—illustrated here from the collection of Cora Ginsburg LLC (New York), other issues can be raised. Some of these were status-conscious purchases to signal cosmopolitanism and success; others were worked by close female relatives and therefore inscribe chains of attachment and possibly also eroticism (color plates 5–10). Eighteenth-century women frequently worked waistcoats and made sword knots for their husbands.

TAKING MEASURE

In 1666 Charles II announced his intention to introduce a new three-piece suit of woolen "cloth," with a "vest" that might derive from Persian costume or the theater. This change was a repudiation of the doublet, stiff collar, and cloak that had preceded it. From the late seventeenth century, British aristocrats preempted the middle-class and puritanical challenge that their rule was tainted by luxury by promoting a more moderate appearance than their French and other Catholic Continental counterparts (color plate 11). Other Protestant nations such as the Low Countries and Sweden also developed distinctive fashions for elite men in the seventeenth century that were conscious rejections of Francophile display. The matter of moderation, explicit in the numerous conduct books that followed Castiglione's, was a common organizing idea for men's dress in the early modern period. Instruction manuals for the young English gentleman demanded neat and modest moderation in dressing with due consideration to social status:

> Be neat withour gawdiness, gentile [sic] without affectation: In fine, the Taylor must take measure of both your purse and of your quality, as well as of your person: For a sute [sic] that fits the character, is more à la mode than that which fits well on the body ... I have seen some Fops over-shoot extravagance; ... a man of war might be rigged up with less noise, and some-times at less expense.[21]

This approach was entirely rejected in fops' dressing practice, wherein there was no character other than that fitted along with the "sute." In the view of this guidebook it was equally damning to adopt a slovenly air—"this is to sacrifice one vice to another, to attone [sic] for vanity with nastiness,"[22] exactly the type of precept advocated by Lord Chesterfield later in his famous *Letters* written to his son in Paris.

FOPS: "OF A MIXT SPECIES"

In the early eighteenth century terms such as *fop, beau,* and *coxcomb* were used to describe the singularly refined dressed man; the suggestion was made that they were an unnatural hybrid, containing a mingling of male and female attributes. Fops wore powdered hair (color plate 12) and court dress that might be embroidered or "laced" with gold and silver braid; they sported accessories such as snuff boxes and canes. Upper servants and men in the appearance industries wore variants of these expensive clothes and sometimes carried new accessories such as silver watches, which dropped in price over the course of the century due to new methods of production. The anonymous author of *A Gentleman Instructed in the Conduct of a Virtuous and Happy Life: Written for the Instruction of a Young Nobleman* noted of the fop and the beau:

> had their mothers made a voyage to the Indies, I should suspect they had some relation to an Ape: For certainly they are of a mixt species, and often the beast predominates, but always the coxcomb.[23]

Similarly, *The Gentleman's Library, Containing Rules for Conduct in All Parts of Life, Written by a Gentleman* (1715), preached restraint and moderation, describing fashion as "a spreading contagion, and epidemical foolery of the age":[24]

> the greatest pride and affectation in apparel, are lodg'd with persons of the most substantial ignorance. The souls of idiots are actuated merely by frail sense, their eyes are made their principal directors.[25]

This text used Ciceronian exemplars to chastise both rusticity and foppery and to advocate for a medium between the two extremes. Such exhortations to common sense and suitability were very prevalent in eighteenth-century England.[26] A useful example is entitled *The Man of Manners: or, Plebeian Polished. Being Plain and Familiar Rules for a Modest and Genteel Behaviour, on most of the ordinary occasions of Life. Whereby the many Vanities, Weaknesses and Impertinences incident to Human Nature, (which expose Persons to Contempt and Ridicule) may be easily avoided. Written chiefly for the Use and Benefit of Persons of Mean Births and Education, who have unaccountably plung'd themselves into Wealth and Power.* This text includes many directions about apparel:

> we must proportion them to our Shape, our Condition, and our Age: The glittering Buckle upon the gouty Foot must be avoided; the white Stocking tightly garter'd upon the lame Leg; the pink-colour'd Waistcoat, richly embroidered and unbutton'd, where a Flannel one is absolutely necessary, and is certainly as ridiculous as grey Hairs decorated with Ribbons ... Gaudy Grandmothers and gay Grandfathers, are equally contemptible in the Eyes of all People.[27]

The conditions of early modern life, with increased travel and dislocation, contributed to new meanings of fashion:

> Handsome Apparel is a main Point, and People, where they are not known, are generall [*sic*] honoured according to their Cloaths; because from the Richnesse of them we judge o [*sic*] their Wealth; ... but who ever pretends to dazzle Men of Sense into Respect, merely with *Scarlet* and *Gold-lace,* will fall short of his Pretensions.[28]

LOOKING AT MEN

Most scholars of dress agree that the male dress of the elite was as colorful, flamboyant, and sumptuous as the female dress from the mid-fourteenth century (the beginning of the development of the Western fashion system) until the "renunciation" of such flamboyance at some point in the second half of the eighteenth century. The theory is often advanced that for much of this time men were in fact more gorgeously appareled than women. Surviving waistcoats and banyans in the mid- to late eighteenth century and even slippers in the mid-nineteenth century provide ample proof of an incredibly varied sartorial vision for men (color plates 13–14). François Boucher argues that whereas men in pre-eighteenth-century Europe were as, or more, splendidly dressed than women, in the eighteenth century women surpassed men in rich clothing.[29]

The theorist Kaja Silverman draws a theoretical conclusion from this issue; the richness of male dress surpassed that of females at times, "so that in so far as clothing was marked by gender, it defined visibility as a male rather than a female attribute."[30] Silverman writes that the history of Western fashion poses a serious challenge to the "naturalized" equation of spectacular display with female subjectivity and the assumption that exhibitionism is synonymous with woman's subjugation to a controlling male gaze. She notes that ornate dress was a class rather than a gender prerogative from the fifteenth to the seventeenth century, a prerogative protected by law. Sartorial extravagance was thus a mark of power and privilege, a mechanism for tyrannizing rather than surrendering to the gaze of the (class) other. The "Vauxhall Affray," a public dispute in which the act of looking at others was key, considered in both Peter McNeil and Olga Vainshtein's essays in this *Reader,* indicates that subject/object relationships were a significant part of the cultural anxiety attending male appearance. The art historian Ewa Lajer-Burcharth has also argued that the extreme fashions cultivated immediately after the French Revolution, the so-called male *Incroyables,* indicated a renegotiation of the self. Refuting Flügel, Lajer-Burcharth argues that the new extreme fashions for both men and women of 1790s Paris indicated a withdrawal from the ideals of stoic masculinity among men, who more and more set themselves amid the gaze of both men and women. The male body, barely disguised under tightly cut cloth and sheer buckskin, became a beautiful object to survey for pleasure and also a narcissistic agent that frequently solicited another man's look.[31] Many conservative straight men still complain today that they do not care to be "looked at" by other men, for whatever reason, and they sometimes resort to violence to stop the gaze.

SPECTACULAR MEN

Foppery in the seventeenth and eighteenth centuries was also a complex cultural pose. It was not unified but could range from the insistent negligence and untidiness of a Restoration rake, to the fastidious Francophile affectation of a macaroni, to the strict control of the Regency dandy, who is not strictly a fop. The stage figure of the fop frequently derived his charge from the fact that he was too old for his fashion and his airs—age literally betrayed him. The macaroni of the 1760s–1770s, explored in an essay by Peter McNeil in this volume, brings together ideas of male behavior, fashion, deception, the staging of a life, and nationhood. Several questions can be posed. Were the macaronies men who refused to relinquish finery because they feared a new form of power in which they could not share? Or were they willingly contesting that power with some remnant of the allure of aristocratic luxury? Questions such as these problematize the theories of sartorial renunciation. Foppery signaled a courtly male elegance in which elegant technologies of the body and dress were fused in a seamless performance. The fop's effeminate behavior, the *philosophes* argued, led to a corruption of the corporeal body and the body politic, and a set of moral and health discourses was mobilized against him. In *Emile* (1762) Rousseau links his theory of gendered education to a critique of contemporary manners.

Women's toilette he advances as caused not by "vanity but lack of occupation."[32] The dancing master is discussed as particularly pernicious:

> I wish there were fewer of these dressed-up old ballet masters promenading our streets. I fear our young people will get more harm from intercourse with such people than profit from their instruction, and that their jargon, their tone, their airs and graces, will instil a precocious taste for the frivolities which the teacher thinks so important, and to which the scholars are only too likely to devote themselves.[33]

Here history and postmodern theory might be brought together in a creative way to understand certain meanings of fashion. The contradictions and multivocal meanings associated with foppish types such as the English macaroni resound in Dick Hebdige's argument that the "meaning of subculture is, then, always in dispute, and style is the area in which the opposing definitions clash with most dramatic force."[34] The reiteration of signs in the caricature genre—the hairstyle, the cane or sword, the pumps, the snuffbox—indicate that these objects had a powerful charge for male participants in this type of dressing. Feminist theory can be used to understand the meanings of style politics—using "rituals of consumption in dress, cosmetics, hairstyle, and gesture to bend the norms ordained by the market and to flout family and other authority."[35]

In the last third of the eighteenth century the types of practical clothes worn by men in the country came more and more to influence fashion (color plate 15). Henry Meister, in his *Letters Written during a Residence in England* (1799), noted, "In England gentlemen employ all the time they can spare from public affairs, or private business, in the exercise of riding or walking, in the diversions of hunting or shooting, at the theatres, or in tavern clubs or societies."[36] Linking fashion with spaces, he noted that less gallantry was expected as there were no *levées* conducted in a lady's bedchamber.[37] The anglophilia expressed by wearing practical country clothes carried a political charge of notions of freedom of the self and the voice. To this was added the neoclassical focus on unencumbered form, popular throughout Europe from Germany to Russia. It inspired new products from fashions in soft broad-brimmed hats to simpler clothing for children, from ambitious art to pictorial jokes (color plates 16a–16b).

The editors' intention is that through the parts of this volume, readers will make connections between different times and cultures when they consider men's fashion. A number of essays have been newly commissioned to support the other authors in this volume, on topics ranging from the allure of the nineteenth-century uniform, to the introduction of the suit in Meiji Japan, and the politics of scrutinizing the Regency dandy's clothes. These new essays are accompanied by extensive illustrations, some of which are previously unpublished.

Peter McNeil and Vicki Karaminas

NOTES

1. "Are Men Afraid of Being Too Beautiful? Slaves to Dress. Sex Differences in Modern Attire. 'Snobbery.' Women's Costumes Indicted by a Professor," *Herself in Australia's Affairs* 1, no. 12 (December 5, 1929): 10.
2. Keith Thomas, "Introduction," in *A Cultural History of Gesture,* ed. Jan Bremmer and Herman Roodenburg (Ithaca, NY: Cornell University Press, 1991), 2.

3. Ibid., 10.

4. J. C. Flügel, *Men and Their Motives: Psycho-Analytical Studies, with Two Essays by Ingeborg Flügel* (London: Kegan Paul, Trench, Trubner & Co., 1934).

5. Ibid., 64–65.

6. J. C. Flügel, *The Psychology of Clothes* (London: Hogarth, 1930), 110–11.

7. Ibid., 117–20.

8. Ibid., 149.

9. John Harvey, *Men in Black* (London: Reaktion, 1995), 10.

10. I take this subheading from the exhibition amusingly entitled *Conspicuous Waist: Waistcoats and Waistcoat Designs 1700–1952,* curators/editors Everett P. Lesley Jr. and William Osmun, New York: The Cooper Union Museum for the Arts of Decoration, 1952.

11. Désirée Koslin and Janet Snyder, eds., "Introduction," in *Encountering Medieval Textiles and Dress: Objects, Texts, Images* (New York: Palgrave Macmillan, 2002), 2.

12. Odile Blanc, "From Battlefield to Court: The Invention of Fashion in the Fourteenth Century," in Koslin and Snyder, *Encountering Medieval Textiles and Dress,* 159.

13. Ibid., 167–70.

14. Ibid., 165.

15. Thomas, "Introduction," 2.

16. On this point see Thomas da Costa Kaufmann, *Court, Cloister and City: The Art and Culture of Central Europe 1450–1800* (Chicago: University of Chicago Press, 1995), 119–20.

17. Anne F. Sutton, "Order and Fashion in Clothes: The King, His Household and the City of London at the End of the Fifteenth Century," *Textile History* 22, no. 2 (1991): 253–76.

18. Lawrence Stone, *The Crisis of the Aristocracy* (Oxford: Clarendon, 1965), 257–58.

19. Johannes Pietsch and Karen Stolleis with a contribution by Nadine Piechatschek, *Kölner Patrizier- und Bürgerkleidung des 17. Jahrhunderts: Die Kostümsammlung Hüpsch im Hessischen Landesmuseum Darmstadt* (Abegg-Stiftung: Riggisberger Berichte, Volume 15, 2008).

20. Baldesar Castiglione, *Etiquette for Renaissance Gentlemen,* trans. George Bull (1967; abridged ed., London: Penguin, 1995), 10.

21. [William Darrell], *A Gentleman Instructed in the Conduct of a Virtuous and Happy Life: Written for the Instruction of a Young Nobleman* (London: E. Evets, 1704), 39–40.

22. Ibid., 40.

23. Ibid., 45.

24. *The Gentlemen's Library, Containing Rules for Conduct in All Parts of Life, Written by a Gentleman* (London: W. Mears and J. Brown, 1715), 59.

25. Ibid., 52–53.

26. For a useful summary of conduct books see Peter Burke, *The Fortunes of the Courtier: The European Reception of Castiglione's Cortegiano* (Cambridge: Polity, 1995), 124–32.

27. *The Man of Manners: or, Plebeian Polished* ... (London: Printed for J. Roberts, n.d.), 10.

28. Ibid., 12.

29. François Boucher, *A History of Costume in the West,* new ed. (London: Thames and Hudson, 1987), 291.

30. Kaja Silverman, "Fragments of a Fashionable Discourse," in *Studies in Entertainment: Critical Approaches to Mass Culture,* ed. Tania Modleski (Bloomington: Indiana University Press, 1986), 139.

31. Ewa Lajer-Burcharth, *Necklines: The Art of Jacques-Louis David after the Terror* (New Haven, CT, and London: Yale University Press, 1999).

32. Jean-Jacques Rousseau, *Emile* (1762; London: J. M. Dent, 1993), 402.

33. Ibid., 405.

34. D. Hebdige, *Subculture: The Meaning of Style* (London: Methuen, 1979), 3.

35. V. de Grazia, "Introduction," in *The Sex of Things: Gender and Consumption in Historical Perspective,* ed. V. de Grazia and E. Furlough (Berkeley, Los Angeles, and London: University of California Press, 1996), 7.

36. Henry Meister, *Letters Written during a Residence in England* (London: T. N. Longman & O. Rees, 1799), 285.

37. Ibid., 283–84.

PART I

A Brief History of Men's Fashion

INTRODUCTION

In the present confusion between the sexes it is almost a miracle to belong to one's own sex.

Jean-Jacques Rousseau, *Emile,* 1762[1]

The body is offered as a picture in a place where glances intersect.

Georges Vigarello[2]

This section introduces readers to ideas about men's fashion, novelty, and stylistics from the early modern period in Western Europe to the closing years of the British Empire. Fashion is considered as a complex social practice in which challenges to reform male appearances are sometimes made by figures with the power to expect obedience. Men have also used their appearance as a strategy of refusal or disinterest in the dominant culture that surrounds them. Others have been reformers who tried to convince the populace that their model of dress would lead to better social relationships. The section includes readings that assess court society and its expectations of flamboyant and sumptuous fashion, the changing notion of black as a fashion fabric and device, foppery as a cultural pose, the development of the Protestant and sober suit, the style war of the foppish English macaroni, and the cultural pose of the early nineteenth-century dandy. Suits, waistcoats, eyeglasses and spying glasses, canes, and wigs are explored by various authors as a set of clothing objects, as well as the stylistics of deploying those objects, including the act of inspecting others' appearances. Olga Vainshtein, in "Dandyism, Visual Games and the Strategies of Representation," examines a series of optical devices used by the Regency dandy that firmly separated looking from touch. That iconic aspect of men's fashion, the bow tie, is traced by Rob Shields as an ambiguous symbol of male (or indeed lesbian) dress extending from the period of Louis XIV to the 1950s and the present day. The section concludes with the challenge laid down to norms of masculine dress by the international Men's Dress Reform Party of the interwar years. This movement, endorsed and adopted by the famous writer on men's fashion J. C. Flügel, advocated the simplification of men's dress within the context of eugenics, practicality, health, and athletics. It failed at the time to change the appearance of the "city gent" but found many of its demands met in the adoption of new types of mass-produced clothing created with new synthetic fabrics and for the increased rate of leisure in the post–World War II period, but without the left-wing and generally radicalized social setting that the reformers might have envisaged.

The *Reader* commences with an analysis of men and that "noncolor," black, explored by the literary historian John Harvey, who notes of dress that "if any human practice is 'over-determined', it is clothing." Black, Harvey notes, has tended to signify a series of paradoxical values in the West. Examining the spread of Spanish black from the self-image of Philip II, son of Charles V, he proposes that Philip's wearing of black, partly out of desire to appear like his fellow citizens and the Spanish merchants, who affected stoic impersonality, may have also been determined by his state of mourning, an interest in astrology (black is linked within astrology to Saturn), and a reference to the black fashions of the Burgundian court, as well as the church. The general effect of such dress was to enclose and encase the body, to compress it; black, Harvey notes, is disciplined, "death-ready," self-effacing. Wartime regimes and religions are ascetic; armor was once painted black; black is the color of the earth to which the fatally wounded return. Harvey suggests that Philip's black indicated a desire to recede, as a monarch who controlled but wished to be unseen, perhaps to "assert a power as frightening as that of his God." Philip's patronage of the Inquisition and the Dominican Inquisitors lent his adoption of black a sinister overtone. Black suggests an office and an officeholder; it enables a shift from a fashion to a uniform, Harvey notes. Reforming preachers wore black not for ritual intention but as the avowal of their inner human sinfulness. Harvey shows how the image and resonance of black has been transferred in the twentieth century to the totalitarian regime and the presidential motorcade, how black can efface self and sometimes even humanity, when people become "the utensil of a power."

Black to a Renaissance mindset can be pious and humble but also sinister and, in the case of the black man, rapacious and diabolical. Blackness and darkness tend to a negative ethical imagery, linked to animality, sexuality, violence, and death—but not always, Harvey reminds us. The devil might be black, but the African *Magus* in the nativity scene is often the most beautiful, the youngest, and the best dressed. Within a nuanced argument, and despite the enormous amounts of negative comments, Harvey suggests that even in the Renaissance, black might have been a beautiful and elegant color to be.

The historian David Kuchta, in "The Three-Piece Suit," argues for the development of a "new aesthetics of masculinity" in the period around 1670. He sees "renunciation" of fine clothing and the adoption of the three-piece suit for men taking place in England long before the late eighteenth century. He argues that Charles II's advisers suggested that setting a new modest standard at court, made up of English woolens, would result in thrift among the courtiers and a falling away of sumptuary law, and would also overthrow the tyranny of "foreign" models. The new "vest," the famous diarist Samuel Pepys wrote on October 15, 1666, resembled "a long cassock close to the body, of black cloth and pinked with white silk under it, and a coat over it, and the legs ruffled with black ribbon like a pigeon's leg."[3] So with its long tail and ribbons, it had very little visual resemblance to a modern suit, but nonetheless became a means to legitimize monarchical power through dress.[4]

The suit has details too. Magnifying and viewing devices such as monocles, lorgnettes, and quizzing glasses for men were, as literary historian Olga Vainshtein argues, central to the dandy of the next generation "for scrutinizing the decisive details [of dress] and judging the appropriateness of them." Such devices conveyed both "interest and contempt." Rather than dwelling on dandies as precursors of aesthetic modernity or camp style, Vainshtein considers the visual codes and games that were both played out in life and extended to a range of truly exquisite male accessories.

Thomas Carlyle's famous essay on the dandies, "The Dandiacal Body," is interpreted by anthropologist and dress studies scholar Michael Carter as a comment on the decline of a collective religious sense; it fills the "gap left by the withdrawal of the sea of faith." Carter writes in this volume on Carlyle's *Sartor Resartus* (which was published in serial form in 1833) and makes a case for Carlyle being the founding father of contemporary dress studies. Carlyle, a critic of mechanization and materialism, argued that the social being was now a "clothes" being, that clothes become the outward manifestation of our sociality and ideals. Clothes to Carlyle are not about protection or modesty, but ornament and decoration, and they relate to the style or "patterning" of human forms. Carlyle, Carter argues, worked within the context of German Romantic thought in which *Geist,* that is, mind or spirit, discovered "a distinctive material embodiment for this collective mental entity."

Following the French Revolution, male citizens in Europe acquired new civil rights and duties, privileges that women could not enjoy and that manifested male preeminence. New concepts of manliness and male beauty emerged. Elisabeth Hackspiel-Mikosch argues in this volume that gender differences became more explicit during the course of the nineteenth century and focuses her attention on military uniforms. She finds the new image of superior male physical strength and masculine intellectual and moral character to be most clearly expressed in military and civilian uniforms, which enjoyed increasing popularity during that century.

A counter to the rigid envelope of the militarized male body is found in two further essays, one on the meaning of the bow tie, the other on the politics of men's dress reform. Rob Shields's "A Tale of Three Louis: Ambiguity, Masculinity and the Bow Tie" argues that the bow tie is among the most ambiguous objects in the male wardrobe, that thing most "concealing of intention." The neck, Shields explains, is a vulnerable part of the body, tender, partial to cold, with a fragile adjacent spine and exposed jugular vein, that must be managed by dress. From a device that functioned as a luck charm against decapitation in the Croatian mercenary armies of Louis XIV, the bow tie shifted to the graceful mode of a flourish garnished with lace, a style established by King Louis XIV. In the twentieth century the bow tie, worn by professionals such as the Chicago modernist architect Louis Kahn or the orator and leader of the Nation of Islam Louis Farrakhan, comes to be used by "the arrogant performer, the maestro," who wishes to indicate superior cultural status, demanding attention on his own radical and sometimes conceited terms. The bow tie, Shields writes, can make patrons look like waiters or clowns and might suggest servitude, but at the same time can suggest grace and lightness. For media campaigns, it is generally photographed on lissome and languid youth. The bow tie, ideally suited to manipulation, is therefore ambiguous; it may suggest lesbian chic or, if lying on the sternum, in the 1920s and 1930s a modern femininity for New Women.

The bow tie reappears as the hanging tie proposed by dress reformers outlined in Barbara Burman's "Better and Brighter Clothes: The Men's Dress Reform Party, 1929–1940." Burman presents examples of attempts to reform men's neckwear, collars, and the general "weight of tailordom" criticized by the radical thinker and homosexual Edward Carpenter in his "Simplification of Life" (1886). Men's dress reform, Burman suggests, was not a fringe activity. Unventilated, heavily constructed, and divided garments—trousers—were criticized by a range of thinkers and 200 branches of men's dress reform parties were established around the world. Some of their ideas were taken up by commercial establishments that were interested in promoting the use of color and the new synthetic fibers, but the craft base of the industry found the attempt to fuse female dressmaking skills with male tailoring to be threatening and absurd. Burman also notes the use of male models, with bare legs and even chiffon tops, in the otherwise very respectable dress reform events conducted in London hotels and at Olympia in the 1930s. She does not comment on the homoerotic charge of the events, which is apparent from looking at the handsome male "mannequins" that populate her original article. The trade was already reforming the options for men's dress as well as providing new construction techniques for sleeveless and buttonless underwear and self-supporting trousers with elasticized waistbands. The movement was also made up of elderly and serious gentlemen reformers who, in their shorts, sandals, and other alternative dress, did little to turn male fashion around except in the arena of holiday and athletic wear. That major shift occurred in the post–World War II period when a range of factors, including the rise of American style, a preoccupation with leisure, and new formations of sexual politics, transformed men's outlooks and appearances.

Peter McNeil

NOTES

1. Jean-Jacques Rousseau, *Emile,* trans. Barbara Foxley (1762; London: J. M. Dent, 1993), 426.
2. Georges Vigarello, "The Upward Training of the Body from the Age of Chivalry to Courtly Civility," in *Fragments for a History of the Human Body,* ed. Michel Feher with Ramona Naddaff and Nadia Tazi (New York: Zone, 1989), part 2, 179.
3. Samuel Pepys, *Diary* (New York: Cassell, 1966).
4. David Kuchta, "The Making of the Self-Made Man: Class, Clothing, and English Masculinity, 1688–1832," in *The Sex of Things,* ed. Victoria de Grazia (Berkeley: University of California Press, 2002), 54–78.

FROM BLACK IN SPAIN TO BLACK IN SHAKESPEARE

John Harvey

By the beginning of the sixteenth century, black was definitely seemly, and could be more or less smart and stately, or more or less reserved, at the wearer's initiative. It was popular in other city-states than Venice. So when Castiglione, in *The Courtier* (1528), addresses the question of what 'the raiment of our courtier' should be, he observes, in Hoby's translation:

> Moreover I will holde alwaies with it, if it bee rather somewhat grave and auncient [sober], than garish. Therfore me thinke a blacke colour hath a better grace in garments than any other, and though not throughly blacke, yet somewhat darke, and this I meane for his ordinarie apparrell.[1]

The courtier defers in his dress, as in other matters: his black or dark clothes have a respectful and self-respectful seriousness in dutifulness, which makes the 'grace' of his courtly loyalty. Black is for his daily wear; over armour, the courtier should have 'sightly and merrie colours', and his garments for pleasure should be 'pompous and rich' (*pomposi e superbi*). But black might be worn by all at court, and by princes as well as by courtiers. The identity of the young man in Bronzino's portrait of the 1550s is not certain: the sitter may be one of the elder sons of Bronzino's main patron, Cosimo de' Medici, Grand Duke of Tuscany. What is certain is that he has distinguished rank, and though his self-possessed gaze is cool, what especially he shows, in person and dress together, is the 'better grace'

of black, which could be worn by young men without needing to imply grief, and could be attractive as well as serious.

Interestingly, at the point where he comments on the courtier's clothing, Castiglione notes the power aspect of dress. He regrets that Italians dress after the French, or Spanish, or Dutch styles, rather than having a style of their own; and he reads this imitativeness as a sign of national weakness, even as 'a prognosticate of bondage'. He cites the case of Darius, who, 'the yeare before hee fought with Alexander, had altered his sword he wore by his side, which was a Persian blade, into the fashion of Macedonie'. When Castiglione speaks of black, it is less clear whom he thinks the Italians are imitating, since he thinks black is intrinsically graceful for courtiers (though few would have worn it a hundred years earlier). The principal inspiration is indicated, however, when he says of the clothes Italians wear that, excepting 'triumphes, games, maskeries', 'I coulde wish they should declare the solemnitie that the Spanish nation much observeth, for outwarde matters many times are a token of the inwarde.'

It was Spain, more than any other nation, which was to be responsible for the major propagation of solemn black both throughout Europe, and in the New World. Spanish black was fed by a grave native tradition, and also, very directly, by the black of Burgundy. For the Emperor Charles V (King Charles I of Spain) had originally been the Burgundian Charles of Luxembourg. He was descended from Philip the Good as well as from the Habsburgs, and when he inherited the Spanish throne in 1516 he brought with him to Spain the black-dominated style of the Burgundian court. In Titian's portrait of 1548 we see the ageing Charles dressed wholly in black: indeed, he seems almost to have no shadow, as though, in his black, he himself is shadow. And he has dressed, for this portrait, very much as Philip the Good had dressed, since the sole decoration he wears, over the black gown, is the Order of the Golden Fleece that Philip had founded. The Golden Fleece was to develop a talismanic character. Charles's father had made him a member before he reached the age of one; and the wearing of black clothes with the Golden Fleece was to become almost the uniform of the Burgundian/Habsburg monarchy. There is an identity in colour spanning two centuries between the clothing Philip the Good wore in the 1450s; the clothing Charles V wears in Titian's portrait; the clothing Philip II wears in almost all the portraits of him; and the clothing worn by Philip IV in portraits by Velazquez.

It is Philip II, however, the son of Charles V, who is something like the pivotal man in black in Europe's history. He ruled Spain from 1556 to 1598 and could seem the archetypal sinister monarch, brooding in plain chambers in the bleak Escorial, procuring murders and patronizing the Inquisition, himself in black and transmitting his will through a secretariat of Black Friars. This was the austere monarch whose taste in art was for the demonology of Hieronymus Bosch. It may, therefore, give some recuperating touch of reality to recall that he struck his contemporaries as a man 'who looked very ordinary, dressed in black just like the citizens'.[2] The citizens were known as the *gente de capa negra,* and had their own tradition of dignified solemnity, preoccupied as they were with the special honour of each native and Christian Spaniard. Philip is modestly dressed even in the sharp-lit apocalyptic vision of El Greco's *Dream of Philip II* of c.1580. The picture shows Philip's

political and religious universes. He kneels with the monarchs and prelates of Europe, while above him, through a break in the stone-grey clouds, the souls of the blest hymn the Holy Name, in a tender light: rose with pale gold. Immediately at Philip's back (he kneels, on his cushions, on the very brink of it), a ravenous, black-dog Hell Mouth yawns, within which the green-grey bodies of the damned writhe in a kind of white ice-fire. And between Heaven and Hell Mouth, in the company of monarchs wearing cloth of gold and ermine, Philip kneels seriously in sober, plain black clothes. If Philip dressed like a citizen—that is, like a merchant—this is perhaps not surprising, since he also was much preoccupied with money, worrying (necessarily) about the costs of court life as well as of the Armada, and about the servicing of the loans he had raised, which threatened bankruptcy on an imperial scale. Since Spanish society was notoriously divided between the courtly feudal world and the mercantile world of the cities, it perhaps shows good instinct on Philip's part to wear a style of black that associated him—the supreme aristocrat—with his somewhat menaced urban citizenry. But the black clothes that Philip was noted for wearing were not in origin mercantile or citizenly. He was extendedly in mourning for his second wife, Elizabeth de Valois, whose death, it is clear, afflicted him with real grief (for two weeks he was wholly shut away, refusing to see even pressing state documents). And there were other deaths, in particular that of his daughter Catalina in 1597, at which he wept, raged and howled in a way that made his courtiers worry for his life. But, as had Philip the Good earlier, he continued to wear black beyond the natural term of mourning, and clearly the colour was congenial to him for more reasons than grief.

Why, in later life, Philip wore black so consistently, it is not possible to know for certain, since he never himself explained his dress. He was interested in astrology, and Geoffrey Parker notes that:

he may, for example, have preferred to wear black because this was a colour associated with the planet Saturn, with which the king felt special sympathy; certainly the treatise on magic known as the Picatrix, of which he possessed a copy, claimed that dressing in black clothes was an effective means of drawing down on the wearer the beneficent influences of Saturn.[3]

There is no proof that this was Philip's motive, but it is a relevant consideration: if any human practice is 'overdetermined', it is clothing. Whatever Philip's particular reasons for wearing black, he would hardly have done so without having some support from a larger tendency of fashion. This, it is clear, there abundantly was. And plain black, with its impersonality, was appropriate wear for a serious governor, who wished to show his strict power was disinterested and just. Philip, working in close conjunction with his secretary, the Dominican priest Diego de Espinosa, replicated the 'picture' of a century before, when Philip the Good, wearing the colour of mourning beyond the period of mourning, governed Burgundy with the black-gowned Nicholas Rolin at his side.

One must not, then, make Philip II too sinister a figure, as is done when he is characterized as a cold spider at the heart of a black web of schemings. He liked gardens and Dutch tiles, and Titian as well as Bosch, and in his later years he worked not only with Black Friars at his beck and call, but also with his daughter Isabella beside him, drying ink and passing him papers. He still was harsh, and given to harsh pleasures. The hunting he relished as exercise consisted of watching from a hide while a herd of deer was netted in front of him, to be torn to pieces by the royal dogs. Even the work of the Inquisition, of which he was a zealous patron, afforded him a serious spectatorial pleasure. Perhaps he did not say the words that Tennyson gives him in his play *Queen Mary:*

The blood and sweat of heretics at the stake
Is God's best dew upon the barren field,

Burn more! (v. i. 46–8)

But Philip liked to preside at *autos-da-fé*, and mused to his secretary about them: 'It is something really worth seeing for those who have not seen one. If there is to be an *auto* during the time I am [in Toledo], it would be good to see it.'[4]

Philip's patronage of the Inquisition included a zeal, informed with a genuine but merciless piety, to see its work extended. The Inquisition tried 'social crimes' such as bigamy, homosexuality and fornication as well as heresy: it was, in effect, both the thought police and social police throughout Philip's possessions. If Philip, in wearing black continuously, was in part taking to himself the colour of the Church, he was specifically adopting the colour of (as it were) the Church Disciplinary, of the Dominican Inquisitors. With the utmost sincerity he used religious faith for social control, in effect making himself not only the supreme magistrate, but the supreme priest-policeman of his strict Christian state. If, then, his black dress had a citizen-like modesty, in keeping with his desire to be addressed simply as 'Sir' ('Señor'), and not as 'Your Sacred Catholic Majesty', this modesty was of the colder kind. It went with his willingness (unlike his widely journeying father) to be a nearly invisible, though most potent, monarch. Philip preferred to stay in Spain, by choice in his simple chambers in the Escorial, governing through intermediaries, and doing as much business as possible on paper rather than in person. His almost permanent black dress fits his desire to recede, to be inconspicuous, a monarch who might be mistaken, as he sometimes was, for a citizen or minor official or priest, but who could still, unseen, assert a power as frightening as that of his God.

Because Philip wore black constantly, his courtiers did also. Perhaps they had not all his severity; black was certainly a good foil for the rich jewellery the gold of the New World made fashionable. Black became the uniform of officials and men of power throughout Philip's possessions—in New Spain as well as Spain, and Naples as well as the Netherlands. The already part-black Burgundian style was in effect both eclipsed and consummated in the new black of Philip's extended administration. Spain was the most powerful nation in the world, and therefore not surprisingly it set international fashion. Nor is it remarkable that the wearing of black should have spread in a period of political change that saw the increasing utilization of a cruel state religion to regiment a resistant empire. Black often has been the colour of asceticism, and asceticism is discipline whether it is inflicted by a hermit on himself, or by an overlord on a nation. One may note here that Philip's great fear was that the Spanish dominions would break apart, as earlier there was fear of Christendom fragmenting. Actually, thanks to Philip's exertions, the Spanish Empire (as it was later called) had still a certain lease on life. Even so, if one is thinking of black and power, it seems one may associate black not so much with power securely enjoyed as with a resolute assertion of power within a period of political anxiety. And one should perhaps see all the features of Philip so far mentioned—the harshness, the religious zeal, the mistrust of his ministers, the procured murders, the empowerment of the Inquisition, the resort to astrology, the desire to withdraw in shadow and to withdraw from view, and indeed the desire to wear black clothes—as the many reflections of a dominating and life-long anxiety. And Philip and his government had real enemies, including the Turks, the Dutch, the French and the English, while they also believed they had enemies within the gates: the Spanish Moors, Spanish Jews and Protestants. They had reasons for anxiety.

This is not to suggest that black-clad officials and men of power must necessarily be anxious. Once a black-clad hierarchy has become established, black seems rather the expression, by all concerned, of their acceptance of authority's bonds; an acknowledgement, both by those in command and by those subdued to them, of a scale of obligations in the power-relation. But Philip, it is clear, was a workaholic monarch who worried all his life, and was famous too for mistrusting everyone. And if one looks back to the portraits of Philip's predecessor Charles V, and considers Charles's subtle face, with its weight of grave care, one may associate his black too with the anxiety as well as the momentousness of empire. Indeed, the cares of empire contributed greatly to the decision of Charles V, at the age of 55, to abdicate the entirety of his monarchies, dukedoms, principalities and Empire, and retire to a monastery. The principal ceremony of his retirement had been his abdication as ruler of the Netherlands on 25 October 1555, in the great hall of the castle of Brussels: Charles attending all in black, with the Order of the Golden Fleece round his neck.

It is perhaps at this point, having in mind black's association at once with power and with care, that one may note a further association, formed in these years, which has since kept a strong (not universal) hold, one visible more recently in some aspects of both Russian and American dress—in, for instance, the dark suits and black coats and attendant dark uniforms of the presidential entourage. This is the association of black not only with power, but with centralized power and with the power of the state. My purpose in mentioning Russia, however, is, at this moment, to digress. Muscovy had its own historic associations of autocracy and black, which I cite for comparison with those of Spain. For in the years (the 1560s) in which Philip was encouraging the Dominicans in their inquisitorial vigilance, Ivan IV, the Terrible, was in the process of establishing his own distinct regal domain, the enormous Oprichnina, and his personal guard, the black-clad 'men apart' or Oprichniki. Ivan swore the Oprichniki to absolute loyalty, a loyalty that must take precedence over friends, parents, family, and rewarded them with estates and immunity from the law. They wore all-black uniforms and rode black horses, bearing on their saddles the emblem of a dog's head and broom, signifying that they would hound traitors and sweep them away. At Ivan's command they burned, raped and killed.[5]

Scourging Ivan's enemies, and with a licence to wreak havoc on their own account, the Oprichniki must have appeared a sinister troop. There can be no doubt, however, that Ivan's first purpose in making them wear black was to institute them as a kind of secular priesthood. The Orthodox clergy had worn black since the fifth century, and in Russia a man in black was first and foremost a man of God. Ivan swore the Oprichniki to loyalty on the Cross, and intended them to serve him with the absolute devotion with which an ascetic serves the Lord. Indeed, within the dense forests of the Oprichnina, within the fortified town he had built at Alexandrovsk, within its palace surrounded by moats, walls and ramparts, Ivan lived with an inner core of 300 Oprichniki whom he called the Brotherhood: he gave them monastic offices, and governed them as 'Abbot'. The arrangement sounds like a parody of the Orthodox vocation, but the Oprichniki were commanded to attend real matins, and were imprisoned if they did not, while Ivan himself prayed in the morning for two or three hours. Later the Oprichniki feasted and drank, while Ivan stood at a lectern reading from sacred books. When he himself dined afterwards, he argued theology; following dinner he might visit the torture-chambers to witness an interrogation. At ten he retired, and blind men told him stories till he slept; at midnight he was woken, for divine service. The whole schedule seems in part an exaggerated mockery of Philip's rule, commanding his Dominicans and praying and confiding with them, withdrawn in his vast Escorial. On Ivan's part it was an extraordinary combination of religious parody and piety, of carnival and autocracy, of holiness and savagery. From this distance in time it looks like cruel madness; but at all events it shows, precisely by the extreme it presents, how the long association of black dress with the Church

could be augmented and enlisted for secular duties, and could work in the interest of ruthless absolutism, turning the disciplines of piety into totalitarian rigour.

The Oprichniki were perceived by their victims as dark in the sense of terrifying and evil. Prince Kurbsky, in his denunciatory biography of Ivan, consistently calls them 'the children of darkness'—men who wear the black livery of the evil they do. And it must be supposed that, with his odd double perspective on the Church, which meant he could simultaneously mock and yet imitate monastic life, Ivan intended his private priesthood, black-mounted and black-clad, to have the authority of priests and yet be feared as devils: an intention that would show a grisly, but shrewd, power-psychology on Ivan's part, perhaps not wholly out of place in a religion where an omnipotent God has assigned to merciless demons a policing and punitive role in his Universe. The Oprichniki demonstrate, in the starkest combination so far seen, the opposite aspects of black. Black is the sign of their selflessness in devotion to their work, yet the nature of that work, the persecution of the Tsar's enemies, makes them for their victims (which included whole classes of the population) a black terror, Death riding not on a pale horse but on black horses to catch you.

This is perhaps the most horrific aspect of black: when the man in black has effaced, with his own self, his common humanity, in order to be the utensil of a power. The Oprichniki were, however, men apart. Ivan himself is never represented in black, and black does not seem, at this date, to have been fashionable in Muscovy to the degree it was in Western Europe. That fashion—to return from my digression—was a European usage that was frequently thought of as being, and to a good extent was, the Spanish fashion. It was the fashion of the most powerful nation in the world, that nation being at the same time, famously, a 'closed society'. Enforcing that closure, the native Christian population, and its aristocracy and monarchy especially, had increasingly employed the Church, in the form of the Holy Office, to subdue, discipline, terrorize and execute Spanish Jews and Spanish Moors, whether or not they converted to Christianity, and, more recently, Spanish Protestants or supposititious Protestants; and to suppress Protestant books and many humanist books, and indeed many forms of study and science. One should perhaps not too hastily identify the large-scale black fashion with the anxious repressiveness of a closed and ferociously conservative society; but the manner of Spanish dress does suggest such a link, for the Spanish black fashion was at the same time a fashion for rigid, constricting, encasing clothing, which costume historians universally call 'severe'. It tended to adopt forms 'imitating the protective and hostile forms of armour'.[6] A particular feature was the high tubular collar, topped by a starched ruff, which gave the Spanish gentleman no option but to be literally, rigidly, erectly stiff-necked. Philip is wearing such a collar in *The Dream of Philip II*. And this style embodied in the most literal way the Spanish conservatism and opposition to change: that is, it did not change, or changed hardly at all, while the fashions of other nations evolved, so that by the later seventeenth century, Spanish gentlemen in portraits, in their traditional capes and breeches, and high-collared black jerkins, were living costume history museums. Foreign visitors to Spain registered as remarkable the constancy and ubiquity of black. The Frenchman Antoine de Brunel, travelling in Spain in 1655, found it a land of black, the women wearing black lace or black veils, even pages wearing black, not coloured liveries as in France; while foreign envoys visiting the Spanish court were advised that they must put on black clothes before they could see the King.[7] The monarch at that date was Philip IV, who loved the arts and yet also loved the black style. It was he who, in 1623, had formally made black official and obligatory for Spanish court dress. In Velazquez's portrait, made at about the time of Antoine de Brunel's visit, Philip is in black, and black surrounds him. He gazes coolly, with distinct hauteur and a Habsburg thrust, as it were from a tank of blackness. We know his body is there from scattered decorative glimmerings, and of course from the gold chain that carries the badge of the Golden Fleece.

Spanish black is, then, clearly the colour chosen by Spanish society. Peter the Venerable had, 400 years earlier, commented on the special enthusiasm of the Spanish for the use of black in mourning: he was struck by the fact that they not only all wore black at a funeral, but that they even blackened their cattle.[8] One should neither exaggerate nor underestimate the exacerbating effect of the particular initiatives of Philip II. And Philip himself, as noted earlier, had chosen to dress in a style that chimed with, but did not initiate, the style of his citizens. The black capes of the citizens could not, however, have influenced international fashion, while the style of the Spanish Court, and above all of Philip and his clerical and aristocratic administration, did have Europe-wide repercussions. Perhaps what is most striking is that this fashion was transmitted especially to those states most in conflict with Spain—England and the Netherlands: so that from having been the uniform of Spanish Catholicism, black was to become, complementarily, the uniform of anti-Spanish Protestantism. The black-clad combatants look back at us still, from portraits of the Spanish by Velazquez, of the English by Van Dyck, of the Dutch by Hals and Rembrandt. This colour-sharing by enemies should not surprise us, if we consider the bitterness of those wars, and the extent also to which at that time political and national conflict expressed itself in rival forms of sacrificial religion. A wartime religion will be ascetic, and asceticism itself has perhaps always been as much a military as a religious virtue: an operational necessity for an army, or a community, or an individual fighting for life in terrible straits. One must be willing to die to hope to win. Military discipline itself, as against an armed rampage, became obligatory in this period.

Soldiers themselves deal in real death; they have hardly needed to wear black, and often have been far from doing so. When, in the ancient world, soldiers fought hand to hand, there was little purpose in being camouflaged; and perhaps some advantage, for heroes at all events, in being dauntingly splendid and gorgeous. So Caesar had been pleased to lead an army of dandies. And at all times colour is courage, it makes a brave show, and furthermore it identifies your side—and also, of course, deserters: if you saw your colour running the wrong way, you shot at it. The colour red may suggest courage and heart, the roused blood keen to act. It may also, like black, play on fear: your own blood is vulnerable to a man made of blood. But soldiers, too, might wear black: often black lacquer was laid on dress armour, as in Robert Peake's portrait of 1593. It had, in fact, been the practice, since the Middle Ages, for suits of full armour to be painted, and often they were treated with black paint, which protected the metal, and presumably also gave them now the menace, now the protective 'invisibility', of the man in black. The Black Prince was so-named, in some accounts, because his armour was black.[9] The soldier in Peake's portrait exploits the values both of black and of the colours red and gold. The gold edging to each plate and scale of the armour suggests this soldier's splendour and martial nobility; the red scarf tied in a bow on his arm is perhaps his courage, and his willingness, too, to shed his own or his opponent's blood. His black is his discipline and severity, also his intensity, as he threatens death to others and also has made of death an armour.

The wars in which Spain was increasingly involved were the inevitable breaking out, in savage secessionist and suppressive violence, of developing divisions, national, ethnic and economic, which were manifest also in the opening of the greatest rift in Christendom, the separation of the Reformed from the Catholic Church. The war that was fought on the ground with cannons and pikes, at the cost throughout Europe of acres of corpses, was fought also in the mind, in language, in Heaven. It was fought by churches and church organizations that increasingly, in the stress of conflict, resolved themselves into institutional machines, indeed into 'institutions' in something like the modern sense, with economies and rigidities of command-structure, and a new impersonality of organization. It is hardly surprising, then, that both sides, Reformation and Counter-Reformation, came to use the same livery of disciplined, death-ready, ascetic self-effacement—that they came to wear black. On the Catholic side, the main warrior institution had been specifically founded on the military model, in that Ignatius of Loyola, with his soldiering past, wanted the Society of Jesus both to be, and to be organized as, the army of the Church (though the General of the Society was an administrator-general, and was not meant to carry, as he has subsequently been presented as carrying, a military title).[10]

Though the Jesuits now are famous for their black, and though their 'General' came to be known as the Black Pope, it had not been the intention of Ignatius for them to wear black, or any assertively priestly garb. He was as strongly opposed to monastic uniform, as to choirs, chanting and the use of the organ, 'for these things which adorn the divine worship of the other orders, we have found by experience to be no small hindrance to us; since we devote a great part of the day and night to the bodily and spiritual care of the sick'. Ignatius had, in other words, his own un-aesthetic, practical-minded, generous form of puritanism, which included his dismissing as spiritual luxury the customary observances of priestly asceticism, such as 'fasts, scourgings, going bare-footed'. Among these addictive priestly distractions he included 'fixed colours of dress'.[11] The Vatican was less willing for the Jesuits to be so individual, and though the Society avoided a rigid specification of dress—and allowed different wear in different countries, so that Jesuits in China dressed as mandarins—it soon became the practice for Jesuits in Rome to wear black, with a distinctive black cape having a high 'Roman' collar. The strong connection of the Society with Spain meant that Spanish black—clerical style—had a strong influence also; and the fact that the Jesuits were so potent in education, with an extraordinary record of achievement in the founding of schools and universities, meant that many were known by the black gowns they wore as tutors and doctors. These considerations led in due course to the general wearing of black by Jesuits, making them, with the Jansenists, the two main forms of 'noir' in Stendhal's *Le Rouge et le noir*. Given their dress and their militancy together, their willingness to use worldly tactics in dealing with the world, and indeed their willingness, in spite of their constitution, for political intervention, it is not surprising they came to be seen by their opponents as a kind of insidious half-secret army, 'black' in something like the modern, distinctly sinister sense. In the Protestant perspective, they are the fanatic praetorian elite of Romanism, a private papal army and police at once—for they were placed directly at the Pope's command—wearing (when not insidiously disguised) the black of the assassin. It is necessary, then, to remind oneself of the difference between the ministering and educating Society of Jesus and the Church's earlier black-caped disciplinarians, such as the Dominican Inquisitors, and the Knights of St John, who were a good deal more prompt with the rack, sword and stake. The Jesuits, too, practised formidable severities, but they are also represented by the wonderful figure of Francis Xavier, moving on from country to country through the Far East, evangelizing and healing: skipping barefoot through snow with a Siamese hat at a jaunty angle, while throwing an apple up and down; or, very shortly before his death from exhaustion, presenting himself, arrayed in silks, before the Japanese *daimyō* Hirado, and upbraiding him to his face for his sodomy while at the same time placating him with the gifts of a grandfather clock, a

music-box, a musket with three barrels, and a cask of port wine.

If it was true of Ignatius, it was true too of the other great reforming individuals, that it was not their purpose to enjoin their followers to wear black, or any set vestment or uniform. Though the Reformation, like the Counter-Reformation, came to wear black, it was rather because several strains of blackness, running through European history, converged irresistibly in the new urgencies. Martin Luther—who saw the Church itself as a form of spiritual clothing—wore a black habit originally because he was an Augustinian canon. The theology of that order had a pessimistic cast, reflected in their penitential robes; and an element of Augustinian pessimism, tied with a melancholy personal to Luther, runs through his later thought on human depravity.[12] And, as virtually every portrait shows, he continued throughout his life to wear black. He did so when preaching, as in the portrait by Lucas Cranach the Elder. It is the black of the inner human sinfulness, of depravity, worn without in honest contrition; and worn no longer with ritual intention, but rather as the avowal of a personal grim inwardness with human failing.

Calvin, for his part, wore a black gown because he had trained in law: so it chanced that he and Luther wore the differing liveries of the two kinds of 'clerk'. If Ignatius had sought a military discipline, Calvin imposed the strictest legal rigour on the fate of souls, on the government of churches, indeed on the will of God, who seems turned by predestination from being the light of Heaven into a great fixed-term contract with an infinity of non-negotiable clauses. But it was not the practice of either Calvin or his lieutenants to ordain specific vestments for their ministers. Their ordinances were rather negative, a discouragement of clothing that suggested priestliness, of garments 'defiled with infinite superstition'.[13] There was no prohibition on the black gown itself, which many people wore, but rather on white priestly overgarments, such as the surplice. So when, in the 1560s, the Bishop of Winchester, Robert Horn, sent the Swiss Protestant Heinrich Bullinger the Order of Administration of the Church of England, Bullinger replied:

> I do not approve of the linen surplice, as they call it, in the ministry of the Gospel, inasmuch as those robes copied from Judaism, savour of popery, and are introduced and established with injury to Christian liberty ... I wish, however, that the habit in which the minister performs Divine service should be decent, according to the fashion of the country, and have nothing light or fantastic about it.[14]

As a result the Reformed minister, while not wearing a black habit, would wear in the pulpit the black gown of the educated clerk or doctor. Though this practice had originally the shock of a man preaching in ordinary clothes—so Bullinger himself was praised because he mounted to the pulpit 'in seiner burgerlichen kleidung' (in his citizen's clothing)—the black gown and white ruff did become associated with the office of the wearer. In time they became the new priestly uniform, a new black form of sartorial authoritarianism, as the dress of citizens and even doctors changed. More generally, it seems in the nature of the self-effacement of black that it easily suggests an office as much as the office-holder, and thus has something like an inherent tendency to move from being a fashion to being a uniform (as happened also with the dress of lawyers). Moreover, the privileged position of the preacher in a Reformed church meant that his dress, however sober and 'ordinary', was likely with time to become privileged dress. The 'position' of the minister was literally a matter of being in the centre (since there was no altar), and of being set often at a great height in the air. In a watercolour of 1648 of the 'temple' at Charenton, the tiny pastor in black, preaching very much from on high, repeats in his clothing the background black of the prodigious tablets of the Old Testament Commandments set in the roof above him. Doubtless he echoes in his sermon Calvin's own words from the pulpit: 'We are never so guiltless in the eyes of God that he does not have good reason to punish us'; he will, perhaps, conclude with a prayer (like Calvin's) that 'it pleaseth Thee to make our labour prosper'.[15]

It became Protestant practice so consistently to wear black in the pulpit, and so frequently to wear black outside it too, that it would not be wrong to consider the consonance between the black dress of 'Puritans' and their cast of spirituality. And what may be true of Luther seems very likely true of many Lutherans and Calvinists, of Dutch regents and English Roundheads—that their austere black style does reflect the intuitions of Protestantism, and in particular the conviction of depravity. The soul is deep-dyed in sin, and has no option but to wait for a Deliverance no human act can hasten. All one may do is live devoutly, according to the attitude that Max Weber was to call 'intramundane asceticism'. While one must be wary, in trying to read faces in portraits from the past, one can I think see, in the 'expression' of this period, the changing timbre and tone of European inner life. If one looks from Bronzino's young Italian Catholic of the 1550s to Heimbach's young Danish Lutheran of 100 years later, one sees a quietly lively sensuousness, perhaps something sweet, in the first young face that seems quite extinct in the later, which has by contrast a cold mistrustful guardedness, not amiable and not happy. Indeed, the Lutheran's mouth shows more displeasure, is more downturned, than that of the middle-aged Philip IV. One can, of course, find diverse moods in portraits, and there are laughing Calvinists painted by Frans Hals, but still one can see, taking many pictures together, the changed temper of the life of northern Europe, with a gain perhaps in introspection, and a loss of supple vivacity.

Theological and introspective issues apart, one might suppose, as to lay fashion, that a severe style will be in part a response to harsh circumstances: it is the style that will survive a prolonged period of pain, and bitter struggle, and constricted and endangered living. That was certainly the situation of the Dutch Republic in its first 100 years, surrounded by enemies, at war with Spain, and under constant guard also against the sea, which periodically reinvaded the land. Its political system was a challenge to monarchies, its Protestant faith a challenge to Catholicism, and its growing wealth a challenge both to enemies and to allies alike. In its isolation it maintained its morale through the incessant reaffirmation, by its pastors and regents, of its privilege and righteousness as the new chosen people of the Lord. It was a society united by recurring anxiety, and it is hardly surprising that many people, both men and women, and at all levels of society, wore the same colours, the black with white ruff, worn also by the preachers of the Reformed Church. That the Dutch Golden Age was mainly a black-clad age we see in its paintings, from portraits to genre scenes.

The four officers of a guild in Van den Eeckhout's painting of 1657 are not severe like Heimbach's young merchant. They are less solemn indeed than many of the gathered regents in group portraits by Rembrandt, and it may be that their geniality is related to their being officers of the Coopers' and Wine-rackers' Guild. St Matthias, the patron saint of coopers, is depicted in a frame behind them holding his axe. The picture reflects at the same time their serious importance, and their importance as members of a tradesmen's guild, rather than as aspirants to noble station: especially it shows their serious solidarity, their desire to dress identically, with seriousness and propriety (though the younger men wear the collar that was in the process of superseding the older man's ruff). Black in the United Provinces seems different in character from the power-black of the Spanish Empire. One might, as Simon Schama has suggested, think rather, on Durkheimian lines, of a society united in a kind of social church.[16] It was a society marked by extremes of wealth, and a rich Amsterdam merchant might display his prosperity, and his enjoyment of it, in the materials of which his clothes were made, in velvet, satin, silk. But even the rich wore, predominantly, the same colour that most people wore—and the poor wore black fustian. The Dutch clung to their black through the remainder of the seventeenth century, even while the brighter fashions of France percolated through the countries round them. They seem a nation for whom black was important, not as the robe of hierarchic power, and not simply as a tribute to Calvinist morality, but rather as the broad, defining cloak of the whole threatened and thriving, beleaguered and warring, anxious and thrusting new republican bourgeois nation.

England by contrast seems at this date a country containing within itself the wars that raged through Europe, with its successive regimes of Protestant, Catholic and Protestant again, its alternating waves of religious persecution, its swings between Catholic monarchism and Calvinistic republicanism. In England, too, the different black fashions of Europe converge. English Puritans, within the Church of England but of Calvinist allegiance, refused to wear the surplice and would wear only the black cassock. Black was fashionable at court, where it was a Spanish fashion (and Mary I had been for a time, though hardly more than technically, the wife of Philip II). It is true that in Elizabeth's court there was a good deal of white-with-black, the black then taken to symbolize constancy, the white the virginity of the Virgin Queen. But chief ministers of the Crown wore black—as did William Cecil, First Baron Burghley, and as had Thomas Cromwell, First Earl of Essex. Theirs is the black of dedication, of the man made over wholly to the enactment of the princely will he serves. The portrait, after Holbein, of Cromwell suggests the narrow shrewd ruthlessness of a man more than glad to sink his self in that enactment. Black was also the fashion among Protestant merchants, for Calvinism took strong root in the London business community. English parliamentarians would wear, when sitting, the black gowns they also wore for serious occasions in general (as, it should be said, did councillors and senators elsewhere in Europe, notably in Genoa). Parliamentary black was apt, for the parliamentarians too were on serious business, and on God's business also they believed, which was later to include cutting off the King's head. Officers and gentlemen might wear colours other than black, so of course might trades-men, farmers and sailors: black never became universal for men in the way that it virtually did in the nineteenth century. Even the most zeal-ously puritan communities, for instance, those who had crossed the ocean to Massachusetts, did not necessarily wear black. They wore 'sadd' colours, which could include low-toned greens and greys as well as black (though they did wear the black felt steeple hats tradition has always placed on them).[17] It is still true that many kinds of black coincided in late sixteenth- and early seventeenth-century England. That even the smarter wearing of black was the smart surface of an anxious life, where no head was guaran-teed safe on its shoulders, may be suggested by the wary sad-eyed faces in many portraits of those years. Charles I had in his wardrobe, in 1634, ten suits of black satin (to seven of cin-namon, six of fawn, four of green), which doubt-less were smart, in the richly lustrous style we know from Van Dyck's portraits of many nobles of those years, but which also were fit wear for a monarchy fallen on serious times.[18]

A BLACK PRINCE

To move from history to literary history, there appeared at the beginning of the seventeenth century England's symbolic man in black—Prince Hamlet. Shakespeare's own faith, if he determined on one, is opaque to us, but there is reason to think that his father was Catholic, while his mother came from a notable Puritan family. So in Shakespeare the opposed severe ex-tremes of Christianity, which had both recently been persecuted as the political tides changed,

met. There is in his work a strain of ascetic se-verity and revulsion; and Hamlet can seem to mourn a larger evil than his father's death:

'Tis not alone my inky cloak, good mother,
Nor customary suits of solemn black . . .
That can denote me truly . . .
. . . I have that within which passeth show,
These but the trappings and the suits of woe.
(I. ii. 77–86).[19]

In his appearance and stage-presence, Hamlet draws on several currents, for in his black he must have some resemblance to a young prince of the Spanish court, and of many courts; and equally to a young notable in the Calvinist and Lutheran states. I should like at this point to draw closer to *Hamlet,* since it is, I think, still a living text we all half-know by heart, and one in which many elements of the black tradition converge, so that in knowing Hamlet we may glimpse the dark side of his time.

Hamlet's decision, for instance, to continue wearing mourning, when the court has aban-doned its weeds for a wedding, is at once per-ceived, both by the court and by the audience, as dramatic and ominous, and involving more than grief. It is certainly disconcerting to Claudius, who takes him to task for persevering in obstinate condolement, calling him impious, unmanly, and incorrect to Heaven. As the killer of Hamlet's father, Claudius is right to be uneasy, for the nat-ural way to read Hamlet's black clothes would be as contemporaries read the weeds of Philip the Good, another princely son of a murdered father: that is, as evidence that Prince Hamlet did not forget his father's death, did not forgive it, and would avenge it when he could. In modern criti-cism Hamlet—or Shakespeare—is sometimes reproached for being un-Christianly vengeful. But it is clear that in the late Renaissance, at least for princes, the avenging of a father's mur-der was a duty and a virtue. Philip the Good was praised in his lifetime for sustaining a war for sixteen years in order to avenge the outrage done to John the Fearless.[20]

At the same time, Hamlet's black is of grief, and in prolonging his wearing of it, he follows not only Philip the Good but also Philip II, the latter mourning both his father and, even more, Elizabeth de Valois. Hamlet, too, extends his mourning in such a way that the prerogative of grief becomes a moral prerogative also, as if by virtue of his bereavement he is more righteous than colourful worldlings. And Hamlet is full of moral contempt for ordinary people—drinking and hollering and whoring. It is as if grief can make a person a righteous black-clad priest. Hamlet is not, of course, pious, as were Philip II and the black-clad Alfonso, King of Aragon, Sicily and Naples; but Hamlet's nihilistic account of life in this world, and of his own depravity, conforms to that which an ascetic might give (black also was penitential):

> I am myself indifferent honest, but yet I could accuse me of such things that it were better my mother had not borne me. I am very proud, revengeful, ambitious, with more offences at my beck than I have thoughts to put them in, imagination to give them shape, or time to act them in. What should such fellows as I do crawling between earth and heaven? We are arrant knaves all, believe none of us. (III. i. 122–30)

Black was humble—the colour of humility and self-effacement—and Hamlet uses his black wear in a way that both Philip II and Alfonso did: as a form of dressing by which the aristocrat or prince could achieve an emancipation from social hierarchy, without materially disowning its advantages. It was a way of escaping censure for possessing the highest of worldly baubles, royalty, which of course worked more successfully, the more genuine the prince was in his humility. It seems that Philip II had a real humility, and also, for all his recessiveness, something of the common touch: he could dress like his citizens, pray with his citizens, and at intervals he enjoyed being mistaken for one of them. Alfonso, a considerably more attractive monarch, certainly had humility. It does appear that the princes who wore black tended to be, whatever melancholy features went also with their black, princes good at conversing with their subjects. Hamlet can enjoy joking with gravediggers, not saying who he is—so that black, the colour of invisibility, is the colour of incognito too, as it also was for Philip II. Most famously, Hamlet will talk with the players, in a humane, humorous, attractive way, while still telling them what to do, and even how to act.

A notable feature Hamlet shares with Philip II and Alfonso is his amused contempt precisely for elaborate courtly dress. So Osric, when he appears, is for Hamlet a 'waterfly' and 'lapwing', and his flourishes with his hat both amuse and irritate the Prince. Hamlet can laugh at Osric's display, because wearing black is dressing down, not up. In the same spirit he mocks Osric's jargon of courtliness:

> *Osric:* The King, sir, hath wagered with him six Barbary horses, against the which he has impawned, as I take it, six French rapiers and poniards, with their assigns, as girdle, hanger, and so. Three of the carriages, in faith, are very dear to fancy, very responsive to the hilts, most delicate carriages, and of very liberal conceit.
> *Hamlet:* What call you the carriages?
> *Osric:* The carriages, sir, are the hangers. (V. ii. 144–54)

The humour of these exchanges, where the Prince mocks the courtier from the standpoint of common humanity, is in the same spirit as the many anecdotes in which Alfonso exposes the vanities of the rich-living and the affected. Given Hamlet's whole situation, it is not surprising that his remarks belong especially to Death's jest-book: many of Hamlet's jokes are as black as his clothes, and not only in the graveyard scene. For instance, he says of a wholly innocent man whom he has himself killed in a rash mistake:

> *King:* Now, Hamlet, where's Polonius?
> *Hamlet:* At supper.
> *King:* At supper? Where?

Hamlet: Not where he eats, but where a'is eaten. A certain convocation of politic worms are e'en at him ... (IV. iii. 16–21)

Hamlet's humour shades into the caprices of his 'antic disposition'—itself, it has been suggested, not only a disguise but a needed relief. Alfonso, King of Aragon, did not put on an antic disposition; he simply was famous, at one and the same time, for wearing black and for making jokes, so that even jokes he had not made were attributed to him in jest-books.[21] This figure, of the jesting prince in black, joining humanity at once through his humble clothes and through his humour (even when grieving), is one of the more attractive aspects of black.

Perhaps the salient characteristic of Hamlet's dress of humility, and its co-operation with his self-image, is that, at key points, he really seems not to think of himself as a prince, but rather to be imaginatively identified not only with citizens but with people of lesser degree, and in less happy situations:

For who would bear the whips and scorns
  of time,
Th'oppressors wrong, the proud man's
  contumely,
The pangs of dispriz'd love, the law's delay,
The insolence of office, and the spurns
That patient merit of th'unworthy takes,
When he himself might his quietus make
With a bare bodkin? (III. i. 70–6)

How much experience would a late medieval or Renaissance prince have of whips and scorns, oppressors, proud men, delaying lawyers, rude officials, ignored merit? These lines would seem to show a generous largeness of feeling in Hamlet—supposing, that is, that Shakespeare is himself remembering, not forgetting, that it is a prince who is supposed to be speaking (for a poet-actor trying to live mainly by the pen would have his knowledge of whips, scorns, oppression, pride, rude officials, ignored merit).

None the less, there is an element of game-playing, and perhaps of falsity, when a prince chats more or less incognito with subjects, as there is in any modern politician saying warmly 'Hello how are you?' to people he does not know. For all his friendliness, Hamlet is a prince, and knows it and shows it, putting Horatio in his place when he needs to, and revealing quite a different and un-humble perspective when he is unexpectedly challenged by Horatio, after he has related his clever joke-murder of two former companions:

Horatio: So Guildenstern and Rosencrantz go to't.
Hamlet: Why, man, they did make love to this employment.
They are not near my conscience, their defeat
Does by their own insinuation grow.
'Tis dangerous when the baser nature comes
Between the pass and fell incensed points
Of mighty opposites. (V. ii. 56–62)

This brings us to the darker aspect of Hamlet himself, for these are two more corpses to be put to Hamlet's account, as it comes to seem, by this stage of the play, that his black clothes are the sign not only that he mourns the death of his father, but that he is himself a Death, and will bring death to numerous others, as well as to the murderer of his father. In this he resembles Philip the Good, who killed many others while he delayed confronting his enemy. The humble princes in black were not self-effacing to the point of passivity: they were active, each stands before a mound of corpses. Philip II killed very many; Alfonso of Aragon was also a warrior. Hamlet cannot approach their score—he never mounts the throne—but certainly he is dangerous to know, killing indirectly, or directly but by mistake, in what proves to be a grisly black-comedy of errors, not only Ophelia but her whole surviving family, and not only sentencing old schoolfriends to death, but seeing his mother die too before, at very long last, he manages to kill his father's killer. As Horatio says to Fortinbras: 'So shall you hear of ... casual slaughters'.

There are no contemporary illustrations to *Hamlet,* and indeed no illustrations at all of the play for more than 100 years after it was first performed, so I have taken the liberty of side-stepping history and enlisting Shakespeare's best-of-all illustrator, Delacroix. *The Murder of Polonius* catches the tragi-comic spirit of the play, with its elements of grotesque, the feet of Polonius just showing beneath the arras. The young mother holds back her son, who, in this illustration, turns from being what in previous scenes he was, the 'sweet prince' (Delacroix had a woman model for him), and begins to show an aspect of the demonic: caught on the edge of becoming a killer, a person who has conjured death and, maybe, invited damnation. His mouth and face harden, as one hardens before hitting. His eye is strange, almost a fish-eye, both large and with something dead about it: an eye faced with a problem like a cliff, intractable, insurmountable.

One might say that Hamlet was unfortunate, no killer by nature: the black inside him is grieving not murderous. But he is willing to accept the role of a Death, taking it as an appointment on the highest authority:

> . . . For this same lord
> I do repent; but heaven hath pleas'd it so,
> To punish me with this and this with me,
> That I must be their scourge and minister.
> (III. iv. 174–7)

Being a scourge was almost a vocation, just as Tamburlaine was 'the scourge of God'. 'Black' matters are not clear-cut. Black—blackness—is a negative quantity that makes a positive impression, and consequently, almost inevitably, black has tended, in matters both of value and of dress, to be paradoxical. In particular there is a recurring irony, where black may be shown to be not so black—as in dashing, stylish, attractive black, or respectable black, 'decent black', or pious, humble, godly black—and yet does prove, after all, to have sinister elements, as humble, penitential self-punishing black becomes stern judicial black

that will tie people to pieces of wood and burn them. In Hamlet's case we see a person suffering evil and bereavement, and precisely through taking these things so to heart, becoming infected by death and death-dealing. So, on the moral level, the Hamlet who suffers such grief for his father—and who, in his grief, is tolerant of his father's sins—becomes Hamlet the preacher, standing in moral tyranny over his mother:

> Nay, but to live
> In the rank sweat of an enseamed bed,
> Stew'd in corruption, honeying and
>   making love
> Over the nasty sty! (III. iv. 91–4)

For criticism Hamlet has proved paradoxical: for Goethe he was 'a lovely, pure, noble and most moral nature', while August von Schlegel concluded that he 'is not solely impelled by necessity to artifice and dissimulation, he has a natural inclination for crooked ways; he is a hypocrite towards himself.' D. H. Lawrence wrote:

> I had always felt an aversion from Hamlet: a creeping, unclean thing he seems, on the stage, whether he is Forbes Robertson or anybody else. His nasty poking and sniffing at his mother, his setting traps for the King, his conceited perversion with Ophelia make him always intolerable. The character is repulsive in its conception, based on self-dislike and the spirit of disintegration.[22]

Lawrence's reflections were suggested by a provincial Italian performance, in which the itinerant Hamlet 'was absorbed in his own self-important self-consciousness':

> His legs, in their black knee breeches, had a crawling, slinking look; he always carried the black rag of a cloak, something for him to twist about as he twisted in his own soul overwhelmed by a sort of inverted perversity.

Lawrence connects this dislike and self dislike with a sense of corruption in the flesh, nourished in the preceding hundreds of years.

It does seem a deep feature of the sensibility out of which the play comes, that its sense of the body's corruption by death is united with its sense of corruption by sin. Hamlet's fascination with death and the rotting body is moralized in a disgust with the fleshy, sweating, coupling human animal, and he feeds on such thoughts and invites them to possess him, wrapping himself in them as in his black cloak. The whole development of the black fashion, in priests, princes, merchants, courtiers, pious citizens—black never shedding altogether its penitential character—occurred in a culture in which a preoccupation with sin and depravity was merged with a preoccupation with death. The vocation of the monk was a vocation of mourning; Philip the Good was cloaked always, however richly, in his father's death; Philip II made his own cult of death, not only prolonging his mourning for Elizabeth, but making his Palace of the Escorial a grand sarcophagus, where he could sit, in a small chapel beneath his living-quarters, surrounded by the gathered corpses of his ancestors. The black-clad merchants commissioned paintings of themselves, kneeling in prayer for what was to happen to them at death. The painting of Christ that Holbein executed with most conviction is not the 'Noli Me Tangere', but his painting of Christ as a sacred corpse. Hamlet—both the prince and the play—shows Shakespeare as the spokesman, or poet, of a culture's 200 years of fascination with death and sin in one:

> That skull had a tongue in it, and could sing once. How the knave jowls it to th' ground, as if 'twere Cain's jawbone, that did the first murder. This might be the pate of a politician ... Or of a courtier ... and now my Lady Worm's, chopless, and knocked about the mazard with a sexton's spade ... Here's another. Why, may not that be the skull of a lawyer? Where be his quiddities now? ... Alas, poor Yorick ... He hath bore me on his back a thousand times, and now—how abhorred in my imagination it is. My gorge rises at it. Here hung those lips that I have kissed I know not how oft. Where be your gibes now? ... not one now to mock your own grinning? Quite chop-fallen? Now get you to my lady's chamber and tell her, let her paint an inch thick, to this favour she must come. Make her laugh at that ... But soft, but soft awhile. Here comes the King ... Who is this they follow? And with such maimed rites? ... What, the fair Ophelia! ... I lov'd Ophelia ... Dost come here to whine, to outface me with leaping in her grave? Be buried quick with her, and so will I. (V. i. 74–274)

It was at once as the black-clad high-life hero, and as the embodiment of the cult of death, that Hamlet left a mark on the stage of his own day—in, for instance, the figure of Vindice in *The Revenger's Tragedy*, who first appears holding the skull of his dead love. It is as if Tourneur had wanted to elide into a single dramatic tableau the moment when Hamlet, holding a skull, talks about his lady's favour, and the subsequent moment when he turns to behold the dead Ophelia carried before him.

Hamlet is not darkened solely by grief and death, he is in addition, famously, a representation of the Humour of Melancholy. 'Melancholy' means literally 'black bile': of the various human types or Humours, Melancholy was the one most frequently discussed (notably in Burton's *Anatomy of Melancholy*). There was a traditional representation of the melancholy man, both in popular verse and in stage performance, precisely as the man in black—as a man half-hidden by a long black cloak and a large black hat (who then sounds like an English perception of the man of Spanish fashion, complete with solemn style). John Davies, writing of 'yonder melancholy gentleman', cited 'his long cloak ... his great black feather'.[23] By stage tradition, Hamlet is bareheaded, but equally he traditionally employs a black cloak, and certainly he is dressed in black. This is not to make Hamlet a stereotype of Melancholy. He seems rather to represent Shakespeare's offer, in relation to that stereotype, to present the sensation of the deeper melancholia. Death loses its sting for Hamlet, and becomes like a dream, because life is become lifeless and all its roads dead ends. The universe, and man, are dust. As you take arms against your troubles they become a sea not an army, the sword turns back on you as in suicide, but already you are drowned in a death like troubled sleep. An observant psychologist, Shakespeare gives Hamlet symptoms of depressive illness: he can contemplate, and inflict, pain and death without affect. The play's power in this presentment has penetrated subsequent literature deeply, doubtless because the play speaks from a melancholia nurtured by the culture—one cultivated in precisely those places this study has visited, in Europe's many enclosures of dying thoughts, and especially in its high-walled gardens of mourning monks and mourning kings, and its many manses where pastors have pondered depravity.

This is not the place to attempt an aetiology of melancholy: though one may also note, apropos both of Hamlet and of other literary Hamlets to be discussed below, that in Shakespeare's presentation the melancholic's vision goes with a damage to his ability to love, and with a tendency to see—in his particular dark glass—a blank, or fear, or death, when he looks at women. His blackness includes a derogation of the feminine ('Frailty, thy name is woman!'), though the feminine in himself is uncertainly negated. He knows he is no Fortinbras: one might call him Shakespeare's most feminine hero. This is not to say that he is without a princely manliness: rather that he is—as he has always been found—not only the darkest, but also the most sensitive, most whole, the richest and most fascinating personality and persona of all the lead roles in Shakespeare. It was not without reason that Delacroix had a woman model for him. He is the male role in Shakespeare that has, most often, been played by women—most famously by Sarah Bernhardt.

There is something that seems deliberately indeterminate about Hamlet. It does appear that Shakespeare had a generalizing intention for him. When we laugh at the exchange—

> *Gravedigger:* . . . young Hamlet . . . he that is mad and sent into England.
> *Hamlet:* Ay, marry. Why was he sent into England?
> *Gravedigger:* Why, because he was mad. He shall recover his wits there, or if he do not, 'tis no great matter there.
> *Hamlet:* Why?
> *Gravedigger:* 'Twill not be seen in him there. There the men are as mad as he. (v. i. 143–50)

—it may be that for Shakespeare this was so good a joke just because at the same time he was not joking. For there were more Jacobean young Englishmen than John Donne, who shared Hamlet's fascination with death-jokes and sin, with wit and with winding-sheets. But beyond any, as it were, English connection, Hamlet has been identified with the shadow-side of the Renaissance, and not only with its fashion of melancholy, but with its whole sceptical interrogation of an ungoverned universe. His speech is fed by streams of Erasmian and Montaigne-minded thought, attacking the confidences of the late Renaissance world. He lives in a restlessness of suspicion and fear, in a mistrust of courts and kings and elders, and of soldiers and wars as well as of women and the body. If he says at one point, contemplating death stoically, 'The readiness is all', it is only to add a few lines later 'Thou wouldst not think how ill all's here about my heart'. Shakespeare himself seems not to want to tie him down, and makes it impossible, I think, to say where the lines should be drawn between his philosophical pessimism and his sickness of soul. He does seem to personate a final turn of the European ascetic tradition, a rejection of the world and its snares not so much in deference to Heaven as in a facing of the fact that the universe is dark, together with the resolution, ironic and with some humour, to live in it so. It is not surprising that every age since Shakespeare's has found him up to date, or that he has been of such interest to later dark writers like Melville and Beckett. He will remain current, a man whose black clothes, finally, are the dress of his dark ontology.

A BLACK GENERAL

The move to Othello, in the next tragedy Shakespeare wrote, is a move to a different and deeper black: not adoptive black—dressed black—but natural black, the black of black skin, which is wholly of life not death. On the English stage, this black is still in a sense adoptive, since the actors playing Othello have usually been white: but Othello's dark presence on stage has no association of penitence, asceticism, melancholy. Rather, he is a figure of energetic dignity, almost—in his language—of majesty. As the drama accelerates one is likely to associate his blackness with his big intensity, his force of passion, opaque blood. He seems visibly to be, when loving, the dark-night intensity that passion has; later he seems to be, in person, the darker darkness inside passion. It is notable then that he in his jealousy, and Hamlet in his disgusted puritanism, may use the same language about sex.

It was already clear that Hamlet's language of asceticism, whether he was castigating Ophelia or his mother, was as much the language of jealousy as of morality: all he can see in any woman is Gertrude's frailty, and even his own father has to intervene (spectrally) to make him desist when he attacks Gertrude with language more apt coming from her husband than from her son. Jealousy was a part of Hamlet's blackness, and in this sense it is perhaps as though, in Hamlet's black clothes, the looming vague presence of the waiting Othello was starting to show through the earlier protagonist; or as if Hamlet's 'suits of woe' have in the next tragedy passed into the black being of the hero.

This is a fancy, but one that may serve to raise, for proper consideration, the sensitive,

vital issue I have not so far touched on in this study of blackness—the issue of race (there is no suggestion, in the play, that Othello wears black clothes). For it is undoubtedly a fact that the whole negative ethical imagery, whereby blackness and darkness mean 'dead', 'bad', 'not there', made its contribution, over the centuries, to the European disparagement of Africans. Apart from the rapacity and cruelty frequently, and the blithe blind trust in an intrinsic superiority always, with which West Europeans treated the 'salvages' they encountered in their voyages, the fact that the African 'salvages' had black skins meant that they incurred a reduplicated stigma. As Malcolm X has observed, it is clear from a perusal of the *Oxford English Dictionary* that the 'dark' and 'bad' values of 'black' regularly attached to Africans, both in popular and in literary discourse. The *OED* is a useful selection of testimony precisely because its avowed purpose was simply to exemplify neutrally the different words applied to Africans—without prejudice, as it were. And whether or not an element of unconscious bias was present in the minds of the selectors of citations, the various words used for Africans have their own built-in bias, which wanted to find the blackness of Africans distinctly 'other' and ugly: 'Ther was no grace in the visage ... Sche loketh forth as doth a More' (Gower, 1390); 'The uggly Maurians ... ' (Barclay 1509); 'Out there flew, ryght blacke and tedyous, A foule Ethyope' (Hawes 1509).

Of course, not all the references are as insulting as these; the sense of racial 'difference' perhaps shows especially in the recurring proverbial saw, to the effect that the blackness of the African cannot be washed off: 'I wash a Negro, Loosing both paines and cost' (Middleton 1611); 'As sure to miss, As they, that wash an Ethiope's Face' (Villiers 1688); 'In the most elegant language, she labours to wash the Aethiop white' (Wesley Sermon lxviii, 1791). Of course, it never occurs to the European natives that their whiteness, or pinkness, or faded blotchy sallowness, might be a pigment applied to their surface, which could be washed off. But the proverbs about washing or not washing off the Africans' blackness all imply that, first, one would naturally think such blackness had been painted on, because it isn't naturally or rightly human to be so black, and second, the realization—no it can't come off, they really are as black as that. Perhaps the crowning injustice for Africans was that devils were regularly represented as black, facilitating many casually obnoxious equations: 'A kind of fish called Negroes or Sea-Devils' (J. Davies 1666); 'He's dead long since, or gone to the Blackamores below' (Cowley 1663). Moreover, not only devils, but The Devil is often black, or manifest as 'a black man'. 'The Devil in the shape of a black man lay with her in the bed' (Glanvill 1681). The last, and cruellest, twist comes in the other, complimentary, proverb: 'Divels are not so blacke as they be painted' (Lodge 1596); 'For the Devill is not so black as he is painted' (Howell 1642). In other words, the Devil's black could be washed off, whereas the African really is as black as he appears to be painted.

There are some neutral references. But what are harder to find in the *OED* are references unqualified in their admiration of Africans. Popular debate about negroes was prejudicial, and was liable, even up to the eighteenth century, to be detained by such issues as 'Whether Negroes shall rise in the last day'. The answer, given by one popular almanac, was 'He shall not arise with that Complexion, but leave it behind him in the Darkness of the Grave, exchanging it for a brighter and a better.' Individual intelligent commentators had recognized the relativism of the human sense of beauty, among them Sir Thomas Browne:

> Whereas men affirm this colour was a Curse, I cannot make out the propriety of that name, it neither seemingly so to them, nor reasonably unto us; for they take so much content therein, that they esteem deformity by other colours, describing the Devil, and terrible objects, white.[24]

He quotes pertinently from the Song of Songs, 'I am black but comely'. And Ben Jonson wrote, for performance at court in 1605, the *Masque of Blacknesse,* 'because it was her Majesty's will'. On a shore peopled with tritons and sea-maids, Oceanus ('the colour of his flesh, blue') greets Niger ('in forme and colour of an Æthiope'), welcoming to Britain 'the Masquers, which were twelve Nymphs, Negros, and the daughters of Niger'. Niger, in the principal speech, celebrates the beauty of black women: 'in their black, the perfect'st beauty grows … their beauties conquer in great beauty's war'. In particular he celebrates 'the fix'd colour of their curled hair (Which is the highest grace of dames most faire)'. None the less, it is the argument of the masque that the African women will be better accommodated in England, where 'their beauty shall be scorch'd no more'. And near the close Jonson takes away much of what he has given by introducing a white Æthiopia ('her garments white and silver'). Æthiopia personifies the moon, which, Jonson claims, the Æthiopians worshipped by this name. Æthiopia then celebrates Britain, its weather, and especially its sun (and King),

> Whose beams shine day, and night, and are of force
> To blanch an Æthiope, and revive a Corse.
> His light scientiall is, and (past mere nature)
> Can salve the rude defects of every creature.

The black nymphs, it seems, must be white nymphs at last, and so not problematic in this Britain of Jonson's, on which, it appears, the sun never sets. The value of black, in the masque, is its value as spectacle.[25]

It is dangerous, nevertheless, to generalize about a culture on the evidence of words alone. The European visual tradition has a more attractive emphasis. The assumption, for instance, that one of the Magi who attended Christ's nativity was an African meant that in the pictures that truly had pride of place in the culture—altarpieces—there was the recurring representation of a noble and wise African monarch. Such a monarch, handsome, young and dignified, clad both majestically and elegantly in black robes, may be seen in the centre panel of Geertgen tot Sint Jans's *Adoration* of c.1465. Maybe it is apt that it is a Burgundian artist who realizes the beauty of a black man in black. And this king's black gown is not itself African: it is a black gown, lined with brown fur, such as a Duke of Burgundy might have worn. The elegance of this Christian African king is heightened by his erect stance (though his head is slightly tilted towards Christ), and by the long steep diagonal of the hem of his gown. The lines that make his figure are the most decisive of any figure in the picture, while at the same time his conspicuous blackness draws attention to him. In the picture's composition he balances, also, the figure of Mary on the other side, whose own robes, as is frequently the case in Burgundian nativities, are so deeply dark-blue they are nearly black (blue and black, it may be noted, had been ecclesiastically identical).

Yet even so, and in this context, and with all this said, the nobility of the African Magus is not unqualified. For if it is part of the visual tradition that one of the Magi was African, it is also part of the tradition that the other two were European or European-looking, and that they took precedence over the African Magus. Often the African Magus is behind the other two, both in the sense that he is the third or last of them to enter the stable, and in the sense that they are nearer the foreground of the picture than he is. Often again, as in this painting, the African is standing while the other two Magi kneel—standing as if he must wait his turn to kneel: their turn comes first. At the same time, the fact that he is standing makes him appear to be in attendance on the other two. It is true that often the African Magus is the youngest, so he may cede place to the others for reasons of youth, not race; and then his relative youth allows the painter to make him the most handsome of the Magi. On the other hand, the fact that he is younger gives the European-looking Magi the

advantage in authority. Furthermore, it would seem part of the tradition that it is the African Magus who brings the myrrh, the bitter herb, as against the purely attractive gold and frankincense. The features I mention are standard: they maybe seen in this painting, and in most Adorations (consider, for instance, the *Adorations* of Rubens). A further feature of Geertgen's work is that the upright beam at the corner of the stable comes down in such a way as both to frame, and mark off, the African Magus, while the steep perspective of the roof-beam, co-operating with the diagonals of the African's gown, seem almost to displace him to a wing of the altarpiece. Yet, none of these considerations qualify the main impression given, that, at any rate in Burgundy in these years, black could be seen not only as a beautiful and elegant colour to wear, but as a beautiful and elegant colour to be. Fine-looking Africans may be found in other paintings, and not only in Adorations. The few Africans in Bosch's *Garden of Earthly Delights* are handsome and slim-limbed. It is also true that one can find in visual art more or less disparaging visualizations of Africans, corresponding to the linguistic clichés. There is, furthermore, the neutral but hardly honorific use of Africans for visual punning—a use that enrols the African as an unusual creature, maybe fabulous, like a griffin—which we find especially in heraldry, but also in painting. In the portrait of Alexander Mornauer, town clerk of Landshut in Bavaria in the 1470s, the object nearest to us in the picture's foreground is the small ring on Mornauer's thumb, with the device of a Moor's head. Presumably Mornauer wore that ring, and both he and the painter are glad to see it foregrounded, because both enjoy the pun on the first syllable of Mornauer's name. Of course, the pun only has its charge because Mornauer is not a Moor, and it is unthinkable that he should be one. At the same time, the fact that Mornauer is dressed almost entirely in black—both out of civic *gravitas* and out of perfect fashionableness of the 1470s—gives the pun a further, not malign, twist. If Mornauer has the Moor's head on his hand, he has also clothed his own body so as to match the Moor's.

In this context, one might ask more distinctly how the author of *Othello* presents Africa and Africans, not only in that play but in his oeuvre at large. On this question, as on most, Shakespeare is multiple-minded. Racial contempt for black Africans can certainly be found: 'Sylvia ... shewes Iulia but a swarthy Ethiope' (II. vi. 26). Such a reference is hardly substantial, however. A fuller indication of the range and sway of attitudes available to a Renaissance intellectual is given in the early play *Titus Andronicus,* in the presentation of Aaron the Moor, the lover of Titus's captive, Tamora, Queen of the Goths. For the Romans, Aaron's blackness is ugly, abhorrent, and bad, to be spoken about with vehement sarcasm:

> *Bassanius:* Believe me, queen, your swarth Cimmerian
> Doth make your honour of his body's hue,
> Spotted, detested, and abominable. (II. 3. 72–4)

Even the sympathetic Lavinia is contemptuous:

> ... I pray you, let us hence,
> And let her joy her raven-coloured love.
> (II. 3. 82–3)

Given these voicings of traditional attitude, it is worth noting that the young Shakespeare gives Tamora herself—no African—a long and beautiful love-speech to Aaron, which shows that (unlike the noble Romans) neither she, nor Shakespeare writing her part, have any problem:

> My lovely Aaron, wherefore look'st thou sad,
> When everything doth make a gleeful boast?
> The birds chant melody on every bush,
> The snake lies rolled in the cheerful sun,
> The green leaves quiver ...
> Under their sweet shade, Aaron, let us sit ...
> We may, each wreathed in the other's arms,
> Our pastimes done, possess a golden slumber ...
> (II. 3. 10–26)

Aaron, none the less, is the villain of the play, and when the inevitable equation is made between his black skin and evil, the words are put by Shakespeare into his own mouth:

> ... O, how this villainy
> Doth fat me with the very thoughts of it!
> Let fools do good, and fair men call for grace,
> Aaron will have his soul black like his face.
> (III. i. 202–5)

With his own sarcasm, he acknowledges that the Grace of God is a product reserved for fair-skinned fair-thinkers, while the alliteration makes these 'fair' men foolish, good grace to them. In other words, as one might expect of an African villain on the Elizabethan stage, he is presented as wanting, zestfully, to be a black devil. He is then confronted with just these clichés, when the nurse, bringing his own baby on stage, describes it with popular prejudiced superstitious idiocy:

> *Aaron:* ... What hath he sent her?
> *Nurse:* A devil.
> ... A joyless, dismal, black, and sorrowful issue!
> Here is the babe, as loathsome as a toad
> Amongst the fair-faced breeders of our clime.
> (IV. 2. 61–8)

To which Aaron very sympathetically rejoins:

> Zounds, ye whore! is black so base a hue?
> Sweet blowse, you are a beauteous blossom, sure. (IV. 2. 71–2)

And presently he defends his son and his colour with a grandeur of heroic diction that prefigures Othello himself—with, also, at last and justly, a defiance of the white race for its limey colour, pallid or painted:

> I tell you, younglings, not Enceladus,
> With all his threat'ning band of
>   Typhon's brood,
> Nor great Alcides, nor the god of war,
> Shall seize this prey out of his father's hands.
> What, what, ye sanguine,
>   shallow-hearted boys!
> Ye white-lim'd walls! ye alehouse painted signs!
> Coal-black is better than another hue,

In that it scorns to bear another hue; . . .
  (IV. 2. 93–100)

Still, for the action of the play, increasingly he is a black devil. Lucius calls the child, to Aaron, 'this growing image of thy fiend-like face' (V. i. 45). And, like a fiend, Aaron not only commits evil but makes sick-black jokes about the evil others do, saying of the mutilated Lavinia 'Why, she was washed, and cut, and trimmed!' (V. iii. 122). At the end he is arraigned as the black source of black evil in the play, 'Chief architect and plotter of these woes' (V. iii. 122), though actually the most hideous acts have been performed by others. He is sentenced to be buried 'breast-deep in earth' and starved to death. In a late medieval or Renaissance perspective, this was an apt punishment, since black was the colour of earth: according to Jehan Courtois, black represented earth, and humbled us by teaching us that we come from earth, that we are made of earth, and that we will return to earth. ('La couleur noire', Jehan says in his final reference to it, 'nous enseigne comment nous debvons penser que nous sommes venuz de terre en nous humiliant, que nous sommes faictz de terre et que nous retournerons en terre'.) Shakespeare's revelations of an emancipated view are then momentary: the main tendency of his play conforms safely to the European assumption that a black African is likely to be a black devil, an assumption that was also a stage convention—witness Muly Hamet, the 'foul ambitious Moor' in George Peele's *Battle of Alcazar* (1594). There is no suggestion of devilry in Shakespeare's later play *The Merchant of Venice,* where a prince of Morocco appears briefly as one of Portia's suitors. He could indeed seem a preliminary sketch for Othello, since he has a solemnly high notion of his own worth, is not brilliant, and speaks with a grand, picturesque, elevated diction (in other words, he conforms to a stereotype subtler than the black-devil, but still a patronizing one):

The Hyrcanian deserts and the vasty wilds
Of wide Arabia are as thoroughfares now

For princes to come view fair Portia.
  (II. vii. 41–3)

He leaves with the same dignity: so there is a shock for us in the brusque couplet with which Portia, our heroine, sums up the scene we have seen:

A gentle riddance. Draw the curtains, go.
Let all of his complexion choose me so.
  (II. vii. 78–9)

The change, emancipation, brave blow struck, is then momentous when we come to Othello, in which another lady of Venice is wooed by an African, and loves him and marries him, with no suggestion from the playwright of her having any difficulty, or anything mischievous or unnatural in her attraction, or anything other in her than the finest and most admirable whole-hearted love. Others in the play make those insinuations, showing a fair range of the inflections of racist malice, but the effect of all such comments is only to make clearer the pure-heartedness, and courageous persistence, in Desdemona's love. Whether in the presentation of Othello himself there is any element of racial condescension is a more delicate question; we can easily say if we want to that it is an element of his 'character' that he is simple-hearted (though big-hearted), extremely credulous, and solemnly and grandly egoistic, both in general and in his love as well—which has a different accent from Desdemona's:

She loved me for the dangers I had passed,
And I loved her that she did pity them.
  (I. iii. 167–8)

Though his character has a magnificently noble outline, and a noble as well as a jealous-violent intensity, it is not subtle, and it would be hard to argue that Shakespeare enters into Othello's psychology with the same intricate inwardness with which he realizes Hamlet or Macbeth. More so than the other tragic heroes, Othello can seem a case of The Other as Tragic Hero. Critics have felt that even Othello himself, in his soliloquies, does not quite fully enter his own experience, but rather 'is cheering himself up' (T. S. Eliot) or 'contemplating the spectacle of himself ... is overcome with the pathos of it' (F. R. Leavis).[26]

Certainly the play seems, at least as much as *Hamlet,* to rely much on the 'spectacle' of its hero. And the blackness of Othello's skin contributes to theatrical effects that can hardly help being, in performance after performance, magnificently and more-than-magnificently beautiful. In a wonderful critical jump, Emrys Jones, in *The Origins of Shakespeare,* finds an affinity between an entrance of Othello, and the torch-lit scene of Christ's arrest at Gethsemane: the tall dignified hero arraigned but refusing flight or evasion, restraining his supporters' ardour and quietly stilling their swords. 'The scene', Jones writes, 'is usually (in my experience) the most brilliant visual moment in the play ... its swords and torches and chiaroscuro effects ('Dusk faces with white silken turbans wreath'd') make it, despite its brevity and rapidity, intensely memorable and beautiful.'[27] But though the Othello of these scenes is so different from Aaron, the 'black devil' is not wholly forgotten. It is, of course, one of the black–white ironies of the play that even though Othello succumbs to jealousy and vengeful murderousness, still the truly black soul in the play is not his but that of his white lieutenant Iago: he is the profoundly jealous-evil 'demi-devil' and 'hellish villain'. There is in the play a structure of references to angels and devils that expand its love-jealousy-and-murder drama into dimensions of religious grace, damnation and evil. A nineteenth-century illustration by Sir John Gilbert attempts to convey this quality, bathing the vulnerable Desdemona, who lies asleep in bed, with a more than natural light and brightness, and representing Othello, who looks not like an African but like a European in black make-up, as a man at once black, and, as it were, in the darkest shadow.

And it is a part of the structure of heaven/hell references that the figure of the black devil should prove, at the crucial moment, to be Othello himself:

> *Othello:* 'Twas I that killed her.
> *Emilia:* O, the more angel she,
> And you the blacker devil. (V. ii. 131–2)

She says again, 'Thou art a devil.' He has earlier associated his colour with the 'bad' forms of blackness, seeing his reputation (a prominent issue in this play) specifically as blackened:

> ... My name, that was as fresh
> As Dian's visage, is now begrim'd, and black
> As mine own face ... (III. iii. 392–4)

'*My* name' is the Folio reading; the second Quarto has '*Her* name', and Othello can think of Desdemona, unfaithful, as blackened or black. He calls her, for instance, a 'fair devil'—that is, a white version of a black being. At that key stage in a Shakespeare tragedy, when the hero abdicates his soul, Othello is shown, in a posture of prayer, consecrating himself to the black evil he invites to possess him:

> Arise, black vengeance, from thy hollow cell,
> Yield up, O love, thy crown, and hearted
>   throne,
> To tyrannous hate, swell, bosom, with thy
>   fraught,
> For 'tis of aspics' tongues! (III. iii. 454–6)

When Othello learns the hideous mistake he has made, he knows fiends will snatch him, he commands devils to whip him, he belongs with them in hell.

Nor is the issue so metaphysical as I have perhaps made it appear. In the Elizabethan period, the blackness of the black man was popularly associated not only with devilry, but with animality, sexuality, bestiality. There is an endlessness of abusive citations, to the effect that negroes 'are beastly in their living' (Andrew Battell), 'are very greedy eaters ... and very lecherous ... and much addicted to uncleanenesse' (Samuel Purchas), that they have 'large Propagators' (Ogilby), that 'in Ethiopia ... the race of men is very keen and lustful' (Jean Bodin).[28] Iago plays at once on the animal and on the diabolic prejudices in his attempts to madden Desdemona's father: 'Even now, very now, an old black ram / Is tupping your white ewe ... the devil will make a grandsire of you ... you'll have your daughter cover'd with a Barbary horse' (I. i. 88–111). It seems Iago believes his description, since he later announces (somewhat suddenly) 'I do suspect the lusty Moor hath leaped into my seat'. Shakespeare's position is not Iago's: Othello has a generous fineness that moves Iago to hatred. But it does seem also to be in Shakespeare's mind that Othello, being an African, does have strongly in him, for all his nobility, the sexual and animal part of man, which, in jealousy, becomes murderous savagery: '... if there be cords, or knives, poison, or fire ... I'll tear her all to pieces ... Pish! Noses, ears and lips ... I see that nose of yours, but not that dog I shall throw't to ... I will chop her into messes ... Goats and monkeys!' Shakespeare's major tragedies turn on the rising, or raising, of evil, and the horror and thrill of *Othello* is in watching the obscene, tortured, rapt co-operation of Othello and Iago in releasing, conjuring, raising, as one would raise the Devil, the jealous-murderous savage animal in man, hovering in wait below the noblest love. There are manifold ironies in the play: we see an evil white man, who feeds on others' pain, goad a noble black man to murder his white wife. The ironies do not, however, emancipate Othello wholly from the conventional expectation that one would find in a black man both a black devilry and a black animality.

The equivocal residue of colour-mythology in a masterpiece so much about a noble love transcending race and colour barriers—a masterpiece that none the less has by the end affirmed the extreme difficulties of mixed-race marriages—may be taken as an index of how deeply the symbolism of black and blackness was embedded in European sensibility. It must then be with many provisos that one returns to the observation that the different forms of vis-

ible blackness in the consecutive heroes Hamlet and Othello do have a symbolic relation (whatever else is involved of mourning and of race) to the 'darkness' that comes to fill the interior of each of them, and which in each case has a large element of sexual hatred tending to murder.

Shakespeare certainly uses all the resources of theatre to make it clear that both Ophelia and Desdemona are wholly innocent victims of the sombre men who cause their deaths: a reminder again that the black and dark figures I have been discussing have often been figures more of darkness than of light for the women who have stood in their path. A reminder, too, that however self-denying and grave and philosophical the associations of black may be, there is also a recurring connection not only between black and death but more particularly between black and violence. The black of mourning may originate in a violence of grieving, and a violence against the self is part of the whole story of asceticism; but it is violence not only against the self, but against others, including the innocent, that is associated with the black of the Dominicans, and the black of Philip II's court (let alone that of Ivan IV). It is not hard, of course, to associate black with biding anger, with violence stifled, but the violence does not for ever stay stifled. Othello kills Desdemona; and even Prince Hamlet, who can seem the saddest and noblest, and in some ways the most sympathetic, of the many black-clad figures so far mentioned, even he, in those moments when he wakens from his sick sad sombre lassitude of soul, does so usually in order to attack, damage or kill.

NOTES

Reprinted with permission from John Harvey, "From Black in Spain to Black in Shakespeare," in *Men in Black* (London: Reaktion, 1995), 71–113.

1. Baldassare Castiglione, *The Book of the Courtier*, trans. Sir Thomas Hoby [1561], ed. J. H. Whitfield (London, 1974): 116.

2. Quoted in Geoffrey Parker (1979), *Philip II*, London: 177.

3. Parker, *Philip II*: 50–51.

4. Tennyson's *Queen Mary* was published in 1875 and, cut to half its length, produced in 1876 with Henry Irving as Phillip; see Leonée Ormond (1993), *Alfred Tennyson: A Literary Life*, London: 177–83. Philip on the 'autos' is quoted by Parker, *Philip II*: 100.

5. On Russia, I draw especially on Ian Grey (1964), *Ivan the Terrible*, London; also on Prince A.M. Kurbsky's (1965) *History of Ivan the Terrible*, ed. and trans. J. L. I. Fennell, Cambridge.

6. Brian Reade (1951), *The Dominance of Spain, 1550–1660*, London: 10.

7. Antoine de Brunel (1914), 'Voyage d'Espagne', *Revue Hispanique*, 30: 119–375.

8. Peter the Venerable, Letter III: 289.

9. On the black painting of armour, see Claude Blair (1958), *European Armour: circa 1066 to circa 1700*, London: 172. As to the Black Prince, David Hume (1762) refers to 'the heroic Edward, commonly called the Black Prince, from the colour of his armour', in *The History of England from the Invasion of Julius Caesar to the Accession of Henry VII*, London: II, ch. xvi: 232; and another John Harvey notes that there is some rather shadowy evidence that the Black Prince was described in French as clad at the battle of Crécy 'en armure noire en fer bruni', a phrase Harvey translates as 'in black armour of burnished steel', though 'bruni' here, rather than meaning polished, may be closer to its original meaning, to make brown (or dark): see *The Black Prince and his Age* (1976), London: 15. Hubert Cole (1976), in *The Black Prince*, London, refers somewhat indeterminately to 'the sable banners that had given him the name by which he was to be known to history' (9–11). Barbara Emerson (1976) notes more cautiously that 'in 1563 the chronicler Grafton was the first to refer to [Edward of Woodstock] as the Black Prince' (*The Black Prince*, London: 1–2), and the name was given currency by Shakespeare when, in *Henry V*, the Archbishop of Canterbury urges Henry to emulate his 'great uncle . . . Edward the Black Prince' (I. ii. 105). The Clown in Shakespeare's *All's Well That Ends Well* merges Edward of Woodstock and another black and black-clad prince: 'The Black Prince, sir, alias, the Prince of Darkness, alias, the Devil' (IV. v. 45–6).

10. See John W. O'Malley (1993), *The First Jesuits*, Cambridge, MA: 45; O'Malley notes that '*praepositus generalis* is the technical Latin term'.

11. See, for instance, the entry on Luther in F. L. Cross (1958), *The Oxford Dictionary of the Christian Church*, Oxford: 831–3.

12. A Letter from Beza and Others, quoted, with other relevant material, by James L. Ainslie (1940), *The Doctrines of Ministerial Order in the Reformed Churches of the 16th and 17th Centuries*, Edinburgh: 36.

13. See Ainslie, *Doctrines*: 36–7.

14. Revd Hastings Robinson, ed. (1845), *Zurich Letters: 2nd Series*, Cambridge: 357.

15. Calvin's sermon on Micah, and prayer before work, are cited in Alastair Duke, Gillian Lewis and Andrew Pettegree, eds (1992), *Calvinism in Europe, 1540–1610*, London: 30–35.

16. Simon Schama (1987), *The Embarrassment of Riches*, London: 569.

17. See 'Massachusetts Dress Ways' in D. H. Fischer (1969), *Albion's Seed*, New York: 139–46.

18. See Roy Strong (1980), 'Charles I's Clothes for the Years 1633 to 1635', *Costume*, 14: 73–89.

19. Shakespeare quotations are from the *Arden Edition of the Works of William Shakespeare: Hamlet*, ed. Harold Jenkins (1982), London; *The Merchant of Venice*, ed. John Russell Brown (1959), London; *Othello*, ed. M. R. Ridley (1958), London; *Titus Andronicus*, ed. J. C. Maxwell (1953), London.

20. See Johan Huizinga (1998), *The Waning of the Middle Ages*, New York: 12 and 40–41.

21. My remarks on Alfonso's jests draw not only on Vespasiano da Bisticci but also on conversations with Dr Anthony Close, of the Modern and Medieval Languages Faculty at Cambridge, who is at present editing a Spanish jest-collection.

22. Goethe and Schlegel are quoted in the *Casebook, Shakespeare: Hamlet*, ed. John Jump (1968), London: 26–7. In D. H. Lawrence's

Twilight in Italy (first published 1916), see chapter 3, 'The Theatre'; the quotation is from p. 75 in the Penguin edition (1960).

23. 'Yonder melancholie gentleman … his long cloake, or his great blacke Feather', lines 1 and 15, 'Meditations of a Gull', Epigrammes, 47, *The Poems of Sir John Davies,* ed. Robert Krueger (1975), Oxford: 150.

24. On colour at resurrection, *The Athenian Oracle: Being an Entire Collection of the Valuable Questions and Answers in the Old Athenian Mercuries* (1703), London: I: 435–6, quoted in Joseph R. Washington Jr (1984), *Anti-Blackness in English Religion, 1500–1800,* New York: 19; Sir Thomas Browne (1912),

The Works of Sir Thomas Browne, ed. Charles Sayle, Edinburgh: II: 383–4.

25. *Ben Jonson,* eds C. H. Herford Percy and Evelyn Simpson (1941), Oxford: VII, 'The Masque of Blacknesse': 169–80.

26. T. S. Eliot (1951), 'Shakespeare and the Stoicism of Seneca', *Selected Essays,* 3rd edn, London: 130; F. R. Leavis (1962), 'Diabolic Intellect and the Noble Hero', *The Common Pursuit,* Harmondsworth: 152.

27. *The Origins of Shakespeare* (1977), London: 78.

28. I take these quotations from the very full presentation of many aspects of attitudes to Africans in Winthrop D. Jordan's (1968) *White over Black,* Chapel Hill, NC: 33–5.

2

THE THREE-PIECE SUIT

David Kuchta

A cultural crisis shook seventeenth-century England's political, economic, social, and moral fabric. The meanings of consumption were debated by Whig and Tory, country and court, Puritan and Anglican, mercantilist and bullionist. Through the course of this debate, a new ideology emerged to oppose and undermine the cultural and political authority of the Stuart court. Political critics of court luxury saw conformity to fashion as incompatible with traditional English liberties. Religious critics condemned the idolatry of 'soft clothes' and called for the display of modesty. Economic critics promoted the consumption of manly English wool over presumably immoral and effeminate imports. Following fashion meant conceding to the absolutist claims of the crown, to the seductive attractions of the material world, and to the enervating lure of foreign luxuries. Together these critiques combined to create a new public image for England's rulers, a new aesthetics of upper-class masculinity, a new image of the English gentleman centred around purportedly productive and virtuous consumer habits: the hardy beef-eater, the temperate ale-drinker, the wearer of wool. In oppositional ideology, England would be rescued by aristocratic gentlemen changing their consumer practices, changing their image from one of luxury and effeminacy to one of industry and frugality. The good example of the court would stop England from declining into tyranny, luxury, popery, and foppery. 'Most of these evils would be easily pre-vented', Privy Councillor Samuel Fortrey advised the restored Charles II in 1663,

> if only his Majesty would be pleased to commend to his people, by his own example, the esteem and value he hath of his own commodities ... besides it seems to be more honourable for a King of England, rather to become a pattern to his own people, than to conform to the humours and fancies of other nations, especially when it is so much to his prejudice.[1]

Charles I had found the seventeenth-century crisis much to his prejudice. Samuel Fortrey hoped that Charles II, by his good example, would not share the same fate.

Samuel Fortrey was not the only adviser of Charles II who warned him of the dangers of living in sartorial splendour. Like Fortrey, John Evelyn counselled that, rather than a new royal proclamation, a new, modest, and manly example should be the course of sartorial reform:

> when his Majesty shall fix a standard at Court, there will need no sumptuary laws to repress and reform the lux which men so much condemn in our apparel ... Doubtless, would the great persons of England but own their nation, and assert themselves as they do, by making choice of some virile and comely fashion, which should incline to neither extreme, and be constant to it, 'twould prove of infinite more reputation to us, than now that there is nothing fixed, and the liberty so exorbitant.[2]

Though the monarchy was restored in 1660, certainly nothing was fixed, as Charles II had inherited the instabilities and criticisms of his father's reign, including criticisms of the lux which men so much condemned in the court's apparel. In the eyes of contemporaries like Evelyn, sartorial stability was a first step toward political stability. 'Let it be considered', Evelyn advised the king in 1661, 'that those who seldom change the mode of their country, have as seldom altered their affections to the Prince'— words not to be taken lightly one year after the Restoration.[3]

Six years after his restoration, Charles II did attempt to become a pattern to his own people, an attempt that led to the introduction of the modern three-piece suit. If, as we have seen, masculinist ideas about manners were a central ideological component of the seventeenth-century crisis, equally the seventeenth-century crisis was a central cause of the birth of modern men's fashion. The three-piece suit has its origins in the political, economic, religious, and social crises that shook seventeenth-century England, as Charles II attempted to restore the Stuart crown to its role as arbiter of taste in the face of criticism of its arbitrary rule. Unlike the early Stuart court, however, after the Restoration the crown's role as arbiter of taste would be defined in terms of inculcating new yet purportedly timeless virtues: thrift, modesty, economy, mixed with gentility, nobility, and politeness. Though, as we will see, the early modesty of the three-piece suit would be short-lived, and it would take the Glorious Revolution of 1688 to permanently install modesty as a marker of elite masculinity, the introduction of the three-piece suit was an attempt both to present a new masculine image of virtuous consumption and to reaffirm a monarchical political culture based on aristocratic cultural hegemony. In introducing the three-piece suit, Charles II attempted to appropriate an iconoclastic, oppositional ideology and use it to redefine court culture, thereby restoring the crown's moral authority and political legitimacy.

A style that he promised never to alter, the three-piece suit was to be Charles II's permanent fashion statement, a style that attempted to teach the nobility thrift and put a stop to the seemingly constant alteration of styles, so disruptive of political stability, as John Evelyn believed. Whereas old-regime sartorial policy had attempted to regulate fashion by limiting its diffusion, Evelyn counselled Charles to foster the diffusion of a fashion that would end all fashion change. As such the three-piece suit would be a new mode of sartorial sovereignty: cultural authority would be expressed by elite opposition to luxury, not by making conspicuous consumption the exclusive prerogative of the court. As a response to the seventeenth-century crisis, then, Charles II's introduction of the three-piece suit turned political, religious, and economic criticisms of court culture into a new means of legitimating monarchical power. By redefining his cultural authority using the terms of the opponents of court luxury, Charles II made a fashion of anti-fashion.

Charles II's claim to sartorial sovereignty was thus part of his re-assertion of political legitimacy. ''Tis not a trivial remark (which I have somewhere met with),' John Evelyn had written to the king in 1661, 'that when a nation is able to impose and give laws to the habit of another (as the late Tartars in China), it has (like that of language) prov'd a forerunner of the spreading of their conquests there.'[4] 'Twas not a trivial remark that Evelyn had heard, but an oft-repeated trope about the tyranny of fashion, as we have seen throughout my previous chapter. Evelyn agreed with this oppositional critique of fashion, and yet remained loyal to the crown: 'The mode is a tyrant', Evelyn opined in a familiar refrain, yet qualified, 'and we may cast off his government, without impeachment to our loyalty.'[5] Opposition to the tyranny of fashion need not entail opposition to monarchy. The three-piece suit, which embodied the republican virtue of simplicity, thus marks a royalist appropriation of republican opposition to fashion. With a virile and comely monarchy, subservience to the effeminating tyranny of fashion could be eliminated without eliminating loyalty to the crown. Modesty just might be compatible with monarchy.

The issue of crown expenditures had been the immediate cause of the outbreak of the Civil War, and when Charles II received his annual dispensation from Parliament in 1662, he made it clear that the court would no longer be a centre of conspicuous consumption. In language that he would echo four years later, Charles expressed his desire to assert his sartorial leadership while simultaneously living within his means:

> I do assure you, and I pray assure your friends in the country, that I will apply all you have given me to the utmost improvement of the peace and happiness of the kingdom; and will, with the best advice and good husbandry I can, bring my expenses within a narrower compass. Now I am speaking to you of my own good husbandry, I must tell you that will not be enough: I cannot but observe to you, that the whole nation seems to me a little corrupted in their excess of living. Sure all men spend much more in their clothes, in their diet, in all their expenses, than they have used to do ... I do believe I have been faulty that way myself: I promise you I will reform; and if you will join with me in your several capacities, we shall, by our examples, do more good, both in city and country, than any new laws would do.[6]

For King Charles, a reformation of the court's example would do more good than any sumptuary laws to re-establish 'the peace and happiness of the kingdom', and thus assure the political stability of the new regime. Royal and aristocratic example was economically and politically advantageous, more effective than any new laws in bringing about the happiness of the kingdom.

On October 7, 1666, four years later, Charles II announced his intention to introduce a 'vest' into court fashion, thereby inaugurating the era of the three-piece suit. The adoption of the vest has received deserved attention from costume historians, who have attributed its introduction to anti-French sentiment, Puritan concerns about modesty, and the theatrical uses of vests.[7] The origins of the style itself are confusing: John Evelyn claims to have first seen a vest worn in Bologna by a Hungarian man, and suggested its adoption to the king.[8] Andrew Marvell considered the vest Turkish, putting the following verse into Charles's mouth:

> I will have a fine Tunick a sash and a vest,
> Tho' not rule like the Turk yet I will be so drest,
> And who knows but the mode may soon bring
> in the rest?[9]

John Evelyn and others also referred to the vest as 'oriental' or 'Persian clothing.'[10]

Whatever its stylistic origins, however, contemporaries also considered the vest as a distinctly English mode, one made of English wool, as we will see.[11]

The connections between the 1666 vest and the modern three-piece suit are equally cloudy, since various contemporaries noted a return to French modes in the 1670s (as will be discussed shortly), thus possibly breaking any link between the vest and the modern waistcoat. Yet by the 1670s the French court had apparently adopted a vest of its own, perhaps in imitation of the English.[12] In an unconfirmed report, Samuel Pepys wrote that on November 2, 1666, Louis XIV 'hath, in defiance to the King of England, caused all his footmen to be put into vests, and that the noblemen of France will do the like; which, if true, is the greatest indignity ever done by one prince to another.'[13] It is these vague origins, and confusing lineage, that led one costume historian to consider the 1666 vest as a novelty item, 'an ephemeral mode [with] little or no lasting influence.'[14] Despite this lack of clarity, however, most historians agree with Penelope

Byrde's assessment that by 1670, 'a three-piece suit, in the modern sense, had emerged.'[15] Thus although the 1666 vest regained much of its sartorial splendour in the later Restoration period, we can nonetheless consider the introduction of the three-piece suit as a founding moment in the development of a new aesthetics of masculinity.

The vest's introduction was widely reported by contemporaries, precisely because it was not only a fashion statement but a political and economic policy statement as well. In October 1666, calls for fashion reform were being debated in the Commons, discussed in the Privy Council, disgorged by the pulpit, and demanded from the street. Panic, outrage, and paranoia over September's Great Fire in London had prompted a roundup of the usual suspects: God, the French, and conspicuous consumers. On October 3, 1666, the MP John Milward recorded in his diary that two sermons had been preached before the Commons calling for a national reformation after the fire, and a parliamentary committee was formed to draft legislation 'for the suppression of atheism, swearing, cursing, lying, profaneness and luxury.'[16] On October 10, the Rev. William Sancroft, later archbishop of Canterbury, preached before the king, interpreting the Great Fire as a warning from God against English emulation of 'French pride, and vanity.'[17] The fire was 'a scourge from that nation or nations whose fashions they follow', God's 'stinging and flaming check against all fashion-mongers', as the Puritan divine Thomas Brooks later bellowed.[18]

If not the hand of God, a French agent was seen to be behind the great conflagration, and the fire spurred a wave of anti-French sentiment. On October 7, 1666, the Venetian ambassador to France reported a popular clamour for the removal of French fashions from the English court. In the wake of the fire, the ambassador wrote to the Doge, 'the people shouted that they ... desired that all commerce with France should be prohibited; that no one should dress after the fashion of this nation [France], but that

Parliament should select some to devise a new form of clothes which should be peculiar to that country.'[19] The populace may have appealed to Parliament, but the king was quicker to respond, declaring that same monumental day in world history, 'his resolution of setting a fashion for clothes, which he will never alter', as Samuel Pepys recorded in words worth repeating: 'It will be a vest, I know not well how; but it is to teach the nobility thrift, and will do good.'[20]

The king had moved rapidly to assert his cultural leadership, introducing a modest, anti-French fashion before Parliament did, and teaching the nobility thrift before Parliament or 'the people' taught him the same lesson. According to MP Milward, Parliament began a movement toward restraining the importation of French commodities on October 8, but, according to the *Calendar of State Papers,* it did not discuss sartorial reform until Thursday, October 11, when the Commons proposed a bill 'prohibiting the import of all French manufactures, and requesting a proclamation to that effect. The nation having for several years aped the French too much in their fashions, especially at this season, the King, to avoid the like vanity, has specified that he will wear a vest not after that mode, but will not put it on till Monday, the Duke of York's birthday.'[21] Pepys witnessed the Duke of York try on his new birthday outfit on Saturday the 13th ('it is a fashion the King says he will never change'), while the next day Anthony Wood saw the king 'put on his vest, which he intends to keep in the same fashion.'[22]

After a week of primping and preparing, then, the three-piece suit made its grand entry onto the world historical stage on Monday, October 15, 1666, as Pepys noted in his diary:

this day the King begins to put on his vest, and I did see several persons of the House of Lords, and Commons too, great courtiers, who are in it—being a long cassock close to the body, of black cloth and pinked with white silk under it, and a coat over it, and the legs ruffled with black ribbon like a pigeon's leg—and upon the whole, I wish the King may keep it, for it is a very fine and handsome garment.[23]

The earl of Sandwich was at court in late 1666, though apparently confused his dates, for he sketched in his journal 'the habit taken up by the King and Court of England November 1666 which they call a vest'.[24] Writing his diary years later, John Evelyn takes some deserved credit for the new fashion, but records that October 18 was

> the first time of his Majesty's putting himself solemnly into the Eastern fashion of vest, changing doublet, stiff collar, and cloak, etc. into a comely vest, after the Persian mode ... resolving never to alter it, and to leave the French mode, which had hitherto obtained to our great expense and reproach: upon which diverse courtiers and gentlemen gave his majesty gold, by way of wager, that he would not persist in this resolution: I had some time before indeed presented an invective against that inconstancy, and our so much affecting the French fashion, to his Majesty in which [I] took occasion to describe the comeliness and usefulness of the Persian clothing in the very same manner his Majesty clad himself; this pamphlet I entitled Tyrannus, or the Mode, and gave it his Majesty to read; I do not impute the change which soon happen'd to this discourse, but it was an identity, that I could not but take notice of.[25]

The earl of Danby also noted the king's new clothes, as well as his wager that he would persist in this new habit, 'which is intended for good husbandry.'[26]

As Pepys, Wood, Evelyn, and Danby made clear, the king believed he had found a fashion that would never change—a sartorial stability that would signify the restoration of political stability. Equally important, however, were economic considerations: good husbandry, as Charles himself understood, was a key to the peace and happiness of the kingdom. Economic as well as political rivalry with France was clearly

central to the introduction of the three-piece suit: the abandonment of French styles, as Lord Halifax wrote, was an attempt to 'throw off their fashion, and put on vests, that we might look more like a distinct people, and not be under the servility of imitation.'[27] In his 1669 edition of *Anglia Notitia,* Edward Chamberlayne recorded that 'since the Restoration of the King now reigning, England never saw, for matter of wearing apparel, less prodigality, and more modesty in clothes, more plainness and comeliness, than amongst her nobility, gentry, superior clergy; only the citizens, and country people, and the servants, appear clothed for the most part above and beyond their qualities, estates or conditions; since our last breach with France, the English men (though not the women) quitted the French mode, and took a grave wear, much according to the oriental nations.'[28]

In the Restoration atmosphere of protectionism and 'muscular patriotism',[29] good husbandry was equivalent to promoting a positive balance of trade with France. Good husbandry thus meant wearing English wool. Samuel Newton noted in May 1669 that 'the then English mode' was 'an ordinary stuff vest and tunic of a saddish colour',[30] or made of 'black cloth', as Pepys reported—'cloth' in the seventeenth century being synonymous with wool. As the author of *The Ancient Trades Decayed* noted, 'no person can be offended at [the wearing of wool], because his majesty (for the encouragement of the trade of his own people) is graciously pleased to wear nothing but what is of the English make.'[31] As we have seen, Privy Councillor Samuel Fortrey was among the mercantilists who urged the king to wear English cloth. Like Fortrey, John Evelyn looked to Charles II to restore the balance of trade through his own example:

> how glorious be to our Prince, when he should behold all his subjects clad with the production of his own country, and the people universally enrich'd, whilst the species that we now consume in lace, or export for foreign silks, and

more unserviceable stuffs, would by this means be all sav'd, and the whole nation knit as one to the heart of their sovereign, as to a provident and indulgent father?[32]

In the eyes of royalist reformers like Evelyn, the moral example of patriarchal authority would remove from the court 'insignificant triflers, whose brains are as transparent as their clothes,' while simultaneously restoring the 'nerves of the state,' enriching the nation and securing allegiance to the crown.[33] To this extent, the king's adoption of the vest paralleled his mercantilist-inspired Act for Burial in Woollen of the same year: if the nation's consumers had not worn English wool while alive, they would at least be buried in it.[34]

Charles II thus inaugurated a reign in which England would be led by the modest example of crown and court, 'without much show and with little ceremony', as Jorevin de Rocheford described the Duke of York's three-piece suit.[35] The Restoration court at least temporarily reversed the relation between power and display: by renouncing show and ceremony, the crown could reclaim its moral and masculine authority in the face of political and economic opposition to royal splendour. Through the introduction of the three-piece suit, the Restoration court turned the anti-royalist critique of aristocratic culture to its own advantage to redefine and relegitimate aristocracy and monarchy. Modesty had become a claim to power. With the three-piece suit, a counterculture became court culture.

Although it is difficult to trace the use and transformation of the vest throughout England, anecdotal and visual evidence hint at a relatively rapid diffusion beginning in 1666. John Evelyn notes that he first wore a vest on October 30, 1666, when 'his majesty had brought the whole court to it.'[36] Samuel Pepys was in his new three-piece suit by early November,[37] while Anthony Wood was wearing a vest by the end of the year.[38] Samuel Sturmy is pictured in the frontispiece of his *Mariner's Magazine* wearing a vest in 1669. Vests were worn by some of those attending the funeral of the duke of Albemarle in 1670, the vests often covered with mantles rather than overcoats, due to the formality of the occasion.[39] In 1675, John Ogilby pictured men in vests in his *Brittania,* a cartographic guide to the island. By 1676, vests were apparently worn at Cambridge, as David Loggan depicts in his illustrated guide to the university. By the 1670s, then, it appears that England's male elite had followed the king's example.

Yet the new modest masculinity established by Charles II was short-lived, as the crown abandoned its effort to 'teach the nobility thrift' in the 1670s and 1680s. Introduced as part of the Restoration crown's attempt to restore its legitimacy, the three-piece suit was intrinsically linked with the political state of the nation. In the face of revolutionary criticism of the court's presumed luxury and effeminacy, a politically unsure crown had stabilized itself in part by instituting a fashion that Charles literally wagered he would never alter. Three centuries' hindsight tells us that the modest three-piece suit was a safe bet, but in the short run, given the status of the Restoration court, it was quite a gamble: as the Restoration crown gained stability and renewed its links with France, the male modesty of 1666 was gradually left behind. By the 1670s, the political state of the nation was changing. A more confident court began to adopt the aesthetics that had dominated the old sartorial regime, gaining its still current image as a site of sexual intrigue and private vice, rakes and masquerades, luxury and debauchery. The three-piece suit participated in this restoration of splendour. Various authors noted that at some point in the 1670s the English court returned to the mode of France, itself adopting a more ornate version of the three-piece suit. The marquis of Halifax linked a return of French fashions to the 1670 Treaty of Dover, which secretly restored religious and political ties between England and France. The return to French splendour, Halifax regretted, 'gave a very critical advantage to

France, since it looked like an evidence of our returning to their interest, as well as to their fashion.'[40] Edward Chamberlayne's 1672 edition of *Anglia Notitia* repeated his lines about 'the grave mode' introduced since the Restoration, but added: 'but that is now left.'[41] In his 1674 edition, Chamberlayne added that 'the French mode again [was] taken up.'[42] In 1677, Elkanah Settle wrote that 'vests, your seven years love, grew out of fashion,' thus dating the return to splendour to 1673.[43]

Though these authors disagree on dates, they agree in their portrayal of a Restoration court returning to the conspicuous consumption of the pre-Civil War court. The old sartorial regime was not dead, as Restoration courtiers returned to their cavalier fashion of defending elite prerogatives to be finely dressed. The author of *The Courtier's Calling* of 1675 counselled against too much gravity and seriousness, since 'comeliness has great charms to bewitch hearts ... To know how to dress himself advantageously is not an unprofitable science'.[44] Conspicuous consumption was merely an 'innocent delight', as Charles's chief minister the earl of Clarendon had put it in the late 1660s. Throughout the 1670s and 1680s, the aesthetic of conspicuous consumption, with its positive associations of magnificence and liberality, and its negative connotations of luxury and effeminacy, dominated court culture. In the history of the Restoration court, then, the modest vest of 1666 may have been merely a brief act of contrition and humility by an unstable crown worried about its cultural authority. Its memory, however, was kept alive by reforming royalists who regretted the return to regal splendour. The royalist author of *England's Vanity* struck a note of nostalgia in 1683, praising

the incomparable tunic and vest, so very comely in itself, so very advantageous to the drapers of the kingdom, perhaps the most grave and manlike dress that ever England saw, which had the unhappiness to be brought in too late, and the

hard fate to be sent out again too soon ... But we can never hold when it is well, such an influence hath the French pipe to make us caper after them, in all their follies, to our own dishonour and ruin.[45]

Late in life, John Evelyn lamented that the vest was 'a comely and manly habit: too good to hold, it being impossible for us to leave the monsieurs' vanities in good earnest long.'[46] For Evelyn, the vest had been 'the most graceful, virile and useful mode that ever appeared at court.'[47] Despite its decline, then, the 1666 vest remained as a symbol of a new model of court culture, one which redefined upper-class men as graceful, virile, and useful: graceful, because their new social identity was formed around a practice of refined simplicity rather than sartorial splendour; virile, because they were able to deflect criticism of being effeminate fops; and useful, because they were wearing garments which were 'advantageous to the drapers of the kingdom.' Ultimately, dressing in the innocent delights of the old sartorial regime brought only dishonour and ruin to the Restoration court, and the Glorious Revolution of 1688 would return the three-piece suit to the modest form that Charles II had originally vowed he would never change.

NOTES

Reprinted with permission from David Kuchta, "The Three-Piece Suit," in *The Three-Piece Suit and Modern Masculinity: England, 1550–1850* (Berkeley and Los Angeles: University of California Press, 2002), 77–90.

1. Samuel Fortrey (1673), *Englands Interest and Improvement. Consisting in the Increase of the Store, and Trade of this Kingdom,* London: Nathanael Brook: 25–26.
2. John Evelyn (1661), *Tyrannus or the Mode: In a Discourse of Sumptuary Lawes,* London: G. Bedel and T. Collins: 14–15. Unless otherwise stated, I have chosen to use this edition

of Evelyn's *Tyrannus*. According to his *Diary*, Evelyn 'presented my little trifle of *Sumptuary Laws* intitled *Tyrannus*' to the king on December 4, 1661 (Evelyn, *The Diary of John Evelyn*, ed. Guy de la Bedoyere [London: Boydell, 2004], 3: 306).

3. Evelyn, *Tyrannus*: 15.

4. Evelyn, *Tyrannus*: 4.

5. Evelyn, *Tyrannus*: 29.

6. 'His Majesty's most gracious Speech, together with the Lord Chancellor's, to the Two Houses of Parliament, at their Prorogation, on Monday the 19th of May, 1662,' in Walter Scott, ed. (1812), *A Collection of Scarce and Valuable Tracts* (Somers Tracts), London: T. Cadell and W. Davies, 7: 547. The very tone of this speech demonstrates why the king of England cared about the court's public image.

7. Diana de Marly (1985), *Fashion for Men*, London: B. T. Batsford: 56; Penelope Byrde (1979), *The Male Image. Men's Fashion in Britain 1300–1970*, London: B. T. Batsford: 76; and Diana de Marly (1974), 'King Charles II's Own Fashion: The Theatrical Origins of the English Vest', *Journal of the Warburg and Courtauld Institutes* 37: 378–381. For a brief review of the secondary literature, see my '"Graceful, Virile, and Useful": The Origins of the Three-Piece Suit', *Dress* 17 (1990): 118–126.

8. John Evelyn, 'Adversaria,' unpublished manuscript cited by the editor in John Evelyn (1951), *Tyrannus or the Mode*, ed. J. L. Nevinson, Oxford: Luttrell Society Reprints: xv–xvi.

9. Andrew Marvell (1670s?; reprint 1927), 'The Kings Vowes', in *The Poems and Letters of Andrew Marvell*, ed. H. M. Margoliouth, Oxford: Clarendon: 167.

10. Edward Chamberlayne (1669), *Anglia Notitia: or the Present State of England*, 3rd ed., London: J. Playford: 59; Evelyn, *Diary*, 3: 465. Aileen Ribeiro (1986) also wonders whether the vest didn't have French origins, though given the anti-French sentiments expressed in introducing the vest, this seems unlikely (*Dress and Morality*, New York: Holmes and Meier: 87).

11. There is no evidence to support Beverly Lemire's (1991) assertion that Charles II was 'promoting England's trade with the Orient' by adopting the vest (*Fashion's Favourite: The Cotton Trade and the Consumer in Britain, 1660–1800*, Oxford: Oxford University Press: 10).

12. Esmond S. de Beer (1938–39), 'King Charles II's Own Fashion: An Episode in Anglo-French Relations 1666–1670', *Journal of the Warburg and Courtauld Institutes* 2: 105–115. For further discussion of the French use of vests, see Richard Heath (1888), 'Studies in English Costume: A Charles the Second Military Coat', *The Magazine of Art* 11: 11–15.

13. Samuel Pepys (1666), *Diary*, New York: Cassell: 7: 379–380.

14. Francis M. Kelly (1931), 'A Comely Vest after the Persian Mode', *The Connoisseur*, no. 88: 96.

15. Byrde, *The Male Image*: 75. Doreen Yarwood (1961) has argued that the shift 'from beribboned doublets and jackets to more dignified, though dull, coats and waistcoats' was 'a change so lasting that today men still conform to the latter garments, though in a modified form' (*English Costume*, London: Batsford: 159).

16. John Milward (1938), *The Diary of John Milward*, ed. Carole Robbins, Cambridge: Cambridge University Press: 14.

17. William Sancroft (1666), *Lex Ignea: Or the School of Righteousness*, London: Timothy Garthwait: 21: 8.

18. Thomas Brooks (1670), *London's Lamentations: Or, A Serious Discourse Concerning that Late Fiery Dispensation that Turned our (Once Renowned) City into a Ruinous Heap*, London: John Hancock and Nathaniel Ponder: 56. Henry Peacham (1647) linked concerns about modesty with the fire (Peacham, *The Worth of a Penny, Or, A Caution to Keep Money*, London: William Lee: 26–27). Without presenting evidence, Diana de Marly has also suggested a link between the fire and fashion reform (de Marly, *Fashion for Men*: 56).

19. Allen B. Hinds, ed. (1935), *Calendar of State Papers—Venetian*, London: HMSO, 35 (1666–1668): 100–101.

20. Pepys, *Diary*, 7: 315.

21. Milward, *Diary*: 17; Mary Anne Everett Green, ed. (1864), *Calendar of State Papers, Domestic Series, of the Reign of Charles II. 1666–1667*,

London: Longman, Green, Longman, Roberts and Green, 174, no. 139 (1666). In accordance with parliamentary wishes, the king in November 1666 issued 'a proclamation prohibiting the importation of all sorts of manufactures and commodities whatsoever, of the growth, production, or manufacture of France,' an act which was renewed on May 18, 1689 (*Catalogue of the Collection of English, Scottish and Irish Proclamations in the University Library*, London: University of London Press, 192.8, Proclamations 251 and 404).

22. Pepys, *Diary*, 7: 320–321; Anthony Wood (1891–1900), *The Life and Times of Anthony Wood, Antiquary, of Oxford, 1632–1695, Described by Himself*, Oxford: Clarendon, 2: 90. Unlike some of Wood's diary, this passage was written contemporaneously.

23. Pepys, *Diary*, 7: 324.

24. Cited in John Drinkwater (1926), *Mr. Charles, King of England*, London: Hudder and Stoughton, plate 5.

25. Evelyn, *Diary*, 3: 464–465. Evelyn gave his *Tyrannus* to the king in December 1661 (Evelyn, *Diary*, 3: 306). Evelyn repeated his claim in a final note to his unpublished second edition of *Tyrannus*: 'Note that this was publish'd two years before the vest, cravat, garters and buckles came to be the fashion, and therefore might happily give occasion to the change that ensued in those very particulars' (*Tyrannus*: 30). It is unclear when Evelyn made these notes, but his claim that the vest emerged in 1663 (two years after the original publication of *Tyrannus*) suggests that many years had passed before Evelyn attempted a second edition.

26. Thomas Osborne (1944), *Thomas Osborne, Earl of Danby and Duke of Leeds, 1632–1712*, ed. Andrew Browning, Glasgow: Jackson, Son, 2: 16–17. As one of the vices castigated by Puritans, gambling that he would keep his resolution was not a good sign of Charles's resolve, as later events would reveal.

27. George Savil, First Marquis of Halifax (1688), *The Character of a Trimmer*, London: n.p.: 32.

28. Chamberlayne, *Anglia Notitia: or the Present State of England*, 3rd ed.: 58–59.

29. J. O. Appleby, *Economic Thought and Ideology in Seventeenth-Century England*, Princeton: Princeton University Press: 123.

30. *The Diary of Samuel Newton Alderman of Cambridge* (1662–1717; reprint, 1890), Cambridge: Cambridge Antiquarian Society: 43.

31. Dorman Newman and T. Cockrel (1678), *The Ancient Trades Decayed, Repaired Again*, London: 17.

32. Evelyn, *Tyrannus*: 22.

33. Evelyn, *Tyrannus*: 23.

34. R. Steele, ed. (1910), *Tudor and Stuart Royal Proclamations, 1485–1714*, Oxford: Oxford University Press, 18 and 19 Car. II, c.4 (1666). This act was renewed and strengthened in 1678 and 1680.

35. Jorevin de Rocheford (1809), 'Description of England and Ireland, In the Seventeenth Century: By Jorevin', in *The Antiquarian Repertory: A Miscellaneous Assemblage of Topography, History, Biography, Customs, and Manners*, ed. Francis Grose, London: Edward Jeffery, 4: 564. From internal evidence, this tract was written between 1667 and 1672.

36. Evelyn, *Diary*, 3: 467.

37. Pepys, *Diary*, 7: 353. Diary entry for November 4, 1666.

38. Wood, *The Life and Times of Anthony Wood*, 2: 98. Diary entry for January 1, 1667.

39. Francis Sandford (1670), *The Order and Ceremonies Used for, and at the Solemn Internment of the Most High, Mighty and Most Noble Prince George Duke of Albemarle*, London: Francis Sandford, plate 5.

40. Halifax, *The Character of a Trimmer*: 32–33.

41. Edward Chamberlayne (1672), *Anglia Notitia: or the Present State of England*, 6th ed., London: J. Playford: 52.

42. Edward Chamberlayne (1674), *Anglia Notitia: or the Present State of England*, 8th ed., London: J. Playford: 54.

43. [Elkanah Settle] (1677), *Pastor Fido: Or, The Faithful Shepherd*, London: William Cademan: 67.

44. *The Courtier's Calling*: 70.

45. *England's Vanity*: 124–125. Nostalgia for the 'manlike' vest of 1666 continued in the early eighteenth century. See Laurence Echard

(1707–8), *The History of England,* London: Jacob Tonson, 3: 177; John Dennis (1711), *An Essay upon Publick Spirit; Being A Satyr in Prose upon the Manners and Luxury of the Times, The Chief Source of our Present Parties and Divisions,* London: Bernard Lintott: 6, and the many editions of Edward Chamberlayne's *Anglia Notitia* and Guy Miege's (1691) *The New State of England under their Majesties K. William and Q. Mary,* 3 vols, London: Jonathon Robinson.

46. Evelyn, *Diary,* 3: 467. Diary entry for October 30, 1666, written years later.
47. Evelyn, 'Adversaria', xv–xvi.

3

MACARONI MASCULINITIES[1]

Peter McNeil

This chapter discusses aspects of the macaroni persona and phenomenon, with reference to transformations of masculinity and gendered consumption in eighteenth-century London. It considers the way in which the dress prerogatives of the male elite may have passed into the reach of the 'lower' orders, as cast-offs and cheaper versions circulating within the burgeoning fashion economy. As the English macaroni was wearing contemporary courtly fashion, but in a particular social climate and in a particular way, it can be argued that macaronic behaviour is more about the wearing, less about the 'worn'; more about the process, less about the product. This is, of course, true of all fashion; but the macaroni provides a particularly apt case study of this issue. In this chapter I also argue for an alternative or additional derivation of the term 'macaroni' that privileges this very sense of performative burlesque. In these terms, the relevant suits and waistcoats that rest in museums are inanimate leftovers of a performance of a particular type of masculinity. The chapter thus makes a case for the benefits of an approach to eighteenth-century male dress in which the relationship between the early-modern, fashion and representation is foregrounded, and macaroni dress related to evolving models of national and gendered identity.

THE 'MACARONI': DEFINITIONS AND DERIVATIONS

In 1823, when the revised edition of Pierce Egan's *Grose's Classical Dictionary of the Vulgar Tongue* included the term 'macaroni,' it had been circulating in the English language for some sixty years, to denote a type of fop:

> Maccaroni [*sic*], An Italian paste made of flour and eggs; also, a fop; which name arose from a club, called the Maccaroni [*sic*] Club, instituted by some of the most dressy travelled gentlemen about town, who led the fashions; whence a man foppishly dressed was supposed a member of that club, and, by contradiction, stiled [*sic*] a Maccaroni [*sic*] (Egan 1823).

An explanation similar to Grose's dictionary entry has been reiterated whenever historians seek an explanation for the meaning and resonance of this expression. A review of the primary sources on which historians of eighteenth-century culture, dress and manners have formulated their understanding of the macaroni indicates that many definitions of the macaroni found in scholarly and popular texts today are flawed or partial. To reiterate the explanations for the term found in the eighteenth-century press, as some historians have done, is problematic. Useful and amusing as these descriptions are, they occur in the context of a genre that was ironic, arch and designed to amuse. The story of the pasta-eating club is possibly apocryphal; it made a convenient contrast with the real beefsteak club and the symbolic roast beef of England, which in discourse represented nationalism rather than internationalism; the values of liberty and free speech versus absolutism and tyranny. Such fictional clubs circulated in eighteenth-century literature and the press to underline a moral point and satirize pretension and outlandish behaviour. Their use belongs to an older tradition that dates to the early years of the century (Allen 1967 and Chancellor n.d.). No scholar has provided evidence of the existence of a concrete club with members and premises. Clues presented in later memoirs and biographies that discussed macaroni figures are ambiguous on this point (Stirling 1911: 323). It therefore is difficult to ascertain whether a discrete club existed with its own rules and premises, or if the macaroni coterie was situated within the structure of an existing club such as Almack's. Whether the macaroni 'club' existed or not, is on one level not so important as that it circulated within contemporary culture as a vital piece of popular life.

HORACE WALPOLE AND THE 'MACCARONI' CLUB

It is generally accepted by scholars of costume and social history that the first recorded use of the term 'macaroni' occurs amongst the voluminous correspondence of Horace Walpole, although this is not strictly true. The word 'macaroni' as a reference to appearance and character predates Walpole's letters and appears in David Garrick's play, *The Male-Coquette* (1757), which included a foppish character called the Marchese di Macaroni. Miles Ogborn describes Marcourt in George Colman's *Man and Wife* (1770) as the 'first Macaroni character on stage' (Ogborn 1998: 139). That a 'maccaroni' [sic] was also later included in Garrick's *Bon Ton* (1775) indicates the currency of this type within contemporary comedy. Despite its theatrical predecessor, Walpole's piercing eye and trenchant prose did record the first detailed impression of the macaroni phenomenon when it appeared amongst the aristocracy in London. Revealing the topicality and the specific nature of his theme—as not just a 'fop' but a new social type of conspicuous dresser—Walpole

discusses the macaroni as if he were a novelty. In the first relevant letter, dated 6 February 1764, addressed to Lord Hertford, Walpole discussed gambling losses amongst the sons of foreign aristocrats at the 'Maccaroni [sic] club, which is composed of all the travelled young men who wear long curls and spying-glasses' (Lewis 1937–83 vol. 38: 306). Contained here are many of the elements of the macaroni stereotype that would circulate extensively in the London press, satirical prints and plays of the 1770s. Walpole's 'travelled young men' clearly refers to those aristocrats who had taken the Grand Tour; in the context of this quote he is referring to a group of youths comprising either French or Swiss and Modenese aristocrats, a thoroughly cosmopolitan gaming table. These were the Duc de Chaulne's son; 'Virette' (possibly Vivret, a Swiss or Genevan); the Marchese Giuseppe Paolucci, Modenese envoy to England; and the Duc de Pecquigny. Walpole records the names as worthy of note because a feud broke out over the payment of gaming debts (Lewis 1937–83 vol. 38: 306, notes 4–5). Profligate gambling, associated with continental and specifically French manners, was strongly associated with the macaronic type, and was itself the focus of much critical literature. Gaming was highly fashionable and losses had reached epidemic proportions. Charles James Fox's stakes of £3,000, and total gambling debts of £140,000, were public knowledge, included in macaroni ditties and satires (Walpole 1806: 23 and Trevelyan 1880: 484). As in France, the behaviour was widely reported and associated in the public mind with the decadence of a spent aristocracy. Matthew and Mary Darly included *A Macaroni Gambler* in their third suite of macaroni caricatures, a topical image that referred to Alexander Fordyce, a Scottish banker who enjoyed the misfortune of having a name exceptionally apt for punning. *The Macaroni Card Players,* a group of ladies and gentlemen, was published as an illustration in *The Macaroni, Scavoir [sic] Vivre, and Theatrical Magazine,* November 1773. Walpole's 'spying-glass' refers to the type of decorative objects examined in this volume by Olga Vainshtein; the expensive glass sets the holder off from the crowd, casting him as an observer and by extension an outsider. The reference to 'long curls' is perhaps the most significant; fashionable young men in the late 1760s and 1770s replaced the small scratch-wig of the older generation with elaborate hairstyles that matched the towering heights of the female *coiffure*. A tall *toupée* and a club of hair required extensive dressing with pomade and powder. The wig was garnished with a large black satin wig-bag trimmed with bows. The use of a long pig-tail and wig-bag was viewed as a Francophile affectation; so much so that the visual shorthand for all Frenchmen in popular imagery was this device, just as a Dutchman was dressed in clogs and a Spaniard in lace. It was the macaronic attention to wigs that caused the most consternation. As Marcia Pointon so deftly indicates in *Hanging the Head,* the wig can function as a sign of masculinity and masculine authority; men without their wig or with their wig slipping are used in images to suggest disempowerment or castration (Pointon 1993: 117–23). In the engraving *Two Bloods of Humour, returning from the Bagnio, after having Kept it Up* (British Museum), the drunken figures roar: 'I SAY KEEP IT UP—KEEP IT UP—'TIS LIFE MY BOY—SO LET'S KEEP IT UP [*sic*].' The parallel of the erect wig and potency is stressed in that one of them has the wig placed on backwards, so that the hind part hangs over his face. The type of the wig dictated the response; effeminate excess was alarming. Macaronies in popular imagery are tailed by hairdressers with devil-like horns and hideous physiognomies; they are mercilessly lampooned as partners in crime, often effete, wizened and satanic. The cost of these wigs might also have excited dismay; even a modest wig was amongst the most expensive items in a gentleman's wardrobe. The macaroni wig was thus a sign of conspicuous consumption and luxury. If not the clothing, then the general effect of a macaronic hair-style would have been possible to replicate; although wigs were very expensive, real hair could be dressed in the new manner and augmented with false, and there was a trade in second-hand and stolen wigs (Pointon 1993: 120). The ragged-looking confections thrust on the heads of many caricatured individuals in the Darlys' macaroni engravings suggest ridiculous efforts to follow an inherently expensive fashion. Not knowing what was real and what was false was part of the alarm excited by fashion. The wig's symbolism as a potentially deceitful object is indicated in the following incident from the diary of Sophie Von La Roche, 1786. An English customs official she described as 'Hogarthian' (even at this date the English scene was mediated through caricature imagery) insisted upon inspecting the wig-box of a fellow traveller:

> The customs man raised his voice, flashed his eyes with greater fire, and insisted on opening the box; then, looking important meanwhile, lifted out the wig, lying there in blissful content, and dropped it again scornfully. The foreigner said, 'It is only my wig after all, isn't it?' 'Yes,' he replied, 'but a wig often covers a multitude of sins' (La Roche 1933: 80).

Although the existence of the Macaroni club has been freely assumed by several historians of dress, and by the editor of the encyclopaedic Walpole correspondence, none has provided any further proof of its membership or premises.[2] The macaroni club is always something heard of, not entered, and even Walpole does not name its location. Had Walpole known more it would have been uncharacteristic for such a 'voluptuary of gossip' (Tillyard 1994: 12) not to detail its structure and members, in accordance with his penchant for passing on gossip to posterity. As the contemporary press printed articles making similar claims in 1772 (*Town and Country* 1772: 242–3), subsequent historians have tended to accept this explanation of the term. The Edwardian biographer of the macaroni Walter Stanhope wrote that the dish macaroni was 'always placed on the table at their dinners.' Although the scholar had access to Stanhope's papers, he did not note the source of this claim (Stirling 1911: 323). The club Walpole refers to is possibly his amalgam of all the fashionable clubs in St James's Street, and thus indicative of youthful fashionability generally, or one of two clubs known to have been frequented by macaronies such as Charles James Fox. The first is the Robert Adam-designed Boodle's, also known as the 'Savoir Vivre,' where vast fortunes were spent gambling by men including the Fox brothers. The second contender is Almack's. Brooks's, the Whig club attended by Sheridan, Fox and the Prince of Wales and set up to rival Almack's on the opposite side of the street, was not fully established until 1778 (Ayling 1991: 49). Walpole linked Almack's with macaronies several times in his correspondence; there were 'Macaronis lolling out of windows at Almack's like carpets to be dusted' (Lewis 1937–83 vol. 35: 458). The *Macaroni and Theatrical Magazine* also referred to Almack's, describing: 'a compound dish of vermicelli and other pastes, which, unknown in England until then, was imported by our Connoscenti [*sic*] in eating, as an improvement to their subscription table at Almack's' (Stephens and Hawkins 1883: 826). If one had to 'gamble' on the site of the macaroni club, Almack's is thus the most likely contender. The issue of the club established an aristocratic profile for the macaroni when he first appeared. By the 1730s, clubs were in part political, the dual *raison d'être* being represented in the title of the Rumpsteak or Liberty Club (1734), which positioned itself in opposition to Robert Walpole's government. Other clubs included the Mohawks; the Society for the Propagation of Sicilian Amorology; the Wet Paper Brigade, which supposedly read the papers damp from the presses; the Lying Club; the Ugly Club; the Hell-fire Club; and the Dilettanti Society. Walpole's description of the macaroni club is

designed to amuse his correspondents, who were familiar with the ambience of Whig establishments, notorious for gaming, feasting and carousing.

Several other macaroni references enliven Walpole's letters in 1764. In November, he indicated that macaroni dress was a style associated with youth, when he observed at the Opera: 'You see I am not likely, like my brother Cholmondeley ... to totter into a solitaire at threescore' (Lewis 1937–83 vol. 38: 470). He reiterated this observation in 1775: 'The macaronies will laugh out, for you say I am still in the fashionable world.—What! they will cry, as they read while their hair is curling,—that old soul;—for old and old-fashioned are synonymous in the vocabulary of mode, alas!' (Lewis 1937–83 vol. 28: 186). Macaroni colour schemes for various seasons, probably copied from the vibrant combinations deployed in French fashions, and also resembling the preferred interior architectural schemes of Robert Adam, are indicated: 'If I went to Almack's and decked out my wrinkles in pink and green like Lord Harrington, I might still be in vogue' (Lewis 1937–83 vol. 32: 191). In 1775, *Matrimonial Magazine* noted that 'A few months ago most of the Macaronies had got into a sort of jaundiced habit; a kind of orange-tawney ... and of late there has been a most unseasonable rage for GREEN CAPES [*sic*; probably meaning collars at that date]' (Lewis 1937–83 vol. 32: 191, note 8).[3] This is borne out in two letters written by Samuel Johnson, in which he expresses an enthusiasm for this colour scheme as well as a deep orange in that year:

This day I had a new great Coat which am exceedingly pleas'd with; it is a light colour with a light green collar, made in the new fashion; the colour of the Coat depends on one's own fancy but the green Capes are almost universal ...

Went to Mr. Lane to talk about another Suit of Cloaths [*sic*] for a best Suit (I have since chosen a Barri [*sic*] colour, a colour deeper than an orange) from him (Radcliffe 1930: 40–1).

Such letters provide powerful evidence of the pleasures involved in the pursuit of macaroni fashion by young men.

CONSPICUOUS 'WASTE'

Walpole's correspondence thus established the characteristics of the macaroni stereotype when he first appeared, and from the beginning linked the macaroni with the themes that provided part of the impetus for the scurrilous visual and verbal caricatures that were generated in their hundreds soon after [figure 3.1]. These comment on fashion and luxury at a time when those terms were the subject of theoretical and economic debate (Berry 1994). The connection in Walpole's mind between the macaroni and the extravagant Whig circle around Charles James Fox is presented in July 1773. The macaronies become a metaphor for problems with the currency and a draining of the economy:

> Ireland is drained and has not a shilling. The explosion of the Scotch banks has reduced them almost as low, and sunk their flourishing manufactures to low water ebb. The Maccaronis [sic] are at their *ne plus ultra*: Charles Fox is already so like Julius Caesar, that he owes an hundred thousand pounds ... What is England now?—A sink of Indian wealth, filled by nabobs and emptied by Maccaronis! A senate sold and despised! A country over-run by horseraces! A gaming, robbing, wrangling, railing nation, without principles, genius, character or allies; the over-grown shadow of what it was! (Lewis 1937–83 vol. 23: 498–9).

Walpole, as usual, exaggerated; he continued: 'Lord bless me, I run on like a political barber—I must go back to my shop ... ' (Lewis 1937–83 vol. 23: 499). His excessive speech pattern was itself drawn out as macaronic. Walpole revelled in peppering his correspondence with the current term; even the Summer arrives '*à la Maccaroni* three months too late' (Lewis 1937–83 vol. 32:

382). He referred to some women as 'maccaronesses,' but this was as suggestive of their propensity to gamble as their appearance; 'the ladies are all Maccaronies and game too deep for me' (Lewis 1937–83 vol. 32: 158). The caricature industry also produced images of female macaronies, sometimes as part of a suite that paired male and female sartorial absurdity, as amusing counterpoint to the male macaroni, and as an extension of the link between women and vanity. Ultra-fashionable women were sometimes addressed by both actor and audience in the contemporary theatre. In October 1775 in his cross-dressed role in *The Provoked Wife*, Garrick brought down the house with his feather headdress: 'Mr. G.—never play'd better, & when he was in Woman's Cloaths he had a head drest with Feathers, Fruit etc. as extravagant as possible to Burlesque the present Mode of Dressing—it had a Monstrous Effect' (Stone and Kahrl 1979: 497). A newspaper reported that the head-dress included feathers, ribbons, oranges and lemons, and flowers: 'The ladies in the boxes drew back their heads, as if ashamed of the picture' (Thomas 1989: 382). Similarly, Sophie Von La Roche described a group of ultra-fashionable women and fops literally driven from the theatre by the combined attentions of actors and audience. A group of four ladies:

> entered a box during the third play, with such wonderfully fantastic caps and hats perched on their heads, that they were received by the entire audience with loud derision. Their neckerchiefs were puffed up so high that their noses were scarce visible, and their nosegays were like huge shrubs, large enough to conceal a person. In less than a quarter of an hour, when the scene had changed to a market-square in any case, four women walked on to the stage dressed equally foolishly, and hailed the four ladies in the box as their friends. All clapped loud applause. The two gentlemen accompanying the fashionable fools were least able to endure the scorn, for they hastily made away. One of the women held her fan before her

Figure 3.1 Robert Sayer, *A Macarony [sic] at a Sale of Pictures,* London, 1771. Private collection. The joke of this image is carried by the portly size of the fop, whose clothes are meant to be fitted on a more slender fashionable ideal. His country origins are suggested in the boots, riding whip and redingote (coat) with fashionable large buttons. The quizzing glass links him to the later figure of the dandy.

face, and was thereupon called by name—and when the expression of the remarks became too strong, they too departed before the end of the sketch, but they were followed out by a number of people from the pit and gallery, and held up to ridicule (La Roche 1933: 95).

A decade later, in his copy of Mason's *Heroic Epistle* (1777), Walpole mocked the word macaroni, stating that its very novelty was a symbol of the fashion system.

> *Maccaroni* is synonimous [*sic*] to *Beau, Fop, Cox-comb, Petit Maître,* &c. for Fashion having no foundation in Sense, or in the flower of sense, Taste, deals in forms & names, by altering which it thinks it invents. Maccaroni was a name adopted by or given to the young Men of fashion who returned from their Travels in the present reign, and is supposed to have been derived from the Italian paste of that denomination ... The Chiefs of the Maccaronis [*sic*] became known beyond the limits of their fantastic Dominion by their excessive gaming ... (Toynbee 1926: 69–70).

Language and money—two symbolic orders— are treated here by Walpole as mere self-reflexive systems. The words for 'macaroni' were interchangeable; eighteenth-century writers and readers enjoyed the play of synonyms, an excess of signifiers. Excess detaches representation from its purportedly 'real' signified in all cases; macaronies did the same with fashion. From the 1770s men's costume became increasingly self-referential. The elements of male attire—coat, waistcoat, breeches—remained unchanged for formal wear. However, various elements—fringe, frogging, braid, buckles, shoe-heels, hats— were manipulated as part of a sartorial language in neither logical order nor manner. Macaroni dressing thus has a strong relationship to the excesses typical of later *Incroyable* dress, a process hastened in post-Revolutionary France by the destruction of the hierarchical feudal system and its replacement by a society of *nouveaux-riches* composed of speculators or *agioteurs* who had no need of court-dress, but revelled in novel and extraordinary effects (Siegfried 1995: 70–81).

The macaroni's contemporary counterpart across the Channel, the *petit maître,* was also manipulating clothing in such a way that bemused commentators could only describe it as a new age of ephemerality. *Petit maître* was perhaps the most common counterpart for 'macaroni'. The English also understood the macaroni in terms of this French courtier counterpart. In the mid-1770s, buttons on ultra-fashionable men's dress in France lost any functional role and became bizarrely distorted; the Comte d'Artois wore watches mounted as buttons; there were pornographic buttons on sale in the Palais-Royal, and rebus and alphabetical buttons of the type that had previously appeared on screens (Quicherat 1875: 604; d'Allemagne 1928 vol. 1: 59). Some men changed their buttons several times a day; a set *à la Buffon* contained insects or leaves imprisoned in glass (Musée de la Mode et du Costume 1983: 117). By the 1780s, it appeared as if several *gilets* of contrasting fabrics were worn on top of each other, waistcoats of 'conspicuous waste' as Lesley and Osmun wittily noted, but also representative of the scrambling of the logic of fashion (*Conspicuous Waist* 1952: 6). Similarly, two watches were worn simultaneously, hanging from tassels on either side of the breeches, jangling as one walked (Quicherat 1875: 605). Fashion of course had undergone regular change for centuries; but the pace seems to have speeded up, resulting in a dizzying whirl in which seasonal change was replaced by monthly, weekly or even daily change, as clothing and silhouettes were named for events of a public and political nature.

'MACARONIC' POETRY: A NEW DERIVATION?

There are other forerunners for the usage of the word macaroni that revolve around a particular construction of language. This may derive from a pun that parts of the better-educated eighteenth-century public would have enjoyed, that of the paired meanings of 'noodle' and 'macaronic' poetry, which was a burlesque of Latin forms, designed to be witty. Comments on both types survive in the correspondence of Walpole (Lewis 1937–83 vol. 18: 315; vol. 20: 219; vol. 16: 141). The term 'macaronic' had been first used in the 1490s to describe Paduan and other Italian poetry in which Latin forms were mixed with the vernacular, the latter being given correct Latin endings. As Wenzel notes, Teofilo Folengo (d. 1544) 'adopted this practice as a medium for wit, playfulness, and parody', and wrote that 'macaronic poems must have nothing but fat, coarseness, and gross words in them' (Wenzel 1994: 3). The sense of burlesque and admixture, characteristic of the eighteenth-century view of the male macaroni who merged masculine and feminine personae in his appearance, as well as the English and the foreign, gave an added resonance to the term. Wenzel notes that the function of macaronic verse in Middle English was in some cases to satirize the true Latin of, for instance, the Vulgate Bible, and in others to characterize good and evil figures by the language they speak (Wenzel 1994: 4). This helps explain the relish contemporaries took in describing the male macaroni as a type of gender-hybrid. The *Oxford English Dictionary* describes macaronic as 'a burlesque form of verse in which vernacular words are introduced in a Latin context with Latin terminations and in Latin constructions … Hence of language, style, etc.: Resembling the mixed jargon of macaronic poetry' (Wenzel 1994: 3–4). Burlesque by definition makes a mockery of both genre and stable identity, particular preoccupations of the contemporary reaction to the macaroni. Wit was nearly always associated with the macaronic or foppish persona—sometimes through their being attacked for a complete lack thereof—and the word probably entered colloquial English through some combination of these terms in both high and popular culture.

The expression continued to circulate into the nineteenth century, an anthology of macaronic poetry being published in 1831 (Sandys 1831). Latham's *Dictionary* (1870) also recorded the meaning of macaroni as 'a droll or fool' (Latham 1870 vol. II, part 1: 140). Cauldrons of the food macaroni had also featured in some early European carnival parades, accompanying a fat man (Burke 1978: 185). A macaroni caricature played directly with the analogy between food and the fop: *The Salutation Tavern* (H. W. Bunbury, publisher J. Bretherton, 20 March 1773) is subtitled 'Macaroni & other Soups hot every day.' The term 'macaroni' thus conjured meanings referring to burlesque, carnival, carousing, food, excess and satiety. A more perfect term to denote the reign of fashion could not be imagined; might 'macaroni' be the most apt description for a fashion victim ever coined?

Aristocratic macaronies such as Charles James Fox were noted for their wit and urbanity, which was derived from their observations of Paris salon life, a sign of a courtly persona. The use of word-play relies on rhetoric, not reality, for hilarity; the ability of language to construct reality is celebrated. The affected speech of the macaroni circles made extensive use of French and certain pronunciations; cowcumber (cucumber), Jarsey (Jersey), charrit (chariot), gould (gold), bal-cõny (bāl-cony) and Lunnon (London) (Stirling 1911: 322). When this taste is played out in the realm of caricature, the macaronies are portrayed as full of empty speech and of no substance. The notion of the macaroni as superficial, shallow and potentially fraudulent is employed in a line of text attached to a subsidiary scene of a political caricature c.1774, a satire on the coin act. A man in macaroni dress accosts a courtesan, who holds out a scale and states, 'You Maccaronys [*sic*] are light Chaps yr Gold may be as light as yourself I'll weigh first' (George 1935: 171). In another version the macaroni has handed the harlot a guinea; she weighs it and finds it defective; he pouts (C. Bowles, *The Light Guinea, or the Blade in the Dumps,* c.1770). This might refer also to a defective macaroni (hetero)sexuality (McNeil 1999).

In performing the artificiality of language, the macaroni frequently exaggerated the artificiality of its actual production; his speech itself was considered unusual and affected. Macaroni talk is strewn with 'mem' and snuff is often 'snush.' Such speech patterns and inane discussions were also associated in the eighteenth-century mind with satires on wealthy women; they can be found in a satirical account of a woman's day in *The Spectator*, 1712. Botsford quotes this passage, which is clearly satirical, as a concrete source for the typical events of a wealthy woman's day, and their 'aimless existence,' which it clearly is not. This type of 'diary' entry was very popular in the press and was often used to satirize fashionability. Its misappropriation indicates the difficulty of treating macaroni 'documents' as if they are fact, when they appear in the context of a press packed with squibs and fabricated reportage. The events and the cadence of the lady's speech here, as well as the inanity, typify satires of fashion generally and inflect later representations of macaronic behaviour. Pet monkeys, lap-dogs, snuff-boxes, miniatures, self-absorption and vanity are all characteristics transferred to the macaroni, whose behaviour thus had to be read as culturally feminine.

The Spectator example reads:

> *Wednesday.* From Eight till Ten, Drank two Dishes of / Chocolate in Bed, and fell asleep after 'em.
> From Ten to Eleven. Eat a Slice of Bread and Butter, / drank a Dish of Bohea, read the *Spectator.*
> From Eleven to One. At my Toilet, try'd a new Head. / Gave Orders for Veny to be combed and washed. Mem. I / look best in Blue.
> From One till Half an Hour after Two. Drove to the / *Change*. Cheapened a Couple of Fans.
> Till Four. At Dinner. Mem. Mr. Froth passed by in / his new Liveries ...

> From Four to Six. Dressed, paid a Visit to old Lady Blithe, / and her Sister, having heard they were gone out of Town that / Day ...
> *Thursday* ... Sent Frank to know how my Lady Hectick rested after / her Monkey's leaping out at Window.
> Looked pale. Fontange tells me my Glass is not true ...
> From Four to Eleven. Saw Company. Mr Froth's Opinion of / Milton. His Account of the Mohocks. His Fancy / for a Pin-Cushion. Picture in the Lid of his Snuff-Box. Old / Lady Faddle promises me her Woman to cut my Hair ... (Botsford 1924: 274–5).

When in 1786 *The Merry Andrew; or, Macaroni Jester. A Choice Collection of Funny Jokes, Merry Stories, Droll Adventures, Frolicksome Tales, Witty Quibbles, Youthful Pranks* ... was published, macaroni in itself must have meant something comical, for this text contains no other reference to macaronies apart from a poem in which a monkey is transformed into a Beau (*Merry Andrew* 1786: 50–1). As late as the 1930s a novel used the notion of macaroni as a type of nonsense to mock regulation (Plunkett 1934). The term 'macaroni' thus enjoyed a long after-life within English popular culture.

MACARONIES AND METHODOLOGY

The macaroni was remembered in the nineteenth century as a colourful oddity representative of a romantic past (Chambers 1864: 31–3), until the cataloguers of the British Museum's eighteenth-century satirical prints put the study onto a more documentary footing. The macaronies are best known today through their representation in visual caricature. Dorothy George's revised catalogue of the collection lists about 150 prints that include the word 'macaroni' in their title; there are many more that allude to the macaroni by their iconography or in the accompanying text (George 1935). The macaronies thus form the most substantial sub-grouping of the caricatures of manners produced in England in the 1770s. Indeed, classed as a genre the macaronies are only outnumbered by the very large body of political caricatures published in the late eighteenth century. Of this category they also form a sub-set, as political identities like Charles James Fox were widely known and caricatured as macaronies. Notably, macaroni satires are more numerous than caricatures of the absurdities of women's dress at this time, an interesting inversion of the persistent Western cultural association of females with vanity and fashion (Donald 1996: 76–8). Despite what is often said regarding the complementary nature of eighteenth-century male and female fashion, women participated differently in the fashion system even at this date. Although there is no comparable English study, Daniel Roche's analyses of French inventories indicate that noble women and female servants nearly always had larger and more valuable wardrobes than their male counterparts; the values of wardrobes of 'ordinary' people were very comparable between genders (Roche 1994: 96–9). It is reasonable to suppose that this trend was also manifested at least as clearly in English society at large, a culture generally more suspicious of male sartorial splendour than the French. Although women's reputed propensity for excess and social emulation was derided, there was also a body of discourse that argued that ornament and adornment were natural to the female sex. Rousseau's famous pronouncement in *Emile* is paradigmatic: 'Here is a little girl busy all day with her doll ... there is no mistaking her bent ... She is more eager for adornment than for food ... in due time she will be her own doll' (Rousseau 1993: 396). The appearance of a sub-culture of such gaudily dressed men as the macaronies upset this cultural understanding, and accounts in part for the satirical invective directed against them.

The approach of pioneering historians of the caricature such as George Paston (actually a woman) and M. Dorothy George was to match caricature with real events and individuals in an unproblematic manner (Paston 1905 and George 1935). Twentieth-century social history used the macaronies as mirrors of contemporary events and fixations; costume history to illustrate the excesses of fashion. A study of the macaroni can utilize a broad range of sources in order to elucidate a form of representation that functioned simultaneously as actuality and fiction. Caricature as a genre needs to be treated cautiously, so that the figure of the macaroni might emerge in a more nuanced way from the exaggerated, fantastic and comic elements of these lampooning images. Men as disparate as Sir Joseph Banks, Dr Solander, the politician Charles James Fox, the preacher William Dodd and the painter Richard Cosway were caricatured as macaronies in their day. Topical interest in the macaroni peaked in the first half of the 1770s, when descriptions and images of the macaronies were published in the principal periodicals such as *Town and Country Magazine, The London Magazine, The Universal Magazine* and *The Lady's Magazine*. A group of macaronies featured in the so-called Vauxhall Affair (1773), in which young men insulted a woman, an event that generated a great deal of periodical and newspaper discussion. The episode has been analyzed as one of Miles Ogborn's case-studies of London's eighteenth-century 'geographies' of modernity. Ogborn reads the promenading macaronies at Vauxhall Gardens as emblematic of the contemporary mapping of masculinity with new spaces of consumption, fashionability and commodified leisure (Ogborn 1998: 133–42). Macaronies and their representations also spilled over in the space of the streets and the print-sellers. In 1772 *The London Magazine* noted of the macaroni: 'The only thing to be said in defence of it is, that the character is harmless; it is rather foolish than vicious. As it is now at its height, our print-shops are filled with Macaronies of a variety of kinds, representing with much drollery the absurdity of this species of character in various professions' (Stephens and Hawkins 1883: 827).

Throughout 1772, *Town and Country Magazine* printed satirical letters to the editor and articles that brought the existence of the macaroni to the reader's attention. From the beginning the macaroni was posed as a hot-house exquisite who was corrupted by urban mores and in turn inflicted them on his country cousins. On return to his provincial home, this macaroni is reported to note, 'Not a moment's felicity can I enjoy with such shocking wretches—hem—where's my shiff box?,' a reference both to that essential accessory the snuff box and to the affected tone that became a hallmark of the macaroni (*Town and Country*, March 1772: 152). A periodical, *Macaroni and Theatrical Magazine,* capitalized on their topicality and ran in 1773. Interest extended beyond the middle-class literature represented by these journals to a songbook that included a tune on the subject of the macaroni around this time. This text was very cheaply printed and may have circulated amongst less affluent areas of the community, its rhyme perhaps drawn from a popular song or ditty ('Bottle and Friends [*sic*] Garland' c.1765). The tune 'The Macaroni' included the following paradigmatic lines:

> With little hat and hair-drest high
> And whip to ride a pony,
> If that you take a right survey
> Denotes a Macaroni ...
>
> Five pounds of hair they wear behind,
> The ladies to delight oh,
> Their senses give unto the wind,
> To make themselves a fight oh!
> (Anon, c.1765: 7).

A study of the macaroni provides an opportunity to study the slippage between the 'reality' and representation of a sartorial system and the distinction between the two. Costume historians throughout the twentieth century have seized on the more piquant and amusing descriptions of macaronies that circulated in ladies' and other middle-class magazines of the early 1770s. Indeed, it is hard to resist these colourful and amusing passages, which cast light on male dress and act as a counter to the preponderance of description and information on and analysis of women's dress in the same period. Rather than deploying them simply as evidence, they can be scrutinized as fictions and representations. As certain 'real' historical figures were labelled 'macaronies' there is a strong temptation to discuss the phenomenon in these terms. But the term was generated, spread and expanded in popular discourse; it thus also functions as a fiction, like the *précieuses* of the seventeenth century and the *Incroyables* and *Merveilleuses* of the *Directoire*. We can only conjecture exactly what a macaroni may have looked like; this endeavour is made possible through the comparison of respectful and scurrilous representations of the same individuals who were considered macaronies. Fortunately, this can be done very easily in the cases of the politician Charles James Fox, the naturalist Sir Joseph Banks and the artist Richard Cosway, and yields different results and issues related to class and political affiliation in each case. The macaroni case thus highlights how different types of visual 'evidence' might be mobilized in costume history.

The social politics of the macaronies is complex. Many of the first macaronies were extremely wealthy, but the most famous of all, Charles James Fox, did not side with the Court, and came from a Francophile and Jacobite background, later becoming a radical Whig. Others such as the painter Richard Cosway and the court preacher the Reverend Dodd were court followers, sycophantic in their dress and their motives. Macaroni caricatures of Julius 'Soubise', the 'Mungo' macaroni, parodied a foppish upstart whose outfits and entertainments, financed by the Duchess of Queensbury, affronted both racial and social expectations of an African male. The court was peripatetic, moving between St James's, Kensington, Hampton Court and Windsor. Yet the macaronies kept court dress in the streets whether the Royal family was in residence or not. Like gambling debts, dress was a very visible part of conspicuous consumption.

A lavish dress, like the sumptuous Whig country estates and town-houses (Spencer House was built in the 1760s), indicated that here was the true power in England. As the Whigs' forebears had opposed absolutism, there was an irony in this re-importation of French court dress, wit and manners as a style detached from its original premise. The young Whigs wore aristocratic dress without the autocratic agenda inherent in the French original. The French had standardized dress and manners as a hegemonic gesture; re-imported into England they had new meanings. Fox loved Paris and her society but hated the Bourbon autocracy (Derry 1972: 295). Thus his adoption of macaroni dress was not a tribute to monarchy but a statement of a cosmopolitan outlook and Whig confidence. Fox himself does not appear to have used the term 'macaroni' to describe himself but preferred the term *petit-maître,* a term that was negative in the hands of a *philosophe,* but affectionate within salon society. In a letter to his father requesting that he stay on at Eton he half-jokingly suggested, 'the *petit maître* de Paris is converted into an Oxford pedant' (Mitchell 1992: 9).

The macaroni sources often employ the notion of John Bull's being affronted and unseated by the 'new' male fashionability. This reflects less the idea that an interest in fashion on the part of men was new, than the notion that more men were being fashionable. The overall impression of the caricatures is that both sexes were becoming more infected with the 'vice of fashion,' a fact that has been confirmed in English and French socio-economic research into the nature of eighteenth-century consumption (McKendrick, Brewer and Plumb 1982; Brewer, Porter, Staves and Bermingham 1993; Roche 1994; Vickery 1998; Weatherill 1991 and 1996). If some members of the lower orders emulated macaroni dress, as sources suggest, then the question of motive becomes even more complicated. That social inferiors might ape the dress

of their betters indicates that the early-modern pattern of a hierarchical dress system underpinned by sumptuary law had collapsed. As Ogborn argues in his analysis of eighteenth-century pleasure-garden culture, fashionable male dress was played out 'within the streets of a commercial city and nation rather than among the ornate displays of the Renaissance court' (Ogborn 1998: 138). Commenting upon this shift, *Universal Magazine* noted of the macaronies: 'was it not for an awkwardness in the gait, a clownishness of manners, and a solecism in speech, the Gentlemen of birth and fortune would not be known from him' (*Universal Magazine* 1772: 209). This is a charge that was more commonly directed at women, particularly merchants' wives and courtesans who could afford fine clothing; but it also extended to upper servants. Cheaper copies of dress and fabric types previously bought by the wealthy, and increased expenditure on clothing by the middling sorts, complicated the visual imagery of dress in England. Accessories were often the key to fashion modulation [figure 3.2].

As Barker-Benfield notes, fashion demanded display as well as purchase (Barker-Benfield 1992: 176). The culture of display was no longer limited to the higher echelons of court society but was spreading rapidly into other ranks and urban spaces. This was partly encouraged by the necessity for the aristocracy and the gentry to integrate socially, and marry for financial reasons, the *raison d'être* of the establishment of the resort town of Bath, at which macaronic behaviour flourished in the 1760s and 1770s (Varey 1990: 101–2). Mrs Montagu complained of Bath 'Misses who strut about in morning in Riding dresses and uniforms and the Maccaronis [*sic*] who trip in pumps and with Parasols over their heads . . . ' (Buck 1979: 100). Bath was a stage for the display of clothing and manners, more or less fine, as the daughters of merchants tried to tempt those less wealthy but more titled than themselves. As the old money and the *nouveaux riches* arrived for the season, so too

SNIP's WAREHOUSE for Ready made CLOATHS___ Great Variety of FANCY WAISTCOATS.

"Does it come up high in the Collar M?.___ O! yes Sir.___ it sits to a charm___ 'tis ease & Elegance itself.___ can Your Honor button it.___ Yes M?.___ but don't You think it too full.___ not at all Your Honor, You wou'd'nt wish to be pinch'd to be sure_____ (M? Snip) And Sir I hope the Young Gentleman's Breeches will be quite to his satisfaction Sir, do ye see, tho to be sure they comes on a little stiffish or so at first___ but You know Sir every thing gets easier in time as a body may say____ I desires him to thrust himself well in___ and I am sure they'll do. Publish'd Dec?.10?.1791. by Rob? Sayer & C? Fleet Street London.

Figure 3.2   Robert Sayer, *Snip's Warehouse for ready made Cloaths [sic]. Great Variety of Fancy Waistcoats,* London, 1791. Private collection. One of the features of macaroni dress was the attention paid to the whimsical waistcoat. This caricature features the types of neo-classical fashions popular in the early 1790s. Here a grotesque scene is played out in which Mrs Snip, the female shop owner, attempts to fit a man in his buckskin breeches; 'to be sure they comes on a little stiffish or so at first ... I desire him to thrust himself well in'. The development of ready-made clothing, vanity, accessibility by larger numbers of men to fashions, the deception of ill-fitting clothes that are passed off as fine, and the connection between female attendants and eroticism are all suggested in this image.

did the purveyors of luxury and the appearance trades, as Daniel Roche so aptly calls them. Their own appearances were walking advertisements for fashions of excess. Bath had its own print-shops in which the latest engravings were displayed (Fawcett 1990: 62); the town itself was fertile ground for the satirist. The Darlys played up these associations, producing several images of Bath macaronies. *The Emaciated Bath Macaroni* (George 1935: cat. no. 5032) depicted one of the invalids of Bath, whose dress was as grotesque as his gouty body; *The Bath Macaroni* shows an elegant man with exaggerated wig-bag and hanger (dress-sword). Christopher Anstey was amongst those who penned hilarious satires upon the Bath macaroni, and H. Bunbury produced drawings for caricatures of Bath macaronies and fashionability (Anstey 1994 and 1997).

Those above the level of the labouring poor, such as artisans and servants, also had access to genuine and copied articles of the types of clothing previously reserved for the gentry and aristocracy, and wore them in a jaunty and insouciant manner that complicated the sartorial hierarchy, and enraged social conservatives. As well as including clothing as part of wages it was common to leave clothing in a will; Horace Walpole left his whole wardrobe to his servant (Lewis 1937–83 vol. 30: 360). The poem 'Time Was in Town Ecologues', by C. Jenner (1773) mocked the pretension of those who follow the dress and manners of their betters by indulging in the pursuit of fashion and leisure:

AVARO.

Time was, when satin waistcoats and
  scratch wigs,
Enough distinguish'd all the city prigs,
Whilst ev'ry sunshine Sunday saw them run
To club their sixpences at *Islington;*
When graver citizens, in suits of brown,
Lin'd ev'ry dusty avenue to town,
Or led the children and the loving spouse,
To spend two shillings at *White*
  Conduit House:
But now, the 'prentices, in suits of green,
At *Richmond* or at *Windsor* may be seen;
Where in mad parties they run down to dine
To play at gentlefolks, and drink bad wine …

PRUDENTIO.

'Tis true my friend; and thus throughout the
  nation
Prevails the general love of dissipation:
It matters little where their sports begin,
Whether at *Arthur's*, or the *Bowl and Pin;*
Whether they tread the gay *Pantheon's* round,
Or play at skittles at *St Giles'* pound,

The self-same idle spirit drags them on,
and peer and porter are alike undone:
Whilst thoughtless imitation leads the way
And laughs at all the grave and wise can say
(George 1928: 166–7).

The reference to 'children and the loving spouse' denotes the emergent bourgeois family; 'Avaro', The Miser, 'Prudentio', Prudence, the enemy of excess; green was the popular macaroni colour. 'Thoughtless imitation' mocks the 'grave and wise', suggesting also death and Judgement of 'true' character. A nineteenth-century periodical recorded a similar theme in a song entitled *The Macaroni,* set to the air 'Nancy Dawson', which may reflect a lost eighteenth-century tune. In the case of the macaroni such popular sources are part of the archaeology of popular culture and attitudes, otherwise almost impossible to retrieve:

… The cits that used, like Jerry Sneak,
To dress and walk out once a week,
And durst not to their betters speak,
Are all grown jolly crony;
Each sneak is now a buckish blade,
When in the Park, but talk of trade,
He thinks you mean him to degrade—
Each cit's a macaroni (Chambers 1864: 32).

As well as those in service, the sector involved with the appearance industries was large. E. P. Thompson notes a growing confidence amongst some workers, and observes:

the enlargement of that sector of the economy which was independent of a client relationship to the gentry. The 'subject' economy remained huge: not only the direct retainers of the great house … but the further concentric rings of economic clientship—the equestrian trades and luxury trades … But the century saw a growing area of independence within which the small employers and labourers felt their client relationship to the gentry very little or not at all (Thompson 1993: 39).

These 'employers and labourers' included clothing workers and urban artisans who had access to fashionable goods, who 'escaped from the social controls of the manorial village and were not yet subject to the discipline of factory labor' (Thompson 1993: 40). Their growing confidence might be expressed sartorially. Although information about this group is more limited, it is possible that some of them adopted a macaronic persona, particularly in urban areas. Many artisans were of course prosperous themselves; the famous cabinet-maker John Cobb, contemporary with the macaronies, was later described as a 'singularly haugty [sic] character ... one of the proudest men in England ... he always appeared in full dress of the most superb and costly kind, in which state he would strut through his workshop giving orders to his men' (Jackson-Stops 1985: 328). The press was full of complaints of men of 'mean station' getting their hands on superior fashions and making macaronies of themselves, the exhibition of 'abominable vanity in the little' (*Universal Magazine* 1772: 209). *Macaroni, Scavoir [sic] Vivre and Theatrical Magazine* reported upon a masquerade at Carlisle house at which 'a maccaroni [sic] tallow chandler, and another of the same trade with his basket, as greasy as the best of them' were present (*Macaroni, Scavoir [sic] Vivre, and Theatrical Magazine*, February 1774: 205). The grease of the tallow trade alludes here variously to a slickness of manners and the social stain that association with such types might leave behind, as well as to the grease of the cheap or rancid wig. The new macaroni hair-styles spread quickly to less affluent youth. Sir Joshua Reynolds' young provincial nephew, Samuel Johnson (b. 1754), convinced by friends to visit an Assembly at Islington (1775), was lent lace ruffles and 'They persuaded me to wear a bag and a sword, but I found myself not singular in a twisted tail' (Radcliffe 1930: 92–3). He must have become accustomed to the style, for in a letter that year to his dismayed mother, who was horrified at the thought of her son's Devonshire curls being plaited and dressed, he wrote:

This is in defence of my tail, which I must wear in London where none but clergymen and boys wear their hair untied; the place only makes the difference; a tail here is the same as curls in the country, and silk stockings the same as worsted; but if it is only for my hair and not for my head that you are concern'd I can assure you that it is in better order than it has been for months ... (Radcliffe 1930: 96).

As this young man had to leave London each weekend for lack of a decent suit (Radcliffe 1930: 119) this indicates that elements such as the hairstyle were sufficient to mark one out as a macaroni. Although Walpole referred generally to the high-born in his discussion of the macaroni, in an intriguing letter of 1775 he provided a rare insight into the persona of another non-noble macaroni. He discusses the death of 'One of our Maccaronis', 'Captain Mawhood, the teaman's son' (Lewis 1937–83 vol. 39: 250). Lewis identified the Captain as James Mawhood (died 1775), brigadier and lieutenant, and the son of a tea-merchant in the New Exchange (Lewis 1937–83 vol. 39: 250, notes 7–8). Mawhood is a tantalizing reminder that not all men of fashion were high-born; Walpole notes that Mawhood was mocked as Captain 'Hyson' (a green tea) by his fellow officers—green recurring as a colour favoured by the macaroni, possibly because traditionally it was a more technically difficult and expensive colour. As the print industry and the popular press indicate, a macaroni persona spread into the general population with different effects and results.

As caricatures went up in print-shop windows, and macaroni figures appeared on the boards in Drury Lane, viewers may have found these images to be riotous critiques of the nobility in general. Thompson's masterful study of 'the view from below' indicates that the 'lower orders' in England did not simply accept the aristocracy in wondrous admiration, but had been involved for generations in activities that ranged from gentle mocking to urban terrorism: 'There is a sense in which rulers and crowd needed each other, watched each other, performed theatre and countertheatre to each other's auditorium, moderated each other's political behaviour. This is a more active and reciprocal relationship than the one normally brought to mind under the formula "paternalism and deference"' (Thompson 1993: 57). Thompson's study sounds a warning to the costume historian: 'No-one is more susceptible to the charms of the gentry's life than the historian of the eighteenth century. His major sources are in the archives of the gentry or aristocracy ... The "labouring poor" did not leave their workhouses stashed with documents for historians to work over nor do they invite identification with their back-breaking toil' (Thompson 1993: 17–18). The macaroni figure and the macaroni caricature may have achieved such currency because they were the perfect vehicle for Thompson's notion of the 'countertheatre of the poor' (Thompson 1993: 67). As the lower orders gazed at macaroni caricatures displayed in print-shop windows and pasted up in taverns and latrines, or watched such figures tread the boards, they could not have failed to make the connection with the toffs around them. The sins of an idle aristocracy or court elite were set out in an engraving from M. Darly's second macaroni suite, *Venison & Claret, or Sr Humpy Haunch Bart of Glutton Hall*, in which an obese nobleman struts along the street in the latest fashionable hair-style and suit trimmed with galloon.

Harassment and jesting were a part of life for over-dressed gentlemen who ventured into hostile territory. Reports survive of over-dressed *émigrés* in London being continually harassed for their hairstyles in the early 1790s (Chrisman 1997: 5–6). The theatre of sartorial display is made all the more interesting as young male workers in the appearance industries—tailors, peruke-makers, hairdressers—adopted elements of the dress as walking advertisements for the trade in court dress upon which their livelihoods depended. Although it is tempting to suggest that members of the appearance industries always attempted to wear lavish clothes, this probably depends upon the place and the trade. Lou

Taylor, in her useful review of Harvey's *Men in Black*, notes that research by Lesley Miller on the wardrobes of Lyons silk designers indicates that their dress 'was muted, based upon the "classic" colours and fabrics deemed appropriate for the middling ranks of society ... The little black (or grey or brown) suit was both utilitarian and self-consciously low-key, suitable for a job in which personal contacts with rich clients made competitive, showy dressing inadvisable' (Taylor 1996: 302). As Miller refers to designers, different findings might be made for the wardrobes of high-fashion purveyors, particularly in Paris. Were they always respectful, or did elements of parody emerge? Were they considered sycophants by other workers, or did they laugh at the sight of these 'apes' and 'monkeys,' to use the standard terms that mocked fashionable pretension?

GARMENTS AS EVIDENCE

Surviving examples of male dress that correspond to the 'macaroni' description indicate the splendour and sensual appeal of such garments. Most museum costume collections that include eighteenth-century menswear hold garments related to the contemporary descriptions of macaroni dressing. This is not surprising, as these are the types of lavish garments retained and collected in the nineteenth and early-twentieth centuries as technical and aesthetic exemplars of textile design. There is difficulty in extricating or distinguishing surviving examples of 'court dress' from 'macaroni' dress, a very real problem considering the lack of *provenance* in this period. Elsewhere I have described holdings relevant to macaroni dress held at the Royal Ontario Museum, most of which were collected in the early years of the twentieth century (McNeil 2000a). These include an English apple-green silk suit finely embroidered with swags of pink flowers and tassels, the favoured macaroni colour scheme cited previously, and a spectacular

French gold silk lampas waistcoat, with pink and green brocading and silver sequins.

Macaroni dress-swords survive in collections including that of the British Museum. The swords were decorated with large tassels or rosettes; an elaborate pair of embroidered and painted sword-knots, English, c.1770, with a design of cornflowers and daisies, hand-painted and outlined in chain stitch in silver and gold, edged with *passementerie* lace, is held at Spencer House, London. Sword-knots held an erotic charge and a reference to potency; they were often worked by ladies for their gentlemen. In France the noble bride at her wedding gave gifts of expensive sword-knots for men, and fans for ladies (Chaussinand-Nogaret 1985: 120). The dress-sword also held an erotic charge, in France at least; in Baudouin's *Le Carquois épuisé* (engraving by N. de Launay, c.1771), a dress-sword with attached ribbons lies discarded on the floor, the sign of sexual contact (d'Allemagne 1928: vol. 1, pi. CCCIV). Like the dress-sword, the over-sized macaroni sword-knot may function as a joke, as many macaronies were in fact considered defective in the matter of virility. Other macaroni accessories include the snuff-boxes and cane-handles of precious and semi-precious materials that survive in the decorative arts collections of most European museums, the glamour of which can be gauged from the relevant plates in Diderot's *Encyclopédie* (1762). The British Museum holds a sumptuous male *châte-laine à breloquet* of green enamel and gold, from which a watch is suspended. This object, which was hooked over the belt, often with a *fausse montre* (false watch) at one end, is the type of extravagant object associated with the macaroni stereotype. In England this fashionable manner of wearing a watch was passing from the male into the female wardrobe by the late 1780s (Tait 1984: 86).

Corsages or 'nosegays' also recur in macaroni caricatures; they were part of aristocratic male attire in the eighteenth century, but the subtle messages were in the styling. The key to the macaroni was excess. Walpole characterized the macaronies as sporting massive nosegays or corsages: 'Lord Nuneham's garden is the quintessence of nosegays: I wonder some macaroni does not offer ten thousand pounds for it—but indeed the flowers come in their natural season, and take care to bring their perfumes along with them' (Lewis 1937–83 vol. 28: 105). These probably resembled the style of the substantial corsages worn at the French court, illustrated in Jean-Michel Moreau le Jeune's drawings for Nicolas-Edmé Restif (Rétif) de la Bretonne's *Monument du Costume Physique et Moral de la Fin du Dix-huitième Siècle* (several series and editions, 1775–1789), which depict a nobleman's toilette.

CONCLUSION

The macaroni contradicted the notion that masculine clothing expressed a stable, continuous and inherent self, overturning early-modern dress hierarchies. Rather, he posited a self that exists only in performance, brought into being by such performative factors as gesture, speech and dress. The macaroni cannot therefore be fully understood simply by analyzing the clothes he wore, deposited as surviving samples in the world's museums. In the same manner, the text of a play languishing unrealized on stage, or in studies that do not refer to performance productions, is diminished in its meaning. Nevertheless, just as much can be deduced from the text of a play, analysis of surviving macaroni costume exposes the visual flux such clothing brought to the spaces of a city such as London, redefining it as a modern centre of international trade and commodity culture. While an emphasis on performance means the constructed histories of the individual wearers of macaroni clothing must be analyzed, it is as records of performance that their lasting depictions in text and image must be read, not as some stable identifier of what their characters were 'actually' like. Any meeting of macaronies could be the 'macaroni club'; it was more a process than a real place. A macaroni need not be a gilded Whig enjoying clubland, but could be a male of any order adopting some element of the macaroni persona. This spread of fashionability accounts for part of the contemporary fascination with the macaroni figure. Men who dressed above their station in ultra-fashionable modes were subjected to a triple mockery, that of transgressions of status, gender and sexuality. They could be viewed as upstarts asserting a social status above their 'true' station. They could be pilloried as effeminate and invoke anxieties about a blurring of gender distinction. They could pejoratively be identified, or possibly even identify themselves, as sodomites (McNeil 1999). The macaroni also disrupted stable notions of national identity at a time when these were being deployed in the interests of British social cohesion, with his exaggerated Francophile performance. He exposed Englishness, too, as a performance.

To analyze the macaronies is nothing less than to ask, what is fashion? The answer may be that fashion is no 'thing' at all, but a process, an endless series of reflections between image and reality. A 'real' macaroni saw exaggerated images of 'himself' on stage, in the print-shops and on the streets, and emulated them; perhaps seeking to outdo the image in his own reality. Caricature actually helped create the identity, its derision making a space for a resistant subjectivity. This may be something fundamental to the development of subcultures; in taking an image of ridicule and exaggerating it an identity was formulated. The deconstruction of the dichotomies of image/wearer, clothing/human in the real and unreal figure of the macaroni is the key to the conflation of this character with 'fashion'. For a few years in the late eighteenth century the macaroni was nothing less than fashion itself. It is the power of fashion as modern commodity that invoked the anxieties that saw the macaroni simultaneously mocked and celebrated in public discourse and popular culture.

NOTES

Reprinted with permission from Peter McNeil, "Macaroni Masculinities," *Fashion Theory: The Journal of Dress, Body and Culture* 4, no. 4 (2000): 373–404.

1. Parts of the research were conducted with the assistance of the Veronika Gervers Research Fellowship in Textiles and Costume History, Royal Ontario Museum. I wish to thank Ms Anu Liivandi, Ms Shannon Elliott and Dr Alexandra Palmer, the Royal Ontario Museum, Toronto; Ms Kay Spilker, Los Angeles County Museum; Mr David Thompson, Curator of Horology, and Ms Judy Rudoe, Assistant Keeper, Department of Medieval and Later Antiquities, at the British Museum.

2. At one point Lewis claimed that the macaroni club was located in King Street, St James's Square (Lewis 1937–83 vol. 38: 306, note 6). In a later note Lewis admitted that the reference to the club was probably a newspaper squib (Lewis 1937–83 vol. 10: 139, note 11).

3. 'Capes' refers here to collars; a turned-down collar, however narrow, was called a cape: C. Willett and Phillis Cunnington (1972), *Handbook of English Costume in the Eighteenth Century,* Boston: Plays Inc.: 38.

4

THOMAS CARLYLE AND *SARTOR RESARTUS*

Michael Carter

Perhaps only a German savant could do the subject full justice.

(James Laver, *Style in Costume,* 1949)

One night, at some point early in the nineteenth century, a rather strange individual called Professor Diogenes Teufelsdröckh stands at his study window high above the German city of Weissnichtwo. Teufelsdröckh is the hero of Thomas Carlyle's book *Sartor Resartus* and at this particular moment he is looking down on the sleeping city which is visible to him below, where 'Upwards of five hundred thousand two-legged animals without feathers lie round us their heads all in nightcaps, and full of the foolishest dreams'.[1]

His is a good vantage point from which to study the affairs of humans situated, as it is, midway between the 'life-circulation' of the town's citizens below and the eternal stars of the heavens above. Indeed, it is partly from his musings upon the city below that the good professor has formulated his novel vision of the universe and of our place in it, which he calls the 'Clothes-Philosophy'. That all might not be as it seems in this scene may be surmised from the fact that 'Weissnichtwo' translates as 'Know-not-where'; that the professor's lodgings are sited on the 'Wahngasse', or 'Fantasy Lane', and that his surname translates variously as 'Devil's Shit', 'Devil's Dirt' or 'Devil's Dust'.[2]

Sartor Resartus is Thomas Carlyle's first book-length publication and the one in which many of the major themes of this most Victorian of writers are first discernible. After its initial appearance in serial form in 1833, the book gradually gained in popularity and fame until it became recognized as one of those magical texts that seems to embody the entirety of an epoch's interests and aspirations. While the work is, and has been, cited within the context of the study of dress and costume history, such references range from the exceedingly brief to the exceptionally dismissive. Certainly, *Sartor Resartus* is unlike any of the other classic texts examined in this book. Its booming prose, the fact that it is, ostensibly, a work of fiction together with its overt religiosity makes sure of that. And yet, it is my contention that *Sartor Resartus* may be seen as a founding text, one that imaginatively prefigures the discourse on dress that follows.[3]

Before we look at the details of Professor Teufelsdröckh's clothes philosophy, something has to be said about the nature of Carlyle's book as a whole as well as his relationship to its overt theme. *Sartor Resartus,* though a work of fiction, is quite unlike other English novels of the nineteenth century. It is not a 'realistic' story if, by that, is meant the unfolding of a tale in which recognizably human characters interact in recognizably real situations. *Sartor Resartus* is a drama of ideas and these ideas are placed before the reader often with little regard for the creation of realistic contexts. Nor may the book be said to be a scientific or philosophical treatise in which the writing style is subservient to its information. The book steadfastly refuses a simple and open proclamation of its message, preferring instead to adopt a number of oblique approaches such as satire, caricature and irony. Everything that happens in the book, everything that is proclaimed by the principal protagonists, has to be interpreted for its 'other' meaning. At the centre of this complex shuffling of the explicit and the metaphorical lies Carlyle's extraordinary notion of clothing. A sense of just how flavoursome the clothes metaphor is for Carlyle comes very early on when the character of the English editor launches into one of the book's many rolling observations on the nature of clothing:

> That ... grand Tissue of all Tissues, the only real Tissue ... the vestural Tissue, namely, of woollen or other Cloth; wherein his whole other tissues are included and screened, his whole Faculties work, his whole Self lives, moves, and has its being.[4]

Metaphor this may be, but there is something about the relish with which the speaker elaborates upon, and returns to, his subject that suggests that it is aspiring to be more than just a simple figure of speech. As the book unfolds the reader is quickly made aware that the author has meditated for a long time upon what the importance of this 'vestural tissue' might be.

The use of clothes as metaphor is hardly original. Ever since Adam and Eve covered their sensitive parts, clothing has served as a rich allegorical resource. Clothes had proven to be a vivid means with which to dramatize our complex natures. There is something about the way in which clothing and the human body flow into each other that enables metaphorical correspondences between the two to acquire a particular force. Most importantly, it becomes (certainly in the West) one of the prime ways of making tangible the differences between a determinate order of nature and the non-natural

dimensions of human existence. Indeed, at one point Teufelsdröckh defines humans as 'two-legged animals without feathers'.[5] As well, clothing has been regularly cast in the role of either a screen, or a sensitive register, of what lies within.[6]

Carlyle's use of clothes as metaphor is more complex than this well-worn path. The first thing to strike the reader is that it is not just garments that Carlyle lights upon as a way of formulating his philosophy. Each stage of the 'social life' of clothing seems to present him with equally rich sources of metaphorical suggestion. Cloth in general as well as its material variability is returned to repeatedly. Cloth's mode of production—that is, spinning and weaving and crucially the transformation of these processes into mechanized factory production—became for Carlyle one of the most important ways in which he could give shape to the blight of 'materialist externality'. Just prior to the publication of *Sartor Resartus,* Carlyle had published his great essay 'Signs of the Times' (1829) in which he highlighted the consequences of industrialization for the traditional weaver. This seems to have suggested to Carlyle a way of particularizing the misery of mechanization.

> On every hand, the living artisan is driven from his workshop, to make room for a speedier, inanimate one. The shuttle drops from the fingers of the weaver, and falls into iron fingers that ply it faster.[7]

This is a critical moment in human affairs. When the animate is displaced by the inanimate our souls are changed and if the soul changes, so too will those 'vestural tissues' that enfold our bodies and our being. This fascination with clothing is carried through to their decomposition into rags. At the end of their lives as garments Carlyle again senses that more is happening than just the decay of matter. Now the metaphor can be turned, with devastating effect, on the otiose social institutions Carlyle sees all around him. Here he is 'ragging' established religion.

For the last three centuries, above all, for the last three-quarters of a century, that same Pericardial Tissue ... of Religion, where lies the Life-essence of Society, has been smote at and perforated, needfully and needlessly; till now it is quite rent into shreds.[8]

Toward the end of the book he will describe the plight of the Irish poor and their spiritual condition as the 'Shock of Rags'.[9]

SOUL, BODY, CLOTHES

We have seen that one of the distinctive characteristics of Carlyle's use of the clothes metaphor is the breadth and the intensity with which he pursues it. One of the most convincing descriptions of Carlyle's uniqueness in *Sartor Resartus* is that advanced by G. B. Tennyson.[10] Rather than settling on any fresh content in Carlyle's deployment of the clothes metaphor, Tennyson tries to identify the source of the metaphor's extraordinary power, a power that is capable of supporting a whole book. Tennyson's answer is that what Carlyle glimpses at the beginning of the metaphor is a way of meshing together the three grand generalities of vesture (clothes), body and spirit:

the meaning with which Carlyle began *Sartor* appears as the clothes metaphor itself; just as clothing covers the body, which in turn houses the soul, so the visible world covers an invisible one, which has as its animating spirit the mind of God. What gives *Sartor* an organism to grow on also gives it dynamism. *Sartor* in operation is the expansion of the clothes metaphor to analogy, the elaboration of an initial perception of likeness to a detailed working out of similarities in *relations*.[11]

Starting from an observation that one line of relations can be used to illuminate a second line of relations, Carlyle erects a complex structure embracing each of its terms in a web of multiple interrelationships. With this insight in place

he can elaborate, imagine and organize his vision of the universe and our place in it. One of Carlyle's favourite ways of dramatizing this metaphorical structure is to snap one the many possible relational permutations between clothes, body and spirit to see what eventuates. As we shall see in a moment, this produces some of the book's most startling passages.

Carlyle, at least early in his career, was a radical critic not simply of industrialization and mechanization but of the spiritual conditions that encouraged these new social tendencies to flourish and become a blueprint for life in general. Whatever name put to the disease ailing Britain— utilitarianism, materialism, functionalism, 'mere externality' or the 'Age of Machinery'—for Carlyle the cause was always the same; a degradation in the quality of religious faith. Without religious faith, soul (or spirit) is absent from the hearts of men and as a consequence they would build a world in which humans were imagined to be nothing more than complicated pieces of machinery. As Carlyle remarks, 'Men are grown mechanical in head and heart, as well as in hand'. There is a moment in the story of Teufelsdröckh's coming of age when, trapped inside a mood of crushing despondency, he has a vision of the universe without faith and it is hellish.

To me the universe was all void of Life, of Purpose, of Volition, even of Hostility: it was one huge, dead, immeasurable Steam engine, rolling on, in its dead indifference, to grind me limb from limb. O the vast, solitary Golgotha, and Mill of Death![12]

For Carlyle, the world around him was full of concrete situations where the proper relations between soul, clothing, and spirit had come unstuck, and the author of *Sartor Resartus* delights in bringing these to our attention by grotesquely manipulating clothing. In another of his moments of illumination, Teufelsdröckh has a vestimentary epiphany, suddenly seeing clothes as pure unmediated materiality severed from any inner significance.

It was in some such mood ... that I first came upon the question of clothes. Strange enough, it strikes me, is this same fact of there being Tailors and Tailored. The Horse I ride has his own whole fell: strip him of the girths and flaps and extraneous tags I have fastened around him, and the noble creature is his own sempster and weaver and spinner: nay his own bootmaker, jeweller and man-milliner; he bounds free through the valleys, with a perennial rainproof court-suit on his body; wherein warmth and easiness of fit have reached perfection ... While I—Good heaven!—have thatched myself over with the dead fleeces of sheep, the bark of vegetables, the entrails of worms, the hides of oxen or seals, the felt of furred beasts; and walk abroad a moving Rag-screen, overheaped with shreds and tatters raked from the Charnel house of nature, where they would have rotted, to rot on me more slowly![13]

The extraordinary power of this passage comes from its ability to see us, and our 'stuff', through the eyes and mind of an alien. It is a sort of anti-transcendentalism where any kind of elementary sublimation has failed to take place.

Carlyle repeats this strategy of illumination-through-negation when Teufelsdröckh meditates upon the importance of clothing to the lives of humans as social beings, that is, the relationship of clothes to politics. In a remarkably contemporary assertion the character of the English editor observes that 'Teufelsdröckh, though a Sans-cullottist, is no Adamite'. The professor will have nothing to do with the notion that if we were to strip off our outer casings truth, equality and justice would blossom. He knows that social being is 'clothed-being' and drives this point home by asking us to imagine the political order naked.

Often in my atrabiliar moods, when I read of pompous ceremonials, Frankfort coronations, Royal Drawing-rooms, Levees, Couchees; and how the ushers and macers and pursuivants are all in waiting; how Duke this is presented by archduke that, and Colonel A by General B, and innumerable Bishops, Admirals, and miscellaneous Functionaries, are advancing gallantly to the anointed presence; and I strive, in my remote privacy, to form a clear picture of that solemnity,—on a sudden, as by some enchanter's wand, the—shall I speak it?—the Clothes fly off the whole dramatic corps; and dukes, Grandees, Bishops, generals, Anointed Presence itself, every mother's son of them, stand straddling there, not a shirt on them; and I know not whether to weep or laugh.[14]

Who hasn't, at some point, wished something similar on the rich and powerful? Remove these external emblems of our communality and what eventuates is farce, not truth. It must be stressed, however, that this is no unthinking endorsement of the status quo on Carlyle's part. Always the three elements of his vision need to be kept in touch with one another; otherwise the relation between an emblem and its life-source becomes distorted. Take the spirit out of clothes and the bodies inside them and they can still hold power over us long after their occupants have any claims to political legitimacy. These emblems of defunct authority eventually die and decay, no longer possessed by an inner spirit, but there are times when this dying can take an age. Nowhere is Carlyle more frightening, and more savage than when he attacks the established Church for its lack of spirit.

Meanwhile, in our era of the World, those same Church-Clothes have gone sorrowfully out at the elbows: nay, far worse, many of them have become mere hollow shapes, or Masks, under which no living figure or Spirit any longer dwells; but only spiders and unclean beedes, in horrid accumulation, drive their trade; and the Mask still glares on you with its glass-eyes in ghastly affectation of Life,—some generation and a half after religion has quite withdrawn from it, and in unnoticed nooks is weaving for herself new vestures, wherewith to reappear, and bless us, or our sons or grandsons.[15]

Clothes, literal and metaphorical, have proved fruitful for Carlyle. Bodies without wrappings become entities devoid of signs of human order and this is because clothes are the outward manifestation, the external condition, of our sociality, our ideals, or what Carlyle would call our 'spirit'. Dead emblems may command obedience but they will never inspire reverence.

CLOTHES, THEIR ORIGIN AND INFLUENCE

We first encounter the clothes philosophy in the magnum opus of Diogenes Teufelsdröckh entitled *Die Kleider ihr Werden und Wirken* or *Clothes, Their Origin and Influence* (hereafter referred to as *Die Kleider*).[16] Some clarification of the structure of *Sartor Resartus* is necessary in order to distinguish between the several voices that are in play at various times in the book. In Book One a fictional 'English editor', whose name and biographical details remain unspecified, introduces his English readers to the professor and his book, *Die Kleider*. Most of what the reader encounters at this stage are comments made by the editor on Teufelsdröckh's eccentric project, together with numerous extracts from the book itself. Throughout, the English editor maintains an ambivalent attitude toward the ideas being put forward by the professor. Admiration there certainly is but also a healthy scepticism toward what he regards as the excesses of German thought. In Book Two a more complex fictional conceit is let loose. We learn some of the details of Teufelsdröckh's life, in particular those experiences which lead him to formulate the clothes philosophy. An acquaintance of the professor from Weissnichtwo, Hofrath Heuschrecke, responds to a request from the English editor for details of the life of the author of *Die Kleider*. Some time later, six paper bags arrive in England. Each bag is marked with a zodiacal sign and consists of 'miscellaneous masses of Sheets, oftener Shreds and Snips', all written in Teufelsdröckh's hand. The account we are given of his life is one that the editor himself has compiled from the disordered material found in the six bags. The final volume assumes a more straightforward form. The English editor at last opens *Die Kleider* and, by way of extensive quotation, discusses in detail the ideas to be found therein. If the present context of writing were one of a work of literary criticism then it would certainly be important to distinguish between the voices of all these characters as well as that of the author Carlyle. While the prospective reader should be aware of the existence of these numerous characters, most of the explicit 'clothing ideas' that are looked at here derive from the Book-within-the-Book. The exact contents of *Die Kleider* are never fully spelt out by the English editor; however, the book's subtitle 'their origin and influence' gives a good indication of how the topic of clothing is generally organized and discussed. I begin with origin and for simplicity's sake refer simply to Carlyle.

Carlyle was never much taken with the notion that clothing was something secondary to the essence of human being. 'Nature is good but she is not the best'.[17] Take clothing off our backs and you also remove that which is the emblem of our unity. '*Man is a Spirit,* and bound by invisible bonds to *All Men . . . he wears clothes* which are visible emblems of that fact.'[18] He refers to this belief in a state of clothesless primal beneficence as 'Adamitism' and his disagreements with this philosophy show just how contrary to established religious ideas this advocate of spiritual renewal had become. Christian Europe had had its own explanation of the origin of clothes in the story of Adam and Eve and their expulsion from the Garden of Eden. Carlyle unequivocally rejects this view of pre-lapsarian naked perfection:

> Nay, now when the reign of folly is over, or altered, and thy clothes are not for triumph but for defence, hast thou always worn them perforce, and as a consequence of Man's Fall; never rejoiced in them as in a war immoveable

House, a Body round thy Body, wherein that strange THEE of thine sat snug, defying all variations of Climate?[19]

Clothes do not derive, argues Carlyle, from shame, modesty, or any of the other sexual anxieties supposed to have arisen as a consequence of the Fall. Instead, he advances an explanation that single-handedly establishes the genre of the dress studies in a manner which persisted well into the twentieth century.

The first purpose of Clothes, as our Professor imagines, was not warmth or decency, but ornament.[20]

In that simple statement can be found perhaps the most seminal clothes idea in the whole of *Sartor Resartus*. Not functionality, since that would make of clothes 'mere externalities'. Not the empty dogmas of established religion, but ornament. 'Decoration', Carlyle asserts, is 'the first spiritual want of a barbarous man' and in making this claim he turns the scrutiny and comprehension of clothing into a matter for anthropology; a move that would be more than confirmed in the second half of the nineteenth century.

HISTORY AND STYLE

One element, remarkable for its almost complete absence from *Sartor Resartus,* is clothing's figurative cousin, fashion. One reason for this is that our contemporary sense of the meaning of fashion contains a strong, perhaps dominant, sense of time's passage. Fashion is equated with the sequence of clothing styles that have characterized Western dress since the end of the Middle Ages. Put specifically, fashion is that dynamic force that propels changes in clothing, come what may. When fashion is discussed in *Sartor*—as happens in the famous chapter on Dandies—it is used in the sense of 'being in fashion'; that is, being dressed *à la mode* with the emphasis falling on modish conformity rather

than rapid and arbitrary changes in clothing styles over time. This might lead us to assume that the element of time is absent from Carlyle's musings on clothes but this is not the case.

It should be remarked, if the reader has not already guessed, that Carlyle was a rare specimen in the British intellectual scene of his day. One source of this distinctiveness was his fluency in German, to the extent that he produced some of the first translations of Goethe in English. As well as his familiarity with the German language he was also an admirer of contemporary German literature and thought and, crucially, of German Idealist philosophy. This intellectual debt shaped Carlyle's thinking about clothes in two ways. First, he comprehends that the changes that happen over time to human 'stuff' are unitary in character. Change there may be, but it is change that, beneath the surface, partakes of a profound coherence and is never just a set of events isolated from one another. When the English editor attempts to describe what is going on in *Die Kleider* he cites, in support of his argument, the extraordinary diversity of costumes over space and time. He is of the opinion that it is the manner in which Teufelsdröckh attempts to explain this diversity that constitutes the most notable feature of the professor's method.

Walking by the light of Oriental, Pelasgic, Scandinavian, Egyptian, Otaheitean, Ancient and Modern researches of every conceivable kind, he strives to give us in compressed shape ... an *Orbis Vestitus*, or view of the costumes of all mankind, in all countries, in all times.[21]

What Carlyle has absorbed from German philosophy is a belief that historical time needs to be distinguished from clock time. To understand human life is to understand that it eventuates within a temporal continuum that is both cumulative and progressive. This means that the human species is never fully present to itself at any one moment but is in a constant process of 'becoming itself'.[22] Time, therefore, is of the essence. Another strong debt to German thought can be detected in Carlyle's notion of the unity and distinctiveness that typify human making. This idea, namely that what issues forth from human manufacture is neither unmediated functionality nor 'mere accident', is of course the sense carried by the idea of style. Style, together with the notion that historical time has quite specific characteristics, became the foundation of what, later in the nineteenth century, became known in German thought as 'Geisteswissenschaften' or 'human sciences'. Although Carlyle does not use the word 'style', preferring instead the phrase 'an Architectural Idea', the manner in which this is subsequently elaborated leaves little doubt that it is 'style' that he has in mind. The section of *Die Kleider* where the notion of the 'Architectural Idea' undergoes elaboration is worth examining in some detail as it could stand as a manifesto for the study of dress almost up until the present day.

Teufelsdröckh begins with a plea for there to come into being an Esprit de Costumes which would match in the seriousness of its intent Montesquieu's *Esprit de Lois*. Clothing is no longer to be the province of the anecdotal, of the dilettante, or of indifference—what he later refers to as 'a comfortable winter-evening entertainment'. This desire to institute a proper study of clothing is possible because of certain crucial characteristics that mark all human endeavours, the most notable being that of 'patterning' or of a certain constant manner of form. This 'styling' would be the proper object of study because 'neither in tailoring nor in legislating does man proceed by mere Accident, but the hand is ever guided on by mysterious operations of the mind'.[23] By the time of the publication of *Sartor Resartus*, mind, spirit or *Geist* had become one of the key concepts of German Romantic thought. Zygmund Bauman has observed that 'what had been the individual *Seele* (Soul) turned into a collective *Geist* and later *Kultur*'.[24] Each *Geist* struggled to discover a distinctive material embodiment for this collective mental entity. 'Style'

was the name given to the specific patterns that emerged within material 'stuff as it was appropriated by *Geist* for its expressive ends. Carlyle exactly reiterates this notion of style. Inside, animating the products of human labour, 'lurks' the architectural idea. If we are to understand the bewildering variety of human 'Modes and habilatory endeavours' it is to this inner impulse that our eyes and minds must be turned. As the professor remarks later in this passage 'every snip of the Scissors has been regulated and prescribed by ever active Influences'.[25] 'Ever active', but also ever changing. This constant shifting in the inner disposition of the human collective is what causes such diversity in human ways of living. At this point we get another of Carlyle's wonderful rolling comparisons.

> Whether he flow gracefully out in folded mantles, based on light sandals; tower up in high headgear, from amid peaks, spangles and bell-girdles; swell out in starched ruffs, buckram stuffings and monstrous tuberosities; or girth himself into separate sections, and front the world an agglomeration of four limbs,—will depend on the nature of such Architectural Idea.[26]

The task of the Clothes Philosopher is to describe and to tabulate the variety of 'habilatory modes' but he, or she, must also be able to move into the heart of the product, or work, if they are to locate the source of its distinctiveness. That is, they must approach, and enter, *Geist*. As Carlyle comments 'If the Cut betoken Intellect and Talent, so does the Colour betoken temper and heart'.[27]

DANDIES AND DRUDGES

The final topic that I want to discuss is the notorious chapter entitled 'The Dandiacal Body'. I have left this until now as a way of countering some of the misconceptions that have formed about Carlyle's ideas about clothing. These,

I suspect, have arisen due to this chapter being interpreted in isolation.

On the whole Carlyle's attack upon dandies has not received a sympathetic hearing. Typical is the comment made by that very minor talent, Max Beerbohm, that 'anyone who dressed so very badly as did Thomas Carlyle should have tried to construct a philosophy of clothes has always seemed to me one of the most pathetic things in literature'.[28] James Laver castigates Carlyle for his moralism:

> If Carlyle had really been an 'Inquirer in to Clothes', and not merely concerned to emphasize the scandalous difference between the luxury of a dandy and the poverty of an Irish peasant he might have found meat for meditation in the pages of Pelham, as well as in those of another young author who was just coming into prominence.[29] (Here Laver is referring to Disraeli.)

Even Ellen Moers, whose account of the anti-dandiacal movement of the 1830s is otherwise fair and balanced, misinterprets the clothes philosophy of *Sartor Resartus* when she states:

> In Carlyle's morality it was not enough to value the soul over the exterior ... True merit lay in the renunciation of surface adornment altogether.[30]

Moers's statement is contradicted by what Carlyle has to say in his essay about Jean-Paul Friederich Richter, a figure he much admired. Richter was a German thinker and scholar and at a certain point in the late eighteenth century he began to deviate quite seriously from the dress codes of his contemporaries. Carlyle is quite explicit about both his fascination with, and his admiration for, Richter's odd behaviour and in a comment, particularly telling for his 'anti-dandy' attitude, he remarks that 'It was a species of pride, even foppery, we will admit; but a tough, strong limbed species ...'[31] *Sartor Resartus* was never a renunciation of clothes, or

even a criticism of elaborate costume. It was a manifesto for authenticity, a plea for the outer 'vestural tissue' to become the true embodiment of spiritual and social renewal: 'blessed he who has a skin and tissues, so it be a living one, and the heart-pulse everywhere discernible through it.'[32] Much more is being articulated in 'The Dandiacal Body' chapter than a dismissal of Regency 'fancy pants'.

The circumstances of how and why that chapter came to be written have been more than adequately covered by scholars such as Moers, Tennyson and Kaplan. It must be admitted that there is undoubtedly an element of personal animosity, as well as intellectual disagreement, fuelling Carlyle's anti-dandy manifesto.[33] But having said this, the reasons for the dispute becoming personal fade away when one realizes that what was happening in this instance was just one small example of the revolution taking place in the social mores and intellectual convictions of a whole section of the nation. Daily life for the British middle and upper classes was changing and changing fast. Part of this change was the rejection, and then demonization, of the values and manners associated with George IV and William IV. What was coming into being was Victorianism with its, at least, overt espousal of personal abstemiousness, social and individual improvement, hard work and earnest desire to be useful and do good. One further matter somewhat complicates things. The ostensible cause of the chapter being written was the encounter that Carlyle had had with Bulwer-Lytton's dandy novel, *Pelham*.[34] In fact, Carlyle includes in his chapter an extract from that novel—the section titled 'Articles of Faith'—which are a list of rules by which the hero organizes his daily life. They are very funny and are in the tradition of camp humour which stretches (at least) from Beau Brummell, through to Wilde, and up to the present day. Carlyle's response at the end of the list is anything but po-faced. To assertions such as 'THERE IS SAFETY IN A SWALLOW

TAIL!' he replies, 'All of which propositions I, for the present, content myself with modestly but peremptorily and irrevocably denying.'[35]

Carlyle's argument with the dandiacal philosophy and the class with which it was associated—what G. B. Tennyson somewhat abruptly dismisses as 'the do-nothing aristocracy'—is that they invert the principal tenet of the clothes philosophy. Others 'dress to live', the dandy 'lives to dress'.[36] But having established their fundamental difference to the normal relationship between life and clothes, Carlyle sets out to explore the nature of this 'Poet of Cloth' and in so doing unravels the vernacular philosophy at work in the appearance and demeanour of the dandy. He might not like what he finds but his ability to put before the reader dandyism's 'Architectural Idea' ranks with Charles Baudelaire's comments on dandyism in his essay 'The Painter of Modern Life' and Susan Sontag's 'Notes on Camp'.[37] Like the latter two critics, Carlyle senses that the emergence of the dandy is related to the arrival of novel historical circumstances, in particular the decline of a collective religious sense. Teufelsdröckh puts it so:

> In these distracted times when the Religious Principle, driven out of most Churches, either lies unseen in the hearts of good men, looking and longing and silently working there towards some new revelation; or else wanders homeless over the world, like a disembodied soul seeking its terrestrial organisation,—into how many strange shapes, of Superstition and Fanaticism, does it not tentatively and errantly cast itself![38]

Dandyism arises, therefore, to fill the gap left by the withdrawal of the sea of faith. Only on the body of the dresser and its immediate vicinity can the world be given any reliable meaning. However, within this narrow horizon Carlyle glimpses all the usual attributes of the cult.

> ... these people, animated with the zeal of a new Sect, display courage and perseverance, and what force there is in man's nature though never

so enslaved. They affect great purity and separatism; distinguish themselves by a particular costume ... and, on the whole, strive to ... keep themselves unspotted from the world.[39]

Carlyle's problem is that the group he is talking about are drawn from the ruling class as well as the ruling-class-in-waiting and it is his opinion that these are not at all the sorts of disposition that will be adequate for the world that is coming into existence. For Carlyle beautiful, futile retreat is simply not a good enough philosophy for those who would claim political legitimacy. It is at this point that he starts to draw a comparison between the dandies and the poor.

Carlyle fails to match his sensitivity to the subtleties of the dandy idea when he attempts to grasp the 'Architectural Idea' of the poor. What might have been witty and amusing when applied to the wealthy loses its humour when turned upon the 'Bogtrotters', 'White-Negroes', 'Ragged-Beggars' or 'Poor-Slaves'; all names he uses to describe the (Irish) poor. Assertion substitutes for elucidation: ' ... the original Sect is that of the *Poor-Slaves*; whose doctrines, practices, and fundamental characteristics, pervade and animate the whole Body, howsoever denominated or outwardly diversified.'[40] Carlyle then launches into one of his grotesque descriptive passages as he tries to do justice to the unruly combination of materials and styles that constitute the typical appearance of the 'Poor-Slave Sect'.

> Their raiment consists of innumerable skirts, lappets, and irregular wings, of all cloths and of all colours; through the labyrinthic intricacies of which their bodies are introduced by some unknown process. It is fastened together by a multiplex combination of buttons, thrums, and skewers; to which frequently is added a girdle of leather, of hempen or even straw rope, round the loins ... In head-dress they affect a certain freedom: hats with partial brim, without crown, or with only a loose, hinged, or valved crown, they sometimes invert the hat, and wear it brim uppermost ... with what view is unknown.[41]

While Carlyle recognises that there can be a style in—and of—poverty, the final admission of defeat in the quotation above would suggest even Teufelsdröckh is unable to go beyond the banal observation that grinding penury is awful, that it leaves no time or energy for the elaboration of the faculties and that those who suffer from this condition tend to lead lives of resentful obedience punctuated by outbreaks of savage destruction. What is important here is not the accuracy of Carlyle's reading of the appearance of the poor, although a great deal of what he says confirms Engels in his study of the Manchester working class.[42] What we have here is the birth of an important trope through which the class divisions of Britain will be played and replayed over the next hundred years. In the differences between these two 'Sects', Carlyle discerns a possible future for the nation and it is not a comforting one: 'I could liken Dandyism and Drudgism to two bottomless boiling whirlpools that had broken out on opposite quarters of the firm land.'[43] This is the beginning of the idea of the 'two nations' that, if left in their divided state, will eventually result in the kind of biological apartheid envisioned by H. G. Wells in his book *The Time Machine*. At the back of this criticism of dandyism a fight is being conducted, not just about the redefinition of ruling-class masculinity, but about what being a ruling class in this new order means. Not least of these considerations is to discover an appropriate external form that could embody the new high seriousness imposed by the duties of government and the leadership of civil society.

THE LEGACY OF THE CLOTHES PHILOSOPHY

Apart from the ten or so pages (out of two hundred and twenty) that deal with dandyism it cannot be said, with any confidence, that Carlyle's book exerts a great influence on any of the thinkers that we look at subsequently. Other than the specialised literature on dandyism, *Sartor Resartus* is, now, seldom cited in dress studies. Yet the book, I believe, can be regarded as the founding text for the emergence of the serious and organized study of clothing.

It would not be difficult to demonstrate that, in *Sartor Resartus*, Carlyle's concept of clothes is modern, just as it would not be difficult to argue that his concept of clothing is also archaic. The 'archaic' element is that aspect of Carlyle's text that is 'pre-social', or better perhaps, 'pre-sociological'. While there is a strong sense of clothing and its styles being collective, there is little indication on Carlyle's part that this collectivity is subject to 'social laws'. It takes the work of Herbert Spencer to place this idea centre stage. But in one respect what Carlyle is doing is transparent to the modern reader and that is his vision of the world, but especially the human world, as being a conjoining of spirit and matter which can only be grasped by the labour of interpretation, not measurement. Given his enormous debt to German Idealist philosophy, could we say that Carlyle is engaged in a kind of hermeneutic activity? If we allow that this is happening, then much of what Carlyle is up to in *Sartor Resartus* becomes comprehensible. Although not overly influenced, or impressed, by Hegel, I find it worth noting that the latter's *The Philosophy of History* was published in 1837.[44] In the 'Introduction' to that work Hegel advances the idea of the 'Spirit of a People' and a 'Spirit of a Time' existing in the form of a pervasive ethos which imparts to both a people, and an historical epoch, a distinctiveness. These non-material aspects of culture, those supra-individual entities that infuse the lives of a nation press with equal intensity upon all elements within a particular life-world. Remember that Diogenes Teufelsdröckh's official position within the University of Weissnichtwo is the 'Professor of Things-in-General' and we should read that title as meaning the study of the particular *in light of* the universal, as well as someone whose curiosity encompasses the trivial, the mundane and the everyday. I am tempted to claim that many of the elements that make up today's Cultural Studies are present in that summary, but perhaps that is going too far. Certainly, much of what might be termed the 'German antecedent' to Cultural Studies—thinkers such as Simmel, Kracauer and Benjamin—would be happy with a great deal of that characterization, but that is not quite what I am claiming for *Sartor Resartus*.

The reader should recall that *Sartor Resartus* is a work of fiction, albeit an unusual one. We also saw that there was nothing at all novel in the way the author used the idea of clothes as a metaphor for human life. Carlyle's *Sartor Resartus* is not strictly speaking the founding text of an 'Esprit des Costumes': it is Teufelsdröckh's *Die Kleider ihr Werden und Wirken* that can claim this title. It was perhaps only in a work of fiction that one could summon up the imaginary spaces in which the professor and his book could appear. Carlyle takes a clichéd trope—clothes as metaphor for human life—and distends it into a luxuriant analogy. In one of the clearings that opens up in the complex structure of *Sartor Resartus*, Carlyle engages in some further elaboration in which analogy becomes (almost) scientific discipline. *Sartor Resartus* founds dress studies not because it causes what comes later but because it is the first to imagine what comes later.

NOTES

Reprinted with permission from Michael Carter, "Thomas Carlyle and Sartor Resartus," in *Fashion Classics from Carlyle to Barthes* (Oxford and New York: Berg, 2003), 1–18.

1. Thomas Carlyle (1987), *Sartor Resartus* eds K. McSweeney and Peter Sabor, Oxford: Oxford University Press: 1.
2. The derivation of Teufelsdröckh's name is still a matter of dispute among Carlyle scholars. One possibility is suggested by Engels (1892) in *The Condition of the Working Class in England in 1844*, London: Allen and Unwin. At one point while describing the poor quality of clothing available for working men he remarks, 'And, if a working-man once buys himself a woollen coat for Sunday, he must get it from one of the cheap shops where he finds bad, so-called "Devil's-dust" cloth manufactured for sale and not for use, and liable to grow threadbare in a fortnight ...' (101). This would certainly enable Carlyle to remain within the metaphor of clothing. For a useful discussion of Carlyle's visit to Manchester in 1838 and the effects that his encounter with the textile industry had upon him see Steven Marcus (1975), *Engels, Manchester and the Working Class,* New York: Random House: 32–6.
3. See William Keenan's (2001) excellent 'Introduction: *Sartor Resartus* Restored: Dress Studies in Carlylean Perspective', in W. J. F. Keenan (ed.), *Dressed to Impress: Looking the Part,* New York and Oxford: Berg.
4. Carlyle, *Sartor*: 4.
5. Ibid.: 18.
6. Anne Hollander (1980), *Seeing through Clothes,* New York: Avon: 445. This text has an extremely useful discussion of the various tropes that use clothing. See pp. 444–54.
7. Thomas Carlyle (n.d), 'Signs of the Times', in *Carlyle, Critical and Miscellaneous Essays,* vol. 1, Boston and New York: Colonial Press: 465. Originally published in 1829.
8. Carlyle, *Sartor*: 176.
9. Ibid.: 212.
10. G. B. Tennyson (1965), *Sartor Called Resartus: The Genesis, Structure and Style of Thomas Carlyle's First Major Work,* Princeton: Princeton University Press.
11. Ibid.: 166.
12. Carlyle, *Sartor*: 127.
13. Ibid.: 44–5.
14. Ibid.: 48.
15. Ibid.: 164.
16. Tennyson, *Sartor*: 186–7, has reconstructed the contents of *Die Kleider*, as far as possible, in the following way:

   'Die Kleider Ihr Werden und Wirken'
   Part I. *Werden*

Chapter 1. 'Paradise and Fig-leaves'.
Several historical chapters
c. Chapter 5. 'Aprons'.
Several historical chapters
c. Chapter 8. Medieval and Renaissance clothing
Several historical chapters up to the nineteenth century
Part II: *Wirken*
Chapter 1. 'World out of Clothes'
Chapter 2. 'Adamitism'
Chapter 3. 'Pure Reason'
Probably several other chapters
c. Chapter 6. 'Perfectibility'
c. Chapter 7. 'Church-Clothes'
Chapter 8. 'Symbols'
Chapter 9. 'Organic Filaments'
Chapter 10. 'Natural Supernaturalism'.
For some reason Tennyson omits from this schema the last two chapters of *Sartor,* 'The Dandiacal Body' and 'Tailors'.

17. Carlyle, *Sartor:* 47.
18. Ibid.: 48.
19. Ibid.: 46.
20. Ibid.: 30.
21. Ibid.: 29–30.
22. The Carlyle scholar John Holloway (*The Victorian Sage,* New York: W. W. Norton, 1965) has summarized the notion of time held by Carlyle and the German Idealist school of thought in the following manner:

   1. the universe is fundamentally not an inert automation, but the incarnation of a cosmic spiritual life;
   2. world history is the expression of spiritual life analogous to that of the individual consciousness;
   3. the principle of cosmic life is progressively eliminating from the universe everything inimical to its inner purpose;
   4. man's duty is to further this process, even at the cost of his immediate happiness.

23. Carlyle, *Sartor:* 28.
24. Zygmund Bauman (1978), *Hermeneutics and the Social Sciences,* London: Hutchinson: 24.
25. Carlyle, *Sartor:* 28.
26. Ibid.
27. Ibid.
28. Max Beerbohm (1964), 'Dandies and Dandies', in *The Incomparable Max Beerbohm,* London: Icon: 18.
29. James Laver (1968), *Dandies,* London: Weidenfeld & Nicolson: 50.
30. Ellen Moers (1960), *The Dandy: Brummell to Beerbohm,* Lincoln: University of Nebraska Press: 181.
31. Carlyle (1827), 'Jean Paul Friederich Richter', first published in the *Edinburgh Review.* See Carlyle (1872), *Critical and Miscellaneous Essays,* Vol. III, London: Colonial Press: 27.
32. Carlyle (1906), *Past and Present,* London: Chapman & Hall: 109.
33. Tennyson, *Sartor;* Moers, *Dandy;* Fred Kaplan (1983), *Thomas Carlyle: A Biography,* New York: Cornell University Press.
34. Edward Bulwer-Lytton (1972), *Pelham or the Adventures of a Gentleman,* Lincoln: University of Nebraska Press. See 'Maxims': 177–80.
35. Carlyle, *Sartor:* 212.
36. Ibid.: 207.
37. Charles Baudelaire (1972), 'The Painter of Modern Life', in *Baudelaire: Selected Writings on Art and Artists,* trans. P. E. Charvet, Cambridge: Cambridge University Press; Susan Sontag (1969), 'Notes on Camp', in Sontag, *Against Interpretation and Other Essays,* New York: Laurel.
38. Carlyle, *Sartor:* 208.
39. Ibid.: 209–10.
40. Ibid.: 212.
41. Ibid.: 213.
42. See Engels, *Condition of Working Class* and Marcus, *Engels, Manchester.*
43. Carlyle, *Sartor:* 216.
44. G. W. F. Hegel (1956), *The Philosophy of History,* New York: Dover. See 'Introduction': 52–3.

5

DANDYISM, VISUAL GAMES, AND THE STRATEGIES OF REPRESENTATION[1]

Olga Vainshtein

To see is only a language.

S. T. Coleridge[2]

Recent critical books and essays about dandyism tend to concentrate on dandies as precursors of modernity, the heroes of urban consumerism, camp style, and self-fashioning.[3] Dandies tell us much about attitudes toward men's fashion, looking at men, and men looking at others. This chapter considers the culture of European dandyism of the nineteenth century in terms of strategies of visualization. By reconsidering the well-known sources for dandyism—the biographies of dandies, fashion magazines and etiquette books, and "fashionable" novels, I argue that the dandyism of the English Regency period established the models of self-fashioning that became stereotypes of men's behavior in society during the nineteenth century. In focusing on the Regency dandy Beau Brummell, I will argue that newly ordered visual games were part of social codes and models of representation introduced by the British dandies. By my own "focus" on newly developed technology, new lenses and glasses, and new fashionable accessories that enabled people to look more closely and with more flourish, I argue for a connection between men's fashion and a wider scopic regime.

Beau Brummell (1778–1840), "England's prime minister of taste," was recognized as "arbiter elegantiarum" by all exquisites. The welcoming glance of the Beau had such value that

in some circumstances it appeared as a type of monetary equivalent. Once, one of his creditors reminded him of a debt, to which Brummell answered that he had already paid. "When?"—"When I said to you, sitting at the window of the White's: 'How are you, Jimmy?'" To understand all of the implications of this episode one must know what the glance and the greeting at the window of White's meant among the dandies of that time. Brummell was a member of an old Tory club White's, one of the few closed and highly prestigious clubs with limited membership. The club was situated in St. James's Street, and in 1811 a bow window was installed and set into the middle of the club's façade, the front door being moved to the left. It was in this window that Beau Brummell sat and held court, passing judgments on passersby, with his inner circle beside him. A company of friends gathered around Brummell, catching his retorts as they flew by. In fact, the circle of participants in this spectacle was actually wider. Knowing that at a certain time Brummell took up his position at the club bow window, many London dandies went out to walk along St. James's Street in order to present their costume to the judgment of Brummell: they could thus indirectly discover his opinion. Because they themselves constituted an audience for the uncrowned king of fashion, even merciless criticism provided a moment of prestigious participation.

There was another feature to this spatial arrangement that was amusing but also created a new dynamic. At the club, Brummell, sitting in the bow window, was himself very clearly visible from the street. He watched—but they also watched him, so he was, to use the Shakespearean phrase, "the observed of all observers." All of those passing by at an unhurried pace could glance at the details of his *toilette,* comparing his own attire with their appearance and evaluating the latest innovations in the costume of the recognized arbiter of elegance. Sharp-witted and sharp-eyed Brummell, sitting near the center of the bow window, appeared from the street as a type of doll or mannequin, although at the beginning of the nineteenth century mannequins did not yet exist. They appeared somewhat later, with the rise of the store windows of the department store.[4] Brummell consciously presented himself to the studying glances, and played his role of fashion doll with professional pleasure. He shared this passion of being seen by and with many of his contemporaries. One of the dandy characters in the novel *The Exclusives* confesses, for instance, that he comes to Hyde Park to see the ladies, but, even more, "to show myself, to be admired."[5]

In this way, a space was established in front of the club window that was full of lightning-quick glances, where the distinction between subject and object of contemplation, the observer and the observed, was instantly erased. There arose a completely unique visual tension, in which two impulses successfully interacted, voyeurism and exhibitionism. In this game of crossing glances there occurred what the philosopher M. Merleau-Ponty calls "the vision ... doubled with a complementary vision or with another vision: myself seen from without, such as another would see me, installed in the midst of the visible, occupied in considering it from a certain spot."[6] The fashionable people of the Regency looked at one another as though looking in a mirror, having taken pleasure in and convinced themselves of the weight and reality of the body as a visible thing. The selectivity of vision automatically postulated its own system of criteria, imprisoning a whole series of things in veritable quotation marks, enlarging or shrinking them according to its scrutiny. The sophisticated gaze could easily perform the function of face control, scanning a person's appropriateness in looks and dress: "Lord Glenmorris ... held out his hand with a stately air of kindly protection, and while he pressed mine surveyed me from head to foot, to see how far my appearance justified his condescension."[7]

The dandy's glance often concentrated on details, exaggerating trifles, inspecting accessories. It is no accident that monocles, lorgnettes, and quizzing glasses were often featured as among the most salient attributes of dandyism.[8] The collection of the College of Optometrists, London, preserves an incredible range of lorgnettes, some with a built-in watch; articulated quizzing glasses; rimless "Waldstein" monocles; opera glasses; and even a Wedgwood single-draw spyglass and a brass "jealousy" glass for surreptitious sideways viewing (figures 5.1–5.17; color plates 26–28). As Peter McNeil has noted elsewhere in this volume, such devices had also characterized the pose of the English macaroni in the period after 1760. The developing taste for such a range of optical accessories within the history of costume points to the principle of significant detail in dandies' fashion. Ulrich Lehman also notes,

> Bodily movement, gesture, and facial expression become rigidly fragmented and mechanical, a representation in miniature of the increasing alienation between subject and object. Therefore, it seems only natural that the "invention" of the monocle in the first decade of the nineteenth century coincided with the rise of commodities and the objectification of modern society.[9]

That details become the leading semiotic code in men's costume of the Regency period

Figure 5.1 Pair of French opera glasses in brass and ivory, with painted enamel decoration depicting an early nineteenth-century ballroom scene, ca. 1850. (British Optical Association Museum, LDBOA1999.2018) © The College of Optometrists, London.

Figure 5.2 Detail. Pair of French opera glasses in brass and ivory, with painted enamel decoration depicting an early nineteenth-century ballroom scene, ca. 1850. This optical device might have been used by a lady or a gentleman. The seventeenth-century fancy dress of some of the men at the ball belies the fact that such optical devices were products of the late eighteenth century. (British Optical Association Museum, LDBOA1999.2018) © The College of Optometrists, London.

is well known—hence the necessity of magnifying visual devices for scrutinizing those decisive details and judging the appropriateness of them. The use of the monocle demonstrated particular sophistication: it could be taken out for close inspection of a remarkable dress detail or for expression of interest or contempt—both by ladies and gentlemen, as seen in a bronze sculpture of an *Incroyable* of the 1790s, made a little later, circa 1830 (figures 5.18–5.19). There existed, for instance, special walking canes with monocles fixed into the handle (figures 5.16–5.17). One can see a man proudly raising such a cane before his eyes in the caricature entitled "Monstrosities" (1822) by George Cruikshank. Here the cane with its attached monocle func-

tions as the grotesque phallic eye of the flâneur, while his glance turned into the refined instrument of dandiacal power, a transparent "scepter."

If we seek another metaphor for men's fashion and visual actions in this part of St. James's Street, we find something reminiscent of a duel, the instant exchange of shots, stinging remarks, or courtesies. Something of this verbal sting passed directly later in the nineteenth century to Oscar Wilde. The novels and memoirs of this period contain numerous detailed descriptions of such visual duels: "My eyes were accidentally fixed on Glanville … he looked up and coloured faintly as he met my look; but he did not withdraw his own—keenly and steadily we gazed

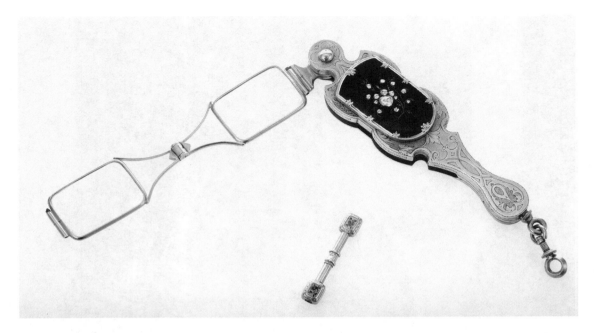

Figure 5.3 Spring lorgnette with built-in watch and elaborate watch key and regulator, early to mid-nineteenth century. From Aiguilles in the Alpine region of southeastern France, this lorgnette has an eighteen-carat gold case decorated with leaf and flower patterns. A rose-spray pattern featuring a diamond is depicted within the blue enamel case lid. The item is accompanied by a gold key and regulator. Such combined devices are rare survivals and would have been very much a luxury product at the time. Ironically, and somewhat fatuously, the lenses of the lorgnette cannot be used to read the watch face. Such an object far exceeds the necessity to tell the time. Long before mobile phone technology, status objects contained multiple functions. (British Optical Association Museum, Catalogue number LDBOA1999.900) © The College of Optometrists, London.

upon each other, till Ellen, turning round suddenly, remarked the unwonted meaning of our looks, and placed her hand in her brother's, with a sort of fear."[10]

One such "stand off" was a famous episode concerning the relationship between the Prince of Wales and Beau Brummell after their quarrel.

The Prince of Wales, who always came out rather before the performance concluded, was waiting for his carriage. Presently, Brummell came out, talking eagerly to some friends, and not seeing the prince or his party, he took up his position near the check-taker's bar. As the crowd flowed out, Brummell was gradually pressed backwards, until he was all but driven against the regent, who directly saw him, but of course would not move. In order to stop him, and prevent actual collision, one of the prince's escorts tapped him on the back, when Brummell immediately turned sharply around, and saw that there was not much more than a foot between his nose and the Prince of Wales's. His countenance did not change in the slightest degree, nor did his head move; they looked straight into each other's eyes; the Prince evidently amazed and annoyed. Brummell, however, did not quail or show the least embarrassment. He receded quite quietly, and backed slowly step by step, till the crowd closed between them, never once taking his eyes off those of the Prince. It is impossible to describe the impression made by this scene on the bystanders. There was in his manner nothing insolent, nothing offensive; by retiring with his face to the regent he recognized

Figure 5.4 Spring lorgnette, with built-in watch and elaborate watch key and regulator. Baudin Freres of Geneva, early to mid-nineteenth century. (British Optical Association Museum, Catalogue number LDBOA1999.899)

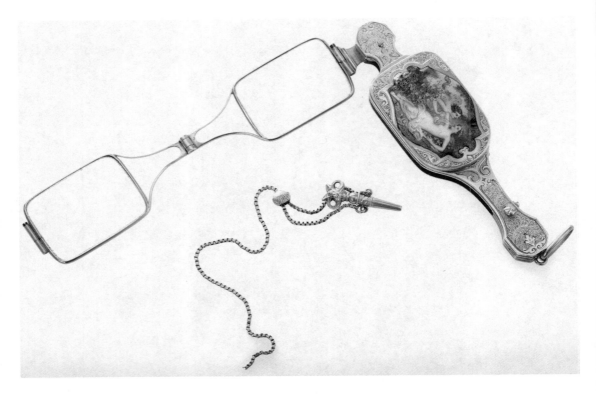

Figure 5.5 Spring lorgnette, with built-in watch and elaborate watch key and regulator. Baudin Freres of Geneva, early to mid-nineteenth century. (British Optical Association Museum, Catalogue number LDBOA1999.899) © The College of Optometrists, London.

his rank, but he offered no apology for his inadvertence ... as man to man, his bearing was adverse and uncompromising.[11]

In such detailed descriptions the exchange of glances functions as a test not only of social status but also of strength of personal character, in Brummell's case fortified by style and pose. It is important to notice that such optical duels also served to affirm gender: the participants behaved "as man to man."[12]

Contemporaries mythologized the power of the dandy's gaze. According to the descriptions, Brummell had a "small gray scrutinizing eye, which instantly surveyed and summed up all the peculiarities of features, dress and manners of those who approached him, so that the weak point was immediately hit"—his gaze seemed to be a "visible manifestation of intelligence."[13] "What a fine eye to discriminate,"[14] Hazlitt noted enthusiastically, and Brummell's biographer Captain Jesse remarked that his eyes were "full of oddity" and "could assume an expression that made the sincerity of his words very doubtful."[15] In the novels of the period, such as *Tremaine* by R. Ward (1825), *Pelham* by E. Bulwer Lytton (1828), *Vivian Grey* by B. Disraeli (1826) and *Cecil, or Adventures of a Coxcomb* by C. Gore (1841), one can find more detailed descriptions of the dandies' gaze. One of the most compelling comes from Lister's *Granby* (1826): "That calm but wondering gaze, which veers, as if unconsciously, round the prescribed individual; neither fixing nor to be fixed; not looking

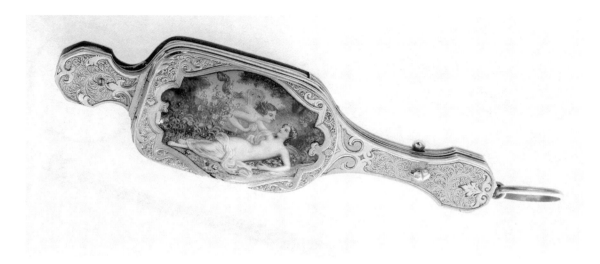

Figure 5.6   Spring lorgnette, with built-in watch and elaborate watch key and regulator. Baudin Frères of Geneva, early to mid-nineteenth century. Enameled case lid. This lorgnette has an eighteen-carat gold case decorated with leaf and scroll patterns. A nude classical love scene in a sylvan setting is depicted on the enameled case lid, suggesting that this object was retailed to a man. This is another combined device in which the lenses of the lorgnette cannot be used to read the watch face. (British Optical Association Museum, Catalogue number LDBOA1999.899) © The College of Optometrists, London.

Figure 5.7   Spring lorgnette with built-in watch formed in the shape of an early guitar, ca. 1830. (British Optical Association Museum, Catalogue number: LDBOA1999.1946) © The College of Optometrists, London.

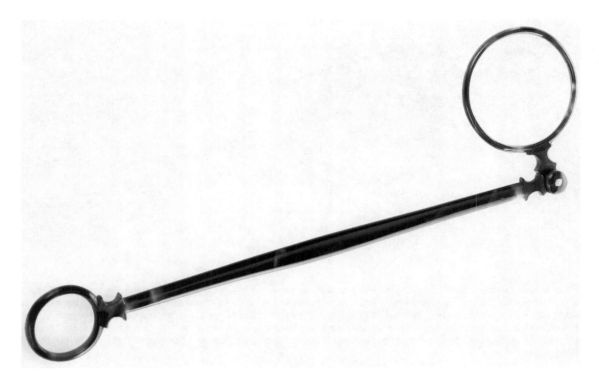

Figure 5.8 Nineteenth-century articulated quizzing glass on the end of a long genuine tortoiseshell handle. Survivals are rare, due to their fragility. (British Optical Association Museum, Catalogue number LDBOA1999.4894) © The College of Optometrists, London.

on vacancy, nor on any object; neither occupied, nor abstracted, a look, which perhaps excuses you to the person cut, and, at any rate, prevents him from accosting you."[16]

As many texts of the period suggest, near-sightedness was almost fashionable among the dandies, so the glass lens was a necessary accessory. Going to the opera without a proper opera glass was impossible, and in Paris there was a special optician, Chevalier, who supplied opera glasses magnifying thirty-two times. Chevalier binoculars were very finely crafted—the handles were typically made of mother-of-pearl or could be decorated with hunting scenes. The firm was established in 1765 by Louis Vincent Chevalier and continued as a family business throughout the nineteenth century.[17]

The lorgnette—a pair of spectacles mounted on a long handle—was worn popularly in the nineteenth century. Sometimes the lorgnette could be used as a piece of jewelry, rather than to enhance vision. Lorgnettes were also widely used by dandies for contemplating the beauties of the ladies and commencing relationships. Félix Deriège, in the aptly named *Physiology of the Lion* (1841), remarks,

You would like, I suppose, to show the lady that you have noticed her beauty ... when you reach for your lorgnette, this movement informs the lady that her charms have produced a favour-able impression. Her attention concentrates on your person. Then you give her a wink. Nothing can be better in creating the provocative look. It would be understood as if you had appreciated

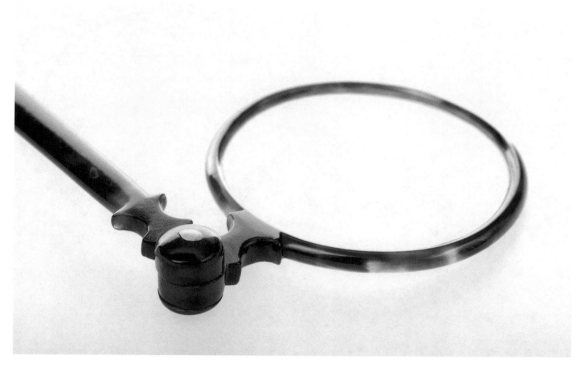

Figure 5.9   Nineteenth-century articulated quizzing glass. Detail. (British Optical Association Museum, Catalogue number LDBOA1999.4894) © The College of Optometrists, London.

every detail and attentively scrutinized all the body lines under the dress.[18]

The lorgnettes and quizzing glasses not only provided the important element of visual games between the sexes, but they also functioned as a costume accessory, decorating the dress and defining the habitual system of the wearer's gestures. As we see from *Physiology of the Lion,* the single gesture of lifting the lorgnette attracted the attention of a lady, thus serving as strategic provocation. The surviving material culture of these objects is incredible. The variety of sophisticated lorgnettes was remarkable—they were frequently made in combination with other accessories, like a fan, a small musical instrument, or a fob chain. Although the twentieth century

considers the accessory to be very much the domain of women, in the early nineteenth century the mannered accessory was central to a gentleman's appearance. The survival of the monocle into the twentieth century for upper-class gentlemen as well as Sapphic ladies and women of great style can be noted here.[19] Observing society through a quizzing glass was a ritual moment in the behavior of every respectable dandy. Lady Morgan describes the entry of the English dandy thus:

I was one evening in the apartment of the Princesse de Volkonski when one of these "fashion-mongering boys" newly arrived in Paris, appeared at the door of the salon, flushed with the conscious pride of the toilette, and reconnoitering

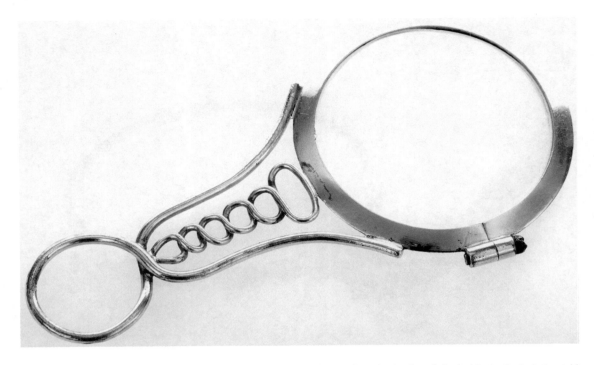

Figure 5.10 Quizzing glass to be held in the hand close to the eye in order to view distant objects, featuring a gold frame with a beveled lens rim. The handle comprises two curving pieces and multiple oval loops and features a suspension ring at the end. French, ca. 1820. (British Optical Association Museum, Catalogue number LDBOA1999.3776) © The College of Optometrists, London.

the company through his glass. I had the honor to be recognized by him; he approached, and half yawned, half articulated some enquiries, which he did not wait to be answered, but drawled on to somebody else, whom he distinguished with his notice.[20]

Apart from the erotic dimension of looking at others, visual games involving judgment and scrutiny were also essentially connected with dandy fashion. Brummell was the first to invent a very important and modern principle of vestimentary behavior, the principle of "conspicuous inconspicuousness." It meant the imperative of dressing elegantly, yet unobtrusively, without attracting undesirable attention. "If John Buhl turns round to look after you, you are not well dressed; but either too

stiff, too tight, or too fashionable," Brummell used to say.

The role of signifying detail as a decisive semiotic message also corresponded to the idea of "conspicuous inconspicuousness." A visual message could be encoded through the careful folds of starched neckcloth, a plain but stylish ring, or blackening the soles of the boots.

In more general terms this idea belongs to the broader concept of aesthetic minimalism. Minimalism can be described as a sign of sartorial understatement manifesting the priority of functional construction and geometry of the basic form stripped of superfluous embellishment. It can be compared with the dandy's stoical rule of economy of emotions—"nil admirari," not to be surprised at anything. In the sphere of body politics, minimalism was declared through the

Figure 5.11 Adams-type folding lorgnette, with real tortoiseshell rims and handle shaped to accommodate the rims when folded. English, ca. 1820. This type of handheld optical device was invented by London optician George Adams I ca. 1770 and described in detail by his son, also named George, in 1789. The item shown here is a later example with oval rims, permitting a slimming of the object's "waistline," and a suspension loop for a neck cord, whereas earlier models were designed to be slipped into the pocket. When the object is shut it resembles a mannered twentieth-century flat sunglasses case. (British Optical Association Museum, Catalogue number LDBOA1999.4762) © The College of Optometrists, London.

Figure 5.12 A rare "Waldstein" rimless monocle with integral fingerpiece to the side, made in Vienna, ca. 1830. (British Optical Association Museum, Catalogue number LDBOA1999.701) © The College of Optometrists, London.

imperative of slow gestures and the static facial expression, the inhibition that prevented running and fussing (what Honoré de Balzac called *virvoucher* in his treatise "Theory of Walking" of 1833). The rhetorical equivalent of minimalism is the genre of aphorism, essentially involving the poetics of silence. Minimalism triumphed in the culture of modernity: suffice it to recall black-and-white photography, constructivism in architecture, cubism in painting, and the modern suit.

Within dandiacal discourse the economy of minimalism worked to a considerable extent through rhetorical figures of intended blindness and selective insight, regulating one's visibility in appropriate contexts. Once, when a follower

Figure 5.13 Detail. Brass jealousy glass for surreptitious sideways viewing. (British Optical Association Museum LDBOA1999.1916) © The College of Optometrists, London.

whom Brummell obviously did not regard very highly, complimented him on the grooming and style of his outfit, Brummell famously replied, "I cannot be elegant, since you noticed me." To be well dressed, one should never be noticed. One of the stories about Brummell runs as follows. One day the Duke of Bedford met him in St. James's Street. "Ah, Brummell," he said, "how do you like my new coat?" The Beau eyed him up and down slowly, and then walked around him. "My dear Bedford," he said, fingering the cloth, "do you call this thing a coat?" The Duke, without a word, went home to change. William Hazlitt enthusiastically commented on this episode: "A distinction ... as nice as it is startling. It seems all at once a vulgar prejudice to suppose that a coat is a coat; the commonest of all common things,—it is here lifted into an ineffable essence, so that a coat is no longer a thing ..."[21]

The principle of "conspicuous inconspicuousness" also implied the blurring of class distinctions, since the new tactics erased aristocratic pretensions to demonstrate wealth and noble origin through clothes and other trappings of status. "When such solid values as wealth and birth are upset, ephemera such as style and pose are called upon to justify the stratification of society," notes Ellen Moers.[22] But this principle did, nevertheless, signal an absolute dominance of persons with good taste. The dandies, these self-proclaimed arbiters of elegance, exercised their power by naming and categorizing, thus

Figure 5.14 Pair of early folding opera glasses, tortoiseshell with four folding lenses. French, ca. 1830. (British Optical Association Museum, Catalogue number: LDBOA1999.1946) © The College of Optometrists, London.

establishing the new order of things. They appropriated the privilege of culturally informed vision, reserving the right to recognize or ignore the existence of a certain person or object. These complicated visual games point to the detachment from the aristocratic life and style based on hierarchical and stable codes of representation. Since the dandy's aim is to be recognized only by his peers, this recognition has to rely on discreet signs. That is why the details become the leading semiotic code in men's costume of the Regency period—hence the necessity of magnifying visual devices for scrutinizing the subtle details and judging the appropriateness of them. According to Richard Sennett,

The clues the initiate reads are created through a process of miniaturization. Details of workmanship now show how "gentle" a man or woman is. The fastening of buttons on a coat, the quality of fabric counts when the fabric itself is subdued in colour or hue. Boot leather becomes another sign. The tying of cravats becomes an intricate business. How they are tied reveals whether a man has "stuffing" or not, what is tied is nondescript material. As watches became simpler in appearance, the materials used in their making are the mark of the owner's social standing. It was, in all details, a matter of subtly marking yourself; anyone who proclaims himself a gent obviously isn't.[23]

The optical strategies cultivated by the dandies indicate the deep shifts in the discourse of visuality in the nineteenth century—the rise of a new art of sign reading, the interpreting of clues. Carlo Ginzburg appropriately calls this

Figure 5.15 Detail. Pair of early folding opera glasses, tortoiseshell with four folding lenses. French, ca. 1830. (British Optical Association Museum, Catalogue number LDBOA1999.1342) © The College of Optometrists, London.

new frame the "conjectural paradigm," implying that apparently negligible details can reveal deep and significant phenomena.[24]

And indeed, the conjectural paradigm had a predictable success in the second half of the nineteenth century. The deductive method of Sherlock Holmes, the fictional character of Conan Doyle, had numerous parallels in real life. F. Galton made a crucial contribution to the analysis of fingerprints; A. Bertillon invented a criminal identification system known as anthropometry; S. Freud founded the discipline of psychoanalysis on the theory that marginal details can be analyzed as symptoms pointing to the hidden cause of illness or unresolved conflict. In male fashion the job of the "detail," relying on the process of miniaturization, allowed the

dandy to escape the masses due to the sophisticated techniques of representation.

Dandies' sartorial experiments did not immediately catch on during the Regency period, and yet they mark certain important tendencies. We might detect some of the mannerisms in the pose of contemporary fashion culture, which eschews the neat and the tidy as intrinsically uncool. For instance, dandies tried to make their coats as thin as possible to reach a perfect clinging fit. For this purpose, according to Barbey D'Aurevilly, they used a sharp fragment of broken glass, scraping the inside of the coat so as to make it almost semitransparent.[25] They also obviously wanted their clothes to look worn out to distance themselves from the rich (figure 5.20).

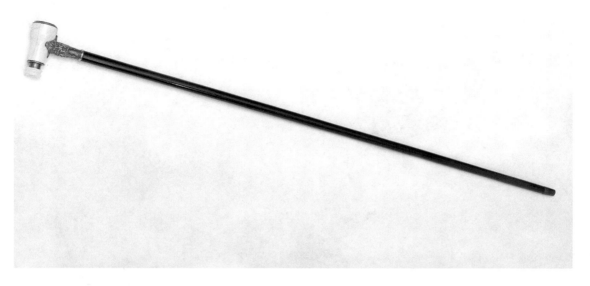

Figure 5.16 Ebony walking stick with an ivory-and-brass spyglass serving as the handle. The ultimate practical accessory for the gentleman around town. Early nineteenth century. (British Optical Association Museum, LDBOA1999.1422) © The College of Optometrists, London.

Some of them ended up making holes in their coats, thus achieving a rather modern look of conspicuous outrage, which could remind us, for instance, of the contemporary fashion for ragged or stonewashed jeans.

When Barbey D'Aurevilly commented on the dandies' attempts to scrape their frock coats with a fragment of glass, he added an aesthetic dimension and motive, noting, "These Gods wanted to walk in the clouds." But allusions to antique culture in men's fashions were often indirect, quite subtle, yet recognizable to the trained eye. This visual model can be explained through the dominance of "nude fashion," providing the new convenient frame for the fashionable body. So the textiles had to be as thin as possible in order to accentuate the silhouette of the body. In a similar way Brummell invented a strap reaching under the foot to achieve the perfect clinging fit of the pantaloons. As Anne Hollander puts it, the male Regency costume offered "a complete envelope for the body that is

nevertheless made in separate, layered, detached pieces ... The separate elements of the costume overlap, rather than attaching to each other, so that the great physical mobility is possible without creating awkward gaps in the composition."[26] This smooth envelope presented the ideal package for visual consumption. It once again connects to aesthetic modernism, like the plates of a streamlined car or a modern enamel stove.

In the context of early nineteenth-century culture, these persistent efforts to refine the fabric also point to the romantic preoccupation with the ideal of transparency, their permanent efforts to transcend material things and play with the effects of translucent layers. Images of transparent things—thin veils, glass, windows, shadows, and mirror reflections—can be found in practically every important Romantic literary text. The stories of the German Romantic writer E.T.A. Hoffman provided a rich variety of such motifs, including crystals, microscopes, and magnifying lenses. In this period the favorite

Figure 5.17 Detail. Ebony walking stick with an ivory-and-brass spyglass serving as the handle. Early nineteenth century. (British Optical Association Museum, LDBOA1999.1422) © The College of Optometrists, London.

entertainment was the magic lantern—*laterna magica*. The most famous "phantasmagoria" showman was the Belgian E. G. Robertson. He placed his projector behind a translucent screen, out of the view of the audience. His lantern, the "phantascope," was mounted on wheels. By moving the projector back and forward, he could rapidly alter the size of the images on the screen, much like a modern zoom lens. The range of reactions to its use in the beginning of the nineteenth century varied from fear and disbelief to amazement, reverence, and admiration. People were fascinated with penetrating vision—the capacity to expand human vision beyond its natural confines. The wide use of the microscope easily produced confusion in unprepared minds. In the caricature by William Heath entitled "Monster Soup Commonly Called Thames Water" (1828), the reaction of a lady observing through a microscope the bacteria in river water carries the joke. This specific interest in visual effects was further supported by the production of optical toys, including stereoscopes, phantascopes, zootropes, and kaleidoscopes, and the installation of large dioramas in Paris and London.[27] As Jonathan Crary remarks, "What takes place from around 1810 to 1840 is an uprooting of vision from the stable and fixed relations incarnated in camera obscura . . . In a sense, what occurs is a new valuation of visual experience: it is given an unprecedented mobility and exchangeability, abstracted from any founding site or referent."[28]

Disrobing, unmasking, laying bare was a fixation that dandified fashion shared with the uncanny fantasies of S. T. Coleridge and E.T.A. Hoffmann. Coleridge's Romantic symbolism

Figure 5.18 Bronze statuette of a dandy using a quizzing glass. Signed on the socle "Gaillemon" and supplied by Maison Alphonse Giroux (founded 1799). Alphonse Gustave Giroux received a silver medal at the 1839 Exposition des l'Industrie Française and produced pieces for the World Exposition of 1855. This example stylistically appears to be ca. 1840 and is therefore a nostalgic recreation of a dandy. © The College of Optometrists, London.

Figure 5.19 Bronze statuette of a dandy using a quizzing glass. Signed on the socle "Gaillemon" and supplied by Maison Alphonse Giroux. Detail showing the type of dress associated with French *incroyables* of the late 1790s. Maison Giroux also produced the first commercial camera and many innovative portraits under the direction of Mr. Daguerre (a relation) himself. (British Optical Association Museum, LD-BOA1999.1494). © The College of Optometrists, London.

implied the optical fetishism: "O! What a life is the eye! What a strange and inscrutable essence!"[29] Yet he constantly tried in his thinking to lift the visible surface of matter, displacing the signs. The final line to "Hexameters" has a startlingly modern conclusion: "to see is only a language."[30] William Wordsworth also wrote about the "bodily eye, in every stage of life the most despotic of senses."[31] This tantalizing fixation on visual experience can also be traced in the popular elite accessory of the period—the painted miniatures set in jeweled brooches, often designed as an intertwined serpent tail. Called the "lover's eye" and made famous by the example of the Prince of Wales's mistress, they featured a perfectly painted miniature of an eye, generally with eyebrow. They represented the eyes of real people as if watching every movement of a person, absent or not. It was a popular variation of sentimental or mourning jewelry from the end of the eighteenth century. Both men's and women's eyes were portrayed in eye brooches (color plate 29). Thus the new discourse of seeing and exploring differences was a cultural experience on all levels: body/vision/dress/style of behavior. In this regime of representation, practiced and promoted by the dandies, the transgressive vision functioned as a correlate to transgressive behavior.

Although the essentially normative codes of self-presentation originally structured the world of "high society" in the Regency period, the dandies dared to violate the existing etiquette. Why, where, and in what form were these social subversions staged? Brummell's special talent was to break social conventions, skillfully violating the rules of politeness and hospitality. Once he came to a ball and, having danced with the most beautiful lady, inquired, "Who the ugly man near the chimney-piece might be." "Why, surely, my good fellow, you know him," said his acquaintance; "that is the master of the house!" "No," replied the unconscious cornet, "how should I? I was never invited."[32] He obviously possessed the sarcastic wit and sufficient self-confidence; reading about his risky tricks, one wonders why he was not shown the first fashionable door he ever entered. On another occasion, when he again came uninvited to the reception of Mrs. Thompson, where he was an undesirable guest, the hostess demanded the invitation card. Brummell searched in his pockets and finally took out the card of another lady, Mrs. Johnson. When his mistake was pointed out, he coolly replied, "'Dear me, how very unfortunate! Really, Mrs. Johns—Thompson, I mean, I am very sorry for this mistake, but you know, Johnson and Thompson—and Thompson and Johnson—are

Figure 5.20 Miniature, probably Austrian, ca. 1800. Private collection. This miniature, typical of a middle-class type throughout western Europe, shows the importance of the black jacket as a foundation of men's fashion, here with the high soft collar fashionable in the late eighteenth century. The black is set off with a red waistcoat and a high white stock, and the hair is unpowdered and cut in the feathery style that marked Romanticism and the cult of the unencumbered body.

so much the same kind of thing.—Mrs. Thompson, I wish you a very good evening;' and making a profound bow, he slowly retired from the room amidst the suppressed anger of intimates, the titter of his own friends, and the undisguised wrath of the lady."[33] Such conspicuous outrage was based on his wish to irritate his former friend, the Prince of Wales, who was expected at that ball; everybody knew he did not want to appear publicly in the same places with Brummell after their quarrel. But Brummell also managed to humiliate a hostess by playing with her "common" name. Such multivalent jokes were a regular pattern with Brummell, displaying a typical variant of the dandy's insolence.

Maurice Blanchot, in his essay on the topic of insolence, notes, "Insolence is quite a useful art. It helps to be true to oneself and superior to others in all circumstances when the others try to dominate. It is also the will to reject the conventional, the customary, the habitual."[34] Since the Middle Ages such liberties were traditionally practiced by court jesters and were socially sanctioned; the fool or jester was expected to insult everybody, subverting all existing hierarchies. Brummell, as his friends testify, "had a happy facility in placing the most ordinary circumstances in a ridiculous point of view and never refrained … from exciting the risible muscles."[35] This type of behavior is sometimes called, in the tradition of the Russian semiotic school, *anti-povedenie*,[36] the reversal of conventional conduct.

The specific form of *anti-povedenie* is what would later be called the art of "cutting," a strategy that became particularly associated with the nineteenth- and twentieth-century English *salonniers*. The dandies elevated a cool and elegant cutting to the rank of high-society rhetorical games. A further anecdote demonstrates how Brummell, expertly using this art, directly expressed his "social superiority" complex. One of his acquaintances, Mr. R., who wished Brummell to notice him, invited him to dinner and let him make up the party himself. So Brummell invited his friends and they had an excellent dinner. The only thing that annoyed him was that "Mr. R. had the assurance to sit down and dine with us!"[37] In other cases Brummell's jokes were directed also at his aristocratic friends, and he acted as the severe arbiter of elegance, correcting the public taste in costume. When the rear view of the Duchess of Rutland offended him, he simply ordered her to leave the ballroom—but moving backwards … His patronizing habits with regard to the Prince of Wales became the talk of London.

What were the reasons for the unprecedented tolerance toward such scandalous behavior? During the period of Regency England, high society, having been shaken by the events in France, adopted a peculiar masochistic attitude toward self-confident individuals from lower classes, allowing them to play the role of sadistic dictators. They all wanted to know Brummell's latest jokes. "Did you hear what Buck Brummell said—or did?" Caught in the pattern of a sado-masochistic relationship, they often involuntarily provoked his double-edged practical jokes or invited direct criticism, exposing their own insecurity. Yet it is worth noting that the majority of Brummell's victims are the assuming parvenus who were very anxious to be well placed among the exquisites. Brummell himself did not belong to the aristocratic families—his grandfather was a valet to a baronet, Sir John Monson. He mixed mainly with young aristocrats, not necessarily wealthy ones, and the rich bourgeois bankers, who were eager to maneuver themselves into higher society.[38] In this sense some of his behavior relates to the *incroyables* across the Channel, who were also partly drawn from a financial speculative group called *agioteurs*.

On another occasion a wealthy young gentleman, then commencing life in society, invited Brummell and a large party to dine. After the party the Beau enquired who could take him to Lady Jersey that evening, and the host offered him his carriage, hoping thus to accompany him and be introduced to Lady Jersey. "Pray how are you to go?—said Brummell—you surely would not like to get up behind? No, that would not be right and yet it will scarcely do for me to be seen in the same carriage with you."[39] This is a classic case of Brummell's cutting, and, what is most interesting, the host laughs good-naturedly with everybody: the conspiracy of players, sharing the same sadomasochistic relationship, is provoked again, although the pretensions of nouveau riche aspiration are dismantled. A similar story provides the object of sarcasm in a more material format: it revolves around champagne. "When Brummell was dining at a gentleman's house, where the champagne was very far from being good, he waited for a pause in the conversation and then condemned it by raising his glass, and saying loud enough to be heard by everyone at the table, 'John, give me some more of that cider.'"[40] The public condemnation of wine serves, surely, to condemn the host, but also points to the normative force of Brummell's judgment.

Such stories about Brummell also demonstrate that he was extremely skillful in self-fashioning. The art of self-fashioning is largely a discursive strategy, the ability to fictionalize the trivialities of daily life and produce a narration out of ephemera. In Brummell's case the effect was often achieved by revealing small secrets, the technology of his success. His pale primrose gloves were famous, and when a friend asked him who his glover was, he answered, "Glover, my dear sir? I have three, one of whom makes the glove, the second—the thumb, the third—the other fingers."[41] Now, what are we supposed to make of such stories? Perhaps three glovers were indeed employed to make the gloves Brummell required. But yet one has to notice that, on the structural level, these stories are all alike, forming a canon of urban folklore about the dandy as cultural type. They are all organized so as to elevate the principal character to the status of a heroic suffering consumer, for whom quality is everything. The narration of consumerism is caught here in its most poetic moment.

Dandyism mastered the strategy of objectifying personality and transforming the individual style into marketable goods. Brummell could fully exploit his authority's potential in order to manipulate the public opinion to his own commercial profit. Once he publicly condemned the best sort of tobacco and then bought it himself—as a bargain. The merchant raised the price immediately afterward, advertising it after his buy.[42] I have argued, however, that the key strategy of representation in dandyism is connected with a special visual experience: a dandy knows how to look at others and to stand up under their looks. He is even especially attuned to these objectifying looks, creating the "to be looked at" situations when out on a stroll, at a ball, in the parlor, sitting by the window of a club. An unhurried gait and immobile face are evidence of self-control, signaling the art of provocative subversion.

In a similar manner Brummell could successfully use hospitality for his own needs and profits. When he served in the army, he was once late for the parade of his regiment, and his general was rather angry. But Brummell managed to correct the situation in his favor by improvising an invitation for dinner from his aristocratic friend the Duke of Rutland. The general was very pleased, but the dandy had to ride to the castle to prepare the host for an unexpected visitor![43] Such games of exchange are more typical of the pragmatic bourgeois approach, in which all symbolic values—and prestigious connections with aristocratic families were certainly highly rated—could become the object of trade or contribute to the social status of a person. Brummell infrequently used his own reputation to avoid paying the debts, as in the joke "How are you, Jimmy?"

The gradual legitimization of scandalous behavior meant the blurring of class distinctions; the expansion of the new bohemian values often signaled the weakness of the accepted aristocratic codes. Thus, the world of dandyism contained the germs of oppositional style, both in clothes and in the models of social self-presentation. The dandies explored the possibilities offered by the new paradigm of vision, being profoundly mapped into a network of visual relations characteristic of urban modernity.

This new paradigm of vision operated through optical accessories creating the new scopic regime for male fashion, in which the principle of conspicuous inconspicuousness implied the art of visible detail. The sophisticated reading of signs became possible due to the cognitive resources of conjectural paradigm. Dandyism also made an art of commodifying personality and so contributed to the formation of the modern subject. At the same time the subversive visual strategies of dandies had opened up a space for the rise of the new bourgeois elite. It was experimental ground on which the demand for changes in male fashion, indeed male lifestyle, could be made.

NOTES

1. This chapter is drawn from my book *Dandy; moda, literatyra, stil zhizni* (Moscow: NLO, 2006). I wish to thank Peter McNeil for his suggestions and revisions.
2. *The Portable Coleridge,* ed. I. A. Richards (New York: Viking, 1950), 161.
3. R. Garelick, *Rising Star: Dandyism, Gender, and Performance in the Fin de Siècle* (Princeton, NJ: Princeton University Press, 1998); S. Fillin-Yeh, ed., *Dandies: Fashion and Finesse in Art and Culture* (New York: New York University Press, 2001); G. Walden, *Who Is a Dandy?* (London: Gibson Square, 2002); A. Cicolini, *The New English Dandy* (London: L. Assouline, 2005); I. Kelly, *Beau Brummell: The Ultimate Man of Style* (New York: Free Press, 2006).
4. See M. Sandberg, *Living Pictures, Missing Persons: Mannequins, Museums and Modernity* (Princeton, NJ: Princeton University Press, 2003).
5. *The Exclusives* (London: Henry Colburn and Richard Bentley, 1830), 1:62–63. The authorship of the novel is attributed to Lady Charlotte Bury.
6. M. Merleau-Ponty, *Basic Writings,* ed. Thomas Baldwin (London: Routledge, 2004), 252. ("Une vision complémentaire ou une autre vision: moi-même vu du dehors, tel qu'un autre me verrait, installé au milieu du visible, en train de le considerer d'un certain lieu." M. Merleau-Ponty, "Tel," in *Le Visible et l'invisible* [Paris: Gallimard, 1964], 177.)
7. E. Bulwer Lytton, *Pelham or Adventures of a Gentleman* (New York: John Lovell, n.d.), 118.
8. Monocles and quizzing glasses were quite popular among the French *incroyables*—so in this aspect the British dandies continued the earlier cultural tradition.
9. Ulrich Lehmann, *Tigersprung: Fashion in Modernity* (Cambridge, MA: MIT Press, 2000), 367.
10. Bulwer Lytton, *Pelham,* 280.
11. W. Jesse, *The Life of George Brummell, Esq., Commonly Called Beau Brummell. In Two Volumes* (London: Saunders and Otley, 1844), 2:388–89.
12. Similar optical games were typical for the culture of the macaroni—there is a famous description of a visual contest in Vauxhall Gardens between Bate, the clergyman, and Fitz-Gerall, a macaroni. They argued "whether any man had a right to look at a fine woman"—the actress Hartley being the object of their attention. The exchange of meaningful glances followed: "I . . . turned around and looked them, in my turn, full in the face; in consequence of which, some distortion of features, I believe, passed on both sides." During the verbal exchange Bate questioned Fitz-Gerall's gender: "You judge of the fair sex as you do of your own doubtful gender which aims only to be looked at and admired." Thus it was the competition for the spectatorial authority but also the field for gender constructing. See *The Vauxhall Affray: Or, the Macaroni Defeated* (1773), as quoted by Peter de Bolla, *The Visibility of Visuality: Vision in Context,* ed. T. Brennan and M. Jay (New York: Routledge, 1996), 77–78. See also P. McNeil, "'That Doubtful Gender': Macaroni Dress and Male Sexualities," *Fashion Theory* 3, no. 4 (1999): 411–49; P. McNeil, "Macaroni Masculinities," *Fashion Theory* 4, no. 4 (2000): 373–405.
13. Quoted from E. Moers, *The Dandy* (New York: Viking, 1960), 37.
14. W. Hazlitt, *Brummelliana: The Complete Works in 22 Volumes,* ed. P. Howe (London: J. M. Dent, 1934), 20:153.

15. Jesse, *Life of George Brummell,* 1:53.

16. Quoted by W. Jesse from the novel *Granby* by Th. H. Lister; see ibid., 1:104.

17. French opera glasses were definitely considered to be the best. They were imported in England, but often the eyecups were replaced with blank rings to cover French brand names, since people did not want to admit to having bought foreign things.

18. "Vous voulez, je suppose, témoigner à une femme que vous la trouvez jolie …; le mouvement que vous faites pour saisir votre lorgnon avertit la dame de l'impression favorable que ses charmes ont produit. Son attention se concentre sur votre individu. Alors vous clignez les paupières. Rien qui donne l'air aussi provocateur. On dirait que vous appréciez chaque détail et que vous suivez attentivement la ligne sous le vêtement." F. Deriège, *Physiologie du Lion* (Paris: Delahaye, 1841), 10–11.

19. The famous monocle wearers were the British actor George Arliss, the architect Sir Patrick Abercrombie, and the British politician and statesman Sir Austen Chamberlain. The monocle was a popular accessory among the bohemian women inhabiting Greenwich Village. In the 1920s it was frequently depicted as a fashionable accessory in the portraits of artistic lesbian ladies (Romaine Brooks, *Una, Lady Trowbridge,* 1924; Otto Dix, *Portrait of a Journalist, Sylvie von Harden,* 1926). Wallis Simpson, in her younger years, used to wear a monocle, as did the Russian poetess Zinaida Gippius. In these cases a monocle functions as a symbol of dignity and power, but it also demonstrates the sustainability of the visual techniques originating in dandyism.

20. Lady Morgan, *France in 1829–1830* (London: Saunders & Otley, 1831), 12–13.

21. Hazlitt, *Brummelliana,* 20:153.

22. Moers, *Dandy,* 12.

23. R. Sennett, *The Fall of Public Man* (Cambridge: Cambridge University Press, 1977), 165.

24. Umberto Eco and Thomas A. Sebeok, eds., *C. Ginzburg, Morelli, Freud, and Sherlock Holmes: Clues and Scientific Method: The Sign of Three: Dupin, Holmes, Peirce* (Bloomington: Indiana University Press, 1984), 81–118.

25. Other sources mention the use of sand for this purpose.

26. A. Hollander, *Sex and Suits* (New York: Kodansha, 1995), 8.

27. See B. Stafford, *Artful Science* (Cambridge, MA: MIT Press, 1994); B. Stafford, *Body Criticism* (Cambridge, MA: MIT Press, 1993).

28. J. Crary, *Techniques of the Observer: On Vision and Modernity in the Nineteenth Century* (Cambridge, MA, and London: MIT Press, 1996), 14.

29. *Portable Coleridge,* 160.

30. Ibid., 161.

31. W. Wordsworth, *The Prelude,* ed. E. Selincourt and H. Darbishire (Oxford: Oxford University Press, 1959), 127.

32. Jesse, *Life of George Brummell,* 1:43.

33. Ibid., 1:106–107.

34. "L'insolence n'est pas un art sans valeur. C'est un moyen d'être égal à soi et supérieur aux autres dans toutes les circonstances où les autres semblent l'emporter sur vous. C'est aussi la volonté de repousser le convenu, le coutumier, l'habituel." M. Blanchot, "De l'insolence considérée comme un des beaux-arts," in *Faux pas* (Paris: Gallimard, 1943), 349.

35. Jesse, *Life of George Brummell,* Vol. 1, 116.

36. See B. A. Uspensky, "Antipovedenie v kulture drevnej Rusi," in *Izbrannie trydi* (Moscow; M. Gnozis, 1994), 320–33.

37. Jesse, *Life of George Brummell,* Vol. 1, 108–109.

38. For an accurate analysis of the social aspects of dandyism, see D. Stanton, *The Aristocrat as Art: A Study of the Honnête Homme and the Dandy in Seventeenth- and Nineteenth-Century French Literature* (New York: Columbia University Press, 1980).

39. Jesse, *Life of George Brummell,* 2:109–110.

40. Ibid., 2:108.

41. Ibid., 2:54.

42. Ibid., 2:102.

43. Ibid., 2:92.

6

A TALE OF THREE LOUIS: AMBIGUITY, MASCULINITY AND THE BOW TIE

Rob Shields

Waiter, Bouncer, Musician, Architect, Magician, Academic ... Who wears bow ties? There is a masculine mythology surrounding the bow tie itself and men who wear it. The bow tie is an accessory or ornament with unrivalled connotations, both positive and negative. It is heavily overcoded with signifiers of both arrogance and enslavement; of both masculinity and femininity; of both nobility and servitude. Even in its cultures of origin, it has been the exception for men to wear a bow tie. It has always been remarkable, extraordinary and provocative. The bow tie is outside the everyday dress codes, what Victor Turner would have called a 'liminal zone' at the neck (Turner 1979). Just wearing a bow tie is to be dressed in a mantle of contradictory signification; it is to locate oneself at an unstable nexus of a contradictory flow of sense and sensuality. No other accessory in the male wardrobe is as ambiguous, as concealing of intention. No other item is as threatening. Surprisingly, however, there is almost nothing in print on this clothing ornament. Where does the bow tie stand in the pantheon of symbols of masculinity or the lack thereof?

This chapter is a 'tale of three Louis' which examines the history of the bow tie and its meanings in relation to male gender and to the male body, stretching back from Louis Farrakhan, through the architect, Louis Kahn, to Louis XIV. These three exemplars, taken *sub speciae aeternitatis*, with a supporting cast of aristocrats and waiters, professionals and hand-puppets, sorcerers and their apprentices, provide the contrasting elements of an interpretation of the ambiguity of the bow tie, rather than a documented history of a form of dress or a specific article of clothing. Thus, we are less concerned with cloth and historical correctness than with the imaginary 'range' of the bow tie; that is, its ability to serve as an indicator of diametrically opposed meanings, wearer-characteristics, and their personae. A Bachelardian phenomenology of clothing is called for (cf. Bachelard 1961). How does the bow tie do this? Could its relation to the body of its wearer provide part of the answer?

LOUIS XIV AND THE BUTTERFLY KNOT

The origin of the bow tie is reputed to go back to the style of a cravat adopted by Louis XIV of France after the uniform of his Croatian mercenaries, called *cravates*. For the soldiers, the bow tie was a lucky charm against decapitation. Louis XIV adopted their white kerchief with added lace and secured it with a small bow at the front (Spooner 1995: 48). Over time, this kerchief narrowed and the lace was removed to become the *'noeud papillon'*, the familiar bow tie, worn in front of the collar. The cravat itself became a separate item worn under the collar, with its bow concealed beneath a larger scarf of material tucked under the shirt.

The roots of the bow tie are thus overwritten with royal associations, and indeed, this may only be one of several origins, and may only be a surviving fragment of aristocratic and fashion-industry myth-making and self-legitimation. Its functionality is also overlaid with superstition. As a result, even as the Croatian-soldiers' kerchief, the knotted cloth about the neck signified something beyond itself, beyond its own presence and possible functionality. This surplus of meaning imbues the bow tie with ambiguity: it is both what I will call 'the uniform' (Joseph 1986) of the servant (for example, the *cravate* soldier or a waiter) and it is also part of what I will call 'the costume' of the aristocratic and extraordinary (for example, Louis XIV, a famous lawyer or a well-known orchestra maestro, might well be seen wearing this sign of the extraordinary in images of their day-to-day work). Reduced to any single meaning at the expense of the others, the bow tie appears ridiculous. Yet, if the constellation of contradictory meanings can be kept aloft, so to speak, then the bow tie and its wearer appear to have a flair that is exactly an ambiguous '*je ne sais quoi*'. The bow tie becomes a sign that there is an ineffable 'something more' to the wearer. The ambiguity of this article of clothing's meaning is transferable to its wearer.

ROUND ABOUT THE NECK

In some ways, the history of clothing is marked out by the treatment of the neck. The bow tie has been as central to this history as the collar itself or the contemporary necktie. Like hemlines, the bows have been bigger or smaller, obscured the neck with high collars, or revealed it with diminutive bows under turned-down collars. Large, soft, velvety bows appear to be associated with femininity and appear often in images of its exemplars. Thus, to limit our discussion to men in Europe and North America, what bow ties can be found in images of culturally exemplary males? Abraham Lincoln is iconically

portrayed as a rugged face sporting a black bow tie and collars turned down. Noble gentlemen and nineteenth-century dandies are said to have sported small bows with winged collars turned up. We find portraits of Oscar Wilde, a famous dandy, sporting such a discreet bow tie (Bristow 1994). A contemporary arbiter of taste, Alan Flusser, notes: 'The general rule of thumb states that bow ties should never be broader than the widest part of the neck and should never extend beyond the outside of the points of the collar' (Flusser 1985, cited in Spooner 1995: 49).

For the purposes of argument, this might serve as a definition of the masculine bow: a performance standard independent of cloth, texture, colour, pattern or even the particulars of the knotting itself and of whether or not the bow tie is clipped on to the collar with mechanical clamps, pre-tied and sewn onto an adjustable strap, or tied and adjusted entirely by hand. Who ties the bow is also not specified, suggesting that the wearer need not actually have tied or even know how to re-tie the bow. Knowledge of the knot itself is presumed, as is knowledge of what a correctly adjusted bow tie might look like—only dimensions and spatial relations are specified.

Most systems for knotting a bow tie drape a strip of cloth around the neck, falling on either side. One end of the cloth is folded back on itself about 15 cm and held across the throat. The other end of the cloth is brought over the centre of this folded portion and looped back under and over it once to form a central knot. The free end is folded itself so that the leading edge of the fold can be tucked, folded edge first, behind the existing fold and through the knot, so that the fold ends up protruding on the opposite side of the knot to the first fold, giving a symmetrically constructed bow tie. Thus most approaches construct a type of double-bow: the two ends of the cloth end up sticking out along with a loop each on either side of the knot. Should these ends be aligned with the folds they fall with in order to adjust the bow neatly?

Should the bow tie be symmetrical about the centre loop? Should the axis of the bow tie be straight (in line with the shoulders)? Flusser limits himself to the extent to which the folds or 'bows' should be pulled out in a concluding adjustment. The 'look' is everything.

What is the importance of the neck? While the Croatian *cravates* of the 1600s wore their bow tie-kerchiefs as a charm against sword cuts, the neck is a famously vulnerable part of the body for any person or mammal. The tenderness of the skin, its vulnerability to cold, the relatively fragile structure of the spine, and the exposure of the jugular vein are all features which make the neck a key area of attention for the comfort and security of the body. The cultural history of the neck extends this pragmatic fuss over this part of the body. It is not only the 'site' of charms, whether the *cravates'* kerchiefs, religious medals, mementos of self-identity or ornamental rings of beaded strands. The neck is also the object of charms itself: an erogenous zone to be stimulated, stroked and gazed upon. It is a fetish zone and object. Hence the 'charm' of the eroticized neck (e.g. some have commented on 'the lesbian neck' fetish). A curious agreement appears to exist about this. This is more than intersubjective: it appears to extend to what might be called an *intercorporeal* agreement (Game 1996), based on generalizing one's own sensations to others.

This excursus on the neck is important for understanding the conventional definitions of the meaning of the bow tie. Flusser describes the contemporary, 'discreet bow tie' worn with turned-down collar tabs (in contrast to the now weddings-only type of formal shirt with a turned-up collar) which does not conceal but rather draws attention to the neck. I will argue that the manner in which the neck is displayed is a crucial detail that inflects the knot with meaning beyond pattern and colour. The relationship between the size of the bow and its wearer's neck appears central to its meaning. Thus,

the 'display' and performance of the bow-tied male is as much a matter of stance, carriage of the head and posture as it is a question of knots and the size of loops. This 'display' may be accomplished either through the cut and size of the collar, or of the bow, or through the angle of the chin itself. The ambiguous social status of the bow-tied-male (servant or patron?) makes the meaning of the bow tie inherently reversible. It can thus be called a liminal signifier, as if on a threshold (*limen*) turned, Janus-like, into both spaces. It is, in Victor Turner's phrase, 'betwixt and between' (1979). Its meaning is susceptible to inversion through rhetoric: the wearer who wishes to appear aristocratic can be lampooned as merely a formally dressed servant. The wearer can make one of the errors in pragmatic dress codes which Flusser warns of. The meaning can also be inverted depending on the performative competence of the wearer: the bow tie is as much the costume of the professional who wishes to be taken seriously and stand out (see below) as the 'uniform' of the comedian. Or, misunderstandings can be the source of unexpected meanings, as the context in which the wearer sports a bow tie moderates its meaning and the 'image' of the wearer (Davis 1992).

If the liminality of the bow tie is in part linked to the liminal charm-zone of the neck, the bow tie also lies on the corporeal *limen* between the torso and head. Therefore, two axes of liminality might usefully be described: one, the vertical axis of relations across a spatial threshold such as the neck; the other, the horizontal axis of symbolic meanings about a transition point of complete ambiguity. In the examples discussed above, this 'symbolic axis' of reversible meanings relates to the vertical axis as time relates to space. The spatial axis concerns the relative position of bodies, places and zones—of the head, the neck and the torso. The horizontal, temporalized axis concerns the reversibility of meaning and states from moment to moment as the bow tie is performed and re-coded, its meaning hijacked and re-coded back to the original meaning once again.

SERVANTS AND MASTERS

As a sumptuary ornament the bow tie has often been used to mark its wearer as someone above the mundane and banal—as a distinguished person. Nobility thus remains a key connotation. The bow tie is 'too special' for most contexts. The contemporary man wearing a bow tie is often accused of snobbery, elitism, of 'putting on airs' and of being 'overdressed'. Being 'overdressed' in a bow tie is hardly to be, for example, too warm or to be simply wearing too many pieces of clothing. The ambiguity of the bow tie is often interpreted within, for example, Anglophone–North American culture, as a signifier of falsity, of Gide-ism, of the dandy whose sincerity is doubted because he cares more for himself than his social relations. Popular opinion suggests that a bow tie shouldn't be worn to a job interview because the wearer may be interpreted as conceited. Is it because its ambiguity is threatening? The 'over'-dressed status relates exactly to the symbolic axis of the bow tie and the reversibility of meaning from one pole (the aristocratic and authoritative) to the other (the servile and uniform). For, in practice, the ambiguity of the bow tie operates in both directions, making the familiar extravagant ... and also making patrons appear like waiters, clowns or another type of servant and vice versa. In a restaurant or at a formal reception, is the wearer a waiter or a noted patron?

As worn by Charlie McCarthy, the 1950s black-bow-tied ventriloquist's dummy or hand-puppet, the bow tie was part of the image of the non-autonomy of a puppet. Ventriloquized, spoken for by a master, and animated by the puppeteer's hand, much of the repartee of this act played on the dummy's direct or indirect proclamations of autonomy and autonomous judgement. The ventriloquist, who operated the puppet as well, played the role of the doubting but dispassionate, reflective interlocutor. Even though the puppet's assumptions of his own autonomy are never directly challenged, the puppet's status is an 'in-joke' shared by the ventriloquist and a knowing audience. The joke is 'on' the bow-tied puppet who is in fact tied hand, foot and mouth to the ventriloquist. Like a clip-on bow tie, the puppet is always clearly just a dummy dressed in the 'costume' of the master.

The bow tie, especially the black bow tie in all its clip-on variations, has proven the preferred *'uniform'* of svelte waiters, obsequious butlers, scrambling bag boys and threatening bouncers: the bow tie is the essential element of a uniform that signifies servitude. It candy-coats the bouncer's threat in the uniform of polite service and chokes off the personal opinions of those in the hospitality industries by clothing them in a uniform and anonymous shell. The 'uniform', below the neck, predominates over any independent thoughts, actions or individual faciality (Deleuze and Guattari 1976) above the neck. The distinction between the 'uniform' and the 'costume' rides on not only the reversible meanings of one axis but the bow tie's associations with the spatial zones of the vertical axis of liminality.

In a performative economy of bodies and signs the bow tie is, in effect, a double-sided index. The instability of its meanings requires a constant effort of maintenance and is always at risk of rhetorical manipulation by *ad hominem* comments. Whereas Flusser discusses the appropriate looping of the bow tie, the key reference is to the wearer's body. His concern is truly *ad hominem*, with the wearer's corporeal embodiment, the co-ordination of body parts and its performance (Shields 1997). The bow-tie-wearer risks being denigrated as attempting to conceal his low economic status or as not having the necessary social status. The bow tie in this case is not just a strategic uniform but an individual *tactic* which has to be 'carried off by the wearer' (DeCerteau 1984). Few of its wearers are fully in control of its meanings. Consider Mickey Mouse—another type of exemplary male (if not by body, by nomenclature and prodigal son-in-the-father's house). In the Walt Disney cartoon *The Sorcerer's Apprentice* Mickey sports the same bow-tied costume as his sorcerer-master, but it proves to be nothing more than a 'uniform' as Mickey loses control of his spells. The apprentice's conjuring commands him and determines his action, rather than the other way around. Mickey is shown to be another type of automaton or dummy. The inept sorcerer is soon a victim of his conjuring—and a 'fashion victim' of the bow tie's duplicitous meanings.

The bow-tie-as-uniform standardizes the human contact-point of large service corporations who wish to evoke a formal tradition of the nineteenth-century man-servant's relation to his aristocratic employer (gender intended). As opposed to those servants merely engaged to carry out a function, the bow-tied man-servant was the personal assistant of the aristocrat and often a trusted proxy in charge of other servants. The contemporary correlate of the bow-tied servant is often tied to the semiotic elevation of the status of customer to that of 'master'. This illusion is not a simple prank that beguiles the flattered client. Like the clip-on bow tie, the taxonomic identity of the 'servant' is also 'clipped-on'. The performance of the master and servant relation consists of a complex and delicate performance fraught with opportunities for shattering the illusion. To remain intact, it must 'float', chiffon-like, on a supporting set of gestures of trustworthiness by the servant and delegation by the customer. These are 'gestural' in that they are knowingly understood to be partial performances. For example, a customer at a restaurant may accept the recommendation of the waiter, or a nightclub patron may defer to the authority or instructions given by bouncers. In this situation of 'ironic complicity'

(Shields 1989) neither interactant abandons his socioeconomic interest, but rather elaborates a tangential, short-term relationship which is no more than evocative of the lifetime association of master and servant. At the close of, for example, a restaurant meal, the performance comes to a ritualized end with the presentation of the bill—with that great consumer flourish—the credit card which allows the monetary transaction to be ritually hidden.

What then of the bow tie's importance in male formal-wear and in lesbian cross-dressing (Doherty 1995; Fillin-Yeh 1995; Polhemus 1978)? How does the appearance of 'elegance' of the bow tie operate? For men, the bow tie is the single most important sumptuary accessory to convey an impression of special dress, of the extraordinary, of the formal occasion and the 'elegance' demanded for such events. While the elegance of a man's dress may arguably lie in the cut of suits or even coats, the bow tie is the element which directly proclaims the importance of the occasion, switching a merely nice suit into a 'formal suit'. Yet, even here, the meaning of the bow tie is ambiguous.

Consider, for example, the case of male formal-wear advertising in the twentieth century. The images in such advertisements depict clean shaven, short-haired and often pomaded young, apparently fit, Caucasian males. In general terms they smile, posed in a relaxed and confident manner often with at least one hand in a pocket. They look directly at the camera (and thus at the viewer), yet they are inattentive. They lounge; contrary to the formal implications of their dress they apparently do not attend to their comportment. Swathed in the constricting clothing of discipline, they are momentarily—arrogantly—undisciplined in their poses. The implication of power and prestige derives partly from the ease and comfort they project even while wearing constricting clothes. The bow ties can even be undone, un-tied, in these images.

But, the models also smile and look downward in these images: their heads tilted down, necks obscured by square chins. Bent slightly forward, the musculature of their torsos is softened by the folds of generously cut shirts which are furthermore often pleated. There is a coy shyness to this pose. The effect is to 'sweeten' their appearance: they are 'sweet guys', generally posed together in homoerotic photographs of camaraderie. They are not attentive servants, their composure belies the restrictions of their unusual costume—it is not their habitual uniform. Carefully posed, only the best image of thousands of photos taken in one fashion-shoot is presented. Their stances, the distribution of weight and the co-ordination between bodies in group photos, indicate their pleasure in the moment: they are at leisure (Rojek 1985; Shields 1997). Elegance achieved in spite of itself, and in this sense 'grace' (understood by Matisse as beauty which has been hidden), is thus a central meaning that can be read from these images. The bow tie or, as more evocatively named, the butterfly-knot, has a long association with grace and lightness.

LOUIS I. KAHN AND THE LOOP

Centuries after Louis XIV's court-dress innovation, an architect equally obsessed with form became one of the definitive professionals to wear a bow tie. Since the nineteenth century, painters and tradesmen had worn forms of the bow tie which did not pose any risk of trailing on a canvas or drawing.[1] While some may be familiar with portraits of the French painter Cézanne wearing a loose bow, the famous architectural 'loop' was that of Louis Kahn, the Chicago architect. Bow ties flourished in the last decades of the nineteenth century—the high point of the 'Chicago-style' where the skyscraper was invented to fit large businesses into the limited central business district of 'The Loop'. This was Chicago's downtown area delimited on either side by the Illinois River and fronting Lake Michigan. Those large buildings fitted an ag-

gressive business style, to which the bow tie was an ideal counterfoil.

Consider, then, this 'aggressive' bow tie wearer, who strikes an entirely different pose from the aristocrat on the one hand, or the waiter, Charlie McCarthy or the coy formal-wear models on the other. The wearer is often caught in a photojournalist's snapshot: standing with weight balanced, often caught in the midst of a gesture. A middle-aged male, sometimes bearded or grizzled, holds his chin up: the bow tie exposes the neck and chest and presides over a sometimes massive gut. On the other hand one expects revulsion as the prime reaction in a weight-obsessed culture. However, this 'overdressed stomach' below the bow tie can also become the embodiment of authority: a signifier of status and corporealized power. This is also a form of conspicuous expression of class power to over-consume.

Rather than elegant, this is an authoritative loop. The aggressive, bow-tied protagonist is a specific assemblage of the body and its ornamentation into a pose completed by the symbolic folds of the bow tie as a marker of prestige. The special significance of this aggressive figure, however, is its link to *bourgeois aggression*. Authority and prestige gloss the nearness of the wearer to the struggle to secure social power and his awareness of this. This is the food-chain struggle to appropriate surplus value and the material wealth which takes the form of not only capital but the *materiel* of reproduction (Lefebvre 1991): the basics of nourishment.

The unusually ambiguous quality of the bow tie has allowed it to act as an affirmation of rebellious individuality. Despite its aggressiveness and assertion of extra-ordinariness and non-conformism, the wearer appears to maintain his investment in social status and thus in the normative regime of the status quo. In opposition to many proletarian radicals' investment in self-effacing everyday garb of collectivism, the bow tie indicates the self-interest and power of the 'maestro'. Power—cultural as much as economic—is not in this case delegated but 'held' and concentrated—much as a sorcerer might 'hold' a magical spell before it is cast. Architects fall into this threshold or liminal category between the servant and the master: they are both. Musicians are another example. On the one hand they are paid servants, yet on the other hand they are masters of a craft, 'geniuses', whose ability is prized beyond their own loyalty to a master. In this reading, they are, by definition, ambitious, for they are driven to excel and distinguish themselves performatively. They hold cultural power in the form of abilities, not just as 'cultural capital' (cf. Bourdieu 1984). The bow tie marks a middle class of men who have higher cultural and social status, above and beyond their often low economic status. They are 'maestros', the shamans of 'Western' culture whose performative competence in orchestrating the meanings of the bow tie is indicative of their competence in other cultural performances.

LOUIS FARRAKHAN
AND THE MAGICAL FOLD

The bow tie thus marks the 'arrogant performer'—the maestro—who *commands* rather than only pleases. Indeed, commanding or performing the role of a commander is central to the service that this servant offers. At the centre of a public event: a trial, hearing, performance or debate, this performance is the opposite of the role of the paid servant for it demands the attention of the audience, rather than signalling the opposite distribution of attention. As an example, we might take only one of a number of contemporary courtroom lawyers, politicians with reputations for 'backroom' influence such as Arthur Schlesinger Jr. was famed for in Washington, DC. Once again, the embodied, physical 'presence' of the wearer and the manner in which he carries off the performance of wearing a bow tie is crucial. That 'presence' is the positioning and

stance of the wearer's body in co-ordination with the bow tie and other sumptuary elements toward the surrounding context and action.

But Louis Kahn is only a way-station on the path to a contemporary example of the ambitious bow-tied male: the powerful orator and leader of the Nation of Islam movement, Louis Farrakhan. Farrakhan graduated from a one-time career singing with a calypso band to the podium of race politics without—in a sense—changing his attire. Nonetheless, there was a change, from the bandsman's bow-tied *uniform* to the maestro's *costume*. The bow tie is a sumptuary proclamation of status, of being a master, marking the hidden power of the sorcerer. It amplifies the rhetorical power of Farrakhan's speeches and a delivery punctuated by sharp, assertive movements. The bow tie claims respectability and demands the audience's attention to Farrakhan at the same time that he attacks the existing social power structure. Symbolically, the bow-tied social critic might be read as seeking membership, but on his own, radical terms. While decrying the status quo, Farrakhan is garbed in the respectability of the establishment and cultural elites. In short a sumptuary tactic complements political and rhetorical tactics.

The bow tie signals a surplus of signification. On the one hand it may be presented for its positive implications and meanings, but it still carries the negative meanings in reserve. But on the other hand, it also suggests that there are even further hidden meanings which are perhaps negative and perhaps positive, which can be conjured out of this sumptuary and semiotic balancing act. There is 'more than meets the eye' and the wearer should therefore be treated with caution.

CROSSING-OVER: CONCLUDING
ADJUSTMENT

A final case of costuming is the adoption of the bow tie as a signifier of masculinity (out of its many possible signifiers) in lesbian cross-dressing. Or is it masculinity? The attraction of the bow tie is its liminality—its threshold, boundary status—and unstable double-coding. The bow tie is firmly anchored within the sartorial repertoire of masculinity despite the constancy of bows in feminine dress over the last two centuries. In contrast to the bow tie, the feminine bow has always tended to fall far below the collar-line, covering the breastbone—even lying as low as the sternum. The two are recognizably different even if they sometimes share the same folds. One is overcoded as 'feminine', the bow tie on the other hand is culturally-gendered as 'masculine'. Yet, because the bow tie is ambiguous it is ideally suited to manipulation. In effect, it is not a simple signifier of masculinity at all. It serves as a liminal device which can reverse the meaning of an entire ensemble of clothing and of poses and gestures, not to mention the gender-meaning of the wearer's body. It is a boundary phenomenon, betwixt and between gender identities. What transforms the 'uniform' into the 'costume'? Attitude and success in carrying it off, is the answer that many give. However, I have argued that it is possible to go beyond a psychological explanation. The answer lies not in the bow or the bow tie, but with the body and the visible co-ordination of the body and the bow. The line of the chin and the display of the neck transform the garb of the lackey into the power suit. Yet this 'costume' can always be reversed back into its rhetorical double of the puppet's uniform. The bow tie requires a constant performance from its wearer; it requires a constant semiotic effort to arrange the body and the bow to signify and connote in the right direction. If the maestro is arrogant, it is an arrogance that is de facto a site of struggle—a constant adjustment—and yet it must be a concealed struggle. The maestro is thus, like every sorcerer, a master of control and of conjuring.

The bow tie is not 'liminal' just because it is outside everyday garb, but because it is a Janus-faced signifier which, like a threshold (a *limen*)

many-times crossed, links the everyday and the extraordinary; the servile and the authoritative; the slave and the master; male and female. It is semiotically unreliable. But, in effect, the bow tie acts as a conduit of semiotic flows: it has a function similar to a lightning rod or conductor, capturing the always approximate arrangement of actants or active elements such as the pose of the body, its posture and comportment, the surrounding context, the other elements worn and the style of bow, into an assemblage glossed as one 'meaning'. These active elements may include what the speaker says and does, stated provocations and the co-ordination of the body with itself as it resolves the mechanics of mobility and gravity into what we blithely call 'stance'. But the body itself is a key factor which makes its appearance independent of intention or of the postulated status of the wearer as maestro or man-servant.

This 'tale of three Louis' is only the beginning of a critical semiotic audit of the changeable signification of the bow tie. To wear a bow tie is to conjure up a point of balance amongst the unstable meanings, or 'assemblages', which we have surveyed. To point out the unstable, 'assembled' quality of the bow tie's signification is to add a level of complexity which reveals the constructed nature of the bow tie as signifier. It reveals that the concept of a 'meaning'—the bow tie as either a 'uniform', or as an elegant or aggressive 'costume'—is a superficial gloss on a fluid arrangement of forces. Balancing the meanings of the bow tie is like adjusting the length of the bow, the final adjustment of the knot.

NOTES

Reprinted with permission from Rob Shields, "A Tale of Three Louis: Ambiguity, Masculinity and the Bowtie," in *Consuming Fashion: Adorning the Transnational Body*, ed. A. Brydon and S. Niessen (Oxford: Berg, 1998), 163–76.

1. This middle class of bow tie is not simply functional. If it is reduced to its function of

'not trailing' then it again appears a ridiculous concession to a social injunction to wear something at the neck: as a friend jokes, 'bow ties make me think of gynaecologists'. The wry hilarity of this comment is that it casts any male in sight wearing a bow tie as 'a gynaecologist', and winks at women's in-group knowledge of the social and bodily discomfort of a gynaecological examination, smuggling another register—what Bakhtin called the carnivalesque 'lower bodily stratum'—into polite conversation (Bakhtin 1973; Cronin 1996). The joke doubles in its destabilizing force amongst those who are part of its knowing-audience by disrupting all semiotic pretence if a bow-tied male interjects with 'I don't understand.' From elegant, authoritative figure, the bow-tied male fails in such cases to juggle all the meanings and interpretations the bow tie can elicit and drops into a category similar to 'Charlie McCarthy', losing face through semiotic ineptitude and performative incompetence.

Plate 1. Anonymous, "Bourgeois Couple." French, miniature painting, c. 1830. Private collection. Facing each other with a rather smug air, this middle-aged couple exemplifies some of the paradoxes of nineteenth-century fashion. Although they wear completely different fashion forms, the artist has captured a sense of complementarity. Thus, both wear garments of fine black cloth, silk in the case of the woman, smooth woolen broadcloth in the case of the man. Both have a detailed and slightly puffed shoulder, expanding their comfortable bodies. The woman's coral jewelry finds a counterpoint in the man's finely striped waistcoat and his more slightly ruddy complexion, which marks him out as being of a different gender. Both of their rather plain profiles and bird-like eyes are clearly defined; were they made for each other? We wonder whether the artist has been a little cruel or whether the couple enjoyed their rather self-satisfied status.

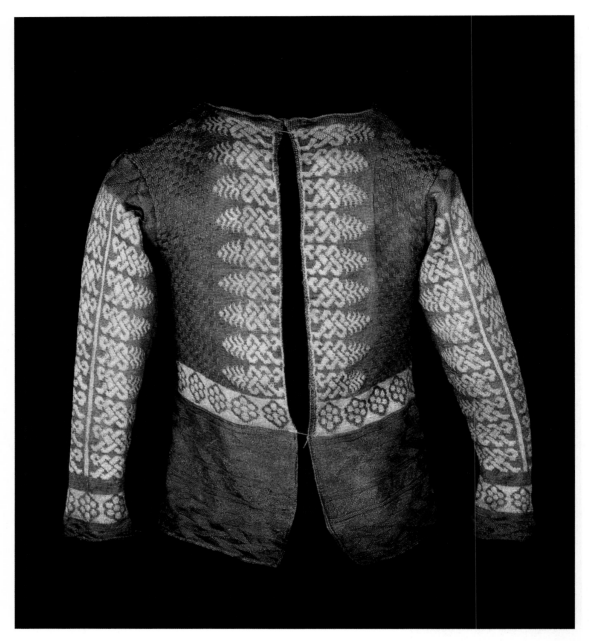

Plate 2. This is a very rare and splendid early seventeenth-century green-and-yellow knitted jacket for a man that indicates how figure-hugging male fashion might be. Such garments were made professionally in several centers including Spain and Italy. The interlace pattern imitates frogging down the center front and down the sleeves. The jacket organizes the man's body into a clearly defined torso, waist, and neckline. The neck was considered a vulnerable and important part of the body and required the added protection of linen. Courtesy of Cora Ginsburg LLC, New York.

Plate 3. Steven van der Meulen, *Erik XIV* (1533–1577). 58 x 31 cm. Nationalmuseum, Stockholm. Erik XIV was the first prince of Vasa to assume the Swedish throne after his father, Gustav I, made Sweden into a hereditary monarchy. Thus, it was imperative for the Vasa family to emphasize its social status in order to legitimize its position. This imposing-looking painting is actually very small in size. Erik's clothes were imported from England and the Netherlands, the black cape indicating Spanish influence. The rich clothes of a king here evoke the effect of damascened armor translated into embroidery. The beard is fashionably cut, the red stockings and the codpiece emphasize his physical assets. The green velvet drapery on which Erik stands is covered with sheaves, the symbol of the Vasa family. The portrait was painted for a proposal of marriage; one version was sent to Queen Elizabeth I of England. Perhaps she did not care for his legs.

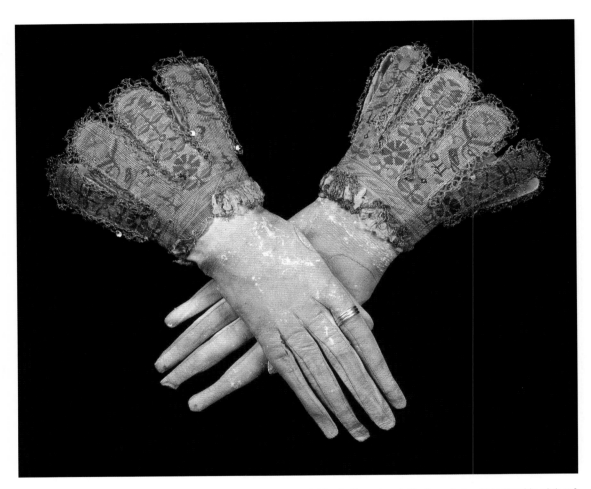

Plate 4. A pair of men's leather gloves with tapestry-woven tabbed silk and metallic thread gauntlets lined in pink taffeta and edged in silver lace with spangles. Rare survivals of tapestry-woven decorative accessories, they are attached to the gauntlet with ruched pink silk and silver lace. The long fingers are padded to add effect. An otherworldly effect is created by this prosthetic device. English, first quarter of the seventeenth century. Courtesy of Cora Ginsburg LLC, New York.

Plate 5. Man's brocaded silk undress cap. Crimson-red Bizarre silk satin damask brocaded with floral design in polychrome silk and metallic (*frisé* and *filé*) threads. Red and gold metallic cord and gold metallic lace trim, silk tuft at peak. Lined in green cotton, diamond quilted with red silk thread, interlined with card. French, early eighteenth century. Such caps were worn as "undress" when the wig was removed and often accompanied a banyan or dressing gown. Men could receive visitors in such attire. Courtesy of Cora Ginsburg LLC, New York.

Plate 6. White linen waistcoat with crewel embroidery, bold floral design in red, green, and purple with yellow borders. English, c. 1735–1740. The vibrant carnations, pansies, and other flowers were possibly rendered by women at home. Such an outfit may have been accompanied by a solid-colored suit. Courtesy of Cora Ginsburg LLC, New York.

Plate 7. Flamepoint wallet in shades of deep reds, olive, deep cream, and celadon with black/brown delineation. Silver, scalloped circular clasp initialed "SM" and dated 1757; crewel wools on canvas, lined in crimson-red silk damask, with two interior pockets. English, 1757. 12.065 x 18.415 cm. A man's wallet was often worked by a female member of his family, to hold documents and currency. Courtesy of Cora Ginsburg LLC, New York.

Plate 8. Man's banyan of Indian painted cotton. Pattern of delicate grapevines, cartouches of thick vines, exotic flowers, and double flowering vases, in shades of red, blue, and purple on white. Indian export, European market, c. 1750. 156.21 x 195.58 cm. A banyan was worn at home for private leisure, writing, and receiving people. Courtesy of Cora Ginsburg LLC, New York.

Plate 9. Man's waistcoat of natural linen embroidered with yellow silk thread, with large stylized foliate sprays and vermicelli-patterned ground; round neckline with yellow silk thread-covered buttons along center front closure; scalloped pocket flaps; long sleeves with embroidery on lower half. English; second quarter of the eighteenth century. This elaborate waistcoat may have accompanied a plain-colored suit, probably as a summer garment. Courtesy of Cora Ginsburg LLC, New York.

Plate 10.   Waistcoat embroidered with fruits, English, c. 1780. Polychrome silk floss on white cotton. Cherries, peaches, strawberries, pears, pineapples, oranges, plums, lemons, figs, and grapes are depicted. Such designs are influenced by the Lyon workshops, which provided thousands of waistcoat designs in the last third of the eighteenth century. Professionally embroidered waistcoats such as this one were eagerly acquired by wealthy macaroni men on the grand tour and are often described as being of "all colours of the rainbow" or in shades of pink, yellow, or green. By 1780 the cut is starting to appear quite different from the fashions of just twenty years earlier, which had wider skirts and were not so tight-fitting. Men of lesser means could replicate these effects by having a simpler example embroidered by their female circle. Museums hold many of the more naïve examples that are rarely displayed. Courtesy of Cora Ginsburg LLC, New York.

Le Jeu du Volant.

On voit souvent une Coquette,   Echauffer plus un jeune Amant
Par un air adroit et charmant,   Que le Volant et la Raquette.
A Paris chez Nicolas Arnoult rue de la Fromagerie a l'image St. Claude aux Halles. Avec Privilege du Roy.

Plate 11.   Nicolas Arnoult, *Le jeu du Volant,* c. 1680–1700. "A Paris chez Nicolas Arnoult rue de la Fromagerie a l'image St. Claude aux Halles. Avec Privilège du Roy." Engraving. 30.2 x 20 cm. Nationalmuseum, Stockholm NMG Orn 4326. This image of gallantry conveys the fashion world that Charles II and his advisers attempted to avoid. The feathered hat and the graceful interaction between men and women in a game of shuttlecock suggest a fluttering world of quixotic appearances. The appended verse suggests that the coquettes playing with the man wish to win him, and not the shuttlecock. Yet the suit worn by the Frenchman at play is quite similar to the suit proposed by Charles II, which was perhaps less national than he in fact claimed. The long wigs are identical in both countries.

Plate 12.   Pehr Nordqvist, *An Audience with a powdered wig,* 1799. Gouache. 36 x 43 cm. Nationalmuseum, Stockholm. This small gouache painting depicts the number of retainers required and the accompanying mess when powdering a wig. This is also an ironic image concerning the luxury consumption of the Swedish aristocracy. The tax introduced in Sweden in 1794 suggested that powder was a luxury as harmful as coffee. The men entering the room are interpreted as collectors, presenting economic claims on the man being powdered. Notice the man's stockings and mule and his *coiffeur,* fashionably dressed. This image mocks the old-fashioned aristocracy, facing a new era with bourgeois ideals. The title makes clear that it is sometimes the dress, rather than the person, which takes center stage. On that level it is a joke about surfaces rather than depth.

Plate 13. Banyan and matching waistcoat of quilted sapphire-blue silk. Standing collar with two-button closure; long curved sleeves, and wide, deep cuffs lined in white linen; long, flared skirts, mid-calf length; extended fronts turn back to fasten to either side with cord loops to a row of matching blue silk-thread-covered buttons; unfastened, banyan closes left over right or right over left; lined in blue silk. Attached waistcoat with round neckline and button closure and flap pockets; thigh-length, back lined in white linen; fine cotton interlining. Chinese export for the European market, c. 1760. An almost identical banyan is in the Brighton & Hove Museum (UK); it belonged to Captain William Fernell, commander of the East India Company Ship *Valentine*. Not only macaroni men aspired to fashionability; this very rare survival with its matching waistcoat might also have suggested success in trade as well as a sensibility for foreign climes and cultures. Courtesy of Cora Ginsburg LLC, New York.

Plate 14.   Pair of men's slippers of dark-blue satin embroidered with polychrome silk thread in long-and-short and satin stitches and French knots with butterflies, pansies, and other floral motifs; monogram embroidered in silver metallic thread on vamp. French; mid-nineteenth century. Courtesy of Cora Ginsburg LLC, New York.

Plate 15.   Ulrika Fredrica Pasch, *Adolf Ludvig Stierneld (1755–1835), friherre, överkammarherre,* 1780. Oil. 78 x 64.5 cm. Nationalmuseum, Stockholm. This charming young Swede wears a fashionable soft Anglophile hat and an elegant chromatic of blue and yellow. He was the chamberlain of Queen Sofia Magdalena (consort of Gustav III) and also the curator of the portrait collection at Gripsholm castle. In this portrait he is twenty-five years old. His high puffed and slashed sleeve refers to the type of "Swedish" dress developed by the Swedish King Gustav III, here translated from a silk court dress to a more easy woolen garment with extra buttons. This particular jacket has been interpreted as part of courtiers' resistance to the dress reform. The hat also refers to reformed Swedish dress. The sense of "esprit" depicts the man as cosmopolitan and capable of taking his place in the urbane world of Enlightenment Europe. As Anne Hollander has noted in *Sex and Suits* (1994), wool, leather, and linen create a harmony with the natural world, rather than the sense of opposition to it created by smooth textiles such as silk and satin.

Plate 16.   Daniel Chodowiecki, *Natur und Afectation,* c. 1780. Engraving, each 8.4 x 4.7 cm. Nationalmuseum, Stockholm. NMG 815/1897. In Germany, Daniel Nikolaus Chodowiecki's engravings for almanacs possess an elegant and animated line that epitomizes the ambiguity of some fashion caricature. His paired contrasting images on the themes of artifice (court dress) and naturalism (neoclassical dressing) do not necessarily castigate the former: perhaps his suggestion is that pastoral dress is just as much an affectation for leisured peoples. This is part of a series of twelve images depicting six scenes with contrasting couples. In the others the unaffected couple is dressed (rather than seminude) in a modest version of fashionable dress, and they use less affected gestures. Chodowiecki's illustrations for Johann Kaspar Lavater's highly influential study of character and physiognomy, *Essays on Physiognomy, designed to promote the knowledge and the love of mankind* (1775–1778, five volumes, translated from the French by Henry Hunter, London, John Murray, 1789), function as explicit attacks on court manners and morals and argue that the new man must reject the set of the courtier in order to be "true."

7

UNIFORMS AND THE CREATION OF IDEAL MASCULINITY

Elisabeth Hackspiel-Mikosch

Uniforms have been frequently described as masculinity at its highest potency. New concepts of masculinity and male beauty emerged in the course of the nineteenth century and still influence thought today.[1] Following the French Revolution, male citizens in Europe acquired new civil rights and duties, privileges that women could not enjoy and that raised the ideal of hegemonic masculinity to a new level. The new status of masculinity was most clearly expressed in military and civilian uniforms, which shaped the male body and mind and enjoyed increasing popularity during that century.[2] Based on the investigation of original sources, this chapter will look at the complex cultural-historical phenomena of masculinity as manifested in men's uniforms during the long nineteenth century (1789–1914/1918). Beginning with a discussion of how the image of the uniformed soldier changed from mercenary to hero during the preceding century, a study of surviving uniforms from the nineteenth century will analyze how this mode of dress constructed the image of superior masculinity through sartorial means. Since the spectacle of uniformed masculinity did not enjoy undivided admiration, the chapter will conclude with a discussion of caricatures and satirical theater plays that reveal contemporary criticism of the adoration of uniformed masculinity. These satires occurred within real events of German militarism under Emperor William II (reigned 1888–1918).

FROM MERCENARY TO HERO—THE CHANGING IMAGE OF THE MAN IN UNIFORM

For centuries, European soldiers were not regarded as an ideal of masculinity. It was quite the opposite. Already the first soldiers of the early modern period, mercenaries like the *Landsknechte* (German mercenary pike men), were widely feared by the population. Being recruited from the lowest sections of the society, they received little salary and frequently had to rely on plundering and pillaging for survival. Although their flamboyant style of multicolored and slashed clothing eventually inspired men's fashion during the sixteenth century, contemporary eyewitness reports reveal that the *Landsknechte* were often treated as social outcasts and scorned as a threat to social peace and public virtue.[3] When standing armies became an integral part of the national defense during the seventeenth and eighteenth centuries in Europe, the regard for soldiers did not necessarily improve. Young peasants and laborers were involuntarily pressed into service, and had no prospects for social advantage, since the officer's career was restricted to members of the aristocracy. As a consequence, desertion was a serious problem for many armies, even though deserters faced draconian punishment. Respected members of the urban middle classes, such as craftsmen and merchants, in general escaped recruitment by claiming to work in reserved occupations.

Martin Dinges has pointed out that the violability of the soldier's body was pervasive and most obvious during the early modern period. Although contemporary pictures may portray soldiers in picturesque uniform, the uniforms did not really protect the soldiers' bodies, neither from the elements nor during combat. Extreme physical drill, unhealthy clothes, insufficient food and living conditions, excessive consumption of alcohol, and whoring endangered the health and well-being of these soldiers. Once injured or crippled, the soldier faced a pitiful life as an invalid.[4]

The low social respect for the soldier and military also becomes evident within social hierarchy. It is most clearly reflected in the court ceremony during this time. Until the eighteenth century, the military in general had to give way to the civil rank at court. According to Julius Bernhard von Rohr's handbook on court ceremony (1733), court officials at most European courts such as the lord chamberlain or chief equerry took priority even over the highest-ranking military officers, including the general field marshal.[5]

During the eighteenth century, several rulers tried to improve the social regard for soldiers. The Prussian king Frederick William I (1688–1744) may be credited with paving the way. Although he avoided fighting wars and never started a war himself, the so-called soldier-king became famous for his comprehensive military reforms introduced in order to improve his army, the economy, and the administration of Prussia. Frederick William I introduced a new drafting system, which was based on regimental cantons and was intended to spread the draft more evenly over the country; all young men of Prussia could be drafted. He enlarged the army to 80,000 soldiers, making it the third- to fourth-strongest and the most modern army in Europe. In order to raise social and political esteem for the military, he gave priority to the military rank at court. Thus, he made the general field marshal rank higher than a state secretary or minister. He also allowed members of the middle class to become officers and awarded peerage to them if they demonstrated merit.[6] The Prussian ruler demanded discipline, obedience, strictness, and frugality from his soldiers, officers, and his own heir to the throne. Thus, he also paved the way for a new canon of masculine virtues, oriented toward military needs and later known as "Prussian" virtues.

When Frederick William I ordered uniforms in a new style for his soldiers in 1718, he publicly renounced the dominating French fashion and set new aesthetic standards for men's fashion in the future. The new Prussian uniforms were more functional and economical. The frugal cut was shorter and tighter. The uniforms needed much less cloth than before and had less decoration.[7] He propagated this new style by wearing military uniform himself during official occasions and in official state portraits.[8]

Receiving considerable international attention, the Prussian reforms and new uniforms inspired other rulers to follow his example. The enlightened German Emperor Joseph II (1741–1790), who saw himself as the first servant of his state rather than as an absolutist ruler, sent an important signal in 1766 when he abolished the Spanish ceremonial dress at his court, preferring to appear in uniform at official occasions. This was strongly criticized by court members, in particular by the *Obersthofmarschall* Count Ulfeld, who was in charge of the court ceremony. As Kurzel-Runtscheiner has shown, the new rule implicitly caused a dramatic upgrading of the military's position at the imperial court, since a person's position at court now only became apparent when he was wearing a uniform.[9] The increasing popularity of the uniforms also caused a change in men's fashion during the second half of the eighteenth century, when men began to adopt the aesthetics of soldiers' uniforms.

That the appreciation for men in uniforms was changing during the eighteenth century is also well documented by court festivals, such as the wedding celebrations that the Saxon ruler Frederick Augustus (known as Augustus the Strong) organized for his heir to the throne in Dresden in 1719. Augustus ordered that an estimated 13,000 men dress in military or civilian uniforms. Soldiers, livery servants, hunters, civic guards, postal servants, miners, and smelters—all were dressed in meticulously prescribed uniforms. Parading in numerous pageants during the month-long festival in Dresden, the men in uniform staged the spectacle of a wealthy and well-organized court and state. Their splendid uniforms manifested the political and social ambitions of Augustus, Elector of Saxony and King of Poland.[10]

Inspired by Norbert Elias's civilization theory, Daniel Roche has suggested that the wide introduction of uniforms for the new standing armies during the eighteenth century was a considerable contribution to the process of civilizing men. As the draft affected wider sections of the male population in Europe, more and more men learned new standards of physical discipline and hygiene, because they were forced to undertake cleanliness and to take meticulous care of their own uniforms.[11]

All of this prepared the way for a more positive image of the soldier. But the idea of the soldier as a hero clearly developed after the French Revolution, in particular, during the Napoleonic Wars. Based on a new concept of the democratic citizen, as opposed to a royal subject, the male citizens of France achieved new political rights and were at the same time expected to defend their nation as part of their civil duty. *Levée en masse* conscription affected hundreds of thousands of young men in France and was soon adopted by other European countries that defended themselves against the French invasion. Clad in dashing, colorful uniforms and fighting for their home country, young men from all sections of society entered the national armies and could now hope for social advancement through a military career (color plate 18).

Uniforms in striking colors became necessary because of new military weapons and strategy. At the same time, the attractive and fashionable uniforms made military service look appealing. The startling appearance of the Napoleonic armies impressed the European population greatly. Fourteen-year-old Carl Schehl witnessed how the Second Carbineer regiment triggered amazement when it entered the city of Krefeld, Rhineland, in 1811. Captivated by the heroic impression of the soldiers with their beautiful horses, splendid uniforms, and impressive music, the boy was eager to join the army despite his young age. In his memoirs he described the well-built men in their sparkling uniforms in full detail, writing, "The reader will easily believe that as a young inexperienced boy, who felt boundless love for horses and did not actually know anything about politics, nor was he a particular friend of the French, I only wished to have such a beautiful horse and such magnificent clothes."[12] It is not surprising that other European armies designed their uniforms following the Napoleonic model.

At the same time, the introduction of civilian uniforms became an important part of administrative reforms, both inspired by the French example and influenced by French dominance early in the nineteenth century. A contemporary German publication showing colored prints of French court and civilian uniforms documents the influence of French uniforms on Germany: *Costumes de la Cour impériale de France. Neueste Hof- und Staatstrachten in Frankreich, vorgeschrieben vom Kaiser Napoleon I* (Leipzig: Industrie Comptoir, circa 1810) (color plates 19–21). The illustrations are identified in French and German, suggesting that the book served as a guide for German uniforms.

During the nineteenth century the hierarchical order in the public administrations became increasingly complex, as officers were sorted into a complicated system of ranks, classes, and subclasses. Civilian uniforms were intended to make public service more effective and enforce general respect for public administrations and their representatives. However, the uniform's internal educational purpose was most important at the time when it was introduced, during the

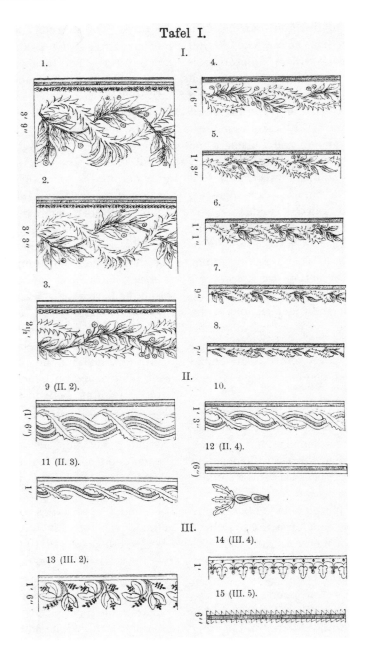

Figure 7.1 Embroidery patterns for different offices and ranks of Bavarian public servants. Numbers 44–47 were for officials of the Academy of Science, numbers 48–49 for officials of the Academy of Art, numbers 50–53 for heads and teachers of secondary schools, and numbers 54–55 for teachers of music schools *(Neue Gesetz- und Verordnungssammlung für das Königreich Bayern,* Munich, 1894).

first decades of the nineteenth century, as Stefan Haas has pointed out.[13] The uniforms served primarily to clarify the administrative hierarchy and to foster the public servant's own working ethos, his discipline, and loyalty to the state. For this reason Haas has called the civilian uniforms *Bekenntniskleidung* (dress of commitment or avowal), clothes that emphatically profess the wearer's commitment to his office and his position within the hierarchical order of the public administration.[14] Meticulous uniform regulations translated these hierarchical distinctions into the size and design of the uniforms' embroidered decoration. Thus, the uniforms visualized another essential aspect of the performance of masculinity, the need for social distinction and strict hierarchical order (figure 7.1).

Military and civilian uniforms made visible and reinforced the new social status of men, who enjoyed new civic responsibilities and privileges that were withheld from women. Unlike women, men of all social classes enjoyed the right to vote and the opportunity to make a career in the military or in public office. In Prussia, military service was propagated as the "school of the nation,"[15] open of course only to the male part of the nation. The military was supposed to foster new male virtues such as discipline, patriotism, courage, physical strength, and pride. Public servants were also expected to follow a new working ethos marked by discipline, incorruptibility, the ability to integrate into administrative hierarchies, pride, and a sense of responsibility. Women, in contrast, had to be humble and docile and practice obedience to men. Therefore, the uniforms can be understood as a symbol and emphatic demonstration of masculine superiority and of gender polarization in the new civic society.

UNIFORMS: THE SARTORIAL CONSTRUCTION OF IDEAL MASCULINITY

The new concepts of male moral virtues blended with new ideas about physical beauty. Toward the end of the eighteenth century, renewed admiration for antique sculpture drew new attention to the aesthetics of the well-proportioned and well-trained nude male body. Johann Joachim Winckelmann, a German writer and archaeologist, wrote rapturous descriptions of antique sculpture, particularly of the *Apollo Belvedere* in Rome. His writings had a tremendous impact on nineteenth-century sensibilities and ultimately on men's fashion. The *Apollo* soon became the most admired antique sculpture. This Roman copy of a late classical Greek sculpture represents the Greek god as a youthful, svelte, and tall athlete with very long straight legs, narrow hips, small waist, and well-toned but not exaggerated muscles. His head is relatively small and his chest broad. Winckelmann thought this antique sculpture to be the epitome of divine and male beauty. For him, it was not only the "utmost perfection of ancient sculpture" but also the perfect expression of male pride, grandeur, serenity, and restraint.[16] Praising ancient Greek art for its "noble simplicity and quiet grandeur," Winckelmann influenced many artists and paved the way for the neo-classical style in art, and ultimately in fashion as well. Toward the end of the eighteenth century, the Greek classical canon of beauty was generally considered aesthetically as well as morally superior to the more plump baroque ideal of beauty that by then had come to be associated with the iniquitous social values of the *ancien régime*.[17]

Physical exercise became popular around the turn of the century. The antique ideal of heroic beauty, which unified physical with mental and moral strength, inspired the founding fathers of physical exercise, Johann Christoph GutsMuths (1759–1839) and Frederik L. Jahn (1778–1852), the latter also known as "Turnvater Jahn." While GutsMuths sought to build up male virtues, such as strength and courage, along the lines of medieval chivalric ideals, Jahn promoted physical exercise and bodily strength as a means to instill patriotism, as well as foster men's mental and physical willingness and ability for combat.[18]

Nineteenth-century uniforms shaped men's bodies and minds, according to this new ideal of beauty. The sartorial construction of masculinity was carried out through the uniform's material, cut, and tailoring. Fashionable variations affected only small details but kept the overall masculine effect throughout the century. The following description of the construction and tailoring of uniforms is based on the investigation of nineteenth-century German civilian uniforms displayed at the exhibition "Nach Rang und Stand" in Krefeld in 2002.[19]

Unlike modern men's suits, which are made of supple cloth and cut generously in order to allow comfortable movement and posture, the uniforms of the nineteenth century tightly encased the body. In order to shape men's body and posture, the uniforms were made of strongly fulled woollen cloth, which was durable and strong. Whereas the patterns of today's suits include allowances for easy movement, tailor handbooks of the nineteenth century recommended that the coat be cut smaller than the body measurement in order to ensure a "correct" and firm fit. Nineteenth-century photos of men in uniform document the tight fit by the appearance of creases around the stomach and armholes (figure 7.2).

Quite different from the modern fit with its comfortable large armholes, the tightly fitted trunk of the nineteenth-century coat demanded small armholes. Placed far toward the back, the armholes pulled the arms back and thrust the chest forward, forcing the man to assume an upright position. Compared with today's form, the coat's chest area was constructed relatively large in proportion to the back. This construction emphasized a protruding chest, which was further enhanced by heavy padding of the front. The central back seam line was straight and slightly indented at the waist, following the straight posture of the back. Modern men's suits, in contrast, show a slightly curving central back line that accommodates the rounded back caused by the modern slouching posture. A drawing compares a modern tailcoat with a tailcoat cut for a civilian uniform around 1900 and illustrates these differences in construction (color plate 22).

It may be surprising that during the nineteenth century the shoulders of men's clothes were not yet artificially broadened. In fact, the shoulder seam reached into the back, which made the fabric's diagonal grain fit snugly around the shoulder's natural shape. This is quite different from modern suits, which have straight, unnaturally extended, and thickly padded shoulders.[20] Some uniforms featured shoulder pieces and epaulets, which gave the impression of particularly wide shoulders. But they were not allowed for all uniform wearers and were stipulated by meticulous ranking regulations. A broad chest was obviously more important than broad shoulders during this period and was therefore artificially enlarged by ample padding in the front and back. The broad chest was understood as a particular sign of manly strength, so that men who entered military service in Germany in 1877 had to have a chest with a circumference at least equal to half the body length.[21] Together with the stiff stand-up collar, which could be as high as two inches, the tailored coat forced the man to adopt an erect posture, pull his arms back, and have his chest thrust out. This rigid stance made the man appear larger than life and gave him an air of pride and superiority.

The uniforms' trousers also made the man look tall and upright.[22] The pants' legs were usually cut very long, and they were pulled straight by straps underneath the foot, which made the legs appear long and straight. Wide borders running along the trousers' side seams reinforced this effect, as did the cut of the tailcoat ending above the waist. The tailcoat was fashionable for civil and uniform clothes during the first half of the nineteenth century and continued to be used in some state uniforms until the twentieth century.

Figure 7.2　Photo of a Bavarian civil officer, ca. 1850 (collection of Jerome Lantz).

The state uniform of a Prussian chamberlain, surviving today in a German private collection, documents how strongly the uniform could shape the body according to the above-described ideal of beauty.[23] The uniform can be dated to the 1840s when narrow waists were particularly fashionable. Its trousers have a built-in waist restraint. Similar to a lady's corset, it is made of firm undyed cotton, tied by drawstrings, and held in place by four whalebone stays (color plates 23–24). The corset-like girdle confirms literary evidence that men in uniform were particularly keen to have a narrow waist and wore corsets and girdles. Hygienists and moralists of the time vehemently attacked the vanity of soldiers who pinched their waist strongly: "Is there not enough steel, lead and exhaustion to cut soldiers down? Do we need to allow the addition of voluntary strangulation?"[24]

The uniforms' accessories also contributed to the image of superior masculinity by influencing the movement and posture of the uniformed man. The head cover, such as the military shako or the bicorn (the latter usually belonging to the civilian uniform), visually increased a man's height and made him keep his head upright. Depending on their rank and function, men of military and civilian office carried sidearms, such as a sword, saber, or hunting knife, which forced them to move slowly and with utmost dignity. Encasing the male body into a "whole-body armor," the uniform and its accessories shaped men's bodies and minds by forcing them to assume a superior physical and mental attitude.[25] The uniformed man presented himself as an image of the utmost possible physical and mental power.

THE AMBIVALENT SPECTACLE OF UNIFORMED MASCULINITY

Contemporary comments reveal that the spectacle of uniforms and the flamboyant performance of masculinity also met with ambivalent reception. This is particularly true in Germany toward the end of the nineteenth century when the rising militarism was facing liberal criticism.

The sexual magnetism of uniformed men was quite obvious and invited satirical comments. Brändli, who has investigated men's dress in the civilian society of the nineteenth century, called the uniform a symbol of heightened virility and a "price tag on the commodity man."[26] Women could read the signs of the uniforms and knew well which regiment and rank corresponded to their own social standing, and which soldier or officer could be a suitable marriage candidate. The uniform enlarged the young man's self-consciousness, making him more aware of his sexual attraction and more courageous in his behavior toward women. Even the young Frederick Engels, serving in an artillery regiment in Berlin in 1841–1842, showed great interest in his uniform, and Arthur Schnitzler as a young man could obviously also not escape the temptation of his uniform's effect on women.[27] Numerous contemporary caricatures poked fun at the narcissistic self-presentation of uniformed men in front of young women. A caricature in the *Fliegende Blätter,* a satirical weekly from Munich, can be dated to the early 1880s. It depicts a young lieutenant swaggering through a ballroom and carries the following text: "'Lieutenant, have you been busy visiting dancing balls during this year's carnival season?' 'Certainly, but I only walked through the ball room once in order to whet the young ladies' appetite.'"[28]

The true story of the so-called "dancing hussars" from Krefeld shows that the widespread popularity of young officers as marriage candidates was not a mere literary stereotype but was actually encouraged by none other than the uniform-loving German Emperor William II. It also reveals that the excessive veneration of men in uniform provoked widespread laughter. In 1906, William II relocated an entire Hussar regiment from Düsseldorf to Krefeld after a young lady had complained to him about the lack of uniformed dancing partners in Krefeld. The minister of war and the German parliament were not amused by the emperor's wayward decision, and some felt that a regiment was more needed at the eastern border of Germany. But Krefeld, then one of the richest towns in Germany thanks to a flourishing textile industry, quickly built new barracks, and the whole city welcomed the regiment in a triumphal pageant, led by the emperor himself clad in a dashing Hussar's uniform. The "dancing hussars" of Krefeld provoked satirical comments from all over Germany. They inspired one of Germany's best caricaturists, Bruno Paul, to draw a cartoon for *Simplicissimus* in 1906, a popular satirical paper published in Munich (color plate 25). He depicts young daughters of rich Krefeld factory owners who are desperately trying to reach a foppish Hussar lounging on a rope high above them. The girl standing on the biggest bag of money, filled with 200,000 Marks, comes closest. The satirical text alludes to the fact that Prussian law required military officers to deposit a considerable sum of money if they wanted to marry. This made young officers often rely on the wealth of a rich father-in-law. Bruno Paul exposes the hussar officer as a choosy prostitute waiting for the bidder with the most assets. The dancing hussars also became the subject of the droll theater play *Husarenfieber* (hussar fever), which made its debut in November of the same year in the capital Berlin. The comedy made fun of the Krefeld story, as well as of the contemporary German fancy for uniforms and of soldiers' role as covetable marriage candidates. The play quickly became popular with all sections of society and helped to rehabilitate the finances of many a theater in Germany.[29] Quite in contrast to Bruno Paul's sharp social attack, this popular comedy neutralized antimilitaristic criticism by transforming it into a harmless and complaisant joke, which even the emperor reportedly enjoyed watching.

Criticism of men in uniform included allegations of effeminacy. In particular, liberal-minded politicians tended to attack the military and its spectacle of uniformed virility. A German caricature from the *Fliegende Blätter,* dated 1848 and titled "Standesunterschiede" (class distinctions), shows an elegant and effeminate-looking officer, clad in a uniform with an extremely tight waist, confronting a portly privy council member dressed in comfortable but unfashionable civilian clothes. They run into each other at an elegant evening party and immediately express their disdain for each other as members of the "opposite class." The liberal Swiss politician Karl Bürkli (1823–1901) excoriated the military and its dashing uniforms, which he felt were modeled after the Napoleonic army. He condemned the "overburdened" multicolored uniforms for their "dazzling" gold decoration and called them "military glitter" and "military crinoline." He felt that they were signs of immoral effeminacy.[30] His anger has to do with the identification of that trait with aristocratic behavior[31], which was considered outdated, decadent, degenerate, and French. Since the eighteenth century, republicans and nationalists in Europe had used anti-French sentiments in order to propagate anti-aristocratic and patriotic feelings. At the same time, the French journalist Victor Tissot indirectly returned this reproach by commenting on the treatment of uniformed men when he visited Germany in 1887. He found it most peculiar that Germans liked to invite well-groomed young officers dressed in provocatively tight and mannered military uniforms to elegant gatherings for the sole purpose of serving as social ornaments. He commented that they were expected to entertain the ladies, just like the dancing masters of the eighteenth century.[32]

What made the uniforms sexually so appealing? It is the "eroticism of power," as Elke Gaugele has pointed out in her study on the fetish of uniform during the second half of the nineteenth century. According to Gaugele, this is the reason why uniforms served as sexual fetishes for homosexual and heterosexual men alike during this time.[33]

The veneration of power goes hand in hand with submission and subservience. Caricatures and satirical literature poignantly expose how the German love for uniforms was closely interconnected with the blind acceptance of hierarchy during the reign of William II. A caricature in the *Simplicissimus* issue of 1904–1905 is titled "Sankt Leutenant." It depicts how numberless citizens pay their devotion to an imposing hussar lieutenant who is towering on a pedestal and displays exaggerated manly proportions. He is crowned by a resplendent halo. Women and men, old and young, from all sections of society, are holding votive candles and form a long procession winding up to the uniformed idol. Those in the front row kneel in devotion. The text of the caricature states that besides the "supreme being," many such saints enjoy divine veneration in Germany at that time. In contrast to the radiant lieutenant, the common people look unglamorous and dull, which makes the officer appear even more daunting. The deliberate misspelling of *Leutenant* (instead of Lieutenant) was intended to suggest that the uniformed officer has become a god for the common people (in German, *Leute*).[34]

Germans' gullible submission to the man in uniform led to another famous incident that made the world laugh at German militarism. In 1906, the destitute cobbler William Voigt, clad in an officer's uniform, which he had bought secondhand at a junk dealer, arrived at the city hall of Köpenick near Berlin. Because of his uniform and his authoritative behavior, he managed to purloin the city treasury, arrest the mayor and the cashier, and have soldiers escort them to the New Guard House in the center of Berlin in order to have them imprisoned. The incident inspired numerous caricatures, comedy sketches, and theater plays, of which Carl Zuckmayer's *Der Hauptmann von Köpenick: Ein deutsches Märchen* (The captain from Köpenick: A German fairytale) from 1930 became the most successful, particularly for its later film adaptations. They held a mirror in front of a nation that overwhelmingly submitted to excessive hierarchical authority and blindly succumbed

to the power of men in uniform. The uniform had become a symbol for the growing militarization and virilization of the political culture in Germany.[35]

Concluding with Robert Connell, who has pointed out that the body assumed a central role for gender practice,[36] the uniformed body demonstrated most poignantly the new male-dominated civic ideals and virtues that were closely connected with power, politics, and the military.[37] This excluded women and forced their social submission. Scott Hughes Myerly considers the spectacle of men's uniforms as an essential foundation of modern mass society, as it offers an attractive ideal for collective identification at times when industrialization causes severe social insecurities.[38] This may be one of the reasons why the ideal of hegemonic masculinity in uniform lasted well into the twentieth century, until feminist gender studies started to question its value and postmodern fashion developed an alternative masculine ideal of beauty.[39]

NOTES

1. Robert W. Connell, *Masculinities* (Cambridge: Polity, 1995); George L. Mosse, *The Image of Man: The Creation of Modern Masculinity* (New York: Oxford University Press, 1996); Thomas Kühne, *Männergeschichte—Geschlechtergeschichte: Männlichkeit im Wandel der Moderne* (Frankfurt/M.: Campus-Verlag, 1996); Wolfgang Schmale, *Geschichte der Männlichkeit in Europa (1450–2000)* (Vienna: Böhlau, 2003); Maren Lorenz, *Leibhaftige Vergangenheit: Einführung in die Körpergeschichte* (Tübingen, Germany: Ed. Diskord, 2000).

2. This article is based on research conducted for an exhibition of German civilian uniforms of the nineteenth century: *Nach Rang und Stand: Deutsche Ziviluniformen im 19. Jahrhundert* (catalog of the exhibition at the Deutsches Textilmuseum Krefeld, March 24–June 23, 2002, curated by Elisabeth Hackspiel-Mikosch [Krefeld: Deutsches Textilmuseum Krefeld, 2002]). See also Elisabeth

Hackspiel-Mikosch, "Beauty in Uniform: The Creation of Ideal Masculinity during the Nineteenth Century," in *On Men: Masculine Dress Code from the Ancient Greeks to Cowboys,* ed. Regine Falkenberg, Adelheid Rasche, and Christine Waidenschlager (Proceedings of the ICOM Costume Committee, 57th annual general meeting in Berlin, June 13–17, 2005 [Berlin: ICOM, 2005]), 63–70.

3.   Richard Baumann, *Landsknechte: Ihre Geschichte und Kultur vom späten Mittelalter bis zum Dreißigjährigen Krieg* (Munich: Beck, 1994).

4.   Martin Dinges, "Soldatenkörper in der Frühen Neuzeit: Erfahrungen mit einem unzureichend geschützten, formierten und verletzten Körper in Selbstzeugnissen," in *Körper-Geschichten,* ed. Richard van Dülmen (Frankfurt/M.: Fischer-Taschenbuch-Verlag, 1996), 71–98. See also Ute Frevert, ed., *Militär und Gesellschaft im 19. und 20. Jahrhundert* (Stuttgart: Klett-Cotta, 1997); Ute Frevert, "Soldaten und Staatsbürger—Überlegungen zur historischen Konstruktion von Männlichkeit," in Kühne, *Männergeschichte—Geschlechtergeschichte,* 69–85.

5.   The priority of rank was only reversed on the battlefield. See Julius Bernhard von Rohr, *Einleitung zur Ceremoniel-Wissenschaft der grossen Herren,* ed. Monika Schlechte (1733; Leipzig, Germany: Edition Leipzig, 1990), 271.

6.   In addition, Frederick William I stated in public that the duties of a military officer should automatically ennoble a person and place him on the same rank as nobility. The author is grateful to Helmut Langhoff, curator at the Prussian Museum in Wesel, for sharing this information.

7.   Klaus-Peter Merta, *Das Heerwesen in Brandenburg und Preussen von 1640–1805: Die Uniformierung,* 2nd ed. (Berlin: Brandenburgisches Verlags-Haus, 2001); Hans Bleckwenn, *Altpreussische Offiziersporträts: Studien aus dem Nachlass,* ed. Bernard Kroener and Joachim Niemeyer (Osnabrück, Germany: Biblio-Verlag, 2000).

8.   See, for example, the double portraits of Frederick Augustus of Saxony and Frederick William I painted by Louis de Silvestre after the meeting of the two kings in Potsdam in 1728 (Staatliche Kunstsammlungen, Dresden). The painting documents the contrast between the new Prussian masculine uniform and the traditional officer's dress in the French fashion that was still worn by the Saxon ruler.

9.   Monica Kurzel-Runtscheiner, "Vom 'Mantelkleid' zu Staatsfrack und Waffenrock: Anfänge und Entwicklung der Ziviluniformen in Österreich," in *Civilian Uniforms as Symbolic Communication,* ed. Elisabeth Hackspiel-Mikosch and Stefan Haas (Stuttgart: Steiner-Verlag, 2006), 83–85.

10. Elisabeth Hackspiel-Mikosch, "Vorläufer der zivilen Uniformen im 18. Jahrhundert: Hofmonturen als Inszenierung fürstlicher Macht im höfischen Fest," in Hackspiel-Mikosch and Haas, *Civilian Uniforms as Symbolic Communication,* 47–79. For a more comprehensive discussion of the dress und uniforms at this festival see Elisabeth Mikosch, "Court Dress and Ceremony in the Age of the Baroque: The Royal/Imperial Wedding of 1719 in Dresden" (PhD diss., New York University, 1999).

11. Daniel Roche, *The Culture of Clothing: Dress and Fashion in the "Ancien régime"* (Cambridge: Cambridge University Press, 1994), 234.

12. A valuable eyewitness, Carl Schehl wrote his memoirs as a member of the French army and survivor of the disastrous Russian campaign: Carl Schehl, *Vom Rhein zur Moskwa, Erinnerungen des jüngsten niederrheinischen Veteranen der großen Armee,* ed. Jürgen Olmes (1812; Krefeld: Obermann, 1957), 39, translation by the author.

13. Stefan Haas, "Vom ständischen zum modernen Staat—Die politische und symbolische Bedeutung der zivilen Uniform," in *Nach Rang und Stand,* 65–72; Jochen Ramming, "Motivation! Disziplin! Autorität! Zu den Lenkungswirkungen der bayerischen Beamtenuniformierung zwischen 1799 und 1848," in *Nach Rang und Stand,* 73–84. For further illustrations of early German civilian uniforms see also *Nach Rang und Stand,* figs. 43–46, cat. no. 22 (p. 226).

14. Stefan Haas, "Der Körper der Beamten," in *Die Kultur der Verwaltung. Zur Umsetzung der*

preußischen Reformen 1808–1848 (Frankfurt/M.: Campus-Verlag, 2005), 354–95.

15. Frevert, *Militär und Gesellschaft*; Karen Hagemann, *"Männlicher Muth und Teutsche Ehre"*: *Nation, Militär und Geschlecht zur Zeit der Anti-napoleonischen Kriege Preußens* (Paderborn, Germany: Schöningh, 2002).

16. Johann Joachim Winckelmann's description of the *Apollo Belvedere,* taken from his *Geschichte des klassischen Altertums* (Dresden, 1764; reprint, Berlin: E-Book Edition, 2003), 309, http://www.math.hu-berlin.de/~mrw/Geschichte_der_Kunst_des_Altertums.pdf; translation by the author.

17. Mosse, *The Image of Man;* Anne Hollander, *Sex and Suits* (New York: A. A. Knopf, 1994).

18. Friedrich Ludwig Jahn, *Die deutsche Turnkunst* (Eiselen, Germany: self-published, 1816); J. F. Gutsmuths, *Gymnastik für die Jugend* (Schnepfenthal, Germany: Buchhandel der Erziehungsanstalt, 1793); J. F. GutsMuths, *Turnbuch für die Söhne des Vaterlands* (Frankfurt/M.: Wilmans, 1817).

19. Kerstin Flintrop, "Die Disziplinierung des männlichen Körpers—Uniformen im historischen Vergleich von Schnittführung und Verarbeitung," in *Nach Rang und Stand,* 28–32.

20. This modern masculine shoulder line emerged only toward the end of the 1920s and markedly in the 1930s, when the ampler cut of men's suits allowed for strong padding of the shoulder and its artificial extension.

21. Sabina Brändli, *"Der herrlich biedere Mann"*: *Vom Siegeszug des bürgerlichen Herrenanzugs im 19. Jahrhundert* (Zürich, Switzerland: Chronos, 1998), 113.

22. Gundula Wolter, *Die Verpackung des männlichen Geschlechts: Eine illustrierte Geschichte der Hose* (Berlin: Aufbau-Taschenbuch-Verlag, 2001).

23. *Nach Rang und Stand,* cat. no. 141. See also Hackspiel-Mikosch, "Beauty in Uniform," 67–70.

24. Philippe Perrot, *Fashioning the Bourgeoisie: A History of Clothing in the Nineteenth Century* (Princeton, NJ: Princeton University Press, 1994), 163.

25. Klaus Theweleit, *Male Fantasies* (Cambridge: Polity, 1987).

26. Brändli, *"Der herrlich biedere Mann"*; Sabina Brändli, "Von 'schneidigen Offizieren' und 'Militärcrinolinen': Aspekte symbolischer Männlichkeit am Beispiel preußischer und schweizerischer Uniformen des 19. Jahrhunderts," in Frevert, *Militär und Gesellschaft,* 201–28.

27. Ute Frevert, "Männer in Uniform: Habitus und Signalzeichen im 19. und 20. Jahrhundert," in *Männlichkeit als Maskerade,* ed. Claudia Benthien (Cologne, Vienna, and Weimar: Böhlau, 2003), 290.

28. Andrea Jentsch, "Der uniformierte Mann im Spiegel der Karikatur," in *Nach Rang und Stand,* 38.

29. *Husarenfieber* was written by Gustav Kadelburg und Richard Skowronnek and was presented at the Berlin Lustspielhaus in the same year, on November 9, 1906. See Joachim Lilla, "'Trost tanzwütiger Jungferlein?'—Streiflichter zu den Krefelder 'Tanzhusaren' und deren Wirkung in der Öffentlichkeit," in *Nach Rang und Stand,* 43–49.

30. Brändli, "Von 'schneidigen Offizieren' und 'Militärcrinolinen,'" 208.

31. "Effeminacy," in *Men and Masculinities: A Social, Cultural and Historical Encyclopaedia,* ed. Michael Kimmel, vol. 1 (Santa Barbara, Denver, and Oxford: ABC-Clio, 2004), 247–48.

32. Bernd Ulrich, Jakob Vogel, and Benjamin Ziemann, eds., *Untertan in Uniform: Militär und Militarismus im Kaiserreich 1871–1914* (Frankfurt/M.: Fischer-Taschenbuch-Verlag, 2001), 100–101.

33. Elke Gaugele, "Uni-Formen des Begehrens, Fetischismus und die textile Konstruktion moderner Genderidentitäten," in Hackspiel-Mikosch and Haas, *Civilian Uniforms as Symbolic Communication,* 269–84.

34. Jentsch, "Der uniformierte Mann im Spiegel der Karikatur," 36; Franz Seidler, *Das Militär in der Karikatur: Kaiserliches Heer, Reichswehr, Wehrmacht, Bundeswehr, Nationale Volksarmee im Spiegel der Pressezeitung* (Munich: Bernard und Graefe, 1982), 47.

35. Hagemann, *"Männlicher Muth und Teutsche Ehre,"* 429.

36. Connell, *Masculinities.*

37. See also Christa Hämmerle, "Zur Relevanz des Connell'schen Konzepts hegemonialer Männlichkeit für Militär und Männlichkeit/en in der Habsburgmonarchie 1868–1914/18," in *Männer—Macht—Körper: Hegemoniale Männlichkeiten vom Mittelalter bis heute,* ed. Martin Dinges (Frankfurt/M.: Campus-Verlag, 2005), 103–21.

38. Scott Hughes Myerly, *British Military Spectacle: From the Napoleonic Wars through the Crimea* (Cambridge, MA: Harvard University Press, 1996), 173.

39. As early as 1930, the English psychoanalyst John Carl Flügel called on men to liberate themselves from the aesthetic restrictions of traditional men's clothes and to display gaiety, exuberance, and beauty in their dress, just as women did. Deploring men's "great renunciation" of fashion, Flügel felt that men's usual civilian dress was uniformly drab and lacked sexual stimulation, which he thought should be the main purpose of clothing and fashion. He insinuates that only the colorful and attractive uniforms come close to the sexually attractive clothes of women. (J. C. Flügel, *The Psychology of Clothes* [London: Hogarth Press, 1930], 200–15).

8

BETTER AND BRIGHTER CLOTHES: THE MEN'S DRESS REFORM PARTY, 1929–1940

Barbara Burman

The truth is that one might almost as well be in one's coffin as in the stiff layers of buckram-like clothing commonly worn nowadays. No genial influence from air or sky can pierce this dead hide. Eleven layers between him and God! No wonder the Arabian has the advantage over us. Who could be inspired under all this weight of tailordom?

(Edward Carpenter, 'Simplification of Life', 1886)

'Look! ... Take yer clothes off an' look at yourselves. Yer ought to be alive an' beautiful, an' yer ugly an' half dead ... An' I'd get my men to wear different clothes ... that alone would change them in a month. They'd begin to be men again ... the women 'ud begin to be women.'

(D. H. Lawrence, Lady Chatterley's Lover, 1928)

Of course there is a sex war; of course women despise men and of course men are jealous of women. They have lived in different worlds; the man's world has gone rotten and the woman's gone silly. Let us start again and, as a symbol of our refounded unity of mind, let us wear the same clothes.

(Eric Gill, Clothes, 1931)

Psychology has taught us to have faith in consciousness, in reason. We have rationalisation in industry. It is time there was rationalisation in clothes. Our motto should be 'Better and Brighter Clothes'.

(J. C. Flügel, speaking at the first rally of the MDRP, London, 3 July 1929)

Melissa Leventon and I published the first account of the Men's Dress Reform Party (MDRP) in 1987.[1] This chapter adds new material and illustrations to a condensed version of the earlier one. My aim here is to explore more fully the ideas and context which informed the MDRP's campaign for change. The MDRP's exclusive focus on menswear makes it unique in the history of British organized dress reform.

We might expect the MDRP to have roots in the various British dress reform groups of the late nineteenth century. It echoed some of their medical and social concerns but it dwelt less on aesthetics and the problems which beset workers in the clothing and allied trades. Equally, it is set apart from the interests of the military who used important research into the biophysics of clothing materials and clothing physiology.[2] The

MDRP had no 'Song of the Shirt' to dramatize its cause,[3] and the menswear trade press criticized their apparent ignorance of trade practices. I would contend that the MDRP is more fairly situated within a loose cluster of progressive individuals and groups whose reform agendas of the first third of this century ranged well beyond dress. The active role taken in the British eugenics movement by men who later became founders of the MDRP was particularly significant. Even in a modest preliminary case study, the MDRP suggests by these connections that we should qualify use of the term movement for British dress reform, recognizing there may have been more diversity and less common cause than is sometimes suggested.

FORMATION, AIMS, AND ACTIVITIES

In the mid-1920s the popular press photographed Dr Alfred Charles Jordan, MD, MRCP, CBE (1872–1956), an internationally renowned radiologist, cycling to work at his Bloomsbury practice.[4] He attracted their interest because he wore tailored shorts with his jacket, at a time when shorts were either for Boy Scouts or holiday, but certainly not for the city or professional life. Partly as a result of his work with convalescent First World War casualties, Jordan became a co-founder of the New Health Society in 1925. From Bloomsbury, until its closure in 1937, the Society campaigned for better awareness of the role of exercise, fresh air, and good diet in improving the health of adults and children and for better conditions in housing and places of work. It published a substantial monthly journal, *New Health,* which provided a platform for Jordan and others to test out ideas on menswear reform later to resurface in the MDRP. For example, campaigns for allowing bathing slips on public beaches and the promotion of shorts for tennis first ran in *New Health* before re-emerging with some success in the MDRP.[5]

Formation of the specialist MDRP derived from discussions amongst members of the Clothing Sub-Committee which the New Health Society had convened in 1927 to consider clothing textiles in relation to health. With widespread national press coverage, the MDRP issued its first call to membership on 12 June 1929 from 39 Bedford Square, London WC1, an address it shared with the New Health Society. Its call was to 'men and women, old and young, rich and poor'—and all 'interested in healthier and better clothes for men' to develop a campaign to 'reform their clothes with as much profit to health and appearance as women have recently achieved'.[6] Jordan was its Honorary Secretary. A steering committee of public figures was formed. Dr Caleb Saleeby, already accustomed to a public role in reform, became Chairman of the Council of the Party.[7]

The MDRP had no journal of its own and so depended for coverage on those of its fellow reform organizations. There was very evident support for it from the New Health Society and equally from the Sunlight League, which had been founded in 1924 by Dr Saleeby who served in both these organizations. At the formation of the MDRP in 1929, the Sunlight League had called its attention to the need for mutual support:

> Members of the MDRP we look to you to help us carry on our work of saving the children of the future from diseases of darkness, dirt and ignorance, and give us the power to secure for you greater facilities for the enjoyment of pure air and sunlight.[8]

The League's quarterly journal *Sunlight* frequently featured men's dress reform. The loss of the New Health Society's support in 1937 was made worse when the offices of the Sunlight League were devastated by a bomb in 1940. When this was followed by the death of Saleeby that same year, the Sunlight League and its journal apparently ceased too, effectively also scuttling the MDRP of which there is no evidence after this date.

In the eleven years before it vanished the MDRP kept menswear reform in the public eye with remarkable consistency. Its opening act was to set up its Design Committee which believed that the design of appropriate reform garments was a collaborative process. It adopted a conciliatory tone in claiming its recommendations for individual garments were reliant on the views of the menswear trade as well as party members. The introduction to its first 1929 report revealed an outlook and language which prevailed throughout the MDRP's literature:

Men's dress has sunk into a rut of ugliness and unhealthiness from which—by common consent—it should be rescued ... Men's dress is ugly, uncomfortable, dirty (because unwashable), unhealthy (because heavy, tight and unventilated). The Committee believe it would be premature to offer fixed and final views; indeed, the men's dress reform movement should have as one of its aims the encouragement of a somewhat greater range of individual style than is possible with men's present very stereotyped costumes. Only through wider individual choice and variation will men's clothes be capable of healthy evolution and reasonable adaptation to progressive social, hygienic and aesthetic ideals. At the same time, it is desirable to guard against the danger of mere change for change's sake, such as has often occurred in women's fashion. All change should aim at improvement in appearance, hygiene, comfort and convenience.[9]

This got considerable national press coverage, mostly supportive.

'Good' menswear at this period, like menswear, was widely understood to require differentiated styles and materials for town and country, work and leisure. Also there was considerably more seasonal variation than now in cloth weight for coating and suiting. The reformers recognized that by 1929 more colourful, soft, open-fronted shirts with shorts were becoming acceptable for holiday wear, but their innovation was to argue that these styles could be worn for town wear and work. They believed this would be acceptable if the styles were available in good materials, preferably made-to-measure.[10] In this, whilst offering some thorough changes in the cut and shape of garments, they were perpetuating the view that, to be taken seriously, menswear still required a degree of substance and structure:

... shirts of rayon or fine poplin; jackets-and-shorts suits (or jacket-and-kilt suits) of fine worsted or cashmere; good stockings to match. The fit and cut must be beyond reproach. The outfit must, in fact, be both smart and attractive. There should be no braces or waistcoat, so that a man might remove his jacket on a hot day and still retain his good looks and his fair name![11]

They thought jackets were mostly unnecessary, ugly, and excessively padded. A knitted jumper would be an appropriate and more attractive substitute. The stiff detachable collar with its studs and the tie were seen as the most objectionable feature of men's dress:

... the time has come when, for instance, the young necks of boys, as well as those of girls, should have their share of light and air not least for the sake of the precious thyroid gland which so largely controls the proper development of body and mind. Unless we give our boys a fair chance, the women of the next generation will surpass the men in a measure that will be of real profit to neither sex nor the nation at large.[12]

Freedom for the neck could be combined with varying degrees of formality by using a 'Byron' collar or a hanging tie, with a lower knot, could still be worn if necessary. The shirt itself could be replaced by a blouse, which, promoted to be a respectable garment in its own right, would release the coat or jacket to serve as an extra rather than an integral part of the ensemble. The abolition of trousers was a high priority. Shorts or breeches were promoted as better alternatives. Hats were unnecessary. Sandals were preferred to shoes. These proposed reforms applied to evening wear as well as sports and work wear.[13] In spite of the call for a broad membership, the reforms being proposed for suits and shirts were clearly most likely to appeal to men with some means and choice in their lifestyles, although in leisure wear some of the reforms would not have been costly to achieve.

From the beginning the MDRP tried to diversify its public image. At its heart was concern for health and hygiene, evidenced by its stream of column inches in the health reform journals, but its drive for publicity and membership always embraced a wide local and overseas network and numerous social events. For example, within four months of its formation the MDRP claimed that enthusiastic contact had been made with them by organizers of potential groups in India, China, Australia, South Africa, the USA, and Canada. They also reported on the existence of a fellow League for reform already well established in New Zealand. There were reports of activities from Costa Rica to Madras, but the closest ties seem to have been with the Viennese and Canadian branches. In the UK decentralization occurred quickly, each of the provincial and London branches urged by Jordan to organize debates and local social events. Eventually almost two hundred branches formed but their rate of formation slowed in 1932.[14]

The summer Rallies and Revels were the MDRP at its most showy. They took place most summers from 1930 until the outbreak of the Second World War. Summer may have been chosen as the best season in which to persuade men to wear less clothing. In 1931, for instance, as well as Sir Henry Wood, Ethel Mannin the novelist served on the organizing committee, as did Mrs A. C. McCorquodale, later known as Barbara Cartland. That year the Revel took place at the Suffolk Street Galleries in London. This 'night of Revelry and Dance will give every man a chance to show how he can LOOK AND FEEL HIS BEST by the costume he will evolve for the UNIQUE OCCASION'.[15] About a thousand people attended, including H. G. Wells.[16] At a similar event in 1933 the unconverted were invited to wear 'Regulation Evening Dress with Starched Collars and Shirt Specially Boiled for the Occasion, in the hope and belief that discomfort will achieve conversion'.[17] The 1935 Jubilee Midsummer Rally was a weekend visit to Stratford-on-Avon with the MDRP Festival Dinner held in the foyer of the Memorial Theatre. The wearing of reform dress on these occasions was encouraged: members were urged to submit their own designs for prizes. The *Daily Sketch* published readers' letters after the first rally; some writers revealed their own dress reform experience, others reported sightings of men in less-than-conventional attire, and one commented: 'In my experience of life—nearly eighty years—unconventional dress leads to unconventional manners and a lower standard of society'.[18]

Despite the considerable resources involved, the MDRP also exhibited at various trade and health-oriented exhibitions. Nineteenth-century dress reformers got plentiful attention when participating, for example, in the 1884 International Health Exhibition in the Albert Hall but it is difficult to judge the response enjoyed by the MDRP. There had been a recent precedent when 'healthy' suits of artificial silk, looking remarkably like the MDRP's idea of reform dress, had been shown at the British Artificial Silk Industries Exhibition in April 1929. The MDRP's first demonstration of reform garments at the New Health Exhibition in November 1929 was followed by their stand and mannequin shows at the major Lancashire Cotton Fair in early 1930, which was part of the industry's drive for exports. The MDRP held demonstrations four times daily, concentrating on washable clothes and on the new open-necked shirt, in designs suitable for town wear rather than just sports wear. It was reported that the Party found many new members there, including 'one of the leading magnates of the industrial North'.[19] The MDRP also exhibited at a Chamber of Trade show in Dewsbury in the same year, at the Ideal Holidays

Exhibition in London and again at the clothing section of the International Hygiene Exhibition in Dresden.

The evidence shows the MDRP as an energetic organization enjoying some rapid, well-publicized successes during its first years, with both the national and the trade press initially on its side. By 1931, for instance, it had the support of Henry Wood and Adrian Boult in what they reported as 'the achievement of the year'—'the reform of the evening dress of the men of the BBC Promenade Orchestra'.[20] It also campaigned to get the bathing slip accepted as adequate for a man when swimming and sunbathing in mixed company.[21]

The MDRP also used radio, film, and TV. Perhaps most elaborate was the Coronation dress reform competition televised in 1937. Entries were for 'office, professional or other vocational wear' and 'ceremonial or evening wear'.[22] This event was an eloquent commentary on the values of the MDRP and some of its typical difficulties. In spite of the offer of a hefty 50-guinea prize, the clothes submitted were neither 'beautiful nor were they practical' and no first prize was awarded. Second prize was for an evening 'costume made of dark blue chiffon velvet; it had a coat with sleeves, the whole lined with white silk, and long trousers of conventional pattern. Under the coat was worn a light blue silk shirt and blue cummerbund'. Third prize went to two day suits with shorts and one with breeches 'on eighteenth century lines'. Dr Jordan contributed several designs including a uniform with shorts for telegraph boys.[23] Despite the apparent bonus in being televised, the MDRP cannot have gained much from the fact that the BBC publications then represented it as unsympathetically as *Punch* had greeted them in 1929. The *Radio Times* published two unflattering and untypical photographs of Dr Jordan in medieval-style tunics[24] and *The Listener* was bluntly unwelcoming: 'Whether man's lower limbs look their best encased in slightly flattened parallel tubes may be open to doubt, but at least there seems no great aesthetic advantage in cutting the tubes short at the knee'. Some interest lay 'in their novel colours', unfortunately not visible on screen, but this limitation was 'fully made up for by the convenience of being able to express our feelings regarding the costumes shown without risk of offending their designers who were safely at Alexandra Palace several miles away', who 'provided viewers with an entertaining ten minutes and plenty of laughter'.[25] This institutional mockery of the MDRP may well have hastened its end.

THE MENSWEAR TRADE AND REFORM

Austin Reed's offer in 1931 of a prize for the MDRP of five guineas' worth of reform clothing suggests the firm not only supported its aims but carried appropriate stock.[26] In 1929 a men's tailor and outfitter in Hastings had dressed its male staff in open-necked shirts.[27] Numerous men's outfitters advertised bespoke or ready-to-wear reform clothing.[28] These are instances from a considerable trade response in the early years of the MDRP. (Reform, however, was a commonly used word in the trade, not necessarily indicating the kind of changes promoted by the MDRP. Any simplification of garment construction and more use of both colour and artificial silk were often also described as reform.) There is no evidence yet of any retailer trading exclusively in reform dress, except the MDRP's own shop in Menton in 1933 and its own London mail order business.[29] So far we have no extant reform clothing, no shop or manufacturing records and no oral testimony about the trade. So the main evidence to date of trade response lies in its journals.

The response to the MDRP in the weekly *Tailor and Cutter* and the monthly *Men's Wear Organiser* to some extent encapsulated the debate and the resistance it provoked. In the *Tailor and Cutter* (founded in 1867 for the mostly bespoke trade) reform dress was represented as interesting but unlikely to have much impact. This journal considered its readers' craft-based trade to be threatened far more by ready-mades and undermined more by devaluation and ignorance of bespoke skills and by the quickening pace of modern life than by reform. It defended the small trader by promoting the specialist and time-consuming skills of cutting, shaping, and fitting fine clothes and the seen and unseen benefits these gave to the wearer. It is here that one of the dilemmas of reform became apparent. Although under threat, bespoke tailoring produced a traditional image of masculine authority, combining substantial physical presence with evidence of the expenditure of time and money. Although the MDRP advocated fine materials and craftsmanship where appropriate, its less structured and lighter garments would have required the skills of the dressmaker as much as the tailor, a challenge to the ancient hierarchy of labour within the clothing trades. It also challenged the long-established differentiation between the appearance of men and women. The *Tailor and Cutter*'s defence of the craftsman tailor became equally an attack on reform.

The Men's Wear Organiser's interests were wider, including all types of menswear, sales techniques, international and national trends in style, travel, business and leisure as they affected menswear. Using progressive design and layout, it cast itself as a forward-looking presence in the trade and at first it welcomed the reformers. However, eventually the *MWO* saw what both the *Tailor and Cutter* and the MDRP failed to see: men were increasingly enjoying the pleasures of modernity and consumerism through the medium of fashion. The *MWO* judged that the concept of reform and its absolutes of health and hygiene, packaged in amateur design, were no match for the variety of choice the conventional trade was now able to offer, using its evolu-

tionary approach, and advertised with increasing sophistication by manufacturers and retailers alike. It criticized the MDRP, with its roots in medicine and social welfare, for overlooking the extent to which the trade's evolution had already produced much lighter, more streamlined, washable and hygienic garments and had balanced demands for tradition and change:

> Comfort and hygiene are very desirable, but that doesn't make such things as style and dignity, and custom and suitability, any the less important … The men's wear trade as it stands today exists to give the public what it wants, but it is quite capable of trying-out something new without waiting to be asked for it. Accordingly it progresses.[30]

Perhaps the worst fault the trade saw in the MDRP was its lack of 'expert knowledge of the materials, the make of garments, and practical considerations of their wear'.[31] For instance, MDRP bathing trunks were compared unfavourably with more stylish versions said to pre-date them on the Riviera:

> We can't reconcile all those well-styled, smartly-knitted trunks with our impression of the M.D.R.P. fabric bathing slip, patched half-navy, half sky blue, at three-and-eight pence in cotton and five-and-eight pence in wool …[32]

The development of artificial silk for garments is sometimes described by historians solely in terms of its effect on womenswear. There was, however, a significant impact on menswear as a result of the new lightweight, colourfast, and washable fabrics. In the 1920s the manufacturers' promotion of artificial silk for menswear exploited the widespread interest in health. It was used for pyjamas, dressing gowns, underwear, and hosiery because of its lightness and washability; it was also used for swimwear. In proliferating markets for new clothing materials, advertisements in the health, fashion, and clothing trade press alike were marrying quasi-scientific language to aesthetics.[33] The liberationist tones adopted by the MDRP seemed more eccentric in such company than they did in the general press. But it was not just language which set it apart.

At the same time that the values of bespoke and good mass-produced tailoring continued to be endorsed for their embodiment of conventional masculinity, the *MWO* also embraced streamlining. It was promoted in terms of garment design, but equally in the appearance of the magazine by means of illustrative techniques and graphic design.[34] Design history has located streamlining as part of the experience of modernism in general, although an account of streamlining as an organizing idea in fashion at this time remains to be written. In menswear it seems to have represented the possibility of both literally sloughing off the layered bulk of the past and grasping a slimmer, more youthful, athletic and informal future, by means, for example, of simplified outer garment construction, such as flexible waistbands, a reduction in the use of buttons and more reliable self-supporting trousers to make dressing and undressing quicker and easier. Underwear was also considered to have been revolutionized by this date, by means of sleeveless, buttonless garments, elasticated waistbands, and new fabrics. The MDRP reforms, on the other hand, were repeatedly photographed in garments of their own design which appeared fussy or amateur in cut, perhaps too pedantic or too soft and, ironically, seldom athletic. They often looked flamboyant, in spite of their interest in simplification for health purposes. Their publicity failed to grasp the attraction of streamlining in content or presentation.

THE BACKGROUND OF THE MDRP

An argument which deserves more space is that the birth in 1929 of the MDRP might have stemmed from envy or fear of the emancipation of women. It could also be understood as a desire for modernity. Undoubtedly the British open air movement and youth movements in Europe also offered parallels. However, I would argue that, though framed within these and committed to a kind of modernity for menswear which would echo that of womenswear and heavily imbued with the concerns of the medical profession, the MDRP was more tinged by eugenics and vestiges of the nineteenth-century Simple Life philosophy. Both these deserve more research in relation to dress reform. In accounts of nineteenth- and twentieth-century dress reform, the Simple Life movement has been unexplored but, arguably, it offered very convincing support for dress reform. Its goal was progressive replacement of the ills of capitalism and industrialization by a socialism based on individual perfection, valuing Ruskinian ideas of manual labour and the cultivation of personal and spiritual liberties.

Although not explicitly socialist, the MDRP and its allied reform groups echoed much of this underlying language and strategy. Edward Carpenter (1844–1929), at the centre of the Simple Life movement, had already articulated a case for the reform of menswear, for example, in his 1886 paper 'Simplification of Life'. In it he covered a range of Simple Life interests, but on clothing he set an agenda and a language very close to that later adopted by the MDRP. Carpenter rejected conventions in menswear, in pursuit of simplicity, frugality, and freedom of sexual expression. He argued for fewer garments 'all simply made, easily washable, and often washed'. To make the case for fewer layers, he advocated unlined coats:

> No one who has had the curiosity once to unpick the lining of a tailor-made coat that has been in wear a little time, will, I think, ever wish to have coats made on the same principle again. The rubbish he will find inside, the frettings and frayings of the cloth collected in little dirt-heaps up and down, the paddings of cotton wool, the odd lots of miscellaneous stuff used

as backings, the quantity of canvas stiffening the tags and paraphernalia connected with the pockets, bits of buckram inserted here and there to make the coat 'sit' well—all these things will be a warning to him.[35]

Carpenter considered the paraphernalia of tailor-made garments the 'coffin' of modern menswear. (The very same tailoring details were summoned later as evidence of its skill and artistry by the bespoke tailoring trade when it tried to defend itself against the threats from the ready-made trade.) Carpenter also anticipated the MDRP's call for sandals to replace enclosed footwear, but not only by reference to the pleasure; like much MDRP language Carpenter wrote in liberationist terms:

As to the feet, which have been condemned to their leather coffins so long that we are almost ashamed to look at them, there is surely a resurrection possible for them. There seems to be no reason except mere habit why, for a larger part of the year at least, we should not go barefoot … (Democracy, which redeems the lowest and most despised of the people, must redeem also the most menial and despised members and organs of the body.)[36]

Just as Carpenter identified dress as both a symbol and a means of reinstating a certain kind of freedom for men, others had followed with calls for social and moral regeneration and the restoration of British youth and manhood in strictly heterosexual terms, citing dress as an agent in this process. The Boy Scout movement was one such case.[37] Immediately prior to the formation of the MDRP, D. H. Lawrence described men as enfeebled by the twin burdens of industrialized labour and sexual hypocrisy. Their restored masculinity could be signalled by their

close red trousers, bright red, an' little short white jackets. Why, if men had red, fine legs, that alone would change them in a month. They'd begin to be men again, to be men! An'

the women could dress as they liked. Because if once the men walked with legs close bright scarlet, and buttocks nice and showing scarlet under a little white jacket: then the women 'ud begin to be women. It's because th' men *aren't* men, that th' women have to be.[38]

Eric Gill quoted from this passage in his 1931 book *Clothes*. Here Gill called for an end to tailored garments for men because the prime purpose of tailoring was to make a close-fitting garment. Fit necessitated the cutting of cloth which Gill saw as the opposite of truth to material; the latter would suppose a return to fuller, less structured garments. The skirt, for both sexes, in tunic or other form, was Gill's recommended solution. 'It is essentially the garment of dignity, and dignity is the essential object of clothes.'[39] Gill's ideas on clothes, like his ideas on art, were rooted in the belief that the modern age was in crisis; like Lawrence and others, he too attacked aspects of industrialization and what he called 'puritanism' and its failings. In *Clothes* Gill seems to have associated sexual differentiation in dress, and sexual conflict, with his idea of 'puritanism'.

Although presumably aware of these and other radical critiques of modern life and its effect on masculinity, the MDRP avoided confrontation with sexual politics. It did this by seeking support wherever possible from establishment figures. It also concentrated social events at venues acceptable to the professional classes. This may have stemmed from a desire to cultivate decision-makers who could effect change and to distance itself from more controversial calls for reform. Effectively it meant women attended the events, thereby helping to uphold apparent probity. One founding member advised an evolutionary strategy to avoid being made targets of fun:

When women want to do anything about their dress they do it. Men are dreadfully afraid of one another. We have to be very careful not to frighten people or cause ridicule. We must not make people think that we want to see a lot of hairy men rushing about the streets in sandals.[40]

The relationship of menswear reform to the wider agenda of sexual politics needs more research.

A significant number of their prominent activists had sought an enlarged social reform through eugenics earlier in their careers. The MDRP appears to have made no public statements about eugenics but there is evidence of substantial investment in eugenics ideas within its ranks. For our purposes here it is useful to note just how widespread and respectable the British eugenics movement had become by the time the MDRP began. It gained political credibility as a project apparently offering satisfyingly coherent and rational solutions to widespread fears about racial degeneration on which the perceived decline in Britain's world strength was frequently blamed. G. R. Searle suggests that whilst eugenics attracted support from a range of different political and philosophical positions, in general it can be seen as one of the impulses in the formation of a new radical right in Britain in the years leading up to the First World War.[41] However, the grip in which eugenics ideas held prominent Fabians and others such as Havelock Ellis underlines the diversity of the anxiety about racial degeneration and the search for reform frameworks.

Dress reform slipped easily enough into a eugenics agenda. For example, in Alexander Bryce's *Ideal Health* (1901) in which eugenics was expounded as an urgent and 'imperative duty ... to conserve the rights of the individual and of the state', he argued for positive help for the healthy to teach them 'the best methods of preserving their manhood and vigour'.[42] Bryce found menswear to be healthier than the then multi-layered clothes of women but argued for all clothing to be looser and less weighty. For Bryce, the purpose of menswear reform was to improve the health of the race, explicitly in the case of the 'ordinary jacket':

It fails ... to protect the loins like a frock coat, and it also leaves the lower portion of the abdomen unnecessarily exposed. This difficulty may be easily overcome if a knitted woollen binder, or what is usually known as a lumbago belt, be worn, or (what is better) if the upright eight inches or so of the trousers be lined with Jaeger or other flannel.[43]

Later on eugenics was embraced in menswear reform but air and sunlight on the skin had become priorities and by 1929 womenswear was perceived as a model of progress in that respect. The career of Dr Caleb Saleeby (1878–1940) illustrates the convergence. Saleeby had founded the Sunlight League in 1924 and later chaired the Clothing Sub-Committee of the New Health Society before becoming chairman of the MDRP.[44] Saleeby was at the heart of one of the differences which arose between eugenicists about the rightful emphasis on hereditary as opposed to social factors. Saleeby argued vigorously for individual responsibility in what he saw as the effective shaping of the right conditions for race regeneration. This belief in progress through individual example and action also defined the MDRP's approach to reform. Saleeby lobbied for an educational approach through legislative support for maternal health, child benefits, and education for good parenthood. In his ideas on this latter point we can see the ease with which he later moved into dress reform. In his view

women's primal and supreme function is or should be that of choosing the fathers of the future ... The natural man and natural woman are Eugenicists at heart. Each of them prefers, in members of the opposite sex, youth and maturity rather than senility, beauty (which has a high degree of correlation with health) rather than ugliness, straightness and efficiency of limbs and feature rather than deformity, optimism rather than pessimism, intelligence, good temper, sympathy, rather than their opposites ... I do not advocate the so-called 'simple life' or the 'return to Nature', but it is possible to accept (modern) civilisation and yet preserve, in personal habits of diet and sleep and exercise and thought and desire, a simplicity and rationality which all these 'modern improvements' may indeed be made to serve.[45]

Saleeby's medical, rationalist position co-existed with criticism of Simple Lifers, another example of difference within the MDRP membership.

Eugenics converged with dress reform in numerous contributions to *New Health*. For example, an article 'Why not beauty for men?' called for men to follow the example of the Women's League for Health and Beauty, founded in 1930 to achieve racial health. Good diet, gymnastic dancing, sun and air bathing, and dress reform would produce a properly graceful masculine physique. In turn this would stimulate and release spiritual beauty and thus win the regard of women. Of women:

Yet, underlying all their so-called modernity, to be devoted to worthy men remains their deepest instinctive need. In the long run, therefore, a renaissance of beauty for men—true masculine beauty of body and mind, the bloom of a joyful spirit—might mean happier marriages, well-born and beautiful children, a healthier and more beautiful race.[46]

William Inge (1860–1954), later to be Dean of St Paul's, was another high-profile eugenicist and Vice-President of the Sunlight League before becoming a founder member of the MDRP. Like many others he was not troubled by supporting eugenics from within the established Church. He was a sharp critic of industrialized and urban life, calling for the recreation of the qualities of rural life. J. C. Flügel was another key player for the MDRP who was already attracted to eugenics. In *The Psychology of Clothes,* a book committed to reform, Flügel called for individuals to change for the sake of the future:

The new science of eugenics, emphasising the importance of sexual selection for future human welfare, adds its own argument to those of hygiene and aesthetics, and demands that we should duly value the body, if not for our own sake, at least for the sake of future generations.[47]

The relation between design and hygiene described by Adrian Forty could also be used to shed light on the MDRP and its eugenic element. Forty cites Mary Douglas's *Purity and Danger* which links pollution anxiety to external social and cultural factors. He suggests a resonance between this and the middle-class energies directed towards its own hygiene and that of the working class:

Even if it is impossible to prove that the fetish for hygiene was caused by bourgeois fears of losing social and political authority, there are enough signs of strong class prejudice in the movement for greater hygiene to suggest some relationship. It seems not implausible that a regimen of cleanliness and order should have been adopted by the middle class as a means of resisting social upheaval and of providing some psychological security against it.[48]

Whilst design history has mapped associations between design and hygiene, it is not yet entirely clear what, if any, can be identified between design and the eugenics movement. However, the membership of the MDRP illustrates that their position was defined in part by eugenics and prompts the question to what extent, if any, eugenics in Britain shaped other fields of design and consumption.

CONCLUSION

Whilst evidence of individual members, activities, and public reception of the MDRP is scattered and fragmentary, there is enough to conclude that it pursued its goals vigorously. It courted publicity successfully for more than a decade. It was a cogent project but the MDRP is less easily evaluated in terms of realization of its goals. It presented frequently unpalatable or amateur designs, in spite of it also arguing for the simple appropriation of open shirts and shorts from holiday wear to work wear. Shorts were problematic for men because of their association with Boy Scouts and juveniles generally. Loose, soft, unstructured clothes were equally problematic because of their approximation to the dominant styles of womenswear.

Until recently menswear history has suggested style fossilization and conservatism were routine until the 1950s. However, it is clear that menswear between the wars was widely characterized, by the trade at least, as undergoing radical changes in style, in retailing, and in the new persuasiveness of fashion and consumerism for men. The trade offered a vision of ever increasing choice of goods of ever better quality, marketed in the rhetoric of modernity. The MDRP offered an ambiguous vision of pedantic concern for hygiene and moments of flamboyance.

The MDRP illustrates the now widely accepted view that significant impetus for change in dress can emerge both outside mainstream fashion and as a result of resistance to it. The MDRP drew its ideas from a wider reform agenda but even a modest case study raises several important questions for menswear history. One of these centres on social class. For example, whilst the MDRP seems to have been predominantly a middle-class professional group whose politics were on the right, the wider British outdoor movement was rooted in working-class self-improvement and the interests of the left.[49] It is still unclear how they related to each other, and what impact the outdoor movement had on masculinity and menswear generally between the wars. Regionalism as a factor in reform and menswear is equally an open question in the period, as too is the role of overseas reformers.[50]

Perhaps more significantly, in masculinity and the hetero- and homosexual politics of the day we would find a fuller understanding of the context of the MDRP, and menswear generally. This merits more attention than has been possible in this essay.

NOTES

Reprinted with permission from Barbara Burman, "Better and Brighter Clothes: The Men's Dress Reform Party, 1929–1940," *Journal of Design History* 8, no. 4 (1995): 275–90.

1. Barbara Burman and Melissa Leventon, 'The Men's Dress Reform Party 1929–1937', *Costume*, no. 21, 1987, was dedicated to Stella Mary Newton on her retirement by her past students. Our contribution was intended to offer an extension of her book *Health, Art and Reason* (John Murray, London, 1974) which provided the first survey of nineteenth-century dress reformers. Our evidence of the MDRP has shown it was not the case that organized reform faded by the start of this century. It is in part a comment on established emphases within dress history that the MDRP did not emerge into the literature earlier but equally it is due to the fragmented and ephemeral nature of the sources. A good deal is known of the nineteenth-century dress reformers and the concepts of reform and opposition now make an accepted framework within recent dress history in general, but there are still important gaps in the evidence about organized reform activity during this century. For example, the Sensible Dress Society and the Hygienic Dress League are known of by name only and further research is needed.

2. For nineteenth-century reform, see Newton, op. cit. Military interest in materials and clothing is apparently unknown in the literature of dress history. See E. T. Renbourn and W. H. Rees (1972), *Materials and Clothing in Health and Disease,* London: H. K. Lewis.

3. Thomas Hood's 'Song of the Shirt' (published anonymously in *Punch,* 1843) focused attention on the plight of needlewomen, whose welfare continued to concern dress reformers throughout the nineteenth century. Mrs C. Meyer and Clementina Black (1909), *Makers of*

Our Clothes: A Case for Trade Boards, London: Duckworth; S. P. Dobbs (1928), *The Clothing Workers of Great Britain,* London: Routledge; reports of the National Anti-Sweating League and other evidence on working conditions and practices seem to have escaped attention from the MDRP.

4. Peter Jordan, son of Dr Alfred Jordan, kindly allowed me to tape record his memories of his father. He also helped identify individuals in MDRP photographs. In general Peter Jordan felt his father's medical career had been hindered because of the medical establishment's disapproval of his dress reform activities.

5. For details of Jordan and Saleeby's campaigns for bathing slips and tennis shorts, respectively (and Saleeby's arguments for artificial silk for most outdoor sportswear), which predated the MDRP, see Burman and Leventon, op. cit.

6. Dr A. C. Jordan, letter to *The Times,* 12 June 1929.

7. The steering committee consisted of Dean Inge, later Dean of St Paul's; Guy Kendall, headmaster of University College School; W. R. Sickert, painter; Ernest Thesiger, actor; Dr Leonard William; Dr Caleb W. Saleeby, Chairman of the Sunlight League. The precise function of the committee is unclear; Sickert and Thesiger seem to have had little to do with running the Party. By August 1929 Dr William, an advocate of evolutionary change and unrestrictive but conventional attire, criticized the Party for excessive zeal and left it (see his letter to editor, *New Health,* August 1929).

8. C. W. Saleeby, *Practical Dress Reform,* report of the Committee on Designs of the MDRP, 1929.

9. *Sunlight,* December 1929: 23.

10. 'Thousands of men spend their holidays in open shirts and shorts. It is perfectly easy to evolve from to-day's holiday dress an ordinary day dress', Dr A. C Jordan, first MDRP Rally, 1929, *Men's Wear Organiser,* August 1929: 70.

11. *Sunlight,* September 1929: 30 (copy of letter written by Jordan to *The Times,* 15 July 1929).

12. *Sunlight,* September 1929: 31.

13. *Sunlight,* December 1929: 23–9.

14. Exact branch or general membership numbers are not known. One of the liveliest branches, in Cambridge University, claimed thirty undergraduates and dons as members by 1930. Jordan claimed initial applications for membership came from a variety of backgrounds, including the military, city clerks 'and university graduates', dentists and doctors, clergymen, 'from a working chap' to a peer's son'. Group applicants included nineteen from 'a Midland University' and '21 from the electricity supply department of a large town' (letter to *The Times,* reprinted in *Sunlight,* September 1929).

15. MDRP pamphlet for the Revel on 24 June 1931.

16. *Men's Wear Organiser,* July 1931: 43.

17. MDRP pamphlet for the Dinner Debate on 21 June 1933.

18. Letter to the *Daily Sketch,* 19 July 1929.

19. The 'magnate' remains unidentified. *Cambridge Independent News,* 4 April 1930.

20. 'Throughout the Season at Queen's Hall (August to October) the men wore soft white shirts with attached soft collars and black Palm-Beach jackets. The men were well pleased with the relief from the starched collar, shirt-front and heavy coat.' This reform, suggested by the MDRP, had been adopted 'very readily'. MDRP newsletter to members, January 1932.

21. Their tactic was the publication of an annual list of all those UK seaside resorts where slips were permitted alongside those where 'regulation' garments were still required. By 1932 the MDRP claimed it had won over several seaside councils and from Aberystwyth to Worthing thirty-eight resorts permitted the slip. There remained twenty-seven against, from Barmouth to Weston-super-Mare. 'Margate still hesitates but has almost come round to the side of health and sense.' *New Health,* November 1932: 22–3.

22. The panel seen on TV was representative of several interest groups: A. S. Bridgland (journalist and menswear expert), Lewis Casson, J. C. Flügel, James Laver, Herbert Norris, and H. A. Rogers (president of the Association of London Master Tailors).

23. *The Listener,* 14 July 1937: 69. Jordan had illustrated his ideas for uniform reform, including for telegraph boys, earlier in *New Health,* November 1932: 22–3.
24. *Radio Times Television Supplement,* 2 July 1937.
25. *The Listener,* op. cit.
26. *Men's Wear Organiser,* July 1931: 43.
27. *Men's Wear Organiser,* August 1929: 103.
28. Firms sympathetic to reform in London included Austin and Smith of Great Portland Street, Dowie and Marshall (shoemakers) of West Strand, Ley and Miller of Edgware Road.
29. The MDRP's Riviera branch opened the shop, but nothing is yet known of how long it lasted or what it stocked. The MDRP Supplies Department expanded so much that it required transfer from Jordan's own home to A. P. Bolland of Warwick Street, London. References to both were made in MDRP newsletters.
30. *Style for Men* (new name for *MWO*), August 1937.
31. *Men's Wear Organiser,* December 1929. S. P. Dobbs, op. cit.: 211, noted an entirely handworked lounge jacket in '3rd class' material could take up to nineteen hours to make, with more than ten hours for extras such as vents or enhanced interfacing.
32. *Style for Men,* August 1937.
33. British Celanese Ltd., for example, advertised their knitted, woven, and printed fabrics in *New Health.* 'Cotton or wool bathing suits leave a "tidemark" of tan; the skin covered by the material remains white, unresponsive to the sun's action. The wearer of a "Celanese" bathing suit will find that the skin is tanned evenly, all over. It is a fact that one can be fully clothed in "Celanese", wearing several layers of the material, and yet be in a state of Lido-like receptivity to ultraviolet rays'. *New Health,* June 1928.
34. *Style for Men* (*MWO*), February 1935.
35. Edward Carpenter (1886), 'Simplification of Life', in *England's Ideal,* reprinted London, 1919: 111.
36. Ibid.: 113.
37. Robert Baden-Powell's pre-First World War belief in the cohesive and inspiring effect of uniform in general and the scouting uniform in particular is recorded in unpublished material held in the Archives of the Scout Association, London. In the earliest days of the Scout movement (founded in 1907), some parents expressed concern about the possible ill-effects on boys of shorts which were seen as innovative replacements for the typical boyswear of knee breeches. By 1929, however, the Scout movement had grown to several million worldwide with adult leaders and boy scouts alike in the then accepted uniform with shorts.
38. D. H. Lawrence (1928), *Lady Chatterley's Lover,* London: Penguin, 1961: 229.
39. Eric Gill (1931), *Clothes,* London: Jonathan Cape: 195.
40. *Men's Wear Organiser,* August 1929.
41. G. R. Searle (1976), *Eugenics and Politics in Britain 1900–1914,* Leyden: Noordhoff International Publishing.
42. Alexander Bryce (1935), *Ideal Health or the Laws of Life and Health,* Bristol and London: 328 (first published 1901, 2nd edn. 1909).
43. Ibid.: 259.
44. Saleeby was already a public figure in reform when he married. His reform wedding suit 'of bright brown gabardine and an open-necked shirt of orange silk' was reported by the *Tailor and Cutter,* 30 August 1929.
45. C W. Saleeby (1911), *The Methods of Race Regeneration,* London: Cassell: 35–7.
46. Dion Byngham (1932), *New Health Journal:* 21–2.
47. J. C. Flügel (1969), *The Psychology of Clothes,* New York: International Universities Press, Inc.: 223.
48. Adrian Forty (1986), *Objects of Desire: Design and Society 1750–1980,* London: Thames & Hudson: 159.
49. See H. R. Walker (1987), 'The Outdoor Movement in England and Wales, 1900–1939', unpublished Ph.D. thesis, University of Sussex.
50. For example, on local examples of menswear style, see Hannah Andrassy (1995), 'Smart but Casual: Masculinity and the Modernisation of Men's Fashion 1930–1950', unpublished MA dissertation, V&A/RCA.

ANNOTATED GUIDE TO FURTHER READING

Brook, Timothy. *The Confusions of Pleasure: Commerce and Culture in Ming China.* Berkeley and Los Angeles: University of California Press, 1998. Considerable attention is paid to men and to fashion within the refined urban life of the towns and cities of Ming China.

Carpenter, John T. "Twisted Poses: The Kabuku Aesthetic in Early Edo Genre Painting." In *Kazari: Decoration and Display in Japan 15th–19th Centuries,* ed. Nicole Coolidge Rousmaniere, 42–49. London: The British Museum Press/The Japan Society, 2002. Compares a "twisted" or mannered pose in seventeenth-century Japanese urban culture with the "swagger" portraits showing the elite men of Van Dyck's England.

Fisher, Will. "The Renaissance Beard: Masculinity in Early Modern England." *Renaissance Quarterly* 54, no. 1 (Spring 2001): 155–87. Using an argument from the theorist Judith Butler, Fisher considers the beard as a prosthetic device that extended the presence of men and helped to shape their identity.

Garelick, Rhonda K. *Rising Star: Dandyism, Gender, and Performance in the Fin de Siècle.* Princeton, NJ: Princeton University Press, 1998. Links dandiacal strategies of the early and late nineteenth century (decadence) to contemporary male style politics.

Huizinga, Johan. *The Waning of the Middle Ages.* New York: Dover Reprint, 1998. First written in Dutch in 1919, this famous history includes several sections that consider men's wardrobes in Franco-Flemish society of the fifteenth century. Sensuality and interrelated meanings were created through textiles, emblems, colors, and the auditory dimension of clothes.

Jones, Ann Rosalind, and Peter Stallybrass. *Renaissance Clothing and the Materials of Memory.* Cambridge: Cambridge University Press, 2000. The key text for considering how new literary readings of the Renaissance theater can be mobilized in order to understand the power and significance of dress in early modern society.

Meyer, Moe, ed. *The Politics and Poetics of Camp.* London and New York: Routledge, 1994. Wide-ranging study of the cultural pose and function of camp style, from the seventeenth-century "arms akimbo" portrait to the twentieth-century performer Liberace. Considers the interventionist politics of ACT UP and examines the "archaeology" of posing.

Murray, Jacqueline, and Konrad Eisenbichler, eds. *Desire and Discipline: Sex and Sexuality in the Premodern West.* Toronto: University of Toronto Press, 1996. A series of essays consider how bodies and mentalities were formed in the late Middle Ages; the linking of contemporary theory with historical case studies is noteworthy.

Myerly, Scott Hughes. *British Military Spectacle: From the Napoleonic Wars through the Crimea.* Cambridge, MA: Harvard University Press, 1996. How did the spectacular appearance and discipline of the British soldier and the martial ideal spread to civilian life? An extended account of British uniform culture.

Orgel, Stephen. *Impersonations: The Performance of Gender in Shakespeare's England.* Cambridge: Cambridge University Press, 1996. Orgel's study of masculine apparel in Elizabethan and Stuart England considers what constituted maleness and glamour in the 1590s. He explains how a king might appear cross-dressed when he represented the goddesses Minerva or Diana in peace, not in war.

Sutton, Anne F. "Order and Fashion in Clothes: The King, His Household and the City of London at the End of the Fifteenth Century." *Textile History* 22, no. 2 (1991): 253–76. Was a king so powerful that he stood outside fashion, or was he influenced by other competing courts?

Vigarello, Georges. "The Upward Training of the Body from the Age of Chivalry to Courtly Civility." In *Fragments for a History of the Human Body,* ed. Michel Feher with Ramona Naddaff and Nadia Tazi, part 2, 148–199. New York: Zone, 1989. How has the male body been disciplined through sports and activities ranging from fencing to horse riding? How were male bodies and ways of appearing transformed when the focus of elite life shifted to a more refined and courtly mode?

Vincent, Sue. "To Fashion a Self: Dressing in Seventeenth-Century England." *Fashion Theory* 3, no. 2 (June 1999): 197–218. In an age before diagrams were common, the language in which clothes were described was essential. Men, too, wrote long and detailed descriptions of what clothes they required.

A selection of these readings feature in Peter McNeil, ed., Fashion: Critical and Primary Sources, *4 vols.* *(Oxford and New York: Berg, 2009).*

PART II

Masculinity and Sexuality: The Making of Fashionable Men

INTRODUCTION

What the study of men's fashion represents, par excellence, is the persistence of gendered attitudes, gendered relations and gendered stereotypes concerning men, masculinity and their place in society.

Tim Edwards, 1997[1]

The study of masculinities and sexualities has become increasingly complex in terms of the field of cultural production. Many of the contemporary writings on men and fashion have been influenced by the work of a number of leading figures, notably Robert Connell, who has been at the forefront of interrogations of the concepts of masculine identities since the early 1980s with the emergence of the "New Man" phenomenon.[2] The construction of masculine identities through the deployment of fashion is an area that has gained much groundwork in the fields of cultural analysis since the growth of the marketing, advertising, and retailing industries in the 1980s. Significant writers from the field of fashion studies whose work examines representations of masculinity, consumption, spectatorship, and identity include Frank Mort, Christopher Breward, Sean Nixon, Tim Edwards, Mark Simpson, and Paul Jobling.[3]

But there cannot be a study of men's fashion without an understanding of the ways in which gender identity constructs meaning in social practices. Definitions of masculinities vary from time to time and from place to place and are contingent on individual and societal interpretations. According to Wilson, "fashion is obsessed with gender, defines and redefines the gender boundary."[4] Similarly, the study of fashion, writes Tim Edwards, "often highlights the very artificial or constructed—as opposed to natural or essential nature of masculinity itself, for in fashion, masculinity, like clothes and accessories, is put on, swapped around and played with, like costumes in a masquerade or theatre."[5] In other words, there is no "natural" masculinity, nor is there a "natural" link between a garment (say a suit) and masculinity; instead, there are sets of meanings that are culturally specific.

The contributors in this section of the *Reader* look at the changing ideas about men's sexuality and the body, at how men's bodies have been constructed as sites of consumption, spectacle, and performativity.

An important point that scholars have raised is that the study of men's fashion still remains marginalized relative to investigations of women's fashion and dress.[6] In *The Empire of Fashion,* Lipovetsky writes that from the fourteenth to the eighteenth century, both sexes were equally extravagant in fashion and ornamentation. Even up until the seventeenth century men's fashion was more playful than women's; it was not until the "great renunciation" of the late eighteenth century that the masculine mode was eclipsed by the feminine.[7] Simply put, it has been claimed that after the decline in court societies, men dressed for comfort and function rather than fashionability and style.[8]

Since the emergence of the "new man" and the rise of style magazines for men such as *GQ* and *Arena* in the 1980s, the study of men's fashion and male buying power has taken a new turn as cultural conceptions of masculinity began to shift.[9] Nixon points to key areas for the "circulation" of the new man: television and press advertising, menswear retail shops, and the magazine press.[10] The new man was the focus of marketing, design, and retailing, all of which targeted the affluent male consumer through a range of retail goods. The growth of marketing and "flexible specialization" in retail also allowed for greater market differentiation in products. Male subjectivity was being constructed through advertising and marketing discourses, which interact with the consumption of imagery, fashion, and cosmetic products to produce a range of idealized and eroticized masculine identities.

Wider social movements of the 1970s such as feminism, movements for sexual liberation, and a range of identity-based political movements, such as gay and civil rights, have also influenced images of contemporary masculinity. These social movements disrupted traditionally held views of race, class, and identity and promoted a model of democratic equality. The outcomes of these movements challenged hegemonic models of masculinity, described as a "crisis in masculinity," and created new ways of conceptualizing and articulating masculine identity.[11]

While these political movements produced and extended representations of men and their bodies, they were not the only sites where masculinity was being challenged. The music industry was operating simultaneously to explore and destabilize conventional representations of gender. A number of musical subcultures, such as punk, glam rock, and the new romantics, opened up a space where stable chains of signification could be broken, creating possibilities for different self-representations among men. The understanding of masculinity as a performance that emerges from the contributions in this section is diverse and encompasses the soccer player, the male model, "superman," and the drag king and drag queen. Each chapter examines notions of the imagination, spectacle, masquerade, and performativity, while also looking at the role that gender and sexuality play in constructing masculine identities within fashion discourse.

The first two contributors in this section examine the marketing and consumption of men's fashion by leisure wear manufacturers and retail industries. William R. Scott's chapter investigates the marketing of Californian leisure wear from 1930 until 1960 and its effect on the transformation of American men's fashion. Tracing the Men's Wear Manufacturers of Los Angeles, established in 1934 (renamed the Men's Apparel Guild in California [MAGIC] in 1948), Scott outlines how Californian marketing practices and cross-promotional relationships with retailers helped to create the conditions for that warm and more bodily region's success in marketing casual apparel. In the chapter, "'Men Don't Wear Velvet You Know!' Fashionable Gay Masculinity and the Shopping Experience, London, 1950–early 1970s," historian Clare Lomas utilizes oral testimony and surviving men's garments in the Museum of London collection to gain insight into fashionable gay masculinity and the shopping experience in London at that time. She examines the mythic status accorded to stores such as Vince Man's Shop, John Stephens's His Clothes, and John Michael and highlights the fact that dress and clothing are part of a series of gay sensibilities that cannot be isolated from their wider cultural, historical, and social context.

The expansion and creation of new markets in fashion, grooming, and related industries that cater to the male consumer have resulted in an increased demand for male models. Joanne Entwistle's contribution, "From Catwalk to Catalogue: Male Fashion Models, Masculinity, and Identity," examines the male modeling industry and how young men negotiate notions of masculinity and employment in a field that focuses primarily on the body. Entwistle asks the question, "How is gender performed and reproduced through aesthetics and strategies of embodiment?" and then proceeds to illuminate the broader relationships between male bodies, self, and society through interviews with male fashion models.

The increased emphasis on the commodified male body in contemporary commercial culture has resulted in a proliferation of images of sexy, muscular, and immaculately groomed young men and celebrities, including British soccer star David Beckham and Australian swimming gold medalist Ian Thorpe selling fashion products. As Stella Bruzzi notes in her chapter, "The Italian Job: Football, Fashion, and That Sarong," "Storm, the London model agency, started signing up footballers in 1995 and those on its books by 1998 included Ruud Gillit, Les Ferdinand and Ian Wright." Other high-profile soccer players include David James, a Liverpool player turned Armani catwalk model, and Chelsea's Dennis Wise. Bruzzi's article examines the emergence of soccer chic and notes how the "style press," such as *Arena, GQ,* and British *Esquire* have utilized soccer celebrities as models for fashion editorials to evoke an aspirational lifestyle. The creation of the soccer player as style icon is yet another example of the shift in the representation of masculinity from the brawny, beer-drinking man, the image of the football hero in the 1970s, to a cool and sexy clotheshorse dressed in Gucci brogues and Zegna suits.

Vicki Karaminas examines masculinity in light of recent work on national identity and its relationship to gender via cinematic representations. Karaminas writes that comic book superheroes have also helped to construct an ideological worldview from the shifting interactions of politics, history, and culture, as well as defining a sense of identity and subjectivity since the 1930s. Yet, for such instantly recognizable icons, she says, little has been written in terms of superhero dress and the collective imagination that sartorial practices produce in framing cultural meanings. Rather than situating male superhero attire in the field of costume design functionality, Karaminas sets out to reposition the discourse of superhero clothing as a vehicle for understanding constructions of masculinity, identity, and nation.

In her seminal text, *Gender Trouble* (1990), Judith Butler writes that gender is not just a social construct but rather a kind of performance, a set of signs that we wear, as costume or disguise. Gender is not a primary category but an attribute, a set of secondary narrative effects that are culturally regulated through a hegemonic matrix that prioritizes heterosexuality as a framework for organizing bodies and desires. As Butler suggests, all gender is a form of performance "drag," a kind of situated form of expression rather than something that is "natural."[12] "If masculinity can be worn in the style of butch or drag kings," says Entwistle, "then gender is stripped of its naturalness and shown to be a set of culturally regulated styles."[13] In other words, masculinity is not a fixed and stable identity but is an identity on the move, challenging and transgressing, breaking and resisting gender paradigms.

The following three contributors explore the relationship between cross-dressing and theatricality and the ways in which garments construct (and deconstruct) gender and gender boundaries. In "The Transvestite Continuum: Liberace–Valentino–Elvis," Marjorie Garber interrogates how culture creates "transvestites." For Garber, transvestism functions to create a "category crisis," rupturing and calling attention to cultural, social, or aesthetic dissonances. By category crisis, Garber means "a failure of definitional distinction, a borderline that becomes permeable, that permits of border crossing from one (apparently distinct) category to another."[14] In celebrated figures like Liberace, Rudolph Valentino, and Elvis, the category crisis focuses cultural anxiety and challenges the hegemonic order. In this way, transvestism opens up a space of possibility, disrupting culture: not just within the binary of masculine and feminine but within the category itself.

Del LaGrace Volcano and Judith "Jack" Halberstam's contribution to this *Reader* examines the intersections between race and class in "Drag King" spaces via the performances of Drag Kings. They note the significance of blackness and the place of lesbians of color in the Drag King scene, while contesting the notion that the latter is predicated on access to an ideal of universal masculinity. According to Halberstam and Volcano, "lesbians produce wildly divergent masculinities in many different cultural arenas." As the feminine embodiment of the masculine, "kinging" is a tool for deconstructing and decentering constructions of masculinity. While Drag Kings subvert gender, they can also reinforce the complexities and stereotypes of male gender roles in their performance. As a marginal identity, the Drag King negotiates and encompasses a range of "desirable" masculinities in order to possess the power afforded to men. Kinging is about transforming hegemonic power into different forms of expression. Such masculine identities include a taxonomy of Drag King types: pimp, suited gentleman, truck driver, rapper, and "daddies," to name but a few.

For Halberstam and Volcano, drag is about "acting out" masculinity; for Mark Simpson, drag is about glamour, travesty, and carnival. Simpson's chapter, "Dragging It Up and Down: The Glamorized Male Body," focuses on three drag performances: the gay drag queen, the male stripper in a gay male venue, and the performance of rock and roll and heavy metal music, examining the way in which drag "acts" as a form of gender rebellion.

Important changes have occurred in the representation of masculinity and sexuality since the 1970s, raising important questions about the construction and representation of men in contemporary culture. These changes have also impacted the expansion of men's fashion, not only in terms of consumption, as a matter of appearances or shopping practices, but also as a topic for serious scholarly investigation.

Vicki Karaminas

NOTES

1. Tim Edwards, *Men in the Mirror: Men's Fashion, Masculinity and Consumer Society* (London: Cassell, 1997), xi.
2. Robert W. Connell, *Gender and Power: Society, the Person and Sexual Politics* (Cambridge: Polity, 1987); Robert W. Connell, *Masculinities* (Cambridge: Polity; St. Leonards, Australia: Allen and Unwin, 1995). See also F. Mort, *Cultures of Consumption: Masculinities and Social Space in Late Twentieth-Century Britain* (London: Routledge, 1996); and S. Nixon, *Hard Looks: Masculinities, Spectatorship and Contemporary Consumption* (New York: St. Martins, 1996).
3. Mort, *Cultures of Consumption;* Christopher Breward, *The Hidden Consumer: Masculinities, Fashion and City Life 1860–1914* (Manchester, UK, and New York: Manchester University Press, 1999); Nixon, *Hard Looks;* Edwards, *Men in the Mirror;* Mark Simpson, *Male Impersonators: Men Performing Masculinity* (New York: Routledge, 1994); and Paul Jobling, *Man Appeal: Advertising, Modernism and Menswear* (Oxford and New York: Berg, 2005).

4. E. Wilson, *Adorned in Dreams, Fashion and Modernity* (London: Virago, 1985), 117.

5. Edwards, *Men in the Mirror,* 4.

6. Farid Chenoune, *A History of Men's Fashion,* trans. Deke Dusinbere (Paris: Flammarion, 1993); Edwards, *Men in the Mirror;* and Anne Hollander, *Sex and Suits: The Evolution of Modern Dress* (New York: Kodansha, 1995).

7. G. Lipovetsky, *Empire of Fashion: Dressing Modern Democracy* (Princeton, NJ: Princeton University Press, 1994), 26–27.

8. J. Craik, *The Face of Fashion: Cultural Studies in Fashion* (London and New York: Routledge, 1994).

9. On the emergence of the "new man," see Edwards, *Men in the Mirror,* and F. Mort, "Boy's Own? Masculinity, Style and Popular Culture," in *Male Order: Unwrapping Masculinity,* ed. Rowena Chapman and Jonathon Rutherford (London: Lawrence and Wishart, 1988), 193–224.

10. Nixon, *Hard Looks.*

11. On the crisis in masculinity, see Chapman and Rutherford, *Male Order*; Edwards, *Men in the Mirror*; Frank Mort, "Images Change: High Street Style and the New Man," *New Socialist* 43 (November 1986): 6–8; Simpson, *Male Impersonators.*

12. Judith Butler, *Gender Trouble: Feminism and the Subversion of Identity* (London and New York: Routledge, 1990), 137.

13. Joanne Entwistle, *The Fashioned Body: Fashion, Dress and Modern Social Theory* (Cambridge: Polity, 2000), 178.

14. Marjorie Garber, *Vested Interests: Cross Dressing and Cultural Anxiety* (New York: Routledge, 1992), 16.

9

CALIFORNIA CASUAL: LIFESTYLE MARKETING AND MEN'S LEISURE WEAR, 1930–1960

William R. Scott

In 1945, *Fortune,* the nation's leading business magazine, documented the rapid growth of Los Angeles from a fashion industry outpost in the early 1930s to the nation's third-largest clothing centre. *Fortune* highlighted the national reach of California's leisurewear industry: eighty-five per cent of production was shipped over the Rockies, while shoppers in all 48 states looked for the 'Made in California' label. California menswear manufacturers, in particular, were poised to play a crucial role in the postwar explosion of American consumption. Indeed Los Angeles would become the world's second-largest fashion capital by the late 1950s, trailing only New York and surpassing older manufacturing centers such as Paris, London, and Chicago.[1]

The dramatic rise of the California clothing industry reflected important transformations in American men's fashion between the 1930s and 1960s. The three-piece suit, once the icon of the self-made man and a symbol of modern masculinity, remained a uniform only among conservative business professionals.[2] By the 1930s, men had stopped wearing hats in urban business districts on hot summer days. By the 1970s, the businessman's fedora was rare; top hats, once a requirement for evenings out, had become a veritable endangered species. In the 1920s, a few middle-class men daringly donned lightweight suits at summer resorts; by the 1960s, a man wearing any kind of suit at the beach looked ridiculous. Casual sportswear had become de rigueur. This new way of

dressing was not limited to the Sun Belt. Men in midwestern suburbs and New England towns enthusiastically adopted styles developed in Los Angeles and Palm Springs.

The rise of leisurewear was a national trend, but the Los Angeles clothing industry was fundamental to its development. 'Los Angeles' Little Cutters', as *Fortune* termed them, designed casual clothing for 'Hollywood's professionally perfect figures', and for people who aspired to the movie stars' casual lifestyle on weekends. Los Angeles manufacturers capitalized on the cultural shift toward informality, reworking masculine style in the process. This new masculine look integrated the high style of Hollywood and Palm Springs resort wear, the toughness of the western frontier, and the informality of the suburb. California leisurewear fused seemingly incongruous references: the same garment might blend stylistic elements from the American ranch and the French Riviera. California leisurewear also lent itself to adaptation. By the late postwar period, west coast clothing had become so widely copied that California casual became synonymous with American vernacular style.

A trade organization played a key role in the sartorial transformation of male America, notably through its innovative marketing practices. In 1934, local clothing producers anxious to lure retail buyers away from the traditional garment centers—Chicago, St. Louis, and New York—formed the Men's Wear Manufacturers of Los Angeles. When the Manufacturers mounted the first men's fashion show in history—the Sports-wear Round Up at Palm Springs in 1942—the Los Angeles menswear industry made serious inroads into the national market. That year, the Manufacturers also helped launch the trade journal *California Men's Stylist*. By 1951, the New York-based trade publication *Men's Wear* started its 'California Dateline' feature, acknowledging the importance of Los Angeles to the national industry. Today the Men's Apparel Guild in California (MAGIC), the successor to the Manufacturers, runs the largest exposition of men's clothing and accessories in the world.

MAGIC and its members forged a range of practices that by the 1960s came to be known as 'lifestyle marketing'. Their Sportswear Round Up attracted retailers from around the country who wanted to experience the 'casual, easy' California 'way-of-life', while they selected casual clothes for their stores. Sportswear manufacturers collectively and individually advertised in national magazines. Their ads associated California casual apparel with youth, celebrity, leisure, and heterosexuality. Los Angeles menswear manufacturers repeatedly emphasized that their designs emanated from the California lifestyle and catered to consumers' desires, rather than the other way around. Lifestyle marketing penetrated all aspects of the Los Angeles sportswear industry: responding to consumer demand and promoting the new casual lifestyle was as much the business as manufacturing apparel. Much earlier than other clothing companies—and thirty years before journalist-historian Thomas Frank documented the phenomenon—Los Angeles sportswear manufacturers oriented their business around lifestyle marketing.[3]

This rise of lifestyle marketing in the menswear industry signalled the ascension of consumerist masculinity during the mid-twentieth century. On the surface, this claim would seem to conflict with recent work on masculinity in this period. James Gilbert's analysis of the era's rhetoric considers how mass culture and suburbia were consistently portrayed as 'feminizing' and 'debasing'.

Clark Davis's study of Los Angeles describes rapidly developing corporate bureaucracies and the concomitant culture of 'white-collar manhood'.[4] Yet it was precisely these white-collar men who supported the California sportswear industry. 'Organization men' who spent their workdays in business hierarchies inhabited less formal social worlds on weekends. Furthermore, marketing tactics that linked products to explicitly masculine values had tremendous appeal to men who shunned consumption's feminine associations. Just as most *Playboy* subscribers in the 1950s were married, California 'frontier' clothes appealed to urban and suburban family men whose fantasies extended to rough-and-tumble living.[5] Men's penchant for fashionable clothing, long 'hidden', was made visible though the simple act of dressing down.[6]

'ON THE MAP AS A GARMENT TOWN'

If Los Angeles appeared 'On the Map as a Garment Town' by 1931, as *Southern California Business* argued, it was still only a lonely outpost.[7] Compared to New York and Chicago, it was at best a regional manufacturing centre in the early 1930s, selling most of its clothes in California and the Southwest.[8] This changed gradually throughout the 1930s and dramatically in the 1940s. Department stores across the country established California departments. A high-end California Shop opened in New York City in 1938, with editors from major fashion magazines dropping in to see the exciting west coast designs.[9] By 1945, an estimated eighty-five per cent of clothing manufactured in California was shipped over the Rockies, with a third of stores nationwide sending their buyers west to order stock.[10]

Other developments speak to California's emergence as a fashion centre. According to the U.S. Chamber of Commerce, the men's sportswear industry was the fastest growing industry in

Los Angeles between 1939 and 1942, outpacing defence spending in the region.[11] This growth accelerated after World War II. In 1934, the men's sportswear industry in Los Angeles had $8 million in sales; by 1957, it manufactured $160 million worth of garments.[12] Annual sales among all Los Angeles clothing manufacturers grew from $50 million in 1940 to $400 million in 1948. By comparison, the New York market, which concentrated on men's suits, women's wear, and children's clothing, dominated the industry, with a $1.5 billion market in 1945.[13] Small next to this giant, the Los Angeles industry nevertheless exerted a powerful influence over American men's fashion.

The rise of Los Angeles as a national sportswear centre was facilitated by historical phenomena not exclusively related to the clothing industry. Federal laws creating the forty-hour working week in 1938 expanded leisure time for middle-class Americans. The dramatic demographic expansion of Los Angeles also certainly played a role. The city more than quadrupled in size from 1920 to 1960, to more than 2.5 million. The swelling population, coupled with the rise of Hollywood, created an image of Los Angeles as the land of limitless opportunity, the hub of commercialized leisure, and a major tourist attraction. Such images, promoted by the mass media, stimulated a nationwide interest in all things Californian. Improved transportation between the west and east allowed manufacturers and retailers to meet the demand for California goods more easily.[14]

World War II played a crucial role in the development of the Los Angeles sportswear industry and the California casual aesthetic. As the largest metropolis on the west coast and a major staging ground for the U.S. armed forces, the city experienced rapid demographic growth and industrial infrastructure development from American military operations in the Pacific. Los Angeles clothing firms, like the Catalina Knitting Company, reaped most of their profits from wartime sportswear production. While other regional clothing centres filled military orders for uniforms, parachutes, and other gear, California sportswear firms expanded their output of civilian clothes.[15] World War II also initiated a lifestyle shift by exposing thousands of soldiers and war workers to the Golden State's informal environment. As *Fortune* noted, workers in Southern California's war plants starting buying and wearing sportswear.[16] Ultimately, this trend spread beyond the factories and proved crucial to the dissemination of California leisurewear. Work clothing and sportswear came to be virtually indistinguishable by the late 1950s, with manual labourers wearing short-sleeved shirts on the job and white-collar workers wearing denim jeans in their free time.[17]

The economic growth of Los Angeles created opportunities for Southern California's industries, including factories that produced women's sportswear. Yet by the 1950s, style leadership in women's clothing remained firmly centred in New York and Paris, with only minor inroads by sportswear manufacturers in California and Italy.[18] The women's wear market had always been larger and more diversified than the menswear industry, and successes of California women's sportswear firms never had a dramatic effect on the transnational industry, except in the niche business of swimwear. In contrast, menswear manufacturers capitalized on these developments to transform men's style and outdistance the local women's fashion industry. In 1971, the region's women's clothing magazine, *California Stylist,* folded, but the trade journal *California Men's Stylist,* created in 1942, was still going strong.

Between 1930 and 1960, California menswear companies moved from making coarse work clothes for the regional market to holding the reins of stylistic leadership for the American sportswear industry. The centre of men's fashion had moved to the west coast. From Manhattan, *Men's Wear* acquiesced in 1948, admitting, 'The conquest of New York goes on steadily but not without some resistance from manufacturers in the east.' Begrudgingly, the trade journal admitted that the 'Pacific coast' was 'largely responsible for the expansion of the leisure apparel market.'[19] *Men's and Boys' Stylist* was even more direct: 'Today California, no doubt, is the men's wear fashion center of the world.'[20] In the short span of twenty years, Los Angeles had been transformed from a regional outpost to the nation's leading producer of men's clothing, by encouraging stores across the country to stock and promote casual sportswear.

Innovative marketing practices contributed to this success. The Men's Wear Manufacturers of Los Angeles, established in 1934, was in full swing by the following year. Representatives from well-established California firms helped create this important organization.[21] The oldest of these firms, Cohn Goldwater and Brownstein Lewis, dated from the 1890s, but most of the founding companies had been established after 1920, during the start-up years of the California leisurewear industry. The trade association grew steadily throughout the 1930s and 1940s. The Manufacturers claimed sixty-two members in 1935; by the time the association was renamed the Men's Apparel Guild in California (MAGIC) in 1948, an additional 179 firms had joined.[22] The association developed an institutional infrastructure, with officers, dues, and regular meetings. In 1941, the organization and its paid staff played a major role in launching the trade journal *California Men's Stylist,* later called the *California Men's and Boys' Stylist.* The next year witnessed the debut of the Manufacturers' premier promotional event, the Round Up, along with its Fall Market Week. Besides promotional activities, the Manufacturers addressed production concerns. In 1944, the organization contributed several hundred thousand dollars to construct independent textile mills in Los Angeles County, and in 1947 it sponsored an apparel training section at a local trade school in response to labour shortages created by the market's growth.[23]

The Manufacturers helped create the conditions for the region's success in apparel. The organization facilitated regional promotions and tie-ins as it marketed sportswear and the 'Made in California' label. It co-sponsored a west coast promotion with women's clothing manufacturers in 1945 and invested thousands in group advertising in 1947.[24] More importantly, the trade association encouraged individual manufacturers and retailers to coordinate their marketing activities with its regional promotional efforts. Los Angeles retailers devoted major window space to tie-ins with the 1947 Palm Springs Round Up.[25] When *Men's Wear* started its 'California Dateline' column in 1951, MAGIC members poured money into this national trade journal, surrounding the new feature with advertisements for west coast leisurewear.[26] In sportswear ads, the A-1 Manufacturing Company, Maurice Holman, and Catalina Knitting Mills proudly proclaimed their MAGIC memberships as they marketed the 'California look'.[27]

These cross-promotions and tie-ins had a synergistic effect. The two trade associations—the Manufacturers and later MAGIC—focused members' attention on the entire region. Relatively small firms began to see themselves as competitors to brand-name manufacturers in New York, Chicago, and St. Louis.[28] Furthermore the association's emphasis on publicity and marketing distinguished it from other manufacturers' organizations in the American clothing industry. For example, at its annual convention in October 1950, the New York-based Clothing Manufacturers' Association focused on government clothing controls and disputes with the Wool Association, discussing advertising and marketing only as an aside. Labour relations, government 'code problems' and industrial research preoccupied its members.[29] Traditional organizations like the Clothing Manufacturers' Association did little to encourage marketing or boost sales. Its 'Buy New York Products' campaign is a case in point. This 1939 effort emerged in response to the buoyant Los Angeles apparel trade, but failed in part because the plea for regional solidarity fell on deaf ears among New York retailers.[30]

A scrapbook found in the MAGIC corporate headquarters in Woodland Hills, California, reveals a very different trade organization—one that took marketing as its primary purpose. Compiled between 1947 and 1950, the scrapbook contains articles covering the group's activities and promotions, culled from an amazing range of local and national publications. While it documents only a fraction of the organization's activities, the scrapbook reveals MAGIC to be an activist association that did everything in its power to expand the California leisurewear industry.

MARKETING A CALIFORNIA LIFESTYLE

The MAGIC clippings show how the association used a wide variety of promotional strategies to generate a relatively cohesive message: buy California casual fashions! A marketing study by the New York-based Men's Apparel Research Guild outlined the basics of 'California Fashion', themes reiterated in MAGIC's advertising, promotions, and articles:

'California Fashion' is best exemplified by:

A—Styled and made in California.
B—Casual, easy fitting apparel.
C—Broader shoulder expression.
D—Tradition slightly sacrificed for comfort.
E—Use of the unusual in colours or colour combinations.
F—Often using motifs and details that stem from the Old West.[31]

California itself proved to be a major selling point for Los Angeles leisurewear, a decade before the mid-1950s when *Gidget* surf movies and Disney marketed the Golden State.[32] Leisurewear represented the 'California lifestyle' among marketers and journalists alike. Nearly every description of Los Angeles sportswear linked it to the 'sunny' and 'carefree' way of life in California.[33] This lifestyle was given expression in the 'casual, easy fitting apparel' and bright colours made by the Los Angeles factories and promoted by MAGIC.

Just as fruit-growers branded Sunkist orange juice and its sunny origins in the Golden State, Los Angeles sportswear manufacturers marketed the idea of casual living through the 'Made in California' label.[34] The 'distinctive styling' of California clothes reflected the close ties of producers and consumers.[35] The chief spokesman for the western apparel manufacturers, P. G. Winnett, noted the principal differences between fashion design in the east and west. 'In New York', he wrote, 'the design may be something picked out of the air, or picked up in Paris … California styles recognize and are an interpretation of the needs of the people.'[36]

The smaller size of western manufacturers enabled the responsive styling for which California producers became known. Rather than focusing on quantity and trying to cut costs when competition got tough, many western operators tried to be nimble all the time. Their small, flexible production plants stood in stark contrast to New York's industry in the mid-twentieth century, which tended toward large manufacturing operations and efficiencies of scale. Their size allowed New York-based factories to undercut the rest of the market in price. Californians parried with nimbleness, 'chang[ing] designs overnight' to satiate consumer desires.[37]

This emphasis on the consumer reflected the distinctive marketing orientation of the California sportswear industry. Los Angeles manufacturers cultivated an image as 'lifestyle' companies that understood the needs of men at play better than did eastern competitors: 'You can't design clothes like that'—casual, fun clothes for weekends in the sun—'huddled over a radiator'.[38] Lifestyle marketing even reshaped the sites of production. When Catalina built a new manufacturing facility, a major feature of the site was an enclosed pool and patio area, presumably so employees could enjoy the California sunshine during their lunch breaks.[39] Perhaps employees also market-tested new product designs as they relaxed around the pool.

The heightened marketing orientation of California sportswear companies placed them at the forefront of American business practice. By mid-century, marketing had achieved status as an academic discipline and was becoming an important factor for companies concerned with satisfying the consumer. Practitioners who launched the 'marketing revolution' in the 1940s and 1950s viewed their discipline as mediating the relationship between businesses and consumers.[40] Since the early 1900s, advertising agencies, mass-circulation magazines, and home economists, among others, had tried to understand, quantify, and respond to consumers' psychology, habits, and desires. Manufacturers also took up the charge of 'imagining consumers', through informal observations of consumers or quantitative analysis of sales data.[41] The postwar marketing revolution codified these ideas and disseminated them to a wider range of companies and industries. New marketing practice aimed to reorganize *all* manufacturing firms to make them more focused on their customers. Like Catalina Knitting Mills, the ideal company would no longer simply be 'production oriented' or even 'marketing oriented', but 'marketing controlled'. In theory, the entire company was to be geared toward creating and meeting consumer demand. The California menswear industry put these theories into action: sportswear firms used innovative promotional techniques to help create demand and responded quickly to consumer taste with batch production and rapid-fire design.

California manufacturers developed advertising campaigns that linked their products to sensual longing, the pleasures of mass consumption, and status enhancement. Female-oriented advertising had used these tropes since 1911, when the Andrew Jergens Company introduced sex appeal to resuscitate Woodbury's Facial Soap, a flagging brand. From 1907 to 1932, Peabody, Cluett and Company commissioned

illustrator Joseph Christian Leyendecker to create the confident and masculine Arrow Man, which graced the firm's advertisements for celluloid collars from 1907 to 1931.[42] Nevertheless, most male-oriented advertisers emphasized durability, practicality, and social correctness to sell their products in the mid-twentieth century. California sportswear manufacturers were among the first men's businesses to foreground sensuality.[43]

MAGIC members emphasized masculine freedom to update the pleasure trope. As early as 1935, California manufacturers paired sportswear with freedom. 'It has at last become good taste to be comfortable', noted the *Los Angeles Times*, 'correct to be free.'[44] Increasingly, California itself came to symbolize the freedom that came from informality and carefree living. Companies like Maurice Holman used California imagery, along with their MAGIC connections, to promote products. Holman's California MultiColored Short Jacket, advertised in *Men's Wear* in 1953, featured the long, pointed collar and the 'broader shoulder expression' that epitomized west coast styling. The sun picture at the top of Holman's ad and the 'rainbow' colours of the clothes evoked California's bright, outdoor image. Maurice Holman typified MAGIC members who simultaneously marketed California *and* California style in trade publications like *Men's Wear*.[45]

This link between leisurewear, sunshine, and California styling became increasingly naturalized throughout the 1940s and 1950s, whether the marketer was on the west coast or in the midwest. Harry B. Pock, sportswear merchandising manager for the William H. Block Company of Indianapolis, launched a promotion titled, 'Perfectly at Home in Indiana: California Shirts and Sport Shirts'. His advertising text connected California styling and sunshine: 'When the mercury soars, the Indiana male naturally turns to shirts from California (where hot weather styling is a year 'round specialty) ... [T]hese sheer cool shirts have a light touch that makes them just right for a Hoosier summer.'[46] The logic ran as follows: when Indiana's weather approached that of Southern California, Indianapolis men would 'naturally' choose Los Angeles shirts. Stores throughout the country advertised similar promotions during the 1940s. In Michigan, Wurzburg's sold 'Leisure Coats' from the 'sunny playgrounds of California', while Hess Brothers in Allentown, Pennsylvania, 'show[ed] men how to be smart, casual and comfortable under California influence.'[47]

Promotions also portrayed the bright colours of California leisurewear as extensions of natural surroundings, including 'native' Mexicans. Writing about women's leisure clothes, *California Stylist* articulated the link between sportswear, the landscape, and the state's colonial settlers. 'The originality of color in California Sportswear is native to the environment', the *Stylist* reported. Chartreuse came 'from the ever new leaves of the citrus groves.' Fuchsia and Dusty Rose owed their hues to the glowing sunset, which gave 'the mountain peaks' and 'the valleys in between' their sensuous colours. 'From the Pueblos come the sombre tones of Tile and Adobe Red, while the gay costume of Mexican inhabitants brings forth an array of brightest red and green and gold.'[48] By reducing Mexicans to the category of the natural, alongside mountain peaks and citrus groves, the leisurewear industry adopted an imagined 'Mexican peasant look' at the moment when racial tensions mounted between Anglos, blacks, and Hispanics in Los Angeles.[49] Naturalization of the Mexican 'peasant' allowed the industry to appropriate Latino culture from a safe distance.[50]

Dusty Rose was perhaps too feminine a hue for menswear manufacturers, who preferred to promote California as 'climate coloured'.[51] Pock framed this vibrant theme in ways that might appeal to men: 'Bold color: The Decisive Masculine Trend in California Sport Shirts.'[52] Colour made the shirt, and hence the wearer, bold, decisive—and manly. *California Stylist* also framed colourful sportswear in masculine terms,

relying on 'nature' to legitimize the dye choices: 'The natural expression of California interpreted in cloth would be the rugged rough types that lend themselves to the active out-of-door life.'[53] Others found the colour choices more shocking than daring. A *Fresno Bee* reporter wrote: 'Hold tight, men. Colors for fall clothes will be gold and bronze, chartreuse and vermillion. The Men's Wear Manufacturers of Los Angeles are throwing the paint pot with wild abandon.'[54] The *Detroit Times* called the California styles 'gaudy'; the *Rochester Democrat and Chronicle* labeled them 'extreme'.[55] Overall, however, sales continued to climb.

California sportswear manufacturers advertised their brightly coloured garments by marketing the 'natural' connection between California's warm climate, vibrant landscape, and California-made leisurewear. The advertisements and commentary repeatedly celebrated the 'outdoor' lifestyle of Los Angeles and environs to explain the 'style leadership' of Los Angeles: sportswear that men in the rest of the country could only wear in summer or at resorts could be tried out earlier and more often in sunny Southern California. Increasingly, it was this lifestyle itself that came to be advertised and marketed along with the clothes. This lifestyle marketing, or as one historian of consumer culture has put it, 'aspirational merchandising', associated men's sportswear so closely with Southern California leisure practices that each came to stand in for the other.[56]

The more men nationally led laid-back, relaxed lives, the more they chose sportswear from Los Angeles (or at least in the Southern California style), a place continually associated with leisure through the rise of tourism to the region and the virtual tourism offered by motion pictures. The connection worked the other way, too: sportswear advertisements sold a leisure-filled lifestyle, or at least the fantasy of such a lifestyle, along with the clothes.

In 1953, one of Southern California's largest manufacturers, Catalina Knitting Mills, published an advertisement in *Men's Wear* illustrating the key elements of lifestyle marketing. Once called the Pacific Knitting Mills, Catalina was a founding member of the Men's Wear Manufacturers of Los Angeles. Established as an underwear manufacturer in 1907, the firm shifted to swimwear in the 1920s. By the 1930s, it began making a popular line of sweaters and sportswear.[57] In the 1945 feature on Los Angeles, *Fortune* deemed Catalina's chief executive Edgar Stewart a 'giant' of the western clothing industry. Under his direction, Catalina sold $5 million worth of apparel each year.[58]

Catalina's advertisement for 'Sun and Swim Fashions' used iconography that reiterated the key themes in lifestyle marketing: leisure, youthfulness, and consumer-inspired plenty (colour plate 30). To twenty-first-century consumers, the advertisement's images of 'beach boys' and 'California girls' look mightily familiar, part and parcel of a culture that values outdoor leisure and bodily display. For viewers in the 1950s, these images would have been new, exciting, and perhaps titillating. For one thing, the advertisement would have been visually arresting because of the five colour photographs taken in 'fabulous Palm Springs', a 'mecca of Hollywood film stars and socialites' and the 'birthplace of fashion trends for summer months'.[59] In 1953, colour images dominated the advertising pages of mass-circulation magazines like the *Saturday Evening Post,* but they were rarer in trade journals like *Men's Wear,* probably due to costs. Second, the images depict scantily clad men and women, enjoying activities such as swimming, sunbathing, and shopping in Palm Springs, which had more pools per capita than any city in the world.[60] For context, it was only twenty years earlier when men first swam without shirts on a public beach in Florida.[61] Regardless of their age, everyone in the pictures looks youthful and tanned, photographs glow with naked legs, shoulders, and chests. 'Catalina', the advertisement stated, 'plays an important role in the Palm Springs resort season picture with styles that

are colourful, comfortable, pretty and practical in the California tradition of casual, easy living.' The name Catalina appears at the bottom, along with the firm's signature flying fish logo.

The imagery in this advertisement linked the 'California tradition of casual, easy living' to bodily display and a barely-under-the-surface sexuality. Other lifestyle advertisers cultivated a meritocracy of the body, but California's clothing and film industries especially pushed these themes. Leisurewear promotions put the body on show along with the clothes. None of the Catalina men resembled celebrity bodybuilder Charles Atlas, who made muscularity popular in 1920s advertisements.[62] Atlas had to work out to look good. In contrast, the skinny, tan good looks of the Catalina models seemed effortless: the product of youthfulness, the right Anglo-Saxon gene pool, and a healthy outdoor lifestyle.[63]

The Catalina models differ from Atlas in another significant way. The Catalina ad steers the viewer's gaze in ways that reinforce heterosexuality and deflect implications of homoeroticism. The presence of women allowed readers to look safely at the men. This tension between advertising men's bodies and clothing while avoiding the threat of homoerotic reading of the images undergirded much of the lifestyle marketing in the pages of *Men's Wear, California Men's Stylist,* and other publications after the mid-1940s. The emergence of this tension reflected a declining acceptability of same-sex sociability, the rising perception that homosexuality was threatening, and, in some cases, a growing discomfort with men being objectified. California menswear marketers borrowed an obvious solution from *Esquire* and *Playboy:* encode the images with ebullient and obvious heterosexuality.[64] Images of young men in family situations and with women deflected suggestions of homoeroticism. Men in advertisements, when pictured together, often appeared looking off into the distance as if to avert homoerotic gazes.

The Catalina advertisement further supported a meritocracy of the body with celebrity tie-ins. For one, Catalina boasted that it provided swimsuits to the Miss Universe Beauty Pageant, held in Long Beach. Palm Springs as a location for the photo shoot implied links to Hollywood movie stars and other beautiful people. California manufacturers were well aware of the boost the entertainment industry gave to their growing businesses.[65] In the ad, bandleader-turned-hotelier Horace Heidt flirts with a young woman, suggesting celebrities were ubiquitous in Palm Springs. Decades earlier, California manufacturers had pioneered celebrity endorsements as a marketing strategy. Celebrity magazines such as *Photoplay* depicted stars lounging poolside in Palm Springs or relaxing in Hollywood; these images served as informal advertisements for California leisurewear and 'easy' living.[66]

Los Angeles manufacturers were so successful at naturalizing the link between California and an informal, 'breezy' lifestyle that eastern manufacturers, eager to capitalize on the move to casual wear, began selling their products as 'California-styled.' West coast manufacturers filed suit to protect the 'Made in California' label, but in 1947 the court ruled against them. The court found that 'California' referred to a type of garment rather than a place of origin.[67] California, casual living, and garment design had been conjoined so closely that outside manufacturers were legally allowed to name their leisurewear after the state. The conflict heralded the dramatic arrival of sportswear on the national picture. By the 1950s, west coast sportswear and the marketing techniques used to sell it were copied by manufacturers throughout the country, transforming the industry in the image of California.[68]

ROUNDING UP CUSTOMERS AT PALM SPRINGS

Perhaps the most novel and important innovation of west coast manufacturers was the Palm Springs Round Up, an annual promotion created by the Men's Wear Manufacturers of Los Angeles in 1942. This Palm Springs event epitomized the sartorial and marketing changes led by Los Angeles apparel producers. Its centrepiece was a fashion show—the first in history to focus on men's clothing—featuring sportswear designed and made in Southern California.[69] More than a style show, the Palm Springs Round Up was also a merchandising forum, a market week, and a real-life demonstration of California living. Visiting buyers selected and ordered their lines, learned methods for promoting California wear, and experienced firsthand the sunny lifestyle. At New York's loosely organized Market Week, individual manufacturers set their own agendas, promoting their own new lines. At the Palm Springs Round Up, the Manufacturers cooperated to plan and host a convention that aimed to boost sales for all its members.

A major success from its start in 1942, the Round Up drew buyers, reporters, and manufacturers from all over the country only a few years later. In 1948, the trade journal *Men's Wear* previewed the Round Up with anticipation: 'Interest in the proceedings is running at high pitch, tempo furioso, inasmuch as the world of men's apparel looks to California for its sartorial stimulation.'[70] A guest register from the 1948 Round Up listed more than 1,200 attendees from cities and towns in every major region of the country: New York, Corpus Christi, Minneapolis, Honolulu, Chicago, Bakersfield, Birmingham, Washington, D.C., and New Orleans, and Vancouver across the border in Canada.[71] The Round Up grew with the leisurewear market. A special American Airlines flight was chartered for attendees in 1950.[72] By the mid-1950s, approximately 2,000 people from 32 states and five countries travelled to Palm Springs for the Round Up. The arbiter of taste in menswear, *Apparel Arts,* called the Round Up the 'talk of the industry', a 'yearly masterpiece' and a 'must on the calendar' for menswear retailers.[73] Today this annual MAGIC convention has moved to Las Vegas and become the world's largest trade show for men's goods.

In 1942, *California Men's Stylist* published a four-page spread of photographs from the first Palm Springs Round Up.[74] The photo essay illustrated the themes and marketing strategies behind California leisurewear. One page showed eight images that conveyed the distinctiveness of California casual. *Esquire* fashion editor O. E. Schoeffler posed with the 'local color', sandwiched between six women to convey a 'playboy' image. The *Esquire* picture linked the Round Up with the nation's most popular men's publication, a 'modern,' lifestyle-oriented magazine whose editors appreciated the 'California way' and helped to publicize it. A poolside picture showed two male runway models in slacks and sport shirts by Duke of Hollywood and Hollywood Sportswear, with Mount San Jacinto rising up behind them.

The style show was perhaps the most innovative event at the Round Up, signifying the incorporation of men into the fashion system. A third photograph of two Hollywood film stars, Charles Farrell and William Gargan, suggested that that men's fashionable presentation was not limited to magazines or staged events. At the event, the Manufacturers honoured Farrell as the country's 'best-dressed sportsman'. Finally, other photographs appropriated cultural icons from Hawaii, Texas, and Mexico to link California to the west and distinguish it from the east: grass skirts, cowboy hats, western scarves, and a horse-drawn stagecoach. The event's title, the Round Up, conjured up images of the Old West as depicted by the movies and is indicative of the sportswear industry's debt to Hollywood.

Perhaps more striking than the beautiful setting, the male models were a major innovation and attraction. In the 1947 Round Up, the models began the fashion show by imitating mannequins in a 'store' window before parading 'out of the window onto the sidewalk, down the center lane of the audience.' Their actions blended stage theatrics with catwalk practices. Clearly, men and their clothes were on display. The businessmen in the crowd watched the models keenly. The organizers of the event were careful in all their promotional material to call this event a 'style show', but little appears to have separated it from a fashion show except that men were the audience and models.[75]

The Round Up's display of men and their clothes had precursors in *Apparel Arts* and in advertisements like Peabody and Cluett's Arrow Man. The all-male fashion show, however, was a markedly new development in the history of men's clothing. More than *Apparel Arts* or even *Esquire,* it symbolized men's entanglement in the fashion system. In this way, the Round Up fashion show prefigured the 'peacock revolution' of the 1960s (colour plate 32), the 'glamorized male body' of the 1980s, and the 'metrosexual' of contemporary parlance.[76] The Round Up show, in encouraging men to look at other men as models of style—which, as we have seen, was intimately connected to broader fantasies loosely captured by the term 'lifestyle'—literalized the homosocial gaze of consumer aspiration. In addition to the clothes themselves, the act of exposure itself came to represent the comfortable, easy California way.

The Palm Springs Round Up had public relations tie-ins with retailers and publishers. Los Angeles department stores created special window displays linked to the event, while *California Apparel News* printed a special edition about it. Throughout Southern California, stores such as Silverwood's in Santa Barbara, Bullock's in Palm Springs, and Mullen and Bluett in Los Angeles launched style events, including community parades and rodeos.[77] While helping to sell California sportswear, this systematic cross-promotion on the local and regional level attracted national media attention.

The Palm Springs Round Up was not only a style forum; it also put forward coherent messages about store merchandising and display.[78] California lifestyle marketing linked clothing style, mass-marketing techniques, retail display, and point-of-sale promotions. Merchandisers who attended the Round Up were convinced by such promotions to return to their hometowns and open up California shops and departments selling sportswear in the ways they had witnessed at Palm Springs.[79] These departments around the country echoed the Round Up's emphasis on masculine leisure, bodily display, and an outdoors lifestyle, for these cultural tropes had become inseparably linked to California sportswear. Marketers' innovative use of scantily clad male models in the Round Up literalized this connection.

The Palm Springs Round Up's style show, along with the inventive advertising of leisurewear, signalled a new relationship to marketing in the menswear industry. The California companies in MAGIC transformed the Round Up into much more than a market week. It was a tour-de-force performance that offered participants—store buyers from around the country—a taste of rodeos, swimming pools, and other symbols of the California lifestyle and the sportswear that was for sale. This reflected an orientation that was very different from east coast manufacturers, at least until the mid-1950s. California sportswear companies may have produced clothes, but the Round Up illustrated that marketing, not manufacturing, drove their businesses. The associations with sexuality, leisure, and status aspiration sold the clothes.

In the 1930s, menswear manufacturers had promoted their clothing as appropriate and correct. The three-piece suit was, after all, appropriate for every occasion, a veritable male uniform. The success of California leisurewear not only changed men's wardrobes, but also changed the way men's clothes were viewed. After the marketing of California sportswear, men's clothing took on greater representational weight: it became symbolic of a lifestyle. The suit did not, of course, disappear. But it increasingly came to represent conventionality, business, and sobriety. Many men, on many more occasions, chose instead to align themselves with the informal ease and sexually laden imagery of leisurewear. California sportswear companies, in

creating these cultural linkages, ensured their success and transformed the marketing of men's consumer goods.

NOTES

Reprinted with permission from William R. Scott, "California Casual: Lifestyle Marketing and Men's Leisurewear, 1930–1960," in *Producing Fashion*, ed. R. Blaszczyk, (Philadelphia: University of Pennsylvania Press, 2007), 169–87.

1. 'Los Angeles' Little Cutters: Their Sportswear Always Had Honor in Its Own Country' (1945), *Fortune* 31, May: 134, 182; 'L.A. Ranks 2nd in World as Apparel Industry Center', 1958, clipping, folder: 'Garment Industry—Los Angeles', Vertical File, Los Angeles Public Library, Los Angeles.

2. For background on men's dress, especially the rise of the three-piece suit, see Christopher Breward (1999), *The Hidden Consumer: Masculinities, Fashion and City Life, 1860–1914,* Manchester: Manchester University Press; David Kuchta (2002), *The Three-Piece Suit and Modern Masculinity: England, 1550–1850,* Berkeley: University of California Press; Michael Zakim (2003), *Ready-Made Democracy: A History of Men's Dress in the American Republic, 1760–1860,* Chicago: University of Chicago Press.

3. Thomas Frank (1997), *The Conquest of Cool: Business Culture, Counterculture, and the Rise of Hip Consumerism,* Chicago: University of Chicago Press.

4. James Gilbert (2005), *Men in the Middle: Searching for Masculinity in the 1950s,* Chicago: University of Chicago Press; Clark Davis (2000), *Company Men: White-Collar Life and Corporate Cultures in Los Angeles, 1892–1941,* Baltimore: Johns Hopkins University Press.

5. 'The Playboy Reader' (1955), *Playboy* 2, Sep.: 36–37.

6. Consumption was coded as feminine in the late nineteenth and early twentieth centuries, leaving masculine consumption hidden in plain sight. But historians should not confuse this gendered understanding of consumption with

the reality, in which men arguably consumed more than women. Breward, *The Hidden Consumer*; Mark A. Swienicki (1999), 'Consuming Brotherhood: Men's Culture, Style and Recreation as Consumer Culture, 1880–1930', in *Consumer Society in American History: A Reader,* ed. Lawrence B. Glickman, Ithaca, N.Y.: Cornell University Press: 207–40.

7. James H. Collins (1931), 'On the Map as a Garment Town', *Southern California Business* 10, Mar.: 13.

8. On the regional nature of California's apparel industry, see Seward C. Simons (1925), 'The West's Greatest Garment Center', *Southern California Business* 4, Oct.: 17.

9. The California Shop's Guest Book from 1938 included visitors from *Vogue, Esquire, Women's Wear Daily, Town and Country, Harper's Bazaar, Parents, Mademoiselle,* and *Glamour.* See box 1, series 3, acc. no. 572, California Shop Records, Archives Center, Smithsonian National Museum of American History, Washington, D.C. (hereafter cited as CS-NMAH).

10. 'Los Angeles' Little Cutters': 134; Charles S. Goodman (1948), *The Location of Fashion Industries with Special Reference to California Apparel Markets,* Ann Arbor: University of Michigan Press: 36.

11. Cited in Phil Lansdale (1942), 'An Unliterary Digest of Los Angeles Sportswear', *California Men's Stylist* 1, Jan.: 45.

12. Robert J. Sullivan (1948), 'Stitch in Time', *Wall Street Journal,* 20 Jan.; Art Ryon (1957), 'Plunging Neckline in Male Styles', *Los Angeles Times,* 28 Oct.

13. 'Los Angeles' Little Cutters': 134.

14. For the image of California, see Kirse Granat May (2002), *Golden State, Golden Youth: The California Image in Popular Culture, 1955–1966,* Chapel Hill: University of North Carolina Press.

15. Gwendolyn June Bymers (1958), 'A Study of Employment in Women's and Misses' Outerwear Manufacturing', Ph.D. dissertation, University of California, Los Angeles.

16. 'Los Angeles' Little Cutters': 134, 186.

17. U.S. Department of Commerce, Business and Defense Services Administration (1961), *Leisure and Work Clothing,* Washington, D.C.: GPO: 3.

18. The women's clothing industry remained more diversified throughout this period. Although California took a lead in many casual styles and was the home to 'star' designers like Edith Head and Adrian, both couture and quantity production remained firmly rooted in the East. For triumphal histories of California women's fashion, see Marian Hall et al. (2002), *California Fashion: From the Old West to New Hollywood,* New York: Abrams; Maureen Reilly (2001), *California Casual: Fashions, 1930s–1970s,* Atglen, Pa.: Schiffer; and 'Iconic to Ironic', Exhibition at the Oakland Museum, Oakland, Calif., Mar.–Sept. 2003. The exhibit presented a celebratory narrative focusing on the influence of beach wear, California jeans, and Hollywood glamour.

19. E. M. Ruttenberg (1948), 'Palm Springs Preview', *Men's Wear* 120, 24 Sept.: 61–67, clipping, MAGIC Archives, Woodland Hills, Calif. (hereafter cited as MA).

20. Fred Grunwald (1947), 'California Futurization', *California Men's and Boys' Stylist,* Nov., clipping, MA.

21. 'Fact Sheet: Men's and Boys' Apparel Guilds in California' (1956), Los Angeles: Men's and Boys' Apparel Guilds in California, MA.

22. Jack Hyde (1948), 'Thorsen Heads Men's Wear Manufacturers of Los Angeles', *Daily News Record,* 9 Jan., clipping, MA.

23. 'Fact Sheet: Men's and Boys' Apparel Guilds in California'; 'Huge Growth Forecast for Apparel Industry' (1944), *Los Angeles Times,* 4 June; 'Manufacturers Plan Training Program' (1947), *California Apparel News,* 28 Nov., clipping, MA.

24. 'California Styles' (1945), *Wall Street Journal,* 27 Aug.; Hyde, 'Thorsen Heads Men's Wear Manufacturers of Los Angeles'.

25. 'Los Angeles Retailers Pledge Bank of Windows for Roundup' (1947), *Boys' Outfitter,* September, clipping, MA.

26. Jack Hyde (1951), 'California Dateline', *Men's Wear* 122, 12 Jan.: 168.

27. A-1 Manufacturing Company (1945), advertisement in *California Men's Stylist* 4, July: 12;

California Sportswear Company (1951), advertisement in *Men's Wear* 123, 27 Apr.: 91.

28. One trade journalist urged menswear manufacturers to act ethically as they built the California industry: 'Ask yourself if, by what you are getting away with, you are building a strong, ethical business for the future, if you are contributing to a greater Los Angeles market … or if you are simply making money.' Will Chappel (1944), 'There'll Come a Day', *California Men's Stylist* 3, Oct.: 85.

29. 'CMA Convention' (1950), *Men's Wear* 122, Mar.: 89–93.

30. '"Buy New York Products" Drive Is Begun to Offset Diversion of the Apparel Trade' (1939), *New York Times,* 6 Apr.

31. Men's Apparel Research Guild (1947), 'The California Market and Its Importance to Men's Wear Retailers', New York: Men's Apparel Research Guild, MA.

32. May, *Golden State, Golden Youth.*

33. See, for example, 'Milady Had Nothing on the Gentlemen' (1947), *American-Statesmen,* 2 Nov.; Fred Grunwald (1947), 'California Futurization'. The link between the California lifestyle and leisurewear marketing dates back at least to the 1920s. See Frank Anderson (1942), 'New Styles Are Set at Palm Springs', *California Men's Stylist* 1, Jan.: 19; Seward C. Simons (1928), 'Dressing Up Los Angeles', *Southern California Business* 7, Feb.: 18; Mary Braggiotti (1940), 'California Clothes Bring Sunshine', *New York Post,* 17 Oct., clipping, box 1, series 3, CS-NMAH.

34. 'California Styles'.

35. Sullivan, 'Stitch in Time'.

36. 'Leadership of California Sportswear Stressed' (1948), *Los Angeles Times,* 28 Apr.

37. Bill Becker (1964), 'California's Sartorial Outlook Is Making Inroads on "Ivy" East', *New York Times,* 9 Feb.; Goodman, *The Location of Fashion Industries:* 36.

38. Sullivan, 'Stitch in Time'.

39. 'Sportswear Concern Opens $2 Million Unit' (1960), *Los Angeles Times,* 25 Sept.

40. Robert Bartels (1988), *The History of Marketing Thought,* 3rd ed., Columbus, Ohio: Publishing Horizons.

41. For seminal texts, see Stuart Ewen (1976), *Captains of Consciousness: Advertising and the Social Roots of the Consumer Culture,* New York: McGraw-Hill; Roland Marchand (1985), *Advertising the American Dream: Making Way for Modernity, 1920–1940,* Berkeley: University of California Press: 52–87. For a revisionist analysis, see Regina Lee Blaszczyk (2000), *Imagining Consumers: Design and Innovation from Wedgwood to Corning,* Baltimore: Johns Hopkins University Press; and, for the British context, Paul Jobling (2005), *Man Appeal: Advertising, Modernism and Menswear,* New York: Berg.

42. Regina Lee Blaszczyk (2008), *American Consumer Society, 1865–2005,* Wheeling, Ill.: Harlan Davidson, forthcoming; Carole Turbin (2001), 'Collars and Consumers: Changing Images of American Manliness and Business', in *Beauty and Business: Commerce, Gender, and Culture in Modern America,* ed. Philip Scranton, New York: Routledge: 87–108.

43. Tom Pendergast (2000), *Creating the Modern Man: American Magazines and Consumer Culture, 1900–1950,* Columbia: University of Missouri Press: 60. His observations are borne out by the slogans in William Borsodi (1910), *Men's Wear Advertising,* New York: Advertisers' Cyclopedia.

44. Robert Fairchild (1935), 'For the Modern Man', *Los Angeles Times,* 20 July.

45. 'Of Course … When You Say CALIFORNIA You're Saying Maurice Holman' (1953), *Men's Wear* 127, 24 Apr.: 133.

46. 'Palm Springs … Countless Promotional Opportunities' (1948), *Men's and Boys' Stylist,* Sept., clipping, MA.

47. 'Promoting California' (1944), *California Men's Stylist* 3, Jan.: 43; 'California "Sells" for You': 39.

48. 'Sportswear: How California Captured the Sportswear Market' (1939), *California Stylist* 3, Feb.: 5. Leisurewear's bold colours and California origins parallel another popular consumer product of the period, Fiesta ware. See Blaszczyk, *Imagining Consumers.*

49. Douglas Monroy (1999), *Rebirth: Mexican Los Angeles from the Great Migration to the Great Depression,* Berkeley: University of California

Press; George Sánchez (1993), *Becoming Mexican American: Ethnicity, Culture and Identity in Chicano Los Angeles, 1900–1945,* New York: Oxford University Press; and Eduardo Obregón Pagán (2003), *Murder at the Sleepy Lagoon: Zoot Suits, Race, and Riot in Wartime L.A.,* Chapel Hill: University of North Carolina Press.

50. On the representational trope of Indians as part of the natural environment, see Philip Deloria (1998), *Playing Indian,* New Haven, Conn.: Yale University Press; and Kerwin L. Klein (1997), *Frontiers of Historical Imagination,* Berkeley: University of California.

51. 'Sheriff of Los Angeles' (1945), *California Men's Stylist* 4, Jan.: 46.

52. 'Palm Springs … Countless Promotional Opportunities'.

53. 'Sportswear: How California Captured the Sportswear Market'.

54. 'Gold and Bronze, Other Vivid Hues Will "Color Men"' (1948), *Fresno Bee,* 21 May, clipping, MA.

55. 'Gaudy Shirts, Slacks Shown for Men, Boys' (1950), *Detroit Times,* 10 Jan.; 'Extreme Styles Shown at Men's Wear Exhibit' (1950), *Rochester Democrat and Chronicle,* 9 Jan., clippings, MA. For the phrase 'sun-ripe', see 'California Fashion Scene, as Viewed by the Matilda Bergman Resident Buying Office of Los Angeles,' 1942 Report, Special Collections Department, Gladys Marcus Library, Fashion Institute of Technology, New York.

56. The term 'aspirational merchandising' is from Daniel Thomas Cook (2004), *The Commodification of Childhood: The Children's Clothing Industry and the Rise of the Child Consumer,* Durham, N.C.: Duke University Press.

57. Frances Anderson (1943), 'The Tale of the Flying Fish', *California Men's Stylist* 2, Jan.: 48–51.

58. 'Los Angeles' Little Cutters': 136.

59. 'Sun and Swim Fashions' (1953), *Men's Wear* 126, 9 Jan.: 39.

60. Anderson, 'New Styles Are Set at Palm Springs'.

61. 'What with Repeal and All, the Shirtless Swimmers Are Going in for a "Nude Deal" All Their Own'; see *Apparel Arts* 4 (1934): 71.

62. *Athletic World* (Aug. 1924): 11, cited by Pendergast, *Creating the Modern Man:* 135.

63. In the pool behind bandleader Heidt is a man with his back to the camera and his hand on a beach ball. His muscular definition approaches that of Atlas. Anne Hollander has called this informal exposed look 'unselfconscious readiness', with a studied 'artlessness' undercutting the exposure's eroticism. See Hollander (1995), *Sex and Suits: The Evolution of Modern Dress,* New York: Kodansha: 175. On the 'double-bind' of female beauty as needing to be both constant and effortless, see Elizabeth Haiken (1999), *Venus Envy: A History of Cosmetic Surgery,* Baltimore: Johns Hopkins University Press.

64. For a critique of using sex to sell to men in the 1950s, see Philip Wylie (1956), 'The Abdicating Male', *Playboy* 4, Nov.: 23–24. On the history of these two men's magazines, see Bill Osgerby (2001), *Playboys in Paradise: Masculinity, Youth, and Leisure-Style in Modern America,* New York: Berg; Pendergast, *Creating the Modern Man;* Kenon Breazeale (2000), 'In Spite of Women: *Esquire* Magazine and the Construction of the Male Consumer', in *The Gender and Consumer Culture Reader,* ed. Jennifer Scanlon, New York: New York University Press: 226–44. On homosexuality and appearance, see 'Fashion Is a Fairy' (1938), *Esquire* 10, Apr.: 35–36.

65. 'Men's and Boys' Market Began Century Ago' (1950), *California Apparel News,* 13 Jan., clipping, MA.

66. *Photoplay,* the original celebrity magazine, was first published in 1911 and followed by a host of imitators. On celebrity magazines, see Richard Dyer (1979), *Stars,* London: BFI; and Richard Meyer (1991), 'Rock Hudson's Body', in *Inside/Out: Lesbian Theories, Gay Theories,* ed. Diana Fuss, New York: Routledge: 259–88.

67. Goodman, *The Location of Fashion Industries:* 29.

68. On east coast manufacturers copying California specialties and turning them into 'strange hybrids', sold as 'California styles', see Ruttenberg, 'Palm Springs Preview.'

69. Earlier California fashion shows focused on women's clothing, with one exception, the

Manufacturers' 1926 'peacock parade'; see 'Styles for the City of Los Angeles' (1926), *Southern California Business* 5, Feb.: 28.

70. Ruttenberg, 'Palm Springs Preview': 61–62.

71. 'P.S.R.U. [Palm Springs Round Up] Guest Register' (1948), *California Apparel News,* 29 Oct.; 'Over 1,200 to Attend Palm Springs Roundup Starting Tomorrow' (1947), *Los Angeles Daily News Record,* 23 Oct., clippings, MA.

72. 'Dignitaries Welcome Visitors' (1948), *California Apparel News,* 29 Oct.; 'MAGIC Arranges for Visitors to Fly to Palm Springs Roundup' (1949), *Los Angeles Daily News Record,* 23 Dec., clippings, MA.

73. 'Fact Sheet: Men's and Boys' Apparel Guilds in California'; William Watts Rose Jr. (1949), 'Palm Springs: Highs in the Roundup', *Apparel Arts,* December, clipping, MA.

74. 'They're Still Talking about Palm Springs!' (1942), *California Men's Stylist* 1, Apr.: 29.

75. 'California Glamour Comes to Life at Roundup Show' (1947), *California Apparel News,* 31 Oct.

76. For accounts of these moments, see Osgerby, *Playboys in Paradise;* Shaun Cole (2000), *'Don We Now Our Gay Apparel': Gay Men's Dress in the Twentieth Century,* New York: Berg; Frank Mort (1996), *Cultures of Consumption: Masculinities and Social Space in Late Twentieth-Century Britain,* New York: Routledge; Mark Simpson (1994), *Male Impersonators: Men Performing Masculinity,* New York: Routledge; Colin McDowell (1997), *The Man of Fashion: Peacock Males and Perfect Gentlemen,* New York: Thames and Hudson; Lynne Luciano (2002), *Looking Good: Male Body Image in Modern America,* New York: Hill and Wang.

77. 'Los Angeles Retailers Pledge Bank of Windows for Roundup' (1947), *Boys' Outfitter,* Sept.; 'P.S.R.U. Guest Register'; 'Roundup Huge Success' (1948), *California Apparel News,* 5 Nov., clipping, MA; 'Sportswear Round Up at Palm Springs' (1942), *California Men's Stylist* 1, Jan.: 51; Jack Hyde (1953), 'California Dateline', *Men's Wear* 125, 20 Mar.: 132–34.

78. Ruth Miller (1948), 'Palm Springs Round Up', *Display World,* Dec., clipping, MA.

79. One such merchant, A. H. Silverman from Minnesota, was profiled in Lois P. Hatton (1948), 'Palm Springs Show Inspires New Shop', *St. Paul Pioneer-Press,* 4 Dec., clipping, MA.

10

'MEN DON'T WEAR VELVET YOU KNOW!' FASHIONABLE GAY MASCULINITY AND THE SHOPPING EXPERIENCE, LONDON, 1950–EARLY 1970S

Clare Lomas

This chapter uses a case-study approach, informed by oral testimony, to explore the relationship between fashion, gay masculinity and shopping, through the experiences of three men during the 1950s to the early 1970s. Focusing on clothing bought by the interviewees from the newly established boutiques aimed at both straight and gay male consumers, such as Vince Man's Shop, John Stephens's 'His Clothes' and John Michael, this research highlights the fact that dress and clothing is part of a series of gay sensibilities that cannot be isolated from their wider cultural, historical and social context.

Focusing on the newly established boutiques catering to young male consumers in London from 1950 to the early 1970s, this chapter utilizes the oral testimony and surviving garments of three men to gain an insight into fashionable gay masculinity and the shopping experience.[1] It is important to acknowledge that this area, within the field of dress and fashion, has received little attention to date. Costume history has often sidelined men's clothing and male consumers, whilst women's dress, particularly haute couture, has received much consideration.[2] Attention to men's clothing, when it has appeared, has been somewhat superficial and dismissive, citing the 'Great Masculine Renunciation'[3] in the nineteenth century as the reason why men's fashion became sombre, devoid of decoration and mainly restricted to the suit. Attempts to examine men's

fashion by dress historians such as Penelope Byrde,[4] Diana de Marly[5] and Doreen Yarwood[6] have produced a chronological typology of male dress, avoiding any discussion of its social and cultural context.

More recent fashion history writing has begun to contextualize menswear by addressing the influence that sportswear, Hollywood films, the music industry, anti-fashion and sub-cultural style have played in the design and consumption of male dress.[7] However, serious discussion of the relationship between sexuality and dress is still relatively limited in this disciplinary field.

QUEER STUDIES AND MID-TWENTIETH-CENTURY LONDON

Gay and lesbian history texts have been useful in establishing the role that clothing has played in sexual orientation and identity. Initially the objective was the search for gay ancestral roots: identifying, reviving and reclaiming narratives that have been lost or hidden from history.[8] This approach clearly had merits in unearthing this forgotten part of social and legal history, along with texts which question whether what is now taken as homosexual activity and behaviour would have had the same connotation and meaning in different cultures and centuries.[9] For example, much has been written on the changing historical conceptions of male homosexuality, from the stereotypical effeminate pansy to the overtly masculine macho man of the 1970s, and the role that clothing and mannerisms played in indicating gender roles and sexual orientation.[10]

Work on gay space and urban history has re-addressed the myth that there was no early gay social culture by deliberately challenging 'isolation, invisibility and internalisation',[11] as well as highlighting the significance of a gay social culture in establishing a recognizable gay identity. The achievement of such texts has been groundbreaking and must be viewed in the context of restoring other voices that have been denied representation in historical records. However, the priority in this politicized agenda has meant that they rarely relate the gay experience to the broader social, economic and political context in which fashion resides.

Research which has used oral testimonies, such as *Between the Acts: Lives of Homosexual Men 1885–1967*[12] and *Walking after Midnight: Gay Men's Life Stories*,[13] is of paramount importance, as it has retrospectively constructed past events from an individual's experiences and offers both descriptive and anecdotal evidence. There was clearly a growing number of cafes, clubs and bars that either catered for, or turned a blind eye to, homosexuality prior to decriminalization in 1967, which were made known to the homosexual community via a growing social network. What is apparent throughout such texts is the anonymity that cities provided and that gay men were leading double lives.[14] Due to a lack of other evidence, a heavy reliance was placed on accounts of deviancy documented in police records and court cases,[15] sidelining accounts that were not as spectacular.

It is these sidelined men's stories that this chapter seeks to explore. The emphasis of this research focuses on the shopping and clothing habits of three interviewees living in Greater London and their memories of the complex negotiations of a covert homosexual identity, but one equally identifiable to others in the same community. It will contextualize their stories against the wider shift in men's fashion from the late 1950s onwards, and will argue that the key to this was both the anonymity that London allowed and the rapid rise of small boutiques that were established as a vibrant draw not just to homosexual men, but all men interested in new approaches to dress and fashion. Prior to the mid-twentieth century, men's dress was very rigid and prescriptive, influenced more by class and social status than sexuality. Wider shifts in masculine clothing styles allowed this covert version of dress greater freedom of expression, with men, both straight and gay, wearing their hair in longer styles and sporting coloured or patterned shirts in a variety of fabrics, alongside the gradual introduction of leisurewear as acceptable everyday clothing.

THE INTERVIEWEES

Peter Viti is in his early sixties, and is the youngest interviewee. During the late 1960s he was a student before going into the antiques business. He lived and shopped in Central London, frequenting the newly established men's boutiques in the West End and Chelsea. Denis Shorrock, now in his seventies, moved to London from Swansea in 1954 to work in the advertising industry on a scholarship. A friend of Peter Viti's, he also shopped in Central London at a variety of the men's boutiques, and still has clothing dating from this period. Walter Wilkins is now in his early eighties, and is the oldest of the men I interviewed. Between 1950 and 1979 he lived in Heston, Middlesex, and shopped both locally in Hounslow and Southall, as well as in Hammersmith and Central London (Oxford Street and Bond Street). It is important to acknowledge the interviewees' relationship between their economic situation and their individual milieu. None of these men could be considered working-class. Peter worked in the antiques business, Denis worked in television advertising and Walter worked in a drawing office for an industrial manufacturer, and this was reflected in their identity in terms of where they shopped in and around Central London in the fashionable boutiques.

These three men span different generations, with twenty years between Walter and Peter; however, all three men lived through the period when homosexuality in England was illegal. Walter, in particular, whilst happy to talk about people accusing him of being 'queer' or 'like that!', was not comfortable about discussing his sexuality openly, hinting at issues, but not being explicit. This was also a concern of other men who were approached to take part in my research: they were ambivalent about talking of a time when they were engaged in a way of life that the law had deemed illegal, particularly as they had kept their sexual relationships hidden from family, friends and work colleagues. It may not have been the only issue that prevented some men from discussing their lives. Steve Humphries and Pamela Gordon, in their book *A Man's World: From Boyhood to Manhood 1900–1960,* noted the difficulty they had in trying to interview men: 'trying to get men of this generation to open up and talk honestly and intimately has not been easy. They are simply not used to talking about themselves and their lives in the way that women are'.[16]

Despite the generational difference between these three men, what is striking about them is that they had shopped for themselves and took an active interest in their dress. Cultural theorist Jennifer Craik notes the stereotypical assumption displayed by many historians when considering men and fashion that 'men dress for fit and comfort, rather than for style; that women dress men and buy clothes for men; that men who dress up are peculiar (one way or another); that men do not notice clothes'.[17] Whilst there has been a tendency to deny men's active participation in fashion, recent work has explicitly acknowledged the presence of the male consumer.[18] However, for the immediate post-1945 period, work from a cultural studies perspective suggests that those male participants were part of the young generation involved in recognizable subcultures, such as Teddy Boys, Mods, Rockers, Skinheads and Punks.[19] The three men I interviewed did not consider themselves to be part of any such recognizable subculture, to the point where one, Denis Shorrock, exclaimed:

> I don't want to be pigeonholed in any respect ... I'm an individual. Don't stereotype me ... don't stick a stereotype veneer on me and I don't want to be judged by stereotypes or assessed ... I try quite hard not to belong to any tribe![20]

It is also worthy of note that my three interviewees, whilst of different ages, all shopped in the newly established men's boutiques, with all of them having bought items from the John Michael[21] shop, contradicting the implications of fashion histories that these boutiques were catering for a predominantly young consumer.[22]

NEW BOUTIQUES FOR MEN

The interviewees remembered the new men's boutiques quite vividly, and whilst there has been much written about the various shops,[23] the quality of the items sold and a discussion of the status of the different shops do not appear to have received much attention. Peter Viti recalled his opinion of the retail outlets he frequented and ranked them:

> ... how can I put it? I think you'd have Vince and then John Stephens. John Stephens was, I suppose, the equivalent of Next today. And above that, slightly smarter, would be John Michael. And then above that would be [Mr] Fish, which was very smart. Cecil Gee would probably be on a par with John Michael. And Turnbull and Asser. But Turnbull and Asser were an old gentleman's outfitters. I don't know when it started, but it's been there for years. And it's for 'nobby' people you know, the aristocracy go there.[24]

This ranking of the outlets by Peter continued at a later interview when he remembered another retailer called Just Men: 'I'd forgotten all about Just Men. I would have said that Cecil Gee, and John, particularly John Michael, was fairly smartish'.[25] Denis, who favoured John Michael, recalled:

I liked John Michael as a shop a lot, over a period of ten years of looking very slick and trendy, and, not that many people could afford his stuff ... you could wear it without any suggestion that you were necessarily gay ...[26]

The use of the word gay by Denis is interesting. The terminology in use to describe someone who was homosexual or considered to be sexually deviant during the 1950s and 1960s ranged from being called an invert, pervert, queer, or, possibly, a pansy. Whilst gay would have probably been used in theatrical or artistic circles for some time, it appears to have entered common usage after the Gay Liberation Movement was established in the United States in 1969 and in the UK in 1970.

What is significant about Denis's use of clothing from John Michael was that it did not imply he was gay, or, during this period, suggest he was sexually deviant. This point reaffirms the fine line of what was an acceptable masculine appearance: that of being smart, but of having no apparent interest in one's appearance. The John Michael clothing that Denis bought appeared to fit this criteria and he even stated that on hearing he had to go to America on a work-related visit in 1962, he 'invested' in suits from John Michael. Under further questioning of what it was about John Michael clothing that he liked, Denis replied that it was partly the fit, describing the suits as being 'slightly waisted' with 'very tight trousers'. Denis's loyalty to John Michael was highlighted in an anecdote about being sent on a last-minute business trip to Jamaica, where on arrival, he realized he did not have enough clothes for the visit, which had been extended from a weekend to a fortnight. He

rang up his secretary and asked her to 'get hold of ... the producer, who was in London, who had some taste, tell him to go to John Michael and tell him to buy five shirts and get them on a plane ... and they were there in twenty-four hours!'[27]

Walter, however, did not remember the John Michael shops specifically, although upon the discovery of a tie labelled John Michael whilst I was cataloguing his clothing from the period, he did recall the name and the store being in Central London, possibly Bond Street. Denis, who revealed that he favoured the store in Bond Street, rather than the one on the Kings Road, confirmed this.

Vince Man's Shop, often associated with a gay clientele, has acquired a quasi-mythical status in accounts of the history of menswear. Nik Cohn,[28] Shaun Cole[29] and Frank Mort[30] all suggest that Vince Man's Shop provided a place where gay men could purchase fashionable clothing, and, as a direct result of the placing of this establishment on the edges of Soho, that it was the catalyst for the whole Carnaby Street phenomenon of the 1960s. In 1954, Bill Green,[31] a London-based physique photographer, opened Vince Man's Shop, one of the first boutiques for men. The music journalist Nik Cohn first raised Bill Green's profile in his influential survey of the menswear business of 1971:

In the beginning, Bill Green was a photographer, specialising in Stage portraiture. Then, during the war, he got involved in weight lifting and, after he'd been demobbed, he began to photograph muscle boys and wrestlers, doing figure studies for the male magazines.[32]

In an interview with Green for his book, Cohn was told about the initial shift from physique photography in the 1950s, a time of stringent anti-homosexual policing, to clothes retailing:

Several photographers had got into serious trouble that way. So I reached a compromise—I made my models wear briefs, and I had them specially made up from cut-down Marks & Spencer roll-ons. They were skimpy but ever so comfy and they caused a terrific reaction among my models and readers ... After a time I began to make the briefs myself and I thought that I should perhaps sell the briefs commercially. So, in 1950, I took an advert in the *Daily Mirror*. It came out on Saturday and, on Monday morning I took 200 pounds worth of orders.[33]

Following the success of these posing trunks in terms of sales, Green opened a shop in 1954 called Vince Man's Shop situated in Newburgh Street, just off Carnaby Street in Soho. Walter did not shop at Vince Man's Shop, but he provided a fascinating insight into Vince's Photography Studio, where, in the early 1950s, he and a friend, Bernard, had some physique photographs taken and purchased the famous posing briefs. He recalled:

We got there [and] this man, he specialized in taking photographs of body builders. I don't know if they still do this ... have a Mr Britain and a Mr England? The idea was that the magazine, you sent a picture of yourself to them and it was judged ... Anyway he [Bernard] fancied himself as a physique you see. Well, I didn't. Anyway, when we got there, he sold these sort of brief things so we had to buy those for the posing point of view ... he'd assumed we had gone knowing what we were going to do and I didn't know anything about it. So anyway, he said, 'Well, have you got your olive oil?' 'Well, what do we want olive oil for?', and then that's of course to put on yourself to make your body shine.[34]

Vince Man's Shop was not liked by Denis, who, upon my clarification that it had opened in 1954, commented,

I don't think I was that aware [of my sexuality], or if I went, I went and had a look, because what he had didn't seem to make sense in terms of what I had, money, that I could afford or in terms of where would I wear those clothes. Because ... you couldn't be that unconventional in the fifties in an advertising agency, but you could be smart with an edge as it were ...[35]

Peter Viti certainly shopped at Vince Man's Shop and recalled he had collected their mail-order catalogues:

I remember Vince very clearly, on the corner of Regent Street, Foubert's Place. Now, I had a whole set of Vince catalogues ... one of the models was Sean Connery[36] ... Those catalogues were quite daring ... Men's fashion photography was very staid. Suddenly to get a good-looking young muscle guy wearing very little was very daring and the poses were very daring, it was all skintight![37]

However, the quality of the clothes from Vince Man's Shop appeared, in Peter's opinion, to be poor, and unlike Denis, he remembered the price of these clothes as being inexpensive: 'Shops like Vince and Dean Rogers were aimed at guys who didn't have much money, the quality was not that good. Maybe I'm being unfair'.[38]

The issue of whether Vince clothing was expensive is obviously subjective, depending on the income of the customer. However, it is worth noting that Nik Cohn claimed Vince sold 'expensive tight sweaters (about £7)'[39] and that John Stephens, previously an employee at Vince Man's Shop, opened the boutique His Clothes in 1957 in Carnaby Street and was 'in direct competition with Vince ... everything that he did, he did it faster and cheaper'.[40]

There appear to be very few surviving Vince Man's Shop clothes that would allow one to confirm Peter's statement regarding the quality of the products.[41] The Museum of London has one Vince item, a casual top acquired in 2002, donated by an actor, who commented that 'there was a tendency for things not to be long-lasting ... one had to be careful when washing not to let the colours run'.[42]

CHANGES TO MENSWEAR 1950 TO EARLY 1970S

Men's clothing was certainly changing in the 1950s and 1960s with the impact of the 'newly enfranchised'[43] teenage consumer and the influence of fashion-conscious subcultures, in particular that of the Mods. The music journalist Richard Barnes observed that 'in the early sixties the climate of opinion was changing, the Mods were wearing more effeminate and colourful clothes of Carnaby Street'.[44] Shaun Cole goes further: 'It is popularly accepted that there was an element of homosexual vanity present in the Mod subculture'.[45] Craik comments that the conservatism in men's clothing 'began to change in the 1960s once some designers decided to take an interest in men's clothes as fashion'.[46] These changes in men's clothes from being conventionally conservative to being more casual and colourful, with the use of fabrics previously regarded as feminine, such as velvets, voiles and lace, were recalled by my interviewees. Peter commented that 'things were getting very much more informal ... Everybody was getting away from the grey and the brown and the beige!'[47]

Denis particularly remembered patterned and coloured shirts:

What I did buy later from John Stephens, and also from Liberty's, was the flowered shirts, which now I see are coming back, very tight here [indicates his waist] with the big collars ... the lawn shirts, oh, the John Michael voile shirts. You really had to have a really smooth chest to get away with them. Men actually grow more hair on their chests as they get older, you probably know. Anyway, I was lucky in my thirties, there wasn't anything that much visible, because there were these tight-fitting voile shirts, see through, and those were a great joy [laughs]. And in lovely shades, tints really of, I was going to say pastel shades, but they were a lot more pastel than tint, although pale colours; I would hardly ever wear a white shirt.[48]

Denis's eye for slightly unusual shirts was evident in three shirts he still owns from that period which he had bought from Mr Fish. Peter remembered the Mr Fish boutique clearly, commenting that 'It was a funny shop. You went in and nobody took any notice of you. They were all in the back

sort of gossiping and having a party. A lot of the shops were very informal'.[49] What is noteworthy of Denis's shirts is the style, which quirkily combined elements accepted in menswear such as fabric choice, merged with the fashionable look of the day, a tailored fit with a polo neck.

Walter also wore coloured shirts as opposed to formal white ones and had two brightly patterned shirts in his clothing collection from this period. When I asked him if the patterns were quite daring for the time, he responded: 'Well, not everyone would wear them, because they said to me [in the shop] in Hammersmith "You're the first customer that wanted them!"'.[50]

Peter remembered that men who wore velvet trousers were 'frowned upon'. When I asked him to explain this comment further he replied:

It was a very young man's thing and older people ... the older generation [were] saying 'Men don't wear velvet you know!' ... When I said it was frowned on, yes, it was frowned on by some people ... it all changed, and young men, like they are today ... started to become very fashion-conscious ... The older generation didn't approve of young men, whatever their sexuality, wearing velvet. You didn't wear a tie all the time. Oh, long hair, a great outcry against long hair, which I had![51]

All three of my interviewees stressed how formal clothing conventions, particularly dressing up to go to the theatre, opera, or out for dinner at a restaurant, from the 1950s onwards were beginning to break down.[52] Alongside this change, there was a greater choice of leisure or casual wear, with *Men's Wear,* a publication aimed at the retailer, claiming in an issue from 1958:

The growth of the casual wear business has been one of the most remarkable developments in menswear in recent times. And the trade is still at its beginnings. The acceptance of clothing that expresses a relaxed, carefree mood is widening and spreading to the older age groups. More and more men now buy clothing not merely to replace necessities, but because of a new found interest—an interest in fashion. That offers the trade tremendous scope for expansion, but also it raises some highly controversial issues.[53]

These so-called 'highly controversial issues' were then discussed in a special feature the following week, outlining the 'issues the trade must face'.[54] These concerns were over the mistaken belief that:

the casual trade is necessarily confined to a particular class of the community and that the better-class business can outlive it without change ... Millions of men are interested as never before in new clothes, different clothes, not just a business suit and a jacket and trousers for the weekend.[55]

Following on from this introduction about casual wear, the use of different fabrics, such as suede cotton, and patterned textiles for shirts was discussed. In an issue from 1960, *Men's Wear* reviewed the 1950s as 'a decade of progress',[56] recalling how the earlier part of the decade was 'a period of austerity' after the ending of clothes rationing and 'the abolition of Utility specifications'[57] which occurred in 1952. The advances in science and technology, such as the new synthetic fibres and new manufacturing techniques, were cited, but most significant was the interest in fashion for menswear:

It began in what was called the 'spiv trade', which a handful of manufacturers pioneered by making unusual—and sometimes monstrous looking—styles as a gimmick to catch the public eye. The more conservative side of the trade was horrified and indignantly declared this to be a further decline in dress standards, which then had hardly recovered from war-time austerity.[58]

Rapid changes to menswear continued throughout the 1950s and 1960s, with *Men's Wear* noting a decade later in 1970 that the men's fashion market had grown at an incredible rate. After a significant drop in its retail profits was reported, the struggle of long-time menswear retailer Montague Burton,[59] previously considered

'the biggest brand in men's suits',[60] was due to changing consumer buying habits, with '... the emphasis ... being placed more firmly on leisurewear, which in fact is becoming a big threat to the traditional suit'.[61]

None of the men I interviewed mentioned Burtons at any time during their interviews or during discussion of men's clothing from this period. All three men discussed the change in men's clothing in terms of menswear becoming less formal. Significantly it was Peter Viti who appeared to embrace the leisurewear styles that were fashionable during this period, possibly as he was the youngest of the men I interviewed.

CONCLUSION

The boutiques which emerged in London during the period from the 1950s to the early 1970s appear to have offered the men I interviewed opportunities for pushing the boundaries in clothing that was acceptable in terms of their masculinity, whilst allowing them to avoid any accusations of sexual deviancy. Denis's comment that 'you couldn't be that unconventional in the fifties ... but you could be smart with an edge, as it were ...'[62] appears to summarize the experience of all three of the interviewees, particularly prior to the change to the law in 1967. It appears that their identity was not defined exclusively by their sexuality; their class, occupation and age also motivated their patronage of the different boutiques. A significant factor during this period appears to be shifts in attitude regarding appropriate attire for men. As Peter explained, as fashions for men became more casual: 'the older generation didn't approve of young men, whatever their sexuality ...'[63] deviating from traditionally accepted men's dress (figure 10.1).

Despite the generational differences between the interviewees, the experiences of Peter, Denis and Walter show through a case-study approach the value of combining oral history with a range of other sources such as photographs and the

Figure 10.1 Rennie Ellis. *Generation Gap,* King's Cross, 1970–71. Courtesy Rennie Ellis Photographic Archive, St Kilda, Melbourne. The Australian social observational photographer Rennie Ellis (1940–2003) took many images that explore the changing face of men's fashion. A part of the weight of this image is conveyed in its place; King's Cross in Sydney, Australia, has been considered since the 1920s a bohemian and socially mixed enclave in which difference is accepted. Rennie Ellis's photograph contrasts a bearded, hatless, hippy wearing a caftan and boots, with an old man wearing a three-piece suit and hat. The cacophony of signage represents references to fashion retailing, and the elderly woman in a head-scarf who appears in the middle distance appears as a type of moderator in the scene. All face the photographer, who captures a scene of generational change.

clothing itself. Their surviving garments, placed alongside their oral testimony, photographs and accounts from the retail trade, such as *Men's Wear*, highlight the changes occurring in menswear during this period, not just through the way clothing was marketed and sold through the new boutiques, but in terms of the types of fabrics, colours and styles available, as well as emphasising that such clothing was not just for the younger man. Unlike the stereotypical view of gay men leading the way in fashion that became a popular rhetoric during the latter part of the twentieth century, changes in men's fashion during this period were due to changes occurring within the menswear clothing trade which underwent an enormous transition due to the introduction of leisurewear and casual wear, and it was this that spearheaded such changes.

ACKNOWLEDGEMENTS

I would like to thank the three interviewees, Peter Viti, Denis Shorrock and Walter Wilkins for their time and generosity in sharing their experiences. I am also extremely grateful to Edwina Ehrman and Oriole Cullen (Museum of London), Geraldine Biddle-Perry (London College of Fashion), and the London College of Fashion, University of the Arts London, for access to the EMap Archive.

NOTES

Reprinted with permission from Clare Lomas, "'Men Don't Wear Velvet You Know!' Fashionable Gay Masculinity and the Shopping Experience, London, 1950–Early 1970s," *Oral History* 35, no. 1 (Spring 2007), 82–90.

1. The testimony of the men interviewed for this chapter is not intended to imply that their particular experiences are representative for all homosexual men from this period, but offers a focused analysis of three individual experiences from men of different ages who were all living in London at a time when homosexuality was illegal. The author is aware of the problem of drawing conclusions from a small sample, but it is important to stress the value of the oral testimony of these men, from differing generations, and this chapter is intended as a case-study approach, offering a springboard for further study.

2. Costume history often focuses on surviving garments which usually belong to the middle and upper classes.

3. Term coined by psychologist J. C. Flügel in his 1930 text *The Psychology of Clothes*, London: Hogarth.

4. P. Byrde (1979), *The Male Image: Men's Fashion in England 1300–1970*, London: BT Batsford.

5. D. de Marly (1985), *Fashion for Men: An Illustrated History*, London: BT Batsford.

6. D. Yarwood (1992), *Fashion in the Western World*, London: BT Batsford.

7. See F. Chenoune (1993), *A History of Men's Fashion*, Paris: Flammarion, and M. Constantino (1997), *Men's Fashion in the Twentieth Century: From Frock Coats to Intelligent Fibres*, London: BT Batsford.

8. For example, M. Duberman, M. Vieninus and G. Chauncey (1989), *Hidden from History: Reclaiming the Gay and Lesbian Past*, London: Penguin.

9. J. Weeks (1985, reprint 1999), *Sexuality and Its Discontents: Meanings, Myth & Modern Sexuality*, London: Routledge.

10. For example, K. Plummer (2000), *The Making of the Modern Homosexual*, London: Hutchinson; P. Nardi (2000), *Gay Masculinities*, London: Sage Publications.

11. G. Chauncey (1994), *Gay New York: The Making of the Gay Male World 1890–1940*, London: Flamingo: 2.

12. J. Weeks and K. Porter (1991, reprint 1998), *Between the Acts: Lives of Homosexual Men 1885–1967*, London: Rivers Oram Press.

13. Hail-Carpenter Archives/Gay Men's Oral History Group (1989, reprint 1990), *Walking after Midnight: Gay Men's Life Stories*, London: Routledge.

14. See D. Higgs (1999), *Queer Sites: Gay Urban History since 1600,* London: Routledge.

15. F. Mort (1999), 'Mapping Sexual London: The Wolfenden Committee on Homosexual Offences and Prostitution 1954–1957', *New Formations: Sexual Geographies, Journal of Culture/Theory/Politics,* no. 37, Spring: 92–113; M. Houlbrook (2000), 'The Private World of Public Urinals: London 1918–1957', *London Journal,* vol. 25, part 1: 52–70; M. Houlbrook (2002), '"Lady Austin's Camp Boys": Constituting the Queer Subject in 1930s London', *Gender and History,* vol. 14, no. 1, April: 31–61; M. Houlbrook (2002), '"A Sun among Cities": Space, Identities and Queer Male Practices, London 1918–57', unpublished PhD thesis, University of Essex.

16. S. Humphries and P. Gordon (1996), *A Man's World: From Boyhood to Manhood, 1900–1960,* London: BBC Books: 9.

17. J. Craik (1994), *The Face of Fashion: Cultural Studies in Fashion,* London: Routledge: 176.

18. See C. Breward (1999), *The Hidden Consumer,* Manchester: Manchester University Press; T. Edwards (1997), *Men in the Mirror: Men's Fashion, Masculinity and the Consumer Society,* London: Cassell; F. Mort (1996), *Cultures of Consumption: Masculinities and Social Space in Late Twentieth-Century Britain,* London: Routledge; S. Nixon (1996), *Hard Looks: Masculinities, Spectatorship and Contemporary Consumption,* New York: St Martins Press.

19. See S. Hall and T. Jefferson (eds) (1995), *Resistance through Ritual: Youth Culture in Post-War Britain,* London: Hutchinson University Library, and D. Hebdige (1979), *Subculture: The Meaning of Style,* London: Routledge.

20. Interview with Denis Shorrock, born in Wales, aged early seventies; recorded by Clare Lomas, 4 February 2003.

21. Denis Shorrock still owns a coat and two jackets from John Michael and considered himself to be a regular customer, including buying shirts and suits; Peter Viti owned three shirts (items now stored at the Museum of London: MOL 85.152/11, MOL 85.152/25 and MOL 85.152/62), a sweater (item MOL 85.152/35), and swimming trunks from John Michael (items MOL 85.152/54 and MOL 85. 152/55); Walter Wilkins still owns a tie bought from John Michael.

22. See N. Cohn (1971), *Today There Are No Gentlemen: The Changes in Englishmen's Clothes since the War,* London: Weidenfeld and Nicolson, and A. O'Neill (2000), 'John Stephen: A Carnaby Street Presentation of Masculinity 1957–1975', *Fashion Theory,* vol. 4, no. 4: 487–506.

23. See Cohn (1971); S. Cole (2000), *'Don We Now Our Gay Apparel': Gay Men's Dress in the Twentieth Century,* Oxford and New York: Berg; Mort (1996); O'Neill (2000); V. Mendes and A. de la Haye (1999), *20th Century Fashion,* London: Thames and Hudson.

24. Interview with Peter Viti, born in London, aged early sixties; recorded by Clare Lomas, 21 July 2003.

25. Interview with Peter Viti, born in London, aged early sixties; recorded by Clare Lomas, 28 July 2003.

26. Interview with Denis Shorrock, born in Wales, aged early seventies; recorded by Clare Lomas, 4 February 2003.

27. Interview with Denis Shorrock, born in Wales, aged early seventies; recorded by Clare Lomas, 4 February 2003.

28. See Cohn (1971).

29. See Cole (2000).

30. See Mort (1996).

31. Vince is called Bill Green in Cohn (1971), but called Basil Green in 'Mr Green's Catalogues Once Had the 007 Look', *Men's Wear,* 21 March 1964: 20 and 'Fashion Pioneer's Creditors Meet: £25,000 Liabilities' *Men's Wear,* 6 February 1969: 7–8. It appears Mr Green was also known as Vince, the name of his successful photographic studio. Legal documents for Vince Green Company (Wholesale) Limited, stored at the National Archives in Kew, Surrey, give the name of the shop's director as 'Basil Joseph Green', BT 31/43605.

32. Cohn (1971): 60.

33. Cohn (1971): 60.

34. Interview with Walter Wilkins, born in London, aged early eighties; recorded by Clare Lomas, 1 January 2000.

35. Interview with Denis Shorrock, born in Wales, aged early seventies; recorded by Clare Lomas, 4 February 2003.

36. *Men's Wear* from 1964 noted that 'Mr Green's catalogues once had the 007 look. Sean Connery may mean James Bond to people nowadays, but the actor was setting trends as long as seven years ago. Vince Green's Spring–Summer catalogue for 1957 contained six pages of casual clothes worn by Sean Connery when he was working as a French polisher', *Men's Wear*, 21 March 1964: 20.

37. Interview with Peter Viti, born in London, aged early sixties; recorded by Clare Lomas, 21 July 2003.

38. Interview with Peter Viti, born in London, aged early sixties; recorded by Clare Lomas, 21 July 2003.

39. Cohn (1971): 61.

40. Cohn (1971): 65.

41. The Victoria & Albert Museum has a pair of jeans from Vince Man's Shop donated by John Hardy, shop assistant and model for the Vince Man's Shop mail-order catalogues. Shaun Cole, curator at the V&A, interviewed John Hardy for his research on Vince (see Cole 2000) and noted that one of the reasons suggested by Hardy for the lack of surviving Vince clothes was the poor quality (Information from Shaun Cole in conversation with the author 2002).

42. Letter to author from J. Beardmore, actor, 24 October 2002.

43. M. Abrams (1959), *The Teenage Consumer*, London: The London Press Exchange Papers.

44. R. Barnes (1979), *Mods!*, London: Eel Pie Publishing: 10.

45. Cole (2000): 76.

46. Craik (1994): 192.

47. Interview with Peter Viti, born in London; recorded by Clare Lomas, 21 July 2003.

48. Interview with Denis Shorrock, born in Wales, aged early seventies; recorded by Clare Lomas, 4 February 2003.

49. Interview with Peter Viti, born in London; recorded by Clare Lomas, 21 July 2003.

50. Interview with Walter Wilkins, born in London, aged early eighties; recorded by Clare Lomas, 1 January 2000.

51. Interview with Peter Viti, born in London, aged early sixties; recorded by Clare Lomas, 21 July 2003.

52. The debate over 'male dress formality' was discussed in *Men's Wear* in June 1960 with a report on clothing attire for Royal Ascot, which claimed 'while formal wear has taken quite a beating in post-war years, it should not be assumed that it is about to surrender', *Men's Wear*, 18 June: 20.

53. Anonymous (1958), 'Casual Wear', *Men's Wear*, 12 April: 11.

54. Anonymous (1958), 'Casual Wear, Special 48 page feature', *Men's Wear*, 19 April: xxiii.

55. Anonymous (1958), 'Casual Wear, Special 48 page feature': xxiii.

56. Anonymous (1960), 'The "Fifties": A Decade of Progress', *Men's Wear*, 2 January: 15.

57. Anonymous (1960), 'The Tales: A Decade of Progress', *Men's Wear*, 2 January: 15.

58. Anonymous (1960), 'The "Fifties"'.

59. Mort (1996): 135.

60. Montague Burton Limited was one of the largest and most renowned multiple tailors. By the late 1930s Burtons owned 600 shops across Britain and remained a market leader until the early 1960s. See K. Honeyman (2002), 'Following Suit: Men, Masculinity and Gendered Practices in the Clothing Trade in Leeds, England, 1890–1940', *Gender and History*, vol. 14, no. 3, November: 426–446 and Mort (1996): 411.

61. Anonymous (1970), 'Burtons' Future', *Men's Wear*, 14 May: 8.

62. Interview with Denis Shorrock, born in Wales, aged early seventies; recorded by Clare Lomas, 4 February 2003.

63. Interview with Peter Viti, born in London, aged early seventies; recorded by Clare Lomas, 21 July 2003.

11

ÜBERMEN: MASCULINITY, COSTUME, AND MEANING IN COMIC BOOK SUPERHEROES

Vicki Karaminas

Much has been written about comic book superheroes and their cinematic adaptations. They are cultural icons recognized in every corner of the world and have featured in the childhoods of most Americans and Australians since the 1930s. Superheroes have also helped to construct an ideological worldview from the shifting interactions of politics, history, and culture, as well as define a sense of identity and subjectivity. Yet, for such instantly recognizable icons, little has been written in terms of superhero dress and the collective imagination that sartorial practices produce in framing cultural meanings. Rather than situating male superhero attire in the field of costume design functionality, this chapter sets out to reposition the discourse of superhero clothing as a vehicle for understanding constructions of masculinity, identity, and nation. By providing a set of cinematic case studies, the chapter also comments on the impact of nanotechnology in the construction of superhero attire in producing techno-augmented überbodies designed to protect the nation's future.

In the fictional world of male superheroes, the dialogue between supernatural abilities and fashion is not new. Since the emergence of comics as a distinct entertainment medium in North American popular culture in the 1930s, the superhero wardrobe has been communicating narratives through a combination of text and sequential illustration that functions within an aesthetic vocabulary of coded symbolism. The superhero wardrobe speaks of the wearer's iden-

tity and serves to highlight the supernatural abilities and attributes of his heroic status. As part of an iconic signifier, the superhero garment and its accessories—armored breastplates, masks, epaulettes, and gauntlets constructed of steel—separate those with superhuman strength from "mere mortals" and set the costume wearers apart from conventional society. As an embodied practice, fashion succeeds in signifying industrial strength associated with the ideal hypermuscular superhero body: the *look* of power, virility, and prowess. In the domain of superheroes, fashion really does matter.

The global release of the animated Pixar movie, *The Incredibles* (2004), which narrates the adventures of a family of "displaced" superheroes who rediscover the source of their powers, has introduced a new theoretical understanding of the superhero wardrobe in the field of cultural theory. The film's introduction of the character Edna Mode, an eccentric fashion designer for superheroes, not only takes the aesthetics of the clothes into account but also their practical uses such as their protective qualities and how these qualities can accommodate and provide functional support to the powers of the wearer.

Rather than situating superhero dress in the domain of the costume and masquerade, *The Incredibles* places superhero attire in the field of fashion. By renaming the costume as a "suit," superhero fashionability now begins to operate within the complex influences of a system governed by notions of realism, performance, gender, status, and power. This chapter draws on cultural theorists such as Roland Barthes, Claude Levi-Strauss, and Mikhail Bakhtin to examine the construction of superhero fashion in contemporary American popular culture. It also investigates the impact of nanotechnology and techno-augmentation associated with the superhero imaginary and comments on the way that the superhero wardrobe constructs notions of masculinity, identity, and nation.

MASKED AVENGERS

In the discourse of clothing, the mask acts as both a material object and a trope for concealment that characterizes all forms of dress. For superheroes, the invisibility offered by the mask is embodied in the formulations of costumes that obscure the body and provide a distinction between the dual secret and private identities that are essential to the superhero genre. Masks and costumes also complicate the undefined nature of the symbolics of dress, by appearing to cover the body while at the same time alluding to and illuminating the hidden powers invested in its adornment that both separate and connect the costume and the wearer to the doubling of dress as both a boundary and a margin.

In *Fashioning the Frame: Boundaries, Dress and the Body,* Warwick and Cavallaro state that within the language of symbolism, one of the key features of all "screening" garments is their ability to conceal and expose, insulate and mediate, which invites the viewer to unmask the secret of the wearer's identity. "The mask magnifies the notion of dress as a structure endowed with autonomous powers, based on the ability either to sustain or shatter the wearer's identity."[1]

Costumes are symbolic constructions denoting the incorporation of the wearer into the symbolic/mythic realm of superheroics by blurring the line between the identity of the hero and the wearer. As Bongco notes, the adaptation of the superhero costume sets the wearer apart from a society that is predicated on conventional fashion, marking the costume wearer as a member of a particular group, in this case superheroes.[2] "Theatricality and deception are powerful agents," Henri Ducard warns Bruce Wayne while undergoing martial arts training in a monastery in China. "You must become more than a man in the mind of your opponent" (*Batman Begins,* 2005).

A consistent totemic appropriation is evident in many costumes that resemble shamanesque figures, who, by summoning their superhuman powers, subsequently ward off or combat societal enemies. In the study of symbols, the wearing of masks is related to the summoning of supernatural agencies, especially those that mediate between ordinary and nonordinary realities in order to transform and endow the wearer with spirit powers, such as the call for protection by ancestors or the summoning of the acute instinct of animals. In *The Way of the Masks* (1998), structural anthropologist Levi-Strauss states that the mask functions as part of a system of diacritical signs (with their origin myths and the rites in which they appear).[3] These signs become intelligible only through the relationships that unite them. In other words, a correlative and oppositional relationship exists between the mask and the function assigned to it. The discourse of superhero fashion (capes, masks, and cloaks) and its reliance on harnessing paranormal energies from totemic animals figuratively marks the body through linguistic and sartorial codes and ushers in new enunciative powers. Superheroes, in this respect, are shamans of sorts, earthbound deities whose costume (complete with accoutrements) allows them to connect with their superhuman strength.

The notion of dress as a hybrid discourse finds similarities between the embodied/disembodied meaning attached to clothing and the shaman process of initiation into *Other* worlds. This process of initiation, state Warwick and Cavallaro,

… may include the dismemberment of the subject's body, the removal and substitution of flesh: a ritual that could be read as metaphorically redolent of the phenomenon of decorporealization triggered by the entry into the symbolic, which dress both ratifies, by positing itself as a substitute skin or flesh, and challenges, by foregrounding its own irreducible materiality.[4]

The significance of the mask as costume and as a potent source of animal force is suggested by Bob Kane's *Batman,* the "Dark Knight" and "Caped Crusader," who assumes the appearance of a bat to fight criminals and develops into a symbol of justice for the community; or Peter Parker's alter ego Spider-Man, who develops "spider powers" when bitten by a radioactive arachnid and who wears a spider-inspired costume as an ultimate metaphor. His unusual accident also grants Peter spider-senses and the ability to detect danger, along with the ability to scale walls and suspend himself high above the cityscape using newly acquired spinnerets, which emit sticky webs from his wrists. His costume in this case is light and functional, perfectly designed for hanging upside down and swinging between buildings. The superhero genre is full of hybrids: creatures simultaneously human and animal that populate worlds ambiguously natural and crafted.

As a garment, the mask conceals while simultaneously revealing the emphatic surfaces and historiographies inscribed on the hypermuscular superhero body. It serves to protect the wearer's subjectivity from the world, yet, at the same time, affectively hints at the *origin* stories and secret identities firmly embedded in the superhero genre. "Identity," states Bukatman, "is the obsessional centre of superhero comics, as revealed by the endless process of self-transformation and the problematic perceptions of others," as identity is negotiated, constructed, and performed.[5]

Efrat Tseëlon explains the constructive aspect of masking, which she uses interchangeably with notions of masquerade and disguise as an analytical tool that creates a subjective space—what she refers to as a "technology of identity." As an analytical category, states Tseëlon, the mask "deals with literal and metaphorical covering for ends as varied as concealing, revealing, highlighting, protesting [and] protecting" in the field where social practices are carried out.[6] Functioning as a means of transgressing one identity to take on another, the superhero mask guarantees the body's passage into the field of the symbolic by marking its liminal presence as a sign of salvation in the doom-and-gloom narrative of modernity gone horribly wrong.

Similarly, the doubling function of the mask is also analyzed by Bakhtin in his examination of the differing ways that masks have been used historically and of shifting social and cultural attitudes. He writes of the mask as an "involvement shield," protecting privacy while at the same time allowing for interaction with others. "The mask," he says, "is related to transition, metamorphoses, the violation of natural boundaries ... it is based on a peculiar interrelation of reality and image."[7]

Borrowing from the analyses of Bakhtin and Tseëlon, the superhero genre and its reliance on visual artefacts (glasses, bat and cat ears, horns, eye masks, and hats), as well as the metaphorical disguises routed in the symbolic ordering of fashion, come to convey the subjective duality of the double identity of superheroes, as they shift from mild-mannered geeks (such as Spider-Man, the Hulk, and Superman) to mercenary vigilantes taking the rules of law and order into their own hands.

FASHIONING THE SUPER-NATION

Fashion speaks a distinct language, which emblematizes the essence of its social and cultural context. Whether local or global, historical or contemporary, dress acts as a "confessional" that offers evidence of the practices and ideals of a given time. Fashion in this sense is not merely a passive reflection on society but serves as a vehicle for circulating patterns of consumption and ideology that are tied to notions of the body and the self.

The superhero costume operates as a language, a mode of communication that functions on numerous levels within a structured system of meanings that speak of the wearer's identity as a champion of liberty and comment on the supernatural abilities and attributes of their heroic status as arbiters of good. Although the design of the superhero garment remains fixed, the values of the society that produces the superhero identity change over time. Superman might have been fighting Communists in the Cold War of the 1950s, but by the beginning of the twenty-first century he was confronting societal fears of technological doom by battling a supercomputer as well as taking on global fears: the nuclear arms race and atomic testing.[8] Most recently, in 2004, Captain America, Daredevil, and the Hulk enlisted as "super-soldiers" in illustrated comic books and were sent to defuse nuclear facilities in Iran and North Korea.[9]

Fighting evil in the form of crime or planet-threatening aliens, superheroes such as Batman, Spider-Man, Superman, and their counterparts are embodiments of hegemonic masculinity; reluctant North American heroes (that is, Western cultural heroes) battling evil characters that are often nonwhite and threatening. These tough, aggressive, and unemotional macho-men and their alter egos, all of whom are quite ordinary, signify the dialectical relationship between what Alan Klein refers to as "Wimp and Warrior" in the constructions of Western masculinities. "If Superman is super, it is in large part a dialectical creation based on the stumbling borderline-incompetent Clark Kent." He continues, "If Batman is the 'Caped Crusader,' it is in relation to the staid, boring (but wealthy) Bruce Wayne."[10] Although the figure of the enemy has shifted and changed across historical and political specificities, the superhero wardrobe remains quintessentially the same, except for the change in fabric.

These larger-than-life heroes who rescue the weak, preserve humanity, and fight evil in "all its forms" invoke discourses about culture and national consciousness and can be located in the mythic narrative construction of the American dream of the late nineteenth and early twentieth century. Constructed around the melting-pot metaphor and narratives of overcoming immigrant hardship on arrival, the United States of America has come to represent a synthesis of peoples, religions, and ethnicities bound by the common ideals of freedom and opportunity. "Wrapped in the flag," writes Kevin Smith, Superman "has come to stand for the American dream."[11]

Like all good immigrants, Superman arrives in America from a distant land and eagerly adopts the nation's enduring values of "truth, justice, democracy, and the American Way." He is a child from the distant planet Krypton who is adopted by American parents and given the name of Clark Kent. Raised in the "safety and security" of rural America, he is taught to respect clean, wholesome living and traditional values and eventually moves to the city of Metropolis, where he lives out the American dream of middle-class ambitions. Clark encapsulates the sacred American right of freedom of speech through his job as an investigative reporter for the *Daily Planet*. Dressed in a white shirt, tie, corporate gray suit, and thick black glasses, Clark successfully blends into the urban environment. His status and identity as a superhero are effectively obscured.

In *Banal Nationalism,* Michael Billig argues that a great deal of nationalist practice is embedded in the rituals and practices of everyday life. Billig states that in the contemporary world, entire peoples are simply embedded in their national symbols. Their flags flutter as adornments to public buildings; the news categorizes events as home affairs or foreign reports; the weather forecast reinforces the awareness of political geography and boundaries; sporting heroes embody national virtues and mobilize collective loyalties; moments of crisis—especially war—produce patriotic addresses from political leaders; and national languages and histories, through their transmission, constitute a sense of communality.[12]

With this kind of formulation, the image of a costumed superhero functions as a cultural articulation of nation and subsequently constructs a series of relations around state and citizen, then of state, then of citizen and *Other*. The national superhero is reduced to a series of enunciations that reverberate around three fundamental concepts: masculinity, identity, and difference.

The contemporary position signaled by, say, Captain America's or Superman's red, white, and blue outfits and the forms they take now circulates in a network of signs, where the actual garment itself is transformed into the *signs* of America. From its existence as an artefact, the superhero costume has evolved into a hybrid form, operating simultaneously in many registers. Whereas it once existed as a single functioning garment, it now proliferates within a larger network of relations that comes to represent the values inscribed on the garment as a sign of "truth, justice, democracy, and the American Way."

BODY TECHNOLOGIES

In *The Fashion System,* Barthes is interested in the way in which sign systems produce not clothing, but the abstract notion of fashion as an independent, autonomous system, an inscription that results from a technique that is normalized by a code. He notes that "real" clothing must not be known by sight, for its visual image does not reveal all its intricacies. It must be known through the mechanical process of its production such as the seams and the pleats, as they are manufactured. In the dress/body relationship, Barthes emphasizes *coenaesthesia* as pivotal to understanding the multiple attributes played by cloth and fabric and stresses the need to think in terms of a coalescence rather than mutual exclusion of bodily effects:

Here is a group of variants whose function is to make certain states of the material signify: its weight, its suppleness, the relief of its surface,

and its transparency ... No variant is in fact literal: neither the weight nor the transparency of a fabric can be reduced to isolated properties: transparency is also lightness, heaviness is also stiffness; in the end, coenesthesia leads back to the opposition between comfortable and uncomfortable ...[13]

The transposition of the garment's attributes and the feelings that it invokes is not simply the effect of the overall garment as a casing, but of the body itself. Barthes stresses the intimate relationship between the body and the garment as one that positions clothing as a kind of surrogate for the body:

As a substitute for the body, the garment, by virtue of its weight, participates in man's [sic] fundamental dreams, in the sky and the cave, of life's sublimity and its entombment, of flight and sleep: it is a garment's weight which makes it a wing or a shroud, seduction or authority; ceremonial garments (and above all charismatic garments) are heavy; authority is a theme of immobility, of death, garments celebrating marriage, birth and life are light and airy.[14]

Sartorial images of superheroes and their associations with nation, the law, and authority advertise them as symbols of loyalty and patriotism. The superhero garment, and its matching accessories, make explicit reference to the symbolism of the American nation by means of color and pattern—most obviously, through stars, stripes, and phoenix motifs. With its emphasis on functionality, male überfashion is intended to be responsive to the hypergendered superhero body and acts as an insulating coat of armor that is suited to the performance-enhancing qualities that are necessary for heroic deeds. According to Michael Carter, a key factor playing over Superman's costume is that of functionalism. As an ensemble, Carter argues that Superman's garments appear as an unchanging suite of highly integrated elements, the result of what he calls "conscious design." "His garments are colour coordinated and each item seems to be constituted by the position it occupies in the whole outfit, rather than being the result of historical accident, irrational fashionability or personal inclination."[15]

The impact of technology is also breeding a generation of male superheroes who are fitted with clothing to which remote-control systems, signal transmitters, and power grids are attached. Although cinematic images of superhero nanotechnologies have been inspired by scientific research, they also encapsulate an entire semiology of visual narratives on military cyborgs and superhuman techno-augmentation associated with the superhero imaginary. Scenes from Christopher Nolan's *Batman Begins* (2005) depict Bruce Wayne's body altered or completely transformed by nanotechnological prostheses of militaristic origin. His symbiotic suit of armor is fitted with carbon-fiber plates to control body temperature and his gloves are made of "memory fabric" whose soft and subtle texture takes on a rigid shape when electrical currents are applied via electrodes embedded within them. The film uses high-tech systems and materials to establish a dialogue between Batman and the environment, while exploring the extent to which cloth, engineering, and science can be integrated in a single design.

Director Christopher Nolan wanted to capture the romantic quality and essence of Batman's cowl while still maintaining subtlety and lightness in cloth. "The finest parachute silk constructed of waterproof nylon was used," states costume designer Lindy Hemming, "and then flocked by tiny hairs so that the cloak ended up looking like a velvet pile. It has an animal feel on the outside and the waterproof nature and lightness [of fabric] allows it to fly" (*Batman Begins,* 2005).

The formal attributes of lightweight "super fabrics" are coupled with the sensation of airiness associated with flight, thus investing the wearer with the attributes of a bat, such as in the case of Batman, or of *a bird or a plane*, as in the case of Superman. The tactile and visual qualities related to the synthetic fibers "favored" by superheroes encase the body in a solid architectural frame, rendering it weightless to the point of transparency as it moves *faster than a speeding bullet,* becoming *more powerful than a locomotive,* and *able to leap tall buildings in a single bound.*

In cinematic adaptations, superhero costumes were traditionally made from natural fibers such as wool or cotton. Tight, figure-hugging fabrics such as the synthetic elastic Lycra, developed beginning in 1958, revolutionized the cinematic superhero wardrobe. Lycra was popularized on television and in film because of its "stretch and recovery" qualities as well as being lightweight, colorful, and moisture-repellent. Similarly, the superhero fashion of underwear as outerwear was popular for certain characters and was a key feature of "action" clothing, because of its flexibility and suitability for high-level action. The Lycra superhero suit was designed to streamline the body's silhouette and to effectively cut down drag and resistance through water and air. It also compressed the muscles and controlled bodily deviations for maximum performance. Microfiber technology has further transformed the properties of many superhero costumes, from bodysuits to masks and capes.

In *The Incredibles* (2004) the animated character Edna Mode, Pixar's "fashion designer to the superheroes," hints at the future of smart-fiber technologies, in the manufacturing of *smart* superhero fashions for a contemporary superhero.

> Your suit can stretch as far as you can without injuring yourself and still retain its shape, virtually indestructible ... yet it breathes like Egyptian cotton. As an extra feature, each suit contains a homing device, giving you the precise global location of the wearer at the touch of a button. (*The Incredibles,* 2004)

These new-age fabrics offer thermal control through quick-absorbing fabric enhancement by pulling perspiration away from the body, drying it quickly, and keeping the body cool and comfortable. Spill-and-stain-resistant fibers (synthetics, wool, rayon) can be used to repel a range of liquids. The developments of permanent static-resistance treatments to reduce cling and deter static substances will also improve the overall appearance and comfort of superhero garments. Nanotechnology also promises performance-enhancing attributes and control mechanisms, in addition to body adjustment or maintenance such as vitamin, perfume, or steroid release. With fabrics such as the aerosol spray-on Fabrican, already being used in fashion to produce supertough street wear, as well as Kevlar-treated or Tyvek-infused fibers to produce practical, lightweight, and extremely durable clothing, the future of male superhero fashion, should it exist, is limitless.

CONCLUSION: DRESSED MALE BODIES

The discourse of male superhero fashion pertains simultaneously to processes of historical, cultural, and ideological structures, which are foremost in the powerful role played by clothing and accoutrements in the construction of male superhero personas. As such, dress is significant in both the development of superhero masculinities and identities and the critical decoding of the languages, practices, and representations enacted by fashion as a signifier of superhuman abilities. Superhero bodies are dressed bodies; dress transforms the body and appropriates it for specific contexts, endowing the superhero psyche with attributes and energies that are beyond the "natural" world. Materials, fabrics, and accoutrements also add a whole array of meanings to the hypergendered masculine superbody that would otherwise not be there. In this way, dress serves as a visual metaphor for identity.

The symbolically encultured body of the superhero is physically translated into the realm of the superhuman by means of a strategy of complete disguise. The functional role of the superhero attire is to conceal, or at least obscure, the wearer's identity, while attracting attention at the same time. Outwardly, the superhero appears to be a normal everyday individual who is not differentiated from others in the crowd. But underneath this commonplace persona lies a shadowy side that possesses all of the hero's superpowers and abilities. "It is not who I am underneath [what I wear]," reflects Batman, "but what I do that defines me" (*Batman Begins,* 2005). The dressed male superbody is always positioned in the in-between space of self and identity, continually vacillating between the human persona and the *Other* side, never living a full existence in either one.

NOTES

1. A. Warwick and D. Cavallaro, *Fashioning the Frame: Boundaries, Dress and the Body* (Oxford: Berg, 1998), 129.
2. M. Bongco, *Reading Comics: Language, Culture and the Concept of the Superhero in Comic Books* (New York: Garland, 2000), 126.
3. C. Levi-Strauss, *The Way of the Masks* (Seattle: University of Washington Press, 1988).
4. Warwick and Cavallaro, *Fashioning the Frame,* 129.
5. S. Bukatman, "X-Bodies (the Torment of the Mutant Superhero)," in *Uncontrollable Bodies: Testimonies of Identity and Culture,* ed. R. Sappington and T. Stallings (Seattle, WA: Bay Press, 1994), 100.
6. Efrat Tseëlon, "From Fashion to Masquerade: Towards an Ungendered Paradigm," in *Body Dressing,* ed. J. Entwistle and E. Wilson (Oxford: Berg, 2001), 108.
7. Mikhail Bakhtin, *Rabelais and His World,* trans. Helene Iswolsky (Bloomington: Indiana University Press, 1984), 40.
8. Danny Fingeroth, *Superman on the Couch: What Superheroes Really Tell Us about Ourselves and Our Society* (New York: Continuum, 2004), 17.
9. S. Botzas, "Biff! Bang! Pow! Captain America Enlists to Fight for Bush in Iraq," *Sunday Herald* (London), November 14, 2004.

10. A. M. Klein, *Little Big Men: Body Building Subculture and Gender Construction* (Albany: State University of New York Press, 1993), 267.

11. K. Smith, "A Superman for all Seasons," *T.V. Guide,* December 8, 2004, 24.

12. M. Billig, *Banal Nationalism* (London: Sage, 1995), 85.

13. R. Barthes, *The Fashion System,* trans. Matthew Ward and Richard Howard (Los Angeles: University of California Press, 1990), 123–24.

14. Ibid., 126.

15. M. Carter, "Superman's Costume," *Form/Work: An Interdisciplinary Journal of Design and the Built Environment, The Fashion Issue* 4 (March 2000): 31.

THE ITALIAN JOB: FOOTBALL, FASHION AND THAT SARONG

Stella Bruzzi

In 1990 Italy hosted its first World Cup since 1938, then under the shadow of Mussolini and the Fascist statues around the Stadio Olimpico in Rome. Italia 90 would be different, a chance to cut a fine figure and, more importantly to Italian football fans, win a third World Cup (*Mondiale*), thus going ahead of Brazil. Expectations were high, Italian club teams had just won all the European trophies, they had in Roberto Baggio—whose recent sale by Fiorentina to Juventus for $20 million had prompted riots in the streets of Florence—the new Paolo Rossi, their hero of 1982, and they were playing at home. Things started well—to a superstitious Italian maybe too well—as Italy, thanks ironically to their new Sicilian striker, Toto Schillaci, arrived unproblematically at a 1–0 lead in their semi-final against an inferior Argentina. Then Argentina scored and the home team choked, losing eventually 4–3 on penalties, ensuring Germany an improbable number of *tifosi* (fans) for the Final. Like the Victorian gentleman who shouted out to Othello before the end of Shakespeare's tragedy that Iago was not to be trusted, this disaster wasn't part of the script. Italy wasn't supposed to end its World Cup campaign slugging it out in a lacklustre, also-rans, third-place play-off in Bari (albeit in a sumptuous, new Renzo Piano-designed San Nicola stadium) against an England team bereft of Gazza, tears and flair; it was destined for the reinvigorated Stadio Olimpico. It was not for this that Italy had designed, re-designed and renovated twelve stadiums, held a national poll to decide the official mascot's name ('Ciao' beating off the challenge of 'Dribbly' and 'Bimbo') and commissioned its film-makers to direct short films about their home towns and cities. As the despairing headline in *La Gazzetta dello Sport* declared the day after the calamitous defeat in the semis: 'Italia Noooo'.

Despite the resulting anticlimax for the host nation and the choice of Giorgio Moroder's 'Un Estate Italiana' as the championship's accompanying pop song, Italia 90 was a turning point for how football was perceived, particularly in the UK where, in its wake, football became synonymous with style, desire, melodrama and spectacle. 'Football' had a new aura; the Pavlovian response to the word was no longer to think of bobble hats and beery, leery men in smelly sheepskin and scarves swaying on the terraces like tinless sardines between other 'white males of little education and even less wit' (Ian Taylor in Williams 1995: 243) on wet, wasted afternoons. Although the pre-Hillsborough and Heysel image of the fan is as much a cliché as the new man with muscles and Italian-cut suits who has replaced him, the shift is monumental and irreversible. Significantly, it wasn't all footballers whose images altered and the new-found football chic was firmly rooted in Italianness—or rather the British reconfiguration of Italianness. There is a marked difference in British attitudes to, for instance, David Ginola's 'Eurotrash' look of jacket, T-shirt, jeans, loafers and no socks than to Gianluca Vialli, player and ex-manager of Chelsea. Ginola is coded as sexy but available: he advertises hair products, he appears with monotonous regularity in the pages of *Hello!* The Premiership reincarnation of Vialli, though, is another matter. On the eve of Chelsea's FA Cup Final against Aston Villa in May 2000, the *Guardian*'s Jim White remarks upon the club's final press day. Unexpectedly for a sports pages feature, perhaps, White begins by dwelling upon the 'Giorgio Armani' press pack that was handed out, in which the squad were pictured donning natty 'three-button, single-breasted suits in charcoal-grey wool worn, according to the blurb, "with light grey tone on tone shirt and tie combination"' (White 2000: 1). White here seems proud of his ability to describe, with admirable accuracy, the Armani garb, whilst simultaneously sneaking in that the journalists themselves were dressed 'in the standard fashion-free manner'. He reserves his greatest admiration, however, for the manager, commenting 'no one wears the ensemble as well as Gianluca Vialli'. This is a curious thing—prior to Vialli's departure from Juventus to Chelsea as a player under his managerial predecessor, Ruud Gullit, Vialli was a favourite target of the Italian sports press, not for his style but his lack of it. As Vialli started to thin on top, so he began tinkering with his mane and his facial hair: from wild curls to crew cut, from clean-shaven chin to designer stubble goatee (ostensibly illustrating the old truism that if you want to change something about your appearance that you'd rather went unnoticed, divert attention to some other feature at the same time). In England, Vialli's very Italianness ensures his fashion status.

Vialli took over at Chelsea from another Serie A export, Dutchman Ruud Gullit. Gullit's arrival at Stamford Bridge under Glenn Hoddle was another key post-Italia 90 moment of transition, although he was nearing the end of his career and had got a bit stocky, slow and ungainly on the pitch. Gullit, however, descended in his Milanese suits (and his own clothes line) and transformed the image of the team of Dennis Wise, London's Gazza. Several factors united to make Gullit such a key icon: his legendary status as a player, particularly at AC Milan; his sartorial panache; his intelligence both as a player and a TV pundit. The English reverence of Gullit (I distinctly recall several minutes of *Match of the Day* being given over to a discussion of the correct pronunciation of his name, as if Alan Hansen *et al.* just liked saying it) was relatively short-lived, as he left Chelsea under a cloud and had little managerial success subsequently with Newcastle United. Alongside his 'culturedness', the other significant facet of Gullit's appeal was that he was black, and like English football has sought a patina of Italian finesse, so it has often been a place for acknowledging black stylishness. Storm, the London model agency, started signing up footballers in 1995 and those on its books by 1998 included Ruud Gullit, Les Ferdinand and Ian Wright. The common factor, of course, is that all three are black, more effortlessly cool and inherently stylish than their pasty-skinned colleagues. Another high-profile footballer-cum-model is David James, the Liverpool then Aston Villa goalie who has done Armani catwalk shows and, in 1996, appeared on a 50-foot-high poster wearing only Armani underpants. Chelsea's transformation from a parochial, technically crude squad pre-Hoddle to one that starts the 2000 FA Cup Final with only one native player is Gullit's lasting legacy. As if to render himself more stylish, Chelsea's only Englishman, Dennis Wise, went up to receive the cup clutching the new century's latest male fashion accessory—his baby.

It was thus more than Gazza's iconic tears of Italia 90 that have cemented the notion of fashionable football in the UK. At the time of the championships, the choice of Pavarotti's rendition of Puccini's 'Nessun Dorma' as the BBC's official Italia 90 anthem was extremely influential in reconstructing football spectatorship as a couch activity worthy of the chattering classes. Although Pavarotti was the masses' opera star, and, alongside Placido Domingo and

Jose Carreras, has become a fixture of British World Cup coverage since, 'Nessun Dorma' was a far cry from Chelsea in 1971 grunting 'Blue is the Colour' or Glenn Hoddle and Chris Waddle appearing on *Top of the Pops* sporting spangly 1980s jackets, feathercuts and quiffs. During the BBC's 1990 coverage there was also the unusual side-tracking commentary by its pundits on the gorgeousness of the Italian stadiums, asides that inevitably contextualized football within society and culture at large. Italy and football were perhaps the significant if unconscious catalysts for the attitude change elsewhere; perhaps it was evident simply from how even designer-clad, middle-class Italians treated football as a significant part of their cultural lives that the sport could be sexy. Certainly in the aftermath of Italia 90 in Britain, more women started to watch and be interested in football, Channel 4 began broadcasting live Serie A action and the accompanying *Gazzetta Football Italia* and footballers became fashion icons. To become fashionable, British football has had to become less parochial and less male, for this was the rite of passage that enabled footballers in general to become objects of pulchritude and aspiration.

There are other less frivolous factors that may have contributed to the need to find the chic in football, the most socially significant being the immediate call for all-seated stadiums after ninety-six fans—the majority from Liverpool—died at Hillsborough, Sheffield on 15 April 1989. The need for such measures had already been signalled by the violence that erupted between Liverpool and Juventus fans at the 1985 European Cup Final at Heysel Stadium where thirty-nine, mainly Italian, fans died. These ugly scenes (that led to English clubs being banned from Europe for five years) have been interpreted as the result of English fans' xenophobia, which is ironic considering their subsequent obsession with the European game. Lord Justice Taylor's official inquiry after Hillsborough stipulated that all stadiums in England, Scotland and Wales would need to become all-seated

by the start of the 1994–5 season. The drop in attendances that this entailed meant in turn that ticket prices had to rise (Manchester United's average receipts per spectator, for example, rose by almost 223 per cent between 1988–9 and 1992–3) and 'raised the spectre, for some, of the sport increasingly becoming distanced, socially and spatially, from its "traditional" audience and being played in soul-less "production-line" concrete bowls in front of passive and affluent consumers (not supporters)' (Williams 1995: 225).[1] This, ironically, is more akin to the dominant European model for viewing football already in place by 1989–90, and it is significant that many commentators on the continental game cite as an important difference between the game in England (or Germany) and France or Italy the fact that in the latter countries it has traditionally been a cross-class activity, for spectators and players alike (Mignon 1999: 82; Lanfranchi 1994: 152–3). The changing image of football chic in the UK coincided, therefore, with the general poshening of the national game. An accurate gauge of this is the changing responses to Graham Le Saux's *Guardian*-reading middle-classness: whereas now he is deemed to fit in, earlier in his career he was ridiculed for being a boffin.

What then happened in the UK during and immediately after Italia 90 that was so radical? First, there was 'Gazza', the contradictory, loaded icon of 1990s English football: a Geordie genius whose famous tears at being issued with another yellow card in England's semi against Germany (which would mean, if England got there, that he wouldn't play in the Final) made him into a national institution, epitomizing the British fixation upon the 'if only' brand of glorious sporting failure. Gazza's image, though, was a complex one; he was likewise renowned for his stupidity, bigotry and bad behaviour, and it was Gazza who declared to Terry Wogan 'I'm norra poof, like', who beat up his wife and got legless on the eve of Glenn Hoddle's selection of England's France 1998 squad. Gazza never lost his Englishness but it was also he who transferred to Lazio in the aftermath of Italia 90 and who, much more than David Piatt who went to Serie A at the same time, exemplified the continuation of the British love affair with *calcio*.

Symptomatic of the essential ambiguity of Gazza's image, the dream combination of Gazza and Italy never took off: at Lazio he was plagued by injury and bad press, he never made efforts to learn Italian and he was swiftly marginalised from his 'news round-up' slot on *Gazzetta Football Italia*, Gazza was as much a symbol of the old image of football as the new; like Maradona and Schillaci, two of the other stars of Italia 90, he was the epitome of the working-class boy made good. There were also parallels to be drawn between Gazza and George Best (with his line of boutiques in the 1970s, one of the few footballers of the pre-1990s era to cash in on the football/fashion intersection): both were resonant icons for their respective generations, both squandered their talents by boozing, womanizing and generally going off the rails. Herein lies the first of many contradictions pertaining to the renaissance of football in the 1990s: that the stylish, fashionable and image-obsessed game is in part a re-fashioning or reclamation of the old drab one. When *Hello!* magazine featured Gazza's wedding to Sheryl in July 1996 (white morning suits and stretch limos), it did so because there was a voracious audience for its kitsch appeal, not because Gazza had suddenly been immortalized into the incarnation of good taste. It was Gazza, the cheeky chappy who farted and belched at the Italian press, who was canonized by the intelligentsia in the UK, and to whom Ian Hamilton dedicated over half an edition of *Granta* in 1993 ('Gazza Agonistes').

As with Gazza's image, the whole issue of football's relationship to style is fraught with anomalies. First, in the fashion pages of men's 1990s style magazines it is often the old image of football that is evoked, obviously out of nostalgia for 1966 and all that but also out of an understanding that 'football chic' will remain a complex and equivocal term to do, for instance, with the inherently ambivalent ways in which designer leisure wear labels have been reappropriated and universalized. The rise of leisure wear as chic is very different from the smartening-up of football by an association with more formal designer wear. As Robert Elms writes in *Arena*, the 'genesis of the footballer as style god' is the sartorially challenged footballer of the 1970s with his collar-length hair and floral shirts, but the 'real style icons' of the mid-1990s football fashion scene are 'the lads on the terraces'; these rather than the Ginolas or the James's on the catwalks are what football chic is about (Elms 1996: 142–4). However much Armani Gazza has worn—and for a 1991 cover article for *GQ* he reputedly wanted a £5,000 fee plus £3,000-worth of Armani clothes—there's still something of the shellsuit brigade about him.[2] This is still where British football chic and its Italian equivalent diverge. In the run-up to USA 94, British *Esquire* ran a fashion article in which several Italian players modelled exclusive ready-to-wear Italian designs by Gucci, Cerruti, Zegna, Armani, Dolce and Gabbana, Valentino and Versace. It's not that all the players selected (who include the hardly stunning—though brilliant—AC Milan defender and national captain, Franco Baresi) are beautiful, nor that they are all super-successful. Indeed, one of the intriguing features of the article, which in June 1994 was prepared reasonably close to team selection time, was that it chose as its models several players—such as Roberto Mancini and Marco Simone—whom few Italians would have tipped to feature in the World Cup squad. The significant 'it' factor seems to be that the footballers are Italian. It's hard to imagine a comparable Italian style monthly running a feature in which David Beckham, Nicky Butt and David Seaman model Paul Smith, Katharine Hamnett and Nicole Farhi.

In Italy there is a clear history of football being seamlessly integrated into the nation's style and culture, and this became one of the lasting legacies of Italia 90 in Britain. Again in June 1994 as their prelude to that year's World Cup, *GQ* studied the form of the countries involved (which didn't include England) in terms of what it calls 'elements of style'. For many of these countries their 'element of style' is related to their footballing chances, so the Cameroon was labelled 'uncontrollable' and the Irish 'optimistic' (although it was Ireland that beat the fancied Italy in their group's opening match). When it comes to the Italians, under 'Style' *GQ* identifies 'Michelangelo, Da Vinci, Verdi, the lot', under 'Strength' it singles out 'gorgeousness' and under 'Weakness' it mentions 'insane media'. Obviously, very little of this has to do with football and much of it has to do with style. This automatic assimilation of leisure and social activities such as football into what's generally held to be attractive about Italy (its art, architecture, people, food, cars) is a recurrent theme in *GQ*. In October 1994, the magazine ran a piece 'Gran Turismo' on Italian cars and clothes featuring the juxtaposition, sensually photographed, of details of the fabric and cut of loose Italian tailoring with close-ups of Alfa Romeo dashboards: the cars are vintage; the clothes soon will be. Then, in December 1998, *GQ* ran a short article again in praise of Italian design in which it yokes together by a sometimes unseemly violence, such eclectic manifestations of this as Leonardo, the Lira notes, the Alfa Romeo badge, the Fiat 500, the Beretta, the Romans, the Cosa Nostra and the Juventus kit. This arbitrary list that ranks Sicilian organized crime alongside a Renaissance artist crudely illustrates the point that Italy is innately fashionable and that we in England want to emulate it. Intriguingly, of the Juventus kit *GQ* says it is as 'Subbuteo as shirts come, which would seem appropriate given that their inspiration came from a visit by Notts County' (*GQ* December 1998: 262). Although the same 'inspiration' on the similarly clad Newcastle United would, perhaps, have been treated ironically, the contradiction of retro English league non-fashion having influenced Agnelli's

slick winning machine is what creates the strip's aura of chic. It is hard to imagine that same British men's style magazine praising the very similar Newcastle monochrome strip, which makes the reverence towards Italian style seem totally uncritical.

In 1982 Mick Jagger, while performing with The Rolling Stones at the Stadio Comunale in Torino after Italy's World Cup victory that summer, donned a Paolo Rossi Number 20 shirt. There is a sense of Italian football having always been cool and evoking effortlessly a whole aura and lifestyle—despite many a naff haircut (Roberto 'the divine pony tail' Baggio's of USA 94 being the most obscene) or the potentially emasculating shots of an entire team in baby blue vests during the shirt-swapping ritual with Brazil after the 1978 third-place play-off. A distinction can be made between the 'full' and the 'empty' footballer as fashion icon image. Whereas a picture of David Beckham in Gucci, for example, is 'empty' because it is just a picture of David Beckham in Gucci, a picture of Gianni Rivera at the height of his fame and powers in the late 1960s/early 1970s, nonchalantly propped up against a bookcase perusing a hefty tome in slim-line black suit and patent Gucci brogues, is 'full' because it evokes not just Rivera and football but an aspirational lifestyle. Beckham's clothes too often wear him, he doesn't look natural in his designer casuals, his 'intellectual' spectacles or indeed posing shirtless on the golf course; he's always self-conscious, always performing and demanding to be looked at. That Italian golden boy Rivera is reading and ignoring us is significant, and the way in which we are invited to view that image (used, for instance, in an *Homme Plus* feature on the fifty most stylish sportsmen of the twentieth century [*Homme Plus* 1996: 89–99]) is as evocative of an unmeasurable cool, a certain lifestyle. The Rivera image is symptomatic of Britain having also caught the Italian need to take football itself so seriously. *Calcio,* one writer suggests, is automatically placed alongside Fellini, Ferrari and wine as something quintessentially Italian, but it is given disproportionate sobriety by, for example, programmes such as RAI 3's weekly post-mortem football analysis programme *Processo del Lunedi* ('Trial on Monday') in which experts adopt absurdly 'lofty tones and flowery language' in their discussion of the matches held the day before (Lanfranchi 1994: 155). The treatment in Britain of football by mainstream culture (as opposed to legitimately interested sports academics) is too frequently ironic or knowing, Nick Hornby being a notably sincere exception. So men's magazines, alongside articles genuinely praising the pervasiveness of Italian style, run features on awful 1970s football haircuts (Kevin Keegan 'the Permed Prince of the Park' [Webb 1998]) and the gaudiness of goalkeepers' strips (see *GQ* June 1994). It is this equivocal response to the pairing of football and style that informs the distressed, trendified Parka image of Fat Les, the trio of Damien Hirst, Keith Allen and Alex James who had a 1998 World Cup hit with 'Vindaloo' and brought out a version of 'Jerusalem' for Euro 2000.

The emergence of football chic in Britain, therefore, has continued to be double-edged. Sartorially speaking, even the more recent history of English football's relationship with fashion is characterized by disasters rather than successes. There was, for instance, the scorn poured on the Liverpool team's emergence for the FA Cup Final of 1996 wearing (ironically) pale beige Giorgio Armani suits. One journalist likened the team to ice-cream salesmen (Greenberg 1998) whilst a fan commented, 'I held my face in my hands in shame. From the moment they stepped out in those suits, I knew we were going to lose' (Blanchard 1998). Then there was the scrutiny of Glenn Hoddle's managerial decision to put the England squad for France 98 in darker beige (or taupe) suits designed by Paul Smith. Smith had suggested navy for the suits but Hoddle wanted something more 'summery'. Not often has what the England squad elected to wear off the pitch been frontpage news, but in this instance the matter was treated with earnest interest, one journalist making the preparation for the big day when the suits would finally be unveiled sound like an important nuptial:

> Final fittings will take place shortly. Because of their training programme, players change shape in a matter of weeks and can only be certain of their final sizes just before the tournament starts (Kennedy 1998).

Here the England squad are described in more feminine terms than normal; more common were references to Paul Ince's thighs bursting out of the flimsy linen-viscose mix trousers or comments such as, 'If the players had their way, they'd arrive [in France] looking like the bad guys in a Tarantino heist movie' (Greenberg 1998). Just as Glenn Hoddle was nicknamed 'Glenda' during his days at Tottenham Hotspur for his silky skills and dainty, leggy appearance, so the unmentionable implication of 'those suits' was that the England team's collective machismo and potential coolness were under threat. In October 1999, David Beckham was stung with a £50,000 fine (later revoked) by the Manchester United coach Alex Ferguson for breaking the club curfew before a Champions League game and turning up at a London Fashion Week show. Although Beckham assured Sir Alex that he and his wife Victoria Adams were in bed by midnight, a taste for fashion has become, like sex before crucial encounters, a factor that can detract from a player's footballing skills. As *The Mirror* put it, 'pictures of him [Beckham] wearing a trendy headscarf put him and United on the spot' (Nixon and Harris 1999).

Apparently most of the squad of France 98 had favoured blue, the colour of the suits Paul Smith had designed for England's Euro 96 team, and although the players were given both the beige and the blue versions of the 1998 suit, this wasn't sufficient—except for the ever-diplomatic and dull Alan Shearer, who thought the beige looked fine against his lads' tanned skin. Although many a critical journalist who attended the taupe extravaganza recalled the Armani/Liverpool embarrassment, none of them seemed to remember Glenn Hoddle's last notable fashion decision as a manager—to put his Chelsea squad for their doomed 1994 FA Cup Final against Manchester United in pale purple because it was, as Hoddle commented at the time, a little bit 'different'. Indeed Paul Smith, who two years previously had simply been given the go-ahead by then England manager Terry Venables, was surprised at Hoddle's interference, remarking, 'I don't think he's well known for his dress sense' (Lee 1998). Several points of emphasis emerge from the coverage in June 1998 of the unveiling of England's off-pitch uniforms: that beige reflected Glenn Hoddle's taste (after all, Hoddle on the touchline was often to be seen in tracksuit bottoms hitched up just a tad high, which made him look like a relaxed version of Reeves and Mortimer's King's Singers); that the suits did not reflect the players' keener fashion sense and masculinity; that this choice suggested the team would fail. Journalists vied with each other to heap the most withering insults on the beige creations: they were not as sharp as the 1966 World Cup winners in 'slim, dark razor-cut' suits—although better than the off-the-peg Burton's numbers of 1970 or the sporty blazers of 1990 (Mouland 1998); they looked like a 'convention of double-glazing salesmen' or a 'pack of Scout leaders at the annual jamboree' (Spencer 1998); they weren't a patch on the French team dressed by Daniel Hechter or the FIFA officials in their Yves Saint Laurent. Even the dubious 'Gallic flair' of the 'former French internationals Eric Cantona and David Ginola' (Webb 1998) was dragged in for comparison. The realm of football and fashion overflows with such exquisite ironies: for Euro 2000 England reverted to suits by Burtons Tailoring, so that they were seen to be wearing clothes that the average fan could afford to emulate.

Paul Smith himself was never blamed for the France 98 sartorial *faux pas,* perhaps because he was Britain's favourite designer and because football coverage is, above all, patriotic (some journalists and fans, for instance, had taken umbrage at both Arsenal and Newcastle walking on to the Wembley turf the day before their FA Cup Final clash just a month before wearing unpatriotic Hugo Boss suits rather than designs by 'local' designer Katharine Hamnett [Blanchard 1998]).[3]

As proof of Smith's worth, it's significant that several of the June 1998 articles estimated the cost and exclusivity of the beige ensemble (£600 suits, £95 dark blue shirts, £55 pound cufflinks, a £50 tie and blue suede shoes from Cheaney of Northamptonshire) as if to deflect criticism. The England team could have—for once—been stylish, but 'Glenda' had thwarted their ambitions. The real problem with the men in beige was that they raised the ugly spectre of the pre-Italia 90 football fashion dark ages, a stigma that the English game has never quite been able to shake off. For whilst the England 98 squad would dearly have liked to resemble their Italian and French counterparts, the images most often evoked throughout the discussions of the beige suits were fellow disasters: John Barnes's shiny suits and unconventional tailoring, Barry Venison's debut as a TV pundit in a silver waistcoat and sporting a 'mop of straggly bleached hair' (Webb 1998)—since dispensed with and replaced with a sombre crop and yet another pair of unshowy 'intellectual' glasses—and Gazza's hair extensions. These were painful reminders of old football and the ridiculously tight shorts of the 1980s, summoning up from the murky depths of fan memory those images of Keegan missing a sitter against Spain in the 1982 World Cup. The *Sun* had asked of David Beckham after the Manchester United midfielder had been spotted in the South of France wearing a sarong, 'Is he trendy, or a twit?' Those suits precipitated a crisis precisely because the English press didn't know what was good fashion and what was Venison fashion and they needed to be told. The maligned Barry Venison himself self-effacingly admitted to being in the dark about this; when questioned about why he'd chosen to look so awful for his television debut, he admitted 'I was not trying to look silly on purpose, it was purely down to my bad taste' (Webb 1998).

Two approaches to the fashion and football intersection have dominated British responses: that footballers are the new Hollywood stars—free, over-exposed and influential clothes horses—and that English football is still 'a style disaster waiting to happen' (Webb 1998). As always, it's a fine line between clever and stupid. Fashion, as the Ferguson–Beckham conflict illustrated, is perceived as a threat to football as well as the salvation of its image, despite the suggestion that the feminization of the male is an essential component of the macho footballer image: Gazza crying, David Beckham wearing a sarong or the Italian Euro 2000 defence keeping their fringes out of their eyes with dainty hair bands. Real men accessorize. However, as Ginola modelled for Cerruti and David James for Armani, or as Marilyn Gauthier Models (MGM; the leading model agency in France) sent scouts to France 98 with the specific brief to get fresh footballing talent on their books, a definite sense emerges of the image being more important than the game. MGM signings include Thierry Henri, Patrick Viera, Emanuel Petit, Ibrahim Ba and Zvonimir Boban, but as a spokesperson for the agency comments, 'Footballers are sexy when they're doing well on the field because they exude confidence and the camera picks that up' (Grey and Lang 1998). No matter how much fashion has radically altered football's public face, nor how differently a wider audience has perceived it since Italia 90, the relationship with the players' real performances on the pitch is still paramount—the bad kits, tight shorts and vests won't go away.

The most prevalent English example of fashion dominating the image of football and con-comitantly of it being hard to erase the negative connotations of football and football chic is David Beckham. He is the archetypal football-fashion icon: successful on the pitch, with a famous and even wealthier wife—Victoria Adams (aka Posh Spice)—a penchant for shopping and bland, malleable good looks. There is, however, the ominous suspicion that, just as his wife is more Essex than posh, Beckham might be more John Barnes than Paolo Maldini: mutton dressed up as lamb. Gianni Rivera later became an MP (for the Christian Democrats); this is probably a fate not awaiting David Beckham, despite the recent lowering, it seems, of his falsetto voice. So, is he trendy or a twit? The Beckhams' wedding on 4 July 1999 at Luttrellstown Castle, near Dublin, would imply the latter (although the ostentatious glamour of the event was not without its fans). Posh went down the aisle in a champagne-coloured Vera Wang satin gown (made of Clerici Duchess satin, 'the finest Italian satin in the world', as *OK!*'s 'David and Victoria: their complete story' Special breathlessly informs us). David wore a complementary three-piece designed by English designer Timothy Everest and shoes by Manolo Blahnik. For the Robin Hood theme reception, the couple changed into matching head to toe purple Antonio Berardi outfits: he wore a double-breasted jacket with quite wide leg trousers over a splayed (shades of George Best) collar shirt, whilst she wore a slim-line, strapless gown of stretch satin with a thigh-high slit that revealed a red lining (to match the swathe of red and purple roses tumbling off her right shoulder) and silver Blahnik strappy sandals. Their uncomprehending baby Brooklyn had matching baby get-ups (two copies of each—in case he was sick down the first); particularly memorable is the purple sheriff's hat he was forced to wear for the reception. Victoria Adams maintained that many of the touches were 'tongue in cheek' (*OK!* 1999: 24), but she omitted to mention walking to the reception marquee to the theme tune from Disney's *Beauty and the*

Beast or intertwining 'VD' on their specially designed coat of arms.

The entire voracious relationship between the press and the Beckhams exemplifies the current state of the relationship between football and fashion that seems to dictate that we forget the Italian, tasteful aspirations and accept football chic's ambiguity and innate tackiness. Apart from feeding us a limitless supply of photos of Posh, Becks and Brooklyn, the contract with *OK!* is characterized by twin revelations: the extent of the couple's designer shopping and how much their respective outfits cost. In the 31 March 2000 edition, under the headline 'David and Victoria's style sensation', the family step out to reveal their radical new haircuts: Beckham and Brooklyn's crew cuts and Victoria's blonde spiky look. In a typically insipid accompanying article, Victoria reveals that she doesn't expect her husband's £300 shave to jeopardise his contract with Brylcreem (*OK!* March 21, 2000: 10) and hairdresser Nicky Clarke is quoted as stating the very obvious—that Beckham's style 'looks like a number one or a number two' (*OK!* March 21, 2000: 9). Posh and Becks have made themselves into consumable fashion icons; what's really on sale in this *OK!* feature is thus a composite image and its concomitant price tags: his Timberlands cost £130, his Hilfiger jacket £100, his Diesel jeans £80, her Gucci leather jacket over £1,800 and her Maharishi orange trousers (or are they Gap Kids as one caption says?) £100. Itemizing and costing their clothes in this way is symptomatically tacky; as Chanel once remarked, good fashion doesn't draw attention to itself, if clothes are truly well designed what they do is subtly and unobtrusively compliment their wearer. The delicious perversity of Chanel has always been that its real signs of class (the braid concealing the join between lining and outer fabric) often remain concealed. This clearly couldn't be further from the point in the case of the Posh 'n Becks phenomenon; their designer labels give them an identity rather than vice versa. They

are contemporary signifiers of power and success, not of taste. Their combined image is an ambivalent one; on the one hand, we know that Beckham and Adams have courted *OK!* and the kind of paparazzi fame it offers, on the other they're rather sweetly gooey, particularly about each other and Brooklyn. One would like to simply hate them for their scowling, posturing expressions when caught on camera, their affluence and their exhibitionism. There is, though, something endearing—if, again, terribly current—about Beckham's tattooed homages to Brooklyn: the boy's name across his lower back, the guardian angel across his shoulder blades watching over him and the promise that 'Et Animus Liber' (Free Spirit) is to follow. As with so many football and fashion fusions, however, there is the hint of a design hiccup here: having told the *Sun* (10 May 2000) and *Esquire* (June 2000) that he intends to have the names of any other offspring likewise tattooed under the angel (presumably between 'Brooklyn' and it) where is 'Et Animus Liber' going to go unless it consciously spoils the symmetry of the design? The Latin could, writ small, go above the angel, but this might look messy peeking out from underneath Beckham's football shirt.

The Beckhams, for all their appropriation of Gucci, are the style descendants not of the Italian aristocracy but of the floral shirts and fast cars of Rodney Marsh and the gold-laden 'Big' Ron Atkinson. The marriage of Gucci in particular and football has a certain resonance. In an interview since his retirement in March 1999, Vinnie Jones the ex-Wimbledon player mentions that he used to have his clothes made for him at Mr Ed in Berwick Street, London (one of the notable 'flash Harry' Soho tailors), and that the Gucci–Versace style of young football celebrities leaves him cold as he's not a label but an 'if I see something I like I buy it' person (Alexander 1999). He since became the 'unofficial ambassador' for Yves Saint Laurent in the UK ('I just go in and tell them what I want and they make it'). Vinnie Jones has classically been pigeon-holed as the hard man of British football, an image immortalized by the snap of him squeezing Gazza's scrotum during a match and refined through many adverts and his acting debut in *Lock, Stock and Two Smoking Barrels*. His conscious distancing of himself from Gucci is especially significant because Gucci in particular epitomized the anomalous affiliation of a certain type of Italianate stylish dress and violence—British football hooligans in pristine Sergio Tacchini, Louis Vuitton and Gucci.

This is all a far cry from the veneration of Rivera, Verdi and Valentino Couture. What has happened as we start the new millennium is that football's fashion-conscious image has once again either dumbed down or got confused. With speculation about a forthcoming David Beckham module at the University of Staffordshire or the domination of the British Premiership by foreign players (in 2000 they numbered approximately 200), the identity of British football chic—whether it's related to the gentrification of the game through an association with Serie A and the rest of Europe or to the continued supremacy of home-grown football wide-boy fashions—is ambiguous. But then, with Vinnie Jones as Yves Saint Laurent's unofficial ambassador and jockey Frankie Dettori as its official one, perhaps the relationship between football and fashion in this country was doomed never to be taken too seriously.

ACKNOWLEDGEMENTS

I would like to thank Mick Conefrey, Stephen Gundle, Barry Langford and Zara Bruzzi for their assistance in the researching of this chapter.

NOTES

Reprinted with permission from Stella Bruzzi, "The Italian Job: Football, Fashion and That Sarong," in *Fashion Cultures: Theories, Explorations and Analysis,* ed. S. Bruzzi and P. Church Gibson (London and New York: Routledge, 2000), 286–97.

1. The Italian model would refute British Premiership claims that lower attendance figures coupled with soaring player salaries have forced ticket prices up: you can still get into a Serie A game for £10.
2. Ironically, Jim White maintains that Armani himself in the Chelsea FA Cup Final press pack 'appears to be wearing a shellsuit' (White 2000: 1).
3. Hamnett, at the time this comment was made, lived in Highbury.

13

FROM CATWALK TO CATALOGUE: MALE FASHION MODELS, MASCULINITY AND IDENTITY

Joanne Entwistle

INTRODUCTION

Modelling is not typically 'masculine' work. In *Glamorama,* Bret Easton Ellis's (1998: 110) tale of models and celebrities in New York, Victor, the central character and a young male model, meets an old friend, Lauren, and their encounter comically captures this:

"Where are you going?" asks Lauren. "Todd Oldham show," I sigh, "I'm in it." "Modeling," she says, "A man's job." "It's not as easy as it may look."

"Yeah, modeling's tough Victor," she says. "The only thing you need to be is on time. Hard work." "It is," I whine.

"It's a job where you need to know how to wear clothes?" she's asking.

"It's a job where you need to know how to— now let me get this straight—walk?"

"Hey, all I did was learn how to make the most of my looks."

"What about your mind?"

"Right," I snicker. "Like in this world"—I'm gesturing—"my mind matters more than my abs. Oh boy, raise your hand if you believe that."

Unlike other display work men do that involves being looked at (such as dancing or acting, for example) modelling is work that has men solely as objects of display—they merely have to 'be on time', 'walk' and 'wear clothes' but nothing more. This apparent lack of activity, the assumed passivity of modelling, make it seem an inappropriate job for a man since a 'real' man is supposed to 'do' rather than 'appear' (Berger 1972). However, the growth of male modelling in recent years, evidenced by the wide usage of male models selling fashion and non-fashion products, and the increasing number of male models represented by model agencies, seem to challenge these assumptions and suggest that, at least for younger men, modelling has lost some of its stigma as 'unmanly'. Since the 1980s there has been an expansion in male modelling, brought about as a result of the opening up of the 'men's markets' in retail and grooming products (Mort 1996; Nixon 1996). This expansion has continued apace in recent years: over the 1990s there was a considerable increase in the numbers of male models represented by model agencies in London and New York.[1] Today, modelling may even represent a very desirable job for some young men. Thus, while older prejudices surrounding male models still linger (as in Easton Ellis's quote above), it would seem that ideas about masculinity are shifting. Men born in the late 1970s and early 1980s have grown up surrounded by images of men selling all kinds of commodities, as well as celebrities, such as British soccer player David Beckham and the pop star Robbie Williams, who both display a quite feminine interest in fashion, the body, and their appearance.[2] It would seem, then, that the taboo that men should not be interested in fashion or in looking good has been eroded to some extent, at least for a younger generation of men.

Thus, one major indication of this change within contemporary understandings of masculinity has been an increased emphasis upon the commodified male body, which has become an established part of contemporary commercial culture. Since the 1970s, and perhaps more significantly, the early 1980s and the rise of the 'new man', attention in the media and popular culture has been focused upon the male body as something to be toned, dressed, groomed, and generally attended to as an object 'to be looked at.' Although, as Gill *et al.* (2000: 100) note, men have been presented as sexually desirable before, what is different today is that codes for the presentation of the male body 'give permission for it to be looked at and desired.' This, they argue, 'is a new phenomenon, which is culturally and historically specific' (ibid.: 100) and they point to a number of developments, which have helped establish a 'cultural milieu' in which a 'new man' could emerge and 'flourish' (ibid.: 102). These include the rise and influence of feminism and new social movements, which have put gender under scrutiny, the rise of the 'style press' such as *Arena, GQ,* and *The Face,* and the expansion of retailing for men. These developments have helped to promote a qualitative shift in representations of men: the displayed male bodies since the 1980s are unlike previous male bodies—young, muscular, sexy, self-consciously narcissistic, and offered for the gaze of women and heterosexual men in the new men's magazines and fashion magazines. This trend is significant because it suggests that the aesthetic appreciation and display of the male body, for a long time associated with gay men and black men, has extended into mainstream commercial culture to include white, heterosexual men. There is growing evidence to suggest that this expansion in images of men is having some impact upon young men, stimulating them to take an interest in how their bodies look (Gill *et al.* 2000). Younger men appear to invest in their bodies more than previous generations of men and this may also go some

way to explain why some of them consider modelling as a career. In 'this world,' as Victor in the quote above puts it, a man's 'abs' (or 'six-pack') have become important.

Taking these developments as evidence of a noticeable change in contemporary masculinities, it is my contention that male modelling is one prominent arena in which these transformations have been played out and can thus be examined. In this chapter, I examine the work of male fashion models in order to explore how young men at the fore of these developments negotiate their masculine identities. I have several overlapping questions about the nature of male modelling as work for men, which focus attention upon the body. The central question is: How is gender performed and reproduced through aesthetics and strategies of embodiment? Recent work on gender has demonstrated how it is inscribed on, and reproduced through, the body (see for example Butler 1990; Gatens 1996). For Butler, gender has no ontological reality; it is an effect of codes of performance, which are endlessly and compulsively repeated within the hegemonic framework of 'compulsory heterosexuality.' Gender, according to Butler, is in fact a product of endless incitements, which serve to maintain the appearance of 'difference.' However, despite their theoretical importance, Butler's arguments are largely abstract and fail to examine how gender is performed and reproduced at the mundane level of everyday social and cultural practices. This research extends Butler's work, focusing on how gender is reproduced in everyday situations by examining how bodies are constantly at work in reproducing themselves as gendered bodies through routine performances in 'situated practices' (Entwistle 2000a). In other words, I am interested in how bodies 'do' gender through various investments in, and techniques of, the body, and through particular embodied performances. Given the nature of male models' work, focusing as it does on appearance, I am particularly interested in how they manage and maintain their body. This raises two particular questions. First, in what ways do male models invest in the body; how do they come to see their body and how do they maintain it? Secondly, in what ways do they 'do' masculinity and how is it reproduced through particular bodily performances in a context, which, as I will argue, potentially disrupts dominant (heterosexuality) masculinity? I contend that male modelling opens up a contradiction between gender and work identities: fashion modelling is dominated by gay men, and is both 'feminine' and 'queer' work that contradicts, or potentially disrupts, what it means to be a 'real' man as defined by the 'regulatory framework' of heterosexuality (Butler 1990, 1993). I am interested in how male models manage this contradiction and orientate their body in order to adapt to the habitus (Bourdieu 1979/1984) of this sphere of work.

Through analysis of these two aspects of embodiment, I examine how, on the one hand, performances of masculinity by male models highlight some of the ways in which dominant masculinity has been (and continues to be) recoded or modified through strategies of embodiment. Unlike other forms of work for men, male modelling requires particular investments in the body: it has to be shaped in terms of a 'look' and thought of as a commodity. However, on the other hand, these performances of gender can also be said to reproduce dominant ideas about heterosexual masculinity, albeit in a modified form. In this way, male modelling sheds light on some contemporary problems and contradictions inherent in contemporary styles of masculinity as it is embodied through the actions and practices of these particular young men.

THE WORLD OF FASHION MODELLING

Before discussing these issues, I want to say a word or two about my sample and methodological approach. I have conducted interviews with twenty-two male fashion models and six bookers in five different agencies in New York and London. Bookers are the people who 'book' the models for jobs and effectively shape their careers. As influential people within the agencies, bookers were my key informants and it was largely through their co-operation that I was able to interview most of my models. In addition, over a two-month period, I spent some time at one of the London agencies, sitting in the open reception area, observing models and their bookers *in situ*. During this time I not only conducted many of my interviews, but I had the opportunity to observe models and bookers at work, witnessing the regular interactions between them, and also with photographers and clients who passed through the agency. On a number of occasions I was at the agency when clients were casting for models and this afforded me the opportunity to see how models deal with this routine part of their job. In addition to these accounts and observations, I also draw on the performances within the interview situation, itself a source of qualitative data. Interviews are performative: the interview situation is an interaction which, in terms of my research concerns, provides evidence of the ways in which male models 'do' masculinity in the context of a heterosexual encounter with me (a young, heterosexual woman). Finally, having befriended a couple of models, I have been able to maintain regular, informal contact over a longer period of time and this has enabled me to gain a long-term perspective on modelling.

The age range of my models was between fifteen and mid-forties; however the majority of my sample were between nineteen and twenty-two (only one model was fifteen, and only one in his mid-forties) and are known as 'New Faces' by the agencies because they are just starting out. The reason I have so many new faces has to do with access: younger models are more likely to stop by the agency where I've been recruiting for interviews and so are easier to get hold of than more successful models who are often travelling and rarely visit the agency. The young age of these men has to be factored into findings and analysis since their experiences of modelling will differ from those of older, more experienced models. So, too, will their relationship to their bodies, to which I shall now turn my attention.

THE BODY OF THE MODEL/ MODELLING THE BODY

Fashion male modelling demands a particular kind of body, one that is largely ascribed by genetics rather than attained through care and work.[3] The male fashion model's body is a very standard one in terms of size and shape: the required height for most agencies is between 180 and 191 cm (5 ft 11 in.–6 ft 3 in.) and the standard measurements are, usually: chest, 96–107 cm (38–42 in.), and waist, 76–81 cm (30–32 in.). Fashion models are, without exception, very slim, even skinny by everyday standards. One booker described male models as 'genetic freaks', although he meant this not in any pejorative sense, but as a description of these men as taller and leaner than most men in the west. Fashion models (male and female) can sometimes look quite unusual, with large or exaggerated features, such as a large mouth or very strong jaw line, although it is essential that these features are 'photogenic'. The quite distinctive bodily features required in male modelling make it something that only a very small minority are 'naturally' predisposed to. The model's body, his look, is the product of nature, although his 'beauty' is most definitely cultural, produced as 'beautiful' by being chosen and valued within the fashion modelling world. Modelling is an aesthetic practice producing some bodies as 'attractive' or 'beautiful', which is internally valorized within the modelling and fashion industries. These bodies are, by definition, rare or unusual. Since, as I have argued elsewhere (see Entwistle forthcoming),

this aesthetic discourse is internal to these industries, the definitions of male (and female) beauty produced do not necessarily correspond to definitions of beauty outside: fashion models are sometimes quite unattractive by conventional standards of beauty found outside fashion modelling. An obvious example of this is the rise of 'heroin chic', which, since the 1990s, has produced extremely thin bodies and often quite extreme or strange looks. This aesthetic for female models has attracted considerable criticism by the press and politicians in the UK, but can also be found, less controversially, in contemporary aesthetics in male modelling since the 1990s as well. The lack of correspondence between the male fashion model's 'beauty' and ideas of male beauty outside is evidenced by the negative reactions, particularly from female students, to footage of male models in the seasonal runway shows which I have shown in class.

The very specific bodily requirements of fashion modelling may account, at least in part, for the surprising lack of body maintenance by a significant number of the models I talked to. Most male fashion models have to do very little to their body in order to become a model. However, age is a factor here since fashion models are very young compared to 'lifestyle' models: they are generally men who have a naturally low body weight and may therefore not need to diet or exercise to maintain it. In a number of interviews some models referred to their age when discussing their body: for example, some argued they are 'lucky' in that they do not need to 'work out' or watch what they eat as they have a fast metabolism. A couple of younger models noted that their body is still changing, as they are still not yet through puberty. Others were aware that as they got older they might have to watch their weight more carefully. Whether these descriptions of the body are entirely true or not, it is interesting that so many male models drew on the notion of the 'natural' body rather than admit to having 'cultivated' their bodies. This may be, in part, a rhetorical strategy to obscure or distance themselves from associations with the cultivation of the body, which might be construed as 'vanity'. This attitude was prevalent among the British models, as discussed in more detail below.

A small number of models did describe how they had to watch what they ate to keep their weight down, and a couple of models had been told by their booker to lose some weight. Only a few models told me they had to 'work out' and of these, the majority were not from the UK. Indeed, many of the British models I spoke to laughed when I asked them about exercise and gym membership and seemed almost proud to say they had never been inside a gym: for example, one model, Simon (in London), told me, 'I don't go the gym, I keep as far away from it as I can.' This attitude, prevalent in the UK, may explain why the London-based models tend to have skinny and 'undeveloped' bodies compared with many of their US counterparts. Indeed, this difference in body styles was noted by a booker in a London agency, who described how UK men are much less sporty than men from the US, South Africa, or Australia, countries renowned for active, outdoor, and sporty lifestyles. According to him, models from these countries have better bodies than UK models and are therefore more likely to do underwear or swimwear jobs. Of the models who do work out, there is still a real concern to maintain a very slim look. Contrary to the perception of male models as muscular 'hunks', the fashion aesthetic favours a very lean look, with some, but not too much muscle, and definitely not 'developed'. 'Fitness' models, for sportswear, may be quite large and developed, but fashion models are advised to maintain a very slim silhouette. Some models described how they had to ensure they did not build up too much, and this might run counter to what they would like to do with their body if they were not a model: for instance, one of these models, Ben, described being a little annoyed to have been told by his booker not to 'build' his arms when he told her he would like to do this.

A cultural variation between UK models and others in terms of body management and aesthetics was also reflected in attitudes to tanning. In New York quite a number of models were concerned to acquire a good colour over the summer and one New Zealand model used sun-beds while in London to acquire a tan. In contrast, the London models took great pride in their pallid complexion and skinny, undeveloped bodies. Indeed, quite a significant number of the UK models claimed to pay little or no attention to how they look, something which may be linked to a particular 'laddish' performance amongst the London models. Two models, Simon and Robbie, interviewed together at a casting in their London agency, typify this. When I referred to Robbie's stubble in many of the images and asked him if he cultivated it, his reply was, 'No, generally I just leave it, because I am so fucking lazy.' When I asked them to talk about their body maintenance, they laughed and joked about their lack of it and appealed, once again, to the 'natural' body:

Q: Do you take much care with your hair and skin?
Robbie: I've always had good skin. I dunno, no I don't. I smoke far too much, I drink far too much [chuckles], I do fuck all exercise. (You don't go to the gym at all?) No.
Q: (to Simon): What about you?
Simon: I don't go the gym, I keep as far away from it as I can. I do the same as Robbie: I smoke and drink too much. And I don't have any problems with my skin.
Q: You are both very lucky then, are you not?
Simon: Yeah.

This cultural variation can, to some extent, be explained in terms of a difference in attitudes toward the cultivation of appearance between models in the UK and the USA. In the UK there is a reticence to appear to take too much interest in your appearance and to appearing like 'you love yourself'. Another London model, Gary, exhibited this attitude when he quite forcefully condemned the sort of men who use gyms. He told me he used to work out 'about four times a week' at home before becoming a model, but after moving to London, he no longer has the space to do this. Although describing himself early on in the interview as 'a bit of a poser', he was critical of any public signs of narcissism and gave this as his reason for disliking gyms:

> I haven't got the motivation to go down to the gym 'cos I hate people like that. You know, if you want to pose and love yourself in front of your own mirror in your own bedroom, that's fair enough. But when you're doing it in front of other people it just makes me feel sick. So that is why I'm not really a great fan of gyms. I go swimming from time to time.

The distinction he draws between the private posing which he deems 'fair enough' and the public posing he describes as making him 'feel sick' seems strange given that his occupation as a male model means he must pose 'in front of other people' all the time. If he sees 'posing' as part of the job of being a model, his relationship to it is obviously quite ambivalent. Comments may be read as a rhetorical strategy to disavow the content of much of his work and perhaps also his enjoyment of it. However, there is more going on here: vanity, posing, and 'loving yourself' are considered moral failings, as Gary's comment indicates. It was frequently noted by the models that people assume models to be narcissistic and arrogant, assumptions these young men try hard to debunk. It would seem, however, that these are particularly 'feminine' failings, since many models described how they encountered female models that were arrogant and vain (or 'love themselves'). Thus, it could be argued that these particular models are keen to distance themselves from any signs of narcissism, and from any possible 'feminization' that may be associated with their work, by disavowing body maintenance altogether. This 'laddish' attitude may therefore be a moral performance to try not to appear as 'vain' or too 'feminine', produced for the benefit of the interview. It may also be read

as part of the models' overall performance of 'masculinity', produced through denial of the overtly 'feminine' aspects of the job.

However, these men may also be in denial about the attention they actually do pay to how they look, since how they look is essential to their careers as models. Although male models may not always be dieting or exercising, this does not mean they are oblivious to their appearance and do not work at it in some way. Most, if not all, models, are aware of the importance of cultivating or maintaining a particular look and develop some distance from their body and the image, objectifying both as part of their career development. Of particular significance to many models, in terms of shaping a look, is hair. Many models described having their hair regularly cut at top salons in London or New York, usually for free in return for modelling. In one instance, Ben, who had very short hair when he was 'discovered', had been told by his booker that he could not grow it longer since this was felt to be 'working' for him at present. However, as hair trends change, canny models will adapt their hair too. Over the time I was conducting the interviews, a number of the models described how many top models in the major shows and campaigns were wearing their hair quite long. In some cases, the models said they were growing their hair to keep pace with this trend and help them get work over the summer, when the castings for major campaigns take place. Gary, for example, said, 'I am growing it 'cos long hair is very in at the moment. Therefore, I think it will benefit me 'cos I'll be more versatile.' Since hair is very malleable, it is one aspect of appearance that can be frequently changed as part of an ongoing process of self-promotion. When asked about how he can cultivate a look appropriate for more fashion (as opposed to commercial) work, Gary returned to the issue of hair, noting that one can transform oneself with different hairstyles: 'A lot of it is to do with the hair at the moment . . . long hair is quite in at the moment. If I have hair coming over like this [pulls hair over his face] it changes the appearance completely.' The aim here is to get a more weird or 'edgy' fashion look, as opposed to the 'clean-cut' look required for commercial work. 'Edgy' is the description often given as appropriate to high fashion: it is 'weird' or 'quirky', as opposed to the more conventionally good looks required for commercial work.

A more radical story of self-transformation was told to me by Tony, an older, experienced model based in New York, who told me he was planning to meet with his booker the following week to totally overhaul his image: his hair, clothes, and the images in his 'book' (his portfolio of images). It was, he said, a 'strategic' way to separate himself from 'all the other models coming through.' He was considering reverting to an earlier hairstyle from a few months previously, a photograph of which he showed me, and described as 'mo-ho', i.e. 'mohican'. The look he was aiming for was 'edgy'. He intended to try this look for a month or two to see if the 1980s made a return to fashion (which it did in the Fall and Spring 2000–1, although I lost track of this model and therefore do not know if this hairstyle was a success as a result).

While such changes in image may be required to renew a model who has been around for a few years, it takes quite a lot of effort and a considerable degree of commitment on the part of the model to reinvent himself so completely. Such a total overhaul demands effort not only in terms of thinking about one's image and making changes, but also in terms of the images in his 'book', which also have to be changed to reflect the new look. A model's book is his main tool for self-promotion and it will contain his best jobs and strongest images. When a model starts out he will only have a few Polaroids to take to clients along with some 'tests' with photographers. These give the model a chance to practise in front of the camera, try out with photographers used by the agency and collect some images for his book. However, as a model gains valuable work experience, his book will be made up of prestigious jobs, good editorial and commercial work, and any campaigns: experienced models do not do 'tests'. If the model's appearance changes significantly, as in Tony's case, a whole series of new 'tests' will need doing to update his book—a considerable investment in terms of time, which he was prepared to make to reinvent himself.

Such an active shaping of one's image requires the model to see his body as a commodity. The model's body is *the* commodity traded by the agency, model, and clients: a model is booked because he has the right look for the client. This point I will return to in a moment. However, important also in male modelling is 'personality.' Many models and bookers argued that male models must be 'nice guys'—friendly, confident, and professional—if they are to become successful. A very arrogant, bad-tempered male model will not last long in a business that is so competitive. In contrast, bookers and models described how female models can get by on looks: a number of very successful female models have reputations for very bad behaviour, which would not be tolerated of male models. As one booker in New York, James, put it, it is 'easy enough to get a good-looking guy booked: what is harder is getting him rebooked', and this will only happen if he has shown himself to be decent and professional. James explained this discrepancy between male and female models in terms of the different values placed on male and female beauty, which has women's beauty more highly valued.[4] As this booker put it to me, guys are not meant to be 'too good-looking' and should not be rewarded for it.

However, while the emphasis on 'personality' is stronger in the case of male models, having the right look/body is still paramount, making modelling a quite unique occupation for men in its total focus on the body. Of course, modelling is not the only occupation in which the body is traded as part of the job: acting and dancing, as well as prostitution, are the other obvious examples. What is different about modelling is the degree of emphasis on the body: in modelling the body is the foremost object of the model's career and his identity as a model. An actor may shape his body as part of his career development, either in order to land work, or as part of his job to develop a particular character, as in the case of Brad Pitt's muscular and toned body for the film *Fight Club,* which he fashioned especially for the role. However, the acting body's appearance is part of a larger commodity transaction, namely acting ability (or celebrity), and alone is not generally enough to ensure an actor's success. Similarly, the dancer's body is a primary tool in his career but, here again, it is shaped as part of a broader concern to make it move and perform in particular ways. In both instances, the body is a body to be looked at, which may also be eroticized in the process, but this attention, and the possible libidinal excesses provoked by it, are by-products of a body that is *also doing something.*

Mulvey's (1975) classic analysis of the female body in Hollywood realist films argues that the woman's body functions primarily 'to be looked at' and in ways that frequently halt the flow of the narrative to allow for erotic contemplation. Men's bodies are rarely photographed as disruptions in the narrative (although, of course, this does not mean they may not sometimes be read in this way). However, the contemporary male model's body displayed in fashion advertisements for Calvin Klein underwear and some commercial advertisements, such as the Diet Coke television advertisement (in which numerous women huddle around a window to watch a male worker outside take off his T-shirt and drink a can of Diet Coke), is a body which functions as a pure (and often erotic) image. This makes modelling a unique occupation for men and this is one reason, I argue, that it serves as a cultural marker of a new kind of masculinity, one that is more self-consciously narcissistic and erotic.

Getting models to talk about this objectification of their body was difficult, if not impossible, in some cases. Most models were quite inarticu-

late when it came to talking about their relationship to the body and some seemed embarrassed when asked about their images and how it feels to be looked at all the time. It is also the case that being looked at constantly becomes so taken for granted that it is not consciously reflected upon by models. The most visible and ubiquitous object, the body of the model, is everywhere, and yet it is almost impossible for models to describe what it feels like to be looked at and objectified in this way. Having said this, I suspect that for the majority of male models, the fact that their bodies, and indeed, their sexuality, are commodified is not a problem: most spoke of enjoying their work and, although pay is not nearly as high as many people imagine, they are paid well enough most of the time and get to travel to interesting places as well. Ben's comments on the commodification of his body probably speak for a good many of the models I interviewed:

> I think if the money was a lot less and the images weren't so great, you would realize you were a commodity, but it's really weird because it's like, Model's 1 is using you, but you then you're using Model's 1, but then the editorials and campaigns are using you, but then you are using them because you're getting so much money off them for doing nothing, posing in front of a camera!

SEXUALITY AT WORK

Having examined the ways in which male models invest in their bodily appearance, I want to consider another important aspect of their embodiment by examining the ways they 'do' masculinity through particular bodily performances in a context which, as I will argue, potentially undermines the conventions of dominant (heterosexual) masculinity. In contrast to increasing numbers of professional women, who must muffle their sexuality at work (see Entwistle 1997, 2000b), and other men whose sexuality is a repressed feature of their work (Collier

1998), male models are sexualized beings at work. Indeed, a model's career prospects may depend upon his ability to project sexuality at work in routine day-to-day interactions: as one model put it to me, models are often asked by a photographer to give 'sex, sex, sex'. Thus, male models have to adapt to a visual arena in which they are the focus of attention that can be quite desirous. Models frequently told me stories of how they were the recipients of sexual advances while at work on the part of the photographer, stylist, or other onlooker. The body of the model, exposed to the gaze of bookers, photographers, and stylists, is an erotic object. The visual arena in which they work is orchestrated predominantly by gay and bisexual men, since most of the bookers, clients, photographers, and stylists in the fashion industry are either openly gay or bisexual, or are commonly thought to be, even if they are not 'out'. Some of the most powerful players within fashion today, such as Calvin Klein, have a reputation as bisexual, while other big names are thought to be gay by models, even though they may have wives and children.

The role played by the homoerotic gaze in defining the codes of masculinity stretches back centuries, as George L. Mosse (1996) has suggested. Since the 1980s, gay photographers, stylists, and designers have been very much at the fore in changing representations of masculinity (Bordo 1999). The body aesthetics of fashion have served to produce gay aesthetics of the male body that have become part of mainstream commercial culture and the iconography of contemporary masculinities. Thus, while Bordo celebrates the intervention of men such as Calvin Klein for producing images that can be enjoyed by heterosexual women, frequently the look for male fashion models does not correspond to dominant ideas of heterosexual male beauty outside the world of fashion modelling: it is often young, boyish, and quite 'feminine', with features such as a large mouth favoured. These looks are quite different from the style of male models in commercial and 'lifestyle'

advertising, which favour a more conventional 'masculine' look that is generally older and more ruggedly 'masculine'.

However, in contrast, male models are predominantly heterosexual. The majority of the models I interviewed self-identified as heterosexual in the course of the interview, referring to their sexuality in comments unsolicited from me. For example, one model told me he was only doing it 'for the girls', while other models told me about their girlfriends. In a couple of interviews, the model alluded to his sexual identity through references to the gay men he encounters at work, sometimes making quite homophobic remarks (for example, telling me that they don't like 'them' but have to 'get on with it'). One model, Gary, summed up this situation:

A lot of people think male models are gay. But not at all, a lot of male models are really big lads if you know what I mean: they want to go out and get laid and whatever. This is where people misinterpret it. A lot of the bookers and stylists and photographers are the gay ones, it's not the models.

The domination of gay men, and the control they have within modelling and fashion, raises interesting questions in terms of the ways in which these (largely straight) male models negotiate their masculinity in an environment where they are frequently the objects of a gay gaze. I therefore argue that male modelling is work with a 'queer' dimension, and the work identity of the male model is, potentially at least, a 'queer' one (Butler 1993). Modelling 'queers' masculinity because of the way it confounds the conventions and expectations of dominant heterosexual masculinity. On the one hand, male models are frequently called upon to perform heterosexual masculinity through poses, gestures, and dress, in the production of images that are often hypermasculine. On the other hand, beyond the image, references to male models as 'poofs' or 'poncers' (see, for example, Freedman in *Guardian*,

March 5, 2002) demonstrate the assumptions people outside the fashion industry have of these men. A male model's 'masculinity', defined as it is in terms of sexuality framed within the 'regulatory framework' of heterosexuality, is compromised or undermined by his work identity, which is associated with homosexuality and effeminacy, and this may partly explain why so many models told me of their reluctance to tell people they model for a living. Given this, how do models handle this contradiction between gender identity and work identity? How do they manage the potential 'threat' posed to their heterosexual masculinity by their work? I want to examine these questions by exploring the accounts given by models of their interactions at work, focusing on the ways in which they describe their performances in routine situations. I also want to consider the performances of gender witnessed in my observations of models at work and in the interview. Two narratives commonly recurred in the interviews and detail two performances drawn on by models to handle their encounters with gay men at work, such as photographers or clients. Both narratives illustrate how male models are sexualized in the process of their work as models and how they respond to this accordingly.

FLIRTING

The first narrative concerns the way in which models interact with those they work with, especially the clients they meet at castings. I am calling this narrative 'flirting' because it describes how models attempt to win over clients in order to increase their chances of landing work. Models, especially new models, spend a considerable part of their work life going to castings, where they meet clients casting for shoots or new campaigns. At any casting there may be twenty, thirty, or many more models, and the issue is how to stand out from the crowd. Canny or 'cynical' models say they exploit their good looks and sexuality by flirting to charm clients; indeed, to make the clients 'fancy' them. This

inevitably means a model has to flirt with male as well as female clients, using his sexuality either by 'queering' it or by overperforming heterosexuality. Simon, a London model, is one such model who is happy to flirt with clients, male and female. Indeed, he demonstrated for me in the interview how he interacts with clients at castings according to their gender. If the client is a woman he will give her a very firm handshake and throw her a direct and confident gaze. If the client is a man, he assumes that he is gay and adopts the stereotypical image of the gay man, camping up his performance, with limp wrists, fey manner, and effeminate voice. Although he claimed not to do this himself, Gary, a model in London, also described this:

> *Gary:* Some of the guys play up to the gay thing, you know so they get the job: they go to the casting [puts on a camp voice], 'oh hi, yeah,' make their voice a bit higher, or whatever, be a bit kinda like that [strikes an effeminate pose]. But it's not really me to do that. If they don't like my look, you know, then they're not going to use me.
> *Q:* So you're not going to play to it?
> *Gary:* Yeah, of course not.

Other models similarly described how they used their good looks as a tool to charm clients, regardless of gender. James said he had no qualms about using his sexuality to get work and spoke quite openly and confidently about being comfortable with his sexuality as a commodity. Although he drew the line at nudity, as do most of the models I spoke to, often the images in a model's book will be quite sexual. On shoots models are required to act sexy by photographers and, here again, they may adopt a flirtatious performance with their photographer. In some cases, models talk about flirting with photographers, especially big names in the industry, many of whom are men reputed to be homosexual. Photographers can be very influential in promoting a new model and thus it makes sense to win them over by being sexy and flirtatious. Here, the aim is, as Simon put it to me, to 'keep them guessing' as to their sexuality. While I have no observational evidence of these performances in the clients' casting or on shoots, I observed models flirting with others at the agency and also found myself on the receiving end of these flirtatious performances in the interview itself, as models would often joke and banter with me in the course of the interview.

It would seem, therefore, that flirting represents a positive adaptation by some models to the sexualized nature of their work. These men are realistic about the work and its erotic content and are not afraid of the gay gaze. This reminds me very much of David Beckham, who has appeared in some highly homoerotic shoots in magazines, such as *Arena Homme Plus* (Summer 2000), and talks of being very comfortable with the idea of himself as a gay icon.[5]

SEXUAL DANGER

The second narrative I call 'sexual danger' because it describes instances where models find themselves in sexual situations that are threatening or problematic. These situations generally occur on shoots, where models may be the recipients of unwanted erotic attention from either stylists or photographers, all of them male (although one model did describe how his booker made sexual advances). Almost all the models I spoke to have been on the receiving end of such attention and it would seem that this is accepted as an occupational hazard. Given the highly sexualized nature of the relationship between model and photographer, as well as the potentially sexual encounter between the stylist and model, it is not surprising that these situations occur. Moreover, as discussed above, there is much room for misunderstanding if models flirt or in other ways use their sexuality while on the job. Narratives of sexual danger describe what happens when the situation becomes untenable for the model. Models told me how they had been 'felt up' by stylists while being dressed, or been asked to strip down or wear

provocative or revealing clothes by the stylist or photographer. For example, Simon told of how he once arrived on a shoot, to be handed a set of wings and nothing else to wear. A couple of models in New York described this behaviour on the part of photographers as 'pushing the envelope' (pushing things a bit too far). Indeed, one model made a very particular point of complaining about the sexual advances of certain photographers, describing his anger at being asked to 'play with himself' on a shoot so as to make himself semi-erect.

Sometimes these instances are contained by the model's insisting on the boundaries within which he wants to work: Simon insisted on wearing a pair of trunks and was given them. A model may also threaten to call his agency to complain if he feels the behaviour is inappropriate. A more radical response came from Emanuel, a model in New York, who described how he handled the unwanted attentions of his desirous booker by punching the wall next to his head. However, sometimes the advances are made after the shoot and may be less overt, implied rather than made directly. Models told me how they handle shoots where they believe the photographer or stylist fancies them: they described imaginary telephone calls to friends in which they brag about a sexual conquest with a woman the night before, or talking to their real girlfriends. Gary described this clearly:

> *Gary:* I've got the vibe, yeah, but I make it quite clear that, you know, if they start I just make a phone call, pretend to make a phone call to my mate sayin' 'Yeah I got laid last night, gorgeous bird', and then they get the message. It happened once and I did do that yeah.
>
> *Q:* What happened to make you reach for the telephone?
>
> *Gary:* I was getting changed and he said, 'Oh you can get changed here if you want.' I don't really care, like. It was him, me, and a girl and a guy so although he wouldn't have done anything I went to the loo and just as I was coming out, he was coming in to the loo and I've noticed, I dunno, I took note that he'd gone

to the toilets about five minutes before that. When I come out he's like, 'Oh I'm sorry' and he kinda like brushed up against me and I am like, right, so I got on the phone.

Q: And made that call?

Gary: Yeah, yeah, I haven't been home since last night.

However, sometimes it may come down to saying something directly to the photographer. Byron described how he handled such situations either by just telling them 'Look, I'm not that way inclined' or '... in the politest way, to fuck off.' Some may go as far as to describe their distaste at these experiences, possibly to ensure that I am in no doubt over their heterosexuality. It would seem, therefore, that models manage these situations by overperforming heterosexuality, in an attempt to reassert their masculine heterosexual identity.

These two narratives may be told by the same model in some form or another: in other words, models may be happy to flirt at work but may also describe situations where the sexual nature of the interaction goes far beyond anything they feel comfortable with. In these situations they may switch from a 'queer' performance to one in which they reassert their heterosexual masculinity. In this way, these performances describe two strategies used by models which, in the case of the first narrative, demonstrate how far removed modelling is from more conventional masculine occupations which do not routinely involve heterosexual men flirting with gay men. However, the second narrative demonstrates how the sexuality of modelling can sometimes threaten a model's heterosexuality, which is reclaimed by overperforming it.

CONCLUSION

To conclude, I have noted how modelling has opened up to men in recent years, affording some young men the opportunity to undertake work that has previously been regarded as 'feminine'. It is work that highlights some important directions within contemporary culture that have taken mainstream masculinity into spheres of activity, in this case new forms of work, which are unconventional and which challenge the straitjacket of conventional white masculinity. It is work that has white, heterosexual men sexualized and commodified in ways that have been associated with women, and to some extent with gay and black men. In addition, it is work which demands men to be sexual beings at work and places them at the centre of attention as erotic objects. Through analysis of the various strategies of embodiment employed by male models, I have argued that these men have to adapt to a habitus which has traditionally been both 'feminine' and 'queer'. This work is not without its problems and contradictions and heterosexual masculinity may be reasserted or overperformed in some situations. Being a male model may involve greater investment in how the body looks, although this investment is often downplayed or disavowed by models, especially those working in London. It would seem that, for some models at least, appearing to care about your appearance is still taboo: either unmanly or too arrogant. It is also the case that while this work has extended or challenged, to some extent, the dimensions of dominant heterosexual masculinity, this asserts itself through the ways in which many models perform their identities while at work, with clients, photographers in particular, and especially with regard to gay men with whom they routinely work.

NOTES

Reprinted with permission from Joanne Entwistle, "From Catwalk to Catalogue: Male Models, Masculinity and Identity," in *Cultural Bodies: Ethnography and Theory*, ed. H. Thomas and J. Ahmed (Cambridge and Oxford: Blackwell, 2004), 55–75.

1. Evidence of this was provided by model agencies, who said they represented significantly more male models in the late 1990s than previously.

2. For example, Beckham is famous for changing his hairstyle (first to a skinhead in 2000 then a mohican in Summer 2001) and this always attracts the attention of the press, who see it as evidence of his vanity. See C. Porter, 'A Cut Above,' *Guardian,* May 25, 2001, for a discussion.

3. There are a number of distinctions between fashion models used in fashion shows and campaigns, such as Versace or Calvin Klein, and commercial or 'lifestyle' models, for furniture, beer, and the other commodities. Fashion modelling uses very young models (teens to early twenties) and some of these may be described as 'edgy' i.e. unusual or distinctive. Commercial models are older (late twenties to thirties or forties) and may be more conventionally 'good-looking'. Fashion models may cross over into commercial work, especially as they get older, but commercial models generally do not do fashion. This project is based on interviews with fashion models.

4. These values are reflected in pay. Modelling represents one of the few occupations in which women are paid significantly more than men (pornography is another). A standard commercial day rate for women starts around £5,000, while shows pay between £5,000 and £20,000. The figures for men are closer to £2,000 for commercial work and a few hundred to perhaps £1,000 for a show appearance.

5. See *OK!* issue 228, September 2000.

14

THE TRANSVESTITE CONTINUUM: LIBERACE–VALENTINO–ELVIS

Marjorie Garber

You don't understand. It's not that there's something extra that makes a superstar. It's that there's something missing.

George Michael[1]

Madonna announced to her screaming fans: 'I want you all to know that there are only three real men on this stage—me and my two backup girls!'

Liz Smith, 'Gossip'[2]

The television show *Saturday Night Live* once featured a mock game show called '*Quien es mas macho?*' in which contestants vied with each other to make gender distinctions. '*Quien es mas macho?*' 'Fernando Lamas or Ricardo Montalban?' In Laurie Anderson's avant-garde film, *Home of the Brave,* this became a contest to distinguish between two objects: '*Que es mas macho?*' Which *thing* is more macho? Pineapple or knife? Toaster or convertible? The choices here were deliberately self-parodic; it was culture itself that was being gendered. And the joke was further perpetrated by Anderson herself, deftly deploying a special microphone, or 'audio mask,' that lowered her voice to a 'male' register. She appeared live onstage in a tuxedo-like black suit and white shirt, but within the film, for one startling moment, she cross-cross-dressed to play Eve in a gold-lamé skirt. *Que es mas macho?*

I have tried both to theorize the question of transvestism and to demarcate certain structures that seem, sometimes surprisingly, to characterize or accompany it. The more I have

studied transvestism and its relation to representation the more I have begun to see it, oddly enough, as in many ways normative: as a condition that very frequently accompanies theatrical representation when theatrical self-awareness is greatest. Transvestite theatre from Kabuki to the Renaissance English stage to the contemporary drag show is not—or not only—a recuperative structure for the social control of sexual behaviour, but also a critique of the possibility of 'representation' itself.

In order to make such large claims for transvestism as a social and theoretical force—in order to argue, as I have, that there can be no culture without the transvestite, because the transvestite marks the entry into the Symbolic—I need to test out the *boundaries* of transvestism, to see it or read it in places other than where it is most obvious. I need to argue, in other words, for an *unconscious* of transvestism, for transvestism as a language that can be read, and double-read, like a dream, a fantasy, or a slip of the tongue. In the domain of theatre, which we have seen to be the self-reflexive locus of much transvestite activity,

I want to hypothesize what might be called 'un-marked' transvestism, to explore the possibility that some entertainers who do not overtly claim to be 'female impersonators,' for example, may in fact signal their cross-gender identities onstage, and that this quality of crossing—which is fundamentally related to other kinds of boundary-crossing in their performances—can be more powerful and seductive than explicit 'female impersonation,' which is often designed to confront, scandalize, titillate, or shock.

But first, let me discuss for a moment the 'normative' case and the issues it raises. One clear space in which to explore the power of transvestism as theatricality is in contemporary popular culture, specifically the pop-rock scene, where cross-dressing, 'androgyny', and gender-bending have become almost de rigueur. David Bowie, Boy George, Kiss, Tiny Tim, Twisted Sister, Siouxie Sioux, the New York Dolls, from glam- and glitter-rock to heavy metal, from the seventies to the nineties, cross-dressing has meant deliberately and brashly—and politically—calling into question received notions of 'masculine' and 'feminine', straight and gay, girl and woman, boy and man. To give one random but suggestive example, Dee Snider, male lead singer of Twisted Sister, was voted one of the worst-dressed *women* of the year in 1984.[3]

When Boy George, in full make-up, wig, and flowing skirts, accepted a Grammy Award in 1984, he remarked to the television audience, 'Thank you, America, you've got style and taste, and you know a good drag queen when you see one.'[4] When he published a book of clothing patterns, complete with make-up instructions, it was immediately snapped up—by his *female* fans.[5] Let us agree to call Boy George (né George O'Dowd) a *marked transvestite,* a cross-dresser whose clothing seems deliberately and obviously at variance with his anatomical gender assignment.

Consider another telling instance of marked transvestism. At an event billed as 'The First Annual Female Impersonator of the Year Contest'

one of the broadcast commentators was short, plain, comic actress Ruth Buzzi, former star of *Laugh-In*. As the curvaceous, stunningly coiffed and made-up contestants in their glittering gowns emerged, on-camera, from a door prominently marked 'Men', and the camera panned back and forth between them and Buzzi, the audience was tacitly invited to speculate on the nature of 'womanhood' or 'femininity'. This may well rank as a species of producer misogyny, but it also frames a question: if 'woman' is culturally constructed, and if female impersonators are *conscious* constructors of artificial and artifactual femininity, how does a 'female impersonator' differ from a 'woman'? The question seems both ludicrous and offensive, but its theoretical and social implications are large and important. Female impersonators are often accused of misogyny (and regularly deny the charge), but in the female impersonator, the feminist debate about essentialism versus constructedness finds an unexpected, parodic, and unwelcome test.

Here is one drag queen's answer, describing the heyday of the London drag balls of the sixties: 'there was a definite distinction then as there is now between the drag queens, who enjoyed masquerading as women, and the sex changes [that is, transsexuals], who regarded themselves, and were regarded, as real women.'[6]

'Masquerading' versus 'real' women. It makes sense that transsexuals, who have invested so much in anatomical alteration, should insist that the ground of reality is the feminized body: the body undergoing hormone treatment to develop breasts and hips, undergoing surgery to translate the penis into a vagina. But this binarism between 'masquerading' and 'real women' has been at the centre of disputes and discussions among psychoanalytic critics, feminist film theorists, and, most recently, lesbian or self-described 'queer theorists'. Drawing on Joan Riviere's classic essay (1986), 'Womanliness as a Masquerade', and on Lacan's revision and extension of that essay in 'The Signification of the Phallus', theorists have sought to define 'woman' as a construct that depends, for reasons social and political as well as erotic, upon masks and masquerade.

Riviere had argued not only that 'women who wish for masculinity may put on a mask of womanliness to avert anxiety and the retribution feared from men', but also that it was impossible to separate womanliness *from* masquerade:

> The reader may now ask how I define womanliness or where I draw the line between genuine womanliness and the 'masquerade'. My suggestion is not, however, that there is any such difference; whether radical or superficial, they are the same thing.[7]

The woman constructed by culture is, then, according to Riviere, already an impersonation. Womanliness is mimicry, is masquerade.

Here is Jacques Lacan, rewriting Riviere to describe 'display in the human being,' not just in the woman:

> the fact that femininity finds its refuge in this mask, by virtue of the fact of the [repression] inherent in the phallic mark of desire, has the curious consequence of making *virile* display in the human being itself seem feminine. ('The Signification of the Phallus', 1997: 291)

What does this mean? Is it that *all* display is feminine, because it is artifactual and displaced, a sign of anxiety and lack? Or that virile display *becomes* feminine because in being displayed it exhibits its own doubt? Or is it that the phallus is that which cannot be displayed? As we will see, the upshot of each of these three scenarios is the same.

As the Lacanian analyst Eugénie Lemoine-Luccioni (1983) explains, in a passage we have already noticed in connection with 'fetish envy', 'if the penis was the phallus, men would have no need of feathers or ties or medals ... Display [parade], just like the masquerade, thus betrays a flaw: no one has the phallus.'[8]

In the same essay ('The Signification of the Phallus') Lacan had talked about the relations

between the sexes as governed by three terms, not two: 'to have' the phallus, which is what, in fantasy, *men* do; 'to be' the phallus, the object of desire, which is what, in fantasy, *women* do; and the intervening term, 'to seem'. This intervention, of 'seeming' (or 'appearing'), substituted for 'having', and protecting against the threat of loss, is, precisely, the place of the transvestite. So that, in psychoanalytic terms, the transvestite does represent a third space, a space of representation, even within a psychic economy in which *all* positions are fantasies. The theatrical transvestite literalizes the anxiety of phallic loss. The overdetermination of phallic jokes, verbal and visual, that often accompany transvestism onstage, is a manifestation of exactly this strategy of reassurance for anxiety through artefactual overcompensation.

Lacan's suggestion about 'virile display' *seeming* feminine is a key one, because it is precisely this 'curious consequence', paradoxical as it may seem, that characterizes the 'transvestite effect' in what I am calling 'unmarked transvestites.' For while it is easy to speak of the power of transvestite display in figures like David Bowie, Boy George, and Annie Lennox, these overt cross-dressers, 'marked transvestites', may in fact merely literalize something that is more powerful when masked or veiled—that is, when it remains unconscious.

I would now like to turn to three figures from popular culture in whom a certain consternation of gender is, to use a distinction from Roland Barthes, 'received' but not 'read.'[9] ('The rhetorical or latent signified,' says Barthes, discussing the ideology of fashion, is 'the essential paradox of connoted signification: it is, one might say, a signification that is *received* but not *read*.') This is another opportunity to look at rather than *through* the transvestite, in this case by regarding the unconscious of transvestism as a speaking symptom, a language of clothing which is, tacitly, both dress and address. Unlike professional female impersonators, or comedians who affect travesty for particular theatrical ends (Milton

Berle, Flip Wilson as Geraldine, Dana Carvey as the Church Lady), these three performers do not think of themselves as transvestites. But—as we will see—the way they are received and discussed in the media, and, increasingly, the way they emphasize their own trademark idiosyncrasies of dress in response to audience interest all suggest that the question of cross-dressing, whether overt or latent, is central to their success, and even to the very question of stardom.

My first example may strike you as a bit too obvious to be considered completely unmarked, but he is, I think, at the origin of a certain theatrical worrying of exactly that borderline. I refer, of course, to the figure 'known variously as Mr. Showmanship, the Candelabra Kid, Guru of Glitter, Mr. Smiles, The King of Diamonds, and Mr. Boxoffice', and described as 'undoubtedly America's most beloved entertainer'[10]: Liberace.

Liberace, pianist, singer, tap dancer, and fashion plate, clearly regarded himself as a direct influence upon the pop stars of the eighties, citing Prince, Michael Jackson, Boy George, and Madonna as among those who had learned from him about 'escapism and fantasy'.[11] 'There was a time', he reminisced, 'when one woman might say to another, "May I borrow your lipstick?" Now, it's not unusual for one male rocker to say to another, "May I borrow your eyeliner?" And practically no man is above borrowing his best friend's skin bronzer' (Liberace 1986: 222). 'I was the first to create shock waves', he said. 'For me to wear a simple tuxedo onstage would be like asking Marlene Dietrich to wear a housedress.'[12]

The genial campiness of these remarks offers the retrospective view of a survivor. Yet Liberace's crossover career in fact tested boundaries with a singular combination of business acumen and purported self-revelation. Strikingly illustrating the notion I have developed above of the transvestite who emerges as sign of a 'category crisis' located in a domain other than that of gender, he straddled the line between classical and popular music, all the while keeping his costume changes one jump (or one jumpsuit) ahead of the competition. A black diamond mink cape lined with Austrian rhinestones, weighing 135 pounds, so heavy that it gave one backstage worker a hernia. An ostrich-feather cape. A hundred-pound cape of pink-dyed turkey feathers for the Radio City Music Hall Easter Show, in which he planned to emerge from a giant Fabergé egg. 'Quite frankly', grumped one critic, 'all that pink and feathers make him look like a female impersonator auditioning for "An Evening at La Cage."'[13] 'A white fox fur cape with a long train which he wore for a command performance for the Queen. A matador's outfit that prefigures George Michael's—and Grace Jones's. A fancy-dress uniform with epaulets and gold braid that anticipates Michael Jackson in 'We Are the World'. Red, white, and blue hot pants that made him look like a drum majorette. His rings and jewellery were as extravagant as his furs and sequins. 'To shake his hand,' said the New York Times, 'was to flirt with laceration.'[14]

Liberace's appeal is often thought to have been largely or exclusively to older women, but at the peak of his popularity he was a culture hero to 'girls and women of all ages—ready to squeal or swoon when they thought the occasion required it of them,' and who responded with 'hysterical adoration' to his appearance in 1956 at the Festival Hall—at least according to the customarily staid Times of London.[15] When the Liberace family—Lee, George, and their mother—arrived in London in 1956, he was welcomed by a crowd of over 3,000, mostly young girls and women, though the Times also notes the presence of 'a few amused policemen [and] some ardent young men.'[16] The British reviews are cautiously admiring, of his 'resourceful' piano playing and 'agreeable' singing and tap dancing as well as his 'fancy dress': 'with all his finery and his almost natural peaches and cream complexion', one noted, 'he is a shy, quiet little man … He did not swank or slobber, or flash diamond rings shaped like grand pianos at his admirers' (Times, October 2, 1956).

His performances were more like fashion shows than piano recitals. Parading up and down the stage in outfit after outfit ('Pardon me while I go slip into something more spectacular') he was in effect the first to mainstream 'voguing'—the eighties dance craze, borrowed from male transvestite drag shows in Harlem in the sixties, that incorporates exaggerated fashion model poses. Liberace dressed for the stage, he said himself, 'just one step short of drag' (Thomas 1987: 215).

Displacing sexual questions onto sartorial ones with practised ease, Liberace used the word 'straight' to describe his 'civilian' or offstage *clothes* (Liberace 1986: 179). Although in his stage performances of the eighties he joked that he'd never wear in the street the clothes he wore on the stage, 'or I'd get picked up, for sure', he preserved a theatrical space in which he could both assert and put in teasing question his heterosexuality and his biological or anatomical maleness. Thus the gag lines in his nightclub act about 'streaking' with sex-symbol Burt Reynolds ('I've got the diamonds, he's got the jewels') and about the necessity of getting up from the piano from time to time ('it straightens the shorts').[17]

While he was not afraid of feminization, and in fact courted it, he steadfastly denied that he was gay, despite clear evidence to the contrary. He even went so far as to sue the London *Daily Mirror* columnist 'Cassandra' (William Neil Connor, writing under a cross-gendered pseudonym) for using words like 'fruit-flavored' and 'it' to describe him. Cassandra had written—bizarrely, we may think—that Liberace was 'the summit of sex—the pinnacle of masculine, feminine, and neuter. Everything that, he, she, and it can ever want.' Masculine, feminine and neuter. He, she and it. Cassandra, oracularly, had consigned Liberace to the space of thirdness, the realm of the Lacanian Symbolic and of the transvestite. The space of desire.

The court case was itself a shrewd performance of transvestite theatre stage-managed for optimal effect. Liberace's London barrister, dressed in his wig and robes, gestured toward the Beefeaters, the Knights of the Garter, and the guards at Buckingham palace as models of 'glamour' 'in these days of somewhat drab and dreary male clothing.' 'Look at me, My Lords and my learned friends, dressed in accordance with old traditions. We do not dress like this in ordinary trial testimony, nor does Liberace' (Thomas 1987: 130–31). As if to make this point, Liberace had arrived in court wearing a conservative blue suit, white shirt, and necktie.

On the occasion of another law case, this one a palimony suit directed at him by a long-time male companion, a judge ruled in Liberace's favour when a woman process server said she had delivered a summons to him when he was dressed in a brown business suit. 'That man wouldn't be caught dead in a brown business suit', said the judge (Thomas 1987: 230). The plaintiff in the case, his former protegé, Scott Thorson, had told the scandal sheet *National Enquirer,* spitefully, that Liberace was almost totally bald and wore hairpieces on stage, and that he had had two major facelifts. 'When he took me in his arms', Thorson testified with self-justifying 'candour,' 'it revolted me at first.' 'I was unaccustomed to his full make-up.' When asked if he himself was wearing make-up at the deposition, Thorson acknowledged that he was (Thomas 1987: 228).

Make-up, wigs, face-lifts. This is the apparatus of 'woman', that is to say, the artefactual creation of female impersonation and the drag queen on the one hand, and the youth culture on the other. 'In fashion', says Roland Barthes, 'it is age that is important, not sex.' 'Both sexes tend to become uniform under a single sign ... that of *youth*' (Barthes 1983: 257, 258). By the end of his career Liberace's face looked as rigid and wooden as those of the mannequins at his Liberace Museum in Las Vegas ('the third most popular attraction in the entire state of Nevada'[18]), to which his old costumes, like Roy Rogers's stuffed horse, Trigger, were retired. As famous for his love of his mother as for supporting single-handedly the entire Austrian rhinestone industry, he had somehow to remain a 'boy', both in his private life as a gay man and in his public life as the crown prince of Mothers' Day.

And this may be a reason for the one extraordinary and unexpected act of female impersonation that did become incorporated into Liberace's act: the aerial flying, back and forth across the stage, that developed into a regular feature of his performance. Already 'ageless', a parodic version of the eternal 'boy', with his face-lifts, hairpieces, and increasingly heavy make-up, he conceived of a desire to become (although he never says so) Peter Pan. Ostensibly this fantasy was triggered by the aerodynamic effect of his cape as he left the stage one night; soon he had enlisted Peter Foy, of the English Flying Foys, the man who had taught two generations of female Peter Pans, including Mary Martin, to 'fly'. Liberace here is, for a moment, a triumph of metonymic transvestism, a middle-aged man imitating a woman who plays a fantasy changeling boy.

It was not Peter Pan, however, who was Liberace's ideal, but rather a male star who had remained forever young by the unlooked-for expedient of dying early—his namesake, Rudolph Valentino. Liberace's mother, a great fan of the Latin lover, named her son Wladziu Valentino Liberace and, for good measure, also named his younger brother Rudolph. In many ways Liberace seems to have been haunted by the phantom of Valentino, 'my namesake', as he described him to reporters (Thomas 1987: 100). He had some of Valentino's elaborate costumes copied for stage performance. He bought Valentino's bed and put it in one of his guest rooms; he collected and exhibited at the Liberace Museum a pair of silver goblets said to have been intended as wedding gifts to Valentino and Pola Negri.

Furthermore, Valentino appears as a major figure in Liberace's personal social history of crossover style: 'Years ago, both male and female movie legends influenced the fashion and cosmetic industries. All over the world, you could find copies of Dietrich's eyebrows, Joan Crawford's shoulder pads and shoes, Valentino's slave bracelet, as well as his slicked-back, glossy patent-leather hairstyle' (Liberace 1986: 222). All of these, we might note, are cross-dressed or cross-gendered examples: a woman's shoulder pads, a man's bracelet, Dietrich's eyebrows.

He-man, heart throb, movie idol, Valentino seems about as distant from Liberace—and from transvestism, marked or unmarked—as it would seem possible to get. Yet he is in fact an exemplary figure of unmarked transvestism, at once feminized and hypermale. His appearance in Arab robes, eyebrow pencil and mascara as the title character in *The Sheik* (1921), as we have noted, set off a frenzy of response among (largely female) filmgoers with its drama of sexual sadism amidst the tents of a 'Middle Eastern' locale.

In fact the cross-dressing elements in Valentino's story are stronger and more omnipresent than the eye-make-up and the flowing robes. A notorious photograph of him as a faun, dressed in fake fur tights and playing a flute was exhibited in court. Valentino apparently tried to explain it as a 'costume test' for a never-produced film called *The Faun through the Ages*, but it is more probable that he was posing in the Nijinsky role from *L'Après-midi d'un Faune* at the behest of his wife, the dancer Natacha Rambova. But then his wife—or rather, his wives—were part of his image problem, at least with men. For Rudolph Valentino, ballyhooed as the Great Lover, had married two women reputed to be lesbians, both members of the coterie surrounding the celebrated Alia Nazimova.[19] Rambova, his second wife, apparently had him prancing about in fur shorts; his first wife, Jean Acker, who according to one account 'favoured a short, very masculine hairstyle, and wore a white blouse and tie under a rather severely cut suit',[20] had locked him out of the marital bedroom and refused to consummate the marriage.

His unusual marital history, coupled with the masterful and pleasurable sadism of the original *Sheik* and the masochism and misogyny of its sequel, have led some recent commentators to speculate about Valentino's own sexual orientation: 'The obvious pleasure he sought from the company of young men, often as handsome as himself', writes one observer, 'should not make us suppose he was homosexual.' And, from the same source, 'There is always something inherently feminine in the "Great Lover", for it is his own narcissistic reflection he seeks in the depths of his beloved's eyes' (Walker 1976: 119). The campy appeal of Valentino to film audiences today exposes an inherent bisexuality in his self-presentation, again emphasized, if not in fact made possible, by the Arab dress he wore in his most famous film.

Valentino, as an immigrant from Italy who had worked as a gardener and a dance partner before making it in films, was first read as a foreign interloper replacing the image of the 'All-American [i.e. Anglo] boy.' This young Italian actor, despite the European specificity of his origins, became the prototype of the so-called 'Latin lover'—the category to which, without saying so explicitly, the wits at *Saturday Night Live* had consigned the contestants for their 'macho' contest, Fernando Lamas and Ricardo Montalban. (The Anglo television actor Jack Lord, star of *Hawaii Five-O,* apparently 'won' the contest.) In this catch-all categorization ethnic and racial distinctions become invidiously blurred, as Latino, Hispanic, Italian and presumably other dark-complected, dark-haired men are deliberately conflated as 'Latin'—smooth, seductive, predatory, irresistible to women. And once again 'hypermale' and 'feminized' become, somehow, versions of the same description: these men are too seductive to be 'really' men. As Miriam Hansen has noted, 'the more desperately Valentino himself emphasized attributes of physical prowess and virility, the more perfectly he played the part of the male impersonator, brilliant counterpart to the female "female" impersonators of the American screen such as Mae West or the vamps of his own films.'[21] The mythical 'Latin lover', like the 'Third World,' was an entity that could be simultaneously invented and manipulated. And

chief among these fantasy figures, in the puritanically xenophobic imagination, was the dangerous Valentino. In other words, Rudolph Valentino was himself a significant figure of *crossover,* disruption, rupture. It was doubtless his foreignness, as well as his eye-make-up, his hair style, and his slave bracelet, that set up the confrontation between Middle East and American Midwest that led to the famous 'Powder Puff' incident.

On July 18, 1926, the *Chicago Sunday Tribune* ran on its editorial page an article headlined 'Pink Powder Puffs,' which is worth reprinting here in its entirety:

A new public ballroom was opened on the north side a few days ago, a truly handsome place and apparently well run. The pleasant impression lasts until one steps into the men's washroom and finds there on the wall a contraption of glass tubes and levers and a slot for the insertion of a coin. The glass tubes contain a fluffy pink solid, and beneath them one reads an amazing legend, which runs something like this: 'Insert coin. Hold personal puff beneath the tube. Then pull the lever.'

A powder vending machine! In a men's washroom! Homo Americanus! Why didn't someone quietly drown Rudolph Guglielmo, alias Valentino, years ago?

And was the pink powder machine pulled from the wall or ignored? It was not. It was used. We personally saw two 'men'—as young lady contributors to the Voice of the People are wont to describe the breed—step up, insert coin, hold kerchief beneath the spout, pull the lever, then take the pretty pink stuff and pat it on their cheeks in front of the mirror.

Another member of this department, one of the most benevolent men on earth, burst raging into the office the other day because he had seen a young 'man' combing his pomaded hair in the elevator. But we claim our pink powder story beats his all hollow.

It is time for a matriarchy if the male of the species allows such things to persist. Better a rule by masculine women than by effeminate men. Man began to slip, we are beginning to believe, when he discarded the straight razor for the safety pattern. We shall not be surprised when we hear that the safety razor has given way to the depilatory.

Who or what is to blame is what puzzles us. Is this degeneration into effeminacy a cognate reaction with pacificism to the virilities and realities of the war? Are pink powder and parlor pinks in any way related? How does one reconcile masculine cosmetics, sheiks, floppy pants, and slave bracelets with a disregard for law and an aptitude for crime more in keeping with the frontier of half a century ago than a twentieth century metropolis?

Do women like the type of 'man' who pats pink powder on his face in a public washroom and arranges his coiffure in a public elevator? Do women at heart belong to the Wilsonian era of 'I Didn't Raise My Boy to be a Soldier'? What has become of the old 'caveman' line?

It is a strange social phenomenon and one that is running its course, not only here in America but in Europe as well. Chicago may have its powder puffs; London has its dancing men and Paris its gigolos. Down with Decatur; up with Elinor Glyn. Hollywood is the national school of masculinity. Rudy, the beautiful gardener's boy, is the prototype of the American male. Hell's bells. Oh, sugar.[22]

Oh, sugar, indeed. Masculine cosmetics, depilatories, sheiks, floppy hats, and slave bracelets, effeminacy and a propensity for crime, pacifism, and communism—blame for all of these is placed squarely at the foot, or the braceleted wrist, of 'Rudy, the beautiful gardener's boy'. Here, without strain, the dark complected, hot-blooded Italian is conflated with the dark-complected, hot-blooded Sheik. No face-saving gesture reveals *this* Sheik as really a blue-blooded, white-skinned aristocrat. Instead his clean-cut looks are attributed to an effeminate use of depilatories.

Valentino's taste for finery, including the infamous slave bracelets, laid him open to this kind of xenophobic attack from middle America in the midst of the summer doldrums. He took it personally, and very badly, issuing a challenge to

his detractor, not to a duel, which the laws of the country forbade, but to a boxing or wrestling match, 'to prove in typically American fashion, for I am an American citizen, which is the better man.' The challenge concluded, 'Hoping I will have an opportunity to demonstrate to you that the wrist under a slave bracelet may snap a real fist into your sagging jaw, and that I may teach you respect of a man even though he happens to prefer to keep his face clean, I remain, With utter contempt, Rudolph Valentino.'[23]

Time magazine, reporting on the editorial and the challenge, described him as 'a closely muscled man, whose sombre skin was clouded with talcum and whose thick wrists tinkled with a perpetual arpeggio of, fine gold bangles, [who] read the effusion with rapidly mounting fury.'[24] *Time* quoted him as saying that his profession required the make-up while sentiment demanded the bracelets. But the editorial writer never revealed himself and after a boxing match with a friendly New York sports reporter (which Valentino won, perhaps by this feat inspiring the mother of Cassius Clay to name her second son Rudolph Valentino Clay [Botham and Donnelly 1976: 200]) he denounced the absent editorial writer as a coward: 'The heroic silence of the writer who chose to attack me without provocation in the *Chicago Tribune* leaves no doubt as to the total absence of manliness in his whole make-up', Valentino wrote, with evident irony and, no doubt, unintended double entendre, his mind still dwelling on the powder puff incident.

Unavenged, the insult continued to rankle to the end of his life. When he was rushed into the hospital for the gastric ulcer and consequent peritonitis that would shortly lead to his death (though some claimed that he had been poisoned by a jealous rival), his first words on awakening from surgery were, reportedly, 'Doctor, am I a pink puff?'[25] And in the final twist of fate, when his body lay in state at Campbell's Funeral Parlour in New York City, where an unprecedented 100,000 people filed by his catafalque, the mortician's art fulfilled his greatest fear: 'Valentino lay in a half open casket, his hair slickered down into the familiar patent-leather imitation of life, his eyebrows freshly pencilled by a make up man and his cheeks rouged in a manner that did indeed recall the gibe about the "pink powder puff"' (Walker 1976: 116).

Xenophobia, classicism, racism, homophobia. Notice that Valentino is not being explicitly described as gay, but as contributing to effeminacy and foppery, sapping the virility of the American Male. Again display and masquerade are perceived as feminine, and feminizing.

We have been looking at Rudolph Valentino as the unlikely role model for Liberace and as the equally unlikely object of what might be called 'transvestification'. Where Liberace was complicit with his cultural classification as a transvestite figure, instinctively understood its relationship to 'star quality', and made it work for him, Valentino was both surprised and appalled, challenging the editorial writer to a boxing match to prove 'which is the better man'. But there is a third figure who stands in significant relation to these two, uncannily linked by circumstances that seem both bizarre and overdetermined, and that is the figure of Elvis Presley.

We have already noted that Liberace thought of himself as the precursor of glitter rock. But of all the show business 'copies' to which Liberace laid claim, the one he most insisted upon was Elvis Presley. In his testimony in a British court in 1959 he maintained that he had to 'dress better than the others who were copying me. One was a young man named Elvis Presley' (Thomas 1987: 131). He made the same claim to the media on the occasion of his twenty-fifth anniversary in show business: 'Because of Elvis Presley and his imitators, I really have to exaggerate to look different and to top them.'[26] Elvis became a *cause* of feminine virile display.

There is a famous moment, a kind of sartorial primal scene, in which Elvis and Liberace themselves change clothes, become each other's changelings. In 1956 they met in Las Vegas, when Elvis appeared in the audience at Liberace's show. Liberace invited the young singer backstage, where, apparently at the suggestion of a press agent, Elvis put on Liberace's gold-sequinned tuxedo jacket, and Liberace donned Elvis's striped sport coat. They then swapped instruments, Liberace on guitar, Elvis on piano, and jammed together for twenty minutes on two of their signature tunes, 'Hound Dog' and 'I'll Be Seeing You'. 'Elvis and I may be characters', commented Liberace, 'me with my gold jackets and him with his sideburns—but we can afford to be' (Thomas 1987: 117).

This crossover moment between two crossover stars (Liberace traversing the boundary between pop and classical, Elvis between 'white' and 'black' music) has important implications beyond those of local publicity. The *New York Times* obituary for Liberace says, succinctly, about his gold lamé jacket, 'Soon Elvis Presley was wearing a suit of gold lamé. Soon Elvis impersonators were wearing suits of gold lamé.'[27] (So that Elvis impersonators are really Liberace impersonators.[28])

Predictably, the keepers of the Elvis legend are less forthcoming about any Liberace connection.[29] The film *This Is Elvis* shows a shot of the Riviera Hotel marquee proclaiming 'Liberace' in large letters, presumably to show what kind of entertainment Las Vegas was used to before the arrival of the King. An off-screen narrator impersonating the voice of Elvis says, 'Liberace and his brother were one of the top acts of the time. I wasn't sure the place was ready for Elvis Presley.' The point is contrast, disruption, not continuity.

Thirteen years later Elvis returned to Las Vegas, heavier, in pancake make-up, wearing a white jumpsuit with an elaborate jewelled belt and cape, crooning pop songs to a microphone: in effect, he had become Liberace. Even his fans were now middle-aged matrons and blue-haired grandmothers, who praised him as a good son who loved his mother; Mother's Day became a special holiday for Elvis's fans as it was for Liberace's.

A 1980 videotape of *Liberace in Las Vegas* (made, therefore, three years after Elvis's death) opens with a lush videotour of his home, including a tour of his closet. This is surely in part a camp joke, but the racks and racks of sequins, rhinestones, and furs—all of which we will shortly see him model onstage—will be oddly but closely echoed in the 1981 Elvis retrospective film, *This Is Elvis,* in which—also quite early in the film—attendants are shown readying his wardrobe for the show. Once again there are racks of clothes, jumpsuits with spangles and rhinestones, a whole rolling rack of jewelled belts. Watching the two films in succession it is difficult to tell whose closet is whose.

But something else, even more uncanny, ties Elvis and Liberace together. Both of them, remarkably, were twins, each born with a twin brother who immediately died. Both, that is to say, were—in the sense in which I have been using the term—changelings, changeling boys, substitutes for or doubles of something that never was.

Elvis Aron and Jesse Garon. *The Rolling Stone Illustrated History of Rock & Roll* notes that 'His twin, Jesse Garon, died at birth, and he was always to be reminded of this absence ("They say when one twin dies, the other grows up with all the quality of the other, too … If I did, I'm lucky"), as if he were somehow incomplete, even down to his matching name,'[30] and almost all his biographers make some version of the same point.[31] Had Elvis's own child, Lisa Marie, been a boy, the parents intended to call him John Baron, continuing the rhyming line.

One biography of Liberace begins with a dramatization of the entertainer's momentous birth:

'One of the babies was born under the veil,' said the midwife in a voice shaded with sadness.

'But the other one, my dear …' her voice suddenly joyful. 'A *big* baby boy!'

How pitiful the dead infant looked, its tiny body almost a skeleton, a film of placenta over its shrivelled face like a cloth for burial …

But the other baby—what a pulsing, squalling, robust piece of humanity. (Thomas 1987: 1)

Uncannily enough, here is a *third* version of this changeling scenario, from the opening paragraphs of yet another biography.

Just before the turn of the present century, two bouncing babies were born who were to bring untold happiness into the lives of men and women all over the world.

One was the fledgling cinema …

The other was Rudolph Valentino.

As the babes grew up together, it was tragically ordained that so they would die.[32]

Jesse Garon Presley, Liberace's unnamed twin, the silent movie: three ghosts that haunt, and perhaps shape, the very notion of contemporary stardom.

Furthermore, Elvis, like Liberace, was obsessed with Rudolph Valentino, to whose celebrity (and spectacular funeral) his own was inevitably compared. The son of his promoter in the early Memphis days remembers that Elvis 'aspired to be a second Rudolph Valentino' (Goldman 1981: 129). Hence the sideburns, the 'sullen, sultry leer' (the adjectives are those of Albert Goldman, a highly unsympathetic biographer), the photo sessions from this period stripped to the waist, the claim to friends that he had Italian blood.[33]

But it is the delicacy and vulnerability of the two men's visual images, as much as their sheer sexual power, that binds them. The pout, the curled lip (about which Elvis would joke onstage in his later Las Vegas years, 'This lip used to curl easier'), the cool stare and contained sexuality, an auto-voyeurism incredibly provocative—all of these can be seen in Valentino's *Son of the Sheik,* an uncanny phantom of Elvis. Indeed Elvis made his own Sheik movie, *Harum Scarum* (1965), in which, dressed in 'Arab' robes and headdress, pursuing the Princess Shalimar (played by Miss America Mary Ann Mobley), he is clearly intended to evoke memories of Valentino. Even the antics of the midget Billy Barty—seemingly gratuitous to the plot—echo, as if for emphasis, the hapless dwarf in *Son of the Sheik*. In an earlier—and better—film, *Jailhouse Rock* (1957), Elvis is stripped to the waist and beaten, in another clear citation from the popular Valentino film. In fact, the example of Valentino is one reason why he chose a movie career, and thus missed out on the early great days of what he himself had started—the theatricalization of rock and roll.

The comparison, explicit and implicit, is everywhere in the press. An article in *McCall's* (presumably a Bible for the matrons of fandom) described Elvis's bodyguards as 'on a scale not seen in Hollywood since the days of Valentino and Fairbanks.'[34] The *New York Times,* reporting on the hysterical scene at his funeral, said, 'Those old enough to remember said there had been nothing like it since Rudolf [*sic*] Valentino.'[35] 'Not since Valentino has a showbiz death so touched the national spirit,' reported *People,*[36] and a Tennessee professor of psychiatry linked Elvis's superstardom with the American propensity for cult figures, suggesting, 'Think of someone like Rudolph Valentino.'[37] In 1989 a retro film was released about teen love in the fifties, which begins with the young hero purchasing Elvis's trademark car, a pink Cadillac; both the car and the film were called *Valentino Returns*—another evocation of the phantom, for Elvis, as we will see, is the other revenant, the other always-expected visitor, too-early lost.

Elvis, like Valentino, seemed to take the world by erotic surprise. Contrasted, again like Valentino, with a notion of the clean-cut all-American boy (represented in his case by Pat Boone), Elvis seemed for a time to stand as the personification of sex. But what does it mean to personify sex? And which sex?

The famous Ed Sullivan story—of how the camera filmed Elvis only from the waist up—has been told and retold, debunked as myth and explained as titillating publicity, a displacement upward that increased desire for a peek below. But what would that peek disclose?

'Is it a sausage? It is certainly smooth and damp-looking, but whoever heard of a 172-lb sausage 6 ft. tall?' This is the beginning of *Time* magazine's review of the film *Love Me Tender* in 1956. The referent, it soon becomes clear, is Elvis himself, not—as one might think—only a part of his anatomy. But Elvis as part-object, Elvis the Pelvis, became, not only a fan's fantasy and fetish but also, perhaps inevitably, his own. 'The Pelvis'—an anatomical region which seems at first specific, but is in fact both remarkably vague and distinctly ungendered—became the site of speculation and spectatorship.

Thus, for example, an admiring male rock critic writing in 1970 praised Elvis as 'The master of the sexual simile, treating his guitar as both phallus and girl … rumour had it that into his skin-tight jeans was sewn a lead bar to suggest a weapon of heroic proportions.'[38] But a boyhood friend of Elvis's tells it somewhat differently, describing a stage ploy from the singer's early career, around 1955:

He would take the cardboard cylinder out of a roll of toilet paper and put a string in one end of it. Then, he'd tie that string around his waist. The other end, with the cardboard roller, would hang down outside his drawers, so as when he got onstage and reared back with that guitar in his hand, it would look to the girls up front like he had one helluva thing there inside his pants.[39]

Lead bar or toilet-paper cylinder, truth or rumour, this tale of Elvis stuffing his own pants with a prosthesis presents the Presley phallus as marionette, the uncanny as canny stage device, one that can manifest its phallic power automatically, so to speak, with the tug of a string or the backward push of the hips. Recall once more Lacan's paradox about virile display. The more protest, the more suspicion of lack. For this is what the phallus signifies: 'its reality as signifier of lack.' It is, as Stephen Heath points out, 'the supreme signifier of an impossible identity.'[40]

Psychoanalytically, transvestism is a mechanism that functions by *displacement* and *through fantasy* to enact a scenario of desire. In fetishistic cross-dressing, particular objects of clothing take on a metonymic role, displacing parts of the body, and especially the maternal phallus—that is, the impossible and imagined phallus which would represent originary wholeness.

What I am going to claim—is that transvestism *on the stage,* and particularly in the kind of entertainment *culture* that generates the phenomenon known as 'stardom', is a symptom for the culture, rather than the individual performer. In the context of popular culture these transvestic symptoms appear, so to speak, to gratify a social or cultural scenario of desire. The onstage transvestite is the fetishized part-object for the social or cultural script of the fan.

One of the hallmarks of transvestic display, as we have seen repeatedly, is the detachable part. Wig, false breasts, the codpiece that can conceal male or female parts, or both, or neither. In the Elvis story the detachable part is not only explicitly and repeatedly described as an artificial phallus but also as a trick, a stage device, and a sham. Not for the first time the phallus itself becomes an impersonator—and, moreover, a female impersonator, for only a female would lack the phallus and need a substitute.

Elvis as female impersonator? Let us look further.

Elvis's appearance at the Grand Ole Opry, at the very beginning of his career, provoked a double scandal. His music was too black, and he was wearing eyeshadow. He was not asked back. For Chet Atkins, soon to become the organizer of Elvis's recording sessions in Nashville, the one lingering memory of Elvis at the Opry was his eye-make-up. 'I couldn't get over that eye shadow he was wearing. It was like seein' a couple of guys kissin' in Key West.'[41] (Notice here once again the conflation of cross-dressing, theatricality, and homosexuality.)

Elvis's hair created even more of a furore. It was like a black man's (Little Richard's; James Brown's); it was like a hood's; it was like a woman's. Race, class, and gender: Elvis's appearance violated or disrupted them all. His created 'identity' as the boy who crossed over, who could take a song like 'Hound Dog' from Big Mama Thornton or the onstage raving—and the pompadour, mascara, and pink and black clothing—from Little Richard, made of Elvis, in the popular imagination, a cultural mulatto, the oxymoronic 'Hillbilly Cat', a living category crisis. Little Richard, defiantly gay, his conked pompadour teased up six inches above his head, his face and eyes brilliantly made-up, his clothes and capes glittering with sequins, appearing, as we have already noted, 'in one show dressed as the Queen of England and in the next as the pope,'[42] was vestimentary crossover incarnate,[43] not passing but trespassing. To put it another way, Elvis mimicking Little Richard is Elvis as female impersonator—or rather, as the *impersonator* of a female impersonator. And it is worth remembering that Richard attributes his adoption of bizarre costume in this period to *racial* crossover. 'We were breaking through the racial barrier ... We decided that my image should be crazy and way-out so that the adults would think I was harmless' (White 1984: 65–66). The year was 1956.

Elvis was the white 'boy' who could sing 'black', the music merchandiser's dream. And that crossover move was (perhaps inevitably) read as a crossover move in gender terms: a move from hypermale to hyperfemale, to, in fact, *hyperreal* female, female impersonator, transvestite.

It was in 1970, only two years after his much-heralded television 'Comeback' performance, that Elvis made a striking vestimentary crossover in Las Vegas:

Not since Marlene Dietrich stunned the ringsiders with the sight of her celebrated legs encased from hip to ankle in a transparent gown had any performer so electrified Las Vegas with his mere physical appearance. Bill Belew [the costume designer], who had been very cautious up to this point about designing any costume that would make Elvis look effeminate, decided finally to kick out the jams. Now Elvis faced the house encased in a smashing white jumpsuit, slashed to the sternum and lovingly fitted around his broad shoulders, flat belly, narrow hips and tightly packed crotch. And then there were his pearls—loads of lustrous pearls, not sewn on the costume but worn unabashedly as body ornaments. (Goldman 1981: 448)

'Not since Marlene Dietrich.' This—in the voice of Elvis debunker Goldman—is Elvis precisely as female impersonator. Critic after critic notices that his sexuality is subject to reassignment, consciously or unconsciously, though the paradox—male sex symbol as female impersonator—remains perplexing and unexamined. 'As for Elvis himself', writes one biographer, 'he'll be gradually castrated into an everlasting pubescent boy. And as movie follows movie, each one worse than the last, he will actually start resembling a eunuch: a plump, jittery figure.'[44]

Elvis moves in the course of his career along a curious continuum from androgyne to transvestite. This male sex symbol is insistently and paradoxically read by the culture as a boy, a eunuch, or a 'woman'—as anything but a man.

His ex-wife Priscilla, the executive producer of the recent television series depicting Elvis's life, wanted in fact to repress, or expunge, the memory of his later years. 'The problem,' wrote one critic sympathetically, 'is that Elvis left in such bad shape: overweight, forgetting the words to his songs, wearing clownish rhinestone-covered jumpsuits. It's that Elvis—the one who keeps cropping up in books and TV-movies—that Priscilla wants to get out of people's minds.' And, 'if only Elvis had paid more attention to his image. Maybe he would have made it through the '70s,

checked into the Betty Ford Center, turned on to aerobics . . .'[45]

Overweight. Reviews and commentaries on Elvis in his last years speak frequently of him as having a 'weight problem', as looking fat, not being able to keep the weight off. Of which gender do we usually speak in these terms? We may think of Elizabeth Taylor and her constant battle with extra pounds: Liz fat, Liz thin, Liz in and out of the Betty Ford Center. This is the spirit in which Elvis watchers watched Elvis watching his weight, as if the eternal boy within could be disclosed by the shedding of pounds, the disappearance of a telltale paunch. The comparable corpulence of wonder-boys Orson Welles and Marlon Brando, though remarked by the press, is not feminized in this way.

Yet the feminization and/or transgendering of Elvis begins much earlier than the Las Vegas jumpsuit days.[46] Whether through his mascara, his dyed hair, or his imitation of black music and style, Elvis was always already crossing over.

The 1990 debut of a weekly TV series on the life of Elvis Presley broke new ground for television programming, as John J. O'Connor noted in the *New York Times*. 'It is', he points out, 'the first weekly series built around the life of an actual entertainment personality'; 'a decided rarity—a half-hour format devoted not to a sitcom but to straightforward biography.' 'Can,' he wondered in print, 'episodic biographies of Marilyn, Chaplin, Dean, *et al.*, be far behind?'[47]

This list of celebrities to be compared to Elvis is instructive: Marilyn Monroe, Charlie Chaplin, James Dean. For all of them have been, like Elvis Presley, objects of imitation, repetition, replication—and re-gendering. (Think of Boy George's former boyfriend, the transvestite pop music figure Marilyn, with his long blond hair and hairy chest; of Lucille Ball's Chaplin [and Chaplin's own cross-dressing films[48]], of James Dean as lesbian butch idol, etc.) Andy Warhol, the master of pop replication, did multiple Elvises as well as Marilyns and James Deans, lots of them: a silkscreened print of Elvis's face reproduced 36 times (six across and six down); *Double* and *Triple Elvis; Red Elvis;* and a work called *Campbell's Elvis*—with Elvis's face superimposed over the label of a soup-can. Elvis was, in fact, the only pop figure Warhol carried over in his work from the fifties to the sixties. Critics have noted the affinities between the artist and the rock star: each 'opted for a blank and apparently superficial parody of earlier styles which surprisingly expanded, rather than alienated, their audience.' '[B]oth took repetition and superficiality to mask an obscure but vital aspect of their work: the desire for transcendence or annihilation without compromise, setting up a profound ambivalence on the part of both artist and audience as to whether the product was trash or tragedy.'[49]

Newsweek read Warhol's interest in Elvis as the recognition of 'an almost androgynous softness and passivity in his punk-hood persona',[50] and the claim to androgyny, as we have seen, is not infrequently made as an explanation of Elvis's powerful appeal to women and men. But one of the things Andy Warhol may have seen in Elvis was the perfection of his status as a pop icon in his condition as always already multiple and replicated. The phenomenon of 'Elvis impersonators', which began long *before* the singer's death, is one of the most startling effects of the Elvis cult.

What, then, is the relationship between transvestism and repetition? For one thing, both put in question the idea of an 'original', a stable starting point, a ground. For transvestism, like the copy or simulacrum, disrupts 'identity' and exposes it as figure. In one of the most famous of twentieth-century cultural analyses, Walter Benjamin noted the effect of mechanical reproduction on works of art like photography and film. 'The technique of reproduction,' he wrote (and think of *Elvis* here),

detaches the reproduced object from the domain of tradition. By making many reproductions it substitutes a plurality of copies for a unique existence. And in permitting the repro-

duction to meet the beholder or listener in his own particular situation, it reactivates the object reproduced.[51]

In the mystical anagram adopted by his followers, 'Elvis lives.' (Or, to cite the slogan employed by Elvis's long-time manager Colonel Parker after his boy's death, 'Always Elvis.' That Colonel Parker deployed this slogan in the form of a rubber stamp says much about the reproduction of Elvis Presley. Had Colonel Parker known or cared anything about literary theory he might have had it read 'Always already Elvis.')

Elvis made his public debut as a performer in 1954. By 1956—only two years later—the warm-up act for his show at the Louisiana Fair Grounds was performed by 'exact replicas of Elvis Presley, doing his songs with his gestures and dressed in his clothes.'[52] In Nashville one Wade Cummings, or 'Elvis Wade', as he called himself, was described as the 'first', or 'original imitation Elvis', complete with paunch and flashy costume slit to the waist. According to him, 'All Elvis impersonators are Elvis Wade impersonators.' (So, in his view at least, there was an original, an original impersonator.) But there are hundreds of others. Notice here the relationship of the 'impersonator' to Freud's 'uncanny'. The impersonator is something alive that seems almost like a machine. Is it possible that this is overdetermination through the dead brother, that all of these impersonators are some version of Jesse Garon Presley?

Most of these acts got their start *before* Elvis Presley's death; they were not only ghostly revisitations but also proliferations, multiplications. Some were even surgically reconstructed, like the man in Florida who had his nose, cheeks, and lip altered to look like the King. The surgeons 'gave a slight millimeter push to the left-hand corner of [his] lip', to approximate the famous sneer.[53]

Indeed, the impersonation of Elvis always seemed to verge on the multiple, the replicated, as if one could never be enough. Two hundred

Elvis impersonators were scheduled to perform at the birthday party for the Statue of Liberty. (Only seventy-five showed up.) What was this insatiable desire that could never be gratified?

After his death the Elvis impersonators assumed the magnitude of a major cult. 'What, other than psychological transference', asked *People* magazine rhetorically one year later, 'can explain the hysteria over the 100 or so ersatz Elvises around the country who are putting on eerie shows—complete with drum rolls from *2001,* sweaty scarfs tossed to screaming women, karate chops, bodyguards, sneers and bathos?'

Time magazine noted the success in Saigon of one Elvis Phuong, who, 'complete with skin-tight pants and sneer, does Presley Vietnamese style.'[54] Two Elvis impersonators in London, one Chinese, the other an Indian Sikh who wears a turban, prompted a two-page feature on the front page of the 'Living Arts' section of the *New York Times* ('Honestly, not too many Chinese people do Elvis,' Paul Chan confides to the *Times* reporter. 'I think I must be the first Chinese Elvis in the world.').[55] And a routine news item in the entertainment pages of the *Los Angeles Times* noted a casting call for Elvis impersonators, 'preferably overweight', for a 'small but fun role' in *Robocop II.*[56]

At the First Annual EP (for Elvis Presley) Impersonators International Association Convention held in Chicago in June 1990, dozens of impersonators put in an appearance, including a female Elvis from Hertfordshire, England, a 'Jordanian–American anesthesiologist Elvis' described by a Chicago newspaper as the 'Hindu Elvis,' and a seven-year-old Elvis from Brooklyn. The event was co-ordinated by a group that eventually hopes to develop a 'Code of Ethics' for Elvis impersonators around the globe. 'If the actual Elvis was at the convention,' one reporter commented, 'he might have been overlooked in the mob of look-alikes.'[57]

One of the most popular sessions at the EPIIA, 'How to Become an Elvis Impersonator', noted the three sartorial stages of Elvis's life as a performer: the fifties, or the Gold Lamé Period, the sixties, or the Black Leather period, and the seventies, or the Vegas Jumpsuit Phase, also known as the Aloha Years. Why do most impersonators choose the third phase, often believed to mark the decline of Elvis's career? This 'question that has plagued Elvologists' was answered by the session leader in two ways: on the one hand, the seventies were the most visually exciting of Elvis's career; on the other, the 'midlife demographics of the impersonator subculture' (largely over 40, largely working class) made the baritone, overweight Elvis an object of more ready—and more convincing-—impersonation. As will be clear, I am suggesting a third reason for the appeal of the Vegas Jumpsuit Elvis, and also a link among the three vestimentary phases—a link for which 'unmarked transvestism' might be thought of as a common term.

Here once again, in a passage of typically purple prose, is Elvis biographer Albert Goldman on the subject of this phenomenon of impersonation:

> What one saw after Elvis's death ... was not just emulation but replication: the rite according to St. Xerox. Like those mythical soldiers sprung from dragon's teeth, there appeared overnight a new class of entertainers who were not so much mimics, impersonators or impressionists as Elvis clones. Some of these human effigies were so fantastically dedicated to their assumed identity that, like transsexuals, they submitted their bodies to plastic surgery so that their natural resemblance might be heightened to virtual indistinguishability. (Goldman 1981: 584–85)

We are very close here to Freud's notion of the uncanny repetition–compulsion, the *heimlich* transformed into the *unheimlich,* castration anxiety, the multiplication of doubles, 'something repressed which *recurs.*'[58] Meantime at Graceland, the Presley home (*Heim?*) and museum in Memphis, his costumes live, too, on mannequins (like Liberace's), for the delectation of the faithful. Elvis as ghost comes home to rejoin the ghostly twin brother whose grave has been moved to the Graceland memorial garden.

And these mechanisms of impersonation lead, with uncanny inevitability, to woman as Elvis impersonator. As Elvis's fame grew, and his looks became as famous as his sound, the hair and make-up began, fascinatingly, to cross *back* over gender lines. When his underage girlfriend Priscilla, later to become his wife, moved in with him in 1962, Elvis took charge of her appearance and turned her into a version of himself, insisting that she tease her hair up about twelve inches and dye it the same jet-black that his own hair was dyed. 'In fact', writes biographer Goldman, 'some people began to insist that Elvis and Priscilla were coming to look alike, that they were becoming twins' (1981: 355). Another set of uncanny twins: changelings.

As early as 1957 Little Richard toured Australia with a package of artists including Alis Lesley, billed as 'the female Elvis Presley', complete with pompadour and low-slung guitar (White 1984: 91). At the 1984 American Grammy Awards Show pop singer Annie Lennox of the Eurythmics, known for her close-cropped orange hair and gender-bending style, made a startling appearance 'in full drag, as a convincing Elvis Presley.'[59] In Jim Jarmusch's film *Mystery Train* (1989) a young Japanese Elvis fan assembles a scrapbook by pairing pictures of Elvis with the Buddha and two women: the Statue of Liberty and Madonna. 'Elvis was even more influential than I thought', says her boyfriend. Canadian rockabilly star k.d. lang, who enjoys particular popularity with lesbian audiences, is famous for her short cropped hair and male attire. Often compared by critics to Elvis Presley, lang, whose lip in performance seems to curl, like Elvis's, of its own accord, did an Elvis impersonation on one of Pee Wee Herman's Christmas shows. And comedienne Roseanne Barr, who has achieved stardom by playing a fat,

lower-middle-class housewife on television, appeared in a one-woman show where she made jokes about her weight, 'handed out scarfs like Elvis', and 'closed the show singing "My Way" arm in arm with an Elvis impersonator.'[60]

So that Elvis is impersonated and evoked on the one hand by female pop and rock stars (Alis Lesley, Annie Lennox, Madonna, k.d. lang) and on the other hand by an overweight comic actress. What I want to suggest is that these particular impersonations, impersonations of Elvis by women, were not only apt but in fact inevitable.

It is almost as if the word 'impersonator,' in contemporary popular culture, can be modified *either* by 'female' *or* by 'Elvis.'

Why should this be? Why is 'Elvis,' like 'woman', that which can be impersonated?

From the beginning Elvis is produced and exhibited as parts of a body—detachable (and imitable) parts that have an uncanny life and movement of their own, seemingly independent of their 'owner': the curling lip, the pompadour, the hips, the pelvis.

Compare him, for example, with an All-American boy like Pat Boone, for whom the only detachable parts are his white bucks. The All-American boy doesn't have a body—or didn't until recently. Again it is useful to compare Elvis to Valentino, who replaced the All-American boy movie star with a model infinitely more dangerous and disturbing—because it had moving parts. Indeed, it could be said that a 'real male' cannot be embodied at all, that embodiment *itself* is a form of feminization. If women, in the Western tradition, have been seen as the representatives of sex itself, then to personify sex on the stage must inevitably be to impersonate a woman.

Elvis is also—like a woman—not only a marked but a *marketed* body, exhibited and put on display, merchandised, not only by his manager Colonel Tom Parker, but also by Steve Binder, who invented the slick look of the 1968 TV *Comeback Special,* leather suit and all, and by David Wolper, who produced the posthumous film *This Is Elvis* and also staged the Statue of Liberty extravaganza.

'The woman of fashion', writes Roland Barthes in a passage we have already had occasion to note, is a 'collection of tiny, separate essences.' 'The paradox,' he says 'is a generality of accumulation, not of synthesis: in Fashion, the *person* is thus simultaneously impossible and yet entirely known' (Barthes 1983: 254–55). Here Barthes says 'person', but earlier, 'woman'. It is 'woman' whom fashion creates as this illusion of parts. And 'woman' is what can be known, exhibited, disseminated, replicated—while at the same time remaining 'impossible'.

Elvis, too, is simultaneously impossible and entirely known. Much as he is exhibited, he is also withheld from view: in the army, in Hollywood, holed up at Graceland. At the end of every performance, while his fans screamed for more, an announcer would solemnly intone, 'Ladies and gentlemen, Elvis has left the building.' Like the changeling boy, Elvis is always absent or elsewhere. Indeed as always already absent, Elvis himself was the best, and the most poignant, of Elvis impersonators, staging a much-heralded 'comeback' in 1968 at the age of 30, and, in another comeback, revisiting his classic crossover rock songs of the fifties from the curious vantage point of Hawaii or Las Vegas in the middle seventies. Like a revenant, he just never stops coming back. (Here we might recall the story of the phantom hitchhiker in the film *Mystery Train*—who turns out, of course, to be the ghost of Elvis heading for Graceland.)

We have briefly noted the fact that Elvis in effect sat out the rock revolution that he himself had started. Instead of taking to the concert stage like the Beatles, he went to Hollywood to become a 'movie star', following the game plan of Colonel Parker, but also, presumably, his own dream of being a Valentino. Like Flaubert writing for the French theatre, he was a genre behind. He missed his own moment—the moment that he had engendered—and spent the rest of his career as he had spent the beginning, being always too early or too late to be the Elvis that he was.

Is it possible that this is the essence of stardom, of superstardom? To be simultaneously belated and replicated; not to be there, and to cover up that absence with representations?

In a recent essay on camp, Andrew Ross has suggested that 'in popular rock culture today, the most "masculine" images are signified by miles of coiffured hair, layers of gaudy make-up, and a complete range of fetishistic body accessories, while it is the clean-cut, close-cropped, fifties-style Europop crooners who are seen as lacking masculine legitimacy' (Ross 1989: 164). As a cultural observation this is shrewd, yet it reinscribes the binary *within* the reassuring domain of the masculine. Ross underestimates the power of the transvestite as that spectral other who exists only in representation—not a representation of male or of female, but of, precisely, itself: its own phantom or ghost.

The argument from 'masquerade' tries to establish 'woman' as artifactual, gestural, a theatrical creature who can be taken apart and put back together. But what has become clearer and clearer is that 'man'—the male person—is at least as artifactual as 'woman.' Mechanical reproduction is the displacement into its opposite of the fear of artefactuality and dismemberment.

'Which is most macho?' The answer can come only from the impersonator. For by enacting on the stage—or the video screen—the disarticulation of parts, the repetition of images that is the breakdown of the image itself, it is only the impersonator who can theorize gender. Let me quote once again from Roland Barthes.

> As for the human body, Hegel had already suggested that it was in a relation of signification with clothing: as pure sentience, the body cannot signify; clothing guarantees the passage from sentience to meaning; it is, we might say, the signified par excellence. But which body is the Fashion garment to signify? (Barthes 1983: 258)

What are the choices? An article in the gay and lesbian journal *Out/Look* called attention to the power of 'The Drag Queen in the Age of Mechanical Reproduction', because the drag queen foregrounds illusion and falsehood as material reality: 'being a drag queen means the constant assertion of the *body*.'[61] But again, *which* body? The fashion garment of the drag queen signifies the absent or phantom body. Paradoxically, the body here is no body, and nobody, the clothes without the Emperor.

It is epistemologically intolerable to many people—including many literary and cultural critics—that the ground should be a figure. That gender exists only in representation. But this is the subversive secret of transvestism, that the body is not the ground, but the figure. Elvis Presley watching *his* figure, as his weight balloons up and down, Elvis deploying his lips and his hips to repeat by an act of will and artifice the 'natural' gestures that once made them seem to take on an uncanny, transgressive life of their own, Elvis Presley, male sex symbol as female impersonator, becomes the fascinating dramatization of the transvestite effect that underlies representation itself.

NOTES

Reprinted with permission from Marjorie Garber, "The Transvestite Continuum: Liberace–Valentino–Elvis," in *Vested Interests: Cross Dressing and Cultural Anxiety* (New York: Routledge, 1997), 353–74.

1. *George Michael: Music, Money. Love, Faith* (MTV Networks, 1988). I am grateful to Nancy Vickers for this reference.
2. *San Francisco Chronicle,* May 9, 1990: El.
3. Mablen Jones (1987), *Getting It On: The Clothing of Rock 'n' Roll,* New York: Abbeville Press: 129.
4. Andrew Ross (1989), 'Uses of Camp', in *No Respect: Intellectuals and Popular Culture,* New York: Routledge: 165.
5. Jones, *Getting It On:* 144.
6. Kris Kirk and Ed Heath (1984), *Men in Frocks,* London: Gay Men's Press: 58.
7. Joan Riviere (1986), 'Womanliness as a Masquerade', in *Formations of Fantasy,* eds Victor Burgin, James Donald and Cora Kaplan, London: Methuen: 38; Jacques Lacan (1977), 'The Signification of the Phallus', in *Ecrits: A Selection,* trans. Alan Sheridan, New York: W. W. Norton.
8. Eugénie Lemoine-Luccioni (1983), *La Robe,* Paris: Seuil: 124.
9. Roland Barthes (1983), *The Fashion System,* trans. Matthew Ward and Richard Howard, New York: Hill and Wang: 231–32.
10. Dustjacket copy for *The Wonderful Private World of Liberace,* by Liberace (1986), New York: Harper & Row.
11. Liberace, *The Wonderful Private World of Liberace:* 171.
12. Bob Thomas (1987), *Liberace,* New York: St. Martin's Press: 243.
13. Dick Maurice (1986), *Las Vegas Sun,* March; Thomas, *Liberace:* 254.
14. William E. Geist (1985), 'About New York: Liberace Is Here, with His Glitter Undimmed', *New York Times,* April 3: B5.
15. *Times of London,* October 2, 1956: 3.
16. *Times of London,* September 26, 1956: 6.
17. *Liberace: Behind the Music,* dir. David Green, writ. Gavin Lambert. The Kushner-Locke Company, 1988 (videocassette).
18. Dick Alexander (1990), 'A Las Vegas Where There's No Better Fun', *San Francisco Examiner,* July 22: T4.
19. Alexander Walker (1976), *Rudolph Valentino,* London: Elm Tree Books/Hamish Hamilton: 32–33, 99. The desire of critics to accept allegations that Acker and Rambova were lesbians may suggest something of their own ambivalence toward Valentino's love-god image; thus one biographer comments, for example, on Valentino's statement that 'a man may admire a woman without desiring her.' 'It has been reported that Natacha construed this as a veiled reference to her Lesbianism, and, on reading it, slapped Valentino's face. But such a report is necessarily hard to confirm' (Walker, *Rudolph Valentino:* 99).

20. Noel Botham and Peter Donnelly (1976), *Valentino: The Love God,* London: Everest Books: 70.

21. Miriam Hansen (1986), 'Pleasure, Ambivalence, Identification: Valentino and Female Spectatorship', *Cinema Journal* 25, 4 (Summer): 25. Hansen also has excellent things to say about the Latin lover, the discourse of exoticism, and the 'repressed desire of miscegenation' in the United States.

22. *Chicago Sunday Tribune,* July 18, 1926: A10.

23. *Chicago Herald-Examiner,* quoted in Botham and Donnelly, *Valentino:* 196–97.

24. Botham and Donnelly, *Valentino:* 200.

25. Jack Scagnetti (1975), *The Intimate Life of Rudolph Valentino,* Middle Village, New York: Jonathan David Publishers: 115.

26. *Time,* the *New York Times* and the *Los Angeles Times* all carried articles on him. Thomas, *Liberace:* 173.

27. James Barron (1987), 'Liberace, Flamboyant Pianist, Is Dead', *New York Times,* February 5: B6.

28. There have, in fact, been numerous Liberace imitators, as Dick Alexander notes in the *San Francisco Examiner,* July 22, 1990: T4.

29. Although at least one, Jac L. Tharpe (1979), points it out in passing. Tharpe, 'Will the Real Elvis Presley . . .', in Tharpe, *Elvis: Images and Fancies,* Jackson: University Press of Mississippi: 4.

30. Peter Guralnick (1980), *The Rolling Stone Illustrated History of Rock & Roll,* ed. Jim Miller, New York: Random House/Rolling Stone Press: 21.

31. Nik Cohn's novel, *King Death* (1975), speculates on what would have happened had Jesse lived. Albert Goldman comments that 'This spirit brother is one of the most important characters in the life of Elvis Presley.' Albert Goldman (1981), *Elvis,* New York: McGraw-Hill: 65.

32. Norman A. Mackenzie (1974), *The Magic of Rudolph Valentino,* London: The Research Publishing Co.: 11.

33. 'This surprising identification with the film idol of the silent era, a man who was dead before Elvis was born', writes Albert Goldman, 'is the first unmistakable sign that Elvis had discovered the essence of his appeal and was starting to cultivate a corresponding image. It is also a sign of prescience, for nothing better defines Elvis' future role than the formula: teen Valentino. If you add to the basic image of the sultry Latin lover the further garnishings of an erotic style of music and dance, the tango for the twenties, rock 'n' roll for the fifties, the parallel is perfect. Soon Elvis would even have crow-black hair' (Goldman, *Elvis:* 129).

34. Vernon Scott (1963), 'Elvis Ten Million Dollars Later', *McCall's,* February: 124.

35. Molly Ivins (1977), 'Presley Fans Mourn in Memphis . . .', *New York Times,* August 18: C18.

36. 'The King Is Dead, But Long Lives the King in a Showbiz Bonanza', *People* 8, 15, October 10, 1977: 29.

37. Werner T. Mays, in John Edgerton (1979), 'Elvis Lives!' *The Progressive* 43, 3 (March): 23.

38. George Melly (1970), *Revolt into Style,* Harmondsworth: Penguin: 36–37.

39. David Houston; Goldman, *Elvis:* 157.

40. Stephen Heath, 'Joan Riviere and the Masquerade', in *Formations of Fantasy:* 53.

41. Goldman, *Elvis:* 122; Patsy Guy Hammontree (1985), *Elvis Presley, A Bio-Bibliography,* Westport, Connecticut: Greenwood Press: 13.

42. Charles White (1984), *The Life and Times of Little Richard,* New York: Pocket Books: 66, 69.

43. White, *The Life and Times of Little Richard:* 69.

44. William Allen Harbinson (1977), *The Illustrated Elvis,* New York: Grosset & Dunlap: 93.

45. J. David Stern (1990), 'The King Is Back', *TV Guide* 38, 7 (February 17): 67.

46. Albert Goldman, whose view of Elvis often borders on the vitriolic, puts the turning point at his army experience, which was traditionally supposed to make a man of him: 'The Elvis who had appeared on the Dorsey, Berle, and Sullivan shows, who had starred in *Loving You* and *Jailhouse Rock,* was butch. He had a chunky, clunky aura . . . After the army, Elvis appears very delicate and vulnerable . . . With his preposterous Little Richard conk, his limp wrist, girlish grin, and wobbly knees, which now turn out instead of in, he looks outrageously gay' (Goldman, *Elvis:* 329–30). Goldman targets, especially, what he describes as 'his queer

showing on *Frank Sinatra's Welcome Home Party for Elvis Presley.*' 'When he confronts the much smaller but more masculine Sinatra, Elvis's body language flashes, "I surrender, dear."'

Goldman's hostility toward (and fascination with) his subject is clear, as is his desire to pop-psychoanalyze and re-gender him. Thus he describes the 21-year-old Elvis's 'Girlish boudoir', full of Teddy bears (picture caption, Goldman: 289ff.), observes that 'throwing things like a hysterical woman was one of Elvis's more dangerous habits' (Goldman: 337) and claims that he was so sensitive about his uncircumcised state that 'instead of pissing in a urinal ... he would always go inside, like a woman' (Goldman: 339). When it comes to accounting for the singer's popularity, Goldman has recourse again to gender and to a kind of instant cultural criticism. 'Much of Elvis's power over young girls came not just from the fact that he embodied their erotic fantasies but that he likewise projected frankly feminine traits with which they could identify. This AC/DC quality became in time characteristic of rock stars in general, commencing with Mick Jagger and the Beatles (who had such ravishingly girlish falsettos) and going on to include Jim Morrison, David Bowie, Elton John and many figures of the punk pantheon' (Goldman: 345).

47. John J. O'Connor (1990), '"Elvis" The Series: Poor Boy Makes Good', *New York Times,* February 6: Bl.

48. *The Masquerader,* 1914; *The Woman* 1915. Of *The Masquerader, Bioscope* wrote, 'Mr. Chaplin gives a really remarkable female impersonation. The make-up is no less successful than the characterization, and is further proof of Mr. Chaplin's versatility.' *The Films of Charlie Chaplin,* ed. Gerald D. McDonald, Michael Conway, and Mark Ricci (1971), Secaucus, New Jersey: The Citadel Press: 62.

49. John Carlin, *The Iconography of Elvis,* as quoted in Victor Bockris (1989), *The Life and Death of Andy Warhol,* New York: Bantam Books: 124–25.

50. *Newsweek,* August 29, 1977. Cited in Tharpe, *Elvis: Images:* 4.

51. Walter Benjamin (1969), 'The Work of Art in the Age of Mechanical Reproduction', in *Illuminations,* trans. Harry Zohn, New York: Schocken Books: 221.

52. Goldman, *Elvis:* 229.

53. 'Elvis Presley Imitations in Spirit and Flesh', *Rolling Stone* 261, March 23, 1978.

54. *Time,* April 9, 1990: 38.

55. Sheila Rule (1990), 'The Men Who Would Be Elvis', *New York Times,* June 26: Bl.

56. 'Beauty Pageant's "Roger & Me" Lesson', 'Outtakes' column, reprinted from the *Los Angeles Times, San Francisco Chronicle,* February 12, 1990: F3.

57. Alice Kahn (1990), 'A Whole Lotta Elvis Going On', *San Francisco Chronicle,* June 11: B3.

58. Sigmund Freud (1919), 'The Uncanny', SE 17: 241.

59. Simon Frith (1988), "Confessions of a Rock Critic," in *Music for Pleasure: Essays in the Sociology of Pop,* New York: Routledge: 193.

60. *San Franscisco Chronicle,* February 12, 1990.

61. Mark Leger (1989), "The Drag Queen in the Age of Mechanical Reproduction," *Out/Look* 6 (Fall): 29.

15

DRAGGING IT UP AND DOWN: THE GLAMORIZED MALE BODY

Mark Simpson

We know, too, to what a degree depreciation of women, horror of women, and a disposition to homosexuality are derived from the final conviction that women have no penis. Ferenczi (19.3) has recently, with complete justice, traced back the mythological symbol of horror—Medusa's head—to the impression of the female genitals devoid of a penis.

Freud, 'The Sexual Theories of Children'

Glamour, n, & v.t. 1. n. magic, enchantment (cast a glamour over, enchant). 2. v.t. delusive or alluring or exciting beauty or charm; (esp. feminine) physical attractiveness.

The Concise Oxford Dictionary

GLAMOUR IN DRAG

In the fifteenth century the war against heresy, the Inquisition, produced the *Malleus Maleficarum,* a book used as the basis of the persecution of millions of women as 'witches'. A charge frequently made by this text of misogyny against feminine witchcraft is its ability to 'disappear' men's *membrum virile*. A typical example of this fiendish sorcery tells of how 'some glamour was cast over him so that he could see or touch nothing but his smooth body'.[1]

Glamour, then, is woman's 'magical' power over man, her power to enchant and allure; and as ever, woman's power is also a castration threat to men: glamour is both desirability and fearsomeness. But more than this, glamour is both the fear of lack *and the disavowal of it;* it is both fear of woman's power, her affinity with nature, and man's early attempts to explain it away as the result of diabolic *artifice:* a man, Lucifer, is at the root of it all. Glamour is Janus-faced, looking towards both feminine power and masculinist plot.

And so it is with that masculine attempt at glamour—drag: is it incitement to gender rebellion or misogynist turn? This is the perennial question, and the answer is, of course, both and neither.

The mother of all glamour, and therefore of drag, is Medusa, who with her serpent hair, tusks of swine and golden wings, could turn her audience to stone with a look: freezing fear in a glance—every drag queen's dream. To appropriate glamour and desirability to the masculine body against the cultural grain, a gay man has traditionally had to put on the appearance of femininity, the point of which is not to become a woman (they wish to keep their penis) but to bind the fear and fascination of the feminine to the male body. This produces a dilemma for the gay man: how to reconcile his own fascination with his own fear—or in other words, how to emulate Athena and fix the Medusa's head in the centre of his shield without himself being turned to stone. The ambiguity of glamour itself is his Perseus here: in the wake of Hollywood, glamour is associated with a masquerade of femininity designed by men, a fetishistic defence against the horror of lack which the Medusa's head represents. Glamour in this fetishistic form can be 'put on' by men very easily.

The respectable men of learning who wrote *Malleus Maleficarum,* in an attempt to counter the manifest irrationality of their charges of castration by witchcraft, explained the effect of the witches' 'glamour' as working 'not indeed by actually despoiling the human body of it [the penis], but by concealing it'; in other words, an effect on the poor man's ability to *perceive.* The Medusa's eyes are the centre of her horror: the active female gaze of the Gorgon rebels against the masculine priority accorded by possessing visible genitalia. The victim bewails his loss of manhood while his friends point out, to no avail, that his *membrum* is still very much *virile.* Likewise the man in drag has his manhood concealed but not despoiled: the 'castration' is *visual.* But this effect is in a reverse order to that experienced by the victim of the witches' glamour—his manhood is concealed not from him but from his audience (albeit only through the suspension of disbelief). The travesty of a man's body that was feared as a result of women's power is disavowed through a travesty of vestments, through *transvestism;* glamour works at man's behest, and his eyes, not the gorgon's, gaze out at us.

This kind of drag draws attention to the concealment of manhood by its crudeness or its exaggeration to make sure that it is taken as concealment and not despoilment. Much of the entertainment of drag depends upon the improbability and inappropriateness of a man in a frock, wig and 'falsies'. But this in turn depends upon not just the improbability of a man dressed as a woman but the 'improbability' of the female body itself. The man in a frock *looks* preposterous but this is just a shadow of the *essential* preposterousness of the female body itself, that which the frock represents (and hides). Likewise the false tits are funny, not just for their falseness, their obvious failure as breasts,

but also because they do in fact represent very well those *innately* inappropriate and therefore humorous accessories. The anxiety that glamour might travesty man's body is thus displaced onto woman's body.

This is the 'misogynist turn' aspect of drag. But true to its ironic heart, drag points glamour in another direction, placing another meaning on travesty, that of carnival. For all its possible denigration of the feminine body, drag has the effect, unwitting or not, of pointing up the foolishness of gender *performance;* by putting a man in a frock, gender itself is defrocked and put in the stocks for a day. As Judith Butler puts it in *Gender Trouble:*

> In imitating gender, drag implicitly reveals the imitative nature of gender itself—as well as its contingency. Indeed, part of the pleasure, the giddiness of the performance is in the recognition of a radical contingency in the relation between sex and gender in the face of cultural configurations of causal unities that are regularly assumed to be natural and necessary.[2]

The travesty of drag can go beyond mere carnival, which can serve in the end merely to shore up the status quo (after all, carnival is really a holiday). It can take the form of an *incitement to rebellion.* It can express a desire to revolt against that most tyrannical of laws, the 'natural' link between sex and gender. This drag-as-rebellion, strange to relate, can even represent a rejection of the denigration of women's bodies on the basis of lack.

Freud suggested that a man's refusal to accept his mother's castration, the improbability of her body compared to his, will often lead to homosexuality. In this castration crisis, he suggests, the non-accepting male's desire for his mother yields to 'ceaseless flight', flight from the 'truth' of her sexual difference. The boy then makes good this lack not through the fetishization of the foot, leg, fur etc., as do heterosexual men, but by substituting his *own body* for the missing phallus.

Kaja Silverman in *Male Subjectivity at the Margins* argues that, rather than being simply the result of a horror of women's bodies on the part of gay men, this process might be the result of an identification with femininity that represents a resistance to 'the whole process of devaluation which is made to follow from a woman's "difference"' and 'a refusal to accede to the equation of the mother with insufficiency'.[3] This is perhaps the basis of some kinds of drag-as-rebellion: gay men dress as women, i.e. women with men's bodies, putting on their subjectivity but refusing woman's castration and becoming themselves a kind of phallic mother (i.e. the mother they desire) and avenging themselves on a tremulous world.

In this model of drag, travesty and glamour are deployed in an attempt to erase misogyny rather than the feminine body's threat. This is no doubt the kind of redemptive drag that gay men and lesbians look to with starry eyes, finding in it phallic heroines and goddesses to champion their *demi-monde* against the heavens themselves; in the queer's dream of the mothers' revolt against the fathers, drag queens are prized for their ball-busting terror; they are Bette Davis and Joan Crawford freed from their studio chains and escaped from the Hollywood zoo, causing panic on the streets.

This is also the origin of the mythology of the Stonewall drag queens leading the resistance to the police raid: the first bottle is thrown from expertly manicured and painted fingers and bursts into a thousand glittering shards and suddenly the drag queens are witches casting a glamour over the uniformed representatives of the masculine Inquisition. In redemptive drag, men in frocks are flamboyant, romantic dissidents in the struggle against gender totalitarianism. But most of all this kind of drag has an enchanting glamour of doomed but splendid resistance; these are faggots who demand to be burned with the witches in a fatalistic challenge in which God's law is itself *travestied,* the majesty of His creation transformed into tragicomedy by the sex heretics:

> ''Oh, yes, my dear'. Miss Destiny said, 'there is a God, and he is one Hell of a joker. Just look—' and she indicates her lively green satin dress and then waves her hand over the entire room. *Trapped* . . . But one day, in the most lavish drag you've evuh seen—heels! and gown! and beads! and spangled earrings!—I'm going to storm heaven and protest! *Here I am!!!* I'll yell—and I'll shake my beads at Him . . . And God will cringe!'[4]

Nature's cruel trick rebounds on Nature's head in the image of the drag queen's revenge. The *'anima muliebris in virili corpore inclusa'* (woman's soul trapped in a man's body) formula becomes the personal drama of the individual struggle against sex–gender tyranny. In this form of drag a female subjectivity really is embraced, inasmuch as this kind of drag queenery places the man in as 'low' a status in God's creation as woman: synonymous with rebellion and sin. But it is a low status that threatens to turn tables any moment, the world of trash that they are regents over may burst upon the 'high' world at any moment: 'I'm going to storm heaven and then protest!' A brazen act of defiance and deviancy; a 'glamour' of hatred so powerful, a 'charm' of beads and heels so strong, that even God will 'cringe'. The naturalness of the sex–gender causality, the imprisonment of desire, is implicitly accepted—'Oh, yes, my dear, there is a God'—in order to assault it. The Miss Destiny model of drag is the flagrant, flaming, final embodiment of Foucault's reverse discourse, irresistible in its sheer verve. 'Yes!' screams the drag queen in bitter pride, 'I *am* a woman's soul trapped in a man's body! *Look at your handiwork and weep!'*

The Miss Destiny model of drag is usually associated with street drag and the misogynist-turn model with pub drag (though both have a little of each other in them). But it was ironically the riot that the drag queens led in the imagination at Stonewall which marked the decline of Miss Destiny: the personal drama became a political one, romance was replaced by realism. Even the drag queenery of the early 1970s, the so-called 'rad-fems' in groups like the Gay Liberation Front, demonstrated its travesty of *social* assumptions by carefully including significations of manhood such as moustaches or beards with their alarming apparel. Miss Destiny became Miss Construed. The *heroic* moment of the drag queen had passed: her heroism had always depended on total surrender to drag rather than self-consciously ironic statements (e.g. the carefully staged street drag of the Sisters of Perpetual Indulgence, gay men who dress as nuns, is occasionally amusing but never *moving*).

Post Stonewall, pub drag became the dominant form. As the gay male body pursued its relentless masculinization, drag queenery that was anything other than cabaret was shunned. Sincere identification with woman's subjectivity, however dubious this might be, was now anathema. Drag was taken off the streets and put on the stage. If beer softens the edges of a sharply condemning world, then drag acts blunt the 'sharp' threat of the feminine for the male patrons of the gay pub. We laugh at what we fear, given the chance, and this is what the drag act offers 'her' audience. 'She' knows very well that is 'her' job to send up the feared sexual difference, to place inverted commas around woman. Between performing songs the 'artiste' will make sure that the audience does not forget that, notionally, 'she' has a vagina. Escalating the 'threat' (and thus its defusion), fake whispered propriety about 'down below' and 'women's problems' gives way to loud and crude references to 'my fucking twat' and 'my bleedin' fanny'. Jokes then come fast and furious about the loss of an endless stream of increasingly unlikely objects—vibrators, bananas, cucumbers, marrows, gasmen—all devoured without trace by the insatiable vagina, but always failing to take even the edge off its

monstrous appetite.[5] The masculine fear of the vagina's ability to swallow up literally everything is avowed through the reference to it, only to be disavowed through the 'joke', through the shared laughter and the shared reassurance that we know very well that this is in fact a man.

This is an inversion of the usual logistics of the disavowal of castration that Freud attributed to children, where the evidence of the child's own eyes about women's bodies is acknowledged on a surface level but denied on another, deeper one. In drag the idea 'all human beings have penises', the primal idea, is no longer held under the secondary, perceptual idea, 'some humans are without penises'—rather the second becomes held under the first: 'I know very well that this person has a penis but I will pretend he is what he appears to be' (this is suspension of disbelief).

The drag queen's invocation of the female body and its terrors in a world of let's pretend is a guaranteed route to comic success. One famous drag queen on the London gay pub circuit exploits this with his famous welcome to lesbian members of the audience: 'Hello all you 1-1-1-l-l-l-l-l-lesbians!', fluttering his tongue in a grotesque parody of cunnilingus, thus conjuring up the gay man's nightmare of being brought face to face with 'the gash'.

Although the glamour invoked, in the form of 1940s Hollywood film stars, is fetishized, even this ambiguous expression of female power, of female enchantment, needs to be travestied. This is often done through the very frocks that invoke the glamour: the ghoulish mysteries of the female anatomy are pointed up by underwear that never fits and must always be adjusted and complained about, apparently reversing the traditional fetishizing use of Hollywood glamour—but only because we know very well that it is a man's body that lies beneath that corset and hoop skirt.

Dame Edna Everage, a misogynist-turn drag queen par excellence, despite Barry Humphries' indignant protestations, also offers her public an opportunity to resolve fears about the monstrous feminine—in this particular case the maternal body. The tag 'housewife superstar' emphasizes that she is a mother at the same time as pointing up the unlikelihood of this; she herself, with all her famous false modesty, constantly refers to herself as a mother who also happens to be an 'international megastar'; the modesty, it is implied, is as false as her maternal femininity. As a hardly petite man in drag who brings to mind aunts who were suspiciously unfeminine beneath their overly made-up faces and blue rinses, Humphries presents his audience with their worst nightmare of femininity-as-drag in women: the fear that mothers might actually be violent bruisers beneath the day-glo and the sweet smiles. Edna is the phallic mother who is also a bad mother; a bad mother, moreover, dissembling as a good one. For all her talk about her 'little chicks' and her love for them, the joke is that she is clearly a *monstrous* mother. This is the basis of her treatment of her guests: instead of being warm and inviting as her 'feminine' appearance might suggest, she often shocks and humiliates. This is the fear of what Melanie Klein would call the bad mother, the fear that she will not satisfy our needs, that she will instead suddenly become as terrifying as she was once loving. Edna is also the fear of the phallic mother, described by Freud, who at any moment might produce a penis instead of a breast. Edna's successful exploitation of bad/phallic mother anxieties is perhaps the reason why she has yet to meet that other performer who has made a career out of the same terrors, the scary auntie with a blue rinse to end all scary aunties: Margaret Thatcher.

In the same way the ambivalent attitude towards the womb/vagina is exploited: her favourite vaginal expression, 'I mean that in a warm, moist, *friendly* kind of way—I do!', is used to envelop the sharpest barbs. This is why criticisms of Edna's racism, sexism and sadism are superfluous. The public want her precisely for her monstrosity and her travesty of nurturing qualities. Again, as a man in a frock these anxieties about the female body are avowed only to be disavowed.

But even the avowal-disavowal of drag is not always enough to eradicate anxieties about the feminine body. The pub drag queen has to cultivate an immobility, an ethereality, in which her body is denied through 'graceful' ghostly movements and she offers up her soul instead through her voice, or, better still, through mime (someone else's voice). For the drag queen, movement is internal and spiritual. This stillness and pathos of the drag queen is *deathly* since death is the most 'sublime' state for the female body. Death is there in the immobility of the drag queen onstage, in the rigor mortis of the frocks, in the funereal, other-worldly quality of sex mismatched with gender; there is something just as mournful about men in frocks as there is something comic. Even the grease-paint, in its ghastliness, is an embalmment.[6]

The ultimate statement of drag as misogynist turn, as male appropriation of female glamour, is portrayed in *Death Becomes Her* (1992), a Hollywood comedy which takes the morbid aspect of the drag myth to its logical conclusion. Meryl Streep and Goldie Hawn play glamorous ballbusting bitches whose feminine power 'casts a spell' over the man they fight each other for (Bruce Willis), making him impotent. After being held up as irresistible, their bodies are then brought low through mutilation: Streep's neck is broken by Willis and Hawn's stomach is blown out by a shotgun. But by the aid of witchcraft, in the form of a potion of youth they took to ward off ageing (*the* threat to their glamour), they become undead: alive in dead bodies. But this also deprives them of the 'beauty' that death brings the female body and they are required to literally drag themselves up in embalming fluid and paint in order to maintain their bodies and their glamour. In keeping with the myth of drag this can be done only by a man: Bruce Willis. They now need the powers of the man they unmanned with their glamour to maintain it for them; this reversal has the effect of curing Willis' impotence. In *Death Becomes Her* death is marked as the route by which woman's power—glamour—is passed into the hands of men, saving them from castration, while woman is reduced to a status below that of drag queens (they can at least do their own make-up).

This is the myth not just of drag but of Hollywood itself: male appropriation of glamour is predicated on the death, the lifelessness of the female body—the Medusa's head needs to be cut off before it can be attached to the aegis.

THE GLAMOUR BOYS

If the ethos of drag is alive and well in Hollywood, it seems to be on the wane in gay pubs. Changes in the representation of the male body in the 1980s have made it possible for a man to appropriate a stagey desirability to the male body without having to avail himself of feminine glamour. These changes are represented, of course, by the phenomenon of the male stripper—and it is the male stripper who is driving drag out of the gay pubs. In the 1990s the number of gay venues advertising male strippers appears to have 'outstripped' those advertising drag acts; some pubs even offer a stripper every night.

In this new-look gay scene the spectacle of the male body, the showing of that which gay men eroticize—the phallus—has replaced the hiding of that which they reject—lack. This contrast is what appears to define this form of cabaret at every turn; it is almost as if the stripper were saying, 'Look how unlike a drag queen I am.'

Drag is a glorious, glamorous celebration of surface over substance, artifice over nature, pretence over authenticity; the carnival of drag overturns the fear of woman-as-nature and replaces it with woman-as-artifice; appearance is held up for approval and essence mocked. The stripper, on the other hand, ostensibly restores order. He presents us with a ritual of substance over surface, biology over artifice, authenticity over pretence; glamour is shunned and appearance is actually stripped away to reveal … essence. In the drag act, clothes are as fussy and frivolous as design and funds will allow and are only removed (off-stage) to be replaced by even more ecstatically diverting costumes. In the strip act, clothes and accessories are devout in their simplicity, and despite their canny multi-layering, loyal in their communication of the male body underneath and—so we are led to believe—they are worn only to be removed.

In contrast to the miming/singing and bitchy patter of the drag queen, language itself is rejected as dissemblance, as something untrustworthy, in the stripper's display of 'truth'. The stripper remains determinedly mute during his performance, and ear-splitting dance music plays over the PA forbidding conversation; when he has to give instructions to members of the audience he puts his hand to their ear and covers his mouth, no doubt to make himself heard but also perhaps to hide his moving lips from us. Wordless corporeality is the only way that the ultimate masculine truth can be told. And once that truth is told there is nothing to do but pick up your clothes and body oil and go home. The penis shown—show over.

This is the myth of stripping that we are invited to participate in: what you finally *see* is what you get and what you finally get is what you wanted to see. In fact the myth of male stripping fascinates by its *dissimulation*; it mesmerizes precisely because it contradicts itself with every discarded item; it enchants by denying the very thing it maintains: it disavows what it avows. The only 'truth' of stripping is that the stripper can never be naked enough, never *stripped* enough, because the phallus can never be shown—instead we are palmed off with a paltry penis. No matter how freakish his genital attributes, no matter how craftily engorged and arranged with rings and elastic bands, no matter how frantically it is waved and waggled in front of the audience's faces, the stripper's penis, once naked, *never lives up to the promise of the phallus*: the climactic finale of the strip is . . . an anti-climax. Next to the phallus the poor stripper's penis is almost no-thing; try as he might the stripper cannot 'see or touch anything but his own smooth body'. The removal of clothes and accessories—leather jacket, shirt(s), T-shirt(s), boots, socks, chaps, jeans, boxer shorts, jock-strap, and even the final posing pouch—can never avow the stripper's nakedness enough. The audience knows this very well and is required (as with the drag act) to suspend disbelief as it watches the strip, as if playing 'Pass the Parcel', knowing that under all the layers of wrapping it will be empty. As with 'Pass the Parcel', the enjoyment of stripping is, of course, in the un-wrapping rather than the revelation.

But once 'revealed', the stripper has to present 'nothing' as 'everything'. In other words he finds himself in the same position as the drag act who has to present nothing (castration) as everything (fetishistic glamour).

Of course the stripper's nakedness is never 'no-thing', it is always some-thing (though not the thing it is supposed to be). The stripper's body, however stripped, is always clothed with preconceptions and conceits. In an attempt to proclaim the nakedness of the male body the stripper accessorizes it. This is the rich irony of male stripping—it is presented as the antithesis of drag *but is in fact part of its thesis*. Surface, artifice and pretence are all celebrated in the strip cabaret. This is, after all, *show-business,* as premeditated, as diverting, as entrancing—as *glamorous* in its masquerade as drag.

The themed outfits (sailor, policeman, leather-man, etc.) frame the stripper in a fantasy that clothes him long after the bell-bottoms and tunic are discarded. The carefully choreographed and rehearsed routines that are the performance of stripping carefully exclude any possibility of 'naked' spontaneity. The artful contrivances on his body, the shaved chest, arms, legs; the clipped balls, whitened teeth; the gym-pampered body, the cock ring, even the glittering oil that

he asks members of the audience to spread over his skin, all weave a spell which idealizes him, and lubricates the passage of the audience's fantasies over him. That is to say they accessorize his body and deny it at the very moment that it appears to be offered unadulterated.

In addition to glamour, travesty and carnival are there in stripping too. The phallus is unwittingly brought low at the very moment of its supposed exaltation by the foolish insufficiency of its signification by the penis on-stage, and wittingly in the way that members of the audience are humiliated and debased for their desire for it. So they are persuaded/forced to perform various acts of sleaze, from simulated acts of fellatio to, in one popular London act, removing their glasses from between the stripper's clenched buttocks with their teeth. Another stripper has his victim lie face down on-stage with his trousers and pants at half-mast, pours baby-oil between the prostrate man's buttocks and then 'fucks' him with a dildo attached to an inflatable man. The phallus, the male body and those who worship these are ridiculed in the strip act, which abases what it appears to hold up (hen parties know this very well, hence the popularity of male strippers with them). As we have seen, the threat of travesty of the male body in putting on women's clothing is displaced onto the female body. But in stripping, ironically, the male body is travestied in the *showing* of it.

Finally it can be said that, contrary to the supposition that drag and strip acts are dichotomous, we can say that they are *homogenous* (sharing the same ancestry). Drag is a pretence, an ecstasy of surfaces (of frocks), that draws attention to the (feminine) body to distract us from it ('I know very well that person has a penis, nevertheless . . . '). Male stripping, it can be seen, is also a pretence, an ecstasy of surfaces (of skins), that draws attention to the (masculine) body and yet distracts us from it ('Is that all there is?'). Thus male stripping works best, and achieves its greatest theatrical and spectacular effect, when it embraces its fate, its continuity with despised drag, and offers the audience self-consciously, not 'nakedness', but *glamour.*

One gay black stripper's act seems to have done just this, and the glorious result is a little epiphany that would surely convince Miss Destiny herself to become a male stripper. The climax of his strip (one of many) is absolutely the finale of a drag act: he presents his back to us, holding out a burgundy red peacock cape at shoulder-length, glittering in the stage-lights. Slowly, slowly, with impeccable grace, he turns towards us, blinding us with an explosion of gold lamé, burning fiery against his ebony skin: the golden wings of Medusa! On his face is a smile that is the soul of glamour, and between his legs, of course, an enormous penis jutting out, pointing at the audience like an accusing priapic finger (a swine's tusk?); this is the male body made improbable, the masculine made Other; naked before us but, in effect, clothed 'in heels! and gown! and beads! and spangled earrings!'

A rush of giddy terror and bliss chills the audience and they know that they are in the presence of the phallic witch-mother, head restored to her shoulders.

And God cringes.

HEAVY METAL—STRAIGHT BOYS DISCOVER DRAG

Stripped to the waist to reveal that fearsome selection of tattoos, drenched with sweat and cycling shorts that leave little to the imagination ..., Axl Rose [lead singer with Guns 'n' Roses] is a very strong stage character. Kilts, leather jackets and a bandana are frequent accessories ...

Axl Rose fanzine

Gay men are not the only ones who are attracted to glamour. Straight men are also enchanted by and afeared of it; they are also keen to fix the Medusa's head in the centre of their shield precisely because her gaze freezes their

blood: the power of glamour is always in direct proportion to the fear of it. As with the drag queen, the problem for the straight man is how to appropriate the power of its countenance—how to be 'a very strong stage character'—without being frozen himself by its gaze.

Rock and roll, of course, provides the answer—rock and roll is male glamour. That it is a form of drag is almost a commonplace. And as with drag, the glamour of rock and roll is controlled by travesty and misogyny. Travesty is there in the carnivalesque world of rock and roll, where Dionysus is worshipped and authority is mocked: glamour is permitted because it is 'far out', and 'zany'; it rebels against humdrum suburban life and upsets your parents. Misogyny stabilizes this male glamour as entertainment, preventing it from spilling over into revolution. This is especially the case in the most 'classical' rock and roll form: heavy metal.

Heavy metal is the most self-consciously Dionysian of all the rock forms and prides itself on what it sees as its 'rassling' nonconformity. In reality the world of heavy metal is a tyrannically conformist one, where rebellion is strictly codified as little more than 'maleness as badness', i.e. the traditional script of fuckin' n' fightin', cussin' n' drinkin'. Most of all, heavy metal is about conformity to the law of the *phallus.* What else could 'cock rock' be but a symphony to phallocentrism?

Ironically it is through masquerade that heavy metal attempts to present itself as a celebration of substance over surface, the phallus over lack. As Kaplan has argued in *Rock Around the Clock,* the male masquerade present in rock and roll differs from that employed in the representation of women in Hollywood in that the accessories do not stand in for lack, rather they attempt to deny that there is any sexual difference that would require the possibility of lack. Thus the dragged-up rock star 'renders the feminine non-male rather than Other ...'[7] The appeal of heavy metal is that it denies difference at the very moment that it appears to be embracing it: heavy metal fans look to their music not just to celebrate the phallus and repudiate lack but also to make them feel both special and ordinary, unique and one of the boys, exceptional and regular all at once. (The reality of the manic denial of difference in heavy metal is most vividly illustrated by the total absence of any black faces either on- or off-stage.)[8]

Little wonder then that the most fascinated heterosexual devotees of male glamour in the form of heavy metal masquerade are teenage boys, who make up the vast majority of heavy metal fans. Teenage boys are required to confront the feminine or else jeopardize their successful graduation into manhood. After years of renouncing them (only sissies play with girls), these boys are often faced with the unknown Other in a setting which bears little relation to the phallic fantasy of the all-conquering studman in which they would like to see themselves. The mundane fact these boys struggle with is that not all girls are simpering 'babes' who will coo in their arms. This can only amplify their anxieties. As Stan Denski and David Sholle have observed in their study of heavy metal fans in 'Metal Men and Glamour Boys':

> These boys are confronted by girls who may be larger, stronger, and smarter than they are, while at the same time these boys are being socialised into the dominant masculine cultural position of pursuer of the female, thus generating a fear of the feminine.[9]

Although heavy metal may wish to deny the possibility of sexual difference and lack at the moment of capturing feminine glamour as much as any gay drag act, the straight boy's anxiety cannot be dealt with through 'ceaseless flight' (or identification)—unless, as he sees it, he is prepared to jettison his manhood completely. Unlike gay men he is required, by definition, to expose himself to the female body in the most intimate and vulnerable way. Instead of flight he must show mastery; woman is a test of his manhood that must be overcome by domination, by *conquest*. This is why aggression is so heavily eroticized in heavy metal. The Gothic iconography popular with this kind of music provides the teen boy with a fantasy-world where he can be Conan the Barbarian winning his mate or He-Man freeing She-Woman with his mighty sword. The violence is not usually directed at women (this would be unmanly), but towards other men in order to win possession of them. But although women are often represented as damsel babes that wait in their castle for 'Bill and Ted', they are just as often portrayed as 'bitches'. Against the 'babes'/'chicks' there is posited the 'groupie', the Whore of Babylon who threatens to literally gobble men up; in the words of Sammy Hagar from Van Halen, explaining why he steers clear of groupies, 'by the time you meet one of those girls she's already sucked about three yards of dick'.[10]

The ambivalent attitude of heavy metal towards women and the body horror the genre attaches to them ('sucked three yards of dick' connotes perhaps the famous tongue scene in *The Exorcist*) is best summed up in the logo used on the singles review page of the main heavy metal magazine *Kerrang!*: a naked curvacious young woman with a rotted skull atop her shoulders. It is the Medusa's head syndrome again.

Women's bodies are desired for what they can bring a man but feared for what they might take away. A famous gesture of 'cock rock', the mock cunnilingus where the artist tilts his head back and flutters his tongue, invokes the same horror as that employed by the drag queen ('1–1–1–1-l-l-l-lesbians!'): the horror of being brought face to face with 'the gash'. And yet its equivalence marks the disjunction of the two forms of drag: on the drag queen's face it is a tease, a whiff of fear resolved through ridicule; on the face of the heavy metal performer it is a challenge, a display of bravado, of *gall*. The threat of the female body is denied: 'I am not afraid,' he says, 'I am master of my emotions and therefore master of the female body.' Woman is rendered non-male rather than Other because rock and roll shows that she has no autonomous power: her glamour, her fearsomeness, her body are all appropriated; desire for the mother is displaced into 'sadistic possession'.

In this drag act of rock and roll woman becomes merely the negative elaboration of the masculine subject. Rock and roll's power and appeal to men is that it devalues woman by rendering her non-male in a phallocentric economy.

> When I was 14 I was over at this girl's house I'd been trying to pick up for months and she played 'Aerosmith Rocks'; I listened to it eight times and forgot all about her. (Slash, lead guitarist with Guns 'n' Roses)[11]

While 'girls' are very much a part of the rock and roll legend they often come behind drinking, drugs and the music itself in priority and then seem to be valued only in terms of what exchange they bring between 'the guys'; as Denski and Sholle, drawing on Irigaray, explain:

> A repressed and, hence, disparaged sexuality (a relationship between men and bonds between men) takes place through the heterosexual exchange and distribution of women. This is particularly evident in the movie, 'Heavy Metal', and in music videos where groups of men divide the spoils, that is, the women. This is especially evident in the Motley Crue video for their song, 'Girls, Girls, Girls.' In it, the women exotic dancers are obvious targets for exchange, yet function only as visual pleasure. The only physical, bodily pleasure in the video takes place in the exchanges between the male band members.[12]

Rock and roll provides an economy of sameness where rock and roll can itself come to stand in for the usual commodity that prevents the economy from lapsing into incest: rock and roll rocks *around* the cock rather than on it.

Put another way, 'cock rock' provides boys with a way to worship the phallus in a fashion that preserves its and their own desired/prized virility—since in Guy Hocquenghem's phrase, the penis is the virile member and what is virile

is not queer. So the prick itself cannot be put on display as in the male strip cabaret since this would 'queer' the economy and bring about incest and the loss of what is desired. Instead it is displaced into phallic accessories (as opposed to the ones that accessorize glamour): tattoos, muscles, and, of course, guitars hoisted between legs clad in skin-tight leather or rubber. The guitars are the key phallic trope and are played in a style that it would be something of an understatement to call masturbatory. Onstage the band 'play' their guitars and the male members of the audience join with them, sharing the experience, either there in the stadium or with a hi-fi in the privacy of their own home, playing the famous 'air guitar'—joining up in one vast crescendoing circle-jerk.

The music itself, with its simple four-bar phrases and its crude repetitive chords, effects a solid, monumental phallicism, the most important feature of which is its *volume,* i.e. its size and power. The ground-shaking, pummelling, gut-wrenching sound of heavy metal is the sound of boys enjoying the barely sublimated fantasy of being on the receiving end of the stupendously virile organ they worship. In the end, no matter how frantically the heavy metal fan fiddles with his air guitar it is just air and his enjoyment of the music is essentially passive.

The hysterically over-amplified sound is the equivalent of the stuffed crotch, a legend which is right at the heart of rock and roll. That the penis is never shown, not only prevents the breakout of incest and shame but also prevents the disappointment that is inevitable in the male strip act when the penis fails to represent the phallus; rock and roll is, and must always be, *larger than life.* By relying on phallicism instead of the penis, the heavy metal band goes from one climax to another.

But the teen boy's desire for the phallus is not completely displaced into the music and the props; he also desires the heavy metal star. This is the other purpose of glamour—not just to abjure the possibility of sexual difference but also to affirm the star's desirability. The disparity between the way the metal star dresses up and the fan dresses down shows that no simple identification is at work here: the rock star is, like the male stripper to the gay pub-goer, glamorous and Other, erotic and alluring.

The careful ambiguity of the masquerade of the metal star, the appropriation of masculine and feminine images, is represented most famously and most successfully in Axl Rose. He is 'stripped to the waist', revealing 'that fearsome selection of tattoos'; he is 'drenched with sweat and cycling shorts that leave little to the imagination'—like the male stripper, before his finale, he presents us the male body in a phantasmic, fetishized form. But unlike the male stripper he also accessorizes 'femininity' to himself: 'kilts, leather jackets and a bandana are frequent accessories'. Even his name spells out the ambivalent masquerade (that sends out the unambivalent message: desire me, I am everything): 'Axl' suggests the axle of a truck or car, something rigid which transmits power and causes movement, while 'Rose' suggests sweet-smelling delicacy and beauty. The name is also an anagram of 'oral sex'.

This is the meaning of his 'confessions' about his childhood sexual abuse: we see before us a rock star, rampant with all the power and technology that such status brings, and yet he carries with him a history that is one of victimization, of humiliation, of forced passivity. This is acceptable, marketable even, because his narrative becomes the narrative of phallic triumph over passive subjection; this is what he acts out every time he takes the stage: 'Yes! I am desirable to men; I know you want to fuck me; watch me tease you—but, aha! *I fuck you!*'

Unlike for gay men, the feminine embodies an added terror for heterosexual or would-be heterosexual men—the fear of homosexuality. For the straight boy, failure to conquer the feminine implies homosexuality, which itself implies 'penetration' by the feminine and thus lack.

This is a powerful equation for the teen boy whose sexuality is bound to be more fluid than it is supposed to be. Thus the need to confront the feminine becomes also the need to master 'the feminine' in himself: his homosexuality. But like the glamour of woman herself, the fear of homosexuality is in proportion to its allure.

So the glamour of rock and roll in general, and heavy metal in particular, is not just the borrowed illusive magic of woman but also the fear/enchantment of homosexuality. The heavy metal star does not just wish to fix the head of the Medusa to his shield but also the colours of Sodom. Queerness is accessorized to the heterosexual male in the same way as is femininity—employing its power but removing most of its threat. Straight boy rock and roll drag assumes implicitly that there is something glamorous about homosexuality (something that gay men themselves seem to have forgotten). In fact, it might even be argued that in rock and roll glamour the phallocentric economy sees to it that the hypermasculine and 'effeminate' (rather than feminine) images the rock star employs are simply fetishistic representatives of *active and passive homo-desire*.

Use Your Illusion (Title of Guns 'n' Roses double album)

NOTES

Reprinted with permission from Mark Simpson, "Dragging It Up and Down: The Glamorized Male Body," in *Male Impersonators: Men Performing Masculinity* (London: Cassell; New York: Routledge, 1994), 177–96.

1. Jane Mills (1991), *Womanwords,* London: Virago Press: 106.

2. Judith Butler (1990), *Gender Trouble,* London: Routledge: 137–8.

3. Kaja Silverman (1992), *Male Subjectivity at the Margins,* London: Routledge: 372.

4. John Rechy (1984), *City of Night,* New York: Evergreen: 116.

5. It is interesting to note that men with a reputation for getting fucked are often teased by their peers about the monstrous appetite of their rectums; gay men, in other words, seem to displace anxieties about the vagina onto 'receptive' gay men's rectums.

6. This was taken to an ironic extreme by a drag act, popular in London a few years ago, called 'Dead Marilyn', in which a man came on stage dressed as a rotting female corpse.

7. E. Ann Kaplan (1987), *Rocking Around the Clock: Music Television, Postmodernism and Consumer Culture*, New York and London: Methuen: 93.

8. Stan Denski and David Sholle (1992), 'Metal Men and Glamour Boys', in *Men, Masculinity and Media*, ed. Steven Craig, London: Sage Publications: 53.

9. Ibid.: 53.

10. Sammy Hagar (1993), *Raw Magazine*, No. 122 (April): 48.

11. Quoted in Denski and Sholle, 'Metal Men and Glamour Boys': 54.

12. Ibid.: 54.

16

CLASS, RACE AND MASCULINITY: THE MACDADDY, THE SUPERFLY AND THE RAPPER

Del LaGrace Volcano and Judith 'Jack' Halberstam

'In my last life, I was a mackdaddy.'

Dred, Winner of the 1996 NY Drag King Contest

Lesbians produce wildly divergent masculinities in many different cultural arenas. As Flipper of the Dodge Bros comments, it is quite possible that Drag King is a black lesbian tradition that has drawn attention only since it has been taken up by a white lesbian community. Since I am examining the various confluences between race and gender in Drag King spaces, I should preface by pointing out that many lesbian scenes are very segregated. Not surprisingly, the clubs which cater to women of colour have a different relation to Drag King performances and to the performances of alternative masculinities in general. While I run the risk of over-simplifying in this section by making distinctions between white clubs and women-of-colour clubs, the risk seems worthwhile because it allows me to suggest that what we recognize as 'Drag King' in one space may pass unremarked in another. In Club Casanova, for example, the woman dressed in drag is usually up on stage and is read immediately as a Drag King, but in other clubs where strict butch–femme codes pertain, as in some Latino/a clubs, for example, a woman in a suit and tie is definitely not on stage, and she is not going to be read as a Drag King.

In London, New York and San Francisco, the pool of Drag Kings who perform regularly in the clubs tends to be white. The Drag King contests, however, do often draw women of colour up on stage to compete. It seems strange then that the contests should feature so many women of colour, but the Drag King clubs actually feature very few acts by black, Asian or Latina Drag Kings. How do we explain the predominance of white Drag Kings in urban scenes? To a certain extent the Drag King clubs represent the same kind of segregation that characterizes urban lesbian scenes in general: the mainstream clubs tend to attract white women, and women of colour populate other lesbian clubs depending upon the neighbourhood and the music that might be played there.

Interestingly, in predominantly women-of-colour queer spaces, in New York at least, many of the women participate in elaborate and creative versions of butch–femme style, while the more white spaces favour a kind of androgynous or alternative aesthetic (piercings and tattoos). Many of the Drag Kings we interviewed in New York attested to a kind of racialized separation of cultural spheres. Since butch–femme already exists within some of the women-of-colour spaces as a noticeable style, one might expect that these clubs would produce more Drag King culture. This was not true. In a club like Escuelitas, a Latino/a drag bar, all of the drag performances are by men, and men perform both male and female drag. In HerShe Bar, the contests, as I have mentioned, did manage to draw women up on stage from the audience, but many of these women had not dressed up in drag; they simply paraded their butchness to great applause and maybe threw in a quick rap or a few dance steps. The HerShe Bar contest induced more women into the Drag King scene, but these did not include a large number of women of colour.

Much lesbian history tries to locate the racial segregation of public lesbian space as a thing of the past, claiming fully integrated queer spaces as representative of today. However, while some women-of-colour spaces do tend to cater to many different ethnic women's groups, a split between white and women-of-colour spaces does linger on. Few of the Drag Kings I spoke to in either New York or London, white kings and kings of colour, were really willing to address the issue of racially split lesbian spaces, but the lack of women of colour in the East Village clubs, for example, and the smattering of white women in the midtown clubs, spoke to the persistence of a colour barrier.

Two black Drag Kings, Shon and Dred, did find their way into regular Drag King performances from the HerShe Bar contests. Shon, twenty-nine, and Dred, twenty-five, have a wide range of performances: Dred's signature act is a 'mackdaddy' from the disco era; Shon is stunning as a hot, crotch-grabbing rapper. Shon and Dred both won HerShe Bar contests and went on to compete in the final showdown against each other. Shon remembers seeing Dred in an early contest: 'I said she's definitely gonna win, she's got it! She was excellent. I liked the name, I liked the presence, and I could tell she was good. As a performer myself, I always look for true dramatic talent.' Dred thinks Shon is a 'smooth' Drag King and remembers seeing Shon as her major competition in the contest; ultimately, the contest came down to the two of them, and it was Dred who walked away with the title. In that contest, she recalls that she was asked to answer a question on stage: 'What does it mean

to you to be a Drag King?' And Shon answered: 'It means showing men and women how women should be treated ... ' This answer is very much in keeping with Shon's smooth Drag King persona and won him plenty of fan support. Shon noticed that more women of colour entered the contests as time went on but she also noted that many of these women did not dress up in drag: 'They went up with what they had rather than in drag; they might be boyish naturally or just butch looking.'

Both Shon and Dred comment upon the dearth of women of colour who are interested in becoming Drag Kings. In a Jackson Five act that Dred and Shon put together, for example, they had to use men for some of the roles. They have a hard time explaining why more women of colour do not get involved but both believe that as time goes on and as Drag King popularity grows, more women of colour will develop stage Drag King acts. In their shows, Dred and Shon mix up the music and the style that each of them favours. In their 'R & B Old School Show' that they performed at HerShe Bar to an audience of screaming women, they performed for about fifteen minutes and included rap songs by Run DMC. They did the duet 'You're All I Need' by Method Man and Mary J. Blige. They also performed a hot and flashy rendition of 'No Diggety' by Blackstreet.

Dred and Shon's show is an extremely entertaining combination of male impersonation, perfectly timed lip-synching, and choreographed dance moves. They manage to pull off close replications of the performers they are imitating, and in many of their shows, parody gives way to homage. If many of the white Drag Kings poke gentle fun at white masculinity, Dred and Shon approach black masculinity from a very different angle. Dred comments: 'We don't make fun of the music of musicians we perform. We respect them.' Shon responds: 'Word. I want to perform an image that I respect and that is respectable.' Dred amplifies on the meaning of 'respectable' here: 'Yeah, I'm not about to pull a dildo out of my pants or whatever; I'm not about that.' So what is their act about? Shon sums it up: 'It's like, I read a book because I am interested in it, and I read a character in the same way.' Shon's analogy to reading makes clear the elements of tribute, faithfulness to the original and interpretation that mark her performances. She wants to conjure up an image of the person that she is performing and capture his aura, but she also transforms him through the Drag King performance into a more complex rendition of sexy masculinity. She attempts to read a particular person or group or style because it holds interest for her and offers something back. Shon describes preparing her act: 'If I'm trying to get Marvin Gaye, or someone like that who has a real aura, I'll try to get his smile, the way he looks at a woman, or his moves. I want people to look at me and say, "Yeah, that's Marvin!"'

People definitely look at Shon and Dred and like what they see. Many nights when they perform, the audience is packed with women moved by their performances, screaming and waving to them, and singing along with the words of the songs. Dred and Shon manage to pull off an incredibly sexy show which appeals less to the crowd's sense of humour and more to their desires. Dred and Shon work the crowd well and set up an exchange between them and what can only be called their fans. Of course, it makes all the difference where any particular act is performed. At HerShe Bar, Dred and Shon often perform to a very active crowd who participate in the songs and interact vociferously with Dred and Shon. When Dred and Shon performed the same R & B Show at Club Casanova, the atmosphere was quite different. The crowd was more subdued and many seemed spellbound by the performances, but less interactive. Dred and Shon ironically performed a Run DMC song at Club Casanova called 'King of Rock,' and one African-American woman from the audience called out: 'Yeah, rock that white bullshit!' The song samples and pokes fun at some white rock anthems, and the spectacle

of black Drag Kings performing 'King of Rock' to a mostly white crowd enacted nicely the satirical dynamic between rap and rock that Run DMC sets up in the song.

Some white Drag Kings perform rap, partly, one assumes, because the stylized moves of the rapper give the Drag King something quite visible to perform. This Drag King act plays off both the Vanilla Ice phenomenon of the white boy rap, and it captures the performability of black masculinity. Drag King DJ Lizerace (Liz Carthaus), twenty-three, cultivates a hip-hop look and a home-boy sensibility. She regularly performs rap songs, sometimes lip synching and sometimes actually singing over the music. Lizerace most frequently performs Rob Base and Run DMC songs but she also throws in some Beastie Boys songs every now and then: 'I do rap songs that I think people will like. I don't try to be the guy, I just take the style . . . ' I asked Lizerace if she thought she was 'dragging' or 'kinging' black masculinity, but she answered, 'No, I definitely don't think I am impersonating black men.' She continued, 'Nor am I impersonating a white boy who impersonates black rappers.' What then? Why did she even choose to do rap? 'It just happened, I like that music and it seemed like the obvious thing for me to do as a Drag King act.' Even though Lizerace has a sense that she is not performing black masculinity, it is hard not to attach a black masculinity to the rap performance. Also, one has to question the urge to disassociate rap from blackness and to try to make it into simply another version of 'pop'. Lizerace, curiously, seems to fear being accused of trying to perform something that she is not entitled to and her reluctance to connect her performance to racial drag speaks to some of the anxiety about identity that crops up when cross-racial performances are in question. Dred relates that she once wanted to perform at Club Casanova as George Michael. She comments: 'I wanted to do a George Michael song; I loved the song, but I wondered if it would be ok and whether it would go over alright. I decided I could pull it off because this particular song had an R & B influence to it … I was concerned because he was white.'

Obviously, cross-ethnic performances raise specific issues about race and authenticity for the kings. Lizerace tries to emphasize the availability of all masculinities to all performers and argues for a kind of universal access. Accordingly, if she does a Rob Base song, that song is multiply translated through her masculinity and her rap performance and becomes something very different; it becomes part of the transformation that the Drag King act brings about. Dred suggests that one should approach such cross-ethnic acts carefully. She emphasizes that she felt she could have performed this particular George Michael song because the song had an R & B feel to it. She too understands herself to be producing an interpretation of an act rather than an impersonation, but she advocates a careful consideration of what the music, the singer and the Drag King performer bring together. Dred's articulation of her translation of the George Michael song provides an intelligent model for cross-ethnic Drag King performance.

Drag King Retro (Kristabelle Munson), twenty-eight, also talks about cross-ethnic performance. Retro is an Asian-American Drag King who often performs as an 'Uncle Louis, a white-trash American truck driver from upstate New York, newly out of prison.' Retro feels that there is real power in performing this character and transforming his racism into other kinds of expression. He says: 'Having experienced a lot of racism as a transgendered Asian–Pacific Islander, I took a lot of pleasure in being able to spoof the visual image of a white-trash guy. I don't play him as a racist guy, however; he has a heart of gold, and he's what gay men like to call a "daddy" or a "bear."' Retro, then, uses his cross-ethnic performance to tap into the homoerotic potential of the white trash guy and to eliminate the almost essentialist racist component with which white-trash masculinity has been associated. Retro also says that he has been developing

an Asian drag character 'along the lines of Kato, the Asian assistant to super-hero character, the Green Hornet.' Uncle Louis loves this character because he is the 'first non-subservient Asian character.'

In San Francisco there are a very few truly racially mixed lesbian spaces, although in the early 90s Club Q perhaps did the best job of creating a dance space which drew white women and women of colour. Club Q even held its own very successful Drag King contests. An original member of the Dodge Bros was Sonny, a Latina Drag King, and at times the Dodge Bros would play with a Cholo aesthetic. Still, as Flipper comments, it made her a little uncomfortable to play with another cultural and racialized form of masculinity. Flipper says: 'Obviously that's not my cultural identity.' Two Drag Kings in San Francisco who consciously play with Italian and Chicano masculinities are Mario from the Barrio (Gina Dominguez) and Vinnie Testosteroni (Malia Spanyol). Mario and Vinnie are gorgeously excessive personalities. Although Mario and Vinnie do not perform on stage as yet, they are a distinctive presence in San Francisco's lounge Drag King club, Club Confidential. Gina and Malia also create white-trash personae and put lots of time and energy into creating their looks.

In London, there are few women of colour doing drag performances in the clubs, although some women of colour do attend the drag shows. Interestingly enough, however, the performers at Club Geezer are diverse in other ways—many of them are non-English, and the regular performers make up a mostly European cast of characters: Stanley is from Greece, Hans is Austrian, Del is American, Hamish is Scottish, Simo is Italian. While these differences play an important role in the kinds of masculinities and performances that the London kings produce, they are all also quite conscious of the lack of women of colour in the club and at a loss to explain it. These Drag Kings, however, do recognize the ways in which their masculinities operate as raced and classed masculinities, and some are quite adept at describing these functions. Stanley, most notably, talks specifically about what form of white masculinity she taps into, especially when she leaves the space of the club and ventures out in the streets in drag: 'My neighbourhood is populated by gays and blacks and some Turkish immigrants. I am Greek, but in drag, I seem to embody a very Anglicized chic masculinity, which I very much desire, but which also sends strange and conflicting messages to the people in the streets.' Stanley elaborates that he is not simply concerned that he may be a target for queer-bashing—'But I really do have questions about what it means to parade my white imitation of upper-class masculinity in this particular neighbourhood.' In this extremely important articulation of the meaning and effects of white masculinity, Stanley manages to reveal how it is that white masculinity becomes visible—either it is turned into a spectacle of working-class masculinity by the Geezer show, or, as in this formulation, it becomes a chic and almost arrogant form of upper-class masculinity. Stanley very bravely states his ambivalence about this performance in terms of both his desire to inhabit that particular form of powerful masculinity, but also in terms of the effects of 'parading' this performance in particular neighbourhoods.

For some white Drag Kings, passing successfully allows them to tap into empowered versions of maleness and gives them at least temporarily some kind of access to the pleasures and liabilities associated with such social approval. Stanley notes the pleasure he takes in such upper-class chic masculinity, but he is also quite aware that this privilege could play out differently in the streets of his mixed neighbourhood where his white maleness and male whiteness become an affront to the less privileged masculinities that he encounters. For the Drag King of colour, the 'pass' only accesses another kind of trouble. Dred tells a story of trying to hail a cab in New York while out in gangsta drag: 'I had my Adidas outfit on and my hat pulled down low. It took me thirty minutes to catch a cab because cabs would slow down, then they would see me and speed by. It felt horrible.' Dred does admit to sometimes feeling safer in drag, but as his cab incident shows, masculinity, at least for the kings of colour, is no guarantee of access to forms of social privilege.

For the time being, the Drag King scene continues to reflect the social stratifications that exist among lesbians in general. The shows of the women of colour and the white kings are different, appeal to different audiences, and are accorded different receptions depending on where they are performed. The Drag Kings who venture out into the world in drag also experience very different treatment depending on whether they are white or black or brown. For this reason, it would be foolish to pretend that racial differences and racial disharmonies do not affect Drag King cultures. The preponderance of white Drag Kings in this book, then, speaks to the cultivation of Drag King theatricality in white spaces and a tendency towards butch–femme within some clubs frequented by women of colour. Shon and Dred, however, represent a bold new horizon for kings of colour, as well as a submerged tradition, and as they tour the club circuit of New York bringing smooth R & B, tough and tight rap and nasty mackdaddy funk, we can be sure that they will inspire others to get down on it and follow their lead.

NOTE

Reprinted with permission from Del LaGrace Volcano and Judith J. Halberstam, "Class, Race and Masculinity: The Superfly, the Macdaddy and the Rapper," in *The Drag King Book* (London: Serpents Tail Books, 1999), 140–52.

ANNOTATED GUIDE TO FURTHER READING

Adams, James Eli. *Dandies and Desert Saints: Styles of Victorian Masculinity.* New York: Cornell University Press, 1995. Draws on queer theory and cultural history to rethink constructions of Victorian manhood. Examines masculine identity in Victorian literature from Thomas Carlyle through Oscar Wilde. Looking at icons of middle-class masculinity (the dandy, the gentleman, the priest, the prophet, and the soldier), this book approaches masculinity as a social norm and a construction, thus arguing that concepts such as the effeminate and the unmanly have been misunderstood.

Chapman, Rowena, and Jonathon Rutherford, eds. *Male Order: Unwrapping Masculinity.* London: Lawrence and Wishart, 1988.

Cicolini, Alice. *The New English Dandy.* London: Thames and Hudson, 2005. A guide to men's dress style and accessories. Includes six chapters that examine six case studies of the twenty-first-century dandy, each featuring a fashion shoot, and eight pages of bespoke tailoring and interviews.

Craig, Steve, ed. *Men, Masculinity and the Media.* Newbury Park, CA: Sage, 1992. This edited volume addresses how the media serve to construct masculinities, how men and their relationships have been depicted, and how men respond to media images. From comic books and rock music, to fashion, to film and television.

Fillin-Yeh, Sarah, ed. *Dandies: Fashion and Finesse in Art and Culture.* New York: New York University Press, 2001. A collection of essays that considers the visual languages, politics, and poetics of dandiacal appearance. Juxtaposes theoretical models with evocative images and descriptions of clothing in order to link sartorial self-construction with artistic, social, and political self-invention.

Jobling, Paul. "Statue Men: The Phallic Body, Identity and Ambiguity in Fashion Photography." In *Fashion Spreads: Word and Image in Fashion Photography since 1980.* London and New York: Berg, 1999. Examines the construction of masculinity and the representation of male bodies in fashion photography and the media industry. Considers the "new man" and "masculinities in crisis."

Malossi, Giannino, ed. *Material Man: Masculinity, Sexuality, Style.* New York: Harry N. Abrams, 2000. *Material Man* is an edited volume with a wide range of interesting articles on fashion, masculinity and the media.

McBride, Dwight A. *Why I Hate Abercrombie and Fitch: Essays on Race and Sexuality.* New York: New York University Press, 2005. This collection of essays investigates topics such as marketing strategies, black gay media representations, gay personal advertisements and pornography and comments on how hiring practices and advertising campaigns affect American culture.

McDowell, Colin. *The Man of Fashion: Peacock Males and Perfect Gentlemen.* London: Thames and Hudson, 1997. Well-illustrated overview of the history of extravagant men's dress.

Nixon, Sean. "Distinguishing Looks: Masculinities, the Visual and Men's Magazines." In *Pleasure Principles: Politics, Sexuality and Ethics,* ed. Victoria Harwood, David Oswell, Kay Parkinson and Anna Ward. London: Lawrence and Wishart, 1993. Nixon, Sean. *Hard Looks: Masculinities, Spectatorship and Contemporary Consumption.* London: UCL; New York: St Martins, 1996. An examination of the new masculine imagery that has developed in relation to popular consumption over the last decade. The author investigates the development of this "new man" imagery and its relationship to contemporary formations of masculinity and masculine culture.

PART III

Icons: The Evolution of Men's Wear

INTRODUCTION

To be well dressed—who does not want to be well dressed?

Adolf Loos, 1898[1]

The European avant-garde identified a number of items of menswear as iconic of modernity and, in some cases, of the evolution of a higher order of design, one timeless and perfectly formed. Do clothing icons begin life as emblems of democratic standardization, or do they develop from eccentric and particular social settings, from "high society" or a college fraternity house? Are these "icons" adopted by the avant-garde because they are already "old-fashioned"? What is the relationship of mass-produced clothing, the boutique, and the media to the idea of singular fashion? In this section readers are introduced to menswear as part of broader modernist debates about the evolution of clothing forms, particularly the modern suit. Aspects of leisure wear, a major site of men's sartorial experimentation in the twentieth century, are also considered. Many of these items of clothing, as well as certain textures and qualities, traveled into formal wear decades later, in part because of generational change, but also as the result of changing social codes after World War II. Iconic pieces of fashion—the turn-up trouser, the unlined suit, the blue jean, the school uniform—can be considered as new types of clothing with parts of their origins in working-class and occupational dress, but also in the dress of elites who refused to conform. Fashion, one concludes after reading the authors selected in this section, not only transforms the way we appear but also the possibilities of being and experiencing life as masculine subjects.

THE BOY PRINCE

Why do men wear striped ties? Who wore the "Windsor knot"? Who would get their jacket and trousers for the same suit made in different continents? In our own era when fashions are set on the catwalk, in clubs, and on the streets, it is difficult to countenance an era when a royal male set trans-Atlantic fashions. Yet that was precisely the role of the Duke of Windsor, already one of the most famous men in the world as Prince Edward of York, later Prince of Wales, before he abdicated after a short reign as King Edward VIII. In his case we see an example of a fashion-conscious aristocrat born in the age of the moving image, who also made extensive use of photography to promulgate his image. As Prince of Wales he brought soft casual sporting wear out of the field and into public space. His youthful squabbles with his father revolved around his appearance and his wardrobe as well as his studied informality, which probably appeared too American, like the sons of the elites at Princeton. He popularized the striped tie in 1920s North America; the Duke's "Windsor knot" is the ideal way to make a tie with a cut-away informal collar. He invented a personal safari suit and stalking trousers that looked like a divided skirt, innovations that relate him to some of the practical proposals of the Men's Dress Reform Party, discussed by Barbara Burman elsewhere in this volume.

In quasi-exile in the 1950s and 1960s, he was a fashion leader but also a follower of postwar American trends, signaled in his adoption of glaring colored checks and multicolored scarves and kerchiefs for Palm Beach resort wear. His accumulation of hundreds of suits, trousers, bow ties, and shoes demanded its own fabric swatch-indexing system for the garments to be moved between residences and countries, contradicting the cliché that men are not fashion consumers. But the frequent explanation that he was "vain" equally does not explain any of this behavior. The Duke was unconventional because of his subject position. He could break sartorial rules because he was the ruler who no longer had to keep up a preordained appearance. All of this was possible precisely because he was a former king; similar eccentricity would not necessarily be tolerated in his eyes if worn by others born to less privilege. He could break the rules because he was fully aware of history, that monarchs once set fashions, instead of following them. Furthermore, he knew that a monarch was also once "cut" by a dandy-innovator, the tale outlined by Olga Vainshtein in this *Reader*. The Duke illustrates Ulrich Lehmann's argument in *Tigersprung* (2000) that modernity in dress is a going backward and forward, back to traditions and leaping forward to newness. That is the ultimate modernity and perhaps the reason the Duke's mode is revered by those who follow male sartorial style.

When the Duke of Windsor died in Paris in 1972, his wardrobe was retained by the Duchess of Windsor, possibly as a type of shrine to her husband. Upon her death in 1986 the contents of "Villa Windsor" were acquired by the Chairman of Harrods of London Mohamed Al Fayed and dispersed at auction at Sotheby's in 1997.[2] The Duke's dressing room revealed dozens of differently patterned kerchiefs and bandannas arranged in glass-topped drawers in chic red-and-white cabinets, hundreds of identical bow ties, and dozens of suits, shoes, and kilts made of a wide range of materials. The collection included Keds canvas shoes, as well as colored slubbed silk and linen trousers from H. Harris (New York). The Duke's modernity was signaled even in his bathing practices; his preference for showers was so extreme that the bathtub in his private quarters was boarded over, becoming a storage place for personal photographs and letters detailing his famous romance with Mrs. Simpson, later Duchess of Windsor, whom he had met in 1931. The bathroom indicates the public/private split that characterized his existence. As a "modern" heir who considered the lot of the worker, visited Hitler's Germany to inspect autobahns and factories, and used the most up-to-date decorators such as Elsie de Wolfe and Syrie Maugham to redecorate his English country residence, the prince would only naturally wish to appear modern. His elegant straw hat, suits, and spectator shoes for the Riviera also matched the machine-age emphasis of the boats and airplanes alongside which he was frequently photographed from the 1930s to the 1950s.

"DRESS SOFT: PANTS ACROSS THE SEA"

In the 1920s the Prince of Wales was probably the most famous man in the world. His ability to relate to the working man, his blond hair, and his small size and rather eccentric posture made him popular with both men and women. He traveled extensively, reaching Canada, Australia, New Zealand, India, South Africa, Argentina, Peru, Chile, and the United States from 1920 to 1929.

In a photograph of him meeting Crown Prince Hirohito of Japan in 1922, the Prince of Wales in uniform reveals a body as curved and as disciplined by military dress as the slightly old-fashioned belle epoque curves of the Japanese Empress [figure 19.2]. The Prince loved uniforms and his military roles, introducing these elements into civilian dress. He popularized the striped tie of the Grenadier Guards, which he was entitled to wear, in the United States in the 1920s. The ubiquitous stripe we see everywhere in men's fashion first had to cross from stiff uniforms to leisure before it became assimilated into formal wear.

The severity and discipline of his masculine style were matched by the sartorial dandyism of the Duchess, who rarely wore patterns and favored superbly cut clothes to highlight her jewels and possibly mask her lack of height. That they were both obsessed with appearances as well as being small and boylike in their body type might go a long way to explain the erotic mutual attraction that has puzzled commentators so often about this love match [figure 18.1].[3] The Duke attached so much importance to fashion that much of his publication *A Family Album* (1960) revolved around dress. As Kerry Taylor notes in her catalogue essay accompanying the dispersal of the Duke's wardrobe, "Not since his forebear King George IV in the 1820s had a monarch lavished so much care and expense on his own personal appearance."[4] Interestingly, the Duke often claimed that his dressing was frugal, a fact not borne out by the contents of the sale. His 1960s records indicate fifteen evening suits, fifty-five lounge suits, and three formal suits. Two pairs of trousers were made for every suit. This claim is reminiscent of one of the current debates in "eco-fashion": that it is better for the environment for men to buy very high-quality bespoke suits that will last the wearer many years. This rather guileless claim is premised on particularly high levels of income as well as a notion of a fixed style that probably suits the ruling class better than others.

The Prince also yearned for practicality. As a child he was brought up in freezing palaces, and his hatred of bundled clothes and his father's refusal to let him put his hands in his pockets led to some of his later informal poses. His father was furious when the Prince appeared in trousers with turn-ups, and the Prince also adopted zip flies in 1934, as well as American low-cut trousers before these were widely worn in Britain. His trousers were made by New York tailor H. Harris and his jackets from 1919 to 1959 by Scholte of London, causing the Duchess to call this manner of dressing "pants across the sea." He wore belts, which were also considered American-style, and also had a type of elasticized girdle stitched into some trousers so that they appeared to stay up with no support. Long before the Armani suit, he wore unlined tweed suits in the 1930s, a mode that he called "Dress Soft." When he acceded to the throne he immediately abolished the wearing of frock coats at court. Of the types of formal dress and Guardsman's tunics that the Prince was required to wear, the Duchess recounts that he once said to her, "I get very bored with all this dressing up." On cruising holidays, "he reverted joyously to the simplest of clothes ... His favourite costume was a pair of shorts, a shirt, and sandals."[5] Photographs of the Duke in Italy in the 1950s indicate the type of studied negligence he preferred: espadrilles, messy hair, artfully knotted bandannas, striped matelots, and belts made from scarves [see figure 21.1].

The Duke's preference for tartans may have influenced that fashion's popularity in 1950s America. For his favorite sport, golf, he shocked the French by wearing a pink shirt, a military tie, a checked suit, red-and-white checked stockings, and black-and-tan shoes. This rather strange combination of garments prefigures the world of rappers and "gangstas" who might wear a suit with no socks. Like today's media stars' clothing, many of the Duke's garments were about effect. Surprisingly, the Windsor knot named for him was not the same as that worn by the Duke, whose ties were in fact padded to achieve the appearance of the effect. The Duke's other aims with his clothes were to look well in photography: he had preferred a blue-black evening suit, as for the purposes of 1930s flash photography a true black would not have looked true. Perhaps this was less about vanity than an aristocrat's attempt to control his representations in an age of mechanical reproduction.

Certain rules could not be broken; black socks, according to the Duke, were for evenings only. In private the Duke wore a dark-green velvet dinner jacket, but when another guest wore innovative clothes to dine, he was swiftly informed that the innovation stopped with the former King. Here the treatises of dandyism must be consulted. Barbey d'Aurevilly's essay on *Beau Brummell* (1843) noted that "Dandies, by virtue of their private authority, establish a rule above that which governs the most aristocratic circles."[6] Françoise Coblence has argued that dandyism represented British and later French anxiety concerning the death of royal power.[7] Ironically, the former monarch had become the bourgeois dandy whose inherent style exceeded that of someone simply born to rule. A dandy's body must also mortify the flesh; the Duke of Windsor's focus on sport and dieting and maintenance of an unchanging figure defy the materiality of the bodies of former princes such as the Prince Regent (later George IV), mocked for his corpulence. Nobody could say to the Duke of Windsor, as Brummell did of His Royal Highness the Prince of Wales around 1800, "Who is that fat man?"[8] Dandies have a curiously disembodied appearance. They tend to or care for themselves, as Garelick notes, in order to "dis-appear." Furthermore, she notes that the dandy cannot reproduce; he is a Promethean figure, never corporeal.[9] No issue could be expected of the Prince of Wales. Perhaps the abdication was indeed necessary in order to acquire true dandiacal status.

We are also reminded here by Roland Barthes that dandyism is both an ethos and a technique. The detail permits the dandy to escape from the masses. Fashion, according to Barthes, killed off this figure when mass production permitted the replication of large amounts of clothing, replacing bespoke menswear. This ready-to-wear, Barthes contends, was the "first fatal set back for dandyism." What ruined dandyism for good was the birth of the boutique—boutique clothing is not mass culture but neither is it "singular." So "fashion" killed the dandy, rather than creating him. This is perhaps the most elegantly put explanation that exists for the relationship of the dandy to fashion in all of the literature.[10]

The Duke of Windsor is but one example of the complex sets of men's fashion played out in twentieth-century life. The cliché that all men were reduced to the same suit and a very limited range of other garments is simply untrue. In the first years of the century the North American elites developed distinctive types of clothing in semiprivate spaces. Thus Deirdre Clemente has argued that the Princeton college men developed their varsity wear as a reaction to their relatively isolated and private campus in which rituals of belonging were enacted through such items as low-cut sporting shoes, corduroy trousers, tweed golfing and sporting wear worn throughout the day, and accessories such as badges, pins, and hatbands.[11] Elites before the 1950s tended to segment their sartorial lives into work and leisure activities. The era before World War I yields striking examples of the quest for male informality and comfort in private spaces such as gardens and walking: the decorator Dorothy Draper's husband Dan Draper, for example, who was photographed in his textured, loose-cut and -fitting, belted "Norfolk Jacket" ca. 1913. Respectability was always invoked, as the comfortable garment is matched with a crisp white short and a bow tie.[12] Men of privilege have also always been able to establish individualistic styles. Bespoke dress invited novel departures: some men had their clothes specially modified to suit their needs, such as the jacket pouches for cigars in the wardrobe of Baron Enrico Di Portanoa, whose jackets were made by Angelo's, Rome.[13] Party dress also generated individualistic dressing, such as the ties inset with ruched gold lamé designed by André Ghekiéré and the black satin jacket with real diamond buttons worn by HH Prince Rajsingh Rajpipla in France and England in the late 1960s.[14]

The "hidden history" of men's fashion also has quirky and eccentric elements, which sometimes had impacts on the mainstream decades later. Some of it was conducted by celebrities, some was published at the time, some was not. Such eccentricity can be recovered from diaries, letters, autobiographies, and photographs. Some of it has a frankly queer dimension and is also associated with the appearance industries, from decorators to photographers and stylists. Much of this clothing was made and worn for leisure spaces and vacations and is frequently presented in settings such as the beach, where the charge of the partly clad body is equally strong. Striking examples include the photographer and stylist Cecil Beaton, the interior decorator Billy Baldwin, and the dilettante and occasional dress designer Bunny Rogers.[15] Historicism in men's shoes also provided opportunities for queer men in the period pre-Stonewall to experiment with alternative but socially acceptable appearances. Cecil Beaton's neo-Edwardianism is well known, with a wasp waist, long coat, and bespoke shoes. Less well known is the dress of Bunny Rogers, a wealthy dilettante of the same era. Over the course of his life Rogers wore Edwardian-style suits, Nehru jackets, 1960s-style jackets in all colors of the rainbow, and, for his famous drag birthday parties, amethyst catsuits and feather headdresses. Rogers's shoes suggest how an extreme attention to a narrow cut and elegant streamlining might point to a fashion consciousness almost fetishistic in its detailing. His dressing also indicates the impossibility of ascribing dandiacal appearance to gay men; a dandy might just as well be a man using his sharp appearance to attract women. The difference generally lies in the detail or the mode of wearing.

Queer men in the United States in the interwar years exhibited an incredibly refined casual style that, decades later, would become associated with collegiate style. Some purposefully drew attention to their clothes in later memoirs. The decorator Billy Baldwin claimed that his 1930s Madras bathing trunks in loud checks were "perhaps the first ones designed in that material in this country."[16] Short-sleeved white shirts, knee-length shorts, and shoes without socks were worn by "Woody," Billy Baldwin's friend, ca. 1940, that appear to our eyes very contemporary.[17] The crossover of textiles and forms normally considered suitable only for one purpose existed well before the postwar period. In addition, Baldwin had made and wore a distinctive bathing costume cut from navy-blue flannel purchased from the tailor Mr. Schantz, at Wetzel's in Saks Fifth Avenue. In another contemporary gesture, this costume of "thin, completely washable, absolutely wrinkle-proof" fabric was also made up as "bathing trunks, a blazer, a couple of pullover shirts, and several pairs of trousers."[18] Baldwin also wore pyjamas that he had designed for him in the late 1930s and wore at the Lido, right up until the 1970s.[19] They were worn on the country estates of rich friends. Similar lounging pyjamas were worn by Cecil

Beaton's circles in the 1930s. The sandal also appears to be significant for informal gay enclaves in Morocco, worn by figures such as Joe Orton.

ICONS OF STYLE

Mass-produced uniforms created for eighteenth-century armies anticipated the nineteenth-century factory-made suits sold through mail-order catalogues and department stores. The development in the mid-nineteenth century of new pattern-grading systems, innovative technological applications such as the sewing machine, and mail-order paper patterns meant that more untrained people than ever before made much of their wardrobe at home, although these tended to be women's and children's clothes. Large amounts of mass-produced clothing for men became available as both access to fashion and the development of ready-made clothing accelerated. The authors assembled in this section see in the development of very different items of mass-produced clothing, from the male suit to the blue jean, specific cultural priorities and agendas.

Anne Hollander's *Sex and Suits* (1994) rather provocatively reads modern men's dress, represented by tailored suiting, as more advanced than women's: "at the Neo-classic moment it was men, not women, who enterprisingly made a radical modern leap in fashion."[20] She argues that in 1675 the creation in France of a female guild for making women's clothes led to a gendered split of the profession, in which male corset makers formed the understructure and shape of women's fashion, leaving women to embellish and trim.[21] Women's clothes, she argues, became a space of surface fantasy rather than technology,[22] whereas male beauty participated in neo-classical aesthetics, which became a more "modern" way of appearing.

Michael Zakim, in "The Reinvention of Tailoring," provides an account of the impact of both the ready-made and bespoke or "custom" clothing trades on the American middle-class fashion system. His essay is part of a larger project in which he argues that "clothing has consistently served as both material and metaphor for the social question" in the United States. Clothing, to Zakim, highlights and contributes to new notions of productive citizenship, a political narrative of capitalist revolution and America's transformation into a democracy. He argues convincingly for a social meaning for the transformation from "homespun" cloth to ready-made clothing. Sartorial virtue, Zakim writes, shifted from homemade to mass-produced; it "no longer signalled the self-sacrifice of elites but, rather, the propertied mobility of all." Luxury in nineteenth-century America was debilitating only when it was exclusive. If luxury might be diffused, then it united opportunity and equality. This was "industrial luxury," Zakim writes, a "middle landscape for the new century which included all citizens." He argues that the standard measure associated with the male suit was "necessary for circulating information in an age when secrecy was no longer good for business." An "American" system overtook one of the oldest crafts. Excess was not banished but more and more relegated to the realm of women. "Sex replaced class as the great social divide in industrial democracies."[23]

Toby Slade considers the transformation and social impact of the suit in Meiji Japan. His essay is a study of modernity and what modern fashion made possible in a society that was almost entirely confined to indigenous fashions before the 1860s. Fashion is analyzed as a piece of statecraft and policy designed to create the modern Japanese citizen by literally redrawing the boundaries of their bodies, their relationships to social and psychic space, and their participation on the newly commissioned "stages" of westernised public life. Slade argues that the suit bears a particular weight in Japan and analyzes its functions across a range of tasks, from imperial image making to office labor to *Rokumeikan* receptions. Fashion is presented as both a social fact and a product of the imaginary that intersected with premodern understandings of hierarchy and propriety. What is most striking about Slade's approach is his foregrounding of fashion aesthetics and a "Kantian veracity of form" in which political, social, and material concerns were only ancillary next to the significance of this aesthetic tendency. The debt to Anne Hollander is clear, but the idea is taken much further. Slade notes of the suit that it "was true to the body and to the garment itself at the same time—as with modern art, the brushstrokes were visible."

Laura Ugolini's analysis of the suit in 1930s Oxford provides a case study that considers the dynamics and politics of men's clothes in the interwar period. In focusing on two disparate groups, Oxford undergraduates and car workers, she is able to associate their clothing politics with larger contemporary debates about the nature of development and modernization of a city. She refutes the notion that the expansion of men's clothing stores led simply to the "manipulation" of consumers. Her finely nuanced argument, in which the way clothes were procured and imagined by their purchasers is explored, reminds us how a vision of a "timeless" set of fashions largely originates in relationships and representations of "modern" interwar and suburban life.

The late Richard Martin, one of the most innovative essayists in the field of male fashion, is represented here with an essay on Jean-Paul Gaultier's leather sailor's middy blouse, designed in 1996. Martin does not proceed from a historical or sociological argument, but rather a sophisticated semiotic one overlaid with the history of ideas, in which one object will suffice. Martin considers how Gaultier's recasting of a sailor's garment into black leather evokes that other icon of male style, the black leather jacket, an object that is simultaneously protective, erotic, and suggestive of rebellion. By manipulating cut and evoking a buccaneer or the leather apron of early-modern industrial men, Gaultier creates a narrative of a rampaging sailor on leave, a type of Jean Cocteau–figure crossed with an urban leatherman perhaps. Designers such as Gaultier, Martin suggests, build their fashion on templates that accrue significance over time. To Martin, this can be an act of the fashion *saboteur;* "to profane apparel is to establish a new connection between that fashion object and its connective cultures."

In the original article as published in *Fashion Theory,* Martin then goes on to consider Calvin Klein's manipulation of jeans through his controversial advertising photography that "evokes the social truant in otherwise affluent American society." These images shock people, Martin suggests, not for their suggestion of underage sex, but because they present a "dismal portrait of class's presence in American society." As Martin notes, if jeans are taken from working-class culture, then why not evoke a slatternly, slack, and sexual world that horrifies the middle class? Martin concludes by noting that contemporary fashion possesses an ability "to be at once what we fear, what we revile, and what we desire."[24]

Jennifer Craik analyzes the rise of the school uniform for boys. She considers how the notion of this uniform developed from welfare motives, charity schools, and Poor Laws in the sixteenth century, to be transformed in the nineteenth century into symbols of either democratic access (France in the 1870s) or elite discipline and order at elite paying schools (the nineteenth-century English great public schools). Uniforms, she notes, instill certain masculine attributes and values that are meant to be "unremarkable" but are also frequently subverted. Finally, she senses that conservative regime persisting in aspects of contemporary male working wardrobes.

George Boeck presents a case study of clothing culture within another male-dominated space, that of Texas cattle livestock auctions in Weatherford in 1980, where the subjects participate in a shared economic activity. Boeck uses an ethnographic model drawn from techniques including the theorists in the Prague Linguistic School of the 1920s, writing within the American field of "folklife," the ethnographic study of ethical and aesthetic expressions of specified groups. Boeck analyzes the setting for the application of these theories of costume in action. He traces ranch dress, which originates in the popular image of the cowboy, later proceeding from the custom-made western boot and shirt. He considers the egalitarian work pants and boots that are available through mail-order houses as the basis for farm costume. Boeck considers how the simple act of wearing an ironed rather than creased work shirt or polished boots can set an older generation apart from the younger men, who are also more likely to wear a wider range of "western-style" shirts, denim pants, and boots. Tidiness, Boeck writes in his finely grained analysis, expressed by the evidence of ironing, "ranks somewhere near a freshly painted barn, conveying mental order and prosperity. The well-worn but clean costume similarly conveys a no-nonsense working ethic. In stark contrast, the disregard for tidiness by the yard boys is benignly approved, granting them station similar to the half-wild cattle they tend." Boeck's comments on Levi's jeans and his telling images find their corollary in Richard Martin's analysis of the effect of suggesting working-class imagery in contemporary jeans advertising.

Beverly Gordon, in "American Denim: Blue Jeans and Their Multiple Layers of Meaning," suggests that the choice of jeans in the first years of the twentieth century did not make "a statement of any kind." Here the reader notes her clashing view with Boeck, who would read in all clothing, no matter how banal, a series of actions and choices. Gordon goes on to analyze the rise of the blue jean as an antifashion statement much earlier than many people would surmise, tracing it to artists' colonies in 1920s Santa Fe. There, anti-establishment figures enjoyed the androgynous and direct image presented by jeans. As early as the 1930s, "dude ranch" vacations and "western chic" were promoted by retailers and advertisers. One recalls here the jeans-wearing episode in George Cukor's *The Women* (1939), the film that is famous for its absence of men. Perhaps their presence is inscribed in the attention paid to the "jeans-wearing" women of all ages and sizes at the "divorce town ranch" featured in the film. Gordon goes on to argue that the association of jeans with war work and patriotism conferred on denim a further positive charge. But jeans could also signal new models of the "juvenile delinquent" explored elsewhere by Alford in this reader, such that a movie about an unwed mother was titled *Blue Denim* (1959). Cold War scenarios were also played out in the 1950s western film, in which good and bad cowboys were marked by the color of their hats.

Gordon sees in the rapid adoption of jeans in 1960s liberal culture the glorification of badges of experience and traces of intensely personal life, for jeans take on the print of the body and proudly carry their rips, tears, and scars. Gordon points out the challenge of seeing in jeans any clear antifashion message, as the couturier Givenchy, for example, designed a denim wardrobe for Audrey Hepburn in the 1970s. As early as 1974 Levi Strauss sponsored an exhibition of customized jeans. Gordon sees in the "distressed" denim movement and the marketing of self-consciously reused and "damaged" jeans from the 1980s an inauthentic jean culture: "Sadly, all of these trends are mere façades." Such a comment prompts our readers to consider their own sartorial position and the different perspectives presented in this *Reader,* to reach their own conclusions about the complex ways in which subjects have assigned meaning to their clothing choices within our network of real and imaginary lives. We might also note here Richard Martin's claim in *Fashion Theory* that garments in contemporary society go beyond any notion of abundance, to be absorbed *"as ideas into our lives and our cultures."*[25]

Peter McNeil

NOTES

1. Adolf Loos, "'Men's Fashion' and 'Men's Hats,'" in *The Rise of Fashion: A Reader,* ed. Daniel Leonhard Purdy (1898; reprint, Minneapolis: University of Minnesota, 2004), 94.

2. See Nicholas Foulkes, "Fit for a King," *Country Life,* October 5, 1995, 40–43.

3. This is most evident in photographs of them in bathing costumes.

4. Kerry Taylor, "Inside the Windsor Style: The Wardrobe of the Duke of Windsor," in *Property from the Collection of The Duke and Duchess of Windsor,* information volume (New York: Sotheby's, September 11–19, 1997), 51.

5. The Duchess of Windsor, *The Heart Has Its Reasons* (London: Readers' Book Club, 1958), 198.

6. Rhonda K. Garelick, *Rising Star: Dandyism, Gender, and Performance in the Fin de Siècle* (Princeton, NJ: Princeton University Press, 1998), 25.

7. Cited in ibid.

8. Ibid., 21.

9. Ibid., 26.

10. R. Barthes, *The Language of Fashion,* ed. Andy Stafford and Michael Carter, trans. Andy Stafford (Oxford, UK, and New York: Berg, 2006).

11. Deirdre Clemente, "Making the Princeton Man: Collegiate Clothing and Campus Culture, 1900–1920," in *The Places and Spaces of Fashion, 1800–2007,* ed. John Potvin (New York and Abingdon: Routledge, 2008), 108–20.

12. Carleton Varney, *The Draper Touch: The High Life and High Style of Dorothy Draper* (New York: Prentice Hall, 1988), 78–79.

13. Slim Aarons photographer, Getty Images 2716839.

14. These clothes were exhibited in the foyer accompanying "Peacocks and Pinstripes: A Snapshot of Masculine Style" (2008), The Fashion and Textile Museum, London.

15. Another good example is Slim Aarons's photograph of W. Clifford Klenk and his wife in their living room at "Island Lookout," Hog Island, May 1968 (Slim Aarons, Getty Images 3095102). Exhibited in "Peacocks and Pinstripes."

16. Billy Baldwin and Michael Gardine, *Billy Baldwin: An Autobiography* (Boston and Toronto: Little, Brown and Company, 1985), 101.

17. Ibid., 150.

18. Ibid., 153.

19. Ibid., 345.

20. Anne Hollander, *Sex and Suits* (New York: Kodansha, 1995), 7.

21. Ibid., 65.

22. Ibid., 69.

23. See Michael Zakim, "Sartorial Ideologies: From Homespun to Ready-Made" *American Historical Review* 16, no. 5 (2001): 1553–86.

24. Richard Martin, "A Note: A Charismatic Art: The Balance of Ingratiation and Outrage in Contemporary Fashion," *Fashion Theory* 1, no. 1 (1997): 91–104.

25. Ibid.

17

HEROES IN WOOL

Anne Hollander

By 1810, the new tailoring techniques had already produced an unornamented sculptured coat, a loose envelope for the male upper body, subtly cut of dull material and sewn with highly visible seams. The essential texture and construction, not the surface richness, created its aesthetic interest. This was a very modern idea; and it was possible only in an ancient tailoring tradition founded on the use of wool. English tailors had long been superior to all others in the cut and fit of woollen garments; and wool was known to be the great staple fabric of England since the earliest period of its history.

Wool was also known to be the common fabric of antiquity, and it was a satisfying fact that not only country coats but heroic togas were properly made of woollen cloth. Consequently, for the creation of a natural man who was both modern and antique, the appropriate fabric was at hand in England, accompanied by materials of equal antiquity and simplicity such as smooth linen and varieties of leather, and colonial contributions such as cotton. Emergent national pride, expressing distance from French and other Continental influences, supported a fashion based mainly on native materials and native skills.

The English had certainly used silk, too; but the firm silk fabrics used for men's clothes had a taut and rigid weave, whereas all wool is flexible and elastic. Under the influence of steam, pressure and careful manipulation, to say nothing of imaginative cutting, wool can be made to stretch, shrink and curve at the tailor's will, to follow and complement the shapes and movements of the wearer's body without buckling and rippling. It truly resembles a sculptural medium, obedient to a designer's creative desire. Silk, on the other hand, asserts its own authority. The more simply cut silk and velvet coats of former days, suitable for the Rococo temper, had wrinkled with every movement of the wearer and with every bit of pressure on the buttons, partly because the fabric refused to stretch at all.

Works of art show that all those rows of buttons and buttonholes, those extra cuffs and flaps and applied embroideries, and all those long waistcoats, full skirts and soft breeches had created a network of little wrinkles over the whole body of the man. This engendered a surface motion that caught the light and made a further embellishment for the suit in wear. The body was always veiled by the rippling surface of its garments, which displayed the elegance of the wearer every time he drew breath.

But by the turn of the century, elegance had shifted entirely away from wrought surfaces to fundamental form, and away from courtly refinement to natural simplicity. And so tailors elevated the unfitted rough country coat into a triumph of art, whereby crude natural man became noble natural man, with references to ancient sculpture built into the structure of his clothes. With the help of nearly imperceptible padding, curved seams, discreet darts and steam pressing, the rough coat of dull cloth was gradually refined into an exquisitely balanced garment that fitted smoothly without wrinkles and buttoned without strain, to clothe what appeared to be the torso of a Greek athlete.

Its collar was forced by clever cut, steaming and stiffening to curve up and around the neck, to fold over and open out in front, and to form lapels that would obediently lie down and align themselves smoothly with the body of the coat. This perfectly tailored collar and flat-lying lapel still forms the most distinctive element of the modern suit-coat, and became the formal sign of modernity in dress. It is now so universal for both sexes that it is almost invisible. The art with which it is accomplished is also invisible, and the lapels of modern jackets look as if they lay flat by natural inclination.

The subtle lines of the coat formed an abstract design based on the underlying curves of human bone and muscle, and the matte texture suggested the smoothness of skin. The careful modelling allowed the actual body to assert itself only at certain places when the wearer moved, to create a vital interaction between costume and person, a nonchalant counterpoint again with echoes of an animal easy in its own skin. The discreet padding in the upper chest and shoulders was carefully thinned out over the chest and back and disappeared in the lower half of the coat, so that the effect was of a wholly unpadded garment, an apparently natural covering.

To go with this apotheosis of rough gear, the plain linen shirt and cravat, which might have been worn soiled and sloppily knotted by rough-living country gentlemen, were laundered into incandescent whiteness, lightly starched, and then folded with a sculptor's care around the neck and jaw, to produce a commanding set of the head on the heroic shoulders. The thick and muddy country boots were refined, fitted and polished to perfection, and the whole ensemble was ready for transfer from the hedgerows to Pall Mall. Adding spice to this potent mixture was the exciting urban contribution from across the Channel, the *sans-culotte* costume of the

Revolutionary labouring classes. This similar Neo-classic 'natural' mode could eventually be blended with the English version, refined and translated from the barricades to the drawing-room, bringing the spirit of revolt and suggestions of plebeian effort to the already powerful combination of ideas embodied in the new masculine costume.

Thus the male figure was recut and the ideal man recast. Formerly the play of light on rich and glinting textures had seemed to endow the gentleman with the play of aristocratic sensibility, and made him an appropriate vessel for exquisite courtesy, schooled wit and refined arrogance without having to reveal the true fibre and calibre of his individual soul any more than that of his body. Now the noble proportions of his manly form, created only by the rigorous use of natural materials, seemed to give him an individual moral strength founded on natural virtue, an integrity that flowers in aesthetic purity without artifice, and made him a proper vessel for forthright modern opinion and natural candid feeling.

His garments made him look honest, since the seams showed and the weave was apparent in the plain fabric—and rational, because of the perfect cut, fit and proportions, which also gave him his artless good looks. The whole achievement had been accomplished entirely by simply reworking the old seventeenth-century scheme of coat, waistcoat, and breeches, with a shirt and some kind of cravat. It replaced the same scheme made of nude muscles that had been the Classical expression of the same virtues, and now gave the impression that the nude hero was even more natural when dressed.

All these new phenomena are associated with the legendary figure of Beau Brummell, who himself embodied the new kind of hero made by tailoring. In the new urban Dandy mode, a man's heroism consisted only in being thoroughly himself; Brummell proved that the essential superior being was no longer a hereditary nobleman. His excellence was entirely personal, unsupported by armorial bearings, ancestral halls, vast lands, or even a fixed address, and he was also known to be able to live on nothing a year. His garments had to be perfect only in their own sartorial integrity, that is, in form alone, unburdened by any surface indices of the worth attached to rank. Brummell himself was known to have wished his clothes to be unnoticeable.

Brocade and embroidery had once indicated the generic superiority even of quite inferior individuals, and had displayed the beauty of the costume, not the man. Careful fit without adornments, on the other hand, emphasizes the unique grace of the individual body—indeed creates it, in the highest tailoring tradition. The man's rank or even his deeds are irrelevant to the fine cut of his plain coat; only his personal qualities are shown to matter. Thus the Neo-classic costume was a leveller in its time, and has since remained one in its subsequent revisions, creating superior beings of all classes. The perfect man, as conceived by English tailors, was part English country gentleman, part innocent natural Adam, and part naked Apollo the creator and destroyer—a combination with an enduring appeal, in other countries and other centuries. Dressed form was now an abstraction of nude form, a new ideal naked man expressed not in bronze or marble but in natural wool, linen, and leather, wearing an easy skin as perfect as the silky pelt of the ideal hound or horse, lion or panther.

Not only the bodily proportions but the ideal colour of the antique was sustained in the newly heroized country costume. In England and Northern Europe, all eighteenth-century Neo-classic art consistently emphasized a lucid monochromy. Suppressing the play of colour led to a better appreciation of fundamental outline and form, and newly admired antiquities were most often reproduced in graphic outlines, the better to celebrate the simple purity of their shapes without irrelevant sensuous distractions.

The originally painted ancient marbles had become colourless by the time they were found, like the ancient buildings. The virtue of their colourlessness had been further supported by Michelangelo and the later sculptors who set out to rival antiquity in white marble. In those days such monochromy was usually offset by chromatic richness in all other modes of art and decoration, and classicizing Renaissance and Baroque painters had continued to use colour and texture when rendering the antique in pictures. David and other French Neo-classic painters were also continuing to evoke the ancient world using the whole spectrum.

But the aesthetic power of antique colourlessness was more thoroughly credited at the end of the eighteenth century than it had ever been before. In England, Holland, Scandinavia, and Germany, rich colour lost its authority for a time—perhaps in part because of its associations with France, now replacing traditional royal licence with tyrannical imperial pomp, after a fearful and bloody interval. The abandonment of colour may have expressed the desire for a certain distance from these vivid developments; and it also seemed to support the idea of the search for Classical authenticity as a kind of purification, in alignment with Protestant impulses.

Sir Joshua Reynolds had written that lavish colour in painting made a base appeal to sensuality, and that the play of light over rich texture had similarly vulgar attractions unworthy of the Great Style in painting, exemplified by Michelangelo. The Sistine Chapel frescoes were already faded and greyish in the eighteenth century; and they were admired all the more for their chromatic dullness, which suggested a much nobler vision of serious ancient events than anything devised in the shimmering styles of Titian or Rubens. Or in the current ones of David and Gerard, at work across the Channel.

Following the prevailing view expressed by Sir Joshua, the Neo-classic English tailors exploited the new prestige of muted colour and matte finish. In clothing, these no longer conveyed sober humility but suggested the same Classical virtues that antique nudity itself embodied, including superior beauty. The new graphic rhetoric for ideal male looks forced the masculine costume not only to classicize its outlines but to lose much of its colour and reflect no light—and to appear more beautiful as a result, not less so.

For men's clothes, clearly defined areas of black, brown, buff and white replaced the spread of fluid and shining coloured stuffs. For coats, dark green and dark blue wool, suggestive of the natural world and the simple country life, might be included in the scheme. But a dull finish and clarity of line were essential. In accordance with the Neo-classic formula for rendering nature truly, a perfect linear composition was a more truthful and a more beautiful, and thus a better achievement than any worked-up, lustrous and multicoloured finish, for artists and tailors both.

In the second act of modernism, during the first quarter of this century, a new radical view of the beauty of form was again accompanied by a certain retreat from colour. The most extreme visions of Cubism tended to eliminate vivid hues in their concentration on the multiple truths of form. In architecture a new respect for the intrinsic beauty of naked steel, glass and concrete helped to revive a taste for formal value uncluttered by busy adornment, including the distracting beauty of colour; and this taste was further supported by masterpieces of black and white photography and cinematography that celebrated only shape, line and surface texture. All this helped to keep the new versions of the modern masculine suit, now celebrating formal abstraction in new ways, on the same path toward muted colour that they had originally taken during their first Neo-classic appearance.

NOTE

Reprinted with permission from Anne Hollander, "The Genesis of the Suit," in *Sex and Suits: The Evolution of Modern Dress* (New York: Kodansha, 1995), 79–115.

18

THE REINVENTION OF TAILORING

Michael Zakim

Ready-made clothing seemed uniquely modern to nineteenth-century observers. 'Procuring the very articles [one] requires all ready-made to his hand' encapsulated the anonymity, the standardization, and the proficiency promised by industrial revolution. That impression was only strengthened by concurrent retail innovations—urban emporiums of grandiose design and an unprecedented volume of merchandise—and the fact that the goods were being made by the principal waged manufacturing force in the city, working on enormous scales of production.

The identification of ready-made with mass production had an important corollary: the equation of made-to-measure, or 'bespoke,' clothing with pre-industrial practices [figure 18.1]. The distinction was perceived as an opposition, representative of the transition from a world of craft singularity to one of market-inspired standardization.[1] By the mid-nineteenth century the made-to-measure business had become known as the 'custom trade.' An old term that once described any customer, 'custom' now denoted a certain type of consumption, namely, the purchase of goods made to personal order. By implication the appellation thus tied bespoke clothing to traditional practices. Of course, no such relationship necessarily existed. It was, in fact, more common in the pre-industrial world than in the nineteenth century for a person to wear clothing originally belonging to someone else, or to leave clothing to others in their wills, or to adapt a garment and then readapt it through innumerable incarnations passed between family members and over generations.[2]

At the same time, the dichotomy between ready-made and custom clothing made sense in an industrializing context [figures 18.2–18.3]. The latter cost more, fit better, and had been associated with craft tradition ever since English tailoring guilds began fighting the encroachments of the ready-made trade in the seventeenth century. The ready-made garment was 'a different species of make', recognizable by clumsy button holes or a 'general misfit' justifiably blamed on the cost-cutting measures taken by proprietors of mercantile habits.[3] Its production was, in general, organized by 'clothiers'—that is, merchants—many of whom had themselves never made a suit and whose artistry was manifest instead in the profitable co-ordination of cloth, labour, and credit. The custom suit, in contrast, was the product of a master tailor who measured his own customers, laid his palms on their shoulders in judging the shape of the shoulder seams, and then leisurely drew his hands down their sides, learning the customer's 'form' in order to successfully model to that particular body a particular suit of clothes. This made custom the legacy of artisanal fastidiousness and seemed also to divorce it from the more aggressive and alienated expressions of commercial life. Rather than something obtained 'much cheaper' from a big shop, it was 'made expressly' for the customer. Certainly, the individual body personally attended by the skilled craftsman was

Figure 18.1 Unknown press photographer, 'The Duke of Windsor looks on as the Duchess of Windsor holds a pair of dogs on their leads, in the grounds of the Hotel Brenner, during the recent visit to Baden-Baden, Germany. With them, on right, is Dr. Schlapper, the Lord Mayor of Baden-Baden'. 9 September 1953. Private collection. Not all suits are equal, and the Duke is able to wear his double-breasted with ease. In the background, uniformed attendants look on, their clothes reflecting more archaic forms that once were high fashion for men.

Figures 18.2 *Theologos Vatousis,* c.1923, Brooklyn, New York. Private collection. Vatousis was an immigrant who arrived in New York from Lesvos, Greece, in the early 1920s. Studio photographs such as this were commonly sent back to Greece as a part of marriage match making arrangements and as a sign of success in the New World. The subject wears a boater hat, lapel pin and pocket square. The suit is probably a heavy wool, single-breasted, two buttoned and cuffed at the trouser hem. The lapels are winged and the breast pocket is angular, adding a relaxed air. The buttoned boots were fashionable at the time.

an obvious antithesis to the anonymous whole-sale trade in ready-mades.[4]

This opposition had other expressions as well. By the 1840s New York City business directories published two separate listings for men's clothing stores: clothiers' 'warehouses' and tailors' 'establishments'. That bifurcation rested on a social taxonomy. Over a quarter of the city's clothiers were located in the distinctly lower-class venues of Chatham Street and the Bowery. Another quarter did business in the old slops neighbourhood bordering the East River wharves. In contrast, a quarter of the tailors had Broadway addresses, and most of the others were to be found in the immediate vicinity. Only one clothier was listed on Broadway, for instance, in *Doggett's New York Business Directory for 1841–42*.[5] The distinction between custom and ready-made, then, appeared to be synonymous with the division between refined and coarse, between bourgeois and proletarian. That opposition reached its apotheosis in a company history privately printed by Brooks Brothers in 1918, celebrating the firm's centenary and staking a credible claim to be one of the oldest surviving clothing firms in America. The company account, however, reinvented Henry Brooks as a tailor, while in fact, as I have noted, neither Henry nor his brother David nor Henry's four sons knew how to make a suit of clothes—as distinguished from knowing how to make money from others doing the same. But such an artisanal pedigree allowed the latter-day firm, having since carefully nurtured an image as purveyor of sartorial refinement to the polite classes, to lay claim to a craft status otherwise refuted by the real nature of their lumpen origins selling low-priced ready-mades along the wharves of the East River. (The company version, however, achieved its aim: the standard

Figure 18.3 *Vassili Karaminas,* c.1909, Boston, Massachusetts. Private collection. Karaminas was an immigrant who arrived in Boston in 1909 from Lesvos, Greece, which was then under Turkish occupation. He settled in the town of Lynn and travelled back and forth from Boston to Greece until the outbreak of World War II. Karaminas wears a single-breasted worsted wool suit with a box cut jacket with pleated trousers. The vest and the trousers are the same shade whilst the jacket appears to be pin striped. Accessories include a rose, tie-pin and pocket pen. The trouser legs are cut close to the ankle exposing polished black shoes. The hat is a fedora with band and the hair is carefully slicked to suggest professionalism and status.

history of the early men's clothing business, Egal Feldman's *Fit for Men,* repeats the fiction.)[6]

In fact, however, the custom trade was the branch of the clothing business that underwent the most far-reaching industrial transformation in the middle of the nineteenth century. For while the ready-made commodity proved originally suited to the new conditions of a mass market, custom tailoring, which was no less exposed to market forces, had a far longer way to go in adapting itself to the economic facts of industrial life. Yet this it did. The result was a new regime of proprietary control over production and the labour force, unceasing competition among merchant tailors for a cut-rate cash business, the replacement of craft secrets with a burgeoning trade in new production technologies, and the attempt, by means of those standardizing technologies, to tap into the huge continental market. All these developments show custom tailoring to have been the full-blooded progeny of industrial revolution rather than the legacy of a less commercial past, and no less a part of the ready-made world.[7]

Tailors' achievements were no less social than economic. As we will see, in adapting their highly personal craft to the exploding market, tailors also effectively integrated the male persona into industry's ceaseless striving for system and predictability without forcing him to consciously surrender his uniqueness. The result was far-reaching. The personally fitted gentleman could now simultaneously embody abstract universal citizenship while honing his individuality, both important desiderata of modern life. Thus, industrial revolution, when it came, was not about the replacement of individual identities with standardized persons. It marked, rather, the simultaneous birth of both.

***

Edgar Allan Poe, who demonstrated an intuitive understanding of the mass character of private life, published a characteristically acerbic parable of commercial foibles called 'The Business Man' soon after moving to New York in the early 1840s, one that exposed the modern nature of custom tailoring. The story was an abbreviated memoir of the insistent efforts of one Peter Proffit, utilizing the twin tenets of 'system' and 'method', to achieve self-made success. While some might consider Proffit's sundry schemes for enriching himself to more closely resemble business scams—and they included an Eye-Sore trade, an Assault and Battery business, and a Cur-Spattering operation—he himself had no doubt that the end of a country seat on the Hudson justified his unorthodox methods.[8]

Proffit's first venture was in the employ of Messrs. Cut and Comeagain, merchant tailors, who dressed him each morning and sent him out for a midday promenade in the city's more fashionable quarters. The 'precise regularity' with which Proffit displayed his personage and brought his suit to bear to the most advantageous view 'was the admiration of all the knowing men in the trade.' Noon never passed without his returning with a new customer to Cut and Comeagain, anxious to be fitted to the same effect. Of course, once back in the shop a customer might be sold a far cheaper milled satinet instead of the broadcloth he had requested. Proffit was responsible for these prevarications as well, and he made certain to charge the tailors for each one he told while in their employ: 25 cents for a 'second class lie', 75 cents for a 'first class lie'. In truth, Proffit's career as a 'walking advertiser' of dubious ethics was the most innocent of all the hoaxes he perpetrated on his road to business success. 'Tailors' tricks' were an old subject of popular suspicion anyway. But Poe knew that they no less belonged in his litany of modern avarice and that the new ethos of system and method, combined with commercial ambition, had overtaken such an apparently timeless relationship as that between a gentleman and his tailor.[9]

In fact, in the same year that 'The Business Man' was published, the *New York Tribune* announced the arrival of a new era in tailoring: 'Within the last few years a revolution in the price of Fashionable Clothing has been effected.' Overcoats that not so long before had cost $40 could now be bought on Broadway for $15. What most impressed the *Tribune,* however, was not the low price of coats per se—'there were always plenty of shops where Clothing could be bought lower'—but that they were being sold at such prices in the centre of *bon ton,* Broadway. Broadway tailors engaged 'the best artists', acquired 'the choicest qualities and most *recherché* styles of goods' from Paris and London, and turned out the very best design and quality of clothing. Nevertheless, they managed to do this 'at prices which ... opened the eye of the public'.[10]

Even before the *Tribune's* pronouncement of the dawning of a new sartorial age, Edward Fox, since 1841 the proprietor of the City Cash Tailoring Establishment at 202 Broadway, embarked on a campaign to refute 'the impression that has heretofore existed in the minds of many that purchasers in Broadway are obliged to pay an exorbitant price for an article of dress.' Fox kept a 'desirable and choice' assortment of French and English broadcloths, cassimeres, and vestings in stock, fabrics that would be turned into garments by 'none but the best cutters and workmen'. Moreover, he promised to sell them at prices as low, if not lower, than those of any other house in the city.[11] Fox advertised in the *Herald,* however, and the *Tribune* preferred to puff its own advertisers. Its notice on the tailoring revolution thus profiled two other Broadway tailors, J. C. Booth and William Jennings. Booth had opened a tailoring business earlier in the decade on Fulton Street, a busy commercial boulevard that crossed Broadway just below City Hall Park and ran east to the Brooklyn ferry. There he offered savings 'of at least 40 per cent from Broadway prices.' He then moved himself to Broadway, a block below Fox, where 'every article requisite to complete a Gentleman's Wardrobe of the latest styles and best fabrics' could still be had for the same low prices. The strategy proved successful. In 1848 observers estimated that Booth, who began in business with little means of his own, had pocketed close to $30,000. Such a reputation for success, of course, made it easier to pocket even more, and Booth had little problem financing the hiring of extra cutters and expanding the business.[12]

William Jennings, whom the *Tribune* actually credited with personally pioneering the revolutionary new price structure, had been tailoring in New York since the twenties. He was popularly considered one of the city's best and enjoyed the endorsement of the consciously fashionable *New Mirror.* Jennings's establishment was located in the American Hotel, at Broadway and Barclay Street, 'opposite the Fountain', a manicured urban idyll peopled with well-appointed strollers that was made the centrepiece of his full-page advertisement in Sheldon's business directory of 1845. But such demonstrative gentility did not keep Jennings from matching the competition: suits 'at a few hours' notice,' winter clearance sales, an assortment of 'FIRST QUALITY' ready-mades, a large selection of furnishings—scarfs, cravats, gloves, suspenders, 'etc. etc.'—and, of course, unprecedentedly low prices.[13]

According to the *Tribune,* the dramatic fall in the price of tailored men's clothing was not attributable to the depressed economy of the early forties. What had transformed tailoring, rather, was the conditions of doing business in modern times: the discovery of a giant market to be reached by lowering prices, or what Jennings pithily captioned 'the system of small profits and quick returns.'[14] The *Tribune* compared the change in tailoring to the birth of the penny press, which had made the heretofore excluded 'carter ... sitting on his cart; a barrowman on his barrow; and a porter at his stand' full participants in the age when they took a break in their workday to read the paper. A parallel could also have been drawn to the falling price of admission to the theatres. All three marked an unprecedented commodification of once exclusive cultural goods. George Foster, the *Tribune's* most notorious exposer of aristocratic pretension, considered cheap theatre a democratic revolution of sorts, a uniquely American success. And Nathaniel Willis, self-anointed copywriter for the city's Upper Tendom (that is, the ten thousand richest New Yorkers), had to admit, albeit with barely disguised regret, that 'the age is, perhaps, forever gone by, when a privileged class could monopolize finery of garb; and of all the civilized nations, it were least possible in ours. I have already seen a dozen at least of cheap-booted apprentices wearing velvet waistcoats, which, a few years ago, would have delighted D'Orsay.' The editor of the plebeian *Aurora* rubbed elbows with the city's gentry at the high-society ball held in Charles Dickens's honour at the Park Theater in 1842. Accoutred in 'faultlessly white' linens and a suitably black coat and pantaloons acquired from Martin's tailoring shop, where one was taught that 'economy is wealth', he mingled with the 'beaux, exquisites, and the dandies at a positive saving of 30 per cent.'[15]

The aforementioned Martin did business on William Street, two blocks east of Broadway, where he made garments 'of the most stylish manner' and sold them exclusively for cash. He was representative of scores of other 'Cash Tailors' who had recently capitalized the adjective in their appellation into a proper noun and begun to aggressively fill the city's newspapers and storefronts with their wares. They could expect cash payment from a broad range of clientele as the urban economy and its waged occupations developed and the expenditures of city households grew steadily through the early decades of the century. Cash meant that there were fewer accounts to keep and fewer debtors to dun, and sometimes to sue. True, sales and gross profits declined in a cash business, but so did expenses and losses at the end of the year. The tailor no longer had to suffer the defaults of persons buying on credit, which was especially appealing in the wake of the 1837 panic. It was indisputably the safest way to do business. Retail advice in the 1840s was adamant on this point: 'As he parts with these goods, again,

he receives the money at once. Unlike the person who sells on credit, there is ... very little risk of his losing his means by the dishonesty, incapacity or misfortunes of others.' The consequent liquidity allowed proprietors to weather the regular downturns in the economy. Ready cash in a period of straitened business conditions even created opportunity, for one could then purchase a new stock of high-quality goods at low prices, turning a potential problem into a profitable situation.[16]

The savings were then passed on to the public. Cash 'economy', in other words, was good for everyone, 'most advantageous to [both] the manufacturer and consumer', as Arthur Levy, proprietor of the Broadway Cash Tailoring Establishment, asserted in his advertisements. 'Purchasers will flock to [cash sales] as instinctively as sharks to a ship', *Hunt's Merchant's Magazine* predicted in 1839, an observation that William Ross repeated verbatim in his business manual a decade later. Ross pointed to those who had learned the hard way that one cannot do a large volume of business at a small profit margin and still give out credit. 'The only inducement for reducing prices below an average standard is a certainty of payment.' Reducing prices made sense because the market proved to be far more elastic than had once been assumed. This meant it was more profitable to broaden one's client base than to foster the loyalty of regular customers who were better trusted with credit purchases. Who could investigate every new customer's credit-worthiness anyway? Indeed, this 'progressive reformation' based on cash and impersonal shopping was a democratic reform: 'As none are credited, so there are none to take offense at a refusal.' And it was just: 'If Mr. Jones failed to pay for his coat,' *Hunt's* explained in pointing out why good customers effectively subsidized the lapses of bad ones in a credit system, 'Mr. Brown must pay double price for his, or the poor tailor must starve, steal, or beg.' Cash tailoring, it turns out, served the Jacksonian hankering for hard money no less than it did the retailer's.[17]

The rush and competitiveness of cash tailoring were heralded by an otherwise unremarkable event. Ever on the alert for corroborative evidence of American industrial progress, *Niles' Weekly Register* had reported in 1822 on the results of a speed competition in upstate New York for producing a man's suit of clothing. A certain General McClure won a fifty-dollar bet that he [*sic*] could turn a fleece of wool into a coat, jacket, and overalls of satinet (a cheap staple of the American woollen industry) within ten hours. *Niles'* duly registered his success: first, the wool was dyed blue, which took 35 minutes; it was then carded, spun, and woven in another two hours and twenty-five minutes, and after that fulled, napped, dried, sheared, and dressed in one hour and fifty-six minutes. At that point someone ran the finished cloth three-quarters of a mile (in four minutes) to Mr. Gilmore's tailor shop, where the suit was completed in 3 hours and 45 minutes, with half a yard of cloth left over (thanks to Gilmore's economy in cutting out the pieces). Gilmore, it was noted, had been assisted by seven extra hands. Flushed with success, McClure offered to double the bet and to accomplish the same, next time in less than eight hours.[18]

Could there be a more innocuous beginning to a world of stopwatches, splintered tasks, and the ceaseless rush to produce? For *Niles'* the effort represented a test of national character. For the locals it had a distinctly sporting air. But the desideratum of speed, together with its corollary of volume, also had a clear commercial application whose lesson was not lost on a clothing market that was becoming ever more competitive.

T. S. Arthur, a best-selling broker of antebellum sentiment, described the situation precisely in his story 'The Seamstress':

'Money don't come in hand-over-fist, as it ought to come,' remarked Grasp, of the flourishing firm of Grasp & Co., Merchant Tailors ... to the junior partner ... A nimble six-pence is better than a slow shilling, you know. We must make our shears eat up cloth a little faster, or we shan't clear ten thousand dollars this year by one third of that sum.'

'Although that would be a pretty decent business these times.'

'I don't call any business a decent one that can be bettered,' replied Grasp contemptuously.

'But can ours be bettered?'

'Certainly!'

'How?'

'By selling more goods.' 'How are we to do that?'

'By putting down prices, and then making a confounded noise about it.'[19]

Such an industrialization of tailoring is to be witnessed in the thirty-year span of Anthoney Arnoux's career. Arnoux opened his business in the twenties, announcing the fact in a notice in the *New York Post* written in French so that no one would mistake him for anything but the source of the most fashionable *habillements*. His posturing had apparent effect. George Templeton Strong, a recent Columbia College graduate and aspiring commercial lawyer with an acute sense of class entitlement, bought his clothing from Arnoux in the thirties. By the next decade, along with everyone else, Arnoux was emphasizing his 'usual moderate prices' in increasingly prolific advertisements. The firm did almost all its 'large and fashionable custom trade' in cash. They also announced their willingness to forward out-of-town orders to any part of the country. By 1851 they were soliciting customers in the South through advertisements in the *New Orleans Daily Picayune*. Arnoux & Co. took pride in the firm's sophisticated commercial operations: its organization into distinct 'departments', each responsible for coats, pants, or waistcoats and each supervised by its own expert cutter. Arnoux, the self-proclaimed *Marchand Drapier et Tailleur*, had become overseer of production. In 1854, not surprisingly, considering Arnoux's business ambitions, the firm became embroiled in a nasty confrontation with the Journeymen Tailors' Society when it went outside the society's ranks in search of cheaper labour.[20]

Cash tailors did not make do with vague promises of unique savings. They filled the dailies with itemized price lists, outbidding one another for the business of the ever-growing public of shoppers interested in affordable prices. The new importance of the popular market was manifest in petitions sent by merchant tailors from New York, Boston, and Philadelphia to Congress in 1832 demanding a reduction in the duty on woollens. Tailors feared that the high price of cloth, which constituted their single largest production expense, was driving away business.[21] Interestingly, four years earlier, during the supercharged tariff debate of 1828, master, merchant, and journeymen tailors had similarly called for a revision of import duties. In 1828, however, their concerns focused on the insufficiently low tariff charged on ready-made clothing imported from Europe. The problem, as all three groups separately contended in almost verbatim petitions to Congress, was that while the duty on woollens had steadily risen over the years to protect American textile manufacturers from cheaper imports, the duty on ready-made clothing had stayed the same. This disparity actually made it cheaper to import many fabrics already made up into clothing, which could then be suitably altered, than to import the raw cloth that still had to be measured, cut, and sewn. In 1828 the profession had demanded, in the face of 'total ruin', that the duty on ready-mades be raised to the same level as that on woollens in order to erase any incentive to import foreign-made garments. Congress complied. But four years later it was obvious that this had not solved the problem. True, the advantages in importing ready-mades were nullified. But the 50 per cent duty on woollens kept the price of clothing in general too high. It was not enough to bring the two duties into line. The cost of imported cloth

had to be reduced so that tailors could then lower their own prices.[22]

This did not happen, and so tailors turned to their next largest production expense—labour—in an effort to maintain their profit margin. T. S. Arthur's fictional account of Grasp & Co. explains what that meant:

'But our prices are very low now.'

'True. But we may reduce them still further, and, by so doing, increase our sales to an extent that will make our business net us beyond the present income quite handsomely. But, to do this, we must cut down the prices now paid for making up our clothes. In this way, we shall be able to greatly increase our sales, with but a slight reduction upon our present rates of profit.'[23]

Tailors, just like clothiers, were left having to rationalize production. A cash business required close management anyway. As profit margins narrowed and volume became the basis of tailoring success, that management increasingly focused on labour. The production process itself stayed the same. The division of tasks—measuring, cutting, basting, stitching, and pressing collars, forearms, coat fronts, and buttonholes—was unaltered. However, its social content was unrecognizably transformed. Class war broke out between masters and journeymen who, by the 1820s, were engaged in a struggle to determine how far property rights allowed one to command the conditions of another's labour. This archetypally industrial confrontation did not begin in those clothing firms that employed hundreds and even thousands at a time, busily mass producing coarse and mid-level ready-made goods for the national wholesale market. The strikes, protests, street confrontations, and subsequent conspiracy trials unfolded in the city's most exclusive tailoring establishments. It was here, in other words, in the highest reaches of the custom trade, that industrial change was most keenly contested.

The industrialization of the custom trade was clearly discernible in an 1827 strike by Philadelphia's journeymen tailors. In contrast to an 1819 turnout in New York provoked by the increasing use of female labour on the part of masters driven to 'accumulate money' at the expense of craft traditions, Philadelphia's journeymen were less directly concerned by the disintegration of producerist mutuality. Indeed, their strike crowned an extended period of instability and work stoppages. Two years earlier, in 1825, an attempt had been made to settle outstanding issues. A carefully detailed bill of prices was drawn up governing payment by masters to their journeymen for work done. The breakdown of this agreement in 1827, however, stemmed less from differences over wages than from a more novel bone of contention: control of the work process.

David Winebrener, a Philadelphia merchant tailor, had assigned six of his journeymen to make up a single riding habit, 'the notice being short' and merchant tailors often advertising the promptest attention to custom orders.[24] The habit was finished satisfactorily, and on time, but Winebrener remunerated the work at a lower rate than his journeymen had expected, namely that, they claimed, prescribed in the trade's recent bill of prices, which Winebrener had signed. Winebrener's journeymen protested by holding up further work until they were paid the difference. In response, Winebrener fired them. Their protest then spread to other shops as Winebrener farmed out his work while the Journeymen's Society sought to keep him from filling his orders. The subsequent conspiracy indictment of twenty-four journeymen tailors addressed the legality—and, by implication, the social legitimacy—of the journeymen's means of redress, namely, the co-operative effort by waged workers to hinder an employer's trade. However, the testimony at the trial itself focused far less on the stuff of criminal conspiracy than on the actual issue at hand: whether the manufacture of the riding habit should cost Winebrener six

dollars, the price he sought to pay, or seven dollars, the price demanded by the journeymen. The problem was that the bill of prices was not clear on the matter. In the tradewide compromise of 1825 journeymen had acceded to their employers' insistent demand that differential rates for making up heavier and lighter garments be instituted. Accordingly, variable prices were listed for making up coats and coatees, explicitly distinguished in the bill of prices on the basis of the type of fabric. Riding habits, however—which were the only women's garments still made by tailors in the nineteenth century, since such garments were the closest in cut and style to men's clothing—were not similarly itemized as light or heavy. As a result, the bill of prices allowed each side its own interpretation. Journeymen could cite the letter of the agreement—namely, the prescribed price of a habit—while Winebrener could no less self-justifiably note its spirit, by which a riding habit made of pongee—a cotton fabric representative of so many of the new cotton or mixed cottons coming into the market for which the public was used to paying less—should cost him less to make up. The stakes were high. The informalities and irregularities characteristic of craft production and earlier market exchange had now become intolerable ambiguities for masters forced to compete in a quickly industrializing environment. Indeed, a new commercial logic could be discerned in these events, one that emptied traditional assumptions of their meaning. Thus, for instance, in seeking to strengthen the virtue of their position in the confrontation, the journeymen actually, albeit implicitly, conceded Winebrener's case. They called a series of expert witnesses to testify that making garments of light cotton fabrics entailed no less, and sometimes even more, effort on the part of the producer. This might have been true—it certainly was the crux of their case—but proportional effort was no longer the principle that informed the structure of their wages, a structure they themselves had agreed to when they signed the differentiated bill of prices in 1825 that was supposed to regularize and thus protect their wages. In any event, the trial resulted in a conviction, although on only one of the three charges brought against the tailors.

The next notable attempt by master tailors to enhance their control over labour occurred in a series of two strikes in New York City in the winter of 1835–36. The strikes marked the culmination of two mutually related processes: first, the heightened mobilization of waged craftsmen into political associations—such as parties or trade unions—that actively opposed the attempts by their employers to reorganize the trades along lines more congenial to market competition; and, second, the growth of a high-flying economy that made New York the country's leading manufacturing city and men's clothing one of the leading branches of manufacturing in the city. During the 1830s these two processes simultaneously pushed capitalists to attempt to 'rationalize' production while giving the producers themselves considerable opportunity to resist those attempts. The result was an ongoing confrontation. Journeymen tailors struck continually throughout the first half of the decade, trying to leverage their craft skills into a suitable social position. By mid-decade it seemed they had succeeded. 'Hands are scarce and work plenty', James Edney wrote in September 1835, upon realizing that his labour costs that year were going to be higher than ever before.[25]

Evidently trying to make the best of the situation, the Society of Journeymen Tailors carried out a long anticipated walkout in October 1835, at the height of the fall production season. The dispute was quickly settled, to the apparent satisfaction of both sides. Industrial peace, however, turned out to be illusory. In January the tailors struck again. This time the turnout lasted for months and was accompanied by vigils outside the shops, confrontations with the scabs hired to finish the work, intimidations and

reputed beatings, newspaper denunciations, and police intervention and arrests—a spiral of mutual recrimination that escalated, at the end of May, into another trial for conspiracy. The trial, which took place in the city's Court of Sessions, resulted in a directed verdict against twenty journeymen tailors.[26]

The January strike ostensibly erupted over wage schedules again, triggered as it was by employers' attempts to pay below the rates agreed upon in October. Certainly, merchant tailors were keenly interested in lowering the costs of their skilled journeymen, upon whom they were dependent, inasmuch as there was still considerable resistance at the high end of the business to hiring women to make up fashionable apparel for men, despite the savings to be derived.[27] But this was not the whole story. Employers had a strategic aim that transcended their immediate interest in the profit equation. They were clearly unhappy with the strike settlement in October, and with their own easy capitulation to the journeymen's society. In response, they organized themselves into an employers' association. They prepared for a long strike and arranged to hire strikebreakers from the city's countless 'irregular shops'. One can credibly suspect that even the arrests for conspiracy 'to the injury of trade and commerce' were not entirely unforeseen. In short, the January strike involved a concerted attempt to break the journeymen's society, not only in order to lower the short-term costs of labour but to affirm employers' singular control over the production process. That is why, for instance, the strike was characterized by 'some features that had never before been presented to employers.' Principal among these was the 'slate rule'. Judge Edwards explained the rule in passing sentence: 'You [the convicted journeymen] would not work for any tailor ... who would refuse to keep a slate hanging up in a public part of his store or shop, on which should be entered the name of every journeymen taking a job from his store, and that no journeyman should take one out of his turn. And also that no member of the said confederacy should go to any such shop for the purpose of getting a job, unless in his turn, under the penalty of forfeiting the price of the job.' For Edwards, the wage workers' insistence on retaining the slate rule epitomized those 'arbitrary by-laws, rules and orders' by which the journeymen's society sought 'to govern not only [them]selves but other journeymen tailors, and persons engaged in the business of tailors', and which constituted criminal conspiracy. Their demand that a public roster of the shop's journeymen should alone determine the distribution of work within that shop—which had been a sacrosanct practice in the English trade for more than a century—clearly delimited the employer's discretion, let alone his control, over a business where he might consider it essential that a particularly important order be made up by his most skilled tailor.[28]

The Panic of 1837 and the depression that followed suppressed the self-assertions of journeymen more effectively than had employers' associations or conspiracy trials. The Union Society of Journeymen Tailors apparently ceased to exist. Or, in the least, its activities became invisible. But the return of prosperity in the mid-forties brought with it renewed agitation. New York tailors struck again in 1844. The main issue of contention was now quite explicitly the question of control over the work process, for which the wage rate was the principal means of expression. But employers were quite clear in the forties that their central concern was to secure an exclusive prerogative regarding the assignment of work to their hired labourers. Nor was the debate any longer confined to the slate rule's prescribed order of jobs. Merchant tailors now sought to combine control over job assignments with a differential rate schedule, whereby they would pay more to a tailor making up a coat of expensive broadcloth than to someone sewing cheaper satinet. The *Herald*, which was critical of the merchant tailors in 1836, was unequivocally understanding of their needs in 1844: 'Where is the justice of compel-

ling, even if the [journeymen] could, employers to pay the good and bad workmen the same amount of wages; or the same prices for every description of work? The same for making a coat worth thirty dollars as for one of forty or fifty dollars?' Thus the issues that first arose in Philadelphia twenty years earlier had reached their resolution. Clothing entrepreneurs—only rarely now referred to by the antiquated appellation of master tailors—could now ensure the highest-quality work on expensive goods while not simultaneously being obliged to pay the same high rate for making up cheaper goods. The importance of such an arrangement in a cash-tailoring business seeking to popularize its market is self-evident.[29]

***

Proprietary authority over the production process was not just necessary for controlling one's work force. It was essential for control over the product itself. This was especially important since male fashion in the nineteenth century was based on a singular, fastidious criterion: fit. 'It is the cut', the *Mirror of Fashion* reminded its readers in 1855, 'that decides the style.' The matte surface of the woollens that were the standard fabric for men's clothing reflected little light, but what the garments sacrificed in colour they gained in malleability. Wool was easily moulded, stretched, shrunk, and shaped to fit the body in a way that silk, for instance, never could be. The goal was a proper fit that facilitated physical mobility and then smoothed itself when back at rest. 'The main argument in favour of the personal appearance of the moderns, is utility,' the *Mirror of Fashion*, that mid-century arbiter of a suitably industrial male aesthetic, continued. A properly fitted garment 'discloses the shape of the figure, and yields to the conveniences of locomotion without restraint to limb, muscle, or joint, and yet without the inconvenience of carrying a surplus of cloth.' This was an apposite vision for the new middle class: 'a quiet pose and graceful fall over the hips, which freedom from extremes generally lends to dress.'[30]

Tailoring success depended on the quality of such a fit. No self-respecting bourgeois, or aspirant to such a status, could be seen in 'spacious-hipped trousers'. Nor could he risk them becoming 'caught on the hip' and thus prevented from falling to his boots in gravitational poise.[31] A business built its reputation on little else but fit. In the competitive conditions of cash tailoring, in fact, a 'warranted fit' became de rigueur. And a 'warranted fit' on the 'most reasonable terms' became an ubiquitous advertising slogan in the 1840s.

On one hand, there was little that was new in these promises. 'Reasonable terms' had been a means of enticing custom since the previous century. And although guaranteeing a fit was a retail innovation of the forties, the promise only made explicit what had always been the traditional assumption of the trade. On the other hand, a contradiction between these two promises now seemed to manifest itself. Cheaper garments meant cheapening the cost of making them up, which employers achieved, as we have seen, by establishing an unprecedented authority over the labour force. But how could the drive toward cheaper labour be reconciled with promises about the quality of the fit when fit traditionally derived from the intuitive skills and practised eye of the artisan? When the merchant tailor had been his own master craftsman there was little problem. But in an age of volume and speed, as J. C. Booth acknowledged, the 'elegance and style for which the establishment has been so long celebrated' rested on 'increasing our help in the cutting department.' In fact, the 'cutter'—who translated the customer's measurements onto the cloth and then cut out the pieces that would be sewn back together into coats, vests, or pantaloons—was the heart of the tailoring enterprise. 'As efficient a corps of cutters as can be found in the country' was the key to success according to William Jennings.

Sometimes the dependence was total, as Edney admitted,

considering the circumstances in which our business is placed, the manner in which it has been carried on, the means we have of keeping it up, the danger that would attend a change of our cutter, the risk of getting one that would cut as well, the uncertainty of getting one that would be willing to devote his whole time to the business, and above all an honest man, one in whom confidence could be placed, in the house with the goods, and in case of my sickness one that would be capable and trustworthy to attend to our business.[32]

How could the artistic, discretionary nature of cutting be integrated into the fundamental logic of a cash business: a higher volume at narrower profit margins? How was the requisite good fit to be achieved when there was far less time to spend on perfecting it, and when repeated fittings were an unwelcome expense, particularly when it came to making up less expensive goods? As Joseph Couts explained in his *Practical Guide for the Tailor's Cutting Room*: 'A gentleman calls to order a coat. He is just on the point of leaving town, or going to a party, and must have his garment ready at a particular hour. You have barely time to get the coat made before he requires to put it on. There can, of course, be no fitting on here. What is the cutter to do?'[33] What's more, how could a proper, fashionable fit be successfully marketed to the majority of American customers who still lived outside the cities?

Such production problems—such business ambitions—were solved by a new technology of drafting systems that came into use in the early 1820s. Each system offered its own patented technique for 'taking the measure of man' and then drafting those measurements onto the cloth so as to achieve the best individual fit on a consistent basis using a minimum amount of cloth and for as varied a clientele as possible. Or, as J. M. Bostian declared in his *Directions for*

Measuring and Drafting Garments (1850): 'The author of this work, in presenting it to the public, does it with perfect confidence in its utility and easy application ... which is most applicable in its various measurements of the human body, overcomes deformity, and renders symmetry symmetrical, approaches nearest to perfect, be it simple or complex in its application.'[34] These systems were a far less dramatic means than strikes and conspiracy trials, but were of no less revolutionary significance in the transformation of tailoring into a mass production business working on a national scale. The number of drafting systems being patented and published proliferated steadily during the 1830s, and then jumped dramatically in the 1840s, by which time methods for drafting men's garments constituted a whole subsidiary trade of competing patents, legal entanglements, regional subscription agents, aggressive advertising, and price wars.

The drafting systems imbued the craft with principles of 'utility and simplicity' that made it possible for 'all who wish [to] be taught to be Practical Garment Cutters' to do so. William Stinemets, a veteran of the labour wars of the thirties who gave up his Broadway tailoring business in 1841 to devote himself to marketing his own system, advertised his desire 'to divest the art of all mystery, and in lieu thereof substitute simplicity and ease.' This meant that 'a person of moderate capacity can, in a few hours, cut with ease and elegance any of the various styles of garments now in vogue.' All those who wanted to get in on the action, whether on Nassau Street in New York, or in Blountville, Tennessee, welcomed advice for 'expediting the work and insuring the fit', as Allen Ward summed up the contribution of his system for drafting the foreparts of coats when he applied for a patent in 1837. Ward's business rival, Francis Mahan, who had unrequitedly challenged him to a public demonstration of their competing drafting systems, quoted a letter he had received from a satisfied tailor in Wheeling, Virginia: 'After having given your system a fair trial I must say it is superior to any system I have used, I have been in business three years, and have tried Sagues, Chappell's, Williams's, Wilson's and others, in using your system, I am always sure of a fit.'[35]

Drafting technology was designed for the 'cutting departments' of city shops and for independent country tailors but not for amateur, that is, household, use. Sewing directions, for instance, were never included in the systems' copiously detailed instructions. As usual, the exceptions prove the rule. A. J. Hunter designed his drafting system, which was published in Kentucky in 1853, 'for the relief of those who have small means, against the extortions and burthens of the professional tailor.' But the focus of Hunter's system was women's clothing, which was more commonly made up at home than were men's clothes. Tellingly, only four of the eighty-four patents issued for drafting systems before 1860 included women's garments at all.[36]

Competition was rife among the inventors of these systems. In 1841 William Fitzmaurice advertised lessons in measuring and drafting techniques 'in the Parisian and London styles' to merchant tailors and clothing manufacturers, supplying vest and pantaloon patterns of 'every size, shape, and style'. In the same year Thomas Oliver touted the popularity of his plan of measuring and drafting among many of New York's leading merchant-tailoring shops. In 1842 the American Institute awarded a prize at its annual industrial fair for the first time to 'the best system for drawing garments'. Oliver, a Broadway tailor, was the honoree, which he must have found particularly gratifying since he was engaged in a bitter public battle with Genio Scott and James Wilson over their accusation that Oliver had infringed on their system. Meanwhile, notices for the second edition of Stinemets's drafting system included a highly reputable list of endorsers from among the city's tailoring elite, and Amos Sherman, author of the *Tailor's Instructor, Professor and Teacher of Cutting*, bragged the next year that his measurement system was used extensively in New York tailoring shops.[37]

The possibility that, as Stinemets already put it, 'a person of moderate capacity can, in a few hours, CUT WITH EASE AND ELEGANCE any of the various styles of garments now in vogue' not only suited metropolitan producers anxious to improve control over, speed up, and reduce the cost of production. It also facilitated provincial initiatives designed to take advantage of the industrial surfeit of cheap cloth, credit, and labour. Sanford & Knowles, Broadway merchant tailors, would send custom suits 'to any part of the United States' as long as customers left their measurements with them. Diagrams for self-measurement began to appear in advertising circulars, so that even those unable to visit the city could nevertheless partake in the sartorial distinction of having one's own custom tailor in New York or Philadelphia.[38] But the main effort came in marketing, not the suits, but the technology. Genio Scott had 136 agents spread over twenty-three states and in Canada selling subscriptions to his *Mirror of Fashion,* which, while peddling urban male style and culture, was also the principal vehicle for Scott in promoting his assorted patented drafting systems. The Wards, in turn, reprinted testimonials from satisfied tailors working with their system in, among other places, Cornesburg, Ohio; Winslow, Indiana; Lexington, Iowa; Rogersville, Tennessee; Little Georgetown, Virginia; Galveston, Texas; Vienna, Georgia; Rutland, Vermont; Watertown, Massachusetts; and Cherry, Pennsylvania. The technologies not only supplied tailors in more remote locations with new economies of production; they also bolstered their businesses by supplying 'the newest fashions from Philadelphia and New-York'. The direct association with New York, and, by implication, with Paris and London, provided popular cachet, and the *Mirror of Fashion,* a trade journal by any other name, adopted a self-conscious tone of high urban sophistication in soliciting the business of America's far-flung tailoring trade, explicit in the hope that its subscribers would 'become the principal teachers of cutting in this country.'

Scott began his publishing venture in association with James Wilson, who received a patent in 1827 for inventing a 'Square Rule System'. Together the two had since bought up related patents and used the *Mirror of Fashion* as the means to market their resulting *Treatise on Cutting Garments to Fit the Human Form,* or their new 'Tractates Nos. 1 and 2,' which contained 'a series of descriptions and illustrations for measuring and drafting.'[39] The reciprocal circulation of fashion and its system of production—the powerful mutuality between the economics and the aesthetics of tailoring—is what contemporaries must have meant by all their talk about the 'utility of fashion'. It certainly makes literal the notion of the mass production of culture, and shows self-fashioning to have been entirely rational, predictable, and constant, and thus potentially common to all.

This trend was already evident in the 1820s as the fashions, like tailoring standards, and together with them, circulated en masse throughout the country. James Douglass, for instance, set up a tailoring business at the west end of Superior Street in Cleveland in the fall of 1825, announcing that 'he has made arrangements to receive the newest fashions from Philadelphia and New-York.' John Wills, another Cleveland tailor, received quarterly reports of the latest fashions for gentlemen's clothing from New York. In Milledgeville, Georgia, A. Cumming regularly acquired 'the latest New York fashions' during the fall of 1827 and promised that his work would be executed according to their designs. One of Scott's agents in Buffalo promised potential subscribers 'New York Fashions at Four Dollars a year only, and including a paper published monthly, and the London plates of Fashions, together with cuts in your paper, representing the Paris Fashions, and the various changes in your city—the whole included at Six Dollars a year.' J. H. Bancker of Nashville sold A. F. Saugues's *Report on Fashions* to tailors in the area 'at the New York prices', together with squares, scales and a book of diagrams, and inch measures. Samuel and Asahel Ward made their colour plates available separately, at a dollar apiece, for adorning the windows of tailoring shops. The new measuring and cutting technologies, while deskilling, or decreasing the need for skilled craftsmen in urban areas, actually gave provincial tailors a new lease on business life. And, of course, the advent of these standard technologies potentially brought customized fashion to the entire citizenry. No wonder, then, as Tocqueville had observed, 'the man you left in New York you find again in almost impenetrable solitudes: same clothes, same attitude, same language, same habits, same pleasures.'[40]

Drafting systems, by their nature, emphasized quantifiable exactitude over subjective judgment. They signalled a new age of 'literacy' in the tailoring craft. Thus, Gabriel Chabot's *The Tailors' Compasses; or, An Abridged and Accurate Method of Measurement* was 'illustrated with Copious and Elaborate Tables and Explanatory Drawings; To which are added Extensive Tables of divisions of heights and breadths to enable every possessor to obtain with true precision every whim of fashion, in a combination of Upwards of 15,000 sizes.' Numbers became the standard of measure, replacing the tailor's personal observation of spatial relations. Deduction of the 'mathematical proportions of the material man' by 'the rule of mathematics' was what distinguished modern times from 'the fantastic days of Elizabeth, or Louis XIV', as B. Read and H. Bodman, highly reputable London tailors who operated a branch store on Broadway, asserted in their *New Superlative System of Cutting*. Public enthusiasm for such scientific conceits was high in the antebellum years, and tailors were in a position to bring the progress of the age to that most popular level—each man's body. One need only look at how these systems promulgated a cartographic ordering of that body into so many discrete provinces of waist, hip, shoulder, back, neck, arm, and leg to understand that the claim to scientific progress was no matter of hyperbole. In fact, science and

system were now the determinant principles of the tailoring craft. It was what Poe had made fun of in his annals of Peter Proffit, except that the pronouncements of patent holders and system sellers were no hoax. Behind all their self-promotion was a basic truth: that tailoring was being driven by the same desiderata of standardization and commercial efficacy as any other industrial-age business.[41]

Prior to that age—in the not too distant past—tailors had each kept their own exclusive set of 'patterns', variably sized and styled paper or cloth cutouts of the constituent sections of sleeves, collars, breasts, and so on, belonging to the various types of garments they regularly made up. When cutting the cloth, the tailor traced designs from the pattern that best matched his customer's size and shape, using the client's personal measurements to particularize the draft. A tailor developed his collection of patterns over the years, the product of his accumulated experience and artistic talents. They were unique to him, although he did occasionally sell patterns and would pass on copies to apprentices at the end of their service. The success of the patterns formed the basis of his own reputation, since they were what translated measurements into a fit. As such, they were carefully guarded trade secrets. Consequently, too, tailors had no need for standard units of measurement. A tailor recorded the length of a person's arm or the circumference of his chest by making notches on a strip of parchment or paper. That strip then contained all the sizing information for a particular customer and could be kept for future reference.[42]

The adoption of the inch tape measure by tailors after 1820 was thus a watershed in the craft's history. Curiously, there is no satisfactory explanation of why the inch measure came into use when it did: the technology was old and was common among other crafts. Nora Waugh, a careful observer of the social details of dress, has argued that the tape measure was invented when it was because it 'drew attention to the comparative relations that exist between the various parts of the body.' This made it integral to a general ethos of interchangeability and proportionality, the systematization of the body requisite for the mass production of raiment. But Claudia Kidwell, the pre-eminent historian of the nineteenth-century clothing revolution, has pointed out that an awareness of comparative relations between body measurements was nothing new. Such knowledge formed the basis of the system of patterns utilized by colonial tailors in their clothing production. Having made that correction, however, Kidwell does not then offer her own explanation for why this technology emerged when it did. She is satisfied with vague allusions to the search for system inherent in a statistical age, an argument curiously akin to Waugh's own.[43]

The truth is that a standard measure was necessary for circulating information in an age when secrecy was no longer good for business. It made it possible to sell what had once been considered trade secrets but now constituted a new opportunity to make money in the exploding clothing market. The practical effect, as Kidwell and Christman have pointed out, was that 'instead of each tailor having his own unique set of markings, now anybody, by following the set procedures for measuring and drafting, could cut for anybody.' An 'American system' of interchangeability had overtaken one of society's oldest and most personalized crafts. Thus, Scott and Perkins could claim that their *Instruction in the Whole Art of Measuring and Cutting* (already in its seventh edition) marked the entry of the 'ordinary mechanical professions' into the same realm of 'useful and practical improvements as steam-driven multiplication and combination of physical power', as contemporaries strained to describe new industrial divisions of labour, even though the physical process of clothing production—the tools and tasks—was actually unchanged. What had changed, of course, was the economic context of production: one now measured and cut garments as part of a new commercial system emphasizing mass volume and speed. This was manifest not only in the escalating number of patents issued for measuring, drafting, and cutting men's clothing but in the clamorous marketing of them. Thus, Samuel and Asahel Ward offered not only their *Quarterly Reports* of the new fashions for sale (an annual subscription costing five dollars a year), but, for an extra dollar, would include coloured plates each spring and fall. They also offered extensive alteration information that allowed for updating fashion details, such as widening the lapels or elongating the skirts of coats. Instructions for learning the Wards' 'Protractor System of Garment Cutting' cost another five dollars. The protractors themselves were twenty-five cents, the essential scales of measurement seventy-five cents each. The special ruler cost a dollar. The Wards also advertised inch measures, tailors' crayons, measure books, shears, trimmers and points, yardsticks, eyelets, squares, scale boxes—all the manufacturing paraphernalia, and all for cash, of course. It is not clear how many provincials in 1853 actually ordered new riding or promenade coats, the kind with large sleeves and edges bound with twilled galloon to match, made of a new style of cashmerette called constelle that, the *Mirror of Fashion* reported, had just appeared in Paris. But the trend was clear, and it was on view in Cleveland, or in Memphis, or almost everywhere else, thanks to Thomas Oliver's 'superb steel plates' that presented unrivalled colour illustrations of the latest fashions.[44]

A growing percentage of the drafting technologies were based on the principles of proportionality, whereby only a minimum number of measurements were taken directly from the customer, the rest being extrapolated from them by means of a patented set of scales or tables. Competing systems touted the superiority of both their actual measurements—which limbs they measured, and with what devices—and the subsequent extrapolations. In a proportional system a tailor would be satisfied with two or three measurements, and sometimes just one. Proportionality, of course, saved time, although just how much time was open to question. More significantly, proportionality seemed to be the basis of mass production, since its logical end was in ready-made clothing, whose sizings were extrapolated from no direct measurements at all.[45]

Standardized production did not have to assume the guise of proportionality, however. A considerable number of the patented drafting systems being published in these years were based on the principle of direct measurement, according to which the tailor eschewed proportional shortcuts and personally took each specific measure, which for a full suit of clothes might reach thirty or forty. On the one hand, these systems approximated popular notions of artisanal tradition. The most exacting personal tailors all claimed to work with direct measurements, which they then favourably compared to proportionality's lazy reliance on patterns and eschewal of fittings—a slothfulness, as one proponent then declared, that reduced the tailoring trade 'to the level of clothes-pin making' or, even worse, made it indistinguishable from dressmaking. But while it assumed for itself the mantle of a higher standard of craft, there was, in fact, little that was traditional about direct measurement as it was practised in the nineteenth century. We have seen how patterns and proportionality predated the industrial age. At the same time, systems of direct measurement were increasingly informed by industrial priorities. They rested no less than did proportionality on newly discovered standards—universally applicable, commodifiable, and aggressively merchandised throughout the land. They represented no less of a systematization of the craft for commercial advantage, promising as they did to deliver a 'definable, repeatable ... procedure' that was utterly at odds with the practices of tailors in the previous century. J. O. Madison, for instance, insisted that taking the measures for a coat using his nonproportional system would

entail less than a minute of time and that the entire subsequent drafting could be completed within five more. The promised result offered a distinct commercial advantage: a more reliable fit utilizing less fabric. Madison went on to explain how direct measurement technologies relied no less than proportional ones on an anthropometric mapping of the human body:

> The body has points that divide the surface; therefore, every point requires a separate measure and each measure must shape the cloth for the part over which the measure was taken; consequently, the envelope for the shoulders and body, like the covering of a ball, must be cut in separate pieces; and then, the great desideratum is to join these several parts or pieces together, in a manner that will produce harmony among the different sections, so that each part will rest at ease without struggling to displace its neighbour.

'Knowledge of the human shape, and ... mathematical science' uncovered anatomical correspondences of a fixed nature that, in turn, became the key for cutting and then reconnecting the cloth so that it matched the individual contours of each body.[46]

And so the myriad drafting technologies all sought to discover the immutable laws that would allow tailors to treat each body as unique while mass producing its raiment faster, cheaper, and more anonymously. This meant that in the new conditions of capitalism, a personalized fit, one that started from measurements taken directly by a tailor, was no less based on a systematization of the buying public—'whereby much labour and expense is saved'—than was the ready-made. Proponents of direct measurement, in fact, made claims that suggested their method was the one ideally suited to a mass market. Proportional measurement, they pointed out, was based on stereotyped patterns. These stereotypes were, by definition, a predetermined assortment of postulated shapes and sizes that did not actually exist in nature. The result was a garment that might or might not fit. For while systems of proportionality rested on the assumption of variation (and thus they needed to establish as wide an assortment of shapes and sizes as possible), their result was singular, that is, a fixed stereotype. The tailor working from 'a successful system' of direct measurements proceeded by the opposite methodology. His system postulated a single standard, a model applicable to all, that, when applied to various persons' measurements, would again and again yield a properly idiosyncratic fit. That is, having uncovered universal truths about body shape, it was capable of suiting everyone. The new tailoring regime thus made a signal contribution to the emerging industrial order by rationalizing that most natural of subjects, the human body. Not only did the personally measured suit, in other words, represent the acme of technological standardization, but standardization proved to be no less than the means of achieving individuation. That individuation, in turn, was what tied the person to the mass market—was what integrated the private body into that market— since it was what made him profitable. If the antebellum economist Henry C. Carey wrote that 'the highest civilization is marked by the most perfect individuality and the greatest tendency to union', it was the custom-fitted suit that in daily practice actually wedded self and society. It did so by a commercial logic that was replacing older, homespun versions of a common identity.[47]

NOTES

Reprinted with permission from Michael Zakim, "The Reinvention of Tailoring," in *Ready-Made Democracy: A History of Men's Dress in the American Republic, 1760–1860* (Chicago and London: University of Chicago Press, 2003), 69–95.

1. On the nineteenth century's clothing revolution, see William C. Browning (1895),

'The Clothing and Furnishing Trade', in *One Hundred Years of American Commerce, 1795–1895*, ed. Chauncey M. Depew, New York: D. O. Haynes & Co.: 561–65; Thomas P. Kettel (1869), 'Clothing Trade', in *Eighty Years' Progress of the United States*, Hartford, Conn.: L. Stebbins: 309–11; Horace Greeley et al. (1872), *The Great Industries of the United States*, Hartford, Conn.: J. B. Burr & Hyde: 587–92. For similar perspectives, see 'The Clothing Trade,' *Hunt's Merchant's Magazine*, March 1864: 233; U.S. Census Office (1865), *Manufactures of the United States in 1860*, Compiled from the Original Returns of the Eighth Census, Washington, D.C.: Government Printing Office: lix–lxv; Isaac Walker (1885), *Dress: As It Has Been, Is, and Will Be*, New York: Isaac Walker: 78–79; Jesse Eliphant Pope (1905), *The Clothing Industry in New York*, Columbia: University of Missouri Press; Egal Feldman (1961), *Fit for Men*, Washington, D.C.: Public Affairs Press; and Claudia B. Kidwell and Margaret C. Christman (1974), *Suiting Everyone: The Democratization of Clothing in America*, Washington, D.C.: Smithsonian Institution Press.

2. On pre-industrial dressing, see, for instance, Jonathan Prude (1991), 'To Look upon the "Lower Sort": Runaway Ads and the Appearance of Unfree Laborers in America, 1750–1800', *Journal of American History* 78, no. 1 (June): 124–59; Carole Shammas (1990), *The Pre-Industrial Consumer in England and America*, Oxford: Clarendon Press.

3. Nathaniel Whittock (1837), *The Complete Book of Trades*, London: John Bennett: 430. On the reputation of ready-made clothing, see Beverly Lemire (1994), 'Redressing the History of the Clothing Trade in England: Ready-Made Clothing, Guilds, and Women Workers, 1650–1800', *Dress* 21: 62–64.

4. See John Pintard (1940), *Letters from John Pintard to His Daughter*, New York: New-York Historical Society: 2:112 (letter of Dec. 7, 1821); Joseph Couts (1848), *A Practical Guide for the Tailor's Cutting-Room*, London: Blackie and Son: 60.

5. See 'tailors' and 'clothiers' in *Doggett's New York Business Directory for 1841–42*, New York: John

Doggett; *Doggett's New York Business Directory for 1844–45*, New York: John Doggett; and *Sheldon & Co.'s Business or Advertising Directory*, 1845, New York: John E Trow & Co. The division of men's clothing stores into 'clothiers' and 'tailors' was less strict in the business directories of the 1830s. See, for instance, *New York As It Is*, in 1833, and *Citizens' Advertising Directory* (1833), ed. Edwin Williams, New York: J. Disturnell.

6. *Brooks Brothers Centenary, 1818–1918* (1918), New York: Brooks Brothers; Feldman, *Fit for Men*: 31–32; advertisement, box 01, BB.1, F10, Brooks Brothers Archive, Chantilly, Va. Henry's transformation from a grocer into a clothier can be followed in his personal listing in the annual editions of *Longworth's American Almanac, New-York Register, and City Directory, 1805–19* (1805–19), New York: David Longworth. Equally revealing was Brooks Brothers' celebration of its 175th anniversary in 1993, which again featured a company history, albeit now in the form of a video produced by the History Factory, Chantilly, Virginia. Revising the earlier version of events, the video, which was shown in all the company's stores, reinstated Henry Brooks's commercial, as opposed to artisanal, pedigree. Apparently in the 1990s there was no longer any reason to conceal the founder's canny entrepreneurialism.

7. Thus the industrial taxonomy used in the manufacturing schedule of the 1850 census perspicaciously assigned clothiers and tailors to the same production category.

8. See Edgar Allan Poe, 'The Business Man', in Poe (1987), *Comedies and Satires,* New York: Penguin Books: 100–108. Charles Baudelaire described Poe as a man 'who regarded Progress, that great idea of modern times, as an idiot's delight.' See 'Edgar Allan Poe', in *Charles Baudelaire, The Painter of Modern Life and Other Essays* (1986), trans. Jonathan Mayne, New York: De Capo: 69–110 (the quote is from p. 73). See also Kenneth Silverman (1991), *Edgar A. Poe: Mournful and Never-Ending Remembrance*, New York: Harper Perennial: 219–30.

9. Poe, 'The Business Man', pp. 102–3. On the early provenance of tailors' tricks, see *Charac-*

ter of a Pilfering Tailor, or a True Anatomy of Monsieur Stitch, in All His Tricks and Qualities (London, 1675). See also *Hunt's Merchant's Magazine,* July 1854: 138.

10. *New York Tribune,* Nov. 15, 1845.

11. *New York Herald,* Sept. 14, 1841 (and see May 7, 1841; and June 2, 1844).

12. *New York Tribune,* Oct. 3, 1845 (and see July 22, 1844). For Booth's $30,000, see *New York County,* vol. 365, p. 102, and vol. 198, p. 127, in the R. G. Dun & Co. Collection, Baker Library, Harvard University Graduate School of Business Administration, Cambridge, Mass.

13. *New Mirror,* Jan. 27, 1844 ('opposite the Fountain'); *New York Tribune,* March 7, 1845. See also William Jennings's advertisement in *Sheldon & Co.'s Business or Advertising Directory, 1845;* Nathaniel Parker Willis (1847), 'Ephemera', in *Dashes at Life with a Free Pencil,* New York: J. S. Redfield: 56–57. Jennings is also mentioned in Edgar Allen Poe's story 'Some Words with a Mummy', *American Review,* April 1845. On the commercialization of Broadway in the 1830s and 1840s, see Eleanor Ewart Southworth (1985), 'Mirrors for a Growing Metropolis: Printed Views of Broadway, 1830–1850', M.A. thesis, University of Delaware: 76.

14. Jennings's advertisement, *New York Tribune,* Oct. 3, 1845. On the growth of demand in these years, even during the deflation of the early 1840s, see Peter Temin (1969), *The Jacksonian Economy,* New York: W. W. Norton. As an English retailer wrote a few years later: 'The same amount of capital is made to do a greater quantity of work than before. In fact, the substitution of quick for slow sales is precisely like an improvement in machinery which cheapens the cost of production.' Quoted in Dorothy Davis (1966), *A History of Shopping,* London: Routledge & Kegan Paul: 259.

15. *New York Tribune* quoted in Asa Greene (1837), *A Glance at New York,* New York: A. Greene: 132–34; Nathaniel Parker Willis (1843), 'Walk in Broadway', *New Mirror,* Oct. 21; *Aurora* (1842), 'Extra' edition, Feb.; advertisements for Martin's tailoring shop, *New York Herald,* Aug. 2, 1841, and May 22, 1842. On George Foster, see Peter Buckley

(1984), 'To the Opera House: Culture and Society in New York City, 1820–1860', Ph.D. dissertation, State University of New York at Stony Brook: 145–46.

16. Advertisement for Martin's tailoring shop, *New York Herald,* May 22, 1842; Samuel Terry (1891), *How to Keep a Store,* New York: Fowler & Wells: 71–72, 149–50 ('As he parts with these goods' is from p. 150). See also Diane Lindstrom (1978), *Economic Development in the Philadelphia Region, 1810–1850,* New York: Columbia University Press: 12; Stephen N. Elias (1992), *Alexander T. Stewart: The Forgotten Merchant Prince,* Westport, Conn: Praeger: 21; David Alexander (1970), *Retailing in England during the Industrial Revolution,* London: Athlone Press: 161–65, 173–85; Ralph Hower (1943), *History of Macy's of New York, 1858–1919,* Cambridge, Mass.: Harvard University Press: 18–21; Carol Halpert Schwartz (1963), 'Retail Trade Development in New York State in the Nineteenth Century, with Special Reference to the Country Store', Ph.D. dissertation, Columbia University: 79–80, 86; and Davis, *History of Shopping:* 187–89.

17. Advertisement for Arthur Levy's Broadway Cash Tailoring Establishment, *New York Herald,* March 23, 1841; *Hunt's Merchant's Magazine,* Dec. 1839: 547; William P.M. Ross (1848), *The Accountant's Own Book and Business Man's Manual,* Philadelphia: G. B. Zieber & Co.: 17 (and see p. 15); *Hunt's Merchant's Magazine,* Dec. 1853: 776.

18. *Niles' Weekly Register,* Oct. 26, 1822.

19. T. S. Arthur (1843), *The Seamstress: A Tale of the Times,* Philadelphia: R. G. Berford: 26–27.

20. *New York Post,* May 9, 1825. See also George Templeton Strong (1952), *The Diary of George Templeton Strong, Young Man in New York, 1835–1849,* ed. Allan Nevins, New York: Macmillan Company, entry for Sept. 26, 1836; *Sheldon & Co.'s Business or Advertising Directory, 1845; New York Tribune,* Sept. 3, 1850; March 18 and March 29, 1854; Egal Feldman (1959), 'New York's Men's Clothing Trade, 1800 to 1861', Ph.D. dissertation, University of Pennsylvania: 24; and *New York County,* vol. 365: 104, in the R. G. Dun & Co.

Collection, Baker Library, Harvard University Graduate School of Business Administration, Cambridge, Mass.

21. Cost estimates of tailors' production expenses are based on Patricia A. Trautman (1982), 'Captain Edward Marrett, a Gentleman Tailor', Ph.D. dissertation, University of Colorado; John Shephard, of New York, N.Y., Merchant Tailoring Accounts, Ac. 861 and Ac. 1721, Special Collections, Rutgers University, New Brunswick, N.J.; James M. Edney, of New York, N.Y., letter book to Francis H. Cooke, of Augusta, Georgia, 1835–37, letter of Feb. 13, 1836, Special Collections, Rutgers University, New Brunswick, N.J.; U.S. Census Office, Seventh Census (1850), Manufactures Schedule, raw data, New York County, N.Y.

22. 'In Favor of Increase of Duties on Ready-Made Clothing', April 28, 1828, 20th Congress, 1st sess., Doc. no. 914; 'Petition of the Journeymen Tailors of Philadelphia', Jan. 30, 1832, 22d Congress, 1st sess., Doc. no. 39. See also related petitions from 1828: 20th Congress, 1st sess., Doc. no. 918; 20th Congress, 1st sess., Sen. Docs. nos. 181, 182, 188 and 191. On cloths and duties, see the *New York Post,* March 27, 1830; Robert Greenhalgh Albion, with the collaboration of Jennie Barnes Pope (1939), *The Rise of New York Port, 1815–1860,* New York: Charles Scribner's Sons: 64; and F. W. Galton (1896), *Select Documents Illustrating the History of Trade Unionism,* vol. 1, *The Tailoring Trade,* London: Longmans, Green.

23. T. S. Arthur (1854), 'The Trials of a Needlewoman', *Godey's Lady's Book,* April: 330.

24. John R. Commons *et al.* (1910), *A Documentary History of American Industrial Society,* Cleveland: Arthur H. Clark: 4:143 (for a full transcript of the trial, see 4:99–264). See also Galton, *Select Documents,* 1:128; and the *New York Post,* Jan. 2, Feb. 18, and Oct. 21, 1822, and April 29 and May 4, 1824. The strike has also received attention from historians, most recently, and perceptively, Christopher L. Tomlins (1993), *Law, Labor, and Ideology in the Early American Republic,* New York: Cambridge University Press: 128–79.

25. Edney to Cooke, letter of Sept. 20, 1835. See also the *New-York Daily Sentinel,* Sept.

7, 1831; and the *New York Post,* Oct. 12, 1833.

26. Commons *et al., Documentary History,* 4:315–33; *New York Sun,* May 26, May 28, and May 30, 1836; Edney to Cooke, letter of June 5, 1835; Tomlins, *Law, Labor, and Ideology:* 128–79.

27. Edney to Cooke, letter of Oct. 21, 1835; *New York Herald,* July 15, 1841.

28. See Commons *et al., Documentary History,* 4:327–33, which reproduces Judge Edwards's ruling. See also the *New York Sun,* May 26, 28 and 30, 1836; *New-York American,* Feb. 9, 1836; *Morning Courier and New-York Enquirer,* May 31, 1836. On the slate rule, see Galton, *Select Documents,* 1.lix, lxxxi, and 89–90; Barbara Taylor (1983), '"The Men Are as Bad as Their Masters ... ": Socialism, Feminism and Sexual Antagonism in the London Tailoring Trade in the 1830s', in *Sex and Class in Women's History,* eds Judith L. Newton, Mary P. Ryan and Judith R. Walkowitz, London: Routledge & Kegan Paul: 206–14.

29. *New York Herald,* July 23, 1844; see also Feb. 25, 1836. On the tailors' strikes of 1844, see the *Working Man's Advocate,* July 27 and Aug. 3, 1844. On a shift in the capital–labour paradigm that could explain the *Herald*'s changed point of view, see Tomlins, *Law, Labor, and Ideology:* 128–79.

30. *Mirror of Fashion,* n.s., vol. 3, no. 1, Jan. 1855: 1–2; and n.s., vol. 1, no. 10, Oct. 1853: 1. See also the *Mirror of Fashion,* vol. 12, no. 5, May 1850: 33; Anne Hollander (1994), *Sex and Suits,* New York: Alfred A. Knopf: 5–9, 88–92; and George P. Fox (1872), *Fashion: The Power That Influences the World,* 3rd ed., New York: Sheldon & Co.: 120–22.

31. Willis, 'Ephemera', in *Dashes at Life with a Free Pencil:* 10, 19.

32. *New York Tribune,* July 22, 1844; *Sheldon & Co's Business or Advertising Directory, 1845,* Edney to Cooke, Oct. 3, 1835. See also Edwin T. Freedley (1858), *Philadelphia and Its Manufactures,* Philadelphia: Edward Young: 221; Francis Wyse (1846), *America, Its Realities and Resources,* London: T. C. Newby: 3:20. In 1835, Edney paid his cutter $1,000 (Edney to

Cooke, letters of Oct. 3, Oct. 25, and Oct. 26, 1835). By the end of the next decade, cutters' salaries had reached $2,000 (*Mirror of Fashion,* vol. 11, no. 11, Nov. 1849: 1). On the importance of a cutter's reputation, see the Ryder Brothers' advertisement in the *New York Herald,* June 25, 1844, and also that for 'a cutter' in the *New York Herald,* March 21, 1855. See also the *Mirror of Fashion,* n.s., vol. 3, no. 3, March 1855: 21–22.

33. Couts, *Practical Guide for the Tailor's Cutting-Room:* 62–63.

34. J. M. Bostian (1850), *Directions for Measuring and Drafting Garments,* Sunbury: by the author: 3.

35. *Mirror of Fashion,* n.s., vol. 1, 1853: 30; Linda Morton (1981), 'American Pattern Drafting Systems for Men in the Nineteenth Century', M.A. thesis, Colorado State University: 34; W. H. Stinemets (1844), *A Complete and Permanent System of Cutting,* New York: Narine & Co.: n.p.; Stinemets advertisement, *New York Herald,* May 1, 1846 (and see May 31, 1844, and May 2, 1845); U.S. Patent Office, letters patent no. 415, Sept. 28, 1837; Francis Mahan (1839), *Mahan's Protractor and Proof Systems of Garment Cutting,* Spring and Summer Report for 1839, no. 8 (Philadelphia), p. 10.

36. Claudia B. Kidwell (1979), *Cutting a Fashionable Fit: Dressmakers' Draftmaking Systems in the United States* (Washington, D.C.: Smithsonian Institution Press: 129–33. See also Morton, 'American Pattern Drafting Systems': 34–35.

37. Fitzmaurice advertisement, *New York Herald,* Aug. 21, 1841; 'List of Premiums Awarded by the Managers of the Fifteenth Annual Fair', American Institute Papers, case no. 4, New-York Historical Society, New York. See also T. Oliver's and H. Levett's advertisements to New York tailors, *New York Herald,* Aug. 27 and Sept. 9, 1841, and April 13, 1848; Feldman, 'New York's Men's Clothing Trade': 190. In addition, see George Gifford (1860), *Before the Honorable Philip F. Thomas ... in the Matter of the Application of Elias Howe, Jr., for an Extension of His Patent for Sewing Machines,* New York: W. W. Rose: 15; B. Read and H.

Bodman (1837), *New Superlative System of Cutting*, London and New York; *J. S. Bonham's Improved Garment Cutter for 1853*, Knoxville, Tenn., quoted in Morton, 'American Pattern Drafting Systems': 34; *New York Herald*, May 1, 1846; and B. T. Pierson (1846–47), *Directory of Newark*, Newark, N.J.: Price & Lee Co.

38. Stinemets advertisement, *New York Herald*, May 1, 1846; Sanford & Knowles advertisement, *Carroll's New York City Directory, 1859*, New York: Carroll & Co.: 80. See also the *Mirror of Fashion*, vol. 11, no. 1, Jan. 1849: 1; *The Gem, or Fashionable Business Directory*, New York, 1844: 82; Charles Stokes and Edward T. Taylor (1864), *Charles Stokes & Co.'s Illustrated Almanac of Fashion*, Philadelphia: 28; and the H. A. Pierson advertisement in the *Floridian*, Oct. 25, 1834, reproduced in Margaret Thompson Ordonez (1978), 'A Frontier Reflected in Costume: Tallahassee, Leon County, Florida, 1824–1861', Ph.D. dissertation, Florida State University: 154.

39. Samuel A. Ward and Asahel F. Ward (1849), *The Philadelphia Fashions and Tailors' Archetypes*, Philadelphia: n.p.; *Mirror of Fashion*, vol. 10, no. 7, July 1848: 8; Genio Scott and James Wilson (1841), *A Treatise on Cutting Garments to Fit the Human Form ... Accompanied by a Periodical Report of Fashions*, New York (for the 'Super Rule System'); *Mirror of Fashion*, n.s., vol. 1, no. 3, March 1853: 63. See also Kidwell, *Cutting a Fashionable Fit*: 129–33; Mary L. Davis-Meyers (1992), 'The Development of American Menswear Pattern Technology, 1822 to 1860', *Clothing and Textiles Research Journal* 10, no. 3 (spring): 12–20.

40. *Cleveland Herald*, Sept. 2, 1825 (and see Oct. 12, 1827); *Georgia Journal*, Nov. 15, 1827; *Mirror of Fashion*, vol. 11, no. 1, Jan. 1849: 1; *National Banner and Nashville Whig*, Jan. 3, 1831; Tocqueville quoted in Marvin Meyers (1957), *The Jacksonian Persuasion: Politics and Belief*, New York: Vintage Books: 131. See also Davis-Meyers, 'Development of American Menswear Pattern Technology': 14–15; *New York Herald*, May 1, 1846; *Mirror of Fashion*, vol. 10, no. 7, July 1848: 8; Ward and Ward, *Philadelphia Fashions and Tailors' Archetypes*;

Morton, 'American Pattern Drafting Systems': 68; *New York Herald*, Aug. 27, 1841; and Scott and Wilson, *Treatise on Cutting Garments*.

41. Gabriel Henry Chabot (1829), *The Tailors' Compasses; or, An Abridged and Accurate Method of Measurement*, Baltimore: J. Matchett: title page; Read and Bodman, *New Superlative System of Cutting*: 3. See also Kidwell, *Cutting a Fashionable Fit*: 4–6; Scott and Perkins (1837), *The Tailor's Master-Piece, Being the Tailor's Complete Guide, for Instruction in the Whole Art of Measuring and Cutting, According to the Variety of Fashion and Form, with Plates, Illustrative of the Same*, New York; Alison Adburgham (1964), *Shops and Shopping, 1800–1914: Where, and in What Manner, the Well-Dressed Englishwoman Bought Her Clothes*, London: George Allen and Unwin: 41; *Mirror of Fashion*, n.s., vol. 3, 1855: 49; and Neil Harris (1973), *Humbug: The Art of P. T. Barnum*, Chicago: University of Chicago Press. On the new entrepreneurial definition of art, see Paul Johnson (1988), '"Art" and the Language of Progress in Early-Industrial Paterson: Sam Patch at Clinton Bridge', *American Quarterly* 40, no. 4 (Dec.): 433–49.

42. See Kidwell, *Cutting a Fashionable Fit*.

43. Nora Waugh (1964), *The Cut of Men's Clothes, 1600–1900*, New York: Theatre Arts Books: 130; Kidwell, *Cutting a Fashionable Fit*: 7–9.

44. Kidwell and Christman, *Suiting Everyone*: 41; Scott and Perkins, *The Tailor's Master-Piece, Being the Tailor's Complete Guide, for Instruction in the Whole Art of Measuring and Cutting*, n.p.; *New York Herald*, Sept. 1, 1841. See also Kidwell, *Cutting a Fashionable Fit*: 4–6; Trautman, 'Captain Edward Marrett': 49–52; Ward and Ward, *Philadelphia Fashions and Tailors' Archetypes*.

45. On proportionality, see Davis-Meyers, 'Development of American Menswear Pattern Technology': 12–18; New York City Tailor, measurement book, 1828–31, New-York Historical Society, New York; Morton, 'American Pattern Drafting Systems': 2, 24.

46. J. O. Madison (1878), *Elements of Garment Cutting*, Hartford, Conn.: Case, Lockwood & Brainard Company: 5–6, 112, and 160 (and

see pp. 6–7, 162). 'Knowledge of the human shape' is from *The Tailor's Director, Containing an Important Discovery for Fitting the Human Shape, by Anatomical Principles,* New York, 1833, quoted in Morton, 'American Pattern Drafting Systems': 23–24. See also Kidwell, *Cutting a Fashionable Fit:* 9.

47. William McWiswell, 'Mode of Cutting the Bodies of Coats in One Piece', U.S. Patent Office, letters patent no. 1119, April 10, 1839; Madison, *Elements of Garment Cutting*: 127–28 (see also pp. 9–17); Henry C. Carey quoted in Angela Miller (1993), *The Empire of the Eye: Landscape Representation and American Cultural Politics, 1825–1875,* Ithaca, N.Y.: Cornell University Press: 69. See also Mark Seltzer (1992), *Bodies and Machines,* New York: Routledge: 49–64.

19

THE JAPANESE SUIT AND MODERNITY

Toby Slade

Even the most casual observer of Japanese fashion will usually come to the conclusion that although men ostensibly dress in suits like their European and American brothers, something different is going on. Closer examination is even more intriguing; modern Japanese menswear somehow uses the suit as its emblem and sartorial workhorse, but it does so for almost none of the reasons usually considered part of the orthodoxy of fashion theory and upon which the explanations of the sequence and causality in men's fashion rest. Japan was unique in its experience of adopting, appropriating, and restyling foreign clothes because it did so without colonization and before extensive industrialization. Furthermore, almost none of the factors traditionally attributed to the refinement of the most common and long-lasting of male dress forms can be applied in the Japanese case. The class arrangements and political revolutions had little equivalence to the French-revolutionary-born sartorial codes based on bourgeois demonstrations of wealth without aristocratic ostentation. Elites' size and response to modernity were entirely different. European and American religious reforms and their clothing expressions were irrelevant, and gender relations were differently demarcated and thus reformed in wholly different ways. What then precipitated the Japanese response—to the crisis of masculine clothing in modern times—to produce the same solutions as in the West? And what does that say about what is universal and what is culturally

specific in the aesthetics of masculine clothing in modernity?

Authenticity, appropriation, and legitimacy were recurring themes and anxieties for the Japanese in the adoption of foreign sartorial schemas like the suit, and this had multiple repercussions for the political agenda in its use of the suit as a potent symbol of cultural equality with late nineteenth-century colonial powers. Furthermore, the sudden jump from feudal social arrangements to modern ones without centuries of enlightenment and reform also shaped very specific social complications played out in clothing. Dissimilar forms of leisure and means of consumption, as well as incompatible furniture and domestic space, not to mention a beautifully efficient and sophisticated male clothing system already in existence, should all have been factors that obstructed the suit from becoming so prevalent in Japan. And yet there seemed to be something so essential to modernity in the aesthetic choice of seriousness and abstraction over frivolousness and ornamentation, the need to repudiate aristocracy and femininity and to disavow sanctioned male vanity, that, despite all the possible social and political enmity, the suit became a universal and irresistible fashion. Masculine sartorial modernity in Japan thus offers a unique interpretive vantage point for the general understanding of the aesthetics of fashion and modernity and a chance to recalibrate the canon of fashion theory to account for the non-Western experience (color plate 31).

The ways in which masculinity could be performed and dressed for were some of the first things challenged by the wave of American and European aesthetics that arrived with the Meiji restoration of 1868. Japanese notions of sartorial femininity, while toyed with by the elite in the 1870s, were essentially untouched until the 1920s. Political and social freedoms were also partitioned in this way, with masculine modernity beginning much earlier and for different reasons from feminine modernity, which, not totally discounting hopeful beginnings, stagnated for much of the Meiji period (1868–1912).

Meiji modernity had a deliberate and methodically discharged political agenda that first attended to the male occupations of the military, the state bureaucracy, and commerce.[1] The clothing forms for these occupations were the first areas to experience reform, although it should be stressed men dressed in modern styles only while performing these occupations, their leisure and domestic wardrobes remaining indigenous. This is the inverse of the central narrative of sartorial modernization in Europe, where men's leisure wear drove clothing reform in modern directions of abstraction, streamlining, simplification, and deliberate dourness, while the state bureaucracy and the military of most European powers remained conservative in their dress agendas.[2] While many European monarchies and militaries entered World War I without really having engaged with modern dress imperatives, the roles of both the Japanese monarchy and military were by then that of models of a new modern agenda rather than examples of hankering after an older aristocratic order and accompanying sartorial aesthetic.[3] Thus, a unique avant-garde drives early Japanese sartorial modernity and indeed Meiji modernity in general—not an artist or intellectual class but an ambitious political class, though this changes by the later waves of modernity in the 1920s. The central narrative of these later waves of modernity belongs to consumption, leisure, and women, but the opening chapters of the story of Japanese dress modernity belong

most definitely to the crisis of Japanese masculinity and its abundant solutions in that most versatile of fashions: the suit.

The penetration and reach of early clothing modernity were greatly limited. There was a definite period of eclectic combinations of kimono and foreign elements, such as hairstyles, shoes, hats, gloves, glasses, umbrellas, and so on, which can be seen in early Meiji photography and prints, but it is logical that this would reflect mainly the urban areas and wealthy social classes that had access to photography and printmaking. Access to a more complete experimentation was also limited by availability, and the compatibility with lifestyle that Western suits lacked until changes to furniture, relaxation regarding the removal of shoes, and other changes allowed for their ample application without too much discomfort.[4]

The essential aesthetic change for Japanese masculine sartorial priorities contrasted with the feminine and indeed reconstructed that very gender demarcation. As in Europe before it, the first modern concern in Japanese masculinity was to rid itself of the feminine; the essential movement is one that disavows sanctioned male vanity—repudiating both aristocracy and femininity.[5] Modernity's inclination toward seriousness and abstraction, over frivolousness and ornamentation, was first naturally exerted by the sex that considered itself, rightly or wrongly, to be serious and nonornamental. Thus, the primary tendencies in clothing modernity were masculine in Japan and bound up with the affairs and priorities of the emerging state, its principal actors, and the identity it wished to fashion for itself.

SUITS: MODERN AND CLASSIC MASCULINITY

The political inequities of the 1858 Harris Treaty[6] provided a heavy incentive to Japanese nationalism but simultaneously reinforced a traditional underlying sense of inferiority, and this contradiction was also at work in attitudes toward male clothing reform. One reason the Japanese government implemented changes so quickly in the Meiji era, adopting Western laws, technology, and clothes, was to demonstrate that they were in fact civilized on Western terms and deserved to be treated as equals—hence the adoption of *Bummei Kaika* (Civilization and Enlightenment) as an official government slogan for the 1870s. As Japan's government lurched into the modern world, there was a tremendous outburst of energy and euphoria for all things Western. Mori Arinori, then a diplomat at the Japanese embassy in Washington, greeted incoming Japanese students by advising them to intermarry and propagate children with superior Caucasian ethnic qualities.[7] The immediate switch to Western clothing was also a self-alienating demand along these lines. These were extremes, but, on the whole, in the beginning, modernization and Westernization seemed to be virtually synonymous.

Japan's willingness to accept Western learning and culture is not without precedent. It reflects a long history of fascination with anything new, foreign, and exotic—perhaps the result of geographic remoteness. In the past this had meant an absorption of continuous waves of influence from China and to a lesser extent from Korea and even, in the late sixteenth century, from Europe. Mori Arinori's debate with the Chinese leader Li Hongzhang in 1876 articulated the central dilemma of practicality and national identity with regard to formal clothing. Li, looking disdainfully at Mori's Western suit, had asked whether Mori's Japanese ancestors had dressed that way. No, Mori replied, they had adopted Chinese dress, but it was no longer practical; Japan had always taken the best of other civilizations for itself, and it was doing so once more. He then went on to remind Li that Li's ancestors had not worn the official robes prescribed by China's Manchu conqueror either; Japan, by inference, had at least made its own choice.[8] The first and longest-lasting of all sartorial choices made by modern Japan had been to adopt a garment—or

a system of garments—that had almost evolved into the suit that is still universally worn for the same reasons 130 years after Mori and Li's terse encounter.

Inoue Kaoru, foreign minister from 1879 to 1887, devoted himself to treaty revision to engender these reforms, designing the first legal modernization, as required by the foreign powers, but devising as well original and highly visible social programs of Westernization and modernization—then understood as the same thing.[9] Inoue, understanding the importance of symbolism, both for domestic and international perception, conceived the Rokumeikan, a European-style mansion in central Tokyo, which was such an important element of early Japanese sartorial modernity and of government policy on cultural direction that it gave its name to the span of years from 1884 to about 1889. Opened in 1883 under the jurisdiction of the Foreign Ministry it was, after the Emperor, the second major tool of sartorial statecraft. The agenda was to forward Inoue's desire that the Japanese be Westernized and that the West should witness that change, such that it would accept Japan as a cultural, and thus political, equal. The Rokumeikan functioned as a space where the new Japanese urban elite could dress like and mingle with, influence and be influenced by, foreign dignitaries.

Anne Hollander's definitive characterization of the suit as a "fluid, multipartite envelope for the body, complementing its shape and movement and establishing a constant visible harmony between the body's structure and that of the clothes without heavily emphasizing either one," is a profoundly modern definition.[10] It touches on many of the defining elements of sartorial modernism: movement, practicality, systematic elements, and a new relationship with the body; and implies important others: the banishment of frivolity and unnecessary ornament, form following function, abstraction, and formal seriousness.

Although the suit became a modern garment rather than one with a particular national association, it did originate in the tailoring of the

English rural gentry, Western European revolutionary movements, and American theology.[11] Central to the suit's Western popularity was the rise of the bourgeoisie, although this term needs clarification. Most often this class is represented as emerging in nineteenth-century England as a class made up of manufacturers. The term has also served to explain various reform movements in England and revolutions abroad; in addition, it is made to account for many things from improved police organization to the popularity of the novel. In clothing it is called upon to account for the rise of the suit and its evolution into the garment that has been adopted universally by government and commerce in the developed world. When the suit was enthusiastically adopted in modernizing Meiji Japan, many of the same explanations were applied, not necessarily appropriately.

The economic and cultural embourgeoisement of most of the first world was a twentieth-century phenomenon;[12] however, the roots of the embourgeoisement of clothing tastes lie much earlier. Although much of what influenced that shift in Europe was irrelevant to the Japanese adoption of suits, there were parallels in the dress practices of Edo merchants and urbanites whose proximity and enrichment—financial and cultural—well predates direct European influence.

Within Japan's agrarian feudal economy, as in feudal Europe, important urban centers developed that were engaged in mercantile operations and manufacturing.[13] One part was the establishment of the *sankin-kōtai* system, whereby regional lords had to maintain an alternative residence in Edo and leave family members there when not in residence themselves—a centralization system not unlike France's at Versailles. In Edo this stimulated unprecedented commercial demand in the urban economy because of the resultant aristocratic consumption of luxury goods in the city and the necessary expenditure on official city residence or *yashiki* maintenance and on frequent travel of households between Edo and their rural domains. Forbidden from legally acquiring agricultural property, Japanese merchants, enriched by the enforced centralization of wealth, could not divert their capital into rural property; thus, the very rigidity of the class system incongruously encouraged the growth of large purely urban fortunes.[14] By the eighteenth century the population of Edo numbered more than a million people, and at least a tenth of the population lived in towns with more than 10,000 residents,[15] demonstrating the demographic concentration of urban, bourgeois economic, and growing cultural dominance.

Despite what seemed to be a demographic and economic inevitability, Tokugawa isolationism meant that merchant capital was constantly constrained and artificially redistributed toward parasitic dependence on the feudal nobility. In contrast, by the beginning of the modern era, inter-European trade was global. The sartorial needs, however, of the class responsible for trade were similar in age-of-discoveries Europe to what they were in Edo Japan. Merchants were becoming much wealthier, but feudal systems—with wealth and status based on land—forbade them from ostentatious displays of wealth or even nonpecuniary sartorial expression and aesthetic self-actualization in their dress. Thus, a code of subtle finery became the vocabulary of trading-class clothing. In Edo Japan the merchant classes used the legal dull colors for their kimonos but used fine silk linings and other means of muted conspicuous display.[16] These same mechanisms were at work in the European merchant princes' gravitation toward the subtle forms of display and class markings that gave birth to the clothing system that became the male suit.

The concept of the "modern" is multidimensional: it is not only a set of ideas that affected the intellectual environment but also the way in which a new industrial, metropolitan, social environment affected the people who inhabited it. Modernity is both the ideas that made new forms and also what those new forms made of ideas—a blending of inner and outer so profound that it had perhaps not been seen since classical times. What made such a formal and conceptual revolution possible was not only new ideas but, more importantly, the tools to make such ideas reality: reason, industrialization, and the urbanization of culture (figure 19.1).

The male three-piece suit was both a remarkable affirmation of belief in a classical aesthetic and the first manifestation of what a new, modern world would be capable of achieving through social and political rearrangement of education, class, and nationality, and, as a result, how people's consciousness would change from defining themselves primarily by class and occupation to defining themselves primarily as educated citizens. This process was actively sought by Meiji rulers, with a mind to turning the passive, ruled, feudal subjects of Tokugawa Japan into active participants in the state and in their own history—in short, modern citizens rather than feudal subjects.[17]

The bourgeois usurpation of aristocracies' role as the economically and culturally dominant class in modernizing society meant that a much larger group took control of the mechanics of state and nationhood. With this change also came the shift of power from the land to the city as the source of wealth creation, through the industrial revolution and the expansions of trade, money markets, and population that preceded it and were accelerated by it. The economic power of the few now rested with the many, and the interests of this larger group had to be accommodated politically.

Japan had a much shorter time to come to terms with these ideas and to transform itself from a feudal state into a modern one, yet it also had many advantages. The level of wealth and the inherent efficiency in the Japanese lifestyle allowed for a rapid economic change. The degree to which religion affected the population was also much less; the dogma of Christianity in such simple things as borrowing money took centuries of enlightenment to reverse in Europe. Literacy and education were also a great boon in the rapid creation of a bourgeois society and meritocratic government. These factors would have allowed the adoption of the suit—a garment already evolved for modern life—to feel more appropriate to the Japanese lifestyle.

Although the suit arrives in the middle of these Western processes, and it is mostly therefore irrelevant to it, Japan also experiences this phenomenon in men's clothing and in performing masculinity, in which the proof of material worth—a measurable and therefore rational scientific imperative—becomes its governing principle. Japan had to emulate the long period of enlightenment in America and Europe in a much shorter time, although it could do this because of certain favorable preexisting social and economic conditions. The political, aesthetic, and sartorial victory of the classical over the baroque has particular relevance for Western history, but its relevance for Japan is far more general and tied up in the need to catch up to nations that had commenced the path to modernity well before it, much more than with internal religious debates. However, the ends had to be the same for the achievement of a truly modern society and state. The *Bummei Kaika* (Civilization and Enlightenment) movement of early Meiji recognized this and saw in the suit the manifestation of modern values that had taken a century to evolve in the West.

EMBOURGEOISEMENT AND THE CIVILIZED CENTER

Essential to the self-conceptualization of the middle class is the idea of a civilized center.[18] Most bourgeois clothing signs are signs of negation: a negative relationship of rejection. The suit is not aristocratic, not decadent, not Catholic, not religious, not part of a hierarchy, and not feminine. For Japan the meaning was slightly different; the suit was not aristocratic (samurai), not primitive, not isolationist, not backward-looking, and not—for the first time—feminine.

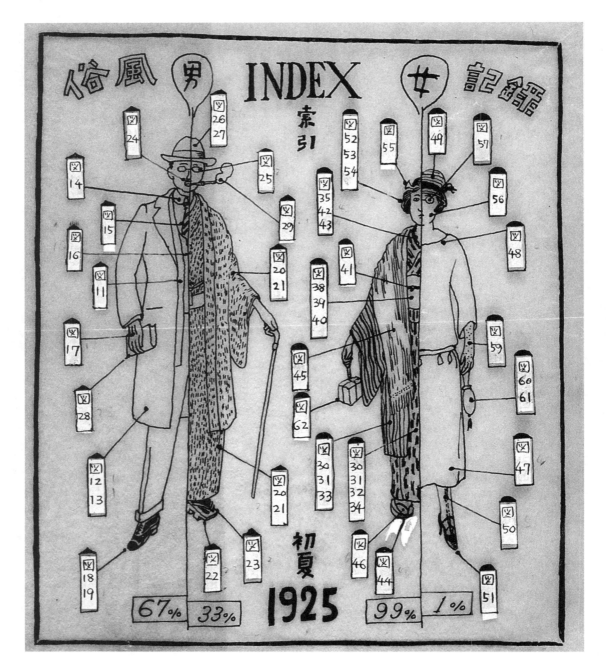

Figure 19.1 Kon Wajirō, *A Record of Styles on a Ginza Boulevard in Tokyo, 1925*. [今和次郎, 東京銀座街風俗記録], *1925*. [工学院大学図書館]. Kogakuin University Library. This is an example of the countless sketches made by Kon Wajirō, an architect and amateur social researcher, who recorded the changing consciousness and evolution of Japanese modernity in the 1920s and 1930s. He noted, in the manner of Walter Benjamin, the role that everyday life plays in life and history, with an expanded notion of what constituted art and what was worthy of serious research. This image records the percentages of people wearing certain fashion details of Western or traditional dress. Kon observed that innumerable identities were being played out daily in shops and cafés and on every street corner, where people could assume different subject positions by the way they dressed and styled their hair and by the choices they made for play and consumption in the rapidly changing metropolis of Tokyo.

The suit pulls away from the movement that sanctioned male vanity, flamboyance, and insouciance: dandyism.

Dandyism was a reaction against this bourgeois sartorial construct that limited male clothing consciousness. Dandyism was a way of being, a particular romantic reaction against the bourgeois prohibition of male sartorial vanity. Kuki Shūzō questioned whether *Dandyisme* had the same structure as the Japanese aesthetic of *iki*. He claims that Baudelaire's *Les Fleurs du mal*[19] expresses a passion close to *iki*, which was born in the urban, wealthy culture of Edo. It was part of the non-profit-making life of the rich man who has become accustomed to enjoying himself.[20] Dandyism, Kuki argued, was the "dogma of elegance," and he claimed that there is no disparity in dandyism having a structure analogous to *iki* but that its semantic content is almost only appropriate to the male sex. As an end in itself, and therefore an aesthetic practice, *iki* was analogous to European dandyism. Nagai Kafū says in *Kanraku* (Pleasure)[21] that the first feature of *iki* lies in the preservation of coquetry without extinguishing it through its completion.[22] The second feature of *iki* is chic—a brave composure (*ikiji*), which is close to the component of cool in dandyism.[23] Self-composed even when starving, *iki* courtesans display a "haughty distain." Through *isagiyosa*—a proud resignation to the truth of life and a disinterest or indifference to its outcomes—coquetry is spiritualized through the "brave composure" produced by idealism. The third attribute of *iki* is resignation (*akirame*), an indifference that has renounced attachment and is based on knowledge of fate. *Iki* must be urbane.

There existed, then, an equivalent to European dandyism in the Japanese context. While some reservations can be placed on its exact equivalence, it can be concluded that some of the aesthetic factors that shaped the suit's development in Europe were at work in the Japanese experience as well. The fact that this aesthetic developed under the same sort of cultural conditions

(increasing urbanization), and among a middle class expanding in power but as yet unrecognized by the state, is important in determining why the suit was deemed so appropriate to modernity in Japan and why it was so widely and quickly adopted.

The streamlining of the suit—from the frock coats and top hats that first arrived in Japan to the simpler suits of Taishō and early Shōwa—mirrors the modernist desire for form to follow function long before anyone had thought to phrase it that way. The suit reflects the gradual progression toward a set of garments that best fit what will be done in them. Therefore, ornamentation is dropped. The form of the body is shown, and the garment is shown in equal measure—the brushstrokes are visible. Streamlining is an essential twentieth-century concept and can be thought of as a product of enlightenment reason.[24] The suit was designed to enable greater movement, and because it is a system of garments, rather than just one, variations could be made to fit certain conditions. Being able to move is part of freedom.

Born out of political ideas, which themselves were born out of the new science and reason, the suit presented the first glimpse of a modern Kantian aesthetic, based on principles of form that are partly classical and partly utilitarian—a formal fidelity. The modern aesthetic was the victory of the classical over the baroque, black and white over color, and formalism over frivolity. The republican values of America and France attempted to remove the artifice and ornamentation of aristocracy from their cultures and replace it with the classical architectural form of noble simplicity and calm grandeur, as their governments removed the arbitrary from their body politics. Humankind's consciousness was to be defined first as a citizenry, and not by occupation or rank, as in premodern times, hence the need for new dress demonstrating this. An international, rational idealism was to replace the tribalism and ethnicity of costume. The risen middle classes of the Western world were to take their place as the new ruling classes of this transatlantic modern world of trade and new money; their puritan faith was both their driving motivation and the shaper of their new cultural values. A social contract was to replace divine right as the central weave of society's fabric. Part of this new and voluntary covenant was display of one's membership in this modern, rational, educated world, through the dark three-piece suit that expressed worldliness.

An essential point in this complex dress evolution is that Japan arrives in the middle of many processes that are largely irrelevant to it. Although changes in dress signaled certain universal trends toward modernity and citizenship, other issues of Protestantism, or Baroque aesthetics, were meaningless to the Japanese in 1868. The European meaning of many elements of male dress, insofar as they had meaning, was unimportant to the elites of early Meiji. This is not to say that the suit did not have meaning, just that the meaning was mostly different. The abolishment of aristocratic rank and the transformation from a feudal social structure to a less arbitrary modern one were shared, but the form this transformation took in Japan was very different. Essentially, the suit was a sign of alignment with a change in policy—the new policy of looking out to the world rather than closing it off. It signaled that the wearer had made a fundamental choice to be part of the change, to be modern, not traditional. The rise of the merchant classes was a similar process to that in Europe and America and had the same implications for male dress, which changed from a feudal theater in which men wore essentially romantic costumes to one where the formerly culturally sanctioned male vanity, flamboyance, and insouciance that allowed for more luxuriant forms of self-expression in clothing declined and were replaced with the imperative of ceaselessly proving one's wealth within a framework of conforming as equal members of a citizenry. This was a universal phenomenon that accompanied the embourgeoisement of peoples everywhere.

In Japan it was a critical field in which the traditional did battle with the modern, socially and aesthetically.

The changes in aesthetic tastes that underpinned the suit's impact were partially universal and partially unique. In the Meiji period, the change in gendering that accompanied the rise of the merchant classes, which restricted male vanity and placed an emphasis on demonstrating wealth but without aristocratic ostentation, was a process that echoed European embourgeoisement. In male clothing, romantic expression was considered in Japan, as in the West, to be an attribute of a feudal ruling class and was thus shunned. Unique to Japan was the question of foreignness, the foundational choices that had to be made by every suit wearer as to whether they should adopt modernity so fully as to change in a totally fundamental way their bodily appearance. That new relationship to the body, not nearly as hidden in a suit as in a kimono, was also part of one of modernity's primary projects, that of physically redefining humanity.

The intentionally fabricated and meaningful sartorial signs of the Meiji state, in the form of the emperor, the civil service, the Rokumeikan, the army, and public schooling, were an essential part of its program of cultural and political modernization and the accompanying desired aesthetic shift to modernity (figure 19.2). It was adopted into masculinity as a Kantian truth in form, with male clothing becoming serious and useful; accordingly, abstract femininity was reconstructed as ever more frivolous and ornamental. Both positions were, of course, abstractions and arbitrary, yet in the universal conditions of modernity, coupled with the particular gendering norms that predated it, in Europe and in Japan, masculinity was the aesthetic that modernized first. The central sartorial form that the new aesthetic took was the various versions of the suit, which repudiated both aristocracy and femininity and was true to the body and to the garment itself at the same time—as with modern art, the brushstrokes were visible.

Figure 19.2 Unknown press photographer, *His Royal Highness the Prince of Wales walking with the Empress [sic] of Japan in Tokio [sic] during the Indian and Eastern Tour of 1921–22.* Private collection. In this artfully composed press photograph of April 1922, the military uniforms worn by Crown Prince Hirohito and the Prince of Wales reveal different posture and gaits, in which the cut of the uniforms alone does not determine the final effect. The Prince of Wales seems both shaped by his uniform and also the embodiment of its elitism. The morning suit and top hat of the prince's attendant provide a foil to the more splendid trappings of the other military officials, possibly including Admiral Sir Lionel Halsey. This is an intriguing scene of a cross-cultural elite encounter. The warmth that the Japanese Crown Prince felt for the Prince of Wales, which was maintained throughout his lifetime in the postabdication period, is palpable. Hirohito's consort is dressed in a slightly old-fashioned *Belle Epoque*–style picture hat, and she carries ermine, a perquisite of European royalty. She also seems to wear her foreign dress with a different bodily imprint compared with a 1920s European woman.

NOTES

1. Carol Gluck, *Japan's Modern Myths: Ideology in the Late Meiji Period* (Princeton, NJ: Princeton University Press, 1985). See also Marius B. Jansen, ed., *The Nineteenth Century,* vol. 5 of *The Cambridge History of Japan,* ed. John Whitney Hall et al. (Cambridge: Cambridge University Press, 1988–1999).

2. James Laver, *The Age of Optimism: Manners and Morals, 1848–1914* (London: Weidenfeld & Nicolson, 1966). See also James Laver, *British Military Uniforms* (London: Penguin, 1948), or, more visually, James Laver, *Costume Illustration: The Nineteenth Century* (London: Victoria and Albert Museum, 1947).

3. Meirion Harries, *Soldiers of the Sun: The Rise and Fall of the Imperial Japanese Army* (New York: Random House, 1991). See also Emiko Ohnuki-Tierney, *Kamikaze, Cherry Blossoms, and Nationalisms: The Militarization of Aesthetics in Japanese History* (Chicago: University

of Chicago Press, 2001), and the *Catalogue of the Yasukuni Jinga Yushukan*, Tokyo, 2003.

4. Jordan Sand, *House and Home in Modern Japan: Architecture, Domestic Space, and Bourgeois Culture 1880–1930* (Cambridge, MA: Harvard University Press, 2003).

5. At the end of the eighteenth century, the bourgeois male underwent what has been called the "great masculine renunciation," which J. C. Flügel describes as "the most remarkable event in the whole history of dress." J. C. Flügel, *The Psychology of Clothes* (London: Hogarth, 1930), 111.

6. Jansen, *The Nineteenth Century*.

7. Marius B. Jansen, *The Making of Modern Japan* (Cambridge, MA: Harvard University Press, 2000).

8. Marius B. Jansen, *China in the Tokugawa World* (Cambridge, MA: Harvard University Press, 1992), 116–18.

9. Julia Meech-Pekarik, *The World of the Meiji Print* (New York and Tokyo: Weatherhill, 1986), 144.

10. Anne Hollander, *Sex and Suits* (New York: A. A. Knopf, 1994).

11. This orthodox account of the development of the suit and the bourgeoisie is seen in Hollander, *Sex and Suits*. See also John Harvey, *Men in Black* (London: Reaktion, 1995).

12. Arno Mayer, *The Persistence of the Old Regime: Europe to the Great War* (London: Croom Helm, 1981).

13. Perry Anderson, *Lineages of the Absolutist State* (London: Verso, 1974), 450.

14. Toshio George Tsukahira, *Feudal Control in Tokugawa Japan: The Sankin-kôtai System* (Cambridge, MA: Harvard University Press, 1966), 96–102.

15. John Whitney Hall, *Japan from Prehistory to Modern Times* (New York: Dell, 1970), 210.

16. Nishiyama Matsunosuke, *Edo Culture: Daily Life and Diversions in Urban Japan, 1600–1868*, trans. Gerald Groemer (Honolulu: University of Hawaii Press, 1997).

17. T. Fujitani, *Splendid Monarchy: Power and Pageantry in Modern Japan* (Berkeley: University of California Press, 1996).

18. This idea of a civilized center came from Dr. Michael Carter at the University of Sydney in a series of lectures on costume, clothing, and fashion given in 1998.

19. Charles Baudelaire, *Les fleurs de mal*, presented by Jean-Paul Sartre (Paris: Flammarion, 1861).

20. Nakaano Hajiimu, "Introduction to the Work of Kuki Shūzō," in *Iki no kōzō* (Reflections on Japanese Taste: The Structure of *Iki*), by Kuki Shūzō, trans. John Clark (Sydney, Australia: Power Publications, 1997), 10.

21. Nagai Kafū, *Kanraku* (Pleasure), quoted in Shūzō, *Iki no kōzō*, 38.

22. Shūzō, *Iki no kōzō*, 38.

23. Susan Sontag, "Notes on Camp," in *Against Interpretation* (1966; New York: Octagon, 1978).

24. Terry Smith, *Making the Modern: Industry, Art and Design in America* (Chicago: Chicago University Press, 1993).

20

CLOTHES AND THE MODERN MAN IN 1930S OXFORD

Laura Ugolini

In 1934 an advertisement in *The Oxford Times* announced that 'rational tailoring' had arrived in town: The Fifty Shilling Tailors had just opened a new shop. This event was presented as more than the prosaic opening of a new branch of a well-known menswear chain store. It was 'another step in the spread of a New Idea in men's tailoring'. All men who cared both for their clothes and for 'their pockets' were invited to call. They would find clothes that were not only in the very latest styles, but also both cheap and of good quality. Cheapness was indeed one of the Fifty Shilling Tailors' main selling points (*The Oxford Times* 25 May 1934; 27 September 1935; 1 November 1935). As with other chain stores, they were careful to emphasize that all men could afford to shop with them, although the low prices were not, it was generally stressed, inconsistent with the provision of good-quality clothing. Montague Burton believed that his own chain of stores had played a vital part in making elegant clothes available to larger sections of the male population than ever before: 'We are justly proud in having made a considerable contribution towards making Britain the best dressed country in the world, so far as men are concerned' (Sigsworth 1990: 89).

The claims of chain stores were to some extent confirmed by contemporary observers, who suggested that, by the inter-war period, changes in the production and distribution of clothes had ensured that working-class and lower-middle-class men and women could afford to dress in very similar ways to the better off among the middle class. George Orwell considered that the 'manufacture of cheap clothes', as well as 'the general softening of manners' had served to tone down 'the surface differences between class and class' (Orwell 1965 [1937]: 133). This was the case in both men's and women's clothes. According to one Sheffield engineering worker, thanks to the new chain stores, 'whereas previously the rich man had a tailor and the poor man bought his clothes off the peg, it became possible for Jack to be as well dressed as his Master, or very nearly' (Benson 1994: 217).

This supposedly new uniformity in dress was viewed with some ambivalence by most (non-working-class) commentators. The new 'democracy' of cheap and easily accessible consumer goods made available by stores such as Woolworth's was one of the themes explored by J. B. Priestley in his influential *English Journey*, first published in 1934. For the first time, 'Jack and Jill are nearly as good as their master and mistress.' According to Priestley, though, the new consumer goods were simply too cheap: 'too much of it is simply a trumpery imitation of something not very good even in the original. There is about it a rather depressing monotony' (Priestley 1997 [1934]: 325–6). In a more positive vein, Lord Elton observed in his autobiography that it was the clothing of 'the underpaid, hat-touching wage-earners' of his boyhood that had been drab and uniform. He commended the transformation of the workers of the past, 'with their class-uniforms of coarse, ill-fitting Sunday black, into the independent young artisan in week-end plus-fours' (Elton 1938: 253).

Despite these claims, the notion of a new inter-class homogeneity in inter-war clothing should be treated with a degree of caution, as the experiences of a certain David Henry Campbell can help to show. On the night between 25 and 26 February 1932, the 21-year-old Campbell broke into the tailoring shop of Castell & Son, in one of Oxford's premier shopping streets, and stole clothing to the value of £1 10s. The stolen items included a jacket, trousers and a bathing suit. There is little doubt that Campbell's subsequent discovery and arrest were aided by the unemployed bricklayer's decision to wear the stolen clothes while residing at Stratton St Mary Public Institution (*The Oxford Times* 15 April 1933). By wearing garments intended for University undergraduates, rather than those suitable for a young man living on the margins of society, Campbell had made himself conspicuous, and had attracted the unwelcome attention of the law. His example may very well be an extreme one; and yet it seems a healthy reminder that despite the spread in the inter-war years of cheap, mass-produced ready-to-wear clothing of reasonably good quality, dress remained an important indicator of status and identity. Boundaries of 'correct' dress had not entirely broken down.

What remains unclear, though, is the exact nature and extent of these boundaries. The emphasis in recent fashion histories has been on the relative 'relaxation' of men's clothing after the First World War, with the abandonment of the stiff formality of the frock coat and of starched collars, in favour of the adoption—at least outside 'business hours'—of lighter materials and the more relaxed style of lounge suits, pullovers and soft collars (Byrde 1979: 92; Chenoune 1993: 163–4; de Marly 1985: 125–8). Such an approach, though, while indicative of changing notions of 'correct' attire, does not shed light on

the relationship between masculine identities and the purchase and consumption of clothes outside a narrow elite, and in the context of the mass production and distribution of menswear. Furthermore, while Christopher Breward and Frank Mort have explored the meanings of fashionable, consuming masculinities in the pre-First World War and post-Second World War periods, the inter-war years have received little attention (Breward 1999; Mort 1996).

This chapter, therefore, aims to shed some light on this period, and to explore the meanings attached to men's clothes in 1930s Oxford. Using the example of Oxford students and car workers, it will consider the role played by clothing in establishing and reinforcing male group identities. It will question whether, and on what terms, by the 1930s such identities could be defined as 'commercialized', and will suggest that consumers were not simply manipulated by retailers and other commercial forces. Using material ranging from local newspapers and periodicals to memoirs, from fictional accounts to 'ephemeral' advertising material, this chapter seeks to provide a snapshot of male clothing styles and patterns of consumption, which takes into account the distinctions between representations (in retailers' adverts, newspaper reports, fictional accounts, and so on) and self-representations (through undergraduate publications, autobiographical accounts, and so on), devoting particular attention to the ways in which all discourses—whether originating from retailers, from supposedly disinterested observers, or from the car workers and students themselves—made inventive use of notions of 'modern' and 'traditional'. Indeed, as a meeting-place between the scholars and citizens of an ancient University town, and the workers in a 'modern' car industry, 1930s Oxford provides a powerful picture of the interplay between status and consumption, tradition and modernization that challenges easy generalizations about the relationship between clothing and masculine identities.

It has become almost a cliché to comment that in the period following the First World War, Oxford rapidly became a city of startling contrasts. Alongside its roles as the home of an ancient and venerable University and as a thriving market town, it had also by the 1920s acquired the role of an industrial centre, with the establishment in Cowley, on the eastern side of Oxford, of Morris Motors and later of Pressed Steel. By 1939, although 19.2 per cent of adults were still employed in domestic service, mostly in connection with the University, roughly 30 per cent were now being employed by the motor industry. Less than 1 per cent had been so employed before the First World War (Whiting 1983: 8–10).[1]

Unsurprisingly, the creation of a new identity for Oxford as an industrial town was neither uncontroversial nor uncontested. The changes—both real and perceived—brought by the growth of the motor industry were widely understood in terms of the arrival of the 'modern' world to the city. The timelessness of the Oxford of the early 1920s, described by the novelist Evelyn Waugh as a city in whose 'spacious and quiet streets men walked and spoke as they had done in Newman's day,' had by the 1930s in the eyes of many been 'submerged ... and obliterated' (Waugh 1980 [1945]: 23). The modernization of Oxford has most often been characterized, both by contemporary and by more recent commentators, as an attack on the very material fabric of the city, which by the 1930s was being ruined in order to cater for a new brand of consumer. Industrialization and changing patterns of consumption and modernization were understood as advancing hand in hand. In particular, the disappearance of the small independent shopkeeper, replaced by multiple stores, was seen as the direct result of the incursion into the city of industrial workers. In her history of Oxford, Ruth Fasnacht lamented what she saw as the dominant trend of the inter-war period: the demolition or 'modernization' of buildings, in order to 'make way for something considered more likely to appeal to the majority of the new working-class citizens.' In Cornmarket, one of the city centre's main shopping streets, individual shops had been crowded out by branches of multiple stores, 'with shop fronts (and with stocks) exactly similar to those found in five hundred other towns' (Fasnacht 1954: 213; Morris 1987 [1965]: 33; Sinclair 1931: 42).

The arrival of a modern world of consumption was heralded not only by chain stores, car parks or the 'garishness ... of big London-controlled enterprises', but was also symbolized by the presence on the main shopping thoroughfares of the car workers themselves, carrying on their persons the fruits of their reprehensible purchasing habits. 'The pale-faced mechanics in Oxford bags and tweed coats [who] walk down the Cornmarket' were complicit, according to John Betjeman, in the destruction of Oxford (Betjeman 1990 [1938]: 9). And yet, a further exploration of the meanings attached to men's clothing in 1930s Oxford shows a more complex picture than a simple assault upon 'tradition' by mechanics dressed in modern mass-produced finery, as local retailers adopted the language of 'modernization' in order to capture the custom of University students, rather than that of car workers.

It seems clear that to some extent at least, despite claims of homogeneity, the cost, value and quality of clothes remained visible and important indicators of social status. As Ernest Baker remarked, having visited Oxford after an absence of twenty-five years, 'caste and humbug' continued to be rampant, and the only way to ensure civil behaviour on the part of residents was by wearing a 50s plus-four suit (*The Oxford Times* 20 May 1932). J. G. Sinclair expressed himself with even greater asperity, claiming that 'Class distinctions in Oxford are as numerous as the legs on a centipede. And as active. A mere shade in the colour of your spats sets up a subtle social standard' (Sinclair 1931: 31).

Nevertheless, the role of clothing does not seem for the most part to have been that of exhibiting one's own, or assessing others' social status and wealth. It also does not seem to have been that of decoding others' private character and moral standing. Indeed, the role of clothing in marking out the individual man from the anonymous urban crowd, either on economic or on moral grounds, seems on the whole to have been hardly in evidence (Gunn 1999: 17–18; Sennett 1974: 20–2; Veblen 1994 [1899]: 103–15). Elizabeth Wilson has suggested that in nineteenth-century Britain, fashion served as a form of classification: 'Individuals participated in a process of self-docketing and self-announcement, as dress became the vehicle for the display of the unique individual personality' (Wilson 1985: 155). There are indications that by the inter-war period the role of clothing had shifted, and had become the means of marking the individual's entry into a more or less well-defined male group. To return briefly to Campbell's experiences as a thief, it is unlikely that the stolen clothes gave him away because they were very expensive (they were not), but rather because they did not 'fit' with his role as an unemployed down-and-out. As George Orwell remarked of his experiences as a tramp, one only needed to wear the 'right clothes' to become one of the 'fraternity', other factors, such as accent, being of far less importance. While begging at back doors, his educated voice never gave him away: 'I was dirty and ragged and that was all they saw' (Orwell 1965 [1937]: 155). In the same way, by wearing clothing inappropriate to the group he belonged to, Campbell ultimately gave himself away. Campbell's vicissitudes were of course not typical of the experiences of most Oxford men. Nevertheless, they do suggest that notions of group, rather than individual, identity might be a useful way of approaching the question of clothing and masculine status.

Historians have most readily identified the importance of clothing as expressing a sense of belonging to a male 'group' in the context of studies of youth and of work-based cultures. Ex-

amples have ranged from the notorious Napoo gang in pre-First World War Manchester, with its distinctive uniform of navy blue suit, trilby hat and pink neckerchief, borrowed from American gangster films (Fowler 1992: 144), to the emblematic figure of the nineteenth-century dustman, with his fantail hat, light jacket, breeches, and colourful stockings (Maidment 1998). Despite these studies, the dynamics of the connection between membership of a male group and the purchase, consumption and display of clothing need further exploration, particularly in terms of the 'commercialization' that this connection is considered to have entailed in the inter-war period (Davies 1992: 97; Fowler 1992). This chapter focuses on two such male 'consumer groups' in Oxford: University undergraduates and car workers. In their case, the development of distinctive clothing styles served to reinforce bonds created by belonging to the same larger body, be it the University (with its associations of tradition and venerability) or the car factory (with its connotations of brashness and modernity), in the context of contemporary debates about the development of inter-war Oxford as a 'modern' city.

Undergraduates and ex-undergraduates recognized the importance of appropriate clothing in marking the assumption of the role of students. Donald Willis was a working-class Oxford youth who successfully competed for a University scholarship. He marked the transition from Cowley to University by opening an account with Walters, a tailoring and outfitting business that specialized in University custom, where he was fitted for his first evening dress and dinner jacket, and acquired a suit of plus-fours (Willis 1987: 71). With characteristic acidity, J. G. Sinclair emphasized that essential for social success in Oxford, alongside things like 'a repertoire of pornographic stories ... and an exhaustless capacity for suppurating self-conceit', was the possession of at least one pair of plus-fours. He considered that there was a good deal of pressure upon undergraduates to adopt a uniform style of clothing, so that even the Ruskin College student soon discarded 'his colliery trousers, or, as the case may be, his porter's cap' and dashed out to buy a pair of flannel trousers (Sinclair 1931: 10, 98).

Trousers (either plus-fours or wide-bottomed flannels), pullovers, college scarves, soft collars and shapeless jackets were the essentials of normal male undergraduate day wear: they were of equal, if not greater, importance in defining 'the undergraduate' than the cap and gown. The Reverend Morse-Boycott, for example, was struck on a visit to Oxford, not only by the undergraduates' 'tattered gowns', but also by their plus-fours and 'fancy' pullovers, a combination which apparently made them look like 'scarecrows' (*The Oxford Times* 23 June 1933). Significantly, the choice and acquisition of clothes seems for the most part to have taken place outside parental control. Angus Wilson, who graduated from Merton College in 1935, stated of his choice of clothes that 'for the first time I could buy the clothes I wanted and I knew that I wanted these' (Thwaite 1986 [1976]: 95).

Students' clothing was nevertheless not uniform. With an estimated half of the undergraduates in receipt of some form of financial assistance or scholarship, financial matters alone must have constrained the choice of a considerable number. At the other end of the financial scale 'the rich men' seem to have been easily recognizable, not only by their fast and fashionable lifestyle, but also by the fact that 'They wear checks. They wear whole suits, well cut ... They are more often seen in a hat than in cap and gown.' Apart from the fact that they must have represented only a tiny minority, it is significant that they were considered to belong more to London, to races and to country houses than to undergraduate Oxford (Betjeman 1990 [1938]: 37). Among the majority of students, individuality seems to have been asserted through the adoption of particular details, rather than a wholesale rejection of the undergraduate outfit. According to John Betjeman, the 'aesthetes'

of the 1920s, such as Harold Acton, Evelyn Waugh, or Betjeman himself, who had clearly stood out with their 'long hair and odd clothes', had by the 1930s disappeared. The aesthete of this decade was 'a little scrubby-looking nowadays; his tie alone flames out' (Betjeman 1990 [1938]: 38). Angus Wilson wore the 'regulation undergraduate grey flannels, sports coats and umbrellas,' but added 'canary-coloured woollen waistcoats with brass buttons ... foulard spotted scarves, and a pleasing selection of bottle green maroon and dark crimson velvet ties.' The ensemble was not meant as the expression of a unique personality, but 'deceptively might have suggested to a stranger that I belonged to a smart Oxford set' (Thwaite 1986 [1976]: 95).

Distinctive clothing was indeed most often associated not with the rejection of the undergraduate identity, but rather with an allegiance to a particular group within it. Items ranged from the ties of particular clubs to sportsmen's outfits. The latter were ridiculed by P.A.S., a contributor to one of the student magazines, who deprecated the way in which sporting undergraduates would in the afternoon change from Harris tweeds, whose 'serviceable nature' no one would dispute, to shorts, '... sweaters ... studded boots ... multicoloured scarves—[which] are vulgar and unnecessary' (*The Isis* 10 May 1933).

Political opinion contributed a further clothing code. Oswald Mosley's black-shirted Fascists were the most obvious example; but it seems clear that all shades of political opinion were attributed a distinctive apparel, even if the reality may have been rather less dramatic. In his advice to first-year students, Michael Sheldon suggested that 'If you are a Right politician, a sober suit is suggested, with possibly, a stiff white collar. A red tie is essential for success as a Lansbury ... and ... rougher tweeds than usual, and your flannels just cannot be clean' (*The Isis* 13 October 1937). By 1933, concern was being expressed at the apparently growing tendency among undergraduates to wear political 'uniforms' (*Oxford Mail* 19 May 1933).

The wearing of politically-motivated cloth-ing was perceived as an exclusively University phenomenon, although in fact this represented one of the exceptional occasions when Town and Gown can be seen to have shared a com-mon clothing code. On May Day 1933, for ex-ample, a meeting of 'Oxford reds' was held in the Oxford Town Hall, with the aim of forming a uniformed body to defend their meetings against Fascist attacks. Among those present were rep-resentatives of both City and University organi-zations: the Oxford Trades and Labour Council, the Oxford City Labour Party and the Univer-sity Labour Club among others. It was decided that the wearing of some form of uniform had become a necessity. Although the colour was never in doubt, there was disagreement as to the nature of the uniform, with some arguing for a red leather jerkin or pullover, while others considered a (red) badge on the arm sufficient. The need for uniforms was expressed in purely practical terms: 'In the case of a rough and tum-ble, you want to know you are not bashing the chap on your side' (*Oxford Mail* 2 May 1933). In the sense of establishing a group identity, the motives for wearing a political uniform do not seem to differ from those lying behind the wear-ing of the distinctive clothing of the sportsman or the aesthete, or indeed more generally of the undergraduate: identities that were established through acts of consumption.

The dynamics that lead a group, in this case University undergraduates, to adopt a collec-tive identity based on a more or less distinc-tive clothing style are difficult to disentangle. While in cases such as that of the Napoo gang, the influence of contemporary cinema is easy to detect, in the case of students the relation-ship with commercial forces is a more complex one. Indeed, films such as *A Yank at Oxford* (1938) seem to have exploited—and possibly reinforced—existing images of undergraduate life and style (Richards 1989 [1984]: 316); it was retailers who had a more direct impact on students' fashionable consumption.

Despite the strong connection made by com-mentators between developments in retailing and the arrival of car workers, there is little doubt that outside East Oxford, traders' (includ-ing menswear retailers') main strategy continued to be to attract University—and in particular undergraduate—custom. Morris Motors could claim that much of the £20,000 paid every week in wages to its workers was spent in Oxford shops (*The Oxford Times* 2 October 1931), but there seems to have been a general agreement that the greatest asset to Oxford trade remained its relationship with the University, and particu-larly with undergraduates (*The Oxford Times* 4 December 1931).

Oxford menswear retailers may have expressed little interest in attracting the custom of indus-trial workers, but this does not mean that they deprecated the development of a modern com-mercial identity for Oxford. By the 1930s, it was common among those writing and commenting on the retailing industry to associate—perhaps unthinkingly—independent shopkeepers with notions of the 'traditional' and the 'old-fashioned', and chain stores with the 'modern' (Levy 1948: 89–90). Independent Oxford traders, though, elaborated a distinctive advertising rhetoric, which blended notions of 'modernity' and 'tradi-tion', and countered the critics of Oxford's 'mod-ernization' by projecting an image of themselves as up-to-date enterprises, but respectful of the ancient fabric of the city.

Cowley's shopping area's claim to be the 'Most progressive quarter of Oxford' was therefore contested by city centre traders (*Oxford Mail* 5 May 1933). The shops in the High Street, one of Oxford's premier shopping areas, were described as 'modern emporiums, yet preserving the an-tiquity of their façades' (*Oxford Monthly* August 1935). The exclusive department store Elliston & Cavell, which in 1933 had established a separate 'Shop for men,' also claimed to be '... an example of modern enterprise allied to restraint in defer-ence to its surroundings' (*The Oxford Times* 20 October 1933). In terms of merchandise, traders were keen to emphasize the way they were able to reconcile 'the well-known Oxford quality' (*The Oxford Times* 20 October 1933) with a responsiveness to 'modern' trends. Walters, a tailoring and outfitting firm based in a lane off the High Street, was typical of a wider trend in rejecting an exclusive concentration on the bespoke trade. 'In keeping with the spirit of the age' they acquired 'a huge stock of styles, patterns and sizes' of ready-to-wear clothes.[2]

Significantly, the new chain stores similarly blended their claims to modernity with an emphasis on their respect for tradition. The Fifty Shilling Tailors were an exception in their relentless claims to modernity, and in their claims to be 'new' and 'up-to-date'. Indeed, those men who resisted its blandishments were dismissed as prejudiced and as 'afraid to try a new idea' (*The Oxford Times* 22 November 1935). Austin Reed, on the other hand, was more representative of other chain stores. In 1935 the firm bought and renovated the Plough Inn, a building originally dating from the late seventeenth century, and re-opened it as a shop. While stressing the novelty and up-to-date nature of the merchandise for sale, the firm's respect for the fabric of the building was also emphasized: the architects had been given 'a free hand to treat the interior of the premises in a style as much in harmony with the original seventeenth century work as possible.'[3]

Retailers may have staked their distinctive place in the 'modern' Oxford, but it is clear that—as was mentioned above—this was an Oxford still dominated by the rhythm of University life. By the 1930s in Britain as a whole, a shopping calendar whereby changes of season were marked by periodic sales and 'events' was well established. While this was also the case in Oxford, here menswear and other retailers at the same time developed a shopping calendar closely connected to the academic year. This was true even of shops unlikely to be patronized by members of the University. In May 1930, for example, the Co-op announced the arrival of 'Eights Week' and issued the call: 'Everyone in flannels!' (*The Oxford Times* 23 May 1930). More specifically, menswear retailers also developed an iconography that made it clear that undergraduates were the customers they aimed to attract.

It remains open to question whether styles of undergraduate clothing were informed and influenced by retailers' adverts. Historians—among others—continue to debate the impact of advertising, and of commercial forces in general on consumers' decision-making (Breazeale 1994; Greenfield, O'Connell and Read 1999; Marchand 1985: 238–54; Mort and Thompson 1994). For periods before the advent of consumer surveys (which have themselves been shown to be blunt instruments), it is practically impossible to determine the relative impact on consumer choice and on personal taste of 'commercial' forces, such as advertising or cinema, and economic factors, such as the accessibility and price of goods. In his study of pre-Second World War working-class culture in Manchester and Salford, Andrew Davies has suggested that 'corner lads' was the most common description of young men, 'reflecting the centrality of street activities in youth culture as late as the 1930s.' It also suggests a pattern of group identity defined by activities other than the purchase and consumption of goods. In the case of Oxford undergraduates, on the other hand, consumption patterns—and in particular, the purchase and use of certain clothes—were of overwhelming importance in creating and sustaining a separate identity (Davies 1992: 97).

In this sense, undergraduates' identity was a 'commercial' one. This does not mean that they were in any simple sense 'manipulated' by retailers. Rather, their relationship seems to have been an uneasy one of mutual dependence, a relationship in which power cannot be stated to be overwhelmingly on either side. By the 1930s, Oxford tradesmen had a well-established and notorious reputation for being far too ready to grant long-term credit to undergraduates only recently emancipated from parental control, encouraging them to contract debts from which they could extricate themselves only with the greatest difficulties (Yee 1944: 5). In 1930, the undergraduate journal *The Isis* had been forced, under pressure from the Oxford Chamber of Trade, to apologize for having accused Oxford traders of 'cupidity' and 'exorbitant prices' (*The Oxford Times* 14 March 1930). In contrast to this image of traders preying upon students, Roger Dataller deprecated 'the insidious influence' on townspeople of their dependence on the University for custom. This, he considered, inevitably sapped 'the dignity of spirit of a full-grown man.' Nevertheless, he himself as a student had been manipulated by a shrewd shopkeeper into paying more than he meant to—in cash—for a lounge coat (Dataller 1933: 95–6, 149).

Boundaries of correct dress were furthermore policed not only by retailers and advertisers. Paul Nystrom has indicated the strength of the forces that compelled men to conform to particular styles of clothing. For those who refused to conform, 'There will be quizzical looks, doubtful stares and critical estimates. He will be thought queer. He will be judged as lacking in brain power and, perhaps, as an undesirable person' (Nystrom 1928: 9–10). Although in Nystrom's analysis such opprobrium was seen to originate from a generalized 'society', in fact the most powerful indictments of non-conformity could come from the group to which the individual was perceived as belonging. Pressures to conform to certain canons could therefore be found within the undergraduate community itself. The flouting of such canons could lead to punishment, including, in some cases, through physical violence: the 'debagging' of aesthetes, or the wrecking of their rooms on the part of athletic 'hearties' being an obvious example (Graves and Hodge 1995 [1940]: 124).[4]

Students themselves could present the connection between their identity and particular styles of clothing as a denial of any link with modern commercialism. Their clothing could serve to align them rather with a sense of tradition and of Oxford's past. D. F. Karaka portrayed undergraduates' clothing almost as part of the ancient fabric of the city: '...with its Gothic structures and dreamy spires, and that drab grey splashed all over—from buildings to bags— Oxford is still as venerable as the Oxford which Arnold knew' (Karaka 1933: 44). In a more open embracing of 'tradition' over the 'modern,' in May 1931 the editors of *The Isis* and *The Cherwell,* the two main undergraduate magazines, united in announcing their intention of wearing the old-fashioned straw boater while punting on the river as '...a symbol of a glorious past'. The boater represented more than a connection with tradition. It also represented a way of differentiating the consumption patterns of students from those of the 'plebeian masses.' 'The triumph of the felt hat over the boater' on the river was seen as embodying '...the indecorous shrieks of the plebeian masses, whose hired punts plough a laborious way through a Sargasso sea of banana skins ... [and have] forever banished from the river the white silk shirts and immaculate flannel trousers of the aristocracy' (*The Cherwell* 9 May 1931; *The Isis* 6 May 1931).

The 'plebeian masses' never acquired the same iconic status as undergraduates in their role as consumers of clothing. There is no doubt that the car workers were by the 1930s a visible, and apparently permanent presence on the streets of Oxford, well beyond the confines of the industrial eastern areas. In terms of representations, though, beyond the role as harbingers of 'modernity' accorded to them by critics of the city's industrialization, Cowley workers remained far less visible than University undergraduates. In particular, car workers' representation and role as purchasers and consumers of clothes continued to be a marginal one.

To some extent, this 'invisibility' reflects the way in which Cowley as a whole remained marginal to representations of Oxford. Alison Light has noted 'the adoration which was afforded to all things Oxford between the wars', an adoration reflected for example in the frequency with which the city was used as a setting for the increasingly popular detective fiction of the 1930s (Light 1991: 77–8). Nevertheless, despite the occasional disturbing hints of the presence of 'another,' less picturesque Oxford—the Coles had their detective, newly arrived from London, remark that the area near the station looked 'like a back street of Birmingham'—the 'whodunits' of the 1930s focused overwhelmingly on the circumscribed world of the Colleges (Cole and Cole 1938: 87). In a similar way, Cowley is largely absent from most inter-war fiction set in Oxford (Dougill 1998: 168–73).

Cowley workers—and the Oxford working-class as a whole—did not have the same opportunities as those afforded to the University undergraduates for self-representation. Students had avenues such as the undergraduate magazines (although admittedly these did not always necessarily reflect the views of the majority of the student population) to create their own image and identity, as well as to respond to attacks from outside. The satirical response in *The Isis* to Richard Rumbold's lampooning of Oxford's 'effeminacy and its young perverts' in the *Sunday Referee* is a case in point (*The Isis* 26 April 1933). In the case of Cowley workers, representations—as harbingers of modern consumerism and chain stores—dominated over self-representations.

In 1965 college servants told Jan Morris that before the Second World War, the town boys had tried to look like undergraduates (Morris 1987 [1965]: 90). Nevertheless, there are some indications that, at least as far as the car workers were concerned, styles of clothing were developed with little reference to the University. Looking back on her East Oxford youth, Phyl Surman described how car workers would generally wear standard dark suits of trousers, jacket and waistcoat, which could be varied by wearing a pullover instead of a waistcoat, or a silk scarf instead of a collar. Caps would be worn for work, but trilby hats and raglan raincoats on a Sun-

day (Surman 1992: 68). Clothing also served to mark distinctions and differences in status between the various Cowley workers. Because of the cleaner nature of their work, for example, Morris Motors employees could wear a 'respectable' jacket and tie at work, while Pressed Steel men were easily recognizable by their greasy overalls (Whiting 1983: 57). Cleaner work and respectable clothing became enmeshed in creating an image of Morris Motors workers as 'superior'. Cowley's dynamism and changing nature as a community were further reflected in the adoption of 'new fashions' by the local young men. These fashions were not copied from cinema stars, often seen as the main focus of working-class emulation, but rather from Welsh immigrants, newly arrived from depressed mining districts. The new fashion could be seen on Sundays, in the shape of 'a smart suit, the most notable feature of which was the double-breasted waistcoat cut straight across the lower front'. Significantly, 'This style was copied and much favoured by the young men but was not approved by their more provincial parents' (Surman 1992: 68).

Despite the relatively high wages that car workers could earn—although irregular, earnings averaged out between 70s. and 80s. per week (Whiting 1983: 40)—in terms of the consumption of fashionable clothing, there is little indication that Oxford retailers outside Cowley made any serious effort to attract their custom. It was left to shops such as the Cowley Road drapery and shoe store Buteers to cater for them, and offer items such as men's khaki shirts as 'very suitable for engineers and mechanics,' or woollen gloves as 'very welcome to cyclists and lorry drivers in wet and cold weather' (*The Oxford Times* 25 September 1931).

Images of working men, or rather of men in working clothes, were extremely rare in adverts in general. Unsurprisingly, the exception was provided once more by Butler's Stores, which advertised its Lybro overalls without attempting to disguise their use in connection with manual work (*The Oxford Times* 28 February 1930). More in general, aside from the image of the undergraduate, much of Oxford retailers' advertising material, while benefiting from improved printing techniques, did not substantially differ from pre-war conventions. The imagery used did not seek to portray realistic figures, but rather ideal 'types'. The prospective buyer was presented with images of desirable, leisured, or even luxurious masculine lifestyles, or, more rarely, of obstacles overcome and success achieved, all through the wearing of a particular set of often inexpensive clothes. The power of these images lies in their inclusiveness. All Oxford men, except the very poorest—and car workers were not among these—could aspire to the images of manly elegance provided by shops such as the Fifty Shilling Tailors (*The Oxford Times* 28 September 1934).

Paradoxically, given the association made by many commentators between car workers and chain stores, the latter's appeal to a working-class clientele was far from explicit, although inexpensiveness was often emphasized: a Burton sale brochure, for example, announced that 'really good clothes' had been reduced in price 'and brought within the reach of every man's purse.'[5] Also, although there is no definite evidence concerning the social status of Burton's customers (or, indeed, of other chain stores), Frank Mort has suggested that the evidence 'points to men in subaltern social groups' (Mort 1996: 137). In 1930s Oxford, though, car workers were not necessarily the social group most strongly influenced by economic considerations in their choice of clothes. It is interesting to find undergraduates in 1935 furtively buying their flannel trousers from Marks & Spencer. According to one observer, 'They were all skirmishing to get to the cheap trousers. As soon as one had made his hasty purchase, another would dive out from behind the fancy goods and take his place' (*The Isis* 5 June 1935). By the 1930s, it was widely acknowledged that undergraduates' spending

power was much reduced in comparison with earlier generations of students (*The Oxford Times* 4 December 1931). For many, then, making their purchases from cheap chain stores may have been a necessity. That such purchases were made furtively, though, seems to confirm the stores' relatively low social status.

The merchandise sold by stores such as Burton was not always necessarily acceptable for students. This is clearly reflected in the difficulties experienced by Ralph Glasser, an ex-presser in a Glasgow garment factory, who had won a scholarship to Oxford just before the outbreak of the Second World War. While sitting with other students in a study group, he observed that the others were mostly wearing 'loose tweed jackets and flannel trousers ... in varying shades of grey or dark blue, with cotton shirts and college ties; a few wore silk shirts in pastel shades and loosely knotted ties of Shantung silk in glowing colours.' Glasser himself 'felt staidly overdressed in my grey worsted suit, my only one, bought in Burtons for fifty shillings ... before leaving Glasgow.' Significantly, he planned to acquire 'the uniform of tweed jacket and bags' as soon as he 'dared spend more money' (Glasser 1988: 18).

While Glasser's own sartorial mistakes were made when attempting to enter a socially more privileged milieu, his scathing comments concerning the socialist and academic Richard Crossman indicate that such mistakes were not exclusive to social 'climbers'. Glasser compared the elegant grey suit and matching silk tie worn by Crossman for a seminar, with the 'shabby flannels ... tweed jacket with leather patches at the elbows, grey or dun shirt and red tie' that he had worn at Socialist meetings, and 'which he must have thought gave him a proletarian appearance' (Glasser 1988: 18–19). In Glasser's opinion Crossman's style of dressing reflected his essential elitism and distance from the working class. It could, though, also reflect the impossibility of defining—and adopting—an accurate and distinctively 'working-class' clothing style. It was certainly the case that Cowley car workers never acquired such easily recognizable symbols as undergraduates' flannel trousers or plus-fours.

It was mostly when rules were transgressed that it became clear that boundaries of 'correct' dress did in fact exist. Among the workers at Morris Radiators, 'dandies' stood out by wearing inappropriately genteel clothing to work, and subverting the distinction between everyday and Sunday clothes. One such 'dandy' was a certain Raoul de Oscar-Thorpe, who, according to a fellow worker, would always be seen with a walking stick, yellow gloves and a trilby hat; most importantly, he 'came to work in them and all.' Although he was a very good workman and obviously likeable, his style of clothing led to thinly disguised reservations in others' estimation: 'He thought he was a gentleman ... he was a proper show-off ... Oh yes, a right dandy. I liked him though' (Exell 1978: 72).

Surveying the inter-war period, Robert Graves and Alan Hodge considered that while in the 1920s Oxford and Cambridge had been 'two main hubs of advanced recreational fashion', by the 1930s they were reduced to the status of 'merely suburbs of London' (Graves and Hodge 1995 [1940]: 122). Notions of suburbanization and of homogeneity, though, are not particularly helpful in examining men's apparel in 1930s Oxford. The main impetus behind men's choice of clothes seems to have been membership of a male group, however at times ill-defined: to some extent at least, consumption was embraced as a way of reinforcing collective masculine identities. Whether this means, though, that such identities had by the 1930s become 'commercialized' is doubtful. Certainly, neither undergraduates nor car workers can easily be pigeon-holed as manipulated by retailers and advertisers: they seem rather to have co-existed in an uneasy relationship of mutual dependence and distrust.

The notion of the 'modern' played an important, if ambiguous, role in male consumer discourses of this period. Critics of Oxford's development as an industrial centre may have lamented the arrival of car workers as the shock troops of modernity. And yet it was the undergraduates, with their flannel trousers and plus-fours, who were by far the most highly visible symbols of the modern Oxford of the 1930s. The 'timeless'—and still very influential—image of Oxford, of 'stone wall retreats where flanneled youths play croquet amidst the oak and the elm' (Dougill 1998: 235), has in fact its origins in representations of the 'modern', fashionable Oxford man of the inter-war years.

NOTES

Reprinted with permission from Laura Ugolini, "Clothes and the Modern Man in 1930s Oxford," *Fashion Theory* 4, no. 4 (2000): 427–46.

1. The population of Oxford had grown from 62,000 in 1911 to 97,000 in 1939. In 1911, about 27 per cent of adults had been engaged in some form of domestic service. Although unemployment reached 3,614 in September 1932, Oxford escaped the worst of the Depression.
2. 'Smoothing the way ...', Walters brochure, n.d., Oxford Trade 6, John Johnson Collection, Bodleian Library, University of Oxford.
3. 'The Plough Inn', Austin Reed brochure, 1935, Oxford Trade 6, John Johnson Collection.
4. These incidents seem to have been more common in the 1920s than the 1930s, possibly as a reflection of the greater general conformity in dress (and possibly behaviour) apparent in the later period.
5. 'Record sale', Montague Burton brochure, n.d., Oxford Trade 6, John Johnson Collection.

21

A NOTE: A CHARISMATIC ART
The Balance of Ingratiation and Outrage in Contemporary Fashion

Richard Martin

Fashion is a charismatic art in its deliberate, decisive equilibrium between ingratiation and outrage. We all know fashion's propensity to seduce us and to morph our social form. Fashion, as the archetypal art of consumption, proves itself essential and desirable only in the context and service of culture's images for itself. In fact, much of the enmity engendered by fashion is because the art is too socially implicated, too socially ambitious, and even too given to social-climbing. Yet, there is another aspect of equal importance to contemporary fashion. In our time, fashion strives to provoke as readily as to appeal. Fashion has taken on the maverick bad-boy self-expression that once was the province of fine-arts bohemianism and Existentialist angst. In this capacity, fashion seeks to disclaim society and to declaim the individuality of its single or exceptional wearer.

The good- and evil-twin in fashion roles can occur in sectors of fashion creation, but can also appear in the work of a single designer. Karl Lagerfeld and Jean-Paul Gaultier have, for example, expressed both gentility and complaisance within the social order, but each has also risked avant-garde and *outré* possibilities in the medium. Conceivably, even an individual garment might offer itself as happy social incorporation and grating social annoyance. Further, a work by Gianni Versace may suggest a parity between the common and uncommon in a single recent garment.

Additionally, fashion surpasses its objects and surrounds them with fashion-specific phenomena of communication and consumerist fulfilment. In these forms, as well, we seem to oscillate between fashion's welcoming and wheedling and fashion's rebarbative insult. Either way, we are assured of fashion's paradoxical intensity: we feel certain that we will be flattered or faked out, reinforced or rebuked, won over or run over.

MÉCHANT MARINE

Like many fashion designers, Gaultier has long been stimulated by the nautical, creating a cast of sailors that could ever populate both *HMS Pinafore* and *On the Town*. But Gaultier's motif is wilfully decadent in his interpretation of the sailor, always more Jean Cocteau or Paul Cadmus than a mere 'few good men'. Gaultier practises an intentional subversion in a man's diabolic black leather sailor middy of spring–summer 1996.

The middy blouse, adapted from the midshipman's top, is well-known in modern sportswear accommodating both men and women. Gaultier traces the garment back to its source in the sailor, but denies the sailor's white cotton middy in favour of the black leather almost as in the manner of Jasper Johns tracing his American flags of the 1950s and 1960s into the absence of colour or the perversion of the accustomed red, white and blue. Indubitably, we recognize the sailor's middy even in its black-leather version.

Black leather may imply another world and another set of values, specifically those associated with rebellion and the renegade. The black-leather jacket is a protective garment suggesting anti-Establishment origins as clearly as the sailor's middy is part of the established order. Gaultier enjoys the good and evil contrast of white and black in convention's middy and his more sinister version.

The sailor's shipshape blouse is confirmed by a fine cut, creating a rectangulation from the upper torso. Gaultier has created a faulty, irregular antipode to the middy's conventionalism. The sleeves end as if with a buccaneer's slash, a pirate's mayhem, and a shipwreck's survivor. The bottom hem is savagely irregular, suggesting Prospero's end, not a sailor's discipline. Gaultier's cut celebrates the leather apron and its basis in hide rather than the proper linens of a sailor. Propriety and discipline are the sailor's life built into his uniform. But Gaultier perceives the reckless sailor on leave, perhaps loose and rampaging, an undisciplined man.

Gaultier's fashion suggests that he fully understands that dress builds upon certain templates using them invariably and with the same or accruing significance. Gaultier works as a saboteur (who, after all, uses apparel as well) to disturb existing ideas and to offer the fashion object a new life. To profane apparel is to establish a new connection between that fashion object and its connective cultures. If a middy in its starched politeness can became raw material for Mineshift mischievousness and dress-up, then Gaultier has successfully perturbed our expected meaning and our secure mooring of the object in culture.

In fact, Establishment culture understands the sailor's middy in one way [figure 21.1]. Even a designer such as Ralph Lauren or Tommy Hilfiger would represent it in such a manner today. Gaultier tosses the middy into the maelstrom of popular culture. Part of what appeals to any viewer in this Gaultier object or any other is its negotiation of the commodity object from its high, posturing position to Gaultier's dispossession of the high order and his replacement of it with a personal, idiosyncratic reading. Contemporary artist Annette Lemieux has reported that some viewers cannot think about an American flag without thinking about Jasper Johns. This entrenched positioning of the common object in a privileged position as art comes about in a late-twentieth-century transfiguration of culture, enabled by pop art but also celebrating pop's forty-year hegemony, into an arena in which new, often rude or enraged, popular values meet and often are quickly assimilated into existing values.

Gaultier's sinister and surprising sailor requires us to understand our culture. Gaultier is observant of history, but he is also equally concerned with the present. His perspective is never deferential or falsely polite. Rather, he offers an informed and adventuresome reinterpretation of the past, imposing upon the past a very contemporary sense of irony or displacement. In his contemporary sensibility, Gaultier is overtly connected to popular culture and youth: rock and roll, partying, media, 'out' gay style, and their aura of dissidence and personal expression. He creates neither a Beavis nor a Butthead, but he is creating in the spirit of such adverse, annoying avatars of popular culture as an instrument of chiding culture at large. In our time, first rock, then rap, media, and advertising have staked out a claim on the territory of raucous, vulgarizing rebellion. Fashion, too.

Gaultier knows that we will indulge him and his wayward sailor perhaps with a willingness not earlier extended to Paul Cadmus's cruising sailors in American art. Contemporary culture is amenable to absorbing outrage and the styles of dissonance. In fact, it depends in some categories of behaviour upon the incorporation of the offensive into the body of the orthodox. Our eagerness to metabolize the antisocial is the decisive social change of the second half of the twentieth century. Gaultier knows by cultural instinct that he can perturb and still

Figure 21.1 Unknown press photographer, The Duke and Duchess of Windsor, Rome, 1952. The Duke wears a *matelot* and a belt possibly made from a scarf, in marked contrast to the formal attire of the Italian gentleman who guides the couple's dogs through a curious crowd. As Richard Martin notes in this *Reader,* garments from the wardrobes of humble occupations such as the sailor can be transformed in multiple ways, from the casual to the erotic.

be immediately accepted by some and suffered by the remainder. In this process, his acclaim of the dissonant, superficially disenfranchised, is even greater because he is demonstrably 'outrageous', yet his work is certain to achieve full acceptance in brief time in the same manner in which, let us say, the Beatles and Rolling Stones shed their initial anti-Establishment profiles to be deemed contemporary 'classics'. Of course, Gaultier teases the viewer by such devices as the zippered breast pockets which tip the balance a little more toward biker's jacket than to sailor's middy.

Understanding that the way 'out' and 'outrageous' is 'through', circulating the quick upheaval of today's surprise and tomorrow's delight, fashion understands in objects such as the Gaultier disobedient sailor's middy that it can readily and rapidly be displaced from the edge to the middle of cultural acceptance. Surely, one knows that

fashion—the personification—and Gaultier—the creator—are sufficiently in touch with and in command of the process of acceptance to know that their venture of first dismay and disruption is destined to achieve quick approbation, perhaps even more intense because of the cultural oscillation at its emergence.

Such a strategy would constitute a knowing simulation of the avant-garde and has been practised at least since the 1960s by advanced visual artists in painting, sculpture, and cognate media.

NOTE

Reprinted with permission from the estate of Richard Martin, "A Note: A Charismatic Art: The Balance of Ingratiation and Outrage in Contemporary Fashion," *Fashion Theory* 1, no. 1 (1997): 91–104.

22

MODERN MASCULINITY AND THE RISE OF SCHOOL UNIFORMS

Jennifer Craik

Give me the boy and I'll give you the man.

Jesuit proverb

The codified concept of school uniforms seems to have developed in Europe with the emergence of civil society (Wagner 2006). The idea of formal schooling was not new with ancient civilizations (such as China) training at least some children in academic, literary, creative, military and religious topics. However, there is little evidence that such children wore a designated uniform—though they may have dressed in similar distinctive ways. During Europe's 'Dark Ages', there is a gap in the record though it is unlikely that schooling would have been a high priority. By the Middle Ages, some education was appearing mostly in monasteries and cathedrals and mostly training boys to enter religious orders. The training was on spiritual and religious matters and the clothing—where adopted—was almost certainly ecclesiastical— probably a surplice (like the novitiates they would become).

This religious basis of modern education had a lasting legacy in the form of academic dress worn in early universities, such as Cambridge and Oxford, dating from the 1300s. University gowns—compulsorily worn by lecturers and students until the 1960s—were based on clerical gowns and surplices traditionally in black and offset by coloured bands, clerical dog collars, trimmings (including ermine), satin linings and elaborate medieval-style headwear.

Later on, customs in ecclesiastical and military uniforms set the scene for the emergence of school uniforms. Broadly speaking, we can identify two main types of school uniform— ecclesiastical-influenced smocks originating in France then spreading to other Mediterranean countries (Belgium, Italy, Portugal and Spain) and military-influenced uniforms emerging in England and adopted in neighbouring countries and most colonies (Scotland, Ireland, Australia, New Zealand, South Africa, Kenya, Malawi, Zimbabwe and India). Military influences were also present in school uniforms in Germany and Austria, later in communist Eastern Europe (Russia, Latvia, the Ukraine) and in totalitarian regimes (Korea, China, Japan, the Philippines, Cuba, for example). Some European counties have tended not to have school uniforms (Scandinavia, Switzerland, Hungary and the Netherlands); nor has the United States (until recently) and generally not in Canada. This chapter concentrates on countries where school uniforms have been adopted.

Although now mostly associated with elite schools and wealthy or aspirational parents, school uniforms of both ecclesiastical and military types originated with 'welfare' motives. In the case of uniforms in England, they were first adopted in charity schools during the sixteenth century and later were codified under the Poor Laws (of 1597 and 1601). The charity schools were essentially workhouses for children and, as they were financed by levies on parish members, were the object of considerable public scrutiny. 'Uniform' clothing was provided to the children in order to clothe them as cheaply as possible and to make them distinctive (rather like present-day prison uniforms). Many were not benign institutions—brutality, hunger, deprivation, punishment and Spartan conditions were the norm. Yet, they did augur the emergence of institutionalized schooling for boys (and girls—although the latter were confined to instruction for assuming 'domestic' employment).

By contrast, in France, school uniforms were adopted much later (in the 1870s) as part of the reforms of the French Third Republic to 'democratize' public education. Uniforms were of a different character, typically a smock worn over everyday clothes (rather like the smocks now worn in art classes). Smocks spread to other European countries (Belgium, Italy, Spain, Portugal, Greece, Morocco, Algeria and Turkey) as well as Latin American countries (like Argentina and Uruguay), although smocks have gone out of favour since the Second World War (Wagner 2002c, 2003a–i).

The introduction of compulsory school uniforms was entirely in keeping with the role of schools as disciplining institutions to shape young boys into citizens. The first of the English charity (or 'Bluecoat') schools to adopt a uniform was Christ's Hospital founded in London in 1552—and other charitable foundations soon followed.[1] Generally, there was little attention to the children in charity care—'welfare' was meant to contain a perceived social decay (abandoned or orphaned children) with the visible sign of the problem being institutionalized and 'hidden' away. The plight of these children was felt to be of their own making ascribed to

the 'hand of the wicked'. A sense of the subordinating intent of charity school 'uniforms' was indicated in this comment by critic Isaac Watts in 1728 when he commented:

> Their clothes are of the coarsest kind, and of the plainest form, thus they are sufficiently distinguished from the children of the better rank, and they ought to be distinguished ... There is no ground for charity children to grow vain and proud of their raiment when it is but a sort of livery. (Watts, cited by Ewing 1975: 23)

It seems that the children of Christ's Hospital may have been more serendipitously provided. Derived from clerical dress, the uniforms consisted of ankle-length bluecoats buttoned to the waist with pleated skirts and dolman sleeves, knee breeches, stockings and clerical-style neckbands. Blue was chosen because it was the cheapest dye available. The Christ's Hospital uniform featured silver buttons on the coat, a narrow leather belt, yellow stockings and a loose-fitting collarless shirt. The uniforms were designed to produce students of a certain type and were copied by other bluecoat schools (The School Uniform Galleries 2002). Boys in bluecoats were expected to exhibit humility as well as agility and grace when wearing these cumbersome outfits. And because they were so distinctive, uniforms also functioned as an effective deterrent to misbehaviour—especially in public.

While most of the bluecoat schools have subsequently abandoned the bluecoat uniforms—or reserve them for special occasions—Christ's Hospital (now located in Sussex) has retained the uniform.[2] Many former pupils recoiled at the memory of the uniform, one describing it as 'ridiculous, uncomfortable and unhygienic Tudor ensemble' (Norman Longmate, *How We Lived Then*), and another reflecting 'I hated the archaic uniform' (Michael Wilding, film star). But others were proud of the curious historic garb—or eventually became 'apathetic' about the 'funny looks' people gave the pupils. As one said: 'it was usually convenient and advantageous to wear the bluecoat and yellow stockings even when at home. It was distinctive and dignified, allowing one to look smart in any surroundings.'[3] A more recent reflection observed that:

> The uniform. Well, it is the oldest school uniform in the world. It is different, and you certainly don't get ignored wearing it ...
>
> When out in public in uniform you sometimes get asked whether you are from a monastery, or by American tourists if you are young vicars or the like. However, I wouldn't have swapped it for a normal uniform ...
>
> The time I most realised what the uniform can mean to people is when I went to South Africa to play cricket for the school. We met up with a number of expatriate Old Blues [ex-Christ's Hospital pupils] and wore our uniforms to meet them. Some of them had not seen the uniform for thirty years and believe it or not many of them were in tears.[4]

But with industrialization taking off in England, charity schools became the precursive model replicated across the expanding education system. It was not until the nineteenth century that the great public schools (elite, fee-paying) in England borrowed the idea of adopting uniforms. But this was for very different reasons:

> The English public school in the 18th and early 19th century had become anarchic, dangerous places in which boys from aristocratic and wealthy families did as they wished and played voluntary games in whatever worn and battered gear was to hand ... Conditions were so bad that many parents refused to send their boys and instead had them educated at home until they were ready for university. The uniformity of clothing was one of the measures designed to replace chaos with disciplined order. (Wagner 2003b: 2)

The reforms were not just superficial. Schools began to supervise behaviour more rigorously, games were organized into formal sports (rugby, football, cricket and baseball), and the curriculum was transformed from an archaic emphasis on the classics to encompass new kinds of knowledge and discoveries. Schooling also adapted to the need to train 'administrators for an expanding empire'. This new approach to schooling was symbolized by the uniform and the fashion spread to preparatory schools as well as other private and (after 1870) government-sponsored schools. As Britain expanded its empire, school uniforms followed and were instituted—with climatic concessions—in most British colonies and dominions, Canada being one of the few exceptions. The result was that 'school uniform was an essential characteristic of the reformed public schools that emerged by the later nineteenth century as some of the most effective and prestigious schools in Europe' (Wagner 2003b: 2).

Perhaps the most generic type of uniform to develop was derived from the so-called Eton suit, the uniform of younger students at Eton College near Windsor. This emerged during the nineteenth century and became popularized in Edwardian times as the 'best wear' of young boys—hence its celebrity. The uniform consisted of a short jacket with black waistcoat and striped trousers. The white shirt featured a broad stiff collar worn outside the jacket with a knotted striped tie. All students wore a top hat until the Second World War, after which it was replaced by a boater hat. The Eton suit captured the popular imagination and has been used as the outfit for many boys' choirs, often worn with a surplice worn over it, and has also featured prominently in films and recreations about boys and schooling.

Other early school uniforms were adopted by military schools that chose modifications of adult military uniforms. These typically featured jackets with braided toggles, a stiff upright collar and black trousers (Davidson 1990). Other choices included khaki shirts and shorts; jackets and kilts with braided decorations and sashes; and 'sailor' suits with cravat. Again many elements of these early uniforms can still be found in present-day school uniforms. Military schools were also important as the first institutions to adopt physical training regimes and exercise as a central part of their curricula. These training methods and sports uniforms were readily adapted to civilian schools as they emerged.

By the early nineteenth century, schools and universities had begun to adopt 'house' colours and badges to indicate membership of different groups and gradually this use of colour was extended to caps, ties, socks and scarves. The custom was subsequently adopted by the armed services, who used colours and badges woven into the design to indicate differences between groups and specialization in roles. The production of ties for school, university and military dress became a major part of the business of silk manufacturers (Hart 1998: 61–2). Concomitantly, ties became a shorthand means of indicating class, status, educational pedigree and distinctive body training—qualities embodied in the term the 'old school tie'.

School uniforms were, then, shaped by ecclesiastical and military influences conjoined with new ideas about masculinity and citizenship. Nowadays, people probably identify the following elements as typical of a traditional Anglo-derived boys' school uniform: boater hat or peaked cap, single-breasted jacket often striped, tie often striped, white, grey or pastel shirt, V-necked jumper, tailored shorts, long socks and black lace-up shoes [figure 22.1]. These school uniforms have become a taken-for-granted part of the training in masculinity where certain attributes and characteristics are instilled and internalized, that is, they become unremarkable. School rules and curricula rest on uniforms and their rules to constitute a comprehensive training for adult masculinity and the roles boys will be expected to play as men.

This is, however, normative and assumes that graduates from these uniforms will adopt a particular set of norms, goals and aspirations as adults. In this sense, the uniform performs the

role of agent provocateur for boys who frequently reject normative codes of adult masculinity and favour alternate constructions. In such cases, these boys must also overthrow the uniform and the trainings and attributes embodied within it. Above all, school uniforms are about the acquisition of a particular form of discipline and specific elements thereof: authority, leadership, hierarchy, status and bonding.

School is not just for the duration of one's school days: attendance qualifies the wearer of the old school tie to life membership of an exclusive and distinctive club. Thus, years later, former pupils will wear their old school tie for certain functions in order to signify their membership and identify themselves as alumni to others from similar institutions. Equally, the camaraderie associated with wearers of the same tie excludes those who were educated elsewhere, creating a hierarchy of 'in' groups and 'out' groups. School ties and insignia are often worn by members long after leaving school (or at certain events or public occasions).[5] Which school one went to is often an initial question in interviews for employment in business and public administration.

The stereotypical school uniform has often influenced post-colonial dress or uniforms at work. These resonances may perform the same function. Hence, in business, the professions, the police force, the armed forces, medical careers and so on, each profession has adopted versions of a uniform as a way of distinguishing its members and excluding others. Most male uniforms still retain elements from school uniforms: tie, coat/blazer, shirt with collar, tailored trousers and lace-up shoes.

As noted earlier, teachers and academics (those closest to schools) have retained or developed formal or ceremonial codes of dress based on ecclesiastical dress, once worn when teaching but now mostly reserved for ceremonial occasions. The adoption of specialist dress to denote the profession of teaching (and research)

Figure 22.1 Queen's College, 1935, Adelaide, Australia. Mayfair Studios, 59 Rundle Street, Adelaide, Private collection. Queen's College Adelaide was the longest-lasting proprietary boys' college in Australia, opening in 1870 and closing in 1946. The schoolboys' uniforms are subdued in colour (most likely grey) and consist of dark trousers or shorts, knee-high socks, a light-coloured shirt, blazer and tie.

not only distinguishes the wearer as a specialist but also conveys to the wearer a confirmation of their specialist skills and membership of a professional community. As a senior academic remarked about wearing academic gown for graduation ceremonies:

> But you do feel different when you put it on. There is a sense when you're processing . . . with a lot of other people in academic gown, there is a sense of academic occasion and a sense of tradition that's associated with the gown . . . you do feel a bit of pride because it represents . . . that you're part of a community of scholars and that's a tradition that goes back quite a long way. (Alan Robson, interviewed by Jane Figgis, ABC 1996)

As this overview suggests, school uniforms have played a dominant role in defining modes of masculinity and as an apparatus for training the body and refining particular techniques.

NOTES

Reprinted with permission from Jennifer Craik, "Modern Masculinity and the Rise of School Uniforms," in *Uniforms Exposed: From Conformity to Transgression* (Oxford and New York: Berg, 2005), 57–64.

1. Many charity schools were badly managed and in the 1850s became the focus of a photographic campaign to address the appalling

conditions of malnourishment and deprivation (Strong 1998: 413–14).

2. Christ's Hospital website: www.christs-hospital.org.uk/main.html, accessed 26 May 2004.

3. Frank Ledwith, 'The Best Of All Possible Worlds', cited by BSU, 'Bluecoat Boys and Their Peculiar Uniform', Bluecoat Schools, www.archivist.f2s.com/bsu/ch/memoirs.htm.

4. 'Some Up To Date Comments From A Pupil Who Recently Left The School', Bluecoat Schools, www.archivist.f2s.com/bsu/ch/memoirs.htm.

5. I recall an event commemorating the construction of a new building at an Australian university where the British High Commissioner was the special guest. Although only recently arrived in the country he was immediately put at ease on discovering that the vice chancellor and heads of two research centres were all wearing their alma mater Oxford University ties. They immediately bonded as a special elite group—a positive for the occasion but alienating many others at the event.

23

RANCHER AND FARMER DRESS IN NORTH CENTRAL TEXAS, AN ETHNOGRAPHIC HISTORY[1]

George A. Boeck, Jr.

Costume has been of perennial interest to folklife scholars. The social relevance of dress and ornament was recognized by as early an ethnographer as Tacitus. In *Germania* he suggests that the German tribes used costume to differentiate social classes (1975: 115–116). The origins of contemporary scholarship, however, appear in the early 1900s. These studies developed into histories of costume by the end of the century. Particularly good examples may be seen in Racinet's spectacular six-volume world history, *Le costume historique* (1888), and Elisabeth McClellan's two-volume *Historic Dress in America* (1917). These predate contemporary approaches, due to their primary emphasis on items of clothing rather than the wearers' social setting.

The modern age of dress and costume scholarship begins in the 1930s with exemplary publications by Matilda Hain and Petr Bogatyrev. Hain's dissertation under the linguist J. Schwietering presents the social function of dress for small-town German farmers. Speaking of costume's capacity to differentiate between social stations in the village, she writes:

Here the communal structure suggests the overlapping social unity of the entire village, the natural division of which is manifested in its various forms of appearance in its costume. Within this village's communal structure the manor residents appear as a separate segment of farming social life and simultaneously as a formulative factor in the life of the costume (Hain 1936: 15).[2]

Bogatyrev's association with the Prague Linguistic Circle gives his scholarship greater currency, especially since the rising popularity of semiotics. Hain's work can be said to precede Bogatyrev's in that hers was an ethnography of costume. Bogatyrev, on the other hand, critiqued existing costume studies, abstracting their ethnographic information. Where hers is a model of reformulation, his is a call to reformulate. His importance derives from the range and subtlety of functions he defines for costume. For the present study we look to him for his theoretical work on everyday costume's capacity to define social status and, to a lesser extent, to exhibit aesthetic choice (1971: 41–51).

Bogatyrev and Hain were speaking of traditional societies. Bogatyrev, in fact, suggests that his approach is most effective when describing slow-to-change phenomena subject to collective sanctions (1971: 33nl). To apply these theories of costume in a modern social sphere, one can look to Roland Barthes' *Système de la mode* (1967). By applying structural linguistic theory to dress, Barthes gives the researcher the concrete means of describing what is occurring in mixed and changing forms.

The livestock auction at Weatherford, Texas, in 1980 provided the setting for the application of these theories of costume in action. The people coming to livestock auctions wear, in their words, clean work clothes. Asked if he dressed the same way at home as he did when he came to auction, one good ole boy (a respectable, older Texan) responded:

> Pretty much. This ain't my best hat; these ain't my worst boots. I just get cleaned up a bit. You never know what you'll have to do out there (interview with a good ole boy, Weatherford Livestock Auction, August 14, 1982).

They are not formal, nor necessarily clothes they would wear around the house. Situated in a self-consciously Western American area, the work clothes are expectably of a Western cut. Since cattle-raising is an aspect of husbandry, the dress on farms and dairies plays a large role as well. A glance at the crowd at an auction reveals, in fact, a range of ranch and farm dress.

The vast majority of the people present wear some mixture of the two (figure 23.1).

Ranch dress results from a variety of changes brought about by historical and popular factors. Terry Jordan, a cultural geographer, presents the history of the cattle trade as a creole of Afro-European influences from South Carolina and Hispanic adaptations to the open range (Jordan 1981: 155–157). Many of the changes instituted related to gathering the animals into pens and handling greater numbers of range-fed cattle at one time. These changes are reflected in their gear (especially the saddle) and their clothing (especially the boot, hat and pants).

In a relatively brief time, these changes in dress were recognized as costume and, as the Wild West shows indicated, exemplified a lifestyle which was well received by the public.

Figure 23.1 View of the stands, Fort Worth Livestock Auction, 1980. Photo by George Boeck, Los Angeles.

Commencing with these shows in the late nineteenth century, the cowboys have periodically engaged the popular imagination. The costume of the cowboy has changed with each of these fads. Prior to these trends, this functional range dress had remained fairly consistent from the 1870s until after the turn of the century. The items of clothing included sharp-toed boots with cut-away heels, long-sleeved full shirts, a kerchief at the neck, a broad-brimmed, high-crowned hat, and work pants (figure 23.2). Both ranchers and farmers preceded city clerks, bankers, and commission men by adopting attached collars sometime in the late nineteenth century. The fairly elaborate stitching on the boots has remained consistent. Denim pants were introduced by the 1920s to fairly remote areas, but were worn loose in the leg.

For modern western wear, the two greatest changes in dress come from the horse-opera. Western movie stars, particularly Gene Autry and Tom Mix, brought the western yoke and tight-fitting pants to the cowboy (figure 23.3). The western shirt was thoroughly presentable by the 1950s, several decades after its arrival on the silver screen. While structurally related, the shirts were considerably more modest than either the movie versions or their predecessors on mounted cowboys. The western fashion prevalent in movies and rodeos seems more related to similar entertainments like Buffalo Bill's Wild West shows. Here the military style adapted from cavalry uniform design continued in high boots and front-paneled shirts, although the style had already disappeared on the range.

Historical antecedents show farm dress to have been a most consistent style of dress throughout this century. Hat or cap, laced work shoes, bib overalls, straight-cut pants and work shirts appear in surviving photographs from the 1880s. The relative frequency of the items and the particular group wearing them do change. Suspenders and fedoras are not likely to be seen currently, although the former sometimes do get worn by elder farmers (figure 23.4). Fedoras, on the other hand, disappeared completely in the 1960s, to be replaced by caps.

Historically, preference for this straight leg and yoke manner of dress can be seen in turn-of-the-century mail-order catalogues (Sears 1969: 987–988, and Eaton 1970: 74ff). Undoubtedly, the style predates this period. The cap, while probably dating at least to the pre-Civil War baseball teams and jockeys, replaced the brimmed hat in the 1970s. According to Roy King, President of Texas and Southwestern Cattle Raisers' Association, these caps were freely given out as advertising by Purina and other feed and seed concerns, resulting in the colloquial name 'Gimme-caps' (interview with Roy King, Fort Worth, Texas, June 1982). The success of the gimmick can be gauged by the absence of unadorned caps (except those caps with ear-muffs worn in winter, which do not include advertisements or logos).

Unlike the range costume style, the clothing market changed radically during the late nineteenth century. Carleton Hayes mentions the mechanization of the clothing industry in the 1880s and, more noticeably, the 1890s. Hand-sewing had been replaced by machine-sewing a decade earlier (Hayes 1941: 95, 96). In 1891, sewing machines for the home provided the first diversification in the Sears catalogue (Sears 1969: viii). The ready-to-wear market was mostly for men, women preferring to make or have made their own clothes (Boucher 1966: 356; Kemper 1977: 137). According to Stuart Flexner, the mail-order catalogue trade was made economically and physically feasible by Rural Free Delivery (1976: 162). In an exemplary description of range life, Agnes Cleaveland discusses the community involvement in placing an order, from perusal and selection to the long wait for sufficient free time to go to town to pick up the order. Cleaveland also mentions that the local merchants were usually turned to first before a catalogue order was considered (1941: 166–168).

Figure 23.2 [Mounted Cowboy]. Library of Congress. As well as boots with cut-away heels, fringed chaps, a canvas shirt (front pleats, full yoke, and breast pocket) and a wide-brimmed western hat, the tools of the mounted working cowboy included a handgun and rifle (both mounted on the left to be drawn from the right), a short rope, what might be a case of field glasses, and a tarp.

Figure 23.3 Anon. photographer. Gene Autry and Champion, c.1942. Gene Autry was among the most popular of film and radio personalities who fashioned themselves as cowboy action figures. For a full description of the phenomenon, see the Autry National Center's History on its website: http://www.autrynationalcenter.org/about.php#history.

Watt Matthews, a prominent local rancher, describes the relationship between small-town merchants and the larger markets:

You know, I brought Levi's to town here. I'd been in Fort Worth, this was in 1927, and had bought some and liked them. I talked our local merchant into stocking them (interview with Watt Matthews, Albany, Texas, March 2, 1982).

The prevalence of the retail outlet in the vicinity of stockyards and its capacity to ship orders is evident in the advertisements in the era's trade journal, The Cattleman (1916, figure 25.5). Both the effect of the small retail outlets on fashion and their prevalence is mentioned by Hough, who also refers to the outlets' role in the introduction of lighter and more varied clothing (1978: 51).

Figure 23.4 Anon. photographer. Informal group of men, c.1930. The variety of hats worn by these older farmers and the laced high-top shoes are indicative of the 1930s in rural America, in this case northeast Kansas.

Farmers and ranchers have shared aspects of their dress. As mentioned above, the sewing machine, mail-order catalogue, and small-merchant marketing influenced those clothes worn in common since the turn of the century. The work shirt was popular with both farmers and ranchers. Khaki and denim pants are occasionally shared as well. Until quite recently, however, some aspects of either manner were not worn by the other. In the last ten years, in fact, significant changes have been occurring. Questioning Roy King about this trend, he said:

> You'll see a man on a horse with a rope wearing a cap, and another man on a tractor with pointy boots and a hat (interview with Roy King, Fort Worth, Texas, June 1982).

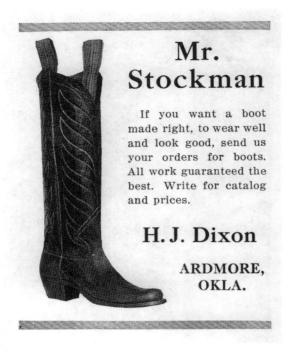

Figure 23.5 Anon. photographer, 'Mr. Stockman' *(Cattleman* 1916: 49). The decorative work on the boot would be worn under trousers and not be seen.

An analysis of the dress at a local auction, while based on the historical precedents outlined here, shows the extent of this change and its basis in the solidarity of the rural community. Anticipating this discussion, two of Bogatyrev's statements on costume might be kept in mind:

> National costume is far more determined by the wearer than the language is by the speaker... For the ethnographer, the question then arises as to what function village dress has when its shape and material have changed (1976: 16, 17).

At the outset, the farmer–rancher distinction should be understood to be a matter of family heritage. Nearly all of the people working for the auction, as well as the order buyers, also have land and own cattle. Similarly, many of the buyers and sellers also have outside jobs. Since World War II, the roles of ranchers, farmers,

and wage earners have steadily converged. The farmer will graze cattle on marginal land; the rancher will feed cattle off planted fields. Their dress increasingly displays a solidarity. Even the order buyers, whose predecessors, the commission men, looked much like prosperous bankers, now dress informally (figure 23.1). In the auction barns most frequently visited, the owner, spotter and auctioneer tend to dress in a western style. To an extent, this may be conscious in that it would imply allegiance with the livestockmen. Order buyers and the men who operate the scales dress more often as farmers do.

A sample of thirty-eight livestockmen at the Weatherford auction provides the basis for a description of the propensities of dress preferences to reveal social alignment. The purpose, following Hain and Bogatyrev, is to consider the social function that costume plays in this community. Seven roles were established with six items of clothing.

Considered as ideal forms, the clothing of ranchers and farmers would appear as easily distinguishable.

Farm and Ranch Wear Compared

Farm	Ranch
Cap	Brimmed hat
Overalls	Shirts with snap pockets and pointed yokes
Lace shoes or square-heeled, round toed boots	Boots with cut-away heels, pointed toes
Suspenders	Belt

On the one hand, the cowboy, western, or ranch style has people wearing a cowboy hat. In the summer, the hat will normally be made of straw, usually off-white or tan in colour. The brim will be three and a half or four inches wide and curled on each side. The band tends to be unadorned and inconspicuous, although the type of band is also a consideration while buying hats. The crown usually has a single crease, although a double crease can tidy a particularly high crown. The sides of the crown will be slightly indented. In the winter, the hat will be a dark shade of brown, grey, or black and made of pressed felt.

On the other hand, farm style has people wearing caps. These generally have a logo of a product for the farm or ranch on the front, mesh sides and back, an adjustable plastic strap in the back, and a bill which extends from the front. Only rarely are plain caps seen and these more likely in winter when ear-flaps may be called for. The term 'gimme cap' would not be appropriate to the substantial winter gear (although most summer caps, it turns out, are also purchased).

Most of these men own several hats suitable for a variety of occasions. In fact, some of the bare-headed men who are at the auction have evidence (a tan line on forehead or hair crimp) of generally wearing hats. Hat etiquette is extremely complicated and follows rules revealing a relationship between formality and revelation of self. For the committed wearer of cowboy hats, a set of complicated rules governs the circumstances of bare-headedness, with different uses in kitchens, banks and offices, churches and evenings at home.[3] For the present purpose, if a man has a hat at an auction, it is on his head. At the auction under study, the ratio of caps to hats to bare heads was 3 to 3 to 1. Checking the tally for the dairy auction shows a similar ratio (4 to 3 to 2) with hats worn a bit less frequently. Dairy-farming has always been an aspect of farming and never a financially relevant part of ranching. The presence of cowboy hats at the Mansfield dairy auction indicates that concerns ancillary to occupation prevail here as well.

The western cut of a shirt depends on their taper and pointed yoke in front and back. According to the salesmen at a local farm and ranch clothier, the two-pointed shirt became popular in the 1950s (interview, Leddy's Westernwear, Fort Worth, Texas, June 1982). The shirts were immediately made in the requisite plaid. Until the late 1970s, snaps were most common; now they are rarely seen. Three pointed yokes in the back are considered proper only for extremely fancy occasions. The shirts are long-sleeved and worn buttoned at the cuff.

Shirts for farm wear are plain-coloured (khaki, green, gray, or dark blue) work shirts of light material. These are usually short-sleeved. Like western shirts, long sleeves are buttoned, collars are not. The rare oxford shirt is generally plaid like the flannel shirts that replace them in the winter. This plaid is so like the western shirt's pattern that the oxford shirt is distinguishable first by its blousiness. Work shirts are fairly straight to the waist. T-shirts, worn exclusively by boys, derive from the popular culture.

Cowboy boots usually are made of leather worn finish-side out and have modest stitching at the toe and on the shank. They tend to be a single colour which is related to that of leather, that is, brown, tan, black, or russet. The heels are slightly higher than those for shoes and somewhat cut-away. The toes tend to be pointier among older men and those young men who are conspicuously range cattle raisers. The rounder toes popular with young men make possible a stance by those relatively few young men who wear pointed toes in adherence to the old-fashioned values. Incidentally, young women prefer the sleeker lines that pointed toes allow.

Work boots and shoes are for the farm. Boots that are not laced are recognizable by the square-cut heel. Like work shirts, these boots and shoes are the mail-order style familiar throughout the country. The ratio of cowboy boots to work boots and shoes is 4 to 1. This corresponds to the dairy auction where the ratio is 3 to 1. Possibly due to the extreme heat during the sampling at the dairy auction, several men were wearing tennis shoes. Usually, canvas shoes are worn only by mature women and young children, and as an alternative by young women.

Pants are either straight-legged blue jeans or work pants in neutral colours like the work shirts above. Blue jeans were preferred 4 to 1 over work pants or the occasional overalls. Again, the dairy was slightly less western, with a ratio of about 3 to 1.

Using these ratios to establish a statistical baseline, one would expect half of the sample to dress purely western, a quarter to dress purely farm and a quarter to be mixed but definitely tending toward ranch wear. In actuality, four-fifths of the people dress in a mixed fashion. It is, in fact, noteworthy that only one-fifth of the people present at these auctions dress in a purely western fashion.

Given this introduction to the history of dress and the combinations most likely to be worn, the focus of attention may proceed to the individuals and their social roles.

Nine-tenths of the people at the livestock auctions are males. These men can be organized into a variety of groupings. Upon questioning, those most relevant to them turn out to be age-related. The four predominant categories, 'good ole boy' (or old boy), bright young man, family man, and young fellow, can be further subdivided by occupation. They run a spread, have a farm, are order buyers, or work for someone. Their dress preferences identify their affiliations and convey something of their attitude.

Good ole boys, a Texas folk category par excellence, have the most complex dress-delineating occupations. They generally dress in looser, light clothes. Chinos, work pants, and even dark polyester pants are most frequently seen. Blue jeans on a good ole boy surely identify a working livestockman. Oddly, a cap rather than a hat can be expected in this case. Good ole boys almost invariably wear light work shirts of a light neutral colour. They are almost always long sleeved and, as with all shirts worn long, tucked in at the waist and buttoned at the cuff. Their hair is worn very short. Overall, they succeed in giving a Spartan look. The extent to which they work out of doors determines the worn durability of their dress. This may account for their preference of blue jeans. Their cowboy hats tend to be conservative, with narrow brims (three and a half inches) and lower crowns. These hats will show age but very little wear and tear. Caps, on

the other hand, tend to be worn more like blue jeans, with some signs of the effects of work in weather. Except for the stitchery on the boot, wedding rings (almost always plain bands), and wrist watches, ornament is missing. Rarely, particularly ostentatious evidence of wealth will be shown in an extra ring (a band with a diamond). A very good hat more appropriately indicates prosperity for a good ole boy.

The choice of comfort over vanity is seen in good ole boy wear. Cultural assumptions abound in these preferences. Tight fit conveys both looking good, in the sense of being sexually active, and the wages of vanity. Vanity is the folly of youth. Some good ole boys will have made the connection that this folly is equating sexual activity with discomfort in dress. More to the point, good ole boys can look dapper by their ironed work shirts, sharply seamed khaki pants, and expensive hats and boots. The differentiation between good ole boy ranchers and farmers appears less in the articles of clothing than in the manner of their wear. An older farmer shows in his shoes and work boots as well as his disregard for crispness that he still works out of doors. His counterpart on the ranch displays equal prosperity by leaving from the house (that is, with a fresh shirt) instead of from the yard. In either case, fashion is eschewed and practical comfort selected.

The kitchen staff dresses much as they would in any café. The cook wears a white shirt, folded apron, black-and-white checked pants, and rubber-soled black shoes. He seems invisible to the community. His cooking is thoroughly appreciated but the praise and blame go to the very visible proprietress.

By their dress the women in the business office, the café proprietress, and the waitresses dress to communicate their acceptance of the rural manner. Their hair has all been 'fixed', although because she works hard, the hair of the proprietress is a bit 'mussed'. Cigarette smoking is sufficiently prevalent among the women that it takes on aspects of ornament. The women's clothing tends to be cotton and polyester blends of bright colours or plaids which match the western shirts of the men. None of the women seen at the auction, regardless of age, station, or affiliation, wear dresses. Age-grade differences do occur. Younger women and girls, both from the café and the office, tend to wear tight blue jeans, crisply tucked shirts, and tennis shoes.

The yard boys all wear blue jeans and boots. Half of them wear western shirts and half wear T-shirts. In this sample, they preferred caps to hats by a ratio of 2 to 1. Notably, their dress was mixed—several of the boys wearing western shirts wore caps and, conversely, several with T-shirts wore hats. By comparing these boys with other employees, it is apparent that T-shirts are correlated with youth.

Strictly attending to style, the yard boys wear their clothing with bravado and disregard. They freely communicate that their labour calls for durable dress, which can withstand thorough ill-treatment. The utility they espouse, expectably, is fictitious. Cowboy boots with cut-away heels are preferred to laced boots, although the latter serve better for running cattle down the alleys between pens. Utility does win out if the weather is cold. Then the boys dress in many layers of loose-fitting clothes. On bitterly cold mornings, they pull on quilted cotton overalls and caps with ear-flaps before going out to work in the pens. Again, however, the bravado they exhibit in their dress elicits praise and concern for them.

All of the adult men working for the auction wear boots and blue jeans; three of them wear western shirts and one wears an oxford shirt. This preference for ranch wear aligns these men with the cattlemen rather than the buyers. An interesting note here concerns the owner. His age and peer group place him as a good ole boy. The importance of the alignment with ranchers, however, seems evident in his dress. Since nearly all of the order buyers are good ole boys, and dress the part, the owner dresses in what would otherwise be an oddly youthful style.

Younger men tend to dress more variously—only the staunchest farmer or rancher will dress

homogeneously. Their shirts are generally plaid and frequently have western yokes. Young men tend to wear blue jeans and boots. Their hair is longer, especially their sideburns, and they are more likely to have a moustache. Younger men are also more likely to have fancy hats. A fancy hat has a broader brim (four inches), a higher crown, and may even have some feathers or a snakeskin band. Younger men are also more likely to have fancy belts. The salesmen at a local clothier catering to farmers and ranchers attest to the fashion changes in these belts, a sure sign that they are worn as adornment (interview, Leddy's Westernwear, Fort Worth, Texas, June 1982). Other adornments include high-school rings and large belt buckles. It would probably not be stretching the point to consider a hat on a farmer or a cap on a rancher as adornment. As stated earlier, the rancher-farmer distinction is rapidly breaking down in this area. The presence of thick belts and work shirts or caps and chinos on men wearing boots and plaid shirts is evidence of this trend.

SUMMARY

Two historical strains can be seen in the heterogeneous dress of the men at auction. Ranch dress, originating in the popular image of the cowboy, proceeds from the custom-made western boot and shirt. Conversely, the egalitarian work pants and boots available through mail-order houses are the basis for farm costume.

Putting these ideal constructs aside in favour of the actual population at the auction, the manner in which the clothing is worn reveals more than the particular items selected. The items of clothing are worn with such disregard for the farmer: rancher dichotomy that the two groups have meaning more as historical antecedents than as current social behavior. For the individual in attendance, age grades and occupational roles carry more importance.

The social roles evident in clothing and its use fall into the age categories: youth, young women, young men, mature men, and mature women.

Cross-cutting these categories are the occupational roles: yard boy, employee, office help, buyers, sellers and café help. By and large, good ole boys dress most simply. Ironed work shirts, creased khaki pants, and polished boots set them apart from the younger men who are more likely to wear western-style shirts, denim pants, and less expensive boots. As a group these mature men exhibit a greater variety of clothing selections. Those good ole boys who wear denim are assumed to be still active in the production of cattle.

The employees of the auction house tend toward a more western style of the most crisp sort. Expectably, yard boys are exempted from this tidiness. As a badge of their station, they are rigidly haphazard in their dress. Young women dress much like young men; the current vogue is away from a blousy look. Women who are office help are most likely to wear more elaborate hair styles and more polyester. Since the 1960s the women have preferred pants; currently they always wear pants.

The implications of these dress styles are fairly evident. The emphasis is on durability and sensibility. The tight jeans of youth and the brilliant man-made fabrics of the office workers seem only acceptable given the situation and station of the wearers. Tidiness, expressed by evidence of ironing, ranks somewhere near a freshly painted barn, conveying mental order and prosperity. The well-worn but clean costume similarly conveys a no-nonsense working ethic. In stark contrast, the disregard for tidiness by the yard boys is benignly approved, granting them station similar to the half-wild cattle they tend.

NOTES

Reprinted with permission from George A. Boeck Jr, "Texas Livestock Auctions: A Folklife Ethnography," American Studies in Anthropology, no. 8 (New York: AMS Press, 1990).

1. This chapter originated in my dissertation 'Texas Livestock Auctions: A Folklife Ethnography', written in the Folklore and Folklife Department of the University of Pennsylvania in 1983 under Don Yoder. Folklife is the ethnographic study of ethical and aesthetic expressions of specified groups. These groups are usually geographical populations, ethnic groups, or, in this instance, people participating in a shared economic activity. As dissertations do, mine carefully set the ethnographic description amidst a theoretical argument before interpreting the observations. The fieldwork setting was Weatherford, Texas, where ranchers and farmers were marketing their cattle at auction. The larger sphere of the study describes the history of auctions and the demographics of range and feeder cattle raising. The nearer sphere describes the rapprochement of ranchers and farmers as evident in their dress, food and speech.

2. 'Diese Gemeinschaft meint zunächst die übergreifende Sozialeinheit des Dorfganzen, dessen natürliche Gliederung in den verschiedenen Erscheinungsformen der Tracht zur Geltung kommt. Innerhalb der dorflichen Gemeinschaftsstruktur erscheint die Hofgruppe als ganzheitliche Zelle bäuerlichen Soziallebens und zugleich als gestaltender Faktor im Leben der Tracht' (Hain 1936: 15).

3.

Hat etiquette

Worn	Sometimes off	Bare-headed
Out of doors (except graveside)		
	Cafés	Churches
Barns	Kitchens	Courts
Stores	Autos and pick-ups	Evenings at home
	Banks and offices	

A spectrum of hat-donning shows a negative relationship between adornment and the revelation of self. The most informal situations (evenings at home) and the most formal and dependent upon ritualized proceedings are those for presenting oneself most directly. Presumably, they are the ones in which the need to be guarded recedes.

24

AMERICAN DENIM: BLUE JEANS AND THEIR MULTIPLE LAYERS OF MEANING

Beverly Gordon

Blue jeans, the now-ubiquitous denim garments that almost constitute a uniform on high school and college campuses, have been an integral part of the American scene for about 130 years. In that time they have embodied many different messages, and functioned in different ways—as symbols of rebellion; outlets for personal creativity; emblems of up-to-date, fashionable awareness; and as evidence of generational longing and insecurity. Changes in jeans styling, embellishment, and marketing are closely tied to changes in the society as a whole, and these changes serve as a subtle but accurate barometer of trends in contemporary popular culture. The jeans phenomenon merits serious attention on the part of the popular culture scholar.

THE BLUE JEAN AS LABOURER: THE WILD WEST AND THE FARMER

Jeans first appeared in their now-familiar form in California in the second half of the nineteenth century. Levi Strauss, a Bavarian immigrant, came to San Francisco in 1850 with a supply of strong canvas cloth that he hoped to sell to people making tents and wagon covers, but when he saw the kind of hard wear the gold prospectors gave their clothes, he had it made into sturdy pants. 'Levi's' were really born when Strauss switched to a heavy denim fabric a few years later. Copper rivets were added at the stress points in 1873 (Ratner 1975: 1–2;

Shea 1975: 31; Brooks 1979: 64–5). Jeans first evolved, then, as practical rather than fashionable clothing, and were associated with hardworking physical labourers, especially those from the rough and rugged west. By the early twentieth century, when Levi's competed with other brands such as Wrangler and Lee, jeans and related denimwear such as protective overalls were the modal garments for farmers. By 1902 the Sears and Roebuck catalogue offered five different denimwear styles (Rupp 1985: 83). Again, individuals who wore these garments were not 'fashionable', they were not making a statement of any kind; they were simply choosing serviceable, affordable clothing.

THE BLUE JEAN AS ANTI-FASHION: THE FIRST ASSOCIATION

Jeans were first adopted as a kind of anti-fashion—a conscious, pointed statement that goes against the fashion norm and says 'I am different, I am different, I am not like you'—by a group of artists in the Santa Fe area in the 1920s (Brooks 1979: 58). Generally well-educated individuals of both sexes took to wearing jeans as a badge of their own group identity and special status. They were identifying themselves with the ruggedness, the directness, and the earthiness of the labourer, and were placing themselves as a part of the western scene. They also adopted a unisex look long before it was the norm.

This group of artists continued to sport jeans in the 1930s, but something of the same impulse was also promulgated in the mainstream fashion world. Levi Strauss executives began encouraging easterners who were taking the newly-popular 'dude ranch' vacations to outfit themselves with jeans or overalls, and the garments even became available for the first time in upscale New York stores. Levi Strauss ran an ad in the April, 1935 *Vogue* that stated, 'true Western chic was invented by cowboys' (Brooks 1979: 70; Berendt 1986: 24). Although the trend did not really take off at this time outside the dude ranch context, this was perhaps the first instance where fashionable consumers were encouraged to take on the aura of a particular lifestyle by wearing jeans.

THE BLUE JEAN AS WAR HERO: WIDENING THE BASE OF SUPPORT

World War II was a turning point for blue jeans in America. Materials were scarce as resources were diverted to the war effort, but with the increasing number of workers in the factories and munitions plants, great quantities of durable work clothes were needed. Jeans were declared 'essential commodities', and to serve the needs of thousands of Rosie the Riveters, the Blue Bell company came out with a special Wrangler dungaree style dubbed 'the Jeanie' (Brooks 1979: 71; Quinn 1978: 19; Shea 1975: 31). Once again, these were not really fashionable garments—they were work clothes. They were still used only in a particular context. Because factory war work was seen in a positive light, however, the garments were perceived as part of the patriotic, all-pitching-in spirit, and were thought of fondly. To women workers who had been used to wearing dresses and more constricting garments, they must have also seemed liberating and refreshingly comfortable. Wartime fashion was changing, also, and taking much of its detailing from the rather unfash-ionable wartime scene. Head wraps or turbans, originally used in the factories to keep long hair out of the machinery, became part of acceptable evening wear. Shoulder pads, originally seen in military uniforms, became an indispensable part of women's civilian garments. Jeans were associated with a particular war-era lifestyle, and were poised somewhere in the middle on the fashion/anti-fashion continuum.

THE BLUE JEAN AS ANTI-FASHION: TOMBOYS, BAD BOYS AND BOHEMIANS

After the war, jeans were no longer just unfashionable; they came to have widespread distinct anti-fashion associations. The hard-edged, square-shouldered female styles gave way in the high-style world to the ultra-feminine and very dressy 'New Look', and the more rugged, 'unisex' denim garments began to be associated with youth, freedom, and rebellion. One of the first things western American servicemen stationed in Europe did when peace was declared was trade their uniforms for blue jeans. They were free, and they were finished with carrying the burdens of the world. Bennington College students, who were generally known as 'artistic' and rather unconventional, adopted jeans as a 'virtual uniform' on their Vermont campus (Brooks 1979: 58). They too used their clothing to symbolize freedom—freedom from the norms of conventional society.

Sometimes this freedom was simply the prerogative of youth, and was seen as innocent and harmless. Eddie Fisher crooned 'Dungaree Doll' in the late 1940s (Rosenberg and Bordow 1978: xi), and evoked the image of a happy-go-lucky bobby-soxer, a tomboy who would eventually, in the words of another post-war era song, 'trade her bobby sox for stockings'. Another type of freedom emerged in the early 1950s, however, which was seen as much more sinister. There was a group of disenfranchised individuals who could not find a place in the conformist climate—and who reacted to it with alienation and disdain. These were the young people symbolized in Marlon Brando's *The Wild One* and James Dean's *Rebel Without a Cause*, the angry or confused or simply no-good 'juvenile delinquents' who at their most extreme flashed switchblades and tire irons and terrorized neighbourhoods. These young people, also, wore jeans: jeans and leather jackets were the anti-fashion wardrobe that symbolically flaunted the mores of the frightened society at large. Jeans were so strongly associated with these outcasts, in fact, that a 1959 movie about an unwed teenage mother was tellingly titled *Blue Denim* (Shea 1975: 30). The good-versus-bad connotations were symbolized by a 'dress right' campaign launched by the American Institute of Men's and Boy's Wear and aimed particularly at blue jeans (Brooks 1979: 72).

Associations with the Wild West actually strengthened or reinforced the anti-fashion statement that jeans made in the 1950s. This was the era of the Gray Flannel Suit and the Organization Man;[1] it was a time permeated by what author Peter Beagle characterizes as 'a strangled, constipated idea of a proper life' (Beagle 1975: 14). It was also the era of the Hollywood and TV Western. Good and bad cowboys were sometimes differentiated by the colour of their hats, but they all wore jeans. The Western simultaneously replayed the good guys/bad guys scenario of the Cold War and represented an escape from it, a foray into a still wild or 'untamed' past where people did not have to fit into such carefully prescribed niches. Baby-boomer children who grew up with western heroes grew up with images of jeans, and wore them for their creative play. They wore them when they wanted to step into a fantasy world that was outside the world of piano lessons, visiting relatives and other dutiful activities.

ANTI-FASHION AT ITS PEAK: THE 'JEANING OF AMERICA' AND THE PERSONALIZED JEAN

It was in the 1960s that the 'jeaning of America' occurred, and jeans took on a new role. The first signs of the shift really began in the late 1950s, when another type of rebel, the bohemian or 'beatnik', began to adopt them with black sweaters for everyday wear. Unlike the Brando/Dean 'bad boy' rebel, this was a dissenter, an urban intellectual who came to an anti-fashion statement of this sort from a thought-out position about the materialistic, conformist society of the day. To wear plain jeans and dark colours was to reject the more-is-better, new-is-better mentality of the Organization Man world. 1962, according to Levi Strauss executive Alfred Sanguinetti, marked the 'breakout' point in jeans sales, with sales figures doubling in just three years. They further quintupled between 1965 and 1970 (Brooks 1979: 73–74).[2] By 1967 the anti-fashion statement was screaming across the land, for jeans were one of the most visible symbols of the rapidly increasing numbers of disenfranchised youth. The late 1960s were, of course, the turbulent period in which there was a marked escalation of the undeclared war in Vietnam, a war that polarized the society and led to a widespread rejection of mainstream social norms on the part of the younger generation. The youth-dominated counterculture, which was made up of the same baby-boomers who had worn jeans as play clothes and had grown up with James Dean and other such cultural icons, turned to jeans very naturally. Jeans were practical, long-lasting, and unchanging; they were the very antitheses of the mainstream 'straight' world where fashion was by its very nature ever-changing and quickly obsolescent. They were cheap, comfortable, and associated with physicality; they represented freedom from dutifulness, and because they were simultaneously associated with work and play, came to stand for a society where there really was no distinction between the two. As Valerie Carnes put it in a 1978 article entitled 'Icons of Popular Fashion':

> Denim jeans became [in the 1960s] the ultimate no-fashion put-down style—a classless, cheap, unisex look that stood for, variously, frontier values, democracy, plain living, ecology and health, rebellion *à la* Brando or Dean, a new interest in the erotic import of the pelvis, or, as Charles Reich suggests in *The Greening of America,* a deliberate rejection of the 'artificial plastic-coated look' of the affluent consumer society (237).

Jeans may have been the common anti-fashion denominator among the young, but all jeans were not alike. Jeans wearers avoided the plastic veneer and the sameness and artificiality it represented by the very act of wearing their jeans. Jeans conformed more and more to their own particular body shapes as they were worn and washed (cotton denim shrinks and stretches each time it is washed and reworn). Over time jeans came to carry particular 'scars'—stains, rips, frayed areas, patches—that could be associated with remembered events and experiences. A pair of jeans became intensely personal. If a small hole developed it might be left alone as a 'badge' of experience, or great deliberation might go into the choice of an appropriate fabric with which to cover it. Soon, counterculture youth were glorifying their jeans—decorating and embellishing them, making them colourful and celebratory, and making them into visible, vocal personal statements. Silk, velvet, leather, feathers, bells, beads, rivets, sequins, paint— anything that could be applied to denim fabric was applied to someone's jeans, jeans jackets, and related accessories. Men who had never learned to sew and who under most circumstances would think of embroidery as unmanly learned the necessary stitches to work on their own clothes. The unisex garment that symbolized the alternative youth culture was an appropriate vehicle for the breakdown of gender

roles, and besides, one's jeans were too personal to trust to anyone else. By 1974 imaginatively adorned jeans were such a pervasive and interesting phenomenon that the Levi Strauss company sponsored a national 'denim art' contest and was deluged with entries. Entrants repeatedly stated that they found it difficult to part with the garments long enough for them to be displayed in the exhibition; they felt they were giving up a part of themselves. 'I feel most myself when I have my jeans on' was a typical comment from an entrant. 'My jeans are an extension of me'; 'my shorts [are] my autobiography on denim' (Beagle 1975: 14, 73).

THE BLUE JEAN AS FASHION: ABSORBING THE COUNTER-CULTURE WITH A DESIGNER LABEL

In some ways it had by this time become almost necessary to dramatically personalize one's jeans in order to still make an anti-fashion statement. Many of the outward signs and even some of the underlying ideas of the counterculture had been adopted (some might say usurped) by the mainstream culture at large. Blue jeans in and of themselves were so well accepted in the establishment that even such political figures as New York City mayor John Lindsay and presidential candidate Jimmy Carter were happy to be photographed wearing them. Anti-fashion had not only been absorbed by fashion, but had become part of its very essence. John Brooks, writing in *The New Yorker* in 1979, attributed the fashionable usurpation of the jeans phenomenon to the early 1970s 'search for the fountain of youth' (Brooks 1979: 60), but it may have been as much a sign of an underlying widespread hunger for life-affirming values in what was a confused and dark time.

Jeans and other denim garments were also seen in the early 1970s as quintessentially *American.* Jeans had been developed in the United States, of course, and had long carried associations of the American West, but once they had filtered into the international fashion scene, they came to stand for the country as a whole. In 1973 the American Fashion Critics presented a special award to Levi Strauss for 'a fundamental American fashion that ... now influences the world.' Nieman Marcus also gave Levi Strauss its Distinguished Service in Fashion Award that same year (Carnes 1978: 236).[3] The popular press began to print rhetorical questions like, 'after all, what's more American than denim?' ('Do It Up Denim!' 1978: 142), and in 1974 American Motors Corporation contracted with Levi Strauss to provide blue denim fabric for upholstery for its Gremlin and Hornet cars (Fehr 1974: 73). The Gremlin, which was promoted as America's answer to the Volkswagen beetle, was meant to be both upbeat and patriotic, and denim furnishings were thought to communicate both qualities.

Jeans sales continued to climb. By 1977 over 500 million pairs were sold in this country alone—more than twice the number of the total population (Brooks 1979: 58).

Fashion and anti-fashion came exceedingly close during this period, but there were continually two thrusts to the jeans craze. The counterculture continued to thrive and maintained and fostered a do-your-own, personalize-your-clothing vision. Numerous instruction books were published between 1973 and 1977 that carried a power-to-the-people message and told people how to fashion and re-fashion their own denim clothing. Publications with such titles as *Clothing Liberation,* and *Make it in Denim, The Jeans Scene, The Jeans Book* and *Native Funk and Flash* (Harlow 1973; Jacopetti 1974; Johnson 1972; Rosenberg and Wiener 1971; Todhunter 1977; Torbet 1973) continued to advocate inexpensive and comfortable clothing that made use of worn garments and other available materials. Cast-offs and odds and ends could not only be salvaged, but creatively used.

At the same time, there was a high-fashion version of this democratic, anti-fashion trend.

Couturiers who saw these creative outfits on the streets and in such legitimizing exhibitions as Wesleyan University's 'Smart Ass Art' (1973) and Levi Strauss' 'Denim Art' at the Museum of Contemporary Crafts (1974) moved in and produced their own high-style versions of counter-culture styles. Givenchy designed an entire denim wardrobe for film star Audrey Hepburn, for example, and Giorgio outfitted Dyan Cannon and Ava Gardner (Fehr 1974: 55, 66; Shea 1975: 29). A $2,325 denim-lined mink jacket and mink-cuffed jeans were shown on the fashion runways in Paris in 1974, and professionally-designed embroidered, sequinned and nail-studded ensembles were going for about $500 in New York boutiques (Fehr 1974: 27, 45). Recycled and well-worn fabrics—hallmarks of the counter-culture look—were part of this style. Giorgio's jeans outfits that sold for $250 were made from already-used denim, for example, and designer shops in department stores like Lord and Taylor sold recycled jeans for three times the price of new ones (Fehr 1974: 46).

By the late 1970s, when the baby-boomer generation had been largely absorbed into the work force and the responsibilities of parenting, and the counter-culture vision had become diffused, the high-style fashion forces won out over the anti-fashion style. Couture denim filtered down into the ready-to-wear market. Designer labels became an obsession; 'designer jeans' were 'the pants in America', according to a Saks Fifth Avenue retailer. Calvin Klein, who drew attention to jeans sporting his label with an erotic advertising campaign, sold 125,000 pairs a week in 1979 (McCord 1979: 115). Designer jeans were in such demand that there was a thriving counterfeit trade, and by 1981 *Good Housekeeping* magazine ran a feature advising consumers how to make sure they were buying the 'real thing' (April: 202).[4]

Designer jeans were often based on anti-fashion prototypes (both Calvin Klein and Oscar de la Renta are known to have sent photographers out into the streets of New York to document what people were wearing) (Carnes 1978: 235–36), but they tended to be subtle: they did not, in the early Reagan era, generally sport embroidered patches and tattered fringe. Often nearly indistinguishable (except by the small designer label sewn on the back pocket), they offered ostentatious but restrained snob appeal. Jeans were no longer the 'great American equalizer;'[5] homemade and recycled garments did not have a place in this less democratic age—or rather, they had a place, but it was back with the poor and have-nots. Designer jeans were made to fit and flatter the body, but they were made to be long lasting and uniform rather than to age and change with the individual. In 1984 several fabric manufacturers came out with new polyester/denim blends that were intended to stretch with the body and keep their shape. The Sydeco company introduced 'Forever Blue', a new fade-resistant jeans fabric that was designed to 'look new longer' ('Institute Report' 1984: 124).

THE BLUE JEAN AS FASHION: PRE-PACKAGED EXPERIENCE

The Aged Jean

It seems fitting to begin the most recent chapter of the jeans saga in 1985, with the story of 'The Authentic Stone'. This was a product developed by Mr Marshall Banks, who got the idea when he discovered a small piece of pumice stone in the pocket of his newly-purchased jeans. Banks learned that the stone was accidentally left behind from the 'stone washing'—the preconditioning process—that the jeans had been subjected to. Small pieces of pumice, which is an abrasive material, had been added to a pre-market wash in order to soften the garment.[6] As the earlier description of innovative 1984 jeans fabrics makes clear, stone washing and other preconditioning treatments were not yet *de rigueur*. Banks stated, presumably with his tongue in his cheek, that he hoped to appeal to the 'do-it-yourselfer' with his Authentic [pumice] Stone packaged in its own

'bed of denim'. He felt his product blended 'the whole 60s look with a status connotation'; it was a symbolic pre-packaging of experience, a fashionable way of referring to the anti-fashion of the past. One hundred thousand Authentic Stones had been sold to leading department stores by 1986 ('A Six Dollar Stone Wash' 1986: 77).

The 1960s anti-fashion style had indeed been a look of well-used, lived-in jeans. The Vietnam years were enormously intense—every day brought the promise of incredible revelation or impending apocalypse[7]—and experience was highly charged. The jeans one wore were part of the experience; they were faithful companions, they had been there. Even if they weren't heavily decorated, they were 'encrusted' with memories (Fehr 1974: 11), and held the accumulated charge.[8] Small wonder that aged, faded, tattered jeans were treasured: they were not only comfortable, but were far richer and more meaningful than those that were new and unmarked.

The best jeans were those that had aged naturally, over the course of time and experience, but there were numerous home-grown or do-it-yourself methods to speed up the aging process in order to look presentable. Folk wisdom suggested the best way to soften and shape one's jeans was to repeatedly get them wet and wear them until they dried. This could be done by soaking in the bathtub, but the sun-and-salt-water of the ocean beach environment was much preferred.[9] New jeans were also home-treated by rubbing sandpaper and pumice stones across the fabric, by burying them, or by adding washing soda or bleach to a tubful of water (Beagle 1975: 39–40; Fehr 1974: 62–4). The bleach treatment was more controversial, largely because it weakened the fabric in the wrong places, and looked bleached rather than worn (Todhunter 1977: 26–7).

The faded look was commercially imitated in a pre-bleached fabric for the first time in 1969, presumably inspired by the sun-bleached denims seen on the Riviera, and the look was popular in France (Carnes 1978: 235; McCord 1979: 115). Some very high-priced customized jeans were pre-faded; items taken to 'Robbie's Stud and Rhinestone Shop', an establishment that serviced fashion-conscious celebrities in Los Angeles, for example, were sent to a denim fading lab before the studding process began (Fehr 1974: 55). A few American laundry companies developed fading treatments in 1973 and jeans manufacturers like H. D. Lee contracted with them for several thousand faded garments (Fehr 1974: 64; Koshetz 1973: 47), but bleached fabrics were still not the norm. More and more 'prewashed' denims were on the market by the late 1970s, but the phenomenon crept in slowly. A 1981 *Mademoiselle* fashion column spoke of the 'new, faded look', but disparaged it for its extra costliness. Readers were advised to use inexpensive commercial colour removers or fading products on their jeans if they liked the look of prewashed fabric ('Denims: Here's How ...' 1981: 258).

The prewashed look was characteristic of jeans manufactured by Guess, Inc., a company started in 1981, interestingly enough, by four brothers who had emigrated to the United States from France. Guess jeans achieved their well-worn look through a stone washing process that took up to twelve hours, and by 1986 the company was already having trouble finding launderers with whom they could subcontract, as the treatments were breaking even the strongest washing machines (Ginsburg 1986: 4–5). Guess products, though expensive, began 'flying off department store shelves' almost as soon as they were stocked (Slutsker 1985: 210), and Guess captured a significant piece of the youth market by the mid-1980s. Other companies quickly found ways to emulate the prewashed look. *Rolling Stone* magazine proclaimed in May of 1986 that the 'best jeans available' were triple bleached and double stonewashed (Schecter 1986: 67–71), but the sentiment was still by no means universally accepted. One commentator writing in *Esquire* protested that hastening the aging process was a form of 'faddish dishonesty'. 'To wear jeans is to create a life mold of oneself in denim,' he exclaimed; pre-worn jeans are not a reflection of the 'person within' (Berendt

1986: 25). Numerous 'upscale' American designers were using denim in their new lines, but were concentrating on less casual items such as dresses and coats, and aging treatments were not part of their design process (Goodman 1986: 48–51; 'Designing the Blues' 1986: 78–9; La Ferla 1986: 60; 'Denim Rides Again' 1986: 76–8).

The Guess prototype and its 'worn to death' look[10] continued to permeate the retail denim market, however, and it effectively dominated the 1987–1988 fashion season. With fierce competition for the many dollars spent on jeans and other denim items (more than thirteen pairs of jeans were sold every second in 1986) ('Denim Rides Again' 1986: 76) it is not surprising that novelty would be at a premium, but there is another, more fundamental reason that such products caught on. The contemporary crop of worn and faded looking denimwear provides its primarily young customers with a costume that has lived. It carries a feeling or ambience, an illusion of experience. It, even more seriously than the Authentic Stone, represents a pre-packaged kind of experience that is risk-free.[11]

The actual intense and heady experiences of the counter-culture Vietnam generation are not available to today's youth. 'Free love' and easy sexuality have been tainted by the terrifying fear of AIDS, and optimistic faith in expanded consciousness through mind-altering drugs has been destroyed by the spectre of crack and other lethal substances.

The world no longer seems full of unending promise. It is no longer possible to take to the road with the certainty that there will be 'brothers' who will provide places to stay along the way; this is the age of the homeless, and people avert their eyes. The realities of child abuse, incest, alcoholism and family violence are ever-more evident. There is no groundswell of passionate feeling to tap into, no clear vision of a better future. Unlike the children of the 1960s, then, the children of the 1980s are cautious and rightfully afraid. I maintain that they have taken to the washed-out tattered garments because they imply experience, adventure and drama, and offer a vicarious (though not really conscious) experience of it. These clothes provide the security of the most up-to-date fashion, but the fashion itself alludes to anti-fashion of an earlier time, and plays upon a longing for the (counter) culture that produced it.

Distressed Denim

The terms used to describe the new denim-wear are quite telling. Denim is now subjected not only to stones, but to acid; it is 'abused', 'distressed', 'sabotaged' and 'blasted'; it has been 'washed out'. It is also cold and frigid: it is 'frosted', 'frozen out', and 'iced'; and 'glacier' or 'polar-washed'. At first these terms seemed reminiscent of the words used in the Vietnam era for the drug experience ('stoned', 'wasted', 'wiped out'), but in reality they have a much harder, more anguished edge. One was stoned or wiped out from an abundance of experience; now one has simply weathered the storm ('Storm Riders', and 'White Lightening' are two contemporary jeans styles). Today's 'Get Used' fashions echo the underlying desperation of the age.

Descriptive labels that come with this aged denimwear try to be comforting. 'This garment is made to look used and soft', one states. 'It is broken in just for you'. Customers are reassured that the jeans are 'inspired by the faded, comfortable character of well worn clothing', or by the 'comfortable good looks and free-wheeling spirit of aviators and prairie hands'. This is 'authentic apparel', state the labels; these garments are 'like three years old'. The underlying message is that the world out there is a tough one, but the clothing has been through it and has already taken it. It is protective, for it acts as a foil and absorbs the shock so its owner doesn't have to. It is soothing: 'worn denim is man's best friend'.[12]

The 1988 season denimwear also borrows from the free-spirited, make-your-own, recycle-it trend of the mid-1970s. Couturiers were beginning to show this look about two years ago,

but now increasing numbers of ready-to-wear garments are designed so as to look as if they were made from several pairs of cut-up and re-used jeans. There are waistband details tucked into bodices or turned upside-down on the bottom of jackets; there are odd pockets and belt loops sewn in at jaunty diagonal angles. Contrasting colour patches, particularly in mattress ticking prints, are also evident.

Sadly, all of these trendy looks are mere façades. Prewashed jeans are not really made 'just for' anyone; they hold no one's individual contours. Jackets may have extra waistbands and added pockets or patches, but they do not have the free-spirited spontaneity and freshness of the make-your own era. Much of the tattered quality of contemporary denimwear, also, looks contrived and unnatural. Wear and tear that develops during consecutive hours of laundering does not necessarily occur in areas that would be naturally stressed or worn, and sewn-in fringed selvages look too regular to be real. When a whole line of jackets even bears a 'rip' in the same place and the rip is always outlined with rows of stitches, the point is exceedingly forced. These clothes may at first allude to another era, and may offer the illusion of experience and comfort, but illusions are all they offer. They are in reality pre-packaged, just like the Authentic Stone. They set up a façade for their wearers, a façade that makes them seem larger than they may be able to be. The look has struck a responsive chord, for it speaks to a yearning on the part of the young jeans customer, a yearning for a time when the world was not just tough, but exciting, and full of promise and imminent discovery.

Selling the Image

Photographs used in magazine advertisements for this denim clothing support the thesis developed above. Jeans manufacturers take it for granted at this point that their product is desirable, but struggle to create memorable images that prospective customers will identify with. Consequently, the photographs do not feature the garments as much as create a mood or tell a story. The stories are dreamy and 'mythic' (Conant 1986: 64)[13] and full of implication. Sometimes they imply a free and uninhibited sexuality—Calvin Klein ads featuring photographs by Bruce Weber consist of ambiguous images such as one woman surrounded by four men, two of whom are shirtless, or an odd tangle of bodies on the grass. Guess advertisements often include unbuttoned and unbuckled garments, and glimpses of lacy underwear beneath. A recent Jordache ad was headlined, 'I Can't Get No Satisfaction', and simulated a young man's internal monologue: 'I don't know what's with you girls ... Your body says yes but your lips say no ... but you, Sandy, you're not like the rest. You wouldn't play with my head ... '. The story had a happy ending, for in the next frame Sandy and the young man are entwined together, and he is peering soulfully into her denim jacket. Even where there is no explicit sexuality, there is a sensual undertone. Characters in Guess ads are always positioned suggestively, leaning, stretching or slouching with studied ease.

Many of the vignettes include references to the adventurous past of the blue jean. There are couples leaning on motorcycles (Calvin Klein) and men in black leather gloves (Guess); rugged rodeo riders or freewheeling western characters with bolo ties or bandana neckerchiefs (Guess, Levi's); and even a young girl with a head kerchief that looks as if she just stepped off the wagon train (Guess). There are aviators and wavy-haired workers from the World War II era (Work Force—the Gap), and sullen bohemian-types dressed in black (Calvin Klein).

The characters in these advertisements are uniformly young and attractive, but they rarely seem full of vitality, joy or optimism. Often, they face completely away from the camera or have their faces totally or partially obscured by unkempt long hair (itself a reference to the 1960s) or by shadow. Where faces are visible, expressions tend to be enigmatic: dreamy or thoughtful, perhaps, or petulant, sad, or weary. This enigmatic quality is quite anonymous, and suitably enough it allows potential customers to project themselves into the scene and become one of the characters. The scenes hint, in a rather desultory way, of experience and adventure, and imply that the worn garments the characters wear will bring that experience within the reach of even the most unadventurous or inexperienced teenager.

Blue jeans and related denim garments have, in sum, come to stand not just for the Wild West or the rugged labourer or the hardworking farmer—they have become an integral part of the whole American (and perhaps the worldwide) scene. They have been bleached, ripped, washed with acid, washed with stones, patched, cut up, decorated, distressed, and 'worn to death', but they are resilient, and seem to always be able to return in yet another guise and take on yet another layer of meaning. They have at different times seemed matter-of-fact and part of the scenery, and at other times have called out for notice and attention. They have served both as symbols of the culture at large and of subsets of that culture, and of rebellious, outspoken counterculture groups; they have been fashionable, unfashionable, and hallmarks of anti-fashion. They have embodied many of the longings, beliefs and realities of the generations that have worn them. We must watch and try to understand them as they continue to evolve.

NOTES

Reprinted with permission from Beverly Gordon, "American Denim: Blue Jeans and Their Multiple Layers of Meaning," in *Dress and Popular Culture,* ed. P. A. Cunningham and S. Vosso Lab (Bowling Green, OH: Bowling Green State University Popular Press, 1991), 31–45.

1. See Russell (1983: 48) for a discussion of the grey flannel suit imagery. The movie by that name came out in 1957. See also Whyte (1956).

2. Brooks reports that the Levi Strauss company commissioned a survey in 1965 that indicated most people still associated the jeans with farmers, but the turning point in the popular association must have occurred very shortly thereafter.

3. Alison Lurie (1981: 87) later came to attribute the popularity of Levi's in Europe to the belief among European teens that 'the power and virtue of America' was contained in the jeans, and would rub off on anyone who wore them.

4. Counterfeiting of jeans had actually begun some time before this date, with the bulk of the bogus products going overseas. Thirty-five thousand pairs of forged Levi's and Wrangler label jeans were confiscated in West Germany in 1977. See 'West Germany: A Booming Market in Counterfeit Jeans' (1977: 38–9).

5. This epithet (and a similar one, the 'great common denominator') had been bandied about considerably in the late 1960s and early 1970s. See Fehr (1974: 35), Shea (1975: 29).

6. Fehr (1974: 63) claims that the original derivation of the phrase 'stone wash' comes from a pre-industrial era when garments were softened by a long exposure to running water. The garments were buried in streams, she says, and held down by rocks or stones. I have been unable to confirm this explanation, and rather suspect it is more likely related to the fact that fabric was long cleaned by rubbing over stones in the stream beds.

7. I speak from memory.

8. The thesis that clothing and other objects can hold a psychic charge has been developed at length by Mihaly Csikszentmihalyi and Eugene Rochberg-Halton in *The Meaning of Things: Domestic Symbols and the Self*. Although this feeling about jeans was probably at its strongest in the Vietnam era when the jeans were still symbolic of counterculture beliefs, it has clearly not died out. In 1985 sculptor Bob Edlund offered to preserve the spirit of one's jeans forever by 'freezing' them in characteristic poses with several coats of fibreglass resin. Edlund said he came up with this idea because jeans 'are the hardest things in the world to part with.' He even planned to coat children's overalls in this manner, much in the spirit of bronzed baby shoes. See *People* ('For A Mere $1,250': 79).

9. Brooks (1979: 80) claims he was given this advice when he bought his first pair of jeans in 1979; jeans 'connoisseurs' had the benefit of years of experience when they told him what to do. Beagle also discusses this process at length (1975: 39–40).

10. This was the actual phrase used by *Rolling Stone* fashion editor Laurie Schecter (1986: 68).

11. It is somewhat outside the parameters of the jeans story, but another type of fashion that caught on in the mid-1980s was the safari-look, made up primarily of cotton khaki garments. The look was spurred on by such popular movies as the *Raiders of the Lost Ark* and *Out of Africa,* but it was first marketed by an innovative company named Banana Republic. When it was a new company, Banana Republic bought up lots of used army and safari clothing and restyled them for its customers. (See feature program on specialty retailers, Adam Smith's *Moneyworld,* airing on PBS network T.V., October 1986). These safari-type clothes also provided a safe fantasy—a vicarious sense of adventure.

12. These adjectives and statements were all copied from labels on denimwear found in a variety of department stores in Madison, Wisconsin, in February 1988.

13. There are even some jeans advertisements that are framed and titled, like slice-of-life or art photographs. *Seventeen* magazine carried an ad for Jeanjer denimwear in September 1986, for example, that featured a snapshot-like image of a sensual girl in jeans and a denim jacket, outlined in black and clearly set off against the page. It was captioned, '"Desert Blues", 1986'.

ANNOTATED GUIDE TO FURTHER READING

Anderson, Fiona. "Fashioning the Gentleman: A Study of Henry Poole and Co., Savile Row Tailors, 1861–1900." *Fashion Theory* 4, no. 4 (2000): 405–26. Case study of the long business life of Savile Row Tailors, including their advertising strategies.

Boucher, François. *A History of Costume in the West.* Trans. John Ross. 1966. new ed., London: Thames and Hudson, 1987. Remains the best accessible illustrated overview of the history of fashion.

Breward, Christopher. "Fashioning Masculinity: Men's Footwear and Modernity." In *Shoes: A History from Sandals to Sneakers,* ed. Giorgio Riello and Peter McNeil. Oxford and New York: Berg, 2006. Breward relates ideas about the standardization of men's shoes to the modernist arguments of architect–polemicists such as Adolf Loos. Men's shoes became associated with the rational world of the machine and the industrial object, whereas women's shoes became more closely identified with irrational impulses.

Breward, Christopher. *The Hidden Consumer: Masculinities, Fashion and City Life in 1860–1914.* Manchester, UK, and New York: Manchester University Press, 1999. Breward shifts the focus within men's fashion from the study of discrete clothing items and production, to a consideration of how prewar British men were transformed into a new type of consumer. He argues that male "elegance" associated with dandyism was not suddenly extinguished but rather that to look fashionable continued to be highly important for Victorian and Edwardian men.

Chenoune, Farid. *A History of Men's Fashion.* Trans. from the French by Deke Dusinbere. Paris: Flammarion, 1993. The most comprehensive illustrated survey of men's fashion, with a focus on nineteenth- and twentieth-century life. This history is organized by clothing types from 1760 to 1990 and has an emphasis on Paris and London.

Farren, M. *The Black Leather Jacket.* New York: Abbeville, 1985. Written by a novelist, the text explores how the "animal" elements of black leather suggest that the wearer is not like others. The jacket can take on a range of associations, from the biker, to the delinquent, to the Third Reich. The queer appropriation of black leather should also be noted here.

Gill, Alison. "Limousines for the Feet: The Rhetoric of Trainers." In *Shoes: A History from Sandals to Sneakers,* ed. Giorgio Riello and Peter McNeil. Oxford and New York: Berg, 2006. In popular media publications and cultural studies literature, the transformation of the casual sports shoe or sneaker into the performance- and lifestyle-enhancing trainer post-1975 is often cited as the preeminent example of postindustrial product as global icon of lifestyle values. Gill examines how, as a powerful sign of performance and aesthetics, each sports shoe can be an expression of skill, speed, power, fitness, sporting history, attitude, and style.

Hoare, Philip. "I Love a Man in Uniform: The Dandy Esprit de Corps." *Fashion Theory, The Journal of Dress, Body and Culture* 9, no. 3 (September 2005): 263–82. Hoare provides an account of the appropriation of aspects of uniforms such as the trench coat. He examines the creative interplay between military style and queer taste-makers, from World War I to Carnaby Street, as well as later glam rock and punk. Readers can reflect further on what happens when clothing with particular connotations of militarism and technology is transformed by adaptation and wearing.

Honeyman, K. "Following Suit: Men, Masculinity and Gendered Practices in the Clothing Trade in Leeds, England, 1890–1940." *Gender and History* 14, no. 3 (2002): 426–46. Why did the majority of British men come to wear a suit for most occasions during the first part of the twentieth century? The article examines the nature of the product and emphasizes the gendered experience of making and buying suits. Using the Leeds tailoring trade as a case study, it concludes that the suit's rise can be attributed to the gendering of production—whereby the intensification of low-paid female labor sustained profitability—and to the gendering of consumption, in which the masculinity of the shopping environment was crucial.

Lehmann, Ulrich. "Language of the PurSuit [sic]: Cary Grant's Clothes in Alfred Hitchcock's 'North by Northwest.'" *Fashion Theory* 4, no. 4 (December 2000): 467–86. In this important analysis of a Hitchcock film, Lehmann argues against reading Cary Grant's clothing changes as simple levers for a plot or as referential quotations. He argues that whether Grant is in his suit or in the leisure wear that appears at the end of the film, the clothes remain about surfaces. The commodified products surrounding the character stand in for linguistic devices that can be read on that level.

Lehmann, Ulrich. *Tigersprung: Fashion in Modernity.* Cambridge, MA: MIT Press, 2000. Lehmann identifies and analyzes the importance of items of men's clothing, from the bow tie to the top hat, within avant-garde stylistics, word play, and painterly practice, from the symbolists to the surrealists. Lehmann argues that clothing objects from the past were deliberately used by modernists in order to create a new modern mythology. His study of *la mode*—fashion, but also "manner" or "type"—within *the modern—the* contemporary—argues that clothes should be accorded a detailed level of analysis that correlates with scholarship on writing and other artistic forms.

O'Neill, Alistair. "John Stephen: A Carnaby Street Presentation of Masculinity 1957–1975." *Fashion Theory* 4, no. 4 (December 2000): 487–506. Case study of the fashion youth-quake in London from the perspective of shifts in marketing and retailing. New shopping habits and practices were shaped not only by entrepreneurs but also by new social spaces.

O'Neill, Alistair. *London: After a Fashion.* London: Reaktion, 2007. Imaginatively interweaves fashions, spaces, and the transformation of modern London life, from the male tattoo parlors of Edwardian London to the taste for chintz and Paul Smith cabbage roses within the postmodernism of the 1980s.

Peacocks and Pinstripes: A Snapshot of Masculine Style. London: The Fashion and Textile Museum, 2008. Short illustrated brochure with links relating to photography of men's fashion within the Getty Images Gallery.

Perrot, Philippe. *Fashioning the Bourgeoisie: A History of Clothing in the Nineteenth Century.* Trans. Richard Bienvenu. Princeton, NJ: Princeton University Press, 1994. Perrot argues that male underwear played a culturally different role from those objects that populated the woman's wardrobe, and he explains why it had to remain white until the 1960s.

Rudofsky, Bernard. *Are Clothes Modern? An Essay on Contemporary Apparel.* Chicago: Paul Theobald, 1947. Reprinted as *The Unfashionable Human Body,* New York: Anchor, Doubleday, 1971, new edition with different plates from the 1947 text *Are Clothes Modern?* Rudofsky argued that men's dress was descended from barbarian cutting techniques and that trousers made men appear like figures from the *commedia dell'arte.* This text should be consulted for the cross-cultural images as well as Rudofsky's proposals for a future for men's wear.

Sanders, Joel, ed. *Stud: Architectures of Masculinity.* New York: Princeton Architectural Press, 1996. Written by an architectural theorist, the book contains stimulating essays on the Playboy residence as well as the uniform management and the training of military cadets.

Shannon, Brent. *The Cut of His Coat: Men, Dress and Consumer Culture in Britain, 1860–1914.* Athens: Ohio University Press, 2006. This study considers how middle-class men made clothing choices to distinguish themselves from aristocratic consumption. The epilogue makes a link with the contemporary notion of the "metrosexual."

Vigarello, Georges. *Concepts of Cleanliness: Changing Attitudes in France since the Middle Ages.* Trans. Jean Birrell. Cambridge: Cambridge University Press, 1988. Vigarello's study of the maintenance of the body and linen helps us understand why men's shirts had to remain white until relatively recently.

Waugh, Norah. *The Cut of Men's Clothes, 1600–1900.* London: Faber and Faber, 1964. Reprint, New York: Theatre Arts Books, 1987. The classic text on cutting and construction enables students to make connections between clothing types.

Zakim, Michael. "Sartorial Ideologies: From Homespun to Ready-Made." *American Historical Review* 16, no. 5 (2001): 1553–86. Through an analysis of cloth, including the cloth made into a suit for George Washington, Zakim links clothing to new notions of productive citizenship, a political narrative of capitalist revolution, and America's transformation into a democracy.

PART IV

Subculture: Style and Resistance

INTRODUCTION

… the construction of a style, in a gesture of defiance or contempt, in a smile or a sneer. It signals a Refusal.

Dick Hebdige (1979)[1]

Subcultures are groups of people who are distinct from mainstream society and are characterized as systematically oppositional to the dominant culture in some way. They are represented as marginal, nonconforming, or dissenting, because of who they are or what they do. Subcultural groups have their own distinct shared conventions, values, and rituals; these may include political, sexual, aesthetic, religious, geographical, and linguistic factors, or a combination of these. Membership in and affiliation to a group are signaled by a distinctive and symbolic use of style that includes mannerisms and argot, which Dick Hebdige describes in *Subculture: The Meaning of Style* (1979) as "bricolage."

Adopting the concept from structural anthropologist Claude Levi Strauss, Hebdige uses the term to describe the act of wearing meaning-laden objects (signs) in ways that seem to violate the dominant hierarchies of the consumerism that binds the many signs into a cultural system. This reworking of dominant signs into styles that generate new meanings is what Umberto Eco has called "semiotic guerrilla warfare."[2] For Hebdige, subcultures represent a challenge to hegemony not through direct means but rather "obliquely" through style. Style is communication, confrontation, homology, and art. At the same time, style is a form of revolt, a tactic and strategy of resistance that he elaborates in his analysis.

Subculture: The Meaning of Style, considered an important text in several disciplines, was a result of the need to understand a growing number of visible subcultures in Britain. Associated with Birmingham University's Centre for Contemporary Cultural Studies (CCCS), Hebdige's analysis of subcultural identity among working-class youths in postwar England, as well as immigrants from former or soon-to-be independent colonies, in particular Jamaicans, is underpinned by readings of age and class.

In "Back to Africa: Reggae and Rastafarianism," Hebdige casts reggae as a unique style that expressed the alienation experienced by most young black Britons in the 1970s. This refracted form of Rastafarian aesthetics was expressed through a combination of "locks," khaki camouflage, and "weed"—a wardrobe of "sinister guerrilla chic," combat jacket, and Afro frizz that came to be known as Rasta and served to position the importance of resistance and young male black identity.[3]

The Birmingham Centre for Contemporary Cultural Studies—comprised of the scholars Hebdige, Cohen, Clark, McRobbie, Hall, Jefferson, Willis, and Grossberg—was very successful in theorizing subcultures as forms of "resistance," "semiotic guerilla warfare," and "authenticity" at a time when Britain was emerging from economic and social changes. Increased migration and rising unemployment also contributed to conflicts based on race and class. Dick Hebdige, Stuart Hall, and Tony Jefferson recognized a growing need to study how young men were affected by these phenomena and their relationship to cultural institutions, society, and social change.

Stuart Hall and Tony Jefferson's 1976 *Resistance through Rituals: Youth Subcultures in Post-War Britain* (reprinted in 2006) theorized subculture as a form of working-class resistance to dominant values.[4] Essentially, by shifting through the symbols attached to consumer goods and "reworking" their meaning, young working-class men (women were seen as marginal to youth subcultures and were omitted at the time; this issue is addressed by Jefferson in this reader) actively constructed group identities that had a different relationship to consumption from the dominant culture's.

The consumption of fashion and music as cultural commodities is expressed through stylistic practice. A style is not about what is worn but rather the way in which garments and accessories are organized to express identity. So, in Tony Jefferson's "Cultural Responses of the Teds," included in the above text, he describes how the Edwardian suit, introduced in 1950 by a group of Savile Row tailors who were attempting to introduce a new style and originally worn by upper-class dandies, was taken up and modified by the Teddy Boys (1953) as an attempt, according to Jefferson, to buy status. The Teds' modifications to the style included the bootlace tie; straighter, less waisted jackets; and skin-tight drain-pipe trousers. In this way, their dress "represented a symbolic way of expressing and negotiating" their social identity.[5] The dandified style of the Teddy Boys, best described as Edwardian retro-fashion, is an example of how dress can act as a powerful form of cultural signification by subverting readings of class and race.

The dandified form of subcultural "refusal," in which dress acts as a framework for political action, is also evident in the zoot suit. The zoot suit was a style of clothing developed and popularized by young male African Americans, Filipino Americans, and Mexican Americans during the 1930s, linked in particular to dance culture. It consisted of very baggy high-waisted pants, pegged around the ankles, worn with a long jacket that came to below the knee. The jacket had high, wide shoulder pads, giving the wearer a broad look. A long chain dangled from the belt, and the suit was trimmed with thick-soled shoes and a wide-brimmed hat. The extravagant style of the zoot suit is believed to have originated in the urban jazz culture of Harlem, Chicago, Detroit, and Atlanta, and it signaled an act of conspicuous consumption.

By this time in the 1940s, studies of subcultures were firmly established by the work of the Chicago School (1892) of sociologists, who were primarily interested in urban social behavior, or "unassimilated" social types: the delinquent, the immigrant, gang members, the "hobo," and other "marginal" identities that were becoming increasingly visible in a pluralized and fractured United States.

On the west coast of America, the zoot suit came to be identified with young African Americans and Mexican Americans. The Mexican Americans, known as pachucos, were mostly second-generation Mexican Americans, the sons of working-class immigrants, who settled in Los Angeles. Pachucos created a subculture with a mysterious argot that incorporated archaic Spanish, modern Spanish, and English slang words. They dressed in zoot suits, creating a distinct style that identified them as neither Mexican nor American but instead emphasized their social detachment and isolation. Because there was a war going on and government restriction on fabric was in place, wearing the zoot suit was considered an unpatriotic act. As Shane White and Graham White write in *Stylin': African American Expressive Culture from Its Beginning to the Zoot Suit* (1998), "at a time of crises … a significant number of young men from the non-white underclasses thumbed their nose at their country's patriotic demands."[6] In her contribution here, Holly Alford focuses on the zoot suit, its history and influence. She looks at the infamous "zoot suit" riots during the summer of 1943, when gangs of sailors and zoot-suiters fought in the streets of Los Angeles. Outraged at the zoot-suit style, sailors chased the zoot-suiters through the streets and undressed them. It is unclear whether this was a race riot or a riot expressing the patriotism of the sailors, who attacked, beat, and stripped young Mexican and African Americans whom they perceived to be disloyal immigrants. For Alford, African American males were trying to make a cultural identification and political statement through the zoot suit. "Living in a society where it is difficult to have a voice," she writes, "African-American men found self-expression through their own personal style."

Holly Alford considers how African American men maintained a voice through the clothing that they wore. Her case study of the zoot suit of the 1930s and 1940s considers how it meshes with a dance cult, politics, and, in some cases, as a disguise. As an example of clothing that sparked a race riot, zoot means something done or worn in an exaggerated manner. Thus the zoot suit continues the semantic interest in a bodily and mannered way of appearing that had been noted by foreigners observing slaves as early as 1800. Zoot suits required an argot to complete the picture, a colloquial culture that was also adopted by the Hispanic American community. The various explanations for the clothing type, which range from a Filipino colony in Los Angeles to a jazz bandleader to Mexican Americans, indicate one of the challenges of attempting to find fashion's "origins." What is clear from the account is that the suit spelled refusal and a certain illicit activity, with some youths hiding their clothes from their parents. To some the suit was a mask for the first "juvenile delinquents." These concerns about black expressive culture can be linked to anxiety about current hip-hop.

The zoot suit became a symbol charged with certain connotations about rebelliousness, nonconformism, and *Otherness.* It has also come to represent a romantic nostalgia for the days of swing when zoot-suited "hipsters" could be found at clubs like the Harlem Savoy, bebopping and jitterbugging to the sounds of jazz musicians such as Cab Calloway. As a garment, the zoot suit also demonstrates how dress, or fashion, music, and subcultural style can emerge as powerful agents of change.[7]

The relationship between popular music, identity, and fashion is a symbiotic one. The fashion industry designs and *creates* garments, while popular music *sells* a lifestyle (aided by pop and rock stars), through the consumption of fashionable merchandise. Fashion and style are the visual counterparts to musical expression—the pose, the "look" merge to create a subcultural spectacle that is coopted by the mainstream via tastemakers, journalists, trend forecasters, fashion buyers, and so on. Businesses often seek to capitalize on the subversive allure of subcultures in search of *cool,* which is valuable in selling any product to a youth consumer.

Quoting Simon Frith, "Pop is nothing if not fashionable," Noel McLaughlin begins his contribution to this *Reader* by addressing the powerful role that fashion plays in how popular music is signified. In "Rock, Fashion and Performativity," McLaughlin examines the main debates about both fashion and pop. He focuses primarily on the performance of gender in pop and the role of clothing in popular music, before moving on to offer a case study of the rock/pop band Suede, which emerged in the early 1990s, a period marked by the rise of "the lad" and the reconceptualization of masculinity.[8]

The centrality of identity to the commodity stylization of rock is the feature that connects it to other postwar subcultures. While explorations of subcultural style as forms of signification, notably the work of Hebdige (1979) and CCCS, are now considered seminal studies, there has been a significant absence of academic inquiry when it comes to exploring the clothed body in popular musical performance. As McLaughlin points out, "while popular music studies can contribute greatly to an understanding of the role of clothing in contemporary culture, there has been a reluctance to consider this." David Muggleton has extended previous studies on subcultural style and identity by positioning them in a postmodern milieu. "Subcultural styles have become simulacra, copies with no originals," he writes, "creative practices such as fashion, art and music become depthless manifestations of post-modern pastiche, where any potential radical politics (identity, resistance or otherwise) is thus erased. If there is no originality there is no authenticity."[9]

If style, in the hands of Hebdige, was considered the active enactment of resistance, one that relied on the creative and dynamic process of bricolage, then style, as argued by Muggleton, involves bricolage without reference to originals' meanings.[10] Style has no underlying message or ironic transformation. It is the look and only the look, pastiche rather than parody.

Rock subculture has also been underpinned by ideologies of "authenticity," not only in terms of subcultural music tastes and commercial production but also in terms of an "authentic" masculinity, one that is constructed via different modes of dress and body performance and reliant on visual images for theatricality and spectacle. Put differently, the criteria for authenticity and the processes by which rock subcultures (alternative, hard, new, and so on) have established and maintained boundaries tend to revolve around gender and sexuality. The discourse of authenticity, argues McLaughlin, "may serve to erect a false naturalism (with masculinity as its centre) sustained by a sex–gender essentialism." This binary between authenticity and inauthenticity not only essentializes notions of identity in rock subcultures but also succeeds in invoking and mythologizing the idea of a "pure" heterosexual masculine libidinal energy.

The cultural politics of sexuality and gender constitute a contested and complex terrain in subcultural studies. Sexuality is regulated through discourses that prioritize and privilege heterosexuality and marginalize homosexuality and other non-heteronormative identities. Gender functions in a similar way, by using its binary of masculinity and femininity to structure social, sexual, and cultural practice. In 'Don We Now Our Gay Apparel', Shaun Cole writes that "the term subculture is often used to refer specifically to youth or delinquent subcultures; but within the context of a gay history, the word does not refer specifically or exclusively to youth," [that] "gay men sit both within and outside a subculture," and that dress choice is an important aspect of expressing gay sexuality, either overtly or covertly within social contexts.[11] In "'Macho Man': Clones and the Development of a Masculine Stereotype," Cole notes that the adoption of an overt gay identity was impossible due to the social and legal climates in Britain and the United States until the 1970s. Dress choice was forced to remain understated and "incognito" but with a reliance on cultural signifiers such as red ties or handkerchiefs. The counterculture movement of the 1960s acted as a catalyst in empowering gay men to challenge public attitudes and revise the signifiers of gay group identities with the subculture ("Bears, sado-masochists, tops and bottoms"). Activist groups such as the Gay Liberation Front called for an end to gender-prescribed behavior and dressing; as a result, a trend arose toward, as Cole describes, a more macho look. Styles that reclaimed and/or subverted the archetypical masculinity of the cowboy and the biker were influential in the adoption of "butch" dress styles. As more gay men adopted the look, they became known as "clones."

Fashion and subculture have always existed in close proximity. Subcultural identity is defined by dress codes (as well as music and argot) and stylistics and symbols, while fashion has been drawn from and influenced by street styles.[12] The contributors in this section examine the relationship between masculinity, fashion, and subculture that marks a discursive space where identity and its products are negotiated, challenged, and redefined.

Vicki Karaminas

NOTES

1. Dick Hebdige, *Subculture: The Meaning of Style* (London: Routledge, 1979), 3.
2. Umberto Eco, cited in Hebdige, *Subculture,* 105.
3. Kobena Mercer, "Black Hair/Style Politics," *New Formations* 3 (Winter 1987): 33–54.
4. S. Hall and T. Jefferson, *Resistance through Rituals: Youth Subcultures in Post-War Britain* (1976; 2nd ed., London and New York: Routledge, 2006).
5. Hall and Jefferson, *Resistance through Rituals,* 70
6. G. White and S. White, *Stylin: African American Expressive Culture from Its Beginnings to the Zoot Suit* (Ithaca, NY: Cornell University Press, 1998), cited in *The Subcultural Studies Reader,* by K. Gelder, 2nd ed. (London and New York: Routledge, 2005), 272.
7. See S. Cosgrove, "The Zoot Suit and Style Warfare," *History Workshop Journal* 18 (Autumn 1984): 77–91; and K. Mercer, "Black Hair/Style Politics," in *The Subcultural Studies Reader,* ed. K. Gelder, 2nd ed. (London and New York: Routledge, 2005).
8. See F. Mort, *Cultures of Consumption: Masculinities and Social Space in Late Twentieth-Century Britain* (London: Routledge, 1996).
9. David Muggleton, *Inside Subculture: The Postmodern Meaning of Style* (Oxford and New York: Berg, 2004), 29.
10. Ibid.
11. Shaun Cole, *'Don We Now Our Gay Apparel': Gay Men's Dress in the Twentieth Century* (Oxford and New York: Berg, 2000), 7.
12. Christopher Breward, *Fashioning London: Clothing and the Modern Metropolis* (Oxford and New York: Berg, 2004); Cole, *'Don We Now Our Gay Apparel';* Mort, *Cultures of Consumption;* Ted Polhemus, *Street Style: From Sidewalk to Catwalk* (London: Thames and Hudson, 1994).

25

THE ZOOT SUIT: ITS HISTORY AND INFLUENCE

Holly Alford

INTRODUCTION

Throughout the twentieth century, African-American men had been discriminated against and stereotyped, but relied on one thing that set them apart from others, and that is the clothing they chose to wear. Living in a society where it is difficult to have a voice,[1] African-American men found self-expression through their own personal style. For African-American men, clothing signifies where they are and more importantly where they want to be (Boston 1998: 15). This is quite evident in the swing era of the 1930s and 1940s when young African-American males were trying to make a cultural identification statement through a suit known as the *Zoot Suit*. Besides cultural identification, young men wore the suit as a part of a dance cult, to make a political statement, and unfortunately, for some, to disguise themselves from criminal activity. The zoot suit's influence was so great that it would have an effect on men's fashion in the future, and it would become one of the first articles of clothing to cause a spontaneous youth movement among African-American, Hispanic-American, and eventually European and Canadian whites. It would have a social and political effect on Fashion in the 1940s, and it was to be the first article of clothing to cause race rioting throughout the United States and Canada.

DESCRIPTION

The zoot suit was best described in Ralph Ellison's *Invisible Man* (1965). The invisible man describes three young African-American men approaching the platform of a New York subway station.

> Tall and slender ... their collars high and tight about their necks, their identical hats of black cheap felt set upon the crowns of their heads with a severe formality above their conked hair?[2] ... Their legs were swinging from their hips in trousers that ballooned upward from cuffs fitting snug about their ankles: their coats long and hip tight with shoulders far too broad to be those of natural men (p. 380).

Zoot, as a verb, means something done or worn in an exaggerated style, but as a noun it is the ultimate in clothes.[3] Mainly young African-Americans and Hispanic-Americans wore this killer diller suit.[4] The craze is said to have begun in lower-class neighbourhoods in major cities such as the borough of Harlem in New York City, Los Angeles, Detroit, Chicago, and Atlanta, and the suit was usually worn by boys aged sixteen to twenty (Z: *Zoot Suit* 1994). Zoot-suitors spared no expense on the suit, which could cost an average of US$78, and the clothing was meticulously worn from the head to the feet. Everything was exaggerated, from the V knot tie, the zoot chain, the tight collar, the wide flat hat, and the Dutch type shoes (White and White 1998: 256). The suit came in various colours, such as lime green or canary yellow, and many suits bore a plaid stripe, or hounds-tooth print.

The zoot suit was but one part of a total look that included not only the suit and accessories but also the way you wore your hair, the walk, and the zoot suit argot (White and White 1998: 255). The hairstyle for African-American men meant slicking back the hair so that it was nice and smooth. This was achieved by either cutting the hair close, or by relaxing or straightening the hair with a process called congolene. This was a process that involved a mixture of lye, eggs, and potatoes. Slicking the hair back was popular, as well, for Hispanic-Americans. Some chose to wear their hair in the signature 'ducktail' (Tovares 2001).[5] The zoot-suitor also had a particular walk or strut. The way you walked and presented yourself enhanced the suit.

Then there was the argot, a secret type of vocabulary or slang that was known in the African-American swing community as Jive, a Harlemese speech. Some define it as a language that was embraced by African-Americans, partly to put the white man off, partly to put him down.[6] To give you an example of the Jive talk, here is an excerpt from Cab Calloway's song 'Are you Hep to the Jive':

> Here's the stone bible for you to collar that
>   apple trickeration
> That will truly get your boots on! Say you cats
>   and chicks,
> Don't be icky. Bust your conk on this mess and
>   you'll be wailin'
> With the mellows. (Brooks 2003a)[7]

> Translation: Here's the solid truth for you to understand, that the big city strut will truly help you know what it's all about or become a hip swinger. Say you swingers (musicians) and girls, don't be stupid, apply yourself to this good thing you will be wailin with the best of them.

The Hispanic-American community, as well, picked up an argot of their own. They used some of the expressions of the African-American zoot-suitors and gave names for the meanings. For example: 'My brother' (friend) is Carnal. 'What's up' is Orale. A 'guy' is called a Vato (Opfer 1999). The argot language, in conjunction with the suit, helped the argot become an important part of colloquial slang for Hispanic-and African-Americans. It also helped to develop the ways and attitudes of the Hispanic-American and African-American youth (Daniels 1997).

ORIGINS

The exact origin of the suit is unknown. There are several different myths as to how the suit originated. Some believe it began with a Georgia busboy by the name of Clyde Duncan who ordered the exaggerated style suit in 1940. Others believe it originated in a Filipino colony in Los Angeles, who then discarded it, to later have the African-Americans and Mexicans pick it up (White and White 1998: 250). Many say it was Hal Fox, a Chicago clothier and jazz bandleader, who invented the suit and who accessorized the suit with the famous chain that he got from a toilet. He is also credited with its rhyming: 'the reat pleat, reave sleeve, ripe stripe, and drape shape', and calling the suit 'the end to end all ends' referring to the letter Z. However, he admits being inspired from the fashions of slum-dwelling teenagers (Eig 1996). Some sources credit two famous white men for the zoot suit: Clark Gable, who wore a version of it in *Gone with the Wind*,[8] and Edward VIII who, in his youth, wore an exaggerated style suit that resembled the zoot suit (White and White 1998: 251).

Although African-American in origin, many Hispanics, especially Mexican-Americans, or Chicanos, believed it to be a way of dressing by Mexicans that caught on with other ethnicities. In an interview for the PBS special *The Zoot Suit Riots* (Tovares 2001), George Sanchez states:

The zoot suit was also worn by black youth ... so there was a sense that the zoot suit was not just a Mexican dress; it was also a connection with other minority youth.

Whatever its origins, there are two things that are for certain: first, mainly Mexican-Americans wore the suit in the western part of the United States and mainly African-Americans in the eastern part of the United States; second, most of these young men were socially and culturally disadvantaged, trying to let people know who they were through their clothing. For these young men, the suit became 'an emblem of ethnicity and a way of negotiating an identity' (Z: *Zoot Suit* 1994). Later, the suit was a refusal of gesture to submit to the norm of not only white society, but of the older generation and black middle-class society who saw the suit as an embarrassment (White and White 1998: 256). They saw the suit as outrageous and many parents forbade their sons to wear the suit. Many young zoot suit wearers had to sneak around wearing their suit. In the PBS special *The Zoot Suit Riots* (Tovares 2001), Carlos Espinoza talks of how his friends would change at a neighbour's house before going to a dance.

JAZZ AND THE ZOOT SUIT

There is no question, however, that music started the craze to wear the elaborate suit. The 1930s brought about a new sound in Jazz called Swing. Persons into Swing were not only into the music, but the newest dance steps, which were usually African-American in origin. Like most dances, such as the tango, or the Charleston, the clothing sometimes changes to accommodate the dance. The suit men wore to do these dances needed to be comfortable and roomy, so many men adopted the idea of wearing full pants, like the English Oxford Bags. H. Daniels states in an article entitled 'Los Angeles Zoot Suit Race Riot, the Pachuco and Black Music Culture' (1997) that:

Eventually, as more and more swingers or hipsters adopted the zoot suit, not only did it become a definite style statement in African-American urban culture, but also an expressive dance cult emerged. Among the hipsters, African-Americans were the most 'cult conscious' spreading their music and the zoot suit to other cultures and ethnicities. The zoot-suitor would be found not only among the poor African-American youth, but Mexican-American and white urbanites as well. This would be fueled by not only swing and later bebop music, but by dances such as lindyhopping and jitterbugging (Daniels 1997: 201–20).[9]

Fritz Redel, a professor of social work, wrote in 1943 that for many zoot-suitors, boys as well as girls, 'jitterbugging' was something very serious (Daniels 1997). These swingers frequented such places as the Harlem Savoy club, where the famous Whitey's Lindy Hoppers were formed. Not only did African-American zoot-suitors frequent the club, but also many white urbanites. 'Harlem zoot-suitors knew no color lines', and because it was a club of racial harmony, the police closed the club down for three months in 1943 due to the mixing of races. The official reason was that US servicemen contracted venereal disease at the club (White and White 1998: 240). Racial mixing could also be seen in downtown Los Angeles clubs, such as: The Million Dollar Theater, the Orpheum, and the Paramount. Many pachucos,[10] who did not fit into Anglo-America, frequented these clubs to listen to the big bands (Swanson 1999).

Swing music defied all racial lines, and as the cult grew, many of these new 'hipsters' began to wear the suit. This included swingers from Austria, Germany, the Soviet Union, Canada, Britain, and France (Tantner 1994). Many of these youths wore versions of the zoot suit. For example, French youths, who were very much into the African-American swing culture, called the suit 'the zazou'. It is said that they eventually wore the suit as a means of defying their Nazi conquerors (Brooks 2003b). In Britain, zoot suit wearers were called spivs, a handle which referred less to the style of dress than the occupation of the wearer (Rushgrove n.d.), which was a racketeer.

The idea of wearing the exaggerated suit caught on by many musical personalities, who became the fashion trendsetters. As Lloyd Boston (1998: 30) states, 'Jazz Musicians became the supermodels of the day.' One of the most famous musicians to wear the suit was Cab Calloway. It is reported that he spared no expense on his zoot suits. He reportedly spent $185.00 on a zoot suit like the one worn in 'Stormy Weather'. The Baltimore Press at Fort Huachua in Arizona reported that, following instructions from the studio, Cab Calloway had to refuse the Black press from photographing him in the garment that he wore in 'Stormy Weather' (White and White 1998: 255). He became such a cultural icon, that the youth movement in France prior to the German occupation named the suit the zazous after Calloway's famous scat singing 'zah zah zaz.' Later those zoot suit wearers would become part of the French resistance, using the song as their anthem during the war (Brooks 2003b). Other musicians who wore the suit were Dizzy Gillespie, Duke Ellington, Stan Kenton, Count Basie, and members of the interracial Jimmy Dale Orchestra. These personalities did not wear the exaggerated version of the suit, but a close copy. This idea of wearing the suit slightly exaggerated could also be seen on Frank Sinatra, who wore wide lapels and extremely baggy pants (Badfads Museum 2000). Some people also believe that some members of the mafia wore a version of the zoot suit.

ZOOT SUIT AND THE GANGSTER

Unfortunately, as more and more youths from the lower class levels started to wear the suit, so did many delinquent youths. There were many young people, especially in the Los Angeles area, who had become members of gangs or involved in racketeering. During World War II, many of the young men's parents were working 'unsocial hours' and 'it became possible for many more young people to gather late into the night at major urban centers or simply on the street corners' (Cosgrove 1984). Many of these delinquent youths were very much into the swing movement and hid behind the zoot suit. By 1942, the zoot suit wearers began to become stereotyped with criminal activity. This is why many youngsters who wanted to wear the suit to be 'hip' had trouble with their parents and the older generation accepting the suit.

There would be two famous zoot suit wearers who were associated with criminal activity. In Los Angeles it would be Cesar Chavez, who in his later years would become a famous Chicano union activist. His wearing of the zoot suit would bring him in contact with community politics. The second was a Detroit pimp by the name of 'Detroit Red'. His participation in some of the zoot-suit riots in Harlem began his political education and transformed him into the Black radical leader Malcolm X (Cosgrove 1984). Both men recalled what it felt like to wear the zoot suit, but both dismissed the suit as they grew up and found themselves. For these delinquent youths, as well as the hipsters, the suit was a 'mask, which permitted adolescents to present themselves as adults and as urban sophisticates' (Daniels 1997). Trying to act like and be adults through the suit, a new term was coined as wartime statistics revealed this new pattern of behaviour, the Juvenile Delinquent (Cosgrove 1984).

WORLD WAR II AND THE ZOOT SUIT

As people began associating criminal youth with the suit, a rationing order was put into place in the United States on March 8 1942. The order placed restrictions on everything from nylon, soap, milk, and the amount of fabric used in certain outfits, especially the suit. The US Government War Production Board issued regulation L-85 that placed restrictions on clothing. The regulation would limit the length of the suit jacket, the number of pleats, number of pockets and pocket flaps, cuffs, and the vest would no longer be a part of the suit. Zoot-suitors, however, continued to wear their elaborate suits, which could take up to as much as five or more yards of fabric in the pants alone (Cats' Corner 1997). The cost of the suit on average was $45–75 during the war years, and could be purchased from a bootleg tailor. Therefore, the Government considered the suit an illicit item and contraband during the war. Many of these zoot suit wearers would continue to flash around town in them as an 'infraction to the expected rules of conduct during the war' (Swanson 1999). This was especially associated with African-Americans and Hispanics who paraded around town displaying their cultural, social, and political freedom, a combination that many would probably find threatening.

In June 1943, fighting broke out between Mexican-American zoot-suitors and navy servicemen on shore leave in Los Angeles. Sixty zoot-suitors were arrested and charged. This created a wave of rumours throughout military bases, and in the weeks to come rioting began throughout the Los Angeles area. Servicemen went throughout the streets throwing and beating Mexican-American and African-American zoot-suitors. Some were beaten with so-called 'Zootbeaters', a two by four with nails, and the popular thing to do was to strip the zoot-suitor of his clothing and humiliate him in public (Cats' Corner 1997).[11] The press did not help matters, calling the young wearers 'Zoot suit gangsters'. They created a devious image of the zoot-suitor, and helped perpetuate the belief that these youth were receiving justly deserved punishment. This was quite evident within the headlines of the *Los Angeles Times* which read on June 2 1943 'Youth Gangs Leading Cause of Delinquency' and on June 9 1943 'Zoot-suitors Learn Lesson in Fight with Servicemen'. By using these references many of the public saw only a conflict between patriotic fighting men and a 'fringe group of maladjusted youth'. Many servicemen stated that they could not stand the so-called 'gamin' dandies', young Mexican-Americans whose cultural norms were an affront to the culture of wartime

America (Swanson 1999). However, if one looks at the time the riots took place in American history, one would observe that many zoot suit wearers wore the suit as a political and social statement against the way African-Americans and Hispanics were being treated in a country that, as a whole, was a segregated society. This was a time when the rights of African-Americans and Hispanic-Americans were limited. These young zoot suit wearers were wearing the suits to violate laws that existed to keep them in their place. The media used its influence to try and keep the zoot-suitors contained, and eventually people started to wonder if these were more race-related riots than politically related riots as many servicemen had suggested.

The riots sparked investigations into what had happened. One was a fact-finding investigation headed by Attorney General Robert Kenny, and the other investigation was by State Senator Jack B. Tenney to determine if the zoot-suit riots were sponsored by Nazi agencies (Cosgrove 1984). The only thing done was that the Los Angeles City Council encouraged the War Production Board to be harsher on the illegal production of the suit and a law was put into effect that wearing or possessing a zoot suit was illegal. Political and racial studies done during the ten-day rioting concluded that most of the 600 youths who were beaten and arrested were Mexican-American and African-American youths, and that it was a blatant display of racial prejudice among not only the servicemen, but the police and press as well. Chester Himes (1943) warned Blacks, in an essay entitled 'Zoot Riots and Race Riots', of police and military brutality and compared the riots to lynching (Cats' Corner 1997).

The effects of the riots in Los Angeles did nothing to stop rioting in other cities. From 1942 to 1944, more riots occurred throughout the United States in areas such as Detroit, Harlem, and also in Canada. In Detroit, the authorities chose to dismiss a zoot-suit riot at a local high school as an adolescent imitation of what occurred in Los Angeles. Within weeks, Detroit witnessed the worst racial riots in its history.

Racial riots raged in Harlem, after a white police officer shot a black serviceman, creating a fully fledged zoot-suit racial war. However, on May 27 1944 in St Lambert, Montreal, riots broke out between zoot-suit youths of Italian and French origin, and Canadian servicemen. The youths' social values clashed with wartime moral standards, similar to the riots which occurred in the Los Angeles area (Durflinger 1998).

In many eastern southern states, rioting was not a major problem, because zoot suit wearers, depending on where you lived, were very few. More than any other African-Americans, Southern African-Americans had to endure the Jim Crow laws, and the Ku Klux Klan. During the 1930s and 1940s, the NAACP was trying desperately to have an anti-lynching law established. Those who dared to wear the zoot suit wore it to state their individuality and did not worry about the consequences. Eighty-three-year-old Theodopelus Mathew Alford, a resident of Norfolk, Virginia, at the time of the riots, discusses wearing his shadow stripe blue zoot suit during the war. 'Anyone who was hip had one. I just loved mine because it was different from the other boys in the neighborhood. The stripes were two hues of blue which caused a shadow effect on the suit.' When I asked him how long did he wear the chain, he stated that 'many southern boys didn't "roll like that" or go out in public with one on. You wore it for special occasions not to parade out in.' I asked if he was fearful of wearing the suit near the Navy base in Norfolk, the largest in the United States, during the time of the zoot-suit riots. He stated, 'Norfolk wasn't a bad place to be. We didn't have any problems with the service boys. Many of the problems with the military occurred in the bigger cities. There were just some places that were rough during those days.'[12]

ITS INFLUENCE

The popularity of the suit was worldwide, and no matter where you lived zoot suit wearers wore their outfits for a number of reasons. They wore the suit as part of an expressive dance cult, as a statement of cultural independence, as part of a spontaneous youth movement, or as a gangster hiding behind the suit. Eventually, the suit, which has been hailed as the first truly American suit, was integrated into the fashions of the late 1940s and 1950s. The influence of the zoot suit can be seen in the generously cut suits worn by American men after the war: their elaborate pin-stripe, herringbone, and plaid suits; their long roomy coats, and generously pleated and cuffed pants. It can be seen on the European youth of the 1950s, like the British Teddy Boys (Rushgrove n.d.). The influence continued into the late 1960s and early 1970s in the long jackets, loud clothing, and meticulous way of dressing. Today we call them 'pimp daddies'.[13] In the 1990s, the influence of the zoot suit returned back into fashion. The coat was longer and the silhouette seemed to fit the big and tall physique. Today, the jackets are still longer, and the pants are still wide and roomy. The suit is still colourful and can contain shadow stripes, plaids, and other prints. Many entertainers have brought the popularity of the zoot suit back to life. The original zoot suit has been seen in various music videos, for example, Janet Jackson's 'Alright' video, in which not only does she wear a zoot suit, but also it features Cab Calloway in a zoot suit. It has also been seen in movies such as 'The Mask' starring Jim Carrey, and on famous American entertainers such as Steve Harvey and Bernie Mac. You can buy the zoot suit custom-made at places such as Zoots by Suavecito's or El Pachuco Zoot Suits, two companies who make some of the most well-known and stylish zoot suits. African–and Hispanic-American men still wear versions of the zoot suit, because it still sets them apart from everyone else, making a definite cultural statement, and proving 'that the styles born of a struggle for self-definition have often been whimsically appropriated by mass-market fashion' (Boston 1998: 15).

CONCLUSION

In conclusion, the zoot suit bore cultural, political, and social implications. It still remains a mystery, not only because its origins are unknown, but also because it comes from a group of peoples whose lifestyle and history remains a mystery, the African-American race. A race of people who tend to conceal those mysteries within their dances and their clothing. A group of people who tend to set themselves apart through their own personal style. The riots themselves prove this theory, indicating that African-American as well as Hispanic-American youth 'found highly charged emotional and symbolic meaning in dress, music, and dance fads', and they spread that lifestyle or philosophy to the American youth (Daniels 1997). This is why it has been deemed the first article of clothing to create a spontaneous youth movement. In the new millennium, once again, we see young people dictating what they are going to wear, wearing their clothes based on political, social or cultural reasons in the new 'hip-hop' generation. Their dances, music, and style have not only caught on with the American popular youth culture, but the international popular youth culture as well. Like the zoot suit, the clothing the hip-hopper[14] chose to wear was first rejected by society. There were many school boards, within the United States, who passed policies prohibiting youngsters from wearing the sexy clothing and the baggy jeans low down on the waist. Even the attitudes that people had about the zoot-suit culture have evolved into the hip-hop culture. Parents, black middle-class society, and white society find the style an embarrassment and outrageous, and the media and law enforcement have once again stereotyped these hip-hoppers with the 'gangster look'. But like the zoot suit, black expressive culture has influenced other minorities and young white urbanites to the point where the garments have become popular and acceptable. The influence, like that of the zoot suit, is now worldwide. The hip-hop generation is now enjoying a new genre of clothing called urban wear, which includes the new version of the zoot suit. In essence, the zoot suit became a symbol for the enigmas of black culture, and those fascinated by that culture have found themselves inspired, and enjoying the pleasures of their newfound identity (Cosgrove 1984).

NOTES

Reprinted with permission from Holly Alford, "The Zoot Suit: Its History and Influence," *Fashion Theory* 8, no. 2 (2004): 225–36.

1. During the early part of the twentieth century African-Americans were discriminated against, and lived in a segregated society where their views and opinions were not heard.
2. A process by which African-Americans relax or straighten their hair.
3. As defined in the *Jive Dictionary* (Brooks 2003a).
4. *The Jive Dictionary* (Brooks 2003a).
5. A hairstyle that became popular with young delinquent males in the 1950s.
6. As defined in Webster's *Ninth New Collegiate Dictionary* (1985).
7. As defined by Calloway Brooks, grandson of Cab Calloway, *Notes of Interest* (2003b).
8. Referring to his exaggerated confederate uniform.
9. Extreme dances that required jumping under and over one another.
10. Referring to a low-status blue-collar Hispanic worker.
11. Taken from an online article 'A Bombs, Bebop, and C Rations: Jazz as Cultural Call to Arms Against 1940's Anxieties' (Vaidhanathan 1997).
12. Mr Theodopelus Mathew Alford, interview with the author, Richmond, Virginia, May 3 2003.
13. Men who love to control fast cars and fast women.
14. A youngster into hip-hop music.

26

BACK TO AFRICA: REGGAE AND RASTAFARIANISM

Dick Hebdige

Are you there Africa with the bulging chest and oblong thigh? Sulking Africa, wrought of iron in the fire, Africa of the millions of royal slaves, deported Africa, drifting continent are you there? Slowly you vanish, you withdraw into the past, into the tales of castaways, colonial museums, the works of scholars; but I call you back this evening to attend a secret revel.

Jean Genet, *The Blacks*, 1966

Even in the *ska* records of the early 60s, underneath the 'rudeness' and the light, choppy metre, there was a thread of Rastafarianism (Don Drummond, Reco, etc.) which became increasingly noticeable as the decade wore on until the Rasta contingent within reggae began, more or less exclusively, to determine the direction the music was to take. Reggae began to slow down to an almost African metabolism. The lyrics became more self-consciously Jamaican, more dimly enunciated and overgrown until they disappeared altogether in the 'dub',[1] to be replaced by 'talk-over'. The 'dread', the ganja, the Messianic feel of this 'heavy' reggae, its blood and fire rhetoric, its troubled rhythms can all be attributed to the Rasta influence. And it was largely through reggae, played at local 'sound-systems' (i.e. discotheques frequented by black working-class youth) and available only through an underground network of small retailers, that the Rastafarian ethos, the 'dreadlocks' and 'ethnicity' were communicated to members of the West Indian community in Great Britain.

For the unemployed black youth, 'heavy dub' and 'rockers'[2] provided an alternative sound-track, infinitely preferable to the muzak which filled the vast new shopping precincts where he spent his days 'doing nothing',[3] subjected to the random tyrannies of 'sus'.[4] But of course the original religious meanings of Rastafarianism suffered adjustment in the transition.

Somewhere between Trenchtown and Ladbroke Grove, the cult of Rastafari had become a 'style': an expressive combination of 'locks', of khaki camouflage and 'weed' which proclaimed unequivocally the alienation felt by many young black Britons.

Alienation could scarcely be avoided: it was built into the lives of young working-class West Indians in the form of bad housing, unemployment and police harassment. As early as 1969, it had been estimated that white youngsters from equivalent backgrounds were approximately five times more likely to find skilled work (*Observer*, 14 July 1968). In addition, throughout the 60s, relations with the police had been deteriorating steadily. The Mangrove trial of 1969 marked the beginning of a long series of bitter confrontations between the black community and the authorities (the Carib trial, the Oval trial, the 1976 Carnival) which led to a progressive polarization.

It was during this period of growing disaffection and joblessness, at a time when conflict between black youths and the police was being openly acknowledged in the press, that imported reggae music began to deal directly with problems of race and class, and to resurrect the African heritage. Reggae, and the forms which had preceded it, had always alluded to these problems obliquely. Oppositional values had been mediated through a range of rebel archetypes: the 'rude boy',[5] the gunfighter, the trickster, etc.—which remained firmly tied to the *particular* and tended to celebrate the *individual* status of revolt.

With dub and heavy reggae, this rebellion was given a much wider currency: it was generalized and theorized. Thus, the rude boy hero immortalized in ska and rocksteady—the lone delinquent pitched hopelessly against an implacable authority—was supplanted as the central focus of identity by the Rastafarian who broke the Law in more profound and subtle ways. Not only did the Rasta fix the dreary cycle of solitary refusal and official retribution within the context of Jamaica's absent history, he broke that cycle altogether by installing the conflict elsewhere on the neglected surfaces of everyday life. By questioning the neat articulations of common sense (in appearance, in language, etc.) the Rasta was able to carry the crusade beyond the obvious arena of law and order to the level of the 'obvious' itself. It was here, quite literally on the 'skin' of the social formation, that the Rastafarian movement made its most startling innovations, refracting the system of black and white polarities, turning negritude into a positive sign, a loaded essence, a weapon at once deadly and divinely licensed. The process of adjustment which simultaneously intensified conflict and turned it inwards was reflected in the music and reproduced exactly in musical form. As has been said, reggae became darker and more African, the patois even more impenetrable, the menace

more overt. At the same time, the 'Battle(s) on Orange Street' (ska record by Prince Buster), literal, bloody and yet humorously described in the 60s, were replaced by full-scale 'War inna Babylon' (Max Romeo, Island, 1976). This 'war' had a double nature: it was fought around ambiguous terms of reference which designated both an actual and an imaginary set of relations (race-class nexus/Babylon; economic exploitation/Biblical suffering), a struggle both real and metaphorical, which described a world of forms enmeshed in ideology where appearance and illusion were synonymous.

Of course, war had its dubious compensations too: a sense of solidarity and purpose, an identity, an enemy more or less clearly denned. Even the tension between violent and religious 'solutions' could be reduced if the conflict between the 'Police and (the) Thieves' 'scaring the Nation with their guns and ammunition' (Junior Murvin, Island, 1977) was taken not only to complement but to *signify* the bloodless battle being waged by the Rastafarians on the terrain of ideology. This displacement was more easily accomplished the further one moved from the original sources of reggae and Rastafarianism. In Great Britain, at every local 'sound-system', in every major city where immigrants had settled in sufficient numbers, a righteous army of militant sufferers would gather to pledge allegiance to the Ethiopian flag.

The 'sound-system', perhaps more than any other institution within working-class West Indian life, was the site at which blackness could be most thoroughly explored, most clearly and uncompromisingly expressed. To a community hemmed in on all sides by discrimination, hostility, suspicion and blank incomprehension, the sound-system came to represent, particularly for the young, a precious inner sanctum, uncontaminated by alien influences, a black heart beating back to Africa on a steady pulse of dub. In clubs like the Four Aces, in the Seven Sisters Road, North London, an exclusively black audience would 'stare down' Babylon, carried along on a thunderous bass-line, transported on 1000 watts. Power was at home here—just beyond the finger tips. It hung on the air—invisible, electric—channelled through a battery of home-made speakers. It was present in every 'toasted'[6] incantation. In an atmosphere shaking with sound, charged with smoke and nemesis, it was easy to imagine that the 'Day of Reckoning' was at hand; that when, at last, the 'lightning flashed', the 'weak heart' would 'drop and the righteous black man stand' ('Lightning Flash', Big Youth, Klik, 1975) armoured in dread,[7] oblivious to his former suffering.

The sound-system thus became associated with the heavier, more 'rootsy' forms of reggae. The two became mutually dependent; indeed they were, for all practical purposes, identical. The music itself was virtually exiled from the airwaves. It could live only in and through the cumbersome network of cabinets and wires, valves and microphones which make up the 'system' and which, though legally the property of an individual entrepreneur, was owned in a much deeper sense by the community. And it was through music, more than any other medium, that the communication with the past, with Jamaica, and hence Africa, considered vital for the maintenance of black identity, was possible. The 'system' turned on sound; the sound was intimately bound up with the notion of 'culture'; and if the system was attacked then the community itself was symbolically threatened. It thus became hallowed ground, territory to be defended against possible contamination by white groups. Police interference was, of course, vehemently resented and in some cases the mere presence of policemen was sufficient to provoke black youths to violent reprisal. The Notting Hill riot of 1976[8] and the Carib Club incident of 1974[9] can be interpreted in this way, as symbolic defences of communal space.

EXODUS: A DOUBLE CROSSING

Fortunately relations with the larger white community were in general rather less fraught. In some parts of London, at least, there existed a whole network of subterranean channels which had for years linked the fringes of the indigenous population to the equivalent West Indian subcultures. Originally opened up to the illicit traffic of 'weed' and jazz, these internal channels provided the basis for much broader cultural exchanges. The bonds were strengthened by time and a common experience of privation, by lives spent in close proximity around a similar set of focal concerns. While each preserved its own distinctive shape, the two cultures could harmonize around the mutual interlocking loyalties of family and street, pub and neighbourhood. With significant exceptions (Nottingham and Notting Hill in 1958, Hoxton and parts of the East End in the 70s) a pattern of relatively peaceful coexistence began to emerge. Certainly this was true of the 50s and early 60s. In general, the first-generation West Indian immigrants held too much cultural space in common with their white working-class neighbours to allow any open antagonism to develop. Confirmed Anglophiles, even when 'at home' in Jamaica, they shared the same goals, sought the same diversions (a pint of beer, a game of darts, a dance on Saturday night) and, despite the unfamiliar accent, drew upon the same 'language of fatalism',[10] resigned to their lowly position, confident that their children would enjoy better prospects, better lives. Of course, things failed to improve at the expected rate and by the early 70s full employment appeared a remote possibility indeed; a moment dimly remembered and by no means representative of Britain's economic fortunes since the War.

Meanwhile black children born and educated in this country were rather less inclined than their parents either to accept the inferior status and narrow options offered them, or to leave unquestioned the dominant definitions of their blackness. Reggae provided the focus around which another culture, another set of values and self-definitions could cluster. These changes were subtly registered in the style of black youth; in the gait, the manner, the voice which seemed almost overnight to become less anglicized.

The very way the black youth moved implied a new assurance—there was more deliberate 'sass', more spring, less shuffle.[11] The clothes had also undergone a series of significant adjustments over the years. The aspirations of the early immigrants had been mirrored in the rainbow mohair suits and picture ties, the neatly printed frocks and patent-leather shoes which they had worn on their arrival in Great Britain. Each snowy cuff had reflected a desire to succeed, to 'make the grade' in the terms traditionally laid down by white society, just as, with tragic irony, all hopes of ever really fitting in were inadvertently belied by every garish jacket sleeve—too loud and jazzy for contemporary British tastes. Both the dreams and the disappointments of an entire generation were thus inscribed in the very cut (ambitious and improbable) of the clothes in which it chose to make its entrance.

The crossing to Great Britain was, like most voluntary migrations, an act of faith: an exodus. It required a peculiar blend of contradictory motivations: desperation or at least impatience with the host country, a belief in the efficacy of action, a desire for increased status, and confidence that the Mother Country would recognize its obligations, would welcome and reward its lost children.

For the first wave of immigrants, which comprised mainly skilled and semi-skilled men, the drive towards improvement was tempered with conservatism: a belief that Britain was bound, by the decency and justice with which it was conventionally associated in Jamaica, to supply a reasonable standard of living for those prepared to work. Typically, the West Indian immigrants of the 50s wanted jobs, homes, respectability, a place for the family to settle once and for all. On the other hand, those who followed in the 60s tended to be unskilled and were, perhaps, more straightforwardly desperate: dissatisfied with the little Jamaica had to offer (Hiro, 1972). For these, the movement to England represented both a last-ditch attempt to salvage something worthwhile

from life and a 'magical' solution to their problems. Perhaps because there was less to lose, more was invested in the transition from the West Indies to Great Britain: hopes of an almost religious nature and intensity were pinned on the outcome. The disillusion felt by this second wave of immigrants therefore tended to be correspondingly deeper, more final and more readily expressed. In any case, as the immigrants began to congregate in the decaying inner rings of Britain's larger cities, a new West Indian style began to emerge. This style was less painfully hemmed in by British-ness, less torn between sobriety and 'colour', and behind it there lay the suggestion (unwelcome to white eyes) that yet another migration had taken place, that Britain had failed to supply the promised goods, and that the disaffected immigrants had psychologically moved out.

On the deviant margins of West Indian society, at least, there were significant changes in appearance. The hustlers and street-corner men, encouraged perhaps by the growth of black clubs and discotheques in the mid-60s, were sharpening up, combining hats and 'shades' and Italian suits to produce a West Indian equivalent of the US 'soul-brother' look; tight-fitting, loose-limbed, black and yet urbane. This soul brother moved on the cool lines of jazz, ska and American r & b. He reproduced the timbre and the scansion of these forms in his walk and argot. He sought refuge in their dark interiors from the world of 'straights' and whites. In these ways, he reassessed the stigmata and turned Caribbean flashiness into a declaration of alien intent, a sign of his Otherness. It was largely under his auspices that blackness was recuperated and made symbolically available to young West Indian men. This blackness was unwrapped from and through the music of the 60s; it was teased up to the surface in *avant-garde* jazz (e.g. John Coltrane, Miles Davis, Pharaoh Saunders, Archie Shepp), and (more importantly here) in dub and heavy reggae.

Of course, this development had its visual corollary in dress. During the 70s, the 'youth' were developing their own unique style: a refracted form of Rastafarian aesthetic, borrowed from the sleeves of imported reggae albums and inflected to suit the needs of second-generation immigrants. This was a Rastafarianism at more than one remove, stripped of nearly all its original religious meanings: a distillation, a highly selective appropriation of all those elements within Rastafarianism which stressed the importance of resistance and black identity, and which served to position the black man and his 'queen' outside the dominant white ideology. The difference around which the whole Rasta style revolved was literally inscribed on the skin of black people and it was through appearance that this difference was to be extended, elaborated upon, realized. Those young blacks who 'stepped' to 'Humble Lion'[12] began to cultivate a more obviously African 'natural' image.[13] The pork-pie hat disappeared, to be replaced by the roughly woven 'tam'. Tonic, mohair and terylene—the raw material for all those shiny suits in midnight and electric blue—were exchanged for cotton, wool and denim out of which more casual and serviceable garments were made. On every other British high street stood an army-surplus store which supplied the righteous with battle dress and combat jackets: a whole wardrobe of sinister guerilla chic. The rude boy crop was grown out and allowed to explode into an ethnic 'Afro' frizz, or plaited into 'locks' or 'knots' (the ubiquitous natty or knotty style). Girls began to leave their hair unstraightened, short or plaited into intricately parted arabesques, capillary tributes to an imagined Africa.

All these developments were mediated to those members of the white working class who lived in the same areas, worked in the same factories and schools and drank in adjacent pubs. In particular, the trajectory 'back to Africa' within second-generation immigrant youth culture was closely monitored by those neighbouring white youths interested in forming their own subcultural options. Of course, in both Britain and America relations between black and white youth cultures have always been delicate, charged with a potentially explosive significance, irrespective of whether or not any actual contact takes place between the two groups. There are strong sym-

bolic links which can be translated into empathy ('For us the whole coloured race was sacred'—George Melly, 1970) or emulation (e.g. hard drug use in the modern jazz era[14]). Both Paul Goodman (1968) and Jock Young (1971) have characterized the Negro as the quintessential subterranean, embodying all those values (the search for adventure and excitement) which co-exist with and undercut the sober positives of mainstream society (routinization, security, etc.). In these terms, the positions 'youth' and 'Negro' are often aligned in the dominant mythology. As Jock Young (1971) writes: They are 'viewed with the same ambivalence: happy-go-lucky and lazy, hedonistic and dangerous'.

Of course, at different times and in different circumstances, this congruence can be more or less apparent, more or less actively perceived and experienced. Put in general terms, identification between the two groups can be either open or closed, direct or indirect, acknowledged or unacknowledged. It can be recognized and extended into actual links (the mods, skinheads and punks) or repressed and inverted into an antagonism (teds, greasers). In either case, the relationship represents a crucial determining factor in the evolution of each youth cultural form and in the ideology both signified in that form and 'acted out' by its members.

At another level, patterns of rejection and assimilation between host and immigrant communities can be mapped along the spectacular lines laid down by white working-class youth cultures. The succession of white subcultural forms can be read as a series of deep-structural adaptations which symbolically accommodate or expunge the black presence from the host community. It is on the plane of aesthetics: in dress, dance, music; in the whole rhetoric of style, that we find the dialogue between black and white most subtly and comprehensively recorded, albeit in code. By describing, interpreting and deciphering these forms, we can construct an oblique account of the exchanges which have taken place between the two communities. We can watch, played out on the loaded surfaces of

British working-class youth cultures, a phantom history of race relations since the War.

NOTES

Reprinted with permission from Dick Hebdige, "Back to Africa: Reggae and Rastafarianism," in *Subculture: The Meaning of Style* (London: Routledge, 1979), 30–45.

1. The dub is the instrumental ridim-track—an unobstructed rhythm without words with the emphasis on the bass. Sound effects and echo in particular are used a lot. It is, in the words of Dermott Hussey, 'a naked dance rhythm', and the producer and the engineer have become the acknowledged 'artists' of the dub. Across the dub, the 'talk-over' artist improvises a spoken 'toast' which is generally organized around 'black' themes.

2. 'Rockers'—'heavy' or 'ethnic' reggae. The term first appeared in early summer 1976.

3. See Gorrigan (1976), who maintains that the major problem experienced by 'kids' is how to 'kill time'.

4. Arrested under the 'Suspected Persons' Act; see *Time Out*, 5 August 1977.

5. The rude boys formed a deviant subculture in Jamaica in the mid- to late 60s. Flashy, urban 'rough and tough', they were glamorized in a string of reggae and rock steady hits: 'Rudy a Message To You'—Dandy Livingstone; 'Rude Boy'—the Wailers; 'Shanty Town'—Desmond Dekker; 'Johnny Too Bad'—the Slickers.

6. The 'toast' is a monologue delivered live by a 'talk-over' DJ as an instrumental dub is being played over the sound system. See note 1.

7. 'Dread' is a polysemantic term. It seems to encompass righteousness, Biblical 'wrath' and the fea r inspired by that wrath.

8. The violence at the 1976 Carnival was triggered off by the conspicuous presence of large numbers of policemen in the Acklam Road area where several sound-systems were positioned under the fly-over. The less serious disturbances of the 1977 Carnival also centred on this officially recognized 'trouble-spot'. When Sir Robert Mark assured the public in the wake of the 1976 riots that he would not tolerate a 'no-go area', one suspects he was referring specifically to the sound-systems in the Acklam Road.

9. A police raid on the Carib Club in the autumn of 1974 triggered off a pitched battle which resulted in the arrest and subsequent acquittal of four black youths.

10. See Tolson (1977), who is concerned with how ideological constructs about 'keeping your place', etc. are manifested in the patterns of working-class speech.

11. Ulf Hannerz has noted a similar transformation in American ghetto-culture, and associated these changing patterns of physical movement with an adjustment in the self-concept of younger blacks. He suggests that the younger blacks are defining themselves against the down-home parent culture and quotes one respondent who explicitly identifies with the outmoded difference and submissiveness: 'They [the 'Uncle Toms'] say "Yes sir", "No sir". They gonna shuffle forever' (Hannerz, 1969).

12. 'Humble Lion' and 'steppers' replaced 'rockers' as the in-term for 'heavy-reggae' and dub, in May 1977 (see *Black Echoes*, 18 July, 1977).

13. The Rasta preoccupation with 'nature' and the 'natural man' is reflected in the lyrics of the songs. Big Youth dismisses Babylon materials in a celebrated mock-serious talk-over 'Natty No Jester' (Klik, 1975): 'Cos Natty dread no jester He wear no polyester...

14. In *The Jazz Life*, Nat Hentoff describes how a mythical association between heroin addiction and inspiration in jazz developed in the 1950s. Young musicians attempting to reproduce the 'hard' sound of Charlie Parker and Fats Navarro (both heroin addicts) were drawn towards what Hentoff calls 'emulation-by-needle'. Le-Roi Jones, in *Blues People*, defines heroin usage as a 'kind of one-upmanship of the highest order', which turns the 'Negro's separation from the mainstream of... society into an advantage'. White hipsters intent on translating their emotional infinities with Blacks into actual terms found heroin appealing at the same symbolic level (see also Harold Finestone, 'Cats, Kicks and Colour', in *The Other Side*).

27

CULTURAL RESPONSES OF THE TEDS

Tony Jefferson

Note: In his review of Teddy Boy culture, Tony Jefferson deals with three related aspects: the way the (sense of group) of the Teds and their low (or near-lumpen) status made them extremely sensitive to insults, real or imagined; the way this over-sensitivity became attacked, primarily to the distinctive dress and appearance of the group; and the elements which the Teds borrowed from the dominant culture and reworked into a distinctive style of their own. This 'proletarianization' of an upper-class style of dress was no mere stylistic flourish: it expressed, Jefferson argues, both the reality, and the aspirations of the group. A longer version of this paper is available (Stencilled Paper No. 22, CCCS).

In the light of growing structural inequalities [argued earlier in the paper] how can we read the Teds' cultural responses as symbolic articulations of their social plight? If we look at the cultural responses adopted, in turn, what becomes apparent in decoding them is an attempt to defend, symbolically, a constantly threatened space and a declining status.

(a)   *Group-mindedness* The group-mindedness of the Teds can be read partly as a response to the post-war upheaval and destruction of the socially cohesive force of the extended kinship network. Thus the group life and intense loyalty of the Teds can be seen as a reaffirmation of traditional slum working-class values and the 'strong sense of territory' (Downes 1966: 119), as an attempt to retain, if only imaginatively, a hold on the territory which was being

expropriated from them, by developers, on two levels:

(1) the actual expropriation of land;
(2) the less tangible expropriation of the culture attached to the land, i.e. the kinship networks and the 'articulations of communal space' mentioned by Cohen (1972: 16).

(b)   *Extreme touchiness to insults real or imagined* If we look at their extreme touchiness to insults, real or imagined, we find that most of these incidents revolved around insults to themselves personally, to their appearance generally, and their dress in particular. To illustrate this point, using one of the more dramatic examples available; the first 'Teddy boy' killing, the Clapham Common murder of 1953, was a result of a fight between three youths and a group of Teds which had been started when one of the Teds had been called 'a flash cunt' by one of the youths. (For a full account of this incident, and the subsequent trial, see Parker 1969.)

My contention is that to lads traditionally lacking in status, and *being further deprived of what little they possessed* (a reference to the declining social situation of the Teds, argued earlier in the fuller version of this paper) there remained only the self, the cultural extension of the self (dress, personal appearance) and the social extension of the self (the group). Once threats were perceived in these areas, the only 'reality' or 'space' on which they had any hold, then the fights, *in defence of this space,* become explicable and *meaningful* phenomena.

If we look closely at the objects of Teddy-boy fighting, this notion of defending their space is, I believe, further amplified. Group fights, i.e. fights with other groups of Teds, are explicable in terms of a defence of the social extension of the self—the group (hence, the importance of 'group-mindedness'). Fights which ensued when individuals insulted Teds are explicable in terms of *a defence of the self and the cultural extension of the self symbolized in their dress and general appearance.* Especially important in this area is the touchiness to insults about dress. This I shall enlarge upon in the next section on 'Dress'.

Whilst many of their fights resulted from extreme sensitivity to insults, even their attacks on the Cypriot proprietors of Cypriot cafes, and Blacks, can be read in terms of defence: a defence of status. Their position as 'lumpen' youths was worsening *independently* of the influx of Commonwealth immigrants in the early 1950s, but in the absence of a coherent and articulate grasp of their social reality, it was perhaps inevitable that they should perceive this influx as causal rather than coincidental. Thus, they rationalized their position as being, in part anyway, due to the immigrants and displaced their frustration onto them. An additional irritant was the perception many Teds had of immigrants as actually making it—the corollary of this, of course, was that they were making it 'at the Teds' expense'. The café-owning Cypriots were one example of those who had 'made it'. Others were the coloured landlords and racketeers. Living, as many Teds did, in dilapidated inner urban areas scheduled for re-development, they came into contact with the minority of coloureds, who, because of the hopelessness of *their* position (being coloured and working class), were forced into positions of very limited options (small-time racketeering and pimping were probably two of the more available and attractive). And so the myth of the coloured immigrants being either pimps, landlords or in

on the rackets, very prevalent among Teds (and many white working-class adults), started and spread. The repercussions of all this, the 1958 'race-riots' in Nottingham and Notting Hill are known, sadly, only too well. That it should have been the Teds who started them lends weight to my thesis. That large numbers of working-class adults responded in the way they did, by joining in, demonstrates that it was not only the young 'lumpen' who were experiencing a worsening of their socio-economic position. But, in an age of 'affluence' the *real structural causes* could not be admitted, and predictably, were not. Instead, the nine *unskilled working-class adolescents* who started the Notting Hill riots were savagely sentenced to four years' imprisonment apiece. The obvious scape-goating involved, as in all similar cases of scape-goat punishments, was, and still is, a sure sign of mystification at work—the protective cloak of the ruling classes being drawn closer to prevent its real interests becoming too visible.

The attacks on youth clubs are perhaps easiest to explain if one remembers that many youth clubs banned all Teddy boys purely on 'reputation'. Simple revenge must then have constituted the basis for some attacks. Additionally, though, there was the chronic lack of public provision of facilities to match the increase in adolescent leisure (see, for example, Fyvel 1963: 120–3). Consequently, much was then expected of what was provided—far too much. When these failed to live up to the expectations, as they invariably did, the disappointment was invariably increased. Thus, ironically, the youth clubs that did exist, far from alleviating adolescent leisure problems actually exacerbated them. (For a fascinating account of the trials and tribulations experienced in this area and of a valiant but shortlived attempt to supply the kids with what they *wanted,* see Gosling 1962.) Finally, the attacks on bus conductors. Since these attacks were usually on conductors on late-night bus routes, this suggests that the opportunity of anonymity, and possibly alcohol, combined to increase the already high level of sensitivity to imagined insults.

(c) *Dress and appearance* Despite periodic unemployment, despite the unskilled jobs, Teds, in common with other teenagers at work during this period, were relatively affluent. Between 1945–1950, the average real wage of teenagers increased at twice the adult rate (see, for example, Abrams 1959). Teds thus certainly had money to spend and, because it was practically all they had, it assumed a crucial importance. Much of the money went on clothes: the Teddy boy 'uniform'. But before decoding this particular cultural articulation, a sketch of the 'style' and its history is necessary.

Originally, the Edwardian suit was introduced in 1950 by a group of Savile Row tailors who were attempting to initiate a new style. It was addressed, primarily, to the young aristocratic men about town. Essentially the dress consisted of a long, narrow-lapelled, waisted jacket, narrow trousers (but without being 'drainpipes'), ordinary toe-capped shoes, and a fancy waistcoat. Shirts were white with cutaway collars and ties were tied with a 'windsor' knot. Headwear, if worn, was a trilby. The essential changes from conventional dress were the cut of the jacket and the dandy waistcoat. Additionally, barbers began offering individual styling, and hair length was generally longer than the conventional short back and sides. (This description is culled from a picture of the 'authentic' Edwardian dress which was put out by the *Tailor and Cutter* and printed in the *Daily Sketch,* 14th November, 1953, in order to dissociate the 'authentic' from the working-class adoption of the style.)

This dress began to be taken up by working-class youths sometime in 1953 and, in those early days, was often taken over wholesale. (The *Daily Mirror* of 23rd October, 1953, shows a picture of Michael Davies, who was convicted of what later became known as the first 'Teddy boy' killing, which would bear this out. In fact the picture shows him in a three-piece matching suit, i.e. without the fancy waistcoat.)

The later modifications to this style by the Teds were the bootlace tie; the thick-creped suede shoes (Eton clubman chukka type); skin-tight, drainpipe trousers (without turn-ups); straighter, less waisted jackets; moleskin or satin collars to the jackets; and the addition of vivid colours. The earlier sombre suit colours occasionally gave way to suits of vivid green, red or pink and other 'primitive' colours (see Sandilands 1968). Blue-suede shoes, post-Elvis, were also worn. The hair-style also underwent a transformation: it was usually long, combed into a 'D-A5' with a boston neck-line (straight cut), greasy, with side whiskers and a quiff. Variations on this were the 'elephant's trunk' or the more extreme 'apache' (short on top, long at sides).

I see this choice of uniform as, initially, an attempt to buy status (since the clothes chosen were originally worn by upper-class dandies) which, being quickly aborted by a harsh social reaction (in 1954 second-hand Edwardian suits were on sale in various markets—see Rock and Cohen 1970—as they became rapidly unwearable by the upper-class dandies once the Teds had taken them over as their own), was followed by an attempt to create their own style via the modifications just outlined.

This, then, was the Teds' one contribution to culture: their adoption and personal modification of Savile Row Edwardian suits. But more important than being a contribution to culture, since culture only has *meaning* when transposed into social terms, their dress represented a symbolic way of expressing and negotiating with their social reality; of giving cultural meaning to their social plight. And because of this, their touchiness to insults about dress becomes not only comprehensible but rational.

But what 'social reality' was their uniform both 'expressive of' and 'a negotiation with'? Unfortunately there is, as yet, no 'grammar' for decoding cultural symbols like dress and what follows is largely speculative. However, if one examines *the context from which the cultural symbol was probably extracted*—one possible way of formulating one aspect of such a grammar—then the adoption of, for example, the bootlace tie, begins to acquire social meaning. Probably picked up from the many American Western films viewed during this period where it was worn, most prevalently, as I remember them, by the slick city gambler whose social status was, grudgingly, high because of his ability to live *by his wits* and *outside* the traditional working-class mores of society (which were basically rural and hardworking as opposed to urban and hedonistic), then I believe its symbolic cultural meaning for the Teds becomes explicable as both expression of their *social reality* (basically outsiders and forced to live by their wits) and their social '*aspirations*' (basically an attempt to gain high, albeit grudging, status for an ability to live smartly, hedonistically and by their wits in an urban setting).

NOTE

Reprinted with permission from Tony Jefferson, "Cultural Responses of the Teds," in *Resistance through Rituals: Youth Subcultures in Post-War Britain,* ed. S. Hall and T. Jefferson, 2nd ed. (London: Routledge, 1993), 67–70.

28

ROCK, FASHION AND PERFORMATIVITY

Noel McLaughlin

INTRODUCTION

Popular music and fashion are frequently used interchangeably in 'everyday' discourse. As Simon Frith puts it, 'pop is nothing if not fashionable (drawing attention to its transience, to the ever familiar shock of the new)' (Frith 1996: 157). In this respect, the popular music and fashion industries are regarded as sharing a close relationship: popular music is taken to play a powerful role in 'shop-windowing' and selling clothes (with certain rock and pop stars regarded as 'fashion leaders') and, in turn, clothing has been viewed as a central part of how popular music signifies. However obvious this may seem, the relationship between popular music and fashion has been much neglected and both areas have been radically under-theorized, especially in comparison to other areas of contemporary culture. If 'dress', as John Street puts it, 'is perhaps the most obvious way in which the formally inarticulate speaks volumes' (Street 1997: 36), then this 'silence' about the dynamic between popular music and fashion is somewhat regrettable as clearly clothing and dress are an important part of how popular music functions and, indeed, a central aspect of popular musical pleasure. In this regard, the lack of detailed consideration about the relationship between popular music and fashion is somewhat surprising, given the centrality of music and clothes to pop's broader 'aestheticisation of everyday life' (McRobbie 1999).

There are a number of reasons for this silence. In relation to fashion, many writers have pointed to how an 'old style' leftism is suspicious, even contemptuous, of fashion and indeed popular culture, seeing these as essentially transient phenomena. Even within the elaborated field of film studies (which has occupied the canonical place in the contemporary study of culture), there has been a reticence to consider the significance and pleasures of costume. As Church Gibson (1998) has poignantly observed:

> Only in the last decade or so has fashion really established itself as a serious academic discipline and as an important area of theoretical debate. The reasons, of course, are well documented: the centuries-old belief in the essential frivolity of fashion, reinforced by the puritanism of many on the left, for whom fashion is the most obvious and ... objectionable form of commodity fetishism, and the conviction of the majority of second-wave feminists that fashion is an arena in which women ... display themselves in order to gratify male desire.[1] (Church Gibson 1998: 36)

This chapter seeks to explore the pop–fashion relationship, to make some general points about how clothing works in popular music culture. This means assessing some of the main debates about both fashion and pop before moving on to offer a case study of the rock/pop band, Suede.[2] I will be focusing primarily on the performance of gender in pop and the role of clothing in the popular music matrix. This is because rock and pop are taken to be 'about sex' (sex, rhythm and the beat and so forth). Before moving on to this, I want to make a few general points about pop and fashion.

Popular music and fashion are casually used terms, but their everyday sense of transparency conceals their complexity. It is frequently claimed 'anything can be fashionable'; that any music can be 'popular'. However, the problem with this type of relativism is that, to paraphrase Richard Middleton, we empty the terms of the meanings which they carry in actual discourse (Middleton 1990: 3). Both pop and fashion cannot be defined in isolation, and the two terms respectively act as 'other': first, pop is other to rock—which can today mean a variety of musics in an increasingly elaborated subcultural field of discriminations (see Thornton 1995)—and second, to something (as yet unnamed—perhaps antifashion or 'normal' dress) that transcends or stands above, or is unconcerned with fashion.

Rock culture has been underpinned by ideologies of authenticity which are antifashion in outlook. As rock was apparently unconcerned with fashion, it could mark itself as superior to a more fashion-centred (and 'superficial') pop. Fashion, then, became associated with 'mere' entertainment and the perceived corrupting ('inauthenticating') effects of consumer capitalism. Put differently: rock culture's difference from pop and the world of fashion enabled rock 'to matter' (Grossberg 1993: 201). Furthermore, as Frith and Goodwin surmise, this distinction between rock and pop

> is a matter of gender, with female (pop) consumers being described as essentially 'passive', in contrast to the discriminating, engaged, male audience for rock ... The essential male address of 'real' rock is thus taken for granted and embodied in the standard history of rock as a succession of bold male heroes.[3] (Frith and Goodwin 1990: 370)

'CLOSE TO HOME?': POP, FASHION AND THE ACADEMY

At the risk of causing offence, academia has never been renowned as a Mecca of male fashion. But, if anything, male dress in the academy has been caricatured as a 'fashion disaster-zone' of tweed jackets and elbow patches, ill-fitting, worn corduroy trousers and Hush Puppies (or their more modern equivalents). Despite the superficiality of this remark, it conceals what is an important point: the masculine academy could be characterized as a host of omniscient spectators—analogous to the male gaze in cinema—who like to look outwards at the world imagining that they cannot be seen in return. Male academics have liked to see themselves (much in the manner of Michelangelo's David) as having their minds on 'higher' things than the flippancy and vagaries of fashion. Moreover, this has been accompanied by a sense that they (we) are beyond scrutiny.[4] This is indicative of a broader trend, where men and male dress have liked to go unnoticed, to function, in Richard Dyer's words, as an 'absent centre' (Dyer 1997) around which 'others'—gay men, women, blacks and Asians (and those 'low' enough to be duped into conspicuous consumption)—revolve. It is important therefore to turn the spotlight back on the masculine academy and on to intellectual agendas themselves. When brought into view, the history of male 'fashions' can prove illuminating. As Fred Davis points out, male dress codes were designed not to be noticed, to be 'not fashion at all':

> [M]en's dress became the primary visual medium for intoning the rejection of 'corrupt' aristocratic claims to elegance, opulence, leisure, and amatory adventure ... Men's dress became more simple, coarse, unchangeable, and sombre, sartorial tendencies that in many respects survive to the present. (Davis 1992: 39)

Fashion has functioned as 'other' to the 'serious' and mainly masculine world of work.

Accompanying this is the lingering sense that fashion and pop can be equated within the feminine. As Bruzzi has argued in her detailed study of clothing in the movies, 'discussions of costume have tended to exclude men and masculine identities, as if attention to dress is an inherently female trait' (Bruzzi 1997b: xv). Similarly, Jennifer Craik has concluded, in surveying the field of fashion literature, that 'most studies of contemporary fashion emphasise female fashion and marginalise attention to male dress'. Accompanying this is the sense that 'men who "dress up" are peculiar' consolidating the 'myth of the "undecorated" male' (Craik 1994: 176).

This, however, goes against the tide of history where, since the 1980s in particular—the period of accelerated de-industrialization and the development of a 'feminized' service sector—masculinity has increasingly come into view, making it no longer feasible to assert that clothes and fashion are essentially a 'feminine' preserve and 'not worth bothering with'. With it, the idea of a 'crisis in masculinity(ies)' has gained increasing currency (see Chapman and Rutherford 1988; Easthope 1992). A key aspect of this has been the introduction of a number of glossy 'style' magazines aimed at men—*The Face, Arena* and latterly *Loaded*—which in their different ways have constructed and placed the male body under the spotlight as an object for sexual consumption (see Mort 1996; Nixon 1996).[5] As a consequence, 'men ... are now more than "disinterested observers"' (Bruzzi 1997b: xv).

This is somewhat general, because it doesn't tell us very much about how masculinities have changed (and the reason for my diatribe against the masculine academy is that by ignoring clothes and music, we may miss the progressive possibilities these so-called superficialities may afford). Furthermore, there has been a reluctance to consider the way that pop has articulated gender identity from the early 1980s onwards; as well as the role of clothing and dress within this. As Frith has argued,

the academic study of popular music has been limited by the assumption that sounds somehow reflect 'a people' ... too often attempts to relate musical forms to social processes ignore the ways in which music is *itself* a social process ... [I]n examining the aesthetics of popular music we need to reverse the usual academic argument: the question is not how a piece of music, a text, 'reflects' popular values, but how—in performance—it produces them. (Frith 1996: 269–70).

While masculinity has come under the spotlight, Frith's insight takes us towards considering the ways this has occurred and what is at stake. He begins to question how different combinations of music, clothing and body in performance articulate different masculine identities. There are obvious but significant differences between performers such as Soft Cell, Boyzone, Oasis and Culture Club, but frequently these are not registered let alone explored in contemporary cultural criticism, where there is an unfortunate tendency to be panglossian in the treatment of pop.

Andrew Goodwin has referred to (and this is the other side of pop nostalgia) a form of 'secret hatred' of popular music within the academy (Goodwin 1993). While popular music studies (which have become a discipline in their own right in recent years) can contribute greatly to an understanding of the role of clothing in contemporary culture, there has been a reluctance to consider this. In fact, rock ideology and popular music studies have colluded together in treating clothes and fashion as the 'gloss' on a performing pop culture that has valued the organic, the natural and the spontaneous.

The notable exceptions have been discussions of punk and subcultural 'style' (Hebdige 1979, 1988). Here, the 'oppositional' moment punk was taken to embody has blinded the academic study of popular music to later moments, which were found 'wanting' contrasted to punk's vitality and authenticity. Indeed, punk has been

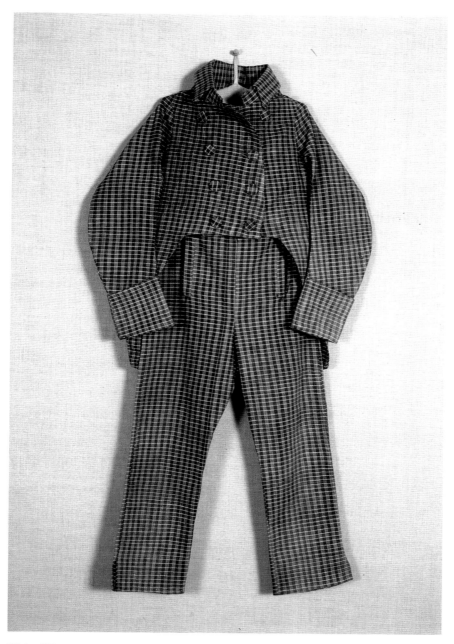

Plate 17. Young boy's suit of blue-and-white cotton; checked fabric; pants: drop front with gold buttons; jacket: double-breasted, cut-away. American, c. 1800–1810. A note in the pocket reads "Found in Lakeville, Ct." Such garments indicate both practicality and an interest in the "unencumbered" nature of children that became popular among the elites in the second half of the eighteenth century. Courtesy of Cora Ginsburg LLC, New York.

Plate 18. Léopold Fertbauer, *Carl Gustaf Löwenhielm (1790–1858), generallöjtnant, landshövding*. Oil. 26 x 21 cm. Nationalmuseum, Stockholm. The sitter was a lieutenant general and a county governor. The painting was made during his appointment as a minister of the Swedish embassy in Vienna. The Swedish uniforms were considered old-fashioned and were not reformed until a few decades later. The uniform—cavalry of the life regiment of the king—is unique for that part of the regiment and dates from 1813.

H.

Grand Costume de Conseiller d'État.

Groß-Costum eines Staatsraths.

Plate 19. Costume drawings of the state uniform for a state council *(Costumes de la Cour impériale de France. Neueste Hof- und Staatstrachten in Frankreich, vorgeschrieben vom Kaiser Napoleon I,* Leipzig: Industrie Comptoir), c. 1810, plate H. Staatsbibliothek zu Berlin—Preußischer Kulturbesitz.

I.

Grand Costume du Maître des Cérémonies.

Grofs-Costüm des Ceremonienmeisters.

Plate 20. Costume drawings of the state uniform for a master of ceremonies *(Costumes de la Cour impériale de France. Neueste Hof- und Staatstrachten in Frankreich, vorgeschrieben vom Kaiser Napoleon I,* Leipzig: Industrie Comptoir), c. 1810, plate I. Staatsbibliothek zu Berlin—Preußischer Kulturbesitz.

K.

Grand Costume du Préfet de Département

Groß-Costüm eines Departement-Präfects.

Plate 21. Costume drawings of the state uniform for a department's prefect *(Costumes de la Cour impériale de France. Neueste Hof- und Staatstrachten in Frankreich, vorgeschrieben vom Kaiser Napoleon I,* Leipzig: Industrie Comptoir), c. 1810, plate K. Staatsbibliothek zu Berlin—Preußischer Kulturbesitz.

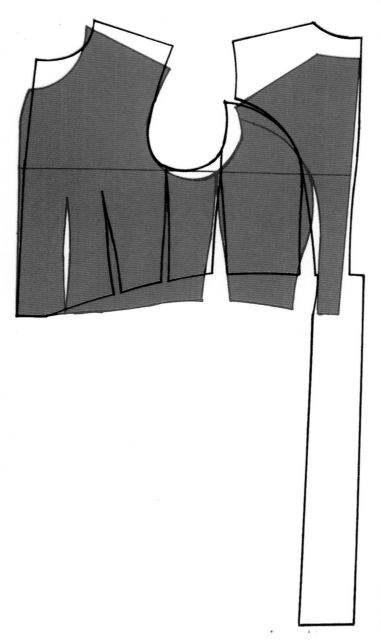

Plate 22. Drawing comparing the pattern construction of a modern tail-coat (1999) with the trunk of tailcoat from around 1900. (Drawing: Kerstin Flintrop, *Nach Rang und Stand* [2002], fig. 17.)

Plate 23. Uniform of a Prussian chamberlain, 1840s. Private collection; photo: Dieter Gasse.

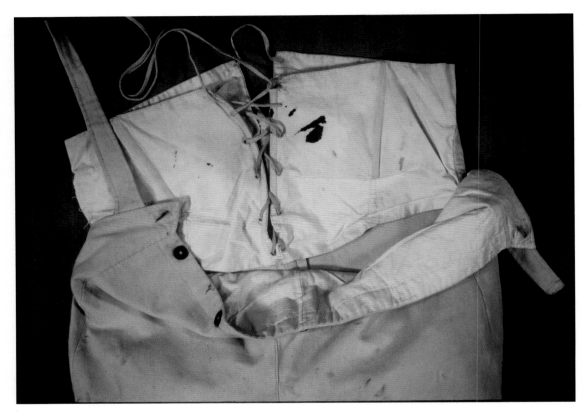

Plate 24. Detail of a Prussian chamberlain's trousers with a corset-like restraint, 1840s. Private collection; photo: Dieter Gasse.

Plate 25. Bruno Paul, *The "Dancing Hussars" from Krefeld.* Caricature for *Simplicissimus,* 1906. Private collection.

Plate 26.   Spring lorgnette with built-in watch formed in the shape of an early guitar, c. 1830. Gold frame and case with a ribbon loop attached to the angled pegboard. The blue enameled lid is studded with rose diamonds. The item was supplied in a genuine tortoiseshell case. This is another combined device in which the lenses of the lorgnette cannot be used to read the watch face. This object was probably for use by a lady, although this is unclear. Perhaps it is the sort of thing an elegant might choose to buy for his lady. (British Optical Association Museum, Catalogue number: LDBOA1999.1946) © The College of Optometrists, London.

Plate 27. An extremely rare single-draw spyglass with blue-and-white Wedgwood barrel, gilt trim, and ivory eyepiece. The decoration depicts the marriage of Cupid and Psyche. The maker's name is engraved on the tube: Watkins & Hill, Charing Cross. English, c. 1820. Watkins & Hill was a small family business but of great repute, with a prestigious location in central London and some leading clients. The company issued its last catalogue in 1845. (British Optical Association Museum, Catalogue number LDBOA1999.1517) © The College of Optometrists, London.

Plate 28. Brass jealousy glass for surreptitious sideways viewing. It features an engraved cap and medallion, depicting a dog and a basket of fruit, and a striped pattern on the barrel, and it incorporates a pill receptacle and scent bottle with brass stopper. Made by Bointaburet of Paris, early nineteenth century. Although it might be assumed today that this was probably made for a lady, this is unclear. The inclusion of the rococo-style dog and basket of fruit and flowers points to a vision of eighteenth-century gallantry also associated with men. (British Optical Association Museum LDBOA1999.1916) © The College of Optometrists, London.

Plate 29. Lover's eye portrait. Miniature in watercolor on ivory of a man's left eye and brow. Set into a round brooch with a surround of graduated natural half-pearls. English, c. 1810–1820. Eye jewelry commonly depicts a female lover or companion; this more unusual example of a man's eye indicates the sensuality with which the male body was also embued in the early modern period. Courtesy The Three Graces. Jewelry of the Ages, www.georgianjewelry.com.

SUN AND SWIM FASHIONS

...Previewed at Palm Springs

Fabulous Palm Springs, mecca of Hollywood film stars and socialites in the national picture, is the birthplace of fashion trends for summer months to come. Catalina, Official Swim Suit of the Miss Universe Beauty Pageant held annually at Long Beach, California, plays an important role in the Palm Springs resort season picture with styles that are colorful, comfortable, pretty and practical in the California tradition of casual, easy living.

when it makes fashion news . . . it's

Catalina

LOOK FOR THE ⟍ FLYING FISH

Plate 30. Catalina's advertisement used images of casual lifestyles in California to promote its clothes. The image appeared in the national trade journal *Men's Wear* in 1953. Courtesy of In Mocean, Inc.

Plate 31. *Japanese Male Youth,* c. 2004. The type of mannerism associated with aspects of Japanese youth culture is better understood when set against an understanding of how Western fashion arrived in Japan, creating a system of blending and bricolage quite unlike the West. In this photograph, taken at a train station in Harajuku, the significance of cut and the space between the body and clothes in creating the effect of fashion is evident. The extraordinary range of mobile phone ornaments take on the ghost of devices formerly suspended by urban men from their robes, the *inroe* and *netsuke*. Labels and insignia range from Louis Vuitton, to Winnie the Pooh, and Santa Fe. The ways in which shoes are worn and thus modified should be noted. Photograph: Gael Pantin, Singapore.

Plate 32. Rennie Ellis, *Mick Treloar fashion shoot,* Melbourne, Australia, c. 1969. Courtesy Rennie Ellis Photographic Archive, St Kilda, Melbourne.

the subject of more academic nostalgia—both simple and reflexive—than any other period or genre in pop history (see Sabin 1999). However, what was important in Hebdige, for example, was the serious consideration of the clothed body in popular music culture and its role in the politics of resignification. But there is a significant absence in this work when it comes to exploring the clothed body *in* popular musical performance (see McDonald 1997: 281). The other exception is the longstanding debate about Madonna (cf. Fiske 1992; Kaplan 1987)—what Frith has termed the 'academic Madonna business' (Frith 1996: 14)—which has been important in opening up discussion about the performance of gender and introducing the role of clothing and fashion in pop performance (against a rock culture suspicious of both pop and fashion). Here though there is a neglect to consider the relationship between clothing and performance within the specificities of popular music culture.[6]

AUTHENTICITY

Authenticity is a central issue in discussions about the value of clothing in popular music culture, as it is a central issue in contemporary cultural studies more broadly. But the notion of authenticity is also a problem and clearly presents difficulties in discussions of popular music (see Thornton 1995). These are most apparent in the extreme ways the term is used: between its unselfconscious use in everyday discourse; and as one of the most perplexing concepts in contemporary cultural criticism. This critical self-consciousness has not extended into popular music culture itself and, indeed, the value judgement that a sound, a performance, the way a particular group is dressed, is 'real' or 'authentic' is a routine designation often made with no more justification than 'I feel it in my gut'—an assertion frequently offered by journalists, musicians and audiences. These inconsistent judgements (about music, performance and dress) take their power from this type of definitional imprecision and, as a consequence, their routine use in day-to-day discourse is obscured and their force left unchallenged.

In rock and popular music, this lack of justification and perpetual mystification of the term makes analysis all the more difficult—a version of 'don't analyze it, feel it!' However, as authenticity is more used of rock and pop than any other cultural form, it is clearly important to investigate the ramifications of these apparently unselfconscious descriptions and judgements. We could ask, following Judith Butler: 'what does "transparency" keep obscure?' (Butler 1999: xix).

Despite the increased prominence of theoretical anti-essentialism in cultural criticism, essentialist ideas and arguments have played a powerful and defining role in the history of popular music. What makes music particularly susceptible to essentialist notions of identity is that music has often been valued within rock ideology precisely for its ability to release repressed desires, to strip away the layers of 'artifice' and reveal the core personality, the essence of race, humanity or sexuality obscured underneath (see Middleton 1990). In 'orthodox' rock history, this ability to facilitate the emergence of an essence of identity has led certain musical attributes— the 'grain of the voice' (Barthes 1977: 181), the characteristics of a performance or body—to be read as the expression of a unique identity. Middleton, for example, has drawn attention to how forms of sexualized or libidinal authenticity have invoked essentialist conceptions of the 'pure' sexual body. This is a common position in rock ideology and 'here libidinal energies are thought to be channelled into musical forms ... radical rock was supposed to provide a direct route to the unconscious, a way to plug in your libido' (Middleton 1990: 259). While this may be powerfully *felt* in certain quarters, its attempted universality masks its situatedness, and frequently sexual authenticity in rock has been underpinned by a particular heterosexual and masculine discourse (see Frith and McRobbie 1990; Frith 1990). Therefore, the discourse of authenticity may serve to erect a false naturalism (with masculinity as its centre), sustained by a sex–gender essentialism that maintains unequal power relations and closes off other ways of envisaging identity, other possibilities of pleasure and performing.

This distrust of fashion is closely related to rock culture's suspicion of the emergence of music video; which has made 'fashion' and 'image', in Will Straw's words,

> more important than the experience of music itself, with effects which were to be feared … the potential difficulty for artists with poor 'images', the risk that theatricality and spectacle would take precedence over intrinsically 'musical' values … [This is part of] a longstanding caution about the relationship between rock music as a culture of presumed resistance and television as the embodiment of mainstream show business and commercial culture. (Straw 1993: 3–4)

However, against the thrust of the positions described by Straw, other commentators have pointed out that rock has always depended on visual images, on fashion, theatricality and spectacle. Shumway (1992) has argued against the orthodox narrative, and suggested that even the early performances and success of Elvis Presley were attributable as much to his visual performance and the significance of the clothed body as to 'the music' itself.

The 'birth' of Anglo-American rock culture marks something of a paradigm shift in the history of fashion, with popular music taking over from cinema as the main source of fashion influence. However, the orthodox narrative of rock history conceals the significance of performers like Little Richard, who played a formative role in articulating the gender-dissonant complexities of performance, the body and dress. Indeed, the performative possibilities of black performers have been overlooked by a more general rock discourse that has validated black music as the authentic expression of racial 'essence', and a key aspect of this has been the longstanding 'necessary connection' forged between black people, black culture (clothes and performance styles) and music-making: between blackness, the body, rhythm and sexuality. This emphasis on validating black music as *the* marker of sexualized authenticity has overlooked the way that black music cultures have used clothes both to undermine conspicuous consumption and to question essentialist notions about the body, gender and sexuality.[7]

What I am describing here is the tendency within a rock culture concerned with authenticity (of music, sexuality, identity) to see clothes as the 'veneer', as essentially fickle, to 'look through them', to value what is *inside*. For rock culture, it is 'others' who wear masks, others who dress up, '"we" just are'. As Paul McDonald has observed, unravelling masculinity is difficult, its false universality hard to pick apart:

> [T]he production of feminine appearance has required cosmetics and clothing to create a glamorous surface—so that it is known that femininity is 'made up' … [D]efinitions of masculinity are in contrast imagined as apparently unconstructed authentic identities … [A]ttempts to read masculinity as performance may be actually more difficult than seeing femininity as a construction. (McDonald 1997: 283)

However, as Bruzzi points out, 'clothes and superficialities *are* identity' (Bruzzi 1997b: 143; emphasis added) and cannot be swept aside by some dubious appeal to the transhistorical body underneath. Even clothing that appears to be unconcerned with fashion, or that seeks to establish itself as beyond (or 'outside') fashion and not draw attention to itself, still has to be 'read' as significant on such terms: 'unconcern' has to be carefully constructed to be read as unconcern.

Therefore, those clothing styles which attempt to conceal their constructedness warrant the most analytical attention (as these are the styles that have sought to evade 'capture').

TENSIONS IN THE POP MATRIX: 'BRING "THE NOISE"'

Riviere's idea of femininity-as-masquerade has acted as a powerful challenge to the essentialism that underpins 'commonsense' thinking about the inter-relationship of sexuality and gender (Riviere 1986 [1929]). Essentialist discourse posits that sex and gender go together: determine, explain and express one another. This, a primary example of Stephen Heath's 'sexual fix'—the way we are *fixed* by the discourse of sexual authenticity—suggests an imaginary unity between biological sex, anatomy, gender, clothing and behaviour (Heath 1982). In other words, gender is the outward expression of some inner sexual 'essence'. As we have seen, 'dress codes have been conditioned by a belief that clothes should solidify gender identity, not question it'; where clothes are simply 'reflective of the dominant, established and unquestioned sex of the wearer' (Bruzzi 1997b: 149).

What has been important about Riviere's argument to debates about gender, clothing and the performing body is that there is no 'original', 'authentic', or primary sexuality behind the mask. If, as Bruzzi asserts, there is 'no difference between womanliness and masquerade' and 'no such thing as "genuine" womanliness, then there is no such thing as "genuine" manliness or a stable subjective male position' (Bruzzi 1997b: 129) untouched by changes in fashion, culture and history. A recognition of the performative aspect of gender helps foreground the 'constructedness' of both sex and gender, prizing open their mutually sustaining necessity and making apparent their relationality; holding sex and gender *apart*. As sex and gender are performative, they must be continuously re-enacted in social situations. 'Identity', as Frith

puts it, 'comes from the outside, not the inside; it is something we put or try on, not something we reveal or discover' (Frith 1996: 273) and popular music plays a powerful role in how we *learn* to be sexed, gendered subjects. However, as Frith moves on to argue, while clothes are

> social signs ... written on the body itself, on its shape, its size, its texture, its curves and bones and flesh and hair ... [s]tage clothes ... do not transcend physical circumstances ... [but] depend, for their effect, as much on the musical relationships between a group's members as on their design features. How musicians look ... clearly affects how at first we hear them ... But we don't just experience a musician's body as costumed. (Frith 1996: 219)

Put differently; the issue in popular music performance is not clothes, but clothing in performance; popular music is about clothes *and* stars, clothing on bodies performing popular music. This means that the *meaning* of dress will be inflected, altered, amplified or contradicted by the musical and performing conventions and associations within which they are placed. Furthermore, clothes work not only within and against musical and performance conventions (the internal conventions of the song) but externally, as contrasted to other work by the same group or singer, as well as along chains of similarity and difference with other music, clothes and performance styles. Popular music has its own history of performances, its own performing discourse, its own way of organizing meaning and value. In validating and finding pleasure in popular music performers, in their music, in their clothes, their bodies, we are considering a performance, not in isolation, but as a performance within a history of performances, the enactment of identity within a series of identities. And often the most interesting, most disruptive music works by articulating the historically and culturally salient contradictions.

Not only does the performance of gender need to be understood within pop-specific discourse, but a further problem in evaluation is the 'artifice-authenticity' binary itself. This binary mutates and changes, meaning that performative artifice may itself be continually reclaimed and ghettoized by essentialist, 'naturalised' heterosexual (and gay) discourse (see Smelik 1998).[8] In this respect, performance that works at a distance from the organic paradigm of the masculine rock centre can be seen as just 'gay music' conforming to the most sedimented notions of gay culture. Gayness may be linked with modes of performing artifice (types of clothing and gesture) and 'playfulness' that may in particular contexts serve the needs of essentialism. Even pop performers such as Divine, Erasure, Boy George, and Marc Almond, who had an historically important role in articulating sex–gender dissonance, may be seen as 'safe', conforming to the broader expectations of heterosexual hegemony. While, as Bruzzi argues, 'lang, Madonna, Lennox and Harvey all, in different ways, are performative; in that they are constantly putting on show the moment of gender construction' (Bruzzi 1997a: 198), this misses telling which performances by the artists mentioned above are performative, for whom, why and how?[9]

A further issue relates more specifically to authenticity and performance. As Frith argues,

[Performance involves gestures which are both false (they are only put on for the situation) and true (they are appropriate to the emotions being described, expressed or invoked) ... [Certain performers] have grasped the camp point that the truth of a feeling is an aesthetic truth, not a moral one; it can only be judged formally, as a matter of gestural grace ... 'Sincerity' ... cannot be measured by searching for what lies behind the performance; if we are moved ... we are moved by what we immediately hear and see. (Frith 1996: 215).

And even though some performers seek to overcome tensions (of gender, sexuality, authenticity and artifice), every performance is at least potentially a combination of sincere and insincere elements.

What I am arguing then is that there is no master performative template. Performativity in pop can only be understood with attention to pop's specific modes of performance and value. In pop, some forms of drag, cross-dressing and androgyny may be overwhelmed by the discursive, rendered 'safe', and seen as the 'innate' expression of 'others' on essentialist terms. Put differently: certain artists may lend themselves to being valued as 'authentically gay'.

Furthermore, as Bruzzi argues, we need to differentiate between terms like 'drag', 'cross-dressing' and 'androgyny' (as these may be used interchangeably), but we need to do so in a popular musical context (Bruzzi 1997b: 149). Also, we need to consider differentiations within these key terms: between misogynistic and anti-misogynistic drag and cross-dressing; between naturalized and performative androgyny. Not all acts of 'drag', cross-dressing or gender-blurring are subversive or radical; not all performances hold sex and gender in distinction. Stella Bruzzi (1997a), for example, in a discussion of k. d. lang, differentiates between that singer's conventional 'naturalized' androgyny after 'coming out', one which has been recouped to essentialist discourse ('fitting "the truth" about lesbians'), and a performative, dissonant androgyny that 'signals and re-signals the space between subject and construction' (Bruzzi 1997a: 205). The knowledge about 'coming out', Bruzzi further argues, creates a narrative within which lang's performance and meaning are anchored—a 'shift in not knowing to knowing' (Bruzzi 1997a: 205), a move from suspense, noise, 'inbetweenness' to coherence, closure and naturalization.

Importantly, Bruzzi's reading pays attention to both the associative semiotics of lang's clothing and how these interact with music conventions, such as genre, as well as discourse about lang (star biography, the music press). In terms of authenticity, what is significant about lang is the 'space' created: how she simultaneously inhabits and departs from these conventions in a combination of sincere and inauthentic elements.

'The pleasure [or lack of it] is in not knowing why and how these elements fit together' (Bruzzi 1997a: 192).

A major part of my argument centres on the importance of considering the pop 'text'. Pop's mobile and shifting textuality (of which clothing and fashion are an integral part) may itself problematize the idea of authenticity, as the rock 'text' is not quite as clear as in other cultural forms. Moreover, rock and pop's mobile intertextuality may set up tensions amongst its various levels.[10] This occurs in three main ways. Tensions may be set up between music, performance, clothing, the body, video and 'star text', where some areas may be regarded as 'authentic' and other areas less so (as between music and video; rock and fashion). Second, tensions may operate historically when a group or performer begins to change sound and style (as in k. d. lang pre–and post–'coming out'). Third, as Frith has argued, any pop performance occurs within a 'history of performances' and what these, over time, are taken to mean, prompting us to consider how performers interpret past performances, evaluating their 'usefulness' to the context in which they find themselves.

This is in part why I have elected to discuss two moments of the fashion–pop nexus in particular (and they are both connected). The first is the so-called New Pop period of the early 1980s. The second is the pop group Suede and in particular their self-titled debut album (*Suede* 1993) and its performance in the video *Love and Poison* of the same year.

NEW POP

New Pop has borne the brunt of rock scorn, regarded as exhibiting an excessive dependence on fashion, and treated with suspicion and disdain—in many ways the popular musical equivalent of the women's picture in film studies. In this respect, pop that was discursively linked to consumer culture was seen as essentially 'feminine' and at odds with the machismo of most mainstream rock. Moreover, rock's 'subsequent corruption and "emasculation" are understood as a straightforward effect of the rock business's attempt to control its market ... The decline of rock 'n roll rested on a process of "feminization"' (Frith and McRobbie 1990: 383). Hence the 'sell-out' narrative of punk's (rock) decline into the consumer co-option of New Pop.

In this way, New Pop was seen as the popular musical counterpart of Thatcherism, as the outward manifestation of Thatcherite ideology, as a cultural form whose 'real' meaning lay in the celebration of conspicuous consumption. There are two problems with this argument. First, it depends on a simple correspondence theory: rock discourse has viewed the music of the period as simply embodying the values of an era. This tendency of seeing music as corresponding to eras in such a way is, of course, problematic. As John Hill has argued, there is a danger of 'reading off meanings in culture from the presumed politics of Thatcherism' (Hill 1999: 28–9). Second, after the 'heroic' resistance to consumer capitalism embodied in punk, New Pop could be constructed as *bourgeois* to punk's apparent proletarianism (or is it with hindsight punk's masculinity to New Pop's 'femininity'?). As punk dress was understood within subcultural theory as 'not really "fashion" at all', the operation of clothing and make-up in punk could be held at some distance from the 'feminine' world of fashion.[11] Even critics such as Peter York could retrospectively join in and attack New Pop's femininity, its 'bad' music, and assert that the significance of the early 1980s was merely as a period for 'dressing up' (York and Jennings 1995). In both cases, this served to displace what was 'noisy' about New Pop—namely New Pop's 'play' on gender expectations. As Paul McDonald has warned,

the difficulty with limiting the reading of gendered performance to items of costume is that it can suggest that while forms of dress are obviously something put on, it could be presumed that the body which lies underneath is a natural and inevitable fact. (McDonald 1997: 282)

What this does is conceal a number of significant changes that the period began to articulate in musical, performance and clothing terms. Here any subversion at the level of clothing and performance is displaced by an appeal to an underlying gender naturalism—clothes are again just the veneer. Of course, the music and performance helped support this, as much of New Pop was defined by a suppression of libidinal conventions. As opposed to strutting, prowess, chest hair, genitals, inconspicuous clothing and the 'bump and grind' of 'the hard rock beat', guitar solos and phallic posturing, New Pop performers comprised a different semiotic: stillness, immobility and camp gestures, and favoured the 'plastic', the 'artificial', the shiny, the conspicuously feminine, over the organic and the natural. Discursively, however, this 'playfulness' was peripheralized and issues about gender and performance were displaced (meaning that New Pop was spoken about within a discourse of kitsch nostalgia—as an era of bad music and making money).

But what was significant about aspects of New Pop was the manner in which clothes came to the fore—not as a layer of 'artifice' that left naturalized (hetero)sexuality intact underneath, but the manner in which gender assumptions were problematized. But New Pop was by no means reducible to the discourses of gender and sexuality. An important feature of New Pop fashion was its 'play' on heritage costume. This was more than nostalgia. As McRobbie has argued, styles such as these 'are neither nostalgic in essence nor without depth. Nostalgia indicates a desire to recreate the past faithfully, and to wallow in such mythical representation' (McRobbie 1989: 41). Therefore, heritage costume was appropriated, rendered excessive, and this was signalled by pop fashion's more general

'knowingness ... wilful anarchy ... irrepressible optimism ... colour, exaggeration, humour and disavowal of the conventions of adult dress' (McRobbie 1989: 42). In this way, New Pop was able to draw attention to the constructedness of heritage, to 'make strange' its pleasures (especially as these clothing styles occurred within a very modern, artificial soundscape and performance mode). Aspects of costume were not only rendered 'strange' by the excessive manner of their 'style' (exaggerated scale, colour and the manner in which they were re-signified with other elements), but in their utilization on performing bodies in the context of sounds that connote the 'future', modernity and so forth. In performance, New Pop artists favoured strategies that downplayed, even exposed, the traditional masculine signifiers required to perform 'powerfully'. As Stan Hawkins has argued, artists such as The Pet Shop Boys 'remind us that music can function as a key vehicle in deconstructing fixed notions of gendered identity in everyday life' (Hawkins 1997: 118).

Thus, the New Pop semiotic worked to form a 'fit' among the different areas of pop's textual matrix, to carefully construct the signification of 'artifice'. This was based on a self-conscious critique of rock in order to counter the organic conventions and masculinist ideology with which rock had become associated. But in time this mode itself became devoid of tension, of contradiction—in other words, the conventions on which signalling the performative depend have to be refreshed, lest they become ghettoized into serving the needs of essentialism.[12]

SUEDE: BEYOND CAMP?

Suede emerged in the early 1990s, a period marked by the rise to prominence of 'the lad' and a new type of 'old' masculinity (see Mort 1996). This, of course, was personified in the rock group Oasis and the 'movement', termed 'New Rock' (Brit-rock) or 'new authenticity', which marked a retreat into a more convention-alised and conservative masculinity and its accompanying rock performance style.[13]

Suede's eponymous debut album went to Number 1 in March 1993, and such was the controversy that the band's every move became much debated in the music press (Savage 1996: 341). The cover, borrowed from the 1970s book of lesbian erotica, *Stolen Glances,* which featured two people of indeterminate gender kissing, announced much of what the band was about: Suede was regarded as offering a 'gleeful trashing of sex and gender boundaries' (Savage 1996: 342), one that is all the more significant given the context into which the band emerged. Discourse in the music press plays a powerful role in framing discussions and interpretations about popular music, mediating between star and audience. The significant and much quoted example here is Brett Anderson's (Suede's lead singer) controversial claim to *Melody Maker* in February 1993, that he 'sees himself as a bisexual man who has never had a homosexual experience' (quoted in Wise 1998). The band here could be recouped to the orthodox position—that Suede is in a long line of male heterosexual pop performers who have colonized aspects of an 'excessive femininity' and the iconographies of 'gay culture' (see Reynolds and Press 1995). However, this accusation of gender-tourism is too neat as it drags us back to essentialism—that sexuality, gender, identity, performance and musical expression all go together.[14] Alternatively, Judith Butler's concept of drag as performative is useful in understanding the group's performance and its significance.

In one vital sense, Anderson's pronouncement supports the indeterminacy of Suede's performance of gender, not in a way that supports heterosexual masculine complexity, but rather undermines it, foregrounding the dissonance between sex and gender and revealing their constructedness. Suede destabilizes the naturalized heterosexism of rock, de-essentializing it. We could follow Bruzzi (1997a) and argue that if

Brett Anderson were to 'come out', this would anchor the narrative about Suede into ontological sex–gender security: to 'fit the fit' ('oh, Anderson is gay, therefore ...') and the music and performance become explained).[15] We can get a glimpse of this line of argument in Suede's debut review in *Village Voice.* The reviewer, Barry Walters, teases out some of the complexity of Suede but argues that he'd 'prefer it if Anderson was a bona fide homo, rather than merely an enthusiastic student' (Walters 1993: 769).[16] But surely the point is that there is no arrival into the essentialized, naturalized world, no point of closure, of sex and gender certitude. We could already conclude that Suede has successfully put on 'the show of gender construction'. However, what interests me is why and how, in what way? How is Suede different from Madonna, New Pop, The Pet Shop Boys or k. d. lang—artists who are taken to be, in some way or other, performative?[17]

To understand this we have to turn to consider the specificities of popular music culture itself. Here, it is important to bear in mind that popular music can be disruptive owing precisely to the tensions set up amongst its various levels and their attendant associations. As we have seen, a great deal of rock and pop strives to form a 'fit' among all the elements concerned, whether into the discourse of authenticity, or of artifice.

There appear to be two main dynamics at work with Suede in its relationship to pop history, costume and performance. The first involves a dynamic with New Pop and a recognition of the limitations of its particular discourse of 'artifice'. The second is a musical appropriation (and critique) of masculinist rock naturalism, the 'New Rock' or 'new authenticity' associated with, say, Oasis. Similarly, in musical terms Suede (circa 1993) did not use synthesisers, sequencing or other forms of 'electronica', which runs in contradistinction to New Pop.

Suede is something of a hybrid of aspects of New Pop performance styles and the codes of British counter-cultural rock and, significantly, occupies the hinterland between rock and pop (between masculine and feminine, authenticity and artifice). A major influence here is David Bowie—perhaps the most famous singer associated with gender-blurring.[18] While, in one way, Bowie is regarded as something of a 'pioneer', it could be argued that for some time he has been valued primarily within a discourse of hagiographic artistry; that Bowie's 'experiments' are subordinate to Bowie as 'great figure'. Pleasure in Bowie's chameleonic elasticity and role-playing, therefore, could be viewed differently: he, more than any other artist, has been able to colonize other identities and their associations, elaborating the already-elaborated subjectivity of the white male (see Dyer 1997). Suede, in the period I am discussing, is, by contrast, a first-album band without the same prominent 'auteur' myth, and no narrative security to ground what is dissonant.

Similarly, Suede's difference from New Pop needs to be understood in relation to the changing dynamics of popular culture and readings of performance, clothing and their performative value. While Suede could be located within a more widely discussed heritage pop/rock trend, exhibiting a self-consciousness about both English pop's (great) past and the codes of counter-cultural rock, this is by no means all the band is about and such a critical trajectory reduces the complexity of pop pleasure and meaning. While these heritage elements are, without doubt, in place, they are utilized in a manner that reveals an increased critical self-consciousness about how popular music makes meaning and, in particular, what music, clothing and the body together signify. Suede's 'gender-as-masquerade' offers few of the traditional signifiers of drag and cross-dressing and is, perhaps, based on an implicit recognition of the limitations of particular drag/cross-dressing practices and their (in)ability to signify sex–gender dissonance.

What is immediately noticeable about the way Suede is dressed is the absence of a conspicuous or clearly signalled male 'dandyism' and its associated shiny, 'inauthentic' apparel. In one sense, Suede avoids the usual camp tropes of dress as 'feminine excess'. What Suede (particularly Anderson) wears is not conspicuously high fashion, or novel or shocking. Anderson is dressed simply in black (black being, of course, the favoured colour of subcultural Bohemia): loose-fitting Levi's and a tight-sleeved top with a low-cut circular neck, and only the latter has feminine connotations. Elsewhere, in terms of music and dress, Suede owes a great deal to rock's past. With regard to movement and posture, hair and clothes, Bernard Butler invokes the image of 'legendary' rock guitarist, Jimmy Page.[19] Sonically, in addition to Page, Butler owes a great deal to Jimi Hendrix (particularly so on the track I have chosen for discussion, 'He's Dead'). This sense of rock traditionalism is carried through to video release, *Love and Poison* (1993): Suede elected to release a 'live' performance video as opposed to video compilation or experimental film, in the manner of their New Pop antecedents.[20]

Musically, 'He's Dead' is convincing (i.e. 'authentic') rock with counter-cultural connotations, with an extended Hendrix-style guitar solo of swirling feedback and distorted 'wah-wah' effects. However, the conventional meanings associated with the form are offset and a number of tensions/contradictions opened up. The first of these relates to the song's address—the use of 'I', 'you', we', 'she'—with Anderson unambiguously singing, mournfully, about a 'he'.[21] The second is how the clothing is inhabited on the performing body in question within this music-performance context, with the tall and slim Anderson invoking the image of the feminine modelesque.

Anderson's Levi's are not figure-hugging or tight, but styled to gather around the hips. Together with his body posture and the figure-hugging top, these tend to signify traditional notions of 'womanliness' (i.e. wider hips and thighs to the normative masculinity). In movement, the singer's style runs against the territorial strut associated with rock and men performing 'powerfully'. Importantly, during the guitar solo—that rock cliché of masculine phallic prowess— Anderson turns his back to the audience and begins a series of non-normative movements. This 'turning away' works in opposition to the thrust of most phallic rock. Attention is taken away from the front of the body, most particularly the genitals, to which, as I argued previously, attention is not drawn either in the framing or by Anderson's dress-code. This fits the more general discourse of avoiding traditional markers of the 'authentically' male.[22]

Instead, Anderson offers his backside to the audience, pushing it out, slowly wiggling it. He also pulls his legs together to construct and accentuate a feminine body shape (traditional sexualized 'womanliness'). Most significantly, utilizing the low-cut top, he pushes his shoulderblades together to form 'breasts', creating the image of a cleavage (significantly swapping the plunged front of orthodox performing masculinity for a plunged back that reveals the constructedness of sexual desire and creates a gap between sex and gender).[23] This invites the gaze on to the cleavage as signifier of male heterosexual desire while simultaneously problematizing it, foregrounding its constructedness, its role in the idea of 'femininity-as-masquerade', as well as revealing the performative aspect of the sexualized, gendered body (Riviere 1986; Bruzzi 1997a, 1997b). Anderson becomes a 'back-to-front' woman, a distorted, 'cubist' composite of constructed sexualized fragments. In this way, Suede signifies gender dissonance/gender confusion, staving off the either–or binary between straight and gay; masculine and feminine; authenticity and artifice. This is accompanied by a self-conscious use of the microphone, which is played with suggestively, with the cable used as a whip at the song's beginning and also pulled, suggestively, across the singer's backside.

In one sense, Anderson is adopting the performance conventions of certain strands of pornography to generate a whole series of uncertainties around the construction of desire: Is this symbolic of anal sex? Is this drag? Is he creating the image of the sexualized woman? Is he gay? Are we, the audience, supposed to feel desire? This confusion is amplified due to an avoidance of traditional drag, as any elements of drag utilized here avoid the 'traditional' signifiers of 'feminine excess' at the level of make-up and costume, and offer a more modern, 'everyday' 'femininity'.[24]

The image here is not simply of transvestism, drag or androgyny, but is something of a hybrid of aspects of all three categories. If the image is mainly androgynous it is not a conventionalised androgyny, but one that simultaneously invokes the constructedness and the 'polymorphous perversity' of sexual desire. As Bruzzi argues,

the blurred ambiguity of the image ... makes androgyny a far more erotic form of transvestism ... than cross-dressing, because it is not defined by an acceptance of the fixity of gender binaries, but rather by the effect of ambiguity.

The androgynous body is never complete because it is innately unstable; it always possesses the capacity for mutability and transformation, And unlike the cross-dressed body, does not hold onto the notion of its single, 'real' sex. (Bruzzi 1997b: 199)

It was certainly rare to see the musical conventions associated with masculine prowess inhabited in a way that rendered ambiguous the performance of masculinity. However, the Suede performance is not just 'playful'; the band does not inhabit the conventions of countercultural rock in a simple ironic, or merely 'playful' way (both of these terms are often used in a way that shuts out their complexity in order to forge a sense of progressiveness). In fact, musically, these conventions are heavily invested in and inhabited convincingly. It can be countered that there is nothing essential in rock's sound that makes it the natural expression of heterosexist masculinity. As Frith and McRobbie (1990: 386) have argued, 'rock's hard beat may not, in itself, speak in terms of male domination, power or aggression'. The musical conventions and their articulation, in their links to authenticity, invoke 'seriousness' which works outside the conventional discourse of camp. Rather, the conventions of sex–gender blurring are pulled to where they wouldn't normally belong—into organic masculinist rock. The gender dissonance created is forceful precisely because it occurs in a 'naturalized', masculine rock space.

Thus, Suede are the more radical for not wholly working within the discourse of artifice, but in the band's articulation of sincere and inauthentic elements; between clothing and the body, the body and performance, clothing and sound, and so on. In one way, rock's 'hard beat' is being 'reclaimed', dislodged from its essentialist masculinist moorings. As Frith and McRobbie (1990: 371) claim in relation to pop, performance and gender: 'the best writers on the subject state the contradictions without resolving them'; it is just as interesting, and more provocative, when popular musical performers do the same.[25] As Judith Butler has argued:

> The moment in which one's staid and usual cultural perceptions fail, when one cannot with surety read the body that one sees, is precisely the moment when one is no longer sure whether the body encountered is that of a man or a woman ... When such categories come into question, the *reality* of gender is also put into crisis: it becomes unclear how to distinguish the real from the unreal. (Butler 1999: xxii–xxiii)

Performers such as Suede represent a brief, if crucial, break 'in the compulsive repetition of normative heterosexuality' and have played a not insignificant part in 'interrogating the binary divide between men and women' (McRobbie 1999: 86).

NOTES

Reprinted with permission from Noel McLaughlin, "Rock, Fashion and Performativity," in *Fashion Cultures: Theories, Explorations and Analysis,* ed. S. Bruzzi and P. Church Gibson (London and New York: Routledge, 2000), 264–85.

1. A significant feature of this 'fashion-neglect', as Church Gibson moves on to point out, is that camera angles and lighting styles have occupied much more serious scholarly attention than the semiotics of costume. This, in one sense, may be read as part of a masculinist agenda that has valued 'the labour of the technical' over fashion labour and the development of a semiotics of dress. In other words, within the history of the academic 'culture disciplines', some codes have been given priority over others.

2. I am greatly indebted to the members of Suede and to Mehelli at Nude Records for their enthusiasm, support and the use of images of Suede in performance.

3. While masculine attire in rock may have been used for sexual display, it was never reducible to this; male rock could set itself up as being about more than 'just clothes and sex'.

4. As Angela McRobbie has pointed out, cultural studies themselves have been seen as 'merely fashionable', as 'feminine', within the masculine academy; that much of the study of culture is focused on the 'trivial' compared to, say, the serious study of 'hard' economic realities (McRobbie 1999: 99). Again, this is regrettable because it overlooks the possibility of where changes might emerge.

5. It is important to point out here that even though I have discussed these magazines together, their construction and treatment of masculinity, in terms of the body and dress, vary greatly.

6. However, not only has the Madonna debate dominated discourse about popular music and gender, it has, like punk before it, pushed out to the margins discussion of other artists' performative moments.

7. For a more detailed discussion of the issues of black musical expression and the operation of authenticity see Gilroy (1993).

8. Smelik notes that essentialism is a powerful discourse within areas of gay culture. By contrast it is important to assert that 'sexuality is not a given of nature but a construct of culture. Thus, the debate shifts from realizing a shared essence to understanding homosexuality as a product of social forces' (Smelik 1998: 144).

9. This is not to dispute that each of the artists mentioned above has at some time articulated radical sex–gender dissonance, but we could take Bruzzi's argument about lang and apply it to Annie Lennox: if there was a performative moment it was *Sweet Dreams,* not the later *Diva.*

10. The study of popular music has needed to be multidisciplinary and attuned to the different areas that comprise popular music culture—audience studies, various forms of textual analysis (performance, video, musicology, the semiotics of clothing: subcultural style) and studies of discourse (debates about popular music, both routine (the music press, the rock biography) and specialist (the journal and textbook)). Here, the role of clothing is clearly of great significance, but needs to be considered in relation to specific musical and discursive contexts and theorized as belonging to a body in musical performance. Arguably, 'reading' the role and function of costume in film and theorizing text–subject relations is less problematic in film studies—the audience's relationship to the form is taken to be clearer. In the cinema the audience is conceived as centred—seated in the dark, fixed and facing the screen. Fashion and popular music by contrast are less anchored in a single (relatively), discrete experience and may be viewed and enjoyed in a variety of different contexts—on the street, club, catwalk, live performance and so on.

11. As Davis argues, much of the objection to fashion within subculturalism is based on 'utilitarian outrage' (Davis 1992: 168), with fashion seen as the height of 'wastefulness, frivolity, impracticality, and vanity' (ibid.). Fashion is constructed as working against the modernist impulse of 'form following function'. Hence, within Hebdige's narrative, punk has to be anchored to its 'function' as subcultural resistance, and distance itself from the 'feminine' (whereas, of course, much of punk (anti)fashion was extremely 'impractical' and expensive).

12. As Richard Middleton has argued, particular musical sounds (guitars signifying warmth, passion and emotion; synthesizers, carrying connotations of coldness, modernity and the future) have particular ideological associations attached to them that once consolidated, become very difficult to dislodge (Middleton 1990: 90). We could add clothing and performance styles to this list: clothes that are shiny and 'feminine' carry connotations of the orthodoxly 'camp' and so forth.

13. In many respects the performing style of Liam Gallagher could be construed as articulating a type of hysterical masculinity; one defined by a lack of movement, an avoidance of anything vaguely 'feminine' and an attempt to stave off sex and gender ambiguity. Liam in performance (as in interview) was surly, sullen and disinterested. As with other types of masculinity that seek to absent themselves, Liam's performance becomes interesting through what it is not. In this way, the masculine boorishness of Oasis relates to Bruzzi's description of 'manliness as masquerade' which can be regarded as 'a desperate, embarrassing, hysterical reaction to encroaching insignificance' (Bruzzi 1997b: 130).

14. As Frith and Goodwin have argued, these assumptions about a 'natural' relationship between sounds, performance and identity 'began to be unpicked by feminists concerned to expose the gender prejudice of 1960s theories of "liberation" through sex, drugs and rock 'n roll' (Frith and Goodwin 1990: 370).

15. Bruzzi argues that there is an anchorage, a closing down brought about by 'the character coming out of the disguise... revealing who s/he really is' (Bruzzi 1997b: 157). Here, any 'noise' is swept away and the performance fixed within the narrative of ontological sexual authenticity.

16. John Gill (1995), in his book *Queer Noises,* notes the importance of Bowie, who for Gill is evidently 'not gay', in articulating Queer possibilities. Despite this, Gill still relies on a

'you have to be one or the other' position and rarely moves beyond the either/or binary into questioning the constructedness of both sex and gender.

17. It is important also in debates about popular music to consider differentiations within dance culture, as dance is often held up as more 'progressive' in terms of the articulation of gender and sexuality. While 'dance culture', in many areas, offers a more asexual iconography than masculinist rock, this is not always the case. For example, the sounds and fashion iconography of 'boozy Big Beat' were criticized for their masculine boorishness by more 'progressive' quarters of the dance music press. Also, aspects of dance culture have valued strains of hip hop, not as a challenge to notions of rootedness and authenticity, but precisely as a marker of masculine and racial authenticity (see Gilroy 1993: 99–101). Therefore, it is not enough simply to celebrate the artistic creativity of contemporary dance culture wholesale in the manner that Angela McRobbie (1999) does (even if I agree). While the turntable is not phallic-shaped in the manner of the electric guitar, it has been put to similar uses, where the DJ skill of mixing may be valued in much the same way as the guitar solo of yore—as an index of predominately male skill. Even though dance presents DIY opportunities, these may become animated by older aesthetics and values. The old codes of prowess and control haven't disappeared, they have just become transferred into new areas (areas where, it is often predicted, they won't belong).

18. For a discussion of Suede's relationship to Bowie and English suburbia, see Simon Frith's (1997) essay, 'The suburban sensibility in British rock and pop'.

19. He significantly also plays the same two guitars most favoured by Page: the Gibson Les Paul and the Gibson ES335. Suede musically favours the authenticity of the pentatonic Blues scale over the decidedly un-R & B inauthenticity of electronic New Pop.

20. Neil Tennant, for example, disliked playing live, and, by contrast, liked to boast about not being able to 'cut it' live as part of the New Pop critique of rock. The Pet Shop Boys and Soft Cell both experimented in terms of video release, as with much of New Pop, avoiding the associations of the 'live'.

21. In discussions of queer artists a frequent criticism, as in Bruzzi's discussion of k. d. lang, concerns the absence of gender-specific address in favour of a universal one (see Bruzzi 1997a).

22. The guitar solo and its conventionalized links to musical and sexual climax are well known. In the video this is acknowledged and parodied: when the solo hits its peak (climax) we see a shot of what we 'read' as cum hitting glass. This, presumably, is included to help expose and undermine the masculinist conventions of 'phallic' guitar rock.

23. As an index of pop's ability to play with and subvert naturalized (heterosexual) notions of desire, Frith argued in 1985 that 'the sexiest performer' he'd seen 'was, in fact, a boy in Depeche Mode, a dyed blonde in mini-skirt and skimpy top. His shoulder straps kept slipping, leaving me a "heterosexual" man, breathlessly hoping throughout the show to get a glimpse of his breasts' (cited in Frith and Goodwin 1990: 419).

24. Significantly, the singer doesn't wear a wig; rather his hair is cut into a bob—cut up at the back and at one side, and with a long fringe at the front that falls over his face—on the fault line between male and female.

25. This discussion of Suede in performance is greatly indebted to David Dunn's paper 'What does it take to turn you on?': Suede, gender and performativity', presented at The School of Art, The University of Northumbria in May 1998. As is customary, the interpretation of the argument here is entirely my responsibility.

29

THE WARHOL LOOK

Mark Francis and Margery King

Andy Warhol's last public appearance before he died was as a runway model in a January 1987 fashion show at the Tunnel club in New York. It was not an isolated occasion, as Warhol had made a career of modelling in his last years, but it poignantly recalls an aspect of Warhol's work that inflects the better-known images of Warhol as painter, filmmaker, publisher of *Interview*, photographer, author and philosopher, television producer, and socialite.

This book, and the exhibition it accompanies, is the first sustained attempt to trace and clarify Warhol's unflagging interests in glamour, style, and fashion throughout his life, from childhood to his untimely death at the age of fifty-eight. When these subjects are followed closely and sympathetically, they reveal a cohesiveness and consistency in Warhol's life and provide a deeper understanding of the influence of his work than emerges from a focus on individual groups or types of work. Glamour, style, and fashion are fundamental threads from period to period and across each of the media he touched. By observing how Warhol moved, with exceptional fluidity and ease, from making photographs, films, and paintings, to performing as a model for hire, overseeing the publication of *Interview* magazine, and going out to Max's Kansas City, or later Studio 54, a complex and nuanced picture of his achievement can be recognized.

The Warhol look is not a fixed entity. It extrapolates in different directions, and it is itself ephemeral and fleeting. It encompasses the look

he engendered, expressed in fashion terms by elements identifiable with Warhol and his entourage; the way he looked, an imitable personal style; and Warhol's way of looking, his gaze, the discerning, ironical, basilisk look caught in Bill King's photograph on the cover of this book, and documented in thousands of Warhol's own photographs.

Alone among his peers, Warhol became a well-known figure beyond the confines of the art world and entered popular culture itself. During the silver Factory years of 1963 to 1968, what Warhol and his entourage wore, said, and did became just as significant as what they produced or exhibited. Their edgy style and the glamour that emanated from it have repeatedly become points of reference for designers of haute couture and for young people on the streets who reject the snobbery and cost of 'designer' fashion.

The Warhol look continues to have widespread influence, evident in popular fashion television and a rash of recent magazine spreads and films (e.g. *I Shot Andy Warhol* or *Basquiat*), which have reinterpreted recent history in the light of current taste. The look of the sixties and that of the eighties have recently been in vogue, and we may expect other moments to be similarly reincarnated.

In their responses to his intense desire to be looked at, other artists, designers, and photographers can be seen to have important roles in the construction and definition of the styles with which Warhol is now associated; in large part they created the Warhol look. That is, War-hol engendered the look, or successive 'looks,' that were then disseminated and promoted by numerous photographers, personalities, and designers through the mass media of print and television. The Warhol look, a repertoire of styles, has evolved from a phenomenon associated with the artist and his entourage into a pervasive influence on taste. No other artist in the past fifty years has had such effect on the symbols and textures of urban life.

The challenge of this project depends ultimately on the ability of the recording media of film and photography, magazines, and objects such as clothing to fix the images and capture the personalities of Warhol and the other volatile characters in his world. Photographs are the principal means by which the Warhol look has been disseminated from the early sixties until today. Warhol had the foresight to recognize how photography could help create his own image when he encouraged, from 1963 onward, talented photographers such as David McCabe, Billy Name, and Nat Finkelstein to record the activities of his entourage. Many of the resulting images have become, through repeated publication, indelibly linked to our nostalgia for this extraordinary moment in cultural history. These photographs convey the mythic fantasy of the Warhol world, in part through their grainy, documentary, 'hand-held' character. They are constituent parts of the Warhol narrative.

Glamour derives from the aural, iconic attraction that was projected in unprecedented ways by Hollywood films and their stars from the twenties onward. The glowing and silvery quality of film was adumbrated by Warhol in his person, his Factory, and his portraits in painting and on film. The allure of the (principally) female stars created and publicized by the Hollywood film studios was classless and democratic for the first time, and it was disseminated through Hollywood's international film distribution system and by posters and publicity stills. For Warhol, the elements of portraiture—dress, make-up, coiffure, lighting—captured in films or photographs, commingled to create collectible fetishes, objects that informed his tastes, his desires, and his own longing for fame and beauty.

Andy Warhol has long been recognized as a major innovator in avant-garde film, but his fervent desire was to create his own Hollywood-like studio and thereby control the production of glamour. He left an enormous body of work in film, video, and television, much of which has not been distributed for over twenty years, or has only been seen briefly on cable, so its significance has been underestimated. Warhol's earliest documented enthusiasm was for relics of the stars he idolized at the movies in the thirties and forties. We can now see how this desire translated first into collections of film stills and publicity photographs, then into silkscreened paintings, and finally, by other hands, into spectacular painted, embroidered, or sequinned costumes, which—to complete the circle—have been worn by a current generation of models and movie stars.

The film industry and the fashion system became templates for Warhol, providing modi operandi for his creation of art. For example, Warhol adopted the methods of film studios for his *Screen Tests*. With the notion that talent and beauty could be found on the street, and employing the lure of becoming one of his 'Superstars', he co-opted the Hollywood practice of subjecting potential talent to the disciplines of make-up and lighting and then capturing them on film. The fame of the Factory in the sixties attracted dramatic beauties like Edie Sedgwick and Nico, and later such characters as Joe Dallesandro and Jackie Curtis. They performed as 'themselves' in Warhol films, including *Kitchen* (1965), *The Chelsea Girls* (1966), *Trash* (1970), and *Women in Revolt* (1974), and they also fulfilled another important function at the Factory by simply hanging out on the studio 'lot', thereby creating irresistible opportunities for magazine image-makers of the day such as Cecil Beaton, David Bailey, and Bill King.

The difficulty of defining style reflects its mutability and immateriality. It is recognized by association and by signs rather than in canonical certainties. Even in his teenage years in Pittsburgh, Warhol established a distinctive style of dress and speech, hesitant and diffident though it was at first. Style was initially for Warhol a means of declaring himself 'different'.

One can see the evident delight with which he discovered kindred spirits almost immediately on his arrival in New York in 1949. Photographs from this period by his roommate Leila Davies Singeles show a carefree and even joyful attitude among Warhol and his friends and colleagues that was to complicate and darken as the fifties wore on. At this time he could 'fit in' to the world he inhabited, yet it was in this decade that Warhol first altered his body and appearance artificially by cosmetic surgery on his nose and by affecting wigs.

In his art, Warhol did not adopt a signature personal or aesthetic style that remained constant over the years. A part of his reputation was the very unpredictability of his style. He did not, for example, continue to celebrate Hollywood stars after *Marilyn* and *Liz* but widened his range with the *Flowers* and *Disasters* series (both later converted into images on clothing). His response to the idea of style was more subtle than most, insofar as he recognized its mobility (of both time and place) and instability. Early on he embraced the constancy of inconstancy.

For Warhol, a style, a look, a fashion each imply first the appraisal of taste and beauty and then a willingness, even a desire, for change, alteration, and embellishment. Warhol's style of dress changed from a deliberately run-down shabbiness in the early fifties, which elicited sympathy for 'Raggedy Andy' in the commercial art and advertising worlds of Madison Avenue, to the more refined well-tailored suit he acquired in Hong Kong on his first trip abroad in 1956, which was more appropriate to his largely gay, cosmopolitan circle at the café Serendipity. His style continued to change; around 1963, he began to wear striped matelot T-shirts, jeans, and black leather jackets, and after 1968 he preferred more sober tailored jackets and Brooks Brothers shirts or black cashmere turtlenecks worn with jeans.

In his later years he was photographed in all of these outfits and others, a testament to the relaxation of taste generally, but more specifically to Warhol's ability to project his own sensibility, even aura, whether wearing a formal evening tuxedo or (on one occasion in 1981) in drag. As a model, Warhol often wore black as a signifier of his authority and power. While never conforming to a conventional definition of stylishness, Warhol was nonetheless an arbiter of taste and style because of his own willingness to change identities, to become a chameleon of changing styles, to surround himself with acolytes attuned to the latest changes in fashion, and to be both participant and discriminating observer in the process. For Warhol, the exemplars of classic style were his close associates and confidants Fred Hughes and Diana Vreeland.

Fashion as a social system, fashion as a means of distinguishing and delighting in nuance and detail, fashion as an ephemeral, seasonal, extravagant spectacle, fashion as an index of beauty—all these were important for Warhol. He delighted in perverse and artificial sensations and in transgressing the boundaries of the different circles in which he moved. And much of this is plainly transmitted in the work Warhol did, whether making paintings and films in the sixties, or photographing and producing programs for television in the seventies and eighties. The fashion world has an omnivorous appetite for disparate inspirations, and Warhol shared this indiscriminate attitude, paradoxically refining his influences into objects for highly discriminating audiences. Many of Warhol's most important works—the *Marilyn* or *Camouflage* paintings, *Interview* magazine, or the film *Women in Revolt!*—attest to this flexible, unencumbered taste and willingness to experiment. Warhol's way of working was thus as vital, as self-confident, and as free of preconceptions as that of the best designers and editors in the fashion world.

Part of Warhol's fascination with the fashion world was the pleasure he took in attending and photographing the runway shows of Halston and other designers. Being publisher of *Interview* gave him access to these spectacles, and the magazine became an important vehicle for communicating Warhol's style and taste to a wide public. Warhol also participated in the creation of clothing, such as his cut-up dresses, made from various designers' clothing, 'Fashion as Fantasy' (1975). These dresses anticipate 'deconstructive' designs by Rei Kawakubo and Martin Margiela.

At present, the world of fashion has absorbed many of the qualities once attributed to avant-garde art and Hollywood. Young fashion models have become the iconic equivalents of glamorous film stars, and the outrageous and provocative behaviour once expected of artists such as Warhol, Candy Darling, or Jean-Michel Basquiat can now be marketed as part of the appeal of Jean Paul Gautier or Stephen Sprouse, John Galliano or Alexander McQueen. Both the art and Fashion worlds have a thirst for novelty and reinvention that is now slaked by the media of glossy magazines and television.

During the past decade the extent of Warhol's cultural legacy has become increasingly apparent. His reputation as a major artist and filmmaker is now assured (except in the moist conservative circles), while references to his status as a public figure, and to his notorious comments on fame, are pervasive. The influence of his work on painters, photographers, designers, editors, scholars, and curators continues to run its various courses. Warhol personified a spectacular fusion of previously distinct cultural fields, and his work embodies the complex range of associations that we expect of the greatest art.

Andy Warhol slipped the moorings of class, race, and gender to reinvent himself as a creative and mercurial artist. He emerged from a working-class, Carpatho-Rusyn, Catholic upbringing in Pittsburgh with an ethic of hard work which translated into an immediately successful career after he moved to New York in 1949.

It was through his self-definition within the gay milieu he discovered there that Warhol was first able to find the freedom to mix work and pleasure, business and nightlife. The narrow and apparently immutable categories of class, ethnicity, and gender imposed by his upbringing crumbled in the delirium of cosmopolitan New York. The same was true for close associates like Fred Hughes, Halston, or Edie Sedgwick. The nightclub Studio 54 became a kind of free zone in the late seventies where socialites and hustlers could mix. Warhol succinctly characterized it as 'a dictatorship at the door, a democracy on the floor.' All could remake their given or inherited identities in a culture that valued individual, unique, or eccentric personalities.

Though he and his predominantly gay associates initially made their contributions in seemingly marginal fields, social and cultural changes over the past forty years enable us to see that the creative 'industries' of window dressing, marketing, display, and commercial illustration, populated as they were (and are) by a relatively high quotient of visible gays, have an enormous impact on popular taste. Historically, dandies have formed an avant-garde of taste, but in an era of mass culture, inheritors of these roles, like Warhol, send ripples far beyond their particular fields. Overall, the enormous profusion of his work is hugely consequential in understanding art, fashion, and popular culture without categorical preconceptions.

For Warhol, these domains, and the creative personalities inhabiting them, nourished one another, and as his career developed from decade to decade, he delighted in the cross-fertilization that occurred as he moved from field to field. As we examined Warhol's achievement, we consciously set aside category distinctions and chronological progression in order to reflect the complex ways in which images and styles traverse fine art, magazines, publicity stunts, studio production, social life, and the popular, vernacular media of photography, film, and video. To introduce eva-nescent and sometimes ephemeral media into the contexts of a book and a museum exhibition, and to integrate and juxtapose them with original paintings and costumes, constitutes a revisionist approach to Warhol's work that is made possible by the availability of the totality of his production, and of his own collections, for the first time.

It is not to diminish the role of Warhol's great paintings as images, or as a form of decor, that we have consciously inverted the traditional hi-erarchy of archival ephemera, costume, photo-graph, film, and fine art. After all, it was Warhol himself who used his epic cycle of paintings *Shadows* (1979) as backdrops for a fashion shoot published in *Interview,* and who described them with his characteristic hilarious nonchalance as 'disco décor'.

An analogy may be found for these blurrings of categories and shifts of taste in the fate of so-ciological terms such as 'subculture.' Whereas the dress, manner, and image of Warhol and his entourage appeared in aggressive opposition to mainstream culture of the Pop era, consumer industries have learned to absorb oppositional subcultures since the late seventies (that is, after punk). No longer do leather jackets and wrap-around shades signify a biker aesthetic; drag poses, styles, and stars have emerged from cult circles; punk fashions and street styles may now be seen in suburban shopping malls. Whereas the uptown and downtown cultures of the fifties re-mained completely distinct from each other, now the boundaries between them are invisible. War-hol's own career is symptomatic of these radical changes, but he also helped bring them about.

From 1961, when he first exhibited his Pop paintings in the windows of the Bonwit Teller department store, his work entered a wide pub-lic consciousness through the mass media. War-hol retained a constantly provocative position in the media through his work, but also through a clearly identifiable persona. Pop culture seemed to appear without precedent, and Warhol's paintings of movie stars, consumer objects,

and traumatic current events were identified as the quintessential Pop art. But he remained enormously prolific and inventive for a further twenty years, though the very glare of media at-tention obscured the real content and qualities of his achievement. Even the fact that Warhol successively took up painting, films, photog-raphy, publishing, or video contributed to the misapprehensions his work suffers from even ten years after his early death in 1987.

Andy Warhol's own books, especially *Andy Warhol's Exposures* (1979), with its mix of fashion and social commentary; the *Index (Book)* (1967), with its high-contrast photographs of his 'scene', and *POPism: The Warhol Sixties* (1980), with its re-imagined autobiography and penetrating di-agnosis of social mores, are highly suggestive of his attitude toward his pluriform activities. With his collaborators Bob Colacello and Pat Hackett, Warhol created new fusions of analysis, gossip, and photography. He subverted standard expec-tations in his own exhibitions, superimposing his *Mao* paintings on decorative wallpaper in 1974, hanging portraits salon-style on glossy brown walls in 1979, and, most important, foreground-ing, as if in a department store, whole cabinets of shoes, umbrellas, and historical wallpaper samples from a museum's collection in his 1969 *Raid the Icebox I.* Warhol's apparently uncritical excess was shocking at the time; subsequently, his unexpected and subversive approach to his task on that occasion has had exceptional influ-ence on museum practice, and he continued to upset conventions in ways that have yet to be fully acknowledged.

Glamour, style, and *fashion* are loaded words. In the vernacular, they have both positive and derog-atory connotations, and yet in the contemporary art world, they have been—until recently—almost exclusively terms of opprobrium. An artist like War-hol whose focus was the passing scene, and who passionately courted novelty, fascinated both by the whims of the *beau monde* and of the flamboy-ant subcultures of the city, consciously risked the denial and disdain of the 'serious' art world. As his

Diaries testify passim, Andy Warhol loved to play with his roles both within and outside this elite.

The influence of the fashion world, the glamour of Hollywood movie stars, and contemporary notions of style informed Warhol's work as a serious and significant artist, and, in turn, his work has affected style and fashion. As an artist and cultural phenomenon, he has shaped the taste of two generations. Warhol maintained these interests throughout his career, long after it was thought that he had left behind the world of commercial illustration for fine art and other arenas. Only now, by looking at the whole range of Warhol's work, are we beginning to see that his fascination with glamour, style, and fashion was not a distraction from his 'real' work, or a debasement of the rarefied, pure world of contemporary art, but an integral part of his multivalent life and work and a complex and productive response to the tensions between art, popular culture, and daily life.

NOTE

Reprinted with permission from Mark Francis and Margery King, "The Warhol Look," in *The Warhol Look: Glamour, Style, Fashion,* ed. M. Francis and M. King (Boston, New York, Toronto, and London: The Andy Warhol Museum/Bullfinch Press, 1997), 23–30.

30

'MACHO MAN': CLONES AND THE DEVELOPMENT OF A MASCULINE STEREOTYPE

Shaun Cole

Nineteenth-century sexologists' theories of homosexuality proposed that male homosexuals had a female soul trapped inside a man's body, and therefore possessed the personality characteristics of women. This emphasis on binary gender divisions had an overwhelming impact upon the development of homosexual identity: effeminacy became the culturally accepted meaning of homosexuality, and the stereotype of homosexuality. The adoption of female clothing or female associated attributes such as plucked eyebrows, rouged lips, powdered face and dyed hair made a very public announcement of a man's sexual orientation and self-identity. In fact, until the 1970s, the history of gay men's dress was dominated by two choices: the adoption of overtly feminine styles or conformity to accepted male dress codes of the day.

Just as there were men who expressed their homosexuality through the adoption of an effeminate appearance in both the gay and the straight worlds, so there were men who would not or could not express their sexuality in this way. They did not identify with the feminine, and regarded themselves as homosexual but not as 'fairies'. The social and legal climates in both Britain and the United States meant that for most gay men the adoption of an overt visible gay identity was impossible, as it could lead to social ostracism or arrest. Dress choice, therefore, followed the conventions of the day and relied on 'secret' signifiers such as suede shoes and red ties to convey a hidden sexual identity to those 'in the know'.

The counterculture movement of the 1960s and the beginnings of sexual liberation prompted men to question their roles. As straight men increasingly moved away from the rigid dress codes of their fathers and adopted a freer outlook, so gay men began to challenge public attitudes towards them and their legal and social position. The gay liberation movement had introduced questions about lifestyle and, as a part of that, acceptable clothing and behaviour. Activist groups such as the Gay Liberation Front called for an end to gender-prescribed behaviour and dressing. While most gay men found gender-fuck too radical, there was a move towards a more masculine look, and they began to be attracted to the 'look of hip masculinity favored in the counterculture' (Humphreys 1971: 8. See also Burke 1969: 72.). Tony Diaman summed up many gay men's disillusionment with society's view of them as effeminate: 'The straight world has told us that if we are not masculine we are homosexual, that to be homosexual means not to be masculine ... one of the things we must do is redefine ourselves as homosexuals' (Diaman 1970). This attitude heralded the masculinization of gay culture. Gay men began to regard themselves as masculine. They adopted manly attire and demeanour as a means of expressing their new sense of self, and in adopting this look they aimed to enhance their physical attractiveness and express their improved self-esteem.

There had of course been overtly masculine gay men in the past. Closeted gay men had often overcompensated for their homosexuality, becoming 'male impersonators'. There was also a tradition of men's attraction to masculine types, epitomized in the attraction (for middle- or upper-class men) to working-class men and to 'rough trade'. Male hustlers, gay and straight, were well aware of the attraction of a masculine image. John Rechy frequently refers to this type of man in his novels.[1] There were also men who frequented the leather or biker bars, projecting an image of extreme rebellious masculinity. The cowboy and the biker were two archetypes that were influential in the adoption of 'butch' dress styles for men. Both had appeared as representations of masculine sexuality in physique magazines and were appearing in gay bars and on hustlers' street corners.[2] They represented a traditional but nonconforming aspect of masculinity and were 'used by the media to play up masculinity and sexuality in ways that are understood by the gay populace' (Fischer 1977: 18). Hal Fischer states that the 'Western or cowboy archetype can be seen as derivative of the natural myth. ... It would be unlikely for an American boy growing up not to have a cowboy hero' and that 'the western image is popular for three reasons. First, movies and television have made it familiar. Second, the cowboy lives a "man's life in a man's world". Third, western dress is easily translated into contemporary dress' (Fischer 1977: 19). Thus gay men were forming a 'site' for their appearance in the present comparable to an image or a point in the past—here, the cowboy in the films of their youth.

As a positive move away from effeminate stereotypes and in search of an 'out' masculine image, gay men looked towards traditional images of rugged masculinity, such as the cowboy or lumberjack, for their dress inspiration. They wore 'blue-collar garb', straight jeans (at a time when flares were all the rage), plaid shirts, hooded sweatshirts, bomber jackets and lace-up work boots; they cropped their hair short and grew moustaches. All these clothes had a clear meaning in the wider American culture: toughness, virility, aggression, strength, potency.

There was a real attempt to dissociate from the ridiculed effeminate stereotyped role of other homosexuals and to become a 'real man', or at the very least to look like a real man. Assumptions about macho masculinity lay at the heart of these manly presentational strategies. The term 'macho' implied overconformity to the traditional male gender role, which was generally regarded as more masculine than the modern male gender role. Many homosexuals imitated the macho role (Newton 1972 and Warren 1974). This attempt to look like a 'real man' reflects many gay men's desire for 'rough trade' or what Quentin Crisp described as 'the great dark man'.[3] It was no longer enough for gay men to 'have men' as their sexual partners; they wanted to (appear to) be these real men. It seems clear, though, that the macho-man is a reaction against effeminacy, and this means that the masculine/feminine binary structure has not gone away, but only been redistributed. John Marshall remarks on 'the extent to which definitions of male homosexuality continue to be pervaded by the tyranny of gender divisions' (Marshall 1981: 154). As this new masculinity became more popular and more gay men adopted the look, these men became known as clones. Andrew Holleran believes that the men who began clone style were not themselves clones. They were 'people who, ironically, prided themselves (consciously or unconsciously) on separating themselves from the crowd' (Holleran 1982: 14). They were, he says, 'breaking away from effeminate homosexual clichés of the Fifties' (Holleran 1982: 16).

The Queer Theorist Judith Butler views the adoption of these hegemonic images as a kind of 'subversive bodily act'. However, clones were not intending to 'pass' as heterosexuals, as their predecessors had. Their appropriation opened up radical and transgressive possibilities. As Joseph Bristow has written: 'stylizing particular aspects of conventional masculine dress, [they could] adopt and subvert given identities, appearing like "real men" and yet being the last thing a "real man" would want to be mistaken for: gay ...'

(Bristow 1989: 70). Clones wore these appropriated clothes differently from heterosexual men, so there could be little doubt about whether someone was a heterosexual macho man or a gay macho man. Straight men wore this attire in an unselfconscious way, usually loosely and for comfort. Their garments might not fit or match; their facial hair might not be perfectly trimmed. In this way, straight masculinity reflected conformity to traditional male norms concerning nonchalance about appearance. Clones rejected this nonchalance and stylized these looks:

> Frank looked like a well-groomed lumberjack. Everything he wore was tailored and matched. His jeans and plaid Pendleton shirt fit perfectly. His black, wool, watchman's cap matched his black Levi's and the black in his shirt. His red thermal undershirt matched the red in his shirt. The brown in his leather belt matched the brown in his hiking boots. No real lumberjack ever looked so well put together, so coordinated in color, his outfit fitting so perfectly. Frank, then *signified* the lumberjack—appropriating the gender conformity that is traditionally associated with lumberjacks, not actually having to cut down trees to do it (Levine 1998: 61).

Martin Humphries believes that 'for many the attraction of machismo is an acceptable way of openly celebrating the eroticism of the male body. It is a safe eroticism in that the images of desire are often those endorsed by society in general; though not endorsed as desirable by men for men. Strong, solid, clearly identifiably masculine men but with a difference—a camp difference.' Clones were interested in sex and dressed both sexily and practically. The practical clothes hid well-toned bodies and 'made sense to an urban homosexual: they were impervious to the depredations of concrete and long hours of walking; they kept you warm; they worked' (Holleran 1982: 16).

Clones wore their garments in a self-consciously tight manner in order to enhance their physical attractiveness. They kept their hair short, beards and moustaches clipped, and clothing fitted and matched. The clothes worn by the clones have a quite different meaning from the clothes' original meaning—or, in Gregg Blachford's words, they 'infuse[d] the style with a new meaning of eroticism and overt sexuality—that is, they [were] used explicitly to make one appear sexy and attractive to other men.'[4] In adopting an image that was based upon a heterosexual macho image, gay men walked a tightrope between straight imitation and an interpretation that could identify them not only as real men but as real gay men. The macho look served a dual purpose, in that whilst attracting other gay men it also acted as a form of self-protection, explained by Ray Weller:

> When you walked down the street dressed as a clone in the early days, what you wanted was straight people to be confused, and they were confused. And slightly menaced as well because it was before these looks had become clichéd. So if they saw someone with a leather jacket on, they didn't think there was a nelly [faggy] leather queen they thought there was someone who might be tough or trouble. So you were pushing [the] straight world away but sending out very specific signals to other gay men which was obviously sexually based. You were making yourself unattractive to the heterosexual world, or menacing, but attractive to the gay world.
>
> I remember feeling like that and talking to people about how, because of the way we appeared, nobody would ever try to mug us because people didn't understand that parody of masculinity was a gay thing.[5]

Gay men moving to major cities, such as New York or San Francisco, quickly adopted the clone look. The Castro and Christopher Street quickly became clone enclaves. Dennis Altman observed that these neighbourhoods 'seem at first sight to be populated almost entirely by men under the age of forty-five, dressed in a uniform and carefully calculated style and dedicated to a hedonistic and high consumption lifestyle' (Altman 1982: 13). Justin Stubbings remembers:

> When I went to San Francisco I just loved the way everyone looked. It was recognizable. You knew. You knew *that* was a gay man because of the jeans and the checked shirt and the moustache and the short hair, and it just seemed that was what you get into if you want to pull and that was the bottom line of it. It wasn't so much about looking good ... it was also about being able to pull on the street. It was a fashion that suited me, it was easy. It was a move away from the perms and T-shirts that were around when I came out and that was what you had to look like. And it was the first time there was a look that said its OK to be a bloke and be gay. That's what I liked about it.[6]

The clone look was, Randy Alfred argued, down to 'sexual selection. Many of these men are simply wearing the costumes that experience has taught them will attract the very men they find sexually attractive' (Alfred 1982: 22).[7] Form-fitting Levi's and T-shirts hugged the body, revealing the contours of genitals, buttocks, and musculature. These features were often highlighted by not wearing underwear, wallets or shirts. Some men even left the top or bottom button of their Levi's undone, in part to signify sexual availability, and in part to suggest that their genitals were so large they had popped a button through sheer size.[8] The crotch of their jeans was often faded through bleaching for a similar effect. A scene from Felice Picano's 1978 novel *The Lure* illustrates these points. Buddy Vega is sent to show Noel (working undercover for the police) how to dress to be accepted in the gay bar scene of New York. 'Jeans', Vega told Noel, 'should hang low on your hips, be tight in the ass and the legs and especially full at your basket.' He selects a pair of jeans that belonged to Noel's girlfriend, which 'had been secondhand when she bought them. The pockets and cuffs were frayed ... they felt tight, too tight to wear.' Vega tells him it is fine for the buttons to remain open, as this will emphasize

the size of his genitals, and then instructs Noel on how to emphasize the bulge of his genitals by making the jeans look more worn around the crotch using a nail file (Picano 1996: 55–6). Outerwear also called attention to these areas of the body. Clones wore waist-length down or leather jackets over their Levi's, which exposed and emphasized the bulge of their genitals and buttocks. These clothes could also be used to camouflage the imperfections of an imperfect body; but on the whole the men who adopted the clone looks adopted a whole lifestyle that involved using the gym and eating the right foods. Having a good body was, at least initially, as important as having the right clothes (Levine 1998: 87).

In an article in the gay magazine *Christopher Street* Seymour Kleinberg identifies 'the uniform of the moment: cheap plaid flannel shirts and jeans, or if it is really warm, just overalls, and boots or construction workers' shoes no matter what the weather is. With the first signs of frost, a heavy leather bomber jacket is *de rigueur*' (Kleinberg 1978: 6). What he neglects to notice, or to mention, is that it wasn't just any jeans or plaid flannel shirt: it had to be the correct colour, style, make or brand. Ray Weller remembers this point only too well:

> When that look is parodied now or people think of the Village People look they think it's almost like a pastiche—it's almost enough to put a check shirt on; but I remember at the time it was much more subtle than that, there were lots of graduations [sic]. You had to have the right tone of check shirt, or the right brand, or certain sorts of sportswear. And certain boots were OK and other boots weren't OK.[9]

The importance of achieving the right look or having the absolutely correct labels, rather than just the generic style, depended upon the clique to which one belonged.[10] The most important item to get right was the jeans. Justin Stubbings illustrates the importance of having Levi's: 'It was the 501 that were the prize. I remember going over to the States to get my first pair and doing the bath thing and the pumice stone just to get the bits looking right. In England it was that look with the 501s that said it—the American jeans said that this was another gay guy.' This was true in America as well as England. Clark Henley's somewhat tongue-in-cheek guide to being a clone, *Butch Manual,* reiterated the importance of Levi's: 'Butch wears pants that show off his bulging calves, his tantalizing thighs, his perfect buns, and of course, his notorious basket. There is only one pair of pants that can fill these requirements: Levi's 501's' (Henley 1982: 55).

As a result of increased cheap transatlantic travel the clone look was soon imported into Britain.[11] This 'stylish thug'[12] soon established himself in London and other major urban centres, and the look became essential in many gay pubs and clubs, especially in London's Earls Court. Ray Weller tells of his first visit to the Copacabana Club in Earls Court in 1979:

I was wearing what was [high street] fashionable for the day; French cut trousers, a heavy grey single-breasted jacket with a shirt with the collar open over the jacket. It really was all checked shirts and 501 jeans and vaguely sports tops and that kind of thing. I remember going there and really enjoying it, but really feeling that I stood out and that nobody was looking at me because I was so obviously, not just provincial, but not part of the scene or the way that everyone wanted to appear or what was considered attractive.[13]

When he returned the next week he was wearing, as was everyone else, 'Levi 501s, a red checked shirt and heavy work boots.'[14]

The gay clone look did have a precedent in Britain, just as it did in America. Some men adopted an overtly masculine look as early as the 1950s. Michael Brown usually dressed in unremarkable clothing during the day, but at night when he was cruising for sex at Notting Hill Gate in London he wore 'a plaid workman's shirt, denim jeans and a heavy leather belt with a large buckle.' This was, he asserts, 'way before

the macho bit came into fashion.'[15] Vince man's shop was selling western-styled clothes, including plaid shirts, jeans and waistcoats, as early as 1952.[16]

While there was a defined basic look for the clone, it did vary from season to season and with the weather. In cold weather they wore the staples of clone wear—construction boots, straight-legged, button-fly Levi's 501s, plaid flannel shirts, and hooded sweatshirts under brown leather flight jackets. During the summer, when it was warmer, 'they wore green-striped, Adidas running shoes, button-fly Levi's, and either Lacoste shirts, tank tops or T-shirts.'[17] Most of the men dressed in accordance with clone fashion codes. Clones often resented intrusions by those who violated these norms:

One afternoon, I was talking to some men at Ty's, a popular circuit bar. A group of suburban homosexuals walked in. These men wore designer jeans, Lacoste shirts with the collars flipped up, and reeked of cologne. They were obviously *not* clones ... To the clones, these gay men were anachronisms, throwbacks to another era of male homosexuality, of blowdried bouffant hairdos, gold pinky rings, and fey demeanor (Levine 1998: 50–1).

In Britain the preppy look that had been so disparaged by New York clones found a place in clone culture. For those who didn't want to dress in the heavily macho looks or didn't feel that they were appropriate to the occasion, there was a more preppy look, which consisted of chinos and Lacoste T-shirts, but still with short hair and moustache. Ray Weller recalls:

I was well enmeshed in the Clone look ... and when you were a Clone and wanted to look smart it was really a kind of preppy look that was the sort of acceptable look ... it started because the people in the Clone world ... went to America for a couple of weeks a year ... What they brought back was a sort of Chinos and Lacoste sort of look which was the ... clone acceptable clothes to go to a restaurant in. That was how you could still be Clone but not look like one of the Village People if you were going to the theatre or something.[18]

As part of the clone image, gay men developed a set of codes to specify their particular sexual interests. Consequently a man could tell if a potential partner would be compatible just by the position of the keys on his belt or the colour of the handkerchief in his back pocket. In his book *Gay Semiotics* Hal Fischer defines the importance of these signifiers.

In gay culture ... signifiers exist for accessibility ... The gay semiotic is far more sophisticated than straight sign language, because in gay culture roles are not as clearly defined. On the street or in a bar it's impossible most of the time to determine a gay man's sexual preference either in terms of activity or passive/aggressive nature. Gays have many more sexual possibilities than straight people and therefore need a more intricate communication system (Fischer 1977: 21).

Along with the sexually loaded codes, specific sign-vehicles were added to the basic look to project an extra butch front. They were typically associated with traditional macho icons, such as the cowboy.[19] Many of the men utilizing these butch sign-vehicles did so with a sense of play inherited from gender-fuck and 'camp' sensibility, referring to their clone clothes as 'butch drag'. It was both a self-conscious, almost parodying reference to traditional stereotypical images of masculinity and a self-conscious embracing of that stereotype.[20]

By the early 1980s, Martin Levine observed that 'strict butch costuming fell out of favour, as clones mixed butch elements for circuit wear and street wear. They wore either black cowboy boots or black leather Patrick sneakers, black or blue button-fly Levi's, plaid flannel shirts, tank tops, or T-shirts, and black leather or down jackets. They also wore their hair longer—down to, but not over, the ears' (Levine 1998: 61). In

London there was a seasonal difference in footwear. John Campbell recalled how 'you have basically the 501s and the Timberlands, the boat shoes for summer, the hiking boots for winter. And it was originally white socks and then, because it became very "Essex", it was no socks.'[21]

Clothes that a man put on to make himself sexually attractive to other men made him, Andrew Holleran says, 'entirely invisible: a non-person.' The clothes became very important; clones would only associate with and have sex with other clones. The proto-clones were quick to move on once their look became the standard dress for gay men, once it became 'clone'. The image became formulaic and tired. Holleran notes that they abandoned their plaid shirts once the majority of gay men adopted them.[22] In London too the clone look became watered down as more gay men adopted the look to be sexually attractive. Ray Weller remembered that:

the Clone world ... that was starting to develop was in a lot of ways ... much more suburban. We often used to joke at the time about Chiswick Clones and about airline stewards about how they had this kind of look, with jeans and checked shirts, but it was all too washed and too clean and too pressed and it was essentially ... it was much more about conforming. I mean I really wanted to conform. You knew that the way to, ehm, get a boyfriend was, kind of, to wear the right clothes in the Clone world. If you had the right shortness of hair, and the right moustache and, you know, the right vest and the right boots then that was very attractive. It didn't make you special but it [did] make you belong.[23]

The straight press had by this time identified that the macho clone was now the prevalent image of homosexuality. 'If women's [sic] image has changed dramatically in recent times, the image of the homosexual has changed out of all recognition. If they were once stereotyped as Julian and Sandy ... they are now Biff and Brad ... coming on ... like everyone's idea of the perfect, ale-swilling Outback wallah from Australia' (Reynolds

1983). Like the reports of the tabloids in the 1950s and early 1960s, heterosexual society did not like the fact that it was hard to identify gay men. As long as gay men kept to their swishy, effeminate and therefore non-sexually threatening stereotypes they could be tolerated, if not actually accepted. Society could find a place for an amusing un-threatening pseudo-woman.

Perhaps ironically, the new gay macho styles began to have an influence on straight fashion. Dennis Altman notes that the 'diffusion of the macho style through advertising (for jeans for example) and entertainers like The Village People led to its being adopted by millions of straight men unaware of its origin' (Altman 1982: 33). Rather than welcome the move, 'straight' men felt threatened by the new overtly masculine homosexual. They felt insecure in their own sexuality because the safe barrier of effeminacy had been torn down. Semiotic signals no longer meant anything. Anybody could be mistaken for a 'poofter' now that sartorial pointers had gone. Straight men began to copy homosexual styles, and leather became commonplace. John Campbell remembered when this happened in London:

And of course everything that the gay scene did within six months it was followed by the straight scene, tentatively followed. Like for instance the crew cuts without the 501s and the clones and the moustaches. The moustaches were very gay, especially the handlebars and the very full growth, but as it became straight the moustaches went. They followed, they started wearing the Lacostes and they started wearing the 501s and the white socks and all the Timberlands.[24]

Andrew Holleran believes that the death of the clones came about once the 'boys from Long Island came into town with their girlfriends on Saturday nights in bomber jackets and plaid shirts, their keys hung on the right side of their belts, like homosexuals looking for a top man' (Holleran 1982: 16).

Elements of the ideas behind the clones' adoption of masculine imagery remained even when younger gay men had begun to reject the clone image and, partially as a result of the influence of punk, look for new forms of self-expression. These were to be seen in the imagery of 'queer nation' and 'act-up' looks in America (and later Britain) and in the gay skinheads and gay rockabillies of London in the 1980s. What the clone did leave was the legacy of the masculinization of homosexuality and an emphasis on overtly masculine images and physiques. This was to become one of the primary modes of self-presentation for gay men during the 1980s and 1990s.

NOTES

Reprinted with permission from Shaun Cole, "'Macho Man': Clones and the Development of a Masculine Stereotype," *Fashion Theory* 4, no. 2 (2000): 125–40.

1. Both in *City of Night* and *Numbers* Rechy describes masculine-type hustlers or trade: Johny Rio 'is very masculine, and has been described recurrently in homosexual jargon as "a very butch number"... A supreme accolade in that world, "butch" means very male and usually carries overtones of roughness' (Rechy, *Numbers*, 1984).
2. 'Looking at Chuck and Miss Destiny—as she rushes on now about the Turbulent Times—I know the scene: Chuck the masculine cowboy and Miss Destiny the femme queen: making it from day to park to bar to day like all the others in that ratty world of downtown L.A. which I will make my own' (Rechy 1964); Herlihy (1970) also features hustlers dressed as cowboys.
3. Cole interview with Quentin Crisp, 2 October 1998.
4. This is the process of 'stylization' that Clarke *et al.* use to describe working-class youth cultures and their 'generated' styles: 'The generation of subcultural styles involves differential selection

from within the matrix of the existent. What happens is not the creation of objects and meanings from nothing, but rather a *transformation and rearrangement* of what is given (and "borrowed") into a pattern which carries a new meaning, its translation to a new context, and its *adaptation*' (quoted in Blachford 1981: 200).

5. Cole interview with Ray Weller, 26 June 1997.

6. Cole interview with Justin Stubbings, 11 July 1997. James Gardiner recounted a similar experience on his visit to San Francisco in 1974: 'I think what happened to me was I first went to America in the early seventies and going to gay places on the West Coast I felt very queeny indeed and that hang over of the floral seventies and the long hair and the bell bottoms and the floral everything, and all that jewellery, all those gold chains and all that stuff had become kind of mainstream gay fashion by 1970. It had become very very femme and I felt very very self-conscious in the gay bars of San Francisco in 1974 and my friend that I was staying with took me aside and said "Darling, we really have got to buy you some real jeans" and I was taken off to one of the shops and bought several pairs of 501s and out went the platforms and on went the construction boots you know, out went the frilly shirt and on came tight T-shirt and so on and so forth and when I came back to London wearing those clothes people used to stare at me.' Cole interview with James Gardiner, 24 September 1997. For a similar New York experience see Levine 1998: 47.

7. See also Iain Finlayson (1990: 113), for his theory on the two conflicting aesthetic appeals of clone style: 'high culture and low sleaze.'

8. Leaving buttons open on jeans was codified to have particular sexual meanings—usually one of availability. See also Clark Henley 1982: 57.

9. Cole interview with Ray Weller, 26 June 1997. Andrew Tomlin recalled how important the 'right' garment was in being accepted in the clone world: 'When I first saw a clone at Heaven [the London nightclub] I thought "I want to wear clothes like that, it's easy," but my first checked shirt wasn't deemed the right one and a cute clone called Paul took me out one day to buy the right ones': Cole interview with Andrew Tomlin, 10 May 1999.

10. Compare the experiences in these two accounts. For John Campbell and his friends, the 'correct label was not the be-all and end-all. It was [important to have the right brand] to a certain extent. I mean it was more of a case of... the uniform was Timberlands, 501s, Lacostes and MAls. You could have that look, but it may not be the real McCoy, provided that you almost fitted in with that, that was fine. If you took it to an extreme, if you wore a lame Lacoste-style polo shirt, that would not have been allowed so to speak. Unless of course you decided to be a queen rather than a clone. It was quite well defined, you were either queens or clones.' Cole interview with John Campbell, 31 July 1997. Ray Weller's clique was much more strict: 'I can remember going to a brunch... there were about 30 men there and it was a sunny summer afternoon, Saturday or Sunday and everyone was wearing a Lacoste top, everybody. There was not a single person who didn't have [one], so every pastel shade imaginable of Lacoste was present. And they had to be right because there were Lacostes that were potentially Far Eastern copies... And it was most important. You really felt bad if you didn't have the genuine article on': Cole interview with Ray Weller, 26 June 1997.

11. James Gardiner maintains that it was cheap airfares offered by companies such as Freddie Laker that allowed gay men to travel easily and cheaply to New York and San Francisco, where they saw the new out, proud and highly visible masculine clone looks and brought them back to England: Cole interview with James Gardiner, 24 September 1997.

12. This is how the poet Adam Johnson described clones (quoted in David 1997: 253).

13. Cole interview with Ray Weller, 26 June 1997.

14. Ibid. 'Right after I moved to the City, I started running with a group I met at the tubs. At first, they made fun of my clothes and haircut.

They really needled me! To get them off my back, I started to change. I looked at what they were wearing and listened to what they said. I started to dress the way they did and talk the way they did. All the teasing stopped after this' (quoted in Levine 1998: 47).

15. Cole interview with Michael Brown, 1 December 1993. Rodney Garland describes a similar look in his 1953 novel *The Heart of Exile*: 'Sartorially [Terry] was typical of at least one section of his generation all over the Western world. He had one suit, a single-breasted garbardine affair for uneasy, representative occasions. He was more at home in blue jeans, lumber-jackets, moccasins and loafers, windcheaters, cowboy shirts, in essentially masculine, revolutionary, anti-traditional, almost anti-capitalist garments. All of which emanate from the most demonstratively and aggressively capitalist state in the world' (Garland 1995: 180).

16. James Gardiner maintains that this was a proto-clone look. British gay men were taking their influence from American western films and images of men (semi) dressed as cowboys and bikers in physique magazines: Cole interview with James Gardiner, 24 September 1997.

17. The athletic look became especially popular after the release of Patricia Nell Warren's novel *The Front Runner*, published in 1974. The hero, Billy Sive, is a young gay athlete who favours Adidas running shoes. Ray Weller and Jonathan Jackson also remember this book's being an influence in London, though much later. 'The first year I went to Heaven on New Year's Eve, which was the first year it opened, I remember I was wearing 501s, which I was very proud of because it was really difficult to get them then, and I think a Fred Perry top and blue Adidas training shoes, and it was that look... it was way before the sports look': Cole interview with Ray Weller, 26 June 1997. As well as the basic, the lumberjack and the athletic looks, there were a number of other clone styles that relied on specific signifying elements of clothing: Cowboy—cowboy hat, cowboy boots, denim jacket, leather chaps; Military—flight jacket, army fatigues, leather bomber jacket, combat

boots, khaki army shirt, army cap; Construction Worker—construction boots, hard hat, cut down Levi's; Uniform—policeman, sailor, army captain; Leatherman—Black leather motorcycle jacket, trousers and cap, studded leather belt and wristband.

18. Cole interview with Ray Weller, 26 June 1997. John Campbell (in interview with Cole, 31 July 1997) also underlined the importance of this 'preppy' look for clones in Britain.

19. The cowboy image was particularly prevalent, as it had figured so heavily for so long as an icon of American masculinity. Picano uses this point in his novel *The Lure*: '[Noel had] always associated homosexuality with feminine gestures and speech. But in here [The Grip—a leather bar of sorts] it was just the opposite: an extreme manliness, unruffled, almost frontiersman calm, as though all those Gary Cooper movies had come to life. Sure! That was it! The rough clothing, the swaggering walk, the drawling speech. They were acting out cowboy fantasies. How easy for him to copy!' (Picano 1996: 64). The Village People (pop group) are a prime example of this.

20. Seymour Kleinberg, however, argues that the advent of an overtly masculine image for gay men was not liberated. By adopting a super-macho appearance gay men were following the strict binary rules of gender division, something that gender-fuck and gay liberation had tried to break away from. He argues that macho looks and associated behaviour were not merely the 'new drag' but a return to the closet: 'Macho, of course, isn't a new closet; indeed, many have suspected that it's the oldest closet in the house' (Kleinberg 1978: 12).

21. Cole interview with John Campbell, 31 July 1997. The type of footwear chosen could be used to send subtly different messages. Ray Weller recalled a friend who 'always wanted to look rough but he was frightened that people would think that he was rough trade, which he wasn't, and his compromise was he used to wear a singlet, a vest and 501 jeans, but he would never wear boots. He used to wear Bass Weegun loafers, which was a kind of an alternative but slightly smarter, but he'd wear

them without socks, and he always used to say he wore them without socks 'cause that would present a rough image but people would actually see that they were actually Bass Weeguns so that they would know that he wasn't rough—that they would be going home to somewhere very nice with clean bed linen and clean kitchen and things': Cole interview with Ray Weller, 26 June 1997. Essex is a county in southern England that borders London; the term 'Essex' became a derogatory term implying that those people were suburban and behind London fashions. It was used in much the same way that New Yorkers refer to people who live outside Manhattan as 'Bridge and Tunnel.'

22. There is a link here to what Dick Hebdige calls 'the process of recuperation,' which takes two forms: the commodity form, 'the conversion of subcultural signs' (dress, music, etc.) into mass-produced objects'; and the ideological form, 'the "labelling" and redefinition of deviant behaviour by dominant groups—the police, the media, the judiciary'. He notes that one of the results of this commercialization and popularization of youth subcultures is the disavowal of the (commercialized/popularized) subcultures by their originators (Hebdige 1987, Chap. 6).

23. Cole interview with Ray Weller, 26 June 1997.

24. Heterosexual men's fashions had been copying gay men for many years. Refer to Chapter 5 in my book *Don We Now Our Gay Apparel* (Berg 2000) for a discussion of Vince and Carnaby Street in the late 1950s and early 1960s.

ANNOTATED GUIDE TO FURTHER READING

Cole, Shaun. *'Don We Now Our Gay Apparel': Gay Men's Dress in the Twentieth Century.* Oxford and New York: Berg, 2000. Examines the subcultural world of gay men in New York and London and analyzes trends in gay men's dress style by addressing the impact of magazines of the 1950s on men.

Cosgrove, Stuart. "Zoot Suit and Style Warfare." *History Workshop Journal* 18 (Autumn 1984): 77–91. Provides a detailed historical account of the zoot suit riots in Los Angeles in 1943 and the cultural forces that shaped the event.

Gelder, Ken, and Sarah Thorton, eds. *The Subcultures Reader.* London and New York: Routledge, 1997. A comprehensive collection of the most important thinking, historically and currently, on the nature and meanings of subcultures.

Halberstam, Judith. *Female Masculinity.* London: Duke University Press, 1998. Provides the first study of female masculinity by examining gender expressions among masculine women from the nineteenth century to contemporary drag king performances. The author discusses the politics surrounding femme–butch roles, transsexuality, and transgender dykes in the lesbian community.

Maffesoli, Michel. *The Time of the Tribes: The Decline of Individualism in Mass Society.* Trans. Don Smith. London: Sage, 1996. The author contends that the insistence on the end of collective ideals masks a complex state of affairs. He demonstrates that while the old determinants of identity such as class have indeed faded, there are new tribal ones. Contemporary identities are now composed of a range of experiences, representations, and everyday emotions. Processes of identification are replacing sexual, political, or professional identities with groups, with sentiments, and with fashions.

McRobbie, Angela, ed. *Zoot Suits and Second-Hand Dresses: An Anthology of Fashion and Music.* London: Macmillan, 1989. A collection of twenty-two articles from the first half of the 1980s that deals with youth cultures through an investigation of the entertainment and fashion industries.

Mercer, Kobena. "Black Hair/Style Politics." *New Formations* 3 (Winter 1987): 33–54. A seminal text on the study of race politics, identity, and resistance. The author interrogates how hairstyle and fashion bear on the changed political, economic, and social circumstances of Black people in the 1980s.

Muggleton, David. *Inside Subculture: The Postmodern Meaning of Style.* Oxford and New York: Berg, 2004. An empirical sociological study of postmodern subcultures that draws on extensive interviews with subcultural stylists.

Muggleton, David, and Rupert Weinzierl. *The Post-Subcultures Reader.* Oxford and New York: Berg, 2004. This reader draws on a wide range of international case studies to investigate the new relationships between youth, music, and the politics of style.

Thornton, Sarah. *Club Cultures: Music Media and Subcultural Capital.* Cambridge: Polity/Wesleyan University Press, 1995. This book discusses youth subcultural groups, such as club and rave cultures, since the 1980s. Discussions concerning media representation facilitate her analysis of the moral panics that surrounded the "acid house" boom.

PART V

Consuming and Creating Style

INTRODUCTION

Cultural production and consumption occupy an important position in the field of fashion. Dress is a powerful marker of gendered discourses and is a site where processes of signification are produced and articulated. The moment of consumption marks one of the processes by which subjectivities and identities are discursively formed as gender is inscribed and reproduced on the body. Mass consumption betrays a location and market, which in turn feeds the production cycle, the inspiration and styling processes. In other words, masculinities are constituted—made, rather than found, by representation. In many ways, the politics of appearance is influenced by cultural conditions that shape and define politics of taste. Displays of taste contribute to the creation of shared identities within groups, but they also allow for the identification and exclusion of outsiders whose standards of taste differ and who therefore do not belong and are not invited inside. Taste cultures are clusters of cultural forms that embody similar values and aesthetic standards to the exclusion of others. Such taste clusters have evolved from the exclusionary to the revolutionary; those that are excluded can now form their own cluster. "Clusters" are no longer few in number but multitudinous and dynamic, with members who capture a specific taste ranging from those of a music band to those of a subcultural group. Such is the regenerative and distorting properties of mass cultural productions of style in the twenty-first century and the flexibility that consumers have applied to the acceptance of differing modes. The boundaries of style and taste are malleable and can no longer be defined as easily as they once were when they "raised eyebrows."

One of the first modern analyses of tastes in the arena of fashion is Thorstein Veblen's study of conspicuous consumption.[1] Veblen argues that invidious distinction and emulation are driving motives of social interaction. The accumulation of wealth is driven not only by a need to ensure basic subsistence but primarily by the honor attached to its possession. In order to confer honor, Veblen argues, wealth must be displayed either through conspicuous leisure (abstention from work or from tasks considered demeaning) or through conspicuous consumption of costly goods. Standards of taste do not reflect autonomous and eternal standards of beauty but a sense of costliness masquerading under the name of beauty.[2] The value attached to the appropriation and consumption of goods determines standards of taste. This is illustrated by the rise, perhaps the acknowledgment, of consumer's desires from the mid-1970s in branded merchandising and licensed fashion by brands such as Pierre Cardin, Burberry, and Louis Vuitton, whose goods were reproduced on a mass scale featuring logos and patterns of distinction. The fashionable wearer would eventually feel overwhelmed by the screaming fabrics, and fashionable society relegated such wearers to the fringes of bad taste or to the music industry, where they were expected to participate in the unique display of wealth and ego.

Like Veblen, sociologist Pierre Bourdieu argues that taste is shaped by status competition: "good taste" is a mark of distinction, in the double sense of setting apart, and conferring honor to, those who claim to possess it. Taste classifies, and it classifies the classifier.[3] As opposed to Veblen, however, Bourdieu argues that taste confers honor not because it signals economic wealth, but rather because it is an expression of wealth, which is cultural in nature. Taste is a distributed capacity for appropriating classes of objects and practices, both symbolically and in a material manner. Along with attitudes, preferences, manners, know-how, and educational credentials, it is a component of cultural capital, which is transmitted by a complex process of socialization through the family and the education system. As part of class habitus, it is one element of a set of dispositions and preferences that are perceived as freely embraced by social actors but that thoroughly reflect their objective class position. In spite of appearances, taste is cultivated rather than being an innate quality.

In tracing modern consumption, Colin Campbell locates different styles or modes of consumption but focuses on the dandy and the romantic bohemian.[4] He argues that the dandy represents an older mode of consumption that privileges an aristocratic preoccupation with self and self-presentation. The dandy was the archetype of an urban man whose appearance was his passion and who inspired admiration and controversy from others regarding his excess and particularity. His devotion to a new style of dress that sanctified understatement augured an era that placed cut and fit ahead of ornament, color, and display and created a fashion that announced a haughty, snobby, and unabashed claim to a higher "class." His style—tight breeches with perfectly polished shoes, finely tailored jacket, crisp white shirt, and expensive cravat—represented a new erotic masculinity that called attention to the male form and inevitably redefined the meaning of masculine power. His manner became stiff to preserve his portrait-like appearance, and he began to deliberately construct his fashion apart with a secret knowledge of the unattainable grace of taste. The romantic bohemian, on the other hand, was relaxed, exuding the same confidence with more understatement and movement in the construction of the garment.

This part of the *Reader* traces the relationship between masculinity and consumption as well as the development of ideas of masculinity, identity, and cultures of taste. It explores how the marketplace dramatizes a series of questions about sexual politics and the meaning of masculinity, fashion, and style politics. Whether we consider the refined taste of the dandy or other masculine forms, it is important to consider the polarization between production and consumption, between appearance and the masculine self. These questions help us understand why the dandy has been an enduring identity beyond the punk and bohemian romantic; despite the claims made for the possibility of the female dandy such as Gabrielle Chanel, dandyism is a style generally suggesting men.

Christopher Breward's contribution to this reader considers the Edwardian male in metropolitan London. He examines masculine forms of selfhood circulated through merchandising and promotions of commercial retailing. Breward compares "Champagne Charlie" and other loud 1860s metropolitan types to the more refined and glamorous dandy or bachelor playboy found in the West End by ca. 1900. He considers the identification with new ideas of manliness present in other aspects of English urban culture such as the theater and print media. Breward asserts that consumption in the nineteenth and early twentieth century has been misread as a unified and feminized domain, which the focus on the department store as an aspect of modern consumption within history and historiography has encouraged. He argues for consideration of a more nuanced and differentiated set of practices and also a wider urban geography to consider upper-working-class and lower-middle-class men between 1870 and 1914. Breward examines masculinities using a case study of Hackney, a suburb that housed a diverse population of working-class men, large numbers of city workers, as well as more suburban men in professional occupations, who were served through a diverse range of outlets that catered to their needs and price points. Outfitters used the imagery of modern design—copious space and hygienic surfaces—to display their fashions. Breward sees in the commodification of surface details, impressions, and external appearances a set of new formulations of modern life; the fashion-conscious West End could also be experienced in Hackney, and Hackney in the West End.

The media and lifestyle magazines have contributed enormously to the impetus with which men's style has been observed and subsequently consumed by the mass market and its distribution channels, including department stores, chain stores, specialty retailers, and digital distribution. In emphasizing the communication of images in print, television, and other modes, the media focus on the visual and continue to falsify the typical by implying the everyday.

Becky Conekin presents an analysis of *Playboy* (from 1953), a magazine that by its third year had an incredible one million readers. The magazine, founded by Hugh Hefner, provided a type of training guide on how to order wine or select trousers for golfing. The stories featured within its pages encouraged a set of reassured male fashion modes, including the types of the playboy, the swinger, and the hip bachelor. They were dressed and prepared for uncomplicated and enjoyable sex, giving the idea of masculinity a caddish and carefree appeal. Conekin compares the magazine to *Esquire,* which promoted ready-to-wear rather than bespoke clothes in the 1930s. Both magazines promoted middle-class fashions based on a preppie college image derived from the uniforms of Oxbridge and the Ivy League. *Playboy* did not endorse the clothes of African-Americans nor those of youthful rebellion such as the T-shirt, blue jeans, and black leather jacket. Hefner wished to promote an image of youthful affluence rather than rebellion and gave men the opportunity to confront their parents' generation, which feigned an indifference to both dress and the body as a signifier of status. Thirty years before the invention of the modern-day men's lifestyle magazines such as *GQ, Arena, Men's Health* or men's *Vogue,* Conekin argues that *Playboy* created a remarkable and enduring method of articulating all aspects of a man's life by making recommendations and rewarding the male reader with his irresistible appeal.

In "New Men and New Markets," Frank Mort describes the media industry's attempt to find a solution to the problem of a general-interest lifestyle magazine for men in the 1980s, an issue that seemed to raise issues of Britishness, as French, Italian, and American men had long read fashion magazines. In this chapter, Mort considers the figure of the new man in mid-1980s Britain and shows that "masculinity" is always in doubt or in crisis. He argues that in the 1980s men were forced to question their social roles. Mort asks whether this was a social fact, or, as Peter York suggested in *The Times,* "nothing more than the advertising industry's dramatisation of its own self-image"? An immense emphasis on consumption marked the pathway to join this new-style elite. Masculinity became more of a matter of how one looked rather than what one did. Whether we consider the "chavs" (working-class and lower-middle-class youths who acquire branded goods) of contemporary Britain in their Burberry caps, or the "brats" (middle- and upper-middle-class boys who aspire to court circles as the ultimate pinnacle) of Sweden with their slicked-back hair, Hermes belt buckles, and Gucci loafers, we still face the "old" issue of the "new" man.

Annette Lynch's contribution to this section of the *Reader* examines the significance of male style within a select African-American community, which she determines is encapsulated by a black expressive culture. Lynch uses a case study of the Young Gentlemen's Beautillion Ball, an esteem-raising ball for high-school graduate-age men held in Iowa since 1995. Although the men wear a uniform tuxedo, their bodily gestures and hairstyles have gradually created the difference between men that have always characterized the synthesis of West African and American aesthetics. West African visual principles, creativity, and spirit have long been used to oppose standardized dress and behavior. African women tended to use clothing and textiles to perform this function; men used the medium of the body itself. Parts of the body became instruments of percussive force. Black male slaves, Lynch writes, "robbed of other forms of resistance, turned to their bodies as modes of expression." African-Americans used kinesic forms of nonverbal activity such as walking and greeting to attract attention and to affirm strength of purpose. Lynch notes that from the early 1800s particular hats and ways of wearing them were noted by foreign visitors, as well as colored waistcoats and canes that drew attention to the wearer in order to create "a more demanding and dramatic presentation." The fusion of body and hairstyles dates to the slave period; generally the styling of the hair was permitted as an expressive medium within the slavery system.

Contributors in this concluding part of the *Reader* analyze the relationship of masculine consumption to the creation of fashion and style systems. The variety of masculinities they describe is as wide-ranging as the commodity culture with which they engage.

Vicki Karaminas

NOTES

1. T. Veblen, *The Theory of the Leisure Class* (1899; reprint, New York: The Modern Library, 1939).
2. Ibid., 128.
3. Pierre Bourdieu, *La distinction: Critique sociale du jugement* (1979; translation published under the title *Distinction: A Social Critique of the Judgement of Taste* [Cambridge, MA: Harvard University Press, 1984]), 6.
4. Colin Campbell, "Understanding Traditional and Modern Patterns of Consumption in Eighteenth Century England: A Character Action Approach," in *Consumption and the World of Goods,* ed. J. Brewer and R. Porter (New York: Routledge, 1993).

31

FASHION AND THE MAN: FROM SUBURB TO CITY STREET
The Spaces of Masculine Consumption, 1870–1914

Christopher Breward

It savours very much of cant and hypocrisy for any man to say that he does not study dress in one form or another. It is absolutely imperative for a man nowadays to study his appearance. As a business, a professional or a social asset it is a very potent factor, and it is the privilege only of the millionaire and the pauper to be able to dress badly.

Dennis Bradley[1]

The fashion writer Dennis Bradley provided a preface to the 1912 catalogue of the progressive tailoring firm Pope and Bradley of Bond Street, London, which stressed the importance of dressing well for all men who lived and worked in the city. Yet despite the crucial role played by clothing in the construction of urban identities, masculine consumption has been overlooked in the developing field of cultural history (figure 31.1). Here I map the ways in which the retailing spaces of metropolitan London shaped fashionable identities for young men in the late nineteenth and early twentieth century. I concentrate on three geographically connected districts in the capital stretching from the East End to the West End, which offered particular models for the creation of modern masculine forms of selfhood. Such social scripts were marked by their fluidity and they were circulated largely through the displays and promotions of commercial retailing. They represented idealised, sartorial versions of manliness which have also been noted in other forms of English urban culture at the turn of the century, from music hall through to the popular novel. Several historians, most notably Peter Bailey, have shown how fictional figures from the theatre and print media encouraged London audiences to identify strongly with the pleasures of new service industries, promoting new strategies for dealing with the speed of change and the promise of choice in urban life.[2] However, spectacular vaudeville performances and the melodramatic images from penny magazines in reality offered rather distorted reflections of the actual possibilities for self-fashioning. Charles Leybourne's appearances on stage as 'Champagne Charlie' and graphic representations of the exploits of 'Ally Sloper' in popular journals represented all of the escapist clichés of conspicuous consumption, and it is difficult to map their fantastic carousings onto the more prosaic opportunities of everyday life. Clearly, by focusing on the material geographies of masculine taste, it is possible to penetrate these rather generalised stereotypes and reach a more nuanced understanding of the shifting tenor of urban life during this period.

It was in the more mundane streets of London, in the windows, fitting rooms and advertisements of clothing retailers, that the finer

Figure 31.1 Robert Lunberg. *Johan Gustaf 'Frippe' Fredrikson (1832–1921), skadespelare, regissör,* 1893. Oil. 50 x 39 cm. Nationalmuseum, Stockholm. In a period before central heating, fur coats were useful and sometimes necessary to stay warm and were frequently worn by men. A fur can suggest either indigenous authenticity or urbane sophistication. Here we have an elegant of Stockholm, the manager of the National Dramatic Theatre, which is depicted beside him. The blackness of his dress contrasts with the white snow. The portrait is both formal and relaxed at the same time.

gradations of masculinity were lived out. These discourses of manliness were heavily reliant on a sense of place and on an understanding of the modernity of city living. They were also mediated through the active decisions made by male consumers themselves. In this sense an examination of masculine consumption choices as they were enacted in the menswear shop can provide a clear indication of the way that innovative commercial displays and marketing strategies, a renewed emphasis on style, encouraged by the rapid expansion of the ready-made clothing sector and the pressures put upon consumers by the emergence of new social roles at home and at work, contributed to a radically altered relationship to commodity culture. The journalist J. W. Cundall, writing in a sixpenny tourist handbook in 1902, considered the complex negotiations involved in buying such commodities in turn-of-the-century London. He remarked that:

> London shops are famous, and at them may be procured almost all, if not every kind of commodity the whole world offers. It may therefore be argued that it is the easiest place possible in which to procure whatever may be desired; but the multiplicity of the shops and the variety and extent of their goods tend to embarrass the would be purchaser. In fact shopping has become almost one of the fine arts.[3]

According to Cundall's guide, the simple supply of life's necessities that characterised traditional retailing in the city had developed into a web of luxurious outlets demanding the attentions of a connoisseur. At first celebrating the positive breadth of provision that London offered, Cundall then warned of a confusion of choice, heightened by the lists of advertisers' shops, ready to answer to the whims and fancies of any hapless browser, which were appended at the end of his book. These included advertisements for: tobacconists, mineralogists, tailors, opticians, Turkish baths, sports outfitters, chemists, philatelists, picture and print dealers, glovers, florists, stationers and travel agencies.

The products and services offered by these businesses reveal a complex system of commodity supply criss-crossing the whole of London. The existence of this network testifies to a burgeoning sphere of masculine consumption, whose domain was spatially defined in terms of a distinctive geography of commerce and was marked by its diffusion into the practices of everyday life in the early-twentieth-century metropolis. In the light of historical readings of consumption practices which have obscured this provision for male needs and desires, how might one best reconstitute the social and economic transactions and the significant cultural meanings which were shaped by such networks?

The assertion that for the Victorians 'acquiring the goods for consumption ... was socially perceived as a feminine task' has become almost routine in much historical writing.[4] Arguing against those claims I suggest that the gendered nature of the task of consuming relied very much on the kind of consumption taking place, rather than on an over-arching conception of sexual and social control which prioritised the highly feminised, but relatively untypical domain of the city centre department store. In that sense nineteenth- and early-twentieth-century material culture needs to be understood not as a unified and feminised whole, but as a more differentiated set of practices marked by particular geographies, in which social identities were formed and sometimes contested. As recent economic histories of retailing and consumption have indicated, this necessitates breaking down the spheres of consumption into their constituent parts. The findings thrown up by this approach can present significant challenges to the accepted picture. For example, beyond the spectacular displays and rather impersonal transactions of large city centre emporia, smaller suburban shops relied on the maintenance of more intimate social connections, established through frequent visits by regular customers. In their fittings and stocking practices such outlets encouraged shopping habits that were more embedded in the work-a-day expectations and rhythms of urban life. Far from endorsing the idea of the shop as an escapist 'dream-world', the suburban shop-keeper contributed directly to the formation of a range of entirely pragmatic and concrete social identities.[5]

An examination of the relationship between masculinity and clothing at this *fin-de-siècle* moment also reveals how the acquisition of fashion goods by men entailed negotiation with a variety of cultural images, many of which were deeply implicated in competing constructions of class.[6] Furthermore, the buying, selling and wearing of clothing, whilst retaining the prerogatives and divisions of social status, carried strong resonances of gender and sexuality. For it was at the point of purchase, in the environment of the shop, that fashionable masculine identities, trends in posture, adornment and bodily presentation, were often most coherently displayed. The relationship between customer and tailor was one of the utmost delicacy and the choices made under the retailer's direction had the potential to define the social standing of the consumer in all walks of life. Finally, retail practice was always tied to the circumstances of location; in the necessarily close relationship to adjacent markets and suppliers and in the need of store proprietors to meet the demands and desires of local customers. This was true for masculine and feminine patterns of acquisition. So to base a cultural history of turn-of-the-century consumption only on the evidence of the West End, or on one or two flagship stores, is to disregard the competing claims of less overtly glamorous retailers in influencing urban identities and attitudes.

The range of outlets for fashionable male consumers during the period was much wider than the tight focus on the department store has implied.[7] There were as many different types of shops supplying items of male clothing as there were elements in the male wardrobe. All of these outlets served a market stratified by social expectations and by location, with many of them boasting an established history which pre-

ceded any notion of a mid-nineteenth-century 'retailing revolution' by several decades.[8] The diffusion of the market across the spaces of contemporary London suggests that the formation of identities through consumption was a plural and frequently an open-ended transaction, drawing into its orbit attitudes towards class, gender, race and sexuality in an urban setting. However, the evidence from clothing and shopping has largely been overlooked by nineteenth- and early-twentieth-century social historians. In most accounts, the ephemera of consuming practices has been dismissed as unimportant in the face of seemingly more durable records of official approaches to the moulding of social behaviour. Yet as George Chauncey has demonstrated in his work on the history of American gay culture in New York, considering the moral or political discourses shaping manliness together with the reflective and creative texts of consumer culture presents a more rounded understanding of historical processes and the part they played in the formation of social identities. Such an examination reveals new maps of social power, which combined official instruction with more informal or quotidian processes. These maps 'guided men's practices even if they were never published or otherwise formalised.'[9]

Popular presentations of the nineteenth-century metropolis made by novelists and journalists frequently mobilised both official and personal notions of 'mapping' in tandem. London was generally conceived of spatially (in architectural and industrial terms) and emotionally (in terms of the author's subjective reactions to geographical difference) through the relationship of east to west and centre to suburb.[10] The stark contrasts which were evoked through this social geography were often illustrated by descriptions of clothing; the grey monotony of East London was deliberately contrasted with the dandyism of the West End. In 1904 the journalist and critic Ford Madox Hueffer imagined the city through its varying genres of masculinity, though in this case architecture deputised for fashion:

Speaking broadly the man who expresses himself with a pen on paper sees his London from the west. At the worst he hopes to end with that view. His London of breathing space, his West End, extends from say Chiswick to say Portland Place. His dense London is the city as far as Fenchurch Street, his East End ends with what he calls 'Whitechapel'. The other sees his London of elbow room extend from say Purfleet to say Blackwall. He is conscious of having, as it were at his back, the very green and very black stretches of the Essex Marshes dotted with large solitary factories and small solitary farms. His dense London, his city, lies along the line from Blackwall to Fenchurch Street. Beyond that the City proper, the City of the Bank and the Mansion House, is already a place rather of dilettante trifling. Its streets are tidied up, its buildings ornamented and spacious. The end of the West End is for him Piccadilly Fountain, and this later quarter of large, almost clean, stone buildings, broad swept streets and a comparative glare of light, is already a foreign land, slightly painful because it is so strange.[11]

The hold of this construct on the popular imagination was a powerful one, but the ways in which different populations, living in different areas of the metropolis, produced their own imaginative maps of the city render its imagery more complex. The writer has adopted a leisurely perspective on the spatial possibilities of his city, defined by the wide streets and green squares of Kensington and Westminster. From the opposite vantage point, the East End of London is imagined as an enclosed and constrictive maze, laid out for the purposes of industrial rather than literary production. These two routes converge on the centre, a site of pleasure marked by its glamorous other-worldly aesthetic, but they progress no further. Any sense of free, uninterrupted perambulation across these zones has been discounted, though the possibilities were clearly intriguing. In considering the retailing of men's clothing across London—from the suburb of Hackney in the east to the City and the West End—I hope to expose both the tensions and the connections which arose between local contexts and the broader characterisations of urban masculinity such as Hueffer's. The sense of urban space projected through this approach prioritises the local character of particular districts, whilst acknowledging the ways in which their inhabitants drew on the associations of all three areas in both positive and negative ways. In this context we might productively conceive of the notion of the shop and its environs as theatre, framing and projecting mobile models of manliness and fashionability to varying audiences. Between 1870 and 1914 proprietors and consumers engaged in a performance of dressing which gained much of its meaning from the retail environment and its extension into the street, the office, the bar and the home.[12]

Suburban life between 1870 and 1914 offers indelible proof that the social and cultural relations of the city were in a state of flux during this period. The 1914 edition of the official guide to Hackney disabused visitors to this inner-London district that they might find much evidence of the rural medieval village from which it took its name. The atmosphere and environment of the area reinforced a notion that urban life entailed constant renewal. Bounded on the north and east by the newer clerks' boroughs of Tottenham, Walthamstow and Leyton, with their endless rows of modest terraced houses, on the south by the heavily industrial and impoverished boroughs of Bow, Bethnal Green and Shoreditch, and on the west by the more affluent districts of Islington and Finsbury Park, Hackney absorbed the influences of all three. At its south-eastern borders at Hackney Wick, Walter Besant observed 'an unsavoury, but a very busy district, with dye, cloth, iron, starch and other works ... the view ... from the railway is indescribably dreary and depressing. Drab walls and drab chimneys rise in mournful monotony.'[13] By contrast, the arterial routes of Mare Street, Kingsland Road and Stoke Newington High Street offered shops and social facilities to rival the thoroughfares of Upper Street and the Holloway Road in the more salubrious neighbouring borough to the west. Residential districts in Clapton, Lordship Park, Cassland Road and Mapledene sported solid and spacious merchants' villas bordering some of the green public spaces which were the legacy of Hackney's eighteenth-century incarnation as a bucolic location of grand country mansions and elite private schools.[14] At the opening of the twentieth century its reputation bore little relation to those former times:

> To the superficial observer the Hackney of today does not, perhaps, suggest itself as a district abounding in historical interest and antiquities. Its name rather conjures up thoughts of a busy and densely populated wing of modern London, intersected by railways and electric tram lines, its main streets thronged almost as densely as the City itself.[15]

The 1914 guide presented a unified and optimistic public face to the area, celebrating the modernity and respectability of a district which provided living space for the families of those men employed in the offices and on the trading floors of the adjacent City of London. The financial district was linked to Hackney by train and tram tracks, and was accessible by foot from the borough's southern end. In this sense the streets of Hackney provide an ideal focus for the study of contemporary suburban shopping habits, replicating similar patterns of middle- and lower-middle-class development which surrounded the central metropolis, from Acton in the west to Brixton in the south. Yet a study of Hackney's shopping spaces also reveals the benefits of locating retailing within its specific social milieu, a milieu which needs to be contrasted with provision in the City and the West End. The district's distinctive images of masculine fashionability and urban experience challenge established understandings of metropolitan consumption during the period, based as they have been on the primacy of the West End. The pages of Hackney's official guide were filled with photographs of broad shopping boulevards and carefully

styled retailers' advertisements which conveyed a form of smart, yet 'buttoned up' fashionability. Such representations sit uneasily both with Walter Besant's and Charles Booth's negative readings of East London deprivation, or with recent interpretations of early-twentieth-century consumption as an overridingly feminine or aristocratic pursuit. A high proportion of the guide's advertisers catered for men rather than women. Its pages presented the reader with an idealised version of Hackney as a discreet concentration of civilised amenities and values, compromised only by the limited salaries of its petty bourgeois inhabitants and marked by social connotations which radically differentiated one street from its immediate neighbour.

The social rhythms of lower-middle-class suburban life were often represented as a pale and anodyne reflection of the true metropolis by contemporary commentators. Suburbans were portrayed as a small-minded rebuke to the excessive follies of fashionable modernity, a view which has persisted in subsequent studies of this stratum.[16] Conformity and aspiration, it was claimed, informed a life that otherwise found its material co-ordinates mapped through an adherence to the hollowness of commodity culture and to the interior world of the home. Leisure and gossip were seen to fill the void once occupied, supposedly, by the exertions of meaningful production. The implications for the sartorial forging of suburban masculine identities were profound, given the weight that such negative rhetoric carried. Undoubtedly, opportunities for the comparison of appearances and attitudes were legion in a culture that devoted great energy and time to socially inclusive activities. For all the criticism of the inward-looking nature of suburban living, the practicalities of travelling to and from work, and the intense engagement with street-life enforced by city-centre occupations encouraged the tendency to observation, emulation and competition evidenced in the Hackney *Guide*. Furthermore, the development of more internalised identities, which drew their influences from the enclosed sphere of the lower-middle-class home, reinforced a characterisation of suburban masculinity as feminised. Suburban men's outfitters thus directed much of their attention to providing a range of clothing which reflected these themes. They offered the finely coded gradations of frock coats, lounge and morning suits that constituted a uniform for the office, together with the soft collars, pyjamas and smoking jackets suitable for the drawing room, and a range of sporting costumes which attested to some attempt at overcoming stereotypical accusations of 'unmanliness'. The consideration of 'respectability' appears to have influenced choice across all of these areas.

In the leisure and retailing section of the guide, opposite a view of Hackney Downs (a space designated according to the journalist George Sims for the promenades of 'the eminently respectable and subdued'), Moss Bros took out a full-page advertisement. This was for its branch at Clarence Road, where the men's department boasted 'tailoring in all its branches and every article sold at wholesale prices'. At Moss Bros a concern for respectability was combined with a recognition of economic expediency and of the social circumstances of modern domestic life. Sims himself noted in his atmospheric observations of Hackney, published in the *Strand Magazine* of 1904, that promenaders in the locale were: 'all neatly dressed; many of the young men wear frock coats and high hats. Among these are the young husbands who are wheeling the perambulators. The young wives who pass us have recognised the beginning of summer with a flower laden hat and a new blouse. But they wear their finery pensively'.[17] A Hackney *Guide* photograph of Kingsland High Street, resplendent under electric lighting, its well-stocked shop fronts protected by deep awnings, focused on the premises of a prominent advertiser, Walkey & Co., 'Ladies and Gentlemen's High Class Tailors', who 'guaranteed style and fit'. Its façade utilised extravagant wrought-iron decoration, ostentatious signage and a sober window display of regimented textile bales and price tickets. Above its frontage the legend 'Our Only Address' promoted notions of exclusivity and local loyalty, though the trousers hanging in the open doorway and the coats and ready-made children's clothes suspended from the next-door drapers conveyed a more commonplace, grittily urban milieu. Promotions in the guide for Thomas Hull & Sons, family drapers of Kingsland Road, and Z. Dudley, fancy & general draper and warehouseman (also known as 'the house of cheapness'[18]) of Kingsland High Street, reinforced the image of this part of Hackney as a focus for shopping. It is instructive to compare the cosmopolitan bustle of Dalston with the more leisured, suburban surroundings of Clarence Road, the former crossed by wide thoroughfares which led directly to the square mile of the City.

A series of commercial illustrations in the *Hackney Guide* focused on the provision and cleaning of collars and shirts for the clerical workers and businessmen who so influenced the atmosphere and reputation of the area between 1870 and 1914. All of the plates presented figures in the process of dressing, positioned in well-appointed domestic interiors more usually associated with the promotion of feminine cosmetics and accessories during the period.[19] Ernest Jay, a hosier of Mare Street and 'maker of the "J" collar', advertised his stock of 'shirts, underwear, half-hose, collars, ties, gloves, pyjamas, handkerchiefs, vest slips, braces, studs, links and pins' with the image of a customer standing with military bearing in his dressing-room, adjusting his tie in front of a heavy dressing-table neatly laid out with brushes, mirrors and shaving pots. The shop remained open from nine a.m. to nine p.m. every day, allowing customers access on the return from work. It was also positioned on the route of the Hackney monkey parade, where local young men would gather in crowds in their best clothes to attract the attention of the opposite sex. The proximity of this display of popular fashionability accounted for the store's extended opening hours on Saturday night, when the shutters came down at eleven p.m. The juxtaposition of the polished promotion of the retailer, with the more chaotic proletarian pleasures which marked the monkey parade is intriguing. George Sims used the parade as an opportunity to comment on the excited attitudes and garish postures of the promenaders: 'There are plenty of people on the pavement and in the roadway. Here and there are groups of typical London lads, cane, cap and cigarette, and we exclaim simultaneously "the monkeys"!' In Sims's account the retailing style of Jay's is clearly absent: 'the feature of the crowd that leapt to the eyes was the complete absence of gloves and umbrellas'.[20] That this hosier remained open for trade whilst the paraders passed by his doorstep perhaps suggests more freedom of movement between the two styles than observers like Sims were prepared to admit.

Capon Bros of Stamford Hill directed its products to a more genteel market, more closely attuned to the finer details of modern menswear. The store rejected the bombastic, 'yellowback' glamour of the Jay image for a spare line drawing in its advertisement, which reflected the more avant-garde advertising style of the West End's Jermyn Street and Savile Row. The strap-line: 'artistic neck wear a speciality' indicated a more urban customer base, with distinctively modish habits. The tone of Capon's promotion indicated the growing reputation of the northern reaches of Hackney, bordering on the picturesque Springfield Park, as a haven for cosmopolitan and relatively wealthy professional families. Besant noted that the lower part of Stamford Hill was 'lined by good middle-class shops, and the upper ... has fair sized dwelling houses standing back in gardens on either side'.[21] The whole area benefited from its healthy hilltop position with spectacular views. A different genre of advertisements from launderers across the borough stressed the social benefits to be had from well-laundered linen. 'The Electric' high-class shirt and collar dresser of Sandringham Road, Dalston boasted three branches in the vicinity. It relied for its trade on the large proportion of single young office workers who were attracted to the area by its lodging houses and the easy City access which Dalston offered. Dalston's collar dresser illustrated its services with a rather risqué image of a housemaid, provocatively thrust into the fashionable 'S' bend, presenting her employer (who peered semiclad around a door frame) with a handful of collars and a fresh shirt. T. W. Copcutt, a dry cleaner of South Hackney, adopted a more sedate approach, in tune with the established expectations of a local population resident in detached 1860s villas, which boasted the largest gardens in the district. In Copcutt's promotion a young 'City gent' in morning wear was shown contemplating the dry cleaning parcel that lay on his dining room table.

What is significant about all of these advertisements is their resolutely homocentric mode of address, their representative spread across the borough and their privileged positions in the *Hackney Guide*. It appears that the retailing of men's clothing in Hackney was confidently geared towards its male markets rather than being subsumed under the general terms of household provision, with its connotations of feminine duties and responsibilities. Local menswear was defined largely by the nature of the local professional population, whose various public identities sustained a buoyant selection of outlets. The consumers depicted in these retail promotions were generally solitary figures whose domestic settings drew attention to the importance of privacy and the authority of the fashioned self, without directly calling on the more sociable images of the female shopper. Most promoted an ideal of muscular corporeal masculinity, accentuated by the shirt-sleeved state of undress and assertive postures, which stood in opposition to contemporary criticisms of the puniness of the office-worker's body and the implied accusations of effeminacy suggested by Sims's familiar description of the perambulator-pushing clerk.[22] In this sense, the profile of men's clothing businesses in Hackney helped to mediate the fine gradations of status and sexuality which permeated the lives of Hackney's male population. What was definitively absent from the commercial imagery was any reference to the more chaotic, carnivalesque images of East-End masculinity, or to the feminising tendencies of family life, or even any acknowledgement of communal working-class leisure.

A clearer picture of the ways in which menswear in Hackney was organised geographically can be gained from an examination of trade directories, topographical postcards and the advertising columns of the local press. At the heart of shopping activity in the area, materially and symbolically, were the majestic façades of Mare Street. Running in the north from the Georgian terraces and parish church abutting Lower Clapton Road, the section of the street formerly called Church Street and later named the Narrow Way still retained something of a village atmosphere in 1914. Custom was increasingly drawn to its narrow incline by the presence of the North London Railway station after 1850 and by the adjacent tram terminus. The drapery emporium Matthew Rose, established in 1852 and expanding along the Narrow Way until its closure in 1936, was Hackney's premier department store. Rose's presence strengthened the fashionable connotations of this end of the street. Moving southwards, the middle section of Mare Street had stronger civic and municipal associations by the turn of the century, with a new town hall, the Hackney Empire music hall, a cinema and Hackney Library all situated along its widened pavements. Trams to Aldgate then passed along a tree-lined stretch of imposing domestic residences, before the road assumed a more rundown, semi-industrial character which announced its decline into Cambridge Heath and Bethnal Green. Along the whole of the length of Mare Street, shops catering for the male wardrobe or for the care of the male body made a significant display. In 1890 Mare Street counted fifteen boot and shoemakers (with

wholesale bootmaking constituting an important local industry), twelve tailors, six hosiers, two shirt and collar dressers, six gentlemen's hairdressers, four hatters, five tobacconists, two outfitters, two sartorial pawnbrokers (sited in the less comfortably situated southern part of the street) and two clothiers.[23]

Other shopping streets in Hackney presented less commercial diversification than Mare Street, reflecting even more closely the demands of local populations through the clustering of particular retail concerns. The streets in Homerton, to the east of the central shopping area, betrayed the more straightened circumstances of their largely working-class inhabitants. The district was the site of chemical and haulage industries, which lined the canal at Hackney Wick, and was served by workers' trains to the City Docks from Homerton station. The journalist Geraldine Mitton, writing in 1908, was appalled by the declining state of Homerton High Street, which had formerly enjoyed a reputation for its rural aspect and distinguished Georgian residences. She lamented that it now revealed an 'unlived in, uncared for aspect. The streets on the south, which go down under the railway, are singularly poor and uninteresting. The shops are small and dirty, the roadway narrow. There is the squalor of an unkempt middle age, but none of the attractiveness of a contented old age such as might have been expected.'[24] In 1901 Kelly's directory could list no tailors in Homerton High Street, its businesses numbering several public houses, fairly humble domestic and food provision stores and many small manufacturers. As far as clothing was concerned, the street accommodated two second-hand dealers and a shirt and collar dresser.

Surrounding streets offered more outlets, though often of a uniform and rather basic quality. Well Street to the south, dominated by the ubiquitous boot and shoe manufacturers and wholesalers (thirty-three in total) and home to a flourishing street market, also included the Direct Clothing Supply Association, a co-operative venture supplying working-men's clothing at reasonable prices. Its trade card promised: 'every description of men's, youth's and boy's clothing supplied to the public direct from factory. Every article marked in plain figures at lowest prices for cash.' A fleeting glimpse of its façade, behind a passing coster's cart in a postcard of about 1890, reveals the most basic signage and shop front decoration.

Close by, the premises of the Bethnal Green workhouse, a hotel for working men, a home for aged Jews, and the Hackney Reform Club reinforced Homerton's reputation as one of the more deprived areas in the borough. Yet even here, between the boot suppliers and the charitable foundations, residents of Well Street could enjoy the services of four gentlemen's hairdressers, eleven drapers including a Home and Colonial stores, a hatter, a tailor, a collar dresser and a hosier. Two pawnbrokers offered loans on clothing. Some of this money was doubtless spent on Saturday nights amongst the twelve tobacconists and beer retailers that serviced the locality. This combination of urban poverty with a plethora of retail outlets, many of them aimed at men, suggests a thriving culture of display amongst the urban poor whose effects were highlighted in the references to proletarian sartorial style at the Mare Street monkey parade. Whilst the images of 'respectable' masculinity peddled to the customers of 'reputable' retailers made strenuous attempts to distance themselves from the implications of mass-production and popular taste, working-class consumers were clearly not denied the opportunity to purchase cheap fashionable clothing on their own doorsteps.

Chatsworth Road, to the north-west of Homerton High Street, bore the same traces of poverty at its southerly end. Three second-hand dealers shared the pavement with a shirt and collar dresser, a tailor and a hairdresser. Significantly though, the presence of the Chatsworth Social and Athletic Club and the Clapton Park Club and Institute along this stretch hinted at the grander pretensions which marked the road as it moved away from industry and slum dwellings towards the respectable and leafy villas of Lower Clapton. Both directories and postcards from the turn of the century record an eclectic mixture of businesses lining this wide shopping street. Extensive displays of collars and ties for young boys, and tailored dresses for local matriarchs, pointed to the lower-middle-class character of local shoppers. It was their patronage of the Chatsworth coffee rooms, haberdashers, outfitters and tailors which distinguished the area from the 'disordered' customers and provisions of Well Street. There was little in Chatsworth Road to hint at the cosmopolitan bustle and robust office culture which drew its male occupants to work every day in the City. The visual character of the street was reticent, undemonstrative, provincial even. It signified a retreat both from the filthy production of heavy industry and from the stressful excitements of the metropolitan centre. The material culture of Lower Clapton seems to exemplify contemporary appraisals of suburban life, famously summarised in 1909 by the historian Charles Masterman, who, in his critique of the social condition of England, stated that: 'no one fears the suburbans, and perhaps for that reason no one respects them. They only appear articulate in comedy ... like the queer people who dispute ... in a recent London play ... the respective social advantages of Clapham and Herne Hill. Strong in numbers and in possession of a ... tyrannical convention of manners, they lack organisation, energy and ideas.'[25]

Yet Masterman overlooked the contradiction lurking in his assessment. For far from lacking any coherent sense of social direction, suburban tastes and cultural inclinations (so far as they existed in the prejudiced opinions of professional observers) were underpinned by a ferocious attention to propriety and 'good form', and by an attention to the character of fashion itself. Whilst this may have resulted in an undeniable conformity to rigid social rules concerning display and public behaviour, it also positioned life on the peripheries of the metropolis in a direct relationship to that enjoyed by those at its centre. Suburban populations were as reliant on the inner city as a focus for both disapproval and emulation, as those West End sophisticates were reliant on the monotony of the suburbs to reinforce their own brilliance. The permeable boundaries between distinct zones of the metropolis, in which men and women acted as couriers of knowledge across the realms of the suburban domestic and the metropolitan public, undercut the dismissive assumptions of writers like Masterman:

> They are the creations not of the industrial, but of the commercial and business activities of London. They form a homogenous civilization—detached, self centred, unostentatious—covering the hills along the northern and southern boundaries of the city ... It is a life of security; a life of sedentary occupation; a life of respectability ... Its male population is engaged in all its working hours in small crowded offices, under artificial light, doing immense sums, adding up other men's accounts, writing other men's letters. It is sucked into the city at daybreak and scattered again as darkness falls. It finds itself towards evening in its own territory in the miles and miles of little red houses in little silent streets ... There are many interests beyond the working hours ... a greenhouse filled with chrysanthemums ... a bicycle shed ... The women find time hangs rather heavy on their hands. But there are excursions to shopping centres in the West End...[26]

This characterisation of the suburban life-style, which stressed a conservative adherence to familiar routines and a dehumanisation of its menfolk into helpless wage-slaves who had forfeited responsibility for their own destinies, provided a prototype for subsequent clichéd renderings of the lower middle class.[27] Masterman's evocative depiction of the gentle and inward-looking leisure occupations of suburban householders, concerned only with the constrained world of family, home and garden, has coloured many assumptions about the world-view and inner lives of suburban men, though it bears a scant relationship to the powerful images of masculine pleasure available in Hackney's commercial sphere. He does allow some freedom for their wives, sisters and daughters, excused the enervating hours at home by occasional trips to city-centre shops, but fashionable consumption is viewed in this sense largely as a feminine sop for a more profound lack of 'authentic' experiences. It is conceived as a pastime removed from the 'dullness' of the periphery and alien to the 'real' activities of men. Versions of this domestic conformity were clearly evident in residential districts such as Clapton, but they informed only part of the inhabitants' lives. In temporal terms lower-middle-class men spent a large proportion of their day away from the suburb. Also, Masterman appears to be referring to men of property, in middle-age. At an earlier stage of the life-cycle, the bachelor with his disposable income was able to draw on a much wider range of outlets both within and outside the suburb, constructing a fashionable identity whose modern energy challenged such closed descriptions.

Elsewhere in Hackney, on the busy arterial routes, away from the suburban enclaves, connections with the inner metropolis were less ambiguous. Shopping for men's clothing provided a clear point of contact and cultural exchange between periphery and centre. Men's clothing retailers, cognizant of the fact that their customers might easily purchase their clothes closer to their place of work, set their services and products in direct competition with city-centre dealers, or attempted to benefit from their close proximity to the square-mile. The hatter Alfred Reid of Mare Street (close to the corner of Well Street) circulated a flyer in 1885 which opened with the sales-lines:

> Don't go to the City to purchase a Hat;
> For nothing you'll gain by a purchase like that,
> Many people are under a fatal mistake
> In choosing the City for fashion and make;
> We own that the sound of 'the City' may claim
> respectful attention—but 'what's in a name?'

Moving from a poetic to a pictorial address, a Hackney Road retailer of roughly the same date circulated a trade card which was shaped like a City hansom cab. A fashionably dressed couple make the unlikely request of the cabbie to: 'Drive us to Abraham's, The Cash Tailor, 63, Hackney Road'.[28] Mention of the City as a venue for the acquisition of clothing also often surfaced in the advertising columns of the local press. The *Hackney and Kingsland Gazette,* far from exclusively supporting the interests of native trade, welcomed the revenue which flowed from the advertising of retailers beyond the borough boundaries who were keen to exploit the custom of Hackney residents. In May 1895 for example, Baker Brothers, wholesale tailors of Eldon Street, close to Liverpool Street Station, promised 'no more ready made clothing' but 'single garments to measure at wholesale prices, saving middlemen's profits'. Such outfits included business suits, morning coats, and cycling suits. Tempting north-east Londoners with work and leisure clothing at bargain prices, Baker Brothers invited readers to call or write for self-measurement forms, reminding them to 'mention this paper'.[29]

The texts of such promotions, together with the actual display of retailing on the street, indicate that men's clothing in Hackney was organised in a variety of ways. It was oriented towards the specific needs of the locality, yet it also looked out towards a broader city-wide picture. Furthermore, the characteristics of the clothing sector also merged with the social reputations of particular districts, their longer histories and outward visual and material profiles inter-weaving with the daily practices of their inhabitants to reveal varied employment patterns, leisure pursuits, life-stages, domestic relationships and class affiliations. How different was the situation in that other space frequented daily by so many of Hackney's men? Although spreading its influence outwards, the retail sector of the square mile represented a sealed and extraordinarily dense arena of sartorial commodification.

What was presented in the City was a more tightly boundaried masculine version of metropolitan modernity.

Journalistic descriptions of the character of City workers displayed a concern both with the spectacular qualities of the urban setting, its aloofness from the districts abutting it, and its heavy reliance on the male populations of those districts to service its industries and man its desks. This was especially marked in articles recording the morning rush hour. In accounts such as that by P. Ryan on 'Going to Business in London' written in 1903, the hierarchical features of the Hackney retail scene were made flesh. From the Homerton docker to the Stamford Hill banker, identities forged with the aid of suburban retailers took on a new intensity in the City. The building trade commuters, arriving on the workmen's trains in the early hours, were depicted as uniform in appearance, but wholesome in effect. Their supervisors were identified by the idiosyncratic adoption of individual symbols of respectability or fashion, which punctuated their functional and constrained site garments: 'it is easy to distinguish the foreman of work. He is comfortably dressed in clothes that seem never to have been new ... his turn down collar is very white and his necktie is a shiny black ... The clerk of works is a superior person ... his hat is nearly always a soft felt; very rarely indeed the stately conventional article.' The company secretary, lounging in his private hansom cab, basked in sartorial splendour: 'His silk hat is drawn slightly over his brows. His small dark moustache is carefully groomed. His legs are crossed, and one foot, poised in the air, shows a patent leather boot tapering with perfect cadence to the toe. His waistcoat is a work of art ... He looks decidedly a dandy, but one with plenty of work in him.'[30] Like the figures shown driving in a hansom to Abraham's the cash tailor, these commuters were seen to inhabit a liminal space between suburb and centre, linking the sartorial and social characteristics of both. Once ensconced in the City, however, the 'modernity' of masculine appearances was sharpened, reflecting the rapid changes which were taking place in this work environment.

The sartorial details which symbolised progress or suggested the appropriate register for manly display and behaviour at work, also formed a material backdrop to the 'nine to five' routine. Take for example the novelist William Pett Ridge's retrospective observations on the presence of German clerks in the City: 'bland persevering-young men' who patronized the German Gymnasium in Pancras Road and 'lodged mainly in the south of London, Catford in particular ... to obtain bed, breakfast and evening meal at 13 and 6d a week'.[31] Or consider the hostile descriptions of women who intruded into the square mile, covered in J. P. Blake's warning that: 'the appearance in a City office of a pretty girl in a summer frock inspires feelings of wonder and delight, but ... is nonetheless untoward and bizarre'.[32] In such accounts it is possible to discern some of the social and sexual pressures which set the stiff suits of City workers in a higher relief. The sociologist David Lockwood has suggested that the worries and frustrations of City clerks and businessmen were largely a product of the pressures of class status. This encouraged an obsession with respectability, as it was enacted in the figure of the 'gentleman'. As Lockwood and others have emphasized, this cultural ideal was: 'so sufficiently vague that it could become curiously confused ... a powerful social control over any intransigence' as well as a 'privilege'. The assumption of quasi-gentlemanly status through demeanour and clothing formed part of the clerk's reward in this period.[33] Together with a desire to differentiate social rank, the occupational uniforms of the City also reflected the daily challenges of a shifting gendered and international context, as well as the demands of new office regimes and settings. Foreign workers, female stenographers, typewriters, imposing new office blocks, imperialist rhetoric, all informed the politics of personal appearances. Their challenge to the traditional rhetorics of City decorum to some extent destabilized the conventions of 'gentlemanly' masculinity which had defined the consuming activities of the City worker, opening up the potential for pioneering clothing retailers to further trade on the shifting meanings of the masculine image.[34]

The City's pre-eminence rested on its reputation as a zone for the production and management of financial wealth rather than its disposal. Despite this fact the *City of London Directory for 1900* projected a landscape littered with provisions for the 'gentlemanly' wardrobe, which made Hackney's teeming shopping streets appear empty. Sixty clothiers, 163 hairdressers, thirty-four hatters, eighty-six hosiers, forty outfitters and over 600 tailors, clustered between the banking halls, exchanges, accountants' offices, churches, chop houses and coffee shops which constituted the shifting architectural backdrop for the late-nineteenth-century square mile.[35] Particular streets retained their character as sites for commercial rather than business ventures. Ludgate Circus and St Paul's Churchyard, together with Cheapside, offered the greatest concentrations of clothing emporia, benefiting from their proximity to the textile and haberdashery warehouses of Wood Street. Such outlets had remained intact, in spite of developments which were transforming many of the area's residential and retailing districts into banking and financial trading quarters. Significantly, the area around the cathedral had a long tradition for clothes retailing and for the buying and selling of fashionable ephemera.[36] By the turn of the century, however, the surrounding streets were being turned into offices for bankers, stockbrokers and clerks, superseding their previous status as sites for merchants' homes and tradesmen's workshops. The journalist Charles Turner summarized the changing ground pattern of the City in an article of 1903, when he noted that older commercial traditions were increasingly being hemmed in by new buildings and workers:

Each centre ... represents an aggregation of allied interests. Of such are the banks of Lombard

Street, the shipping offices of Leadenhall and Fenchurch Street, the accountants of Old Jewry, the clothes and clothing interests of Wood Street and the narrow ways just east of St Pauls ... the curious excrescent growths from the great Bank district to be found in the extraordinary maze of irregular narrow lanes and cul-de-sacs of Austin Friars and Copthall Avenue, where you see an overflow of hatless clerks from Throgmorton Street.[37]

Other City streets were the sites of an older grouping of established trades; Harrow Alley and Middlesex Street boasted a high proportion of clothiers, while tailors' businesses were more plentiful in the region of Aldgate, which was close to the centre of garment production in Whitechapel. However, from the 1880s evidence from photographic images of City thoroughfares and from trade directories reveals new office buildings and business headquarters regularly interspersed with menswear retailers. Turner reflected that 'in Bishopsgate, Old Broad Street and London Wall we get the modern system of great blocks of offices ... cities in themselves with a maze of streets on every floor ... some of them boasting a restaurant, a barber, a tobacconist and even a collar and tie shop'.[38] Views of Cannon Street in 1910, its pavements blocked by top-hatted desk men, showed the palazzo-like façades of shipping assurance companies and trading houses, obscured by overhanging signs for 'haircuts 6d' and 'umbrellas recovered in one hour'.[39] The appearance of Cheapside in the summer of 1900, its inhabitants' top hats laid aside for straw boaters and the masculine tenor of the street enlivened by the presence of several female shoppers, was defined by a row of buildings which clearly reflected the integration of business and consumer activity. Blundell Brothers, the milliners and furriers, sat alongside the offices of the *Draper's Record* and *Men's Wear* magazine. These premises were adjacent to a narrow dining room which adjoined Percy Jones & Co., Time Saving Office Systems, J & H

Meyers Wholesale Furriers, and the Aerated Bread Company.[40]

City clothing retailers thus contributed significantly to the visual environment of the square mile, offering a distinctive focus for the wares of the retailer that complemented the professional identities and working spaces of many City consumers. Traditional tailoring interiors were generally noted for their cramped and utilitarian simplicity, constructed plainly in deal, and providing little more than a changing room for successive fittings and a storage and working area for the handling of cloth. Window displays were minimal. Outfitters and hosiers on the other hand tended to incorporate the most progressive fittings and decorations as a foil for the display of ready-made items, which were themselves indicative of the extraordinary expansion of the menswear industry during this period. Shimmering glass and steel display cases, large windows, black lacquered woodwork and white-washed walls announced a very particular version of modernity, which prioritized hygienic surfaces, copious space and light. In this vein, the hosier Robinson & Cleaver of 101 Cheapside advertised the opening of its new premises opposite St Mary-le-Bow with a pamphlet illustrating the incorporation of its elegant, spotlit façade into the general street scene. The advertising imagery revealed an airy, two-tiered display of plate glass and fine iron work, punctuating the grey monotony of its administrative neighbours, while not over-asserting its own architectural individuality. Robinson & Cleaver's restrained signage and royal crest provided a textbook example of the hosier's preferred mode of address and a clear echo of the decorum of City dressing, whilst also suggesting an element of conscious fashionability and a sleek functional aesthetic which positioned such men's clothing outlets at the forefront of modernist architectural experimentation and innovative retail technique.[41]

As Cheapside moved west through to Holborn Viaduct, directing the crowds towards

New Oxford Street, and Ludgate Hill flowed into Fleet Street and the Strand, the retailing environment underwent a substantial change. The city of work was gradually transformed into the sites of leisure and popular diversion which signalled the arrival of the West End. This was the city of the tourist. It was a world characterized by its playful unruliness in the prose of Edwin Pugh, who in 1908 described the Strand as a collection of:

> brick … granite and stucco … dormer windows and noble stone copings—one coping adorned with a fresco of classical figures … advertising some up-to-date brand of physical culture—plate glass windows, expansive and boldly glittering … hotels that are towns in themselves … one temple of drama which might have sprung from the ruined splendour that was Greece … an ornate restaurant, palatial but popular and cheap, the frivolous Tivoli music hall and sombre Somerset House.[42]

The heterogeneity of this part of metropolitan London signalled a familiar form of modernity pitched around the notion of pleasure and its packaging and presentation for consumption.

A geographical progression from the smaller, older buildings which tended to house the shops of the square mile with their relatively discreet and contained façades, to the large, brash purpose-built bazaars of the West End, was captured in the promotional material of Charles Baker & Co. This retailing outlet was opened in 1877 to keep pace with the Civil Service Stores. By 1895 it had expanded to incorporate four magnificently appointed branches. Baker's city branch at Ludgate Hill opposite the Old Bailey contained only three window bays and limited advertising space at the front of a conventional gabled brick front. The head depot and order department at High Holborn boasted five bays and an exuberantly decked exterior, fronted by company slogans in wrought iron, together with a flag pole. The Tottenham Court Road branch on the corner of Euston Road, near to Maples the famous furniture warehouse, took up the widest expanse of pavement and enjoyed display space on two sides of the building. The Oxford Street store, a few doors from Peter Robinson and entirely devoted to gentlemen's bespoke tailoring, inhabited a fine beaux-arts style structure, with Mansard roofs and sweeping arches. Its architectural confidence was echoed in the flamboyant art nouveau scrolls of its contemporary catalogues.[43]

As men's clothing stores penetrated more deeply into the retailing heart of the capital, their visual features and modes of address took on the characteristics of established genteel consumption. Traditionally, of course, the protagonists of these West End forms of consumer culture were largely female. In his critique of Park Lane, Pugh spoke of a district where 'life moves indeed with an orderly, seemly leisure-liness. In all these streets there are numerous evidences of a polished, cushioned state of being … Beauty regally adorned trips fussily from kerb to Blyth doorway in an aura of sweet perfumes … with modern cavaliers in their modern armour of starch bowing them to and fro.'[44] What was being referred to here were a series of masculine social identities which echoed the geographical shift from business to pleasure. These were scripts which had much stronger links with the ideal of the leisured salon, drawing on established discourses of fashionable feminine consumption rather than the rhetoric of work or familial duty. The romantic notion of the bachelor playboy replaced the figure of the spruce and muscular clerk as a key advertising and retailing referent. This elevation of the West End bachelor 'type' had been a marked characteristic of popular writing on London since the early nineteenth century and reached its apex by 1900.[45] The 1860s in particular were identified with a celebration of the seemingly wealthy metropolitan single-man's 'loud' personal style.[46] This character's existence was seen to revolve around food and drink, night-life and the brash culture of the modern journal. By the turn of the century this louchness had been glossed over in favour of a more glamorous promotion of dandified attributes, connected to the rapid commercialisation of the West End as a site for the new saloon bars and restaurants of entrepreneurs such as Spiers and Pond, and a second wave of huge department stores. The bachelor playboy now represented a profitable and unthreatening niche in the marketing of goods including tobacco, alcohol, theatre productions and clothing.

Drawing on this popular rhetoric the department store Peter Robinson made a concerted effort to attract masculine custom to its elite Oxford Street store by presenting itself as a well-kept secret known only to the most select of customers. In a booklet published in 1912 and illustrated by the modish cartoonist Dudley Hardy, it depicted a conversation between two fictitious West End gents: the author, Arthur Lawrence and his friend, civil servant the Hon. Herbert Blyth. In tone and visual style the copy drew the male customer into a narrative more usually reserved for female aristocratic shoppers. In opposition to the solitary consumption of the Hackney professional, these representations evoked the idea of shopping as a social event shared between male friends. The writer created a very personal exchange which revolved around the merits of a distinctive West End articulation of 'taste':

> Blyth is quite an exemplar in the matter of dress ... 'the cult of slovenliness' he exclaimed as we stood at the corner of Bond Street ... 'ought to entitle the man who is not driven to slovenliness by absolute poverty to wear the broad arrow for the rest of his life.' ... It occurred to me that I had never asked Blyth where he is tailored. On putting the question he replied: 'Peter Robinson'. 'Tut tut!' I responded as Blyth linked his arm in mine and drew me northwards towards Oxford Street. 'I ask for your tailor and

you refer me to a drapery establishment.' Blyth promptly took me to task. 'I am going there now and you cannot possibly have anything better to do than to come along with me. I will introduce you to the finest cutter in London. The majority of my best friends have their clothes made in the tailoring department of Peter Robinson'.[47]

The leading trade paper, the *Tailor and Cutter*, certainly seemed to be aware of these differences between City and West End selling methods when it claimed that Regent Street:

> is 'the' street of the Metropolis where within a few hundred yards, one may see most of the popular styles of garments either in actual wear or exhibited in the shop windows. Yet it is not distinctly a tailor's or an outfitter's street, although there are a few well known establishments whose history has always been connected with this thoroughfare. The most recent invasions of tailordom began about ten or twelve years ago, and shocked the select trades by a display of goods and tickets which is generally associated with the district lying eastwards and towards the City.[48]

Furthermore, the goods on display reflected a clientele with tastes far removed from the office trade that formed the customer-base in the City. Thus:

> The West End clothiers who by some paradox came from the City a few years ago, have a nice display of grey herringbone or feather pattern tweeds, useful either for trouserings or suitings, for plain dressing gentlemen. Those who like 'character' in the designs of the materials they wear may have the pleasure of examining some striking patterns ... The colours cannot be described as 'subdued tints'; they are striking combinations of fawn or grey grounds with dark thread overchecks. They are following a very prevalent custom amongst tailors who make a show in their window by exhibiting three over garments. One of these was made from a black and white herringbone material of loose texture ... This was cut to hang loosely, had a

fly front and Frock Coat lapels … an appropriate garment for a dressy gentleman. The other two garments were very much in the background, but we could observe that the collar of one was trimmed with astrakhan, and the other with seal or plush.[49]

One of two hypotheses can be deduced from this type of trade commentary. Either the loud checks and astrakhan collars of Regent Street served a wholly different constituency of customers from those in the City, or the circumstances and expectations of West End retailing demanded a mode of address and display quite distinct from that employed by City tailors—as different indeed as the broad Nash terraces of Oxford Circus and Regent Street were from the medieval alleys leading off Cheapside and Lothbury. Yet the social type conjured up by the loud style of the West End was arguably positioned as the most enduring representation in commercial and imaginative terms. It supplied a template of modern masculinity which cast the other versions into shadow. Many of the accoutrements of the bachelor type, from his tightly-cut modern suits to his coloured shirts and horse-shoe tie-pins, were precisely the commodities which both characterized the significant shift from old tailoring to new outfitting practices in the men's retailing sector during the period. They found the widest markets across social groupings, attracting the attentions of monkey paraders, clerks, shop-walkers, actors, journalists and young aristocrats alike. The look of the modern man promoted most coherently by the West End retailer provided a clear precedent for twentieth-century ideals of fashionable masculinity. The mannered social scripts carried by the images of men in astrakhan collars and monocles in Regent Street, St James and Mayfair also evoked the etiquette of a new 'smart' society governed by the power of consumer choice.

This atmosphere is very obviously communicated in contemporary guides such as *London and Londoners,* published in 1898:

It is fashionable to be radical in theory and advance women's privileges.

To have an inner knowledge of all classes of society. To know the latest club scandals. To have some particular fad. To wear some particular garment different from anybody else … To telegraph always, but rarely write a letter, unless one has a secretary. To be up in the slang of the day … to know the points of a horse. To have an enormous dog in the drawing room … To know the latest music hall song … To go to Paris twice a year and at least once to Monte Carlo. Never to be in town after Goodwood or to return to it before November … To excel in one's special sport, fox hunting for preference … To subscribe to every journal published. To belong to a club and have some of one's letters and telegrams sent there. Always to fill one's rooms with more men than women.[50]

Whilst such a list of elite social pastimes revelled in the paradoxical nonsense of trivia, its pointed social observations also mapped an accumulated cosmopolitan knowledge which defined the exalted status of the early-twentieth-century London playboy—'the man about town'. In its random citation of modishness, what were registered were the juxtapositions of high and low culture, and reactionary posturing combined with hearty philistinism, which shaped the dominant model of fashionable masculinity at the turn of the century. Here was a dandified persona which could comfortably accommodate advanced taste and commodity fetishism within its remit, without compromising dominant notions of manliness. What was especially resonant in the list of masculine pastimes were the references to music hall, slang, sport, new technology and travel. Gendemen's clubland, along with gambling and hunting, would have connoted aristocratic excess fifty years earlier, but the engagement with the modernity of London now positioned the West End consumer as part of a culture transfixed by the idea of showy masculine pleasures. The figure of the leisured urban male, targeted by the publishers of such guides, had himself come to signify a modern and fashionable style of living by the 1890s, as potent in commodity terms as Marie Lloyd or Princess Alexandra. And like his female counterparts, he was utilized by retailers and consumers alike as a prop on which products could be hung, across from Hackney to Hyde Park.

Yet while these assertive models of masculine consumption proclaimed a bullish adherence to the polished and flourishing style of the bachelor dandy, the co-existence of older, more restrained and 'gentlemanly' versions of manliness in London's retail geography gives some indication of the tensions implicit in the ideal. Confined to the tailoring catalogue, or the society guide, the leisured male consumer epitomized the essence of West End fashionable poise and offered a very modern take on the sartorial options available to the aspirant man-about-town. Yet so ubiquitous did his figure become, through its reproduction in yellow-back novels, advertising campaigns and stage productions, that negative or problematic versions of the type were inevitable. For every clean-cut young Englishman puffing the 'smart' attractions of detachable collars in the Hackney *Guide,* a more derogatory model could be found, espousing the 'wicked' attractions of the East End, or the quick fortunes to be made from venture capitalism. Beyond the fixing of the West End type as a model for an unproblematic if occasionally risqué consumerism, his wider diffusion through urban culture revealed deeper worries regarding masculinity, effeminacy and class. Despite the close association of the bachelor figure with the new energies of a fashionable consumer culture, his dapper persona drew moral accusations of inauthenticity, of hollow obsessions too closely tied to feminized West End consumption. The journalist Thomas Burke, writing in his autobiography in 1915, looked back to a mythical East End for the reassurance of masculine pleasure in more concentrated 'virile' form, untainted by commerce or business:

It is a good tip when tired of the West, and as the phrase goes, at a loose end, to go East young man ... For the East is eternally fresh, because it is alive. The West, like all things of fashion, is but a corpse electrified. They are so tired, these lily-clad ladies and white-fronted gentlemen, of their bloodless, wine-whipped frivolities ... Night, in the particular spots of the East ... shows you life in the raw, stripped of its silken wrappings ... In the East it may be a thinner, poorer body, but it is alive ... There when the lamps are lighted and bead the night with tears, and the sweet girls go by and throw their little laughter to the boys—there you have your true Bacchanale.[51]

The changes in metropolitan life which linked Hackney, the City and the West End, along with structural changes such as the Aldwych street improvement scheme of 1899 which made transit between east and west much simpler, and the opening of an underground railway linking Marble Arch and the Bank of England the following year, show how male clothing in London was marked not by distinction alone, but also by connection.[52] Such a reading makes Burke's appraisal of East and West appear more obviously literary and personal than topographical and objective. Yet his suggestion that the two worlds connect, if only in negative terms, and his own free movement between them, implies that any reading of commercial and material culture in the period needs to take account of these real and imagined links. The suburb itself did not stand outside urban interpretations of fashion and masculinity, but engaged fully with these complex registers of style. Mica Nava has drawn attention to this phenomenon as a symptom of modernity itself when she claims that 'a crucial component of the concept of modernity was the growing importance of external appearances, of surface impressions ... characterised by an escalating instability of class and geographical boundaries'.[53] While it is clear that local sartorial characteristics were not fully dissolved by these shifts, it is necessary to acknowledge the role played by fashion and retailing in new formations of modern life. The menswear shop and its promotions clearly offered a broad and suggestive stage for the fluid negotiation of such changes across all the zones of London, so that through the figure of the fashion-conscious male shopper the West End could be experienced in Hackney and Hackney in the West End.

NOTES

Reprinted with permission from Christopher Breward, "Fashion and the Man: From Suburb to City Street. The Spaces of Masculine Consumption, 1870–1914," *New Formations: A Journal of Culture/Theory/Politics* 37 (1999), 47–70.

1. Dennis Bradley (1912), *Vogue: A Catalogue for Pope and Bradley,* London: 55.
2. Peter Bailey (1986), 'Champagne Charlie: Performance and Ideology in the Music Hall Swell Song', in J. S. Bratton (ed.), *Music Hall: Performance & Style,* Milton Keynes: Open University Press: 61; P. Bailey (1983), 'Ally Sloper's Half Holiday: Comic Art in the 1880s', *History Workshop Journal* 16: 4–31.
3. James Cundall (1902), *London: A Guide for the Visitor, Sportsman and Naturalist,* London: Greening & Co.: 101.
4. Lori Loeb (1994), *Consuming Angels: Advertising and Victorian Women,* Oxford: Oxford University Press: 11.
5. John Benson (1994), *The Rise of Consumer Society in Britain 1880–1980,* London: Longman: 59–81; John Benson & Gareth Shaw (eds) (1992), *The Evolution of Retail Systems c. 1800–1914,* Leicester: Leicester University Press.
6. Christopher Breward (1998), 'Manliness and the Pleasures of Consumption: Masculinities, Fashion and London Life', unpublished PhD thesis, Royal College of Art, London.
7. Rosalind Williams (1982), *Dream Worlds: Mass Consumption in Late Nineteenth Century France,* Berkeley and Los Angeles: University of California Press; Elaine Abelson (1989), *When Ladies Go A Thieving: Middle Class Shoplifters in the Victorian Department Store,* Oxford: Oxford University Press; Lynne Walker (1995), 'Vistas of Pleasure: Women Consumers of Urban Space in the West End of London 1850–1900', in C. Campbell Orr (ed.), *Women in the Victorian Art World,* Manchester: Manchester University Press: 70–88.
8. David Alexander (1970), *Retailing in England during the Industrial Revolution,* London: Athlone Press: 128–146.
9. George Chauncey (1994), *Gay New York: Gender, Urban Culture and the Making of the Gay Male World 1890–1940,* London: Flamingo: 26.
10. Richard Allen (1998), *The Moving Pageant: A Literary Sourcebook on London Streetlife 1700–1914,* London: Routledge.
11. Ford Madox Hueffer (1904), *The Soul of London: A Survey of a Modern City,* London: Alston Rivers: 70–71.
12. Lynda Nead (1996), 'Mapping the Self: Gender, Space and Modernity in Mid-Victorian London', in Roy Porter (ed.), *Reuniting the Self: Histories from the Renaissance to the Present,* London: Routledge: 167.
13. Walter Besant (1911), *London North of the Thames,* London: Adam & Charles Black: 553–554.
14. Benjamin Clarke (1986), *Glimpses of Ancient Hackney & Stoke Newington,* London: London Borough of Hackney.
15. *Official Guide to the Metropolitan Borough of Hackney* (1914), London: Hackney Borough Council: 27.
16. Frank Bechofer (1981), *The Petit Bourgeoisie: Comparative Studies of the Uneasy Stratum,* London: Macmillan: 182; Joseph Banks (1954), *Prosperity & Parenthood: A Study of Family Planning among the Victorian Middle Classes,* London: Routledge: 199–200.
17. George Sims (1904), 'Off the Track in London: Around Hackney Wick', *The Strand Magazine,* September: 40.
18. David Mander and Jenny Golden (1991), *The London Borough of Hackney in Old Photographs 1890–1960,* Stroud: Alan Sutton: 57.
19. Loeb, op. cit.: 130–132.
20. Sims, op. cit.: 41.
21. Besant, op. cit.: 550.

22. William Greenslade (1992), 'Fitness and the Fin-de-Siècle', in John Stokes (ed.), *Fin de Siècle/Fin du Globe: Fears and Fantasies of the Late Nineteenth-Century,* London: Macmillan: 48.

23. *Kelly's Hackney, Dalston, Old Ford & Bow Directory for 1890* (1890), London: Kelly & Co.

24. Geraldine Mitton (1908), *The Fascination of London: Hackney and Stoke Newington,* London: Adam & Charles Black: 18.

25. C. F. G. Masterman (1909), *The Condition of England,* London: Methuen: 68.

26. Ibid.: 69–70.

27. F. M. L. Thompson (ed.) (1982), *The Rise of Suburbia,* Leicester: Leicester University Press; John Carey (1992), *The Intellectuals and the Masses,* London: Faber; Geoffrey Crossick & Heinz-Gerhard Haupt (1995), *The Petit Bourgeoisie in Europe 1780–1914,* London: Routledge.

28. John Johnson Collection of Printed Ephemera, Bodleian Library, Men's Clothing.

29. *The Hackney and Kingsland Express,* May 13 1895.

30. P. Ryan (1903), 'Going to Business in London', in George Sims (ed.), *Living London,* Vol. 1, London: Cassell: 197–200.

31. William Pett Ridge (1925), *I Like to Remember,* London: Hodder & Stoughton: 77.

32. John Blake (1904), *The Money God: A Tale of the City,* London: Heinemann: 20.

33. David Lockwood (1989), *The Blackcoated Worker: A Study in Class Consciousness,* Oxford: Clarendon Press: 29–30.

34. Felix Driver and David Gilbert (1998), 'Heart of Empire? Landscape, Space and Performance in Imperial London', *Society & Space* Vol. 16, No. 1.

35. *The City of London Directory for 1900* (1900), London: W. H. & L. Collingridge.

36. Jane Ashelford (1988), *Dress in the Age of Elizabeth I,* London: Batsford: 44.

37. C. S. Turner (1903), 'The City at High Noon', in G. Sims (ed.), *Living London,* Vol. II, London: Cassell: 126.

38. Ibid.: 125.

39. Walter Besant (1910), *The Survey of London: London City,* London: A. & C. Black.

40. John Usher (1976), *City of London Past & Present,* Oxford: Oxford Illustrated Press.

41. John Johnson Collection, op. cit.

42. Edwin Pugh (1908), *The City of the World: A Book about London and the Londoner,* London: Thomas Nelson: 19.

43. John Johnson Collection, op. cit.

44. Pugh, op. cit.: 24.

45. Pierce Egan (1821), *Life in London,* London: Sherwood, Neely & Jones.

46. Donald Shaw (1908), *London in the Sixties by One of the Old Brigade,* London: Everett & Co.

47. A. Lawrence (1912), *Man in the Making,* London: Peter Robinson: 5, 7; John Johnson Collection, op. cit.

48. *The Tailor & Cutter,* February 5 1903: 87.

49. Ibid.

50. Rosalind Pritchard (1898), *London and Londoners: What to See: What to Do: When to Shop: And Practical Hints,* London: Scientific Press: 323–324.

51. Thomas Burke (1915), *Nights in Town: A London Autobiography,* London: George Allen & Unwin: 75–76.

52. Richard Sennett (1996), *Flesh and Stone: The Body and the City in Western Civilization,* New York: Norton: 317–354.

53. Mica Nava (1996), 'Modernity's Disavowal: Women, the City and the Department Store', in Mica Nava and Alan O'Shea (eds), *Modern Times: Reflections on a Century of English Modernity,* London: Routledge: 47.

32

FASHIONING THE PLAYBOY: MESSAGES OF STYLE AND MASCULINITY IN THE PAGES OF *PLAYBOY* MAGAZINE, 1953–1963

Becky Conekin

Many people believe that there were no general men's magazines, especially none with a marked interest in fashion, until the 1980s. According to Sean Nixon 'advertising and publishing debates' raged in Britain 'between 1983 and 1989' over how to produce a viable formula for general-interest men's magazines, which included some attention to the issue of masculine fashionability (Nixon 1996: 129).[1] On this debate, Nixon quotes Simon Marquis, amongst others, writing in 1985 in the advertising trade's 'Bible', *Campaign*. There Marquis argued that a men's general-interest magazine would not work because:

> While women become 'friends' with their magazines there is an inbuilt male resistance to the idea of a magazine that makes public and shares ideas about being a man. To men it is an unacceptable contradiction. Self-consciousness is permissible, even attractive in a women [sic]; 'it is perceived as weak and unmanly in a man' (Marquis, as quoted by Nixon 1996: 129).

But, of course, beyond the narrower confines of the British publishing industry there were earlier examples of male magazines that addressed men publicly, sharing 'ideas about being a man', often through recourse to debates on fashionable consumption. Examples include the inter-war *Esquire* and the early fifties *Modern Man,* but in the post-war period the most popular one was *Playboy*.[2] Barbara Ehrenreich asserts that *Playboy* 'encouraged the sense of membership in a fraternity of male rebels' and its founder, Hugh Hefner, wrote in the first editorial: 'We want to make clear from the very start, we aren't a "family magazine." If you're somebody's sister, wife or mother-in-law and picked us up by mistake, please pass us along to the man in your life and get back to your *Ladies' Home Companion*' (Ehrenreich 1983: 43). Ehrenreich has brilliantly shown how '*Playboy* was ... like the party organ of a diffuse and swelling movement' which called for a new, single, heterosexual, consuming male, who escaped the trap of marriage or in her words: 'the bondage of breadwinning' (Ehrenreich 1983: 42, 51). Building on Ehrenreich's argument, I am interested in how *Playboy* addressed, and thereby simultaneously helped to create, this new masculine, always (allegedly) heterosexual consumer, especially in relation to clothes and fashion in its first decade. Ehrenreich goes so far as to argue that the nude female centrefolds were only included in Playboy to 'protect it' from the charge of homosexuality—to make it 'impervious to the ultimate sanction against male rebellion'—'queerness' (Ehrenreich 1983: 51). Whether or not we accept this radical account of *Playboy*'s agenda, we can certainly view the magazine, with its one million plus readers by its third year, as an important site in the construction of a particular form of masculinity—or perhaps, more accurately, particular forms of masculinities—known then as the 'playboy', the 'swinger' or the 'hip bachelor'.

Ehrenreich has shown how Hefner believed that by the end of its first decade *Playboy* even had the power to inspire men to work harder than they might otherwise. She quotes him as stating:

'... *Playboy* exists, in part, as a motivation for men to expend greater effort in their work, develop their capabilities further and climb higher on the ladder of success.' This kind of motivation, he went on, 'is obviously desirable in our competitive, free enterprise system', apparently unaware that the average reader was more likely to be a white-collar 'organization man' or blue-collar employee than a free entrepreneur himself (Ehrenreich 1983: 46).

Certainly, Ehrenreich is being ironic here, recognizing that Hefner was not 'unaware' of his readers' socio-economic backgrounds, but actually more interested in creating the illusion and fantasy of a more upscale clientele for his magazine. Anxieties about the class status of its constituency were revealed in the first survey of *Playboy*'s readers, conducted by 'an independent market research organization', Gould, Gleiss and Benn, Inc., and published in the September 1995 edition of *Playboy* (*Playboy*, Vol. 2, No. 9: 36–7). There Hefner and the magazine announced that 'over 70% of *Playboy*'s readers have attended college'. But a closer look revealed that only 29.8% of readers had a college degree at the time of the survey, while 42.1% had attended college for 'less than 4 years'. Under the list marked with an asterisk the text read: 'Over half of the "College" group are students at the present time and a good percentage may be expected to join the "College degree" group later' (*Playboy*, Vol. 2, No. 9: 36). 'The great majority of *Playboy*'s readers are business and professional men and the young men who are in college who will be in business and the professions in two or three years. *Playboy* has a greater percentage of college men in its audience than any other national magazine' (*Playboy*, Vol. 2, No. 9: 36). Hefner clearly desired his readers to be perceived as 'college-educated' whether they actually were or not. Categories such as 'the college man' and 'the professional' were actively promoted as models of a particular kind of aspirational, white, heterosexual American male fashionability in this period, as opposed to the celebration of rougher, working-class masculinities found in Hollywood films such as *The Wild One* or *Rebel Without a Cause* (Votolato 1998: 245).[3]

Hefner also distinguishes the playboy as distinct from outdoor types who spent their leisure time shooting, hunting or fishing. In the very first issue in December 1953, along with the centrefold of Marilyn Monroe, Hugh Hefner gave his readers a sort of manifesto that asserted their masculine right to 'spend[ing] most of our time inside ... mixing up cocktails and an hors d'oeuvre or two, putting a little mood music on the phonograph and inviting in a female acquaintance for a quiet discussion on Picasso, Nietzsche, jazz, sex', rather than 'thrashing through thorny thickets or splashing about in fast-flowing streams' (*Playboy*, Vol. 1, No. 1: n.p.). *Playboy* defined its readers two years later as: 'sophisticated, intelligent, urban—a young man about town, who enjoys good, gracious living' (*Playboy*, Vol. 2, No. 9: 36). The art historian, Christopher Reed, has argued that: 'If the domestic is the main arena for the enforcement of conventional divisions of masculinity and femininity (along with their complement, heterosexuality), however, the modern home has also been a staging ground for rebellion against these norms' (Reed 1996: 14). The playboy's 'bachelor pad', as represented implicitly and explicitly in the pages of the magazine, provides a perfect example of the reinforcement of heterosexuality and conventional masculinity and the simultaneous creation of more rebellious and allegedly liberated forms of both.

As Steven Cohan has written, *Playboy* magazine promulgated the fantasy of the 'bachelor pad' in its 1956 series, with its alliterative title, '*Playboy*'s Penthouse Apartment: A High Handsome Haven for the Bachelor in Town' (Cohan

1996). Cohan contends that: 'The bachelor pad operated as a site of consumerism; it marked the single man's marginal position in relation to domestic ideology of the period, while at the same time allowing for his recuperation as a consumer whose masculinity could be redeemed—even glamorized—by the things he bought to accessorize his virility' (Cohan 1996: 28). What these imagined urban 'playboys' were encouraged to consume in the realm of fashion is one of the main concerns of this article.

PLAYBOY 'WAS WRITTEN AND EDITED FOR HUGH M. HEFNER'

In a piece published in 1991, which was an attempt to revisit the girls' comics she had worked on more than ten years earlier, Angela McRobbie called for scholars to examine 'production values' and the 'ideas and values of those working on magazines' as a way to further understand magazines and their appeal to their audiences (McRobbie 1991: 186).[4] McRobbie's challenge is a good one, especially in relation to *Playboy*. It is difficult fully to understand *Playboy* without considering the character of its creator and editor. This may not always be the case with every text, but Hefner is famous for exercising extraordinary control over all aspects of *Playboy*. That, along with the fact that the magazine was in every way a dream come true for its founder, suggests that some biographical information will shed light on the curious creation that was *Playboy* in its first decade. An early editor, Jack Kessie, has stated that: 'That magazine was written and edited for Hugh M. Hefner' (Kessie, as quoted by Halberstam 1993: 574). So, who was this Hefner in the early fifties?

Hefner had graduated from high school in a Chicago suburb in 1944, where he was more renowned for his extra-curricular than his academic pursuits. He had been raised in a Methodist household that permitted neither smoking nor drinking and observed the Sabbath so seriously that not even the radio was played. After

graduating, he volunteered for the army, but his war duty consisted of working as a typing clerk in Camp Hood, Texas. One biographer reports that Hefner 'found the language and behavior of the military profoundly shocking. For a boy who had only just turned 18, never swore, was a virgin, the infantry came as an exceedingly nasty surprise' (Miller 1984: 27). In the spring of 1946 he returned to Illinois and his girlfriend Mildred Williams, whom he married three years later. He enrolled at the University of Illinois, Urbana through the GI Bill, joining his girlfriend, who was already studying to be a teacher. Hefner hoped to be a journalist, but majored in psychology. He also picked up on his high-school pursuits, contributing cartoons to the university daily newspaper and acting as managing editor of a campus magazine called *The Shaft*. In 1948 he wrote an enthusiastic review of the Kinsey Report for *The Shaft*, in which he expressed his disdain for the hypocrisy of American public attitudes towards sex. The ground-breaking Kinsey Report indicated that 86 per cent of American men had premarital sex, 70 per cent had sex with prostitutes and 40 per cent engaged in extramarital intercourse. From that moment on it seems that Hefner decided that sex was a legitimate area of scholarship, and he began to read everything from medical journals to pornography in the name of such academic study (Miller 1984: 28–9).[5] (In the first issue of *Playboy* the introductory text states: 'We believe, too, that we are filling a publishing need only slightly less important than the one just taken care of by the Kinsey Report' (*Playboy*, Vol. 1, No. 1: n.p.)

He graduated from the University of Illinois in 1949 and applied unsuccessfully to every magazine and newspaper in Chicago. After a brief stint in the personnel department of a carton company, Hefner entered a Master's program in sociology at Northwestern University on Chicago's north shore. He and his wife were living with his parents and she was teaching school. Hefner only lasted one semester in graduate school. However, while he was at Northwestern he built on his new-found cause, writing a paper on 'Sex Behavior and the US Law' in which he argued that a complete re-examination of all laws relating to sex was necessary (Miller 1984: 31). Next, he held the post of advertising copywriter for a large Chicago department store before moving to *Esquire* as a promotional copywriter. According to one biographer, Russell Miller, *Esquire* was Hefner's favourite magazine and he was 'thrilled' to get the job (Miller 1984: 32). In late 1951 *Esquire* moved its headquarters to New York and Hefner decided not to follow. Nevertheless, his employment at *Esquire* left a lasting impact. It explains the seemingly odd, frequent comparisons between that magazine and *Playboy* that appeared in the first few volumes of Hefner's creation (see, for example, *Playboy*, Vol. 1, No. 5, April 1954: 3). In 1957 when *Playboy*'s circulation figures were closing in on *Esquire*'s—the January issue of *Playboy* sold 687,593 copies, while *Esquire*'s sold 778,190—Hefner is featured in a series of photographic cartoons as sitting at a desk, and the caption reads: 'I'm truly sorry Mr. Smart [then publisher of *Esquire*] but at present our staff is at full capacity. Leave your name with the office boy and I'll call if something comes up' (Miller 1984: 59).

The story of *Esquire* is an interesting one, and it highlights the centrality of style and fashion to Hefner's conception of *Playboy*.[6] In 1933 the editorial team who had founded *Apparel Arts,* 'the first male fashion magazine aimed at trade people, manufacturers, wholesalers and retailers,' launched *Esquire* 'in the same spirit ... at the general public' (Chenoune 1993: 188). Subscriptions to *Esquire* reached 728,000 by 1937. The man behind both magazines, Arnold Gingrich, was determined 'to liberate male stylishness from the closed little circle of "high society" with its English traditions, its private schools, clubs and shopping trips to London' (ibid.). Gingrich pitched *Esquire* at the middle-class male consumer, attempting 'to democratize the game of fashion and stylishness' (ibid.). Its broader-based constituency distinguishes this

phenomenon from earlier examples of masculine representations built around conspicuous consumption, such as those outlined by Christopher Breward for late Victorian Britain and Paula Fass for 1920s America (Breward 1999; Fass 1977). In addition, Gingrich's magazines were promoting ready-to-wear, not custom-made, clothing, which the American industry was perfectly placed to provide, as it entered 'a golden age that would last until the mid-1960s' (Chenoune 1993: 188).

Miller claims that Hefner saw *Esquire* as 'the arbiter of taste and style, the very last word in male sophistication. He had bought it for years whenever he could afford it, read it with admiration, laughed at the cartoons and spent many happy hours studying the lustrous girls drawn by Alberto Vargas and George Petty' (Miller 1984: 32). By the forties, in addition to being the most fashionable, *Esquire* was also the most daring men's magazine, with several issues declared obscene by the US Post Office. But by the time Hefner joined its staff its editors had begun what they called the 'rescue of *Esquire* from bawd(try' (Miller 1984: 33). Hefner had been disappointed by this turn of events, finding even the forties version of *Esquire* less bawdy than he would have liked. In 1952, in the fifty-second volume of what he called his *Comic Autobiography,* which he had been writing since high school, Hefner admitted: 'I'd like to produce an entertainment magazine for the city-bred guy—breezy, sophisticated. The girlie features would guarantee the initial sale, but the magazine would have quality too' (Hefner 1952, as quoted by Miller 1984: 36). A work colleague from about this time, Vince Tajiri, says he remembers Hefner talking 'a lot about becoming a publisher himself, but I don't think anyone took much notice. I thought he was very immature for his age. He was totally unsophisticated, but he had an obsession with sex' (Tajiri, as quoted by Miller 1984: 35). Such a characterization of Hugh Hefner appears repeatedly in the reminiscences of people who knew him just prior to and in the early days of *Playboy.*

Having finally moved from his parents' house to a five-room apartment in Hyde Park on the south side of Chicago, Hefner was next employed as circulation manager for *Children's Activities* magazine, running its direct-mail subscription campaign, which taught him valuable lessons in how to distribute a national title. He and a college friend began working in the evenings on the mock-up of a magazine they initially called *Stag Party*. Hefner explained that the idea was a magazine based on the 'contemporary equivalent of wine, women and song, although not necessarily in that order' (Miller 1984: 37). He was able to borrow a little money from a bank and a little more from a loan company, and then he hocked the contemporary living-room furniture that he had bought with money borrowed from his parents. Ray Russell, a writer and editor who worked for *Playboy* in the fifties, has said that: 'A lot of it was good luck, random choice, being carried on the tide of the times ... It was a matter of being the right magazine able to take advantage of a rising economy, more than any degree of conscious planning' (Russell, as quoted by Halberstam 1993: 573–4). The prime example of Hefner's good luck and being in the right place at the right time is that in 1952 he discovered in a trade publication that the famous semi-nude Marilyn Monroe calendar had been printed by a company in Chicago. Hefner went directly the same morning to see that company, the John Baumgarth Company. Because of the fear of prosecution for obscenity, Baumgarth did not believe he could use the pictures of Monroe any more than he had, which consisted of featuring them in a free promotional calendar to be used by garages and similar clients. He agreed to sell Hefner the rights to publish the Monroe semi-nude pictures and threw in the colour separations for a fee of $500 (Miller 1984: 37–8). At that moment Hefner knew he had the key to a winning first issue; in December 1953 Volume One, Issue One appeared on the news-stands.

HEFNER'S FASHION AND CONSUMER CHOICES

David Halberstam, in his best-selling work on fifties America, has argued that 'Hefner's great strength was his lack of sophistication. If he was square, he still longed to share the better world, which was now increasingly available around him; in that he mirrored the longings of millions of young men of similar background, more affluent than their parents, wanting a better and freer life' (Halberstam 1993: 574). Hefner shared other heterosexual, newly college-educated veterans' fantasies of a life with less strings and more pleasure. His subscription pitch in the April 1956 issue of *Playboy* defined 'a playboy' in terms of happiness, taste and pleasure. It ran:

> What is a playboy? Is he simply a wastrel, a ne'er-do-well, a fashionable bum? Far from it. He can be a sharp minded young business executive, a worker in the arts, a university professor, an architect or an engineer. He can be many things, provided he possesses a certain kind of view. He must see life not as a vale of tears, but as a happy time, he must take joy in his work, without regarding it as the end of all living; he must be an alert man, a man of taste, a man sensitive to pleasure, a man who—without acquiring the stigma of voluptuary or dilettante—can live life to the hilt. This is the sort of man we mean when we use the word playboy (*Playboy*, Vol. 2, No. 4: n.p.).

A little over a year later Hefner described himself and his pleasures in *Playboy*. Here we can see both how *Playboy* was produced by and for Hefner, and what sort of fashions and commodities were necessary for 'the playboy' lifestyle. In the June 1957 issue Hefner wrote of himself:

> His dress is conservative and casual. He always wears loafers ... There is an electronic entertainment wall in his office, very much like the one featured in *Playboy*'s Penthouse apartment, that includes hi-fi, AM-FM radio,

tape and television, and will store up to 2000 LPs .... He likes jazz, foreign films, Ivy League clothes, gin and tonic and pretty girls—the same sort of things the *Playboy* readers like—and his approach to life is as fresh, sophisticated, and yet admittedly sentimental as is the magazine (*Playboy*, Vol. 4, No. 6: n.p.).

According to his biographers, however, Hefner's dress style had not always been 'casual and conservative' or Ivy-inspired, as he also called it in *Playboy*. It is reported that in the first year or so of *Playboy*, Hefner sported white socks and 'zoot suits' with his penny loafers. It was the chance encounter with Victor Lownes III, whom Hefner immediately made editor in charge of promotion and advertising, that transformed his style. Lownes's 'Ivy League look' inspired Hefner to change his own (Miller 1984: 64).

The original zoot suits were, of course, worn by stylish African–American musicians in the 1930s. But, they came to be the basis of many an American man's look in the forties and even gave rise to the 'bold look' promoted by the fashion industry in 1947 (Chenoune 1993: 208). This was probably the sort of suit Hefner was wearing in the early fifties, a watered-down version of a zoot suit. Yet this still carried some connotations of rebellion and blackness—two associations he was shedding when he donned his Ivy League look. According to the fashion historian Farid Chenoune, both Oxbridge and the Ivy League were thought of as sites of new male fashion trends in the inter-war period (Chenoune 1993: 156). But, twenty or more years later, the smart-casual look of button-downs, blazers, slacks and loafers could be called conservative. Although an advocate of African–American jazz, both personally and in the pages of *Playboy*, and later a truly equal-opportunity employer in his international Playboy Clubs, Hefner's fashion choices for himself and for his readers were decidedly WASP-ish. They eschewed not only any African–American references, but also any hint of the working

class. Neither the popular fifties clothing code for youthful rebellion—T-shirt, blue jeans and black leather jacket—nor the bohemian Village look of the Beats ever found its way into the world of *Playboy* (Chenoune 1993).[7]

Hefner had by 1954, it seems, a very clear idea of both what he and his readership should look like. The youthfulness of their attire should be represented by their relative casualness, not their rebelliousness. They should not look stuffy or dated, like their fathers, but 'fresh and sophisticated' in their Ivy League clothes. As Jo Barraclough Paoletti has shown for turn-of-the-century American men's fashion, younger men have often distinguished themselves from older men through their clothes choices (Paoletti 1985). Pumphrey has written specifically of how older men in the fifties and sixties displayed 'an aggressive indifference to dress and a silent avoidance of bodily display', 'refusing to take notice of fashion' (Pumphrey, as cited by Craik 1994: 191).

Hefner certainly believed that generational differences were key. In his second instalment of his 'Playboy Philosophy' in January 1963, he claimed that there was a new, positive generation who 'searched for new answers and new opportunities.' Although *Life* magazine had dubbed this group 'The Takeover Generation' the previous autumn, Hefner thought his name, 'The Upbeat Generation', was more apt. Simultaneously revealing his personal sense of American history, Hefner (1963) explained that: 'Actually, the spirit and attitude of the Upbeats is right out of the first part of this century—it's the same optimistic viewpoint and zest for living that made America great in the first place. In the 1930s and 1940s we lost faith in ourselves, we hid our individual identities in groups ...' (*Playboy*, Vol. 10, No. 1: 50). But, according to Hefner, this new generation of the early sixties was 'bringing this country alive again' (ibid.). He was explicit that this 'Upbeat Generation'—'the only hope America has for the future'—did not consist of real radicals or revolutionaries. They were not the 'part of this new generation [who] rejected the old in a negative way, simply turning their backs on society and ceasing to communicate' (ibid.). No, the men who subscribed to *Playboy* were those going to university, heading for decent jobs and moving up the social ladder.

TEXTS ON *PLAYBOY*

Curiously, given *Playboy's* huge popularity at the time—the first issue in 1953 exceeded expectations, selling 53,991 copies, one year later circulation was 175,000 and by 1956 it had passed the one million mark—it has only seldom been looked at seriously by scholars (Ehrenreich 1983: 42; Dines 1995: 257). And when it has been, writers and scholars have most often used *Playboy* to illustrate a larger point about for instance feminism, in Barbara Ehrenreich's case, or 'queer masculinity' in Steven Cohan's (Ehrenreich 1983: 42–5; Cohan 1996: 28–41). But what happens if we refocus and examine *Playboy* more in the way we might a woman's magazine? Such a re-examination of *Playboy* in no way disagrees or detracts from those other angles, it is merely an attempt to set out different parameters for this influential magazine. Cultural studies scholarship on girls' and women's magazines has generally focused on questions of fantasy, desire and aspiration (White 1970; Winship 1987b; Wilson 1985; Walkerdine 1990; McRobbie 1991; Craik 1994). Such are the realms of the current argument regarding *Playboy*.

In these terms the most relevant scholarly article on *Playboy* is by Gail Dines, who looks at the magazine in terms of what she calls 'the sexualization of consumerism' (Dines 1995: 254–62). According to Dines, '"soft porn" or "men's entertainment"' magazines 'offer a "lifestyle" that involves the consumption of numerous upmarket commodities as a way of capturing the ultimate prized commodity: lots and lots of attractive,

young, big-breasted women, just like the ones masturbated to in the centerfold' (Dines 1995: 254). She further argues that: 'As with all advertising, the actual product on offer was not the commodity being advertised but rather the fantasy of transformation this product promised to bring to the consumer's life ... the pages of *Playboy* and *Penthouse* are filled with advertisements from companies such as Seagrams, Bensons [*sic*] and Hedges, Mercedes, Sony and Bugle Boy—a sign of both their upscale readership and mainstream status' (ibid.).

First doubts about Dines's interesting argument arise from reading the early issues of *Playboy*, which she herself states have been her focus (Dines 1995: 256). The editorial in Volume One, Issue Twelve, for instance, announced that *Playboy* would soon be 'opening its pages' to advertisers. In the editorial Hefner explained that advertising was not included in *Playboy's* first year of publication because the editors wanted 'to first create a truly new and distinctive men's magazine' (*Playboy*, Vol. 1, No. 12: 3). Others have written that actually advertisers were quite cautious of appearing in *Playboy* initially, since it was not clear that the US Postal Service would allow such pornographic material to be delivered, much less what the public response would be (see, for example, Miller 1984: 64). But, for whatever reason, there was no advertising in the first twelve issues of *Playboy*. Furthermore, in its first few years the advertising was modest and sketchy, and it certainly does not include companies of the calibre of those listed by Dines. Most frequent were advertisements for mail-order 'show-off' record racks, 'tastefully designed drinkware with an authentic black and gold coin collection ringing the top of the glasses', and an ash tray shaped like a golf club 'ready to whack one down the fairway' (*Playboy*, Vol. 2, No. 10: 57, 61).

On a wider level, although Dines seems to be making an anti-reductionist argument about *Playboy*, her reading still contains a certain literalism that makes the beautiful, semi-clad woman the telos of male consumption. Such a reading underestimates the overall aspirational character of *Playboy* magazine. Yes, of course, it was a 'girlie' magazine, and women's bodies were clearly commodified therein. However, the other commodities presented in what she calls the '"service" features on the latest upmarket consumer products' were not only laid out as a means to an end; they were also a large part of the goal. Dines has truly undervalued the importance of those other 'prizes,' especially for the upwardly mobile, lower-middle-class male in fifties and early sixties America. Moreover, it is surely naive to argue that advertisements in particular periodicals correspond to or even map simply on to their readers' socio-economic status. Does anyone really believe that the majority of women who read fashion magazines can afford to buy designer clothes, for example? Such magazines are the stuff of fantasy, desire and aspiration: 'fashion acts as a vehicle for fantasy', in Elizabeth Wilson's words (Wilson 1985: 246; see also Craik 1994: 50–1). Many of the heterosexual male readers of *Playboy* would have served in the Second World War and/or Korea, and then returned to a newly affluent and increasingly domesticated America, which was rife with and then recovering from McCarthyism. The *Playboy* readers were ready to move from military control and uniforms to personal choice in actions and dress. But, since many had been out of the dressing game for some time and most were attempting to move quickly and quietly up the social ladder, these men would have been happy to find a sexy monthly publication to guide their choices, as well as fuel their fantasies. A magazine that assumed these men had already climbed that ladder—that they owned expensive cars, boats, and apartments, read 'the classics,' knew how to cook, how to dress like East Coast, privately-educated men, how to select wine and liquor, etc.—would have had great appeal. Such a magazine, as many women and girls know, gives you the sense in the act of interpolating you as a reader that you would know

how to do all those things once the opportunity arises. Halberstam has written that:

Playboy shepherded a generation of young men to the good life. It helped explain how to buy a sports car, what kind of hi-fi set to buy, how to order in a restaurant, what kind of wine to drink with what kind of meal. For men whose parents had not gone to college, *Playboy* served a valuable function: It provided an early and elementary tutorial on the new American lifestyle. For those fearful of headwaiters in fancy restaurants, wary of slick salesmen in stores and of foreign-car dealers who seemed to speak a language never heard in Detroit, *Playboy* provided a valuable consumer service: It midwifed the readers into a world of increasing plenty (Halberstam 1993: 575–6).

But, here too, we must beware of literalism. Surely, it is more realistic to say that *Playboy* provided its readers with the satisfaction of thinking that if their dreams came true, they would know how to buy a foreign sportscar or order in an exclusive restaurant.

Barbara Ehrenreich writes of how, in mid-fifties America, Americans were encouraged to enjoy 'a life of pleasurable consumption' and 'fun morality' (Ehrenreich 1983: 46). She quotes the motivational researcher, Dr Ernest Dichter, who told businessmen at the time: 'We are now confronted with the problem of permitting the average American to feel moral ... even when he is spending, even when he is not saving ... One of the basic problems of prosperity, then is to demonstrate that the hedonistic approach to his life is a moral, not an immoral one' (Dichter, as quoted by Ehrenreich 1983: 45). It is clear that *Playboy* was an early proponent of such 'fun morality.' The magazine did 'offer a lifestyle' (not to mention an ideology), as Dines has argued. This was a lifestyle which 'swung' not simply because it encouraged single, heterosexual men to stay single and be sexual, but also because it advocated fun through consumption. *Playboy's* pages were filled with new goods, foods, drink and travel. Included in these new masculine, bachelor purchasing pleasures was the pleasure of shopping for clothes and accessories for himself. If we turn to the fashion and style pages of *Playboy* magazine in its first decade in existence, what do we find?

THE FASHION AND STYLE PAGES OF EARLY *PLAYBOY*

We know from the work of Frank Mort that, by the mid-fifties, British mid-market menswear retailers had begun to address 'a fashion-conscious, young adult man,' and that this 'resulted in a proliferation of styles' (Mort 1996: 140, 142). In many ways the fantasy of the American playboy provided a prototype for the British equivalent. At least as presented in the feature on *Playboy*'s 'bachelor pad' in 1956, the American single male consumer was assumed already to own: 'winter wear, summer wear, sports clothes, dress clothes … terry-cloth robes … flat-lying sweaters and knit T-shirts' (*Playboy*, Vol. 3, No. 10: 70; also reprinted with Cohan 1996: 63–7). But the playboy needed assistance in choosing the right components for his copious wardrobe.

In *Playboy*'s first decade there was a marked shift in the tone of its fashion pages from didacticism to fantasy. The first fashion editor listed on *Playboy*'s masthead was Blake Rutherford. This Ivy League-inspired pseudonym belonged to Jack Kessie, who had contributed a freelance piece to the January 1955 issue, and then 'was hired as an associate editor at $100 a week partly because Hefner liked the way he looked', according to Miller. Kessie was a graduate of Drake University in Des Moines, Iowa, and 'he had the kind of casual elegance which Hefner thought exemplified the *Playboy* style' (Miller 1984: 67), As early as the January 1955 issue, Kessie's article, 'The Well Dressed Playboy: *Playboy*'s Position on the Proper Male Attire,' was accompanied by the byline: 'Jack J. Kessie, *Playboy*'s apparel editor' (*Playboy*, Vol. 2, No. 2: 39). The tone of

Kessie's articles, on style, fashion and accessories, whether written under the name of Kessie or Rutherford, was didactic. For example, in that first piece he started by acknowledging men's confusion over fashion choices:

> Although style changes in the men's fashion world are neither as dramatic nor as frequent as those enjoyed by the female, proper masculine dress can become a very confusing matter. If a man is concerned with how he looks, and he should be, he may find himself caught up in a perplexing, phantasmagoria of colour combinations, patterns, styles, designs, fabrics and cuts (*Playboy*, Vol. 2, No. 2: 39).

Kessie's answer to the bewilderment of his readers was a vision of conservative, elegant, establishment dressing. References to conservatism were repeated again and again in his articles. For example, in the piece on the 'The Well Dressed Playboy' Kessie explained: 'Conservative in all departments we lean heavily towards those distinctive details of styling that point up the man as being quietly well dressed.' 'His business shirts are of three basic collar styles, button-down, round (worn with safety pin) and tab … The Edwardian waistcoat is welcomed by our conservative man as an item of rare distinction … His hosiery follows the solid color line … The final mark of our well-tailored man dictates that his shoes be correctly coordinated to the rest of his apparel' (*Playboy*, Vol. 2, No. 2: 39). And such references to Englishness as the mark of conservatism were far from rare. Actual English ties and hats were advocated by Kessie, but even when writing about black dinner jackets and tailcoats he established a long link with Englishness. In 'Formal Forecast: The Return to Black' 'Blake Rutherford' announced to the playboys that:

> After a brief excursion into gaudier evening plumage last winter, the cocks of the walk who know their formal fashion are reverting to black, and depending on the niceties of fabric, tailoring and accessories to point up their individuality.

Now we said black. Not midnight blue, not maroon, not burnt ochre. Just black. Black looks and feels right for all formal occasions, which is why it has been firmly entrenched among the knowledgeable for nearly 100 years, ever since an inconsolable Queen Victoria prescribed mourning for her court after the death of Albert. We recommend wearing it today for the very good reason that dramatic black, coupled with the tasteful crispness of white, lends an elegance of uniformity to dress-up affairs that no colour can match (*Playboy,* Vol. 5, No. 1: 61–2).

'An elegance of uniformity' was what Kessie generally advocated in his autocratic tone. He claimed that there were '... certain basic tenets of style and cut in men's clothing that are unchangeable' (*Playboy,* Vol. 2, No. 9: 27). The key to that conservative message, not surprisingly given his own and Hefner's fashion choices, was summed up in two words: Ivy League. Be it the article about 'Summa Cum Style' (*Playboy,* Vol. 2, No. 10: 18) or 'Ivy Action: The Right Look for the Beach, Boating, Tennis and the Links' (*Playboy,* Vol. 4, No 7: 20), Kessie recommended that the old East Coast, private universities held the answer to the playboy's style quandaries. According to Kessie, '... few will argue [in the Autumn of 1955] against the fact that it is to the Ivy Leaguers that we owe the current national acceptance of the trim, tapered, natural look in men's clothing' (*Playboy,* Vol. 2, No. 10: 18). This look included: a couple of blazers, complete with university crest, if you liked, a sports waistcoat, a 'duffer' coat or double-breasted greatcoat, a crew neck long sleeve pullover, and a muffler either in cashmere, your 'eastern club or midwestern fraternity' colours or 'an authentic tartan plaid woven in Scotland by the very same fellow (Cambridge '07) who makes them for the British Royal Family' (ibid.). In a later article Kessie argued that 'there is, believe it or not, an authentic Ivy look in active sportswear, just as there is in town' (*Playboy,* Vol. 4, No. 7: 20). He told his readers to eschew 'the kind of gruesome garbage ... touted as the hottest news

from Majorca, the Italian Riviera, Cap d'Antibes and Southern California: Old Testament sandals, ballet-dancer shirts that tie north of the navel, too-short swim trunk laced and latticed up the side, etc ...' (ibid.). Instead, proper playboys should choose white shorts and shoes for tennis, teamed with a red imported French Lacoste knit shirt, for swimming, 'trim, fly-front cotton poplin trunks with side-tabs for waist-clinching fit', and for golf, pleatless, poplin, olive green shorts, worn with 'a good-looking glen, plaid, long sleeved shirt', and 'the best golf shoes you can afford' (ibid.). For boating, Kessie believed the 'Ivy-bred style' consisted of tan slacks from Kenya cloth, a long sleeve 'marine blue sweater-shirt from Allen Solly, London', and 'an additional husky Shetland sweater or a short, zip-up jacket'. 'Blue Topsiders are de rigueur on deck', stated Kessie in his signature alliterative style (ibid.).

In all Kessie's fashion articles there was an implied promise. Dressing 'properly' in the conservative, Ivy-inspired style meant that you were a playboy and as such you were destined for a more successful life at work, as well as in bed. When Kessie wasn't imagining his readers ensconced in Ivy League eating clubs, he envisioned them as 'Madison Avenue advertising executives' (*Playboy,* Vol. 2, No. 5: 27), or 'downtown brokers' (*Playboy,* Vol. 2, No. 9: 28). Acquiring the necessary marks of distinction was never going to be easy, but with sufficient effort, the transformation would become a natural part of the playboy's personality. As Kessie put it in 'The Marks of the Well-Dressed Man':

> As you should know by this time, had you been following these columns zealously, being well-appointed is not a hit-or-miss proposition. It is a carefully planned strategem [*sic*] involving a broad view and a close watch on details. But once mastered, it is a process that becomes as effortless (and rewarding) as sampling 20-year-old Armagnac from a snifter (*Playboy,* Vol. 4, No. 3: 47).

The perfect blazer and the vintage Armagnac merged into a seamless habitus—an image of perfect taste, naturally acquired through a process of aging. Nobody need know how recently the playboy had come by these marks of distinction.

The clothing essentials recommended as 'Marks of the Well-Dressed Man' were: a snap-brimmed hat, button-down shirts in white, yellow, blue, and brown and red with white, a suit made of fabric not with 'too bold pattern, too hairy tweed, too nubby or shiny material', a tie featuring 'restrained paisleys, stripes and all-over designs in warm pleasant colors', and fine Italian boots (*Playboy*, Vol. 4, No. 3: 69). But, as *Playboy* frequently reminded its readers in the early issues, 'however well you select your head-to-toe garb, though, you'll still look like a bum or a bumpkin if you wear it—and treat it—badly' (*Playboy*, Vol. 4, No. 3: 70). Like the didactic literature it was, Kessie's article quoted a letter from Lord Chesterfield ('of overcoat and cigarette fame') to his son as 'sage advice'. He claimed Chesterfield had written: 'Take good care always to be dressed like the reasonable people of your own age in the place where you are; whose dress is never spoken of one way or another, as either too negligent or too much studied' (ibid.). When put into a context more appropriate for business, Hefner's conservative, elegant style was advocated for all the other playboys.

Kessie's conservatism seemed to strike the appropriate note with *Playboy* readers. He generated numerous letters to the editor, some chastising him for omitting a tuxedo and dinner jacket from his Basic Wardrobe. 'What self respecting playboy would be caught dead without a tuxedo and dinner jacket? Why it's almost as bad as finding a Madison Avenue ad-exec without a button-down shirt', wrote Martin Silver of Wantagh, New York (*Playboy*, Vol. 2, No. 12: 3). And more than one reader requested specific store advice on where to buy 'Jack Kessie's "Featherweights for Spring"' suits, which could be purchased for $26.50 at Brooks Brothers in New York or Chicago or at that famous department store in Chicago, Marshall Field's in their 'Young Chicagoan' shop (*Playboy*, Vol. 2, No. 8: 4).

However, by 1959 *Playboy* and its readers were assumed to have grown up in some ways. The sorts of fashion features typically targeted at female teenagers, which dictated the constitutive components of an appropriate wardrobe and reminded readers about the importance of repairing and maintaining their clothes and shoes, were now superseded by articles suffused with fantasies of wealth, luxury and travel. No longer was the *Playboy* reader to be told to polish his shoes. Under the magazine's first fashion director, Robert L. Green, the playboy was encouraged to imagine himself in the perfect 'wardrobe for a jet weekend' to Paris and London, the 'right raiment' at the country or yacht club, and the correct 'sports car fashions', donned for Nassau Speed Week (*Playboy*, Vol. 6, No. 5: 38–9; *Playboy*, Vol. 7, No. 4: 37–8, 101; *Playboy*, Vol. 6, No. 4: 28–30, 89). Just as in up-market women's fashion magazines, in *Playboy*'s late fifties and early sixties style pages the practical was shunned in favour of the fanciful and aspirational. By the end of the fifties the magazine had clearly established itself and its playboy lifestyle firmly enough to move into this other arena of fashion publishing. And although the length and content of the articles changed in the ensuing decades, *Playboy* never really looked back from this formula.[8]

CONCLUSION

The American historian Elaine Tyler May has argued in her book, *Homeward Bound,* that the post-war, Cold War ideology of containment extended to the home, where all sorts of sexualities were to be contained within the domestic dyad of the heterosexual, married couple (May 1988). *Playboy* magazine claimed that it contained the urban, sophisticated, heterosexual man's life. But, as with all magazines, what it really contained was heterosexual men's fantasies, their longings and their desires in post-war America. This was especially true for men like its founder, Hugh Hefner, who had gone to university on the GI Bill and who aimed to achieve more than their parents had in terms of material comforts, as well as sexual experiences. Hefner believed that, if you worked hard, you should be able to play hard, and that heterosexual sex should be a part of that. His long-time executive editor, Arthur Kretchmer, believes that: 'Hefner helped the world to discover toys. He said "Play, it's okay to play."' (Kretchmer, as quoted by Halberstam 1993: 576). This is a very generous reading of *Playboy*. A less generous one would argue that *Playboy* helped to contain the fantasies of men who had fought in US wars and returned home to a country with an extremely circumscribed version of heterosexual, domestic bliss and upward mobility, channelling their discontent and longings into tasteful luxury consumption.

In doing so it contradicted the widely held belief that such publications were profoundly gendered. It has been said that women's magazines claim to contain all aspects of women's lives, while magazines for men address them in terms of their interests—sports, hobbies, cars, etc. Men's lives cannot be contained within the pages of a single magazine, the argument runs.[9] As we saw at the beginning of this article, some editors and publishers began to question this in the mid-1980s. But, as this article has shown, Hefner's *Playboy* magazine achieved this end thirty years earlier. In the sixth issue, for example, a subscription advertisement defined *Playboy* as 'the new entertainment magazine for men', 'edited in the belief that men deserve a magazine of their own, and that such a publication should, properly, devote itself to the real interests of its audience.' Detailing who it considered its audience, the advertisement explained: 'Beyond that, *Playboy* is specifically styled to the tastes of the city-bred man—the man-about-town—the fellow concerned with proper dress, food and drink, art, literature (of the lighter sort, primarily) and, of course, women' (*Playboy*, Vol. 1, No. 6: n.p.). The British socialist and cultural critic, Judith Williamson, contends that for consumers commodities are, in addition to 'congealed labour', also 'congealed longing, the final form of an active wish' (Williamson 1986: 12). She asserts that: 'The need for change, the sense that there must be something else, something different from the way things are, becomes the need for a new purchase ... Consuming products does give a thrill, a sense of both belonging and being different, charging normality with the excitement of the unusual ...' (Williamson 1986: 12–13). One can hardly ask for a more apt description of early *Playboy*'s agenda. Its fashion pages advocated distinction through careful attention to detail, offering the possibility of combining conservatism in dress, success at work, and a new and exciting lifestyle in the realm of leisure. Especially in its first six years, under the tutelage of Jack Kessie, the playboy was assured that if he learned the lessons of how to dress in the Ivy League style, 'like the reasonable people of your own age in the place where you are', his life would be enriched and he would be capable of moving easily up the social ladder (*Playboy*, Vol. 4, No. 3: 70). *Playboy* encouraged men in the fifties and sixties to charge their normal working lives with 'the excitement of the unusual' through a unique, balanced combination of risqué images of beautiful women and conservative fashions.

ACKNOWLEDGEMENTS

I would like to thank the librarians at the New York Public Library for their assistance. The London College of Fashion's (LCF) Research Fund has made this work possible through a part-time Research Fellowship and a travel grant specifically for this project; I am extremely grateful and wish to particularly thank Elizabeth Rouse and Norma Starszakowna of LCF. For advice and support during the research and writing of this article, I wish to thank: the anonymous reader for this journal,

Christopher Breward, Marjorie Bryer, Caroline Cox, Janene Furness, Jack Lechner, Sam Maser, and Adam Tooze, as well as the students on the History and Theory Pathway of the MA in Fashion Studies at LCF, who offered their comments on an earlier version of this piece.

NOTES

Reprinted with permission from Becky Conekin, "Fashioning the Playboy: Messages of Style and Masculinity in the Pages of *Playboy* Magazine, 1953–1963," *Fashion Theory* 4, no. 4 (2000): 447–66.

1. Frank Mort (1996), in his *Cultures of Consumption,* briefly discusses *Man About Town,* established in 1953.

2. To be fair, I should acknowledge that Nixon explains that publishers believed that the "'soft porn" magazine market was not the same as the "general interest men's magazine" market' (Nixon 1996: 129). But, as I hope to show in this article, and as Barbara Ehrenreich (1983) has illustrated in *The Hearts of Men* (p. 42–51) in some very important ways, especially relevant to the 1950s and 1960s, *Playboy* magazine was much more than a soft porn magazine.

3. According to Kidwell, from the 1930s the American retailer and mail order catalogue, Sears, had defined its male customers as fitting into one of four groups: 'the "snappy" dresser with jazzy styling, the "university", or fashion conscious young man, the "business" man and the "conservative"' (Kidwell and Steele 1989: 141). On the mutually reinforcing representations of whiteness and heterosexuality, see Richard Dyer, *White* (1997). There he argues that ' ... there is implicit racial resonance to the idea, endemic in the representation of white heterosexuality, of sexual desire as itself dark ... ' (1997: 13). It seems that in the first decade of *Playboy,* at least, its images of masculinity generally excluded men of colour, as well as working-class men. And, following from Dyer, we can assume that—consciously or unconsciously—it did this to shore up its claims of an exclusively heterosexual readership.

4. In this piece McRobbie also acknowledges the importance of a more reader-centred approach, which she includes and which was already being pursued by people like Janice Radway, Cora Kaplan, David Morley and Charlotte Brunsdon in their work on books, television and film. It was my original plan to interview some older men about the role of *Playboy* in their lives, and especially in relation to their clothing choices and consumption patterns in the mid-1950s and 1960s, but time constraints, so familiar to all scholars, but perhaps particularly so to those working in British institutions, made this impossible. Such work will have to wait for another time or another researcher.

5. On the Kinsey Report, as well as other forties and fifties scholarship on sexual practice and behaviour, see Segal (1994: 87–9).

6. A close comparison of thirties and forties *Esquire* to early *Playboy* should yield some very interesting results and should illustrate that the latter was not as original as Hefner and his biographers would like the world to believe. Unfortunately, these issues of *Esquire* are not available in the UK.

7. Hefner did celebrate the writing and energy of the Beats in *Playboy,* however. See, for example, Gold et al. (1958: 20–6, 50, 74–5, 84–7), and Kerouac (1959: 31–2, 42, 79).

8. For example, in May 1974 and August 1975 Robert L. Green presented two articles on 'attire' entitled 'Loose Threads' and 'Loose Living'. The fantasy at the core of these spreads was overtly heterosexual sex, rather than exotic foreign climes.

9. Such an argument seems to be an oversimplified version of one first published in the late 1970s by Angela McRobbie. She was exploring the construction of what she called 'romantic individualism' in *Jackie,* a British teenage girls' magazine. In the article McRobbie actually wrote: 'In fact, women's and girls' weeklies occupy a privileged position. Addressing themselves solely to a female market, their concern is with promoting feminine culture for their readers. They define and shape the woman's world, spanning every stage from childhood to old age ... There are no male equivalents

to these products. Male magazines tend to be based on particular leisure pursuits or hobbies, motorcycling, fishing, cars or even pornography ... there are a variety of leisure options available, many of which involve participation outside the home' (McRobbie 1991: 83). Other early work on women's magazines made similar points. See, for example, White (1970) and Winship (1987b).

33

'IT WAS STYLE, WITH A CAPITAL "S"'. VERSIONS OF BEING MALE PRESENTED AT THE BEAUTILLION BALL

Annette Lynch

The first male image that I carry is not of my father but of a friend and neighbor, Charlie Burley, the brilliant Hall of Fame prizefighter. A combination of intelligence, the handsome yet bruised face, the swollen knuckles embodying the speed and power and grace of his rough trade. The starched white shirt, the embossed silk tie, the cashmere coat, the exquisite felt fur of the broad-rimmed quintessential hundred-dollar Stetson (the kind Staggerlee wore), and the highly polished yam-colored Florsheim shoes that completed his Friday night regalia. It was style with a capital 'S'. But it was more than being a connoisseur of fine haberdashery; it was attitude and presentation. The men on the corner with their big hats and polished shoes carried and lent a weight to a world that was beholden to their casual elegance as they mocked the condition of their life and paraded through the streets like warrior kings.

Wilson 1995: xi

'Style', it is with this image of a black man that August Wilson chooses to open his foreword to Don Belton's (1995) compilation of essays by black men writing on masculinity. Bouncing off that image are the words of my white teenage daughter walking into the kitchen after school talking about the walk and talk of the lone black male in her junior high English class who far outshines his white peers in mode of presentation. 'He is "hot"', she declares, and goes on to describe his walk, talk, and demeanour. Rollin' back the clock, I remember my first year at the Beautillion Ball. All the Beautillion candidates are dressed in simple formal black, but one black beau raised the roof with his walk, his look, and his coiffure. 'Why', I early asked myself, 'does male style mean so much within the African-American community?'

Writers on American popular culture and the African-American experience have noted the importance and impact of black style on American expressive culture. In particular documentation of the black power movement of the 1960s focused attention upon the role of black style in defining black identity and in affecting national consciousness. From Tom Wolf's (1970) scathing portraits of the New York liberal elite entertaining the Black Panthers in politically correct salons in the 1960s to William Van DeBurg's (1992) academic analysis of the role of black style in African-American self-actualization, scholars and writers have noted the internal importance of appearance to black males and the impact of their deportment and style on wider American culture (see also Mercer 1990 and Kelley 1994).

From the beginning of the black power movement the relationship between appearance and maintenance of cultural integrity and heritage has been stressed in the black community. Barbara Ann Teer, writing in 1968 and quoted by Van DeBurg (1992), stated:

> The way we talk (the rhythms of our speech which naturally fit our impulses), the way we walk, sing, dance, pray, laugh, eat, make love, and finally, *most important* [my emphasis], the way we look, makes up our cultural heritage. There is nothing like it or equal to it, it stands alone in comparison to other cultures. It is uniquely, beautifully, personally ours and no one can emulate it. (Van DeBurg 1992: 192)

It is within this context that the dress and deportment styles of the young beaux must be interpreted and understood. Appearance isn't simply an expression of identity for these young men, it is a formative medium used to create and sustain African-American identity and culture.

OVERVIEW AND DESCRIPTION: YOUNG GENTLEMEN'S BEAUTILLION

The Beautillion Ball in the Iowa community in which I did my research was an outgrowth of the women's Cotillion. Male organizers stressed that they wanted to develop a male version of the coming-of-age ball because they felt the debutante Cotillion Ball had successfully raised self-esteem and aspirations of many young women in the African-American community. The first Young Gentlemen's Beautillion Ball in the community was held in 1995. I attended balls in 1996, 1997, and 1998. The balls are held in a large downtown convention centre the weekend of graduation for the local high schools and were positioned in the community as events honouring outstanding black graduates. Similar male balls also emerged at about the same time period in Detroit, Michigan and Davenport, Iowa, both Midwestern American cities with large African-American populations. Therefore this case study could be interpreted within a larger context of trends within African-American communities in this region of the United States.

The sponsoring organization for the Young Gentlemen's Beautillion in Waterloo, Iowa is an African American men's professional organization entitled The Black Alliance. The mission of the men's organization reproduced below is linked to W.E.B. Du Bois's concept of uplift through education and leadership:

> The Mission of The Black Alliance is to *uplift* [my emphasis], strengthen, and educate our African American community through positive interaction. We are an organization whose members are socially conscientious individuals whose goals and aims are towards the betterment of our African American community.

The structure of the organization is modelled on business rather than social organizations, with a Chief Executive Officer (CEO) and Chairman heading the organization and a President. In addition to the Beautillion Ball, The Black Alliance sponsors economic workshops in the community, provides school supplies for black children, and organizes youth activities such as trips to major league baseball games and campouts. At the 1996 Beautillion Ball all twenty-one of the members of the Black Alliance were brought on stage with introductions including place of employment. All members had a strong history of involvement in the Waterloo black community and had jobs indicating middle- and upper-middle-class positions within the community.

The Young Gentlemen's Beautillion Ball, like the women's Cotillion Ball, is the final stage of a mentoring process between black youth and prominent (same-sex) adults in the African-American community. In contrast to the women's mentoring process, which is more etiquette-based, The Black Alliance emphasizes professional job-related mentoring in an effort to encourage the young men toward setting career goals. Similar to young debutantes, young black men are chosen to participate in the ball on the basis of academic standing and involvement in school and community activities. African-American athletes, who are often the recipients of college athletic scholarships, are the clear favourites of the audience at some balls. However generalizations are difficult as in 1998 a young man with an extremely strong record of community service and minimal participation in athletics was the most roundly applauded young man who walked the stage that night.

The Chairman and Chief Executive Officer of The Black Alliance opens the Beautillion from an elevated stage. The message of the Chairman is action-based and often underscores the activities of the organization. It also strongly emphasizes the role of the ball in recognizing excellence and potential within the ranks of African-American youth as well as hearkening back and taking a bow to strong leaders of the past. These opening words are followed by a prayer. The theme of uplift is emphasized at the beginning of each ball as the audience sings James Weldon Johnson's (1871–1938) 'Lift Every Voice and Sing,' a popular secular hymn. Its theme of advancing black people through democratic ideals and faith has made it a popular inspirational hymn for the American black community:

> Lift every voice and sing
> Till earth and heaven ring.
> Ring with the harmony of liberty;
> Let our rejoicing rise
> High as the listening skies.
> Let us resound loud as the rolling sea.
> Sing a song full of the faith that the dark path
>   has taught us,
> Sing a song full of the hope that the present
>   has brought us.
> Facing the rising sun of our new day begun,
> Let us march on till victory is won.

Following the standing and singing of the Negro National Anthem important guests and members of The Black Alliance are introduced to the audience. Typical important guests can include, but do not always include, elected political officials. The introduction of The Black Alliance members varies from year to year ranging from formal presentation on stage to more informal recognition of members seated in the audience.

Following the introductions is the keynote address. Keynote speakers are inspirational in tone and generally drawn from the ranks of the African-American community. Messages I heard from the stage both stressed the reality of statistics indicating tough roads ahead for young black men, but also the importance of keeping faith, focus, and commitment in the face of these harsh realities. In 1996 Reverend Michael Coleman urged the young people in the audience to use their faith to hone character and craft exemplary lives. Those that fall in the face of adversity, the audience was told, may have many excuses, but they are 'choosing something other than iron to sharpen themselves by' (Lynch 1996, as summarized in my notes). Coleman painted a grim picture of many black men's lives but called for the young men of the community to rise above and defy the statistics. As summarized in my notes, 'The statistics say that some are going to die, but lives are not shaped by statistics; they are shaped by the hearts of great people.' In 1998 the speaker was a man who grew up in the community and had gone on to have a successful career as a lawyer. He presented a story of a life influenced by strong black male leadership and mentoring, and perhaps most importantly the strong role of education in uplift.

The keynote addresses delivered each year were in the spirit of Henry Louis Gates's calls for black leadership to acknowledge the despair haunting large percentages of black males in the United States, while at the same time find ways to motivate individuals to work for personal and community uplift and change. Gates stresses that the 'first mission' of black leadership 'isn't the reinforcement of the idea of black America' but rather, to find 'a way of speaking about black poverty that doesn't falsify the reality of black advancement; a way of speaking about black advancement that doesn't distort the enduring realities of black poverty' (1997: 38). Like Gates, the male leaders sponsoring this event are attempting to narrow the gap between the growing black underclass and the advancing middle class. By recognizing excellence within the ranks of black male youth they are attempting to defy statistics and advance young black males into positions of respect and power in American society.

Following a brief intermission the beaux are introduced to the audience. Beaux, like their female counterparts, are presented on a runway to a mostly African-American audience. The young men wear matching conventional formal suit styles that add unity and decorum to the event. The uniformity of dress is significant, given the African-American community's tendency to use dress to mark individual interpretations of black style. The young men walk down the runway as their accomplishments are announced to the audience. At the end of the runway, each young man takes a bow and acknowledges the audience. Although these young men are dressed in a uniform manner, individual style is expressed in gesture and walk and to a limited extent through hairstyles. While some young men have a conventional presentation style, the solo walk down the runway and finale bow are often used by young men as venues for expressing their own personal style. The audience takes visible and audible delight in the young men who play the audience using body movement and gesture.

After acknowledging the audience the young beaux walk back up the runway to meet their female escorts. The escort's name is announced as she enters the main stage to be walked down the runway by her male partner. Female escorts are generally African-American women from the community and are friends and/or girlfriends of the beaux. Female escorts are also in formal dress styles, but wear a wider range of individually chosen dresses. Typical dresses are black full-length evening gowns that are cut close to the body. They often include a high slit to allow movement and also reveal the leg of the wearer as she walks. Open-back midriff styles and bodice cuts that reveal cleavage are common. Paired, the candidate and his escort present an eveningwear appearance that contrasts with the 'wedding-day look' constructed for the young women's debutante ball. The audience and beaux are frankly appreciative of the beauty and sensuality of the young female escorts. In this sense the event hearkens back to the black beauty contests and fashion shows that showcased black female beauty earlier in the twentieth century. Following the introduction of the female escort, the couple walks down the runway, acknowledges the audience, and is seated at a head table with attending family members. The young beaux are typically more restrained in gesture and movement during the second walk down the runway, perhaps granting attention to the beauty of their female escorts.

While in most aspects the individual presentation of the beaux is similar to the debutantes, the stage show climaxes with a dramatic show of group identity, the 'Salute to the Beaux', that has no comparable equivalent within the debutante ritual. The format of the Salute to the Beaux was different all three years I attended. In 1996 Black Alliance members lined up in two columns, creating a passageway stretching the length of the runway. The beaux then walked through this path between the two lines of male mentors and were welcomed into the brotherhood of adult men often through physical contact in the form of handshaking and shoulder-patting. In the second year, only the young beaux were featured in the Salute. As a group they came to the front of the runway and danced for the audience, taking turns at being centre stage, similar to the way jazz musicians alternate between solo and group performance. Tuxedo jackets were typically dramatically thrown over the shoulder as the young men fell into athletic shows of dancing ability and personal pride. In 1998, the beaux formed a long line up the centre of the runway and displayed personal style through dance, gesture, and eye contact.

The Salute reminded me of the dramatic shows of group pride and cohesiveness that characterize the bonding rituals displayed by many largely black member basketball teams prior to basketball games. An energy is released as the presentation styles of the young men play off each other on stage to the rousing theme by Black Men United. The lyrics of the BMU song express the coming-of-age theme as well as the importance of holding on to dreams and standing tall:

You Will Know
Um, Um, Um, Um
Yeah, Yeah
When i was a young boy
I had visions of fame
They were wild and they were free
They were blessed with my name

And i grew older
And i saw what's to see
That the world is full of pain
That's when i picked up the pieces
And i regained my name
And i fought hard ya'll
To cover my place
And if right now you could ask me
And it all seems in place

Chorus:

Your dreams ain't easy
Just stick by young man
You must go from boys to men
You must act like a man
When it gets hard ya'll
You must grab what you know
Stand up tall and don't you fall
You will know (four times)

And i know you're crying
Cause it's all in his fate
And the things you want you can't have
It just all went away

But life ain't over Ohh...
Just grab the wind

And make the mends
And the vow will take you far

Following the Salute to the Beaux special and lifetime awards are presented to male leaders from the community. Similar to the Cotillion Ball, the stage events close with the beaux leading their female escorts to the dance floor for a formal waltz. The informal dance with music provided by the disc jockey closes the night.

The dress, appearance, and modes of self-presentation of these young beaux express a synthesis of West African and American aesthetics that has a long American history dating back to the slavery period. Four themes emerged as significant as I related what I observed at the Beautillion Ball to the history of African-American male dress and appearance styles: (1) movement as an expression of style, (2) importance of wearing a 'smart' suit, (3) having a hat, having a 'do', (4) importance of street style.

BACKGROUND AND HISTORY: STYLE AND MOVEMENT

Male escorts at the Cotillion and candidates at the Beautillion often use their walk and gestures to express distinct versions of male style that draw enthusiastic responses from the audience. In contrast to the female debutantes, who work hard to conform to conventional styles of formal presentation, males at both balls openly play with and challenge convention through confident displays of stylized movement and gestures. Young men with the most distinct styles of self-presentation are clearly appreciated by the audience, and clearly gain confidence through the movement of their bodies on stage.

Black men's distinct styles of movement and gesture have been noted by observers since the day black slaves landed on the American coastline. In a different form, but working out of a shared body of West African aesthetic principles, black men, like black women, used creativity and spirit to compose an artistic response to imposed standards of dress and behaviour. The medium for women was textiles and clothing, the medium for men included the body itself. The result was a long history of integrating West African and American forms of movement and gesture into a distinct self-presentation style that has echoes and impact beyond the confines of the African-American community.

Robert Farris Thompson's research on dance and movement in West Africa using internal sources to uncover the criteria used to judge and the principles governing body movement revealed distinct and significant contrasts with Euro-American attitudes. Drawing attention to the self through conscious use of distinct styles of movement and gesture is central, argued Thompson, to West African ideals of self-presentation. A thirty-year-old male from the Dan population in Northeast Liberia stated that among his people it is important for him to 'move with flair [and add] something to my dance or walking, to show my beauty to attract the attention of all those around me, even if they are thinking of something else' (Thompson 1974: 16). In the interview this man goes on to stress the importance of bodily movement as a key component of the aesthetic evaluation of a person:

Dan can criticize a handsome person by the way he walks and the way he acts even though this person is otherwise completely beautiful … There is no mistaking a completely beautiful person who walks and talks and acts and looks beautifully. We teach the composing of the face, the right way of walking, the right proportion of standing, the right way of acting with the body when making conversation. (Thompson 1974: 251)

Gender-based differences in preferred modes of walking are noted in Sylvia Boone's research among the Mende of Sierre Leone. According to Mende aesthetic canons, women's carriage should be smoother and more majestic, contrasting with a male style stressing assertive energetic movement (1986: 126). These differences in body deportment translate into the aesthetic underlying West African male dance styles that emphasize 'vital movement' of distinct parts of the body:

The concept of vital aliveness leads to the interpretation of the parts of the body as independent instruments of percussive force. It is not usually permissible to allow the arms to lapse into an absent-minded swaying while the legs are stamping fiercely. The dancer must impart equal autonomy, to every dancing portion of this frame. (Thompson 1974: 9)

Male dancers capable of bold, dramatic movements that draw the attention of the audience are the most heavily lauded among the Dan: 'Shyness in Dan dance is bad; shyness in dancing spoils the effect of the art; a good dancer must be bold' (Thompson 1974: 252).

Early responses to the carriage and deportment styles of black African slaves indicate that differences between deportment styles of male and female slaves existed. While women described in runaway slave advertisements are frequently described as being 'proud' in terms of walking style, males are more frequently described as having 'bold', 'lofty', 'swaggering', and 'strutting' styles of deportment (see descriptions in White and White 1998: 72). Black male slaves, robbed of other forms of resistance, turned to their bodies as modes of expression.

As freed black slaves turned to the street as a venue for self-presentation, black men cultivated a street style highly dependent upon movement as a means of personal distinction. African-American parades were started in northern cities in the early 1800s and became arenas for self-presentation as well. The parades spread to the South and have some of the same character as the masking rituals I observed in Nigeria in 1995 in that individuals played specific roles that were expressed both in movement and dress. By the early twentieth century New Orleans had become a centre of black music, with jazz funerals an important venue for expressing black consciousness through sound and movement. Parade marshals of the early jazz funeral parades were marked not only by distinctive dress, but by strong improvisational movements that surprised and delighted the audience. In Shane and Graham White's (1998) book on style they quote jazz musician Sidney Bechet's description of the parade marshals in the parades he attended as a child:

'And all those fancy steps he'd have' Bechet elaborated, 'oh, that was really something!—ways he'd have of turning around himself. People, they got a whole lot of pleasure out of just watching him, hearing the music and seeing him strut and other members of the club coming behind him, strutting and marching, some riding on horses but getting down to march a while, gallivanting there in real style'. (141)

Improvisational movement, the ability to use the body to cajole and court the audience through spontaneous and often unpredictable response to the crowd and music, was an important dimension of the performance of the marshal. Bechet, quoted by White and White (1998), continues:

When the Grand Marshal reached a street corner, 'He'd have a way of tricking his knee, of turning all around, prancing—he'd fool you. You wouldn't be knowing if he was going left or right ... And that was a big part of it—him stepping and twisting and having you guessing all along. The way he could move, that was doing something for you. He led it.' (141)

The use of stylized movement to confirm and validate black identity continues to be important to African-American men throughout the twentieth century. During an historical period when many black men continue to be blocked from obtaining respected professional positions, public presentation of the body is a means of asserting pride in the self and in African-American identity. Benjamin G. Cooke, a black drummer, published an article in the 1970s showing the role of kinesic interaction in black culture. Within his article he identifies distinct walking and

stance styles of African-American males, arguing that 'Just as clothes and hair consciously affirm black people's strength and unity of purpose for the achievement of control of their lives and destinies, so do the selected kinesic forms of nonverbal communication' (1972: 64). He argues that black male walking styles were consciously performed to attract attention and were more rhythmical and sensual than the walks of other American men. The very fact that he was able to identify distinct and named styles of walk[1] and stance among black men indicates the importance granted to body and movement in the community.[2] As the black underclass has grown in the United States, rap culture, including distinct styles of movement, has grown in expressive strength and salience (Kelley 1994), it isn't just the style of clothes you wear, but how you move in them.

THE WEARING OF A SMART SUIT

Movement, as the free means of attaining style, perhaps came first in America, but soon after came the ability to combine and wear American-style menswear with a distinct African-American flair. Bricolage, the ability to creatively combine dress elements drawn from a wide cultural palate, was characteristic of West African ensembles and became emblematic of a distinct African-American style. It was early observed that black slaves put together ensembles that combined various items of dress in what appeared to their white owners as unorthodox and jarring ways (White and White 1998: 31). The incorporation of elite elements of dress into more common ensembles was in part 'making do' with the clothing that came their way, through exchange with other slaves, or as rewards from their owners. But perhaps more importantly it was an openness to integrating outside cultural influences into aesthetic expression that came with blacks from West Africa. It also arose as a response to the limited range of expression allowed to black male slaves. By creating a stylish presence in the face of adversity, black males challenged the position they were assigned in America, and began to create a positive individual and collective consciousness.

The dress of freed Northern black males in the 1800s is described as more dashing and exaggerated than their white counterparts. A tendency to push a fashion trend to the extreme emerged during this period and continues to be a staple element of black style. In the early 1800s men's formal coats were cut open in the chest area, but a Swedish visitor describes black men's coats as being cut 'so open that the shirt sticks out under the arm-pits' (White and White 1998: 94). Hats worn at a jauntier and more rakish angle and accessories that demanded attention were also noted elements in the dress of this early period. The same Swedish visitor goes on to say, 'The waistcoats are of all colours of the rainbow; the hat is carelessly put on one side; the gloves are yellow, and every sable dandy carries a smart cane' (White and White 1998: 94). To be noted, in all cases the modifications to standard menswear styles of the period serve to draw attention to the wearer and create a more demanding and dramatic presentation.

The perceived relationship between sartorial and kinesthetic excess and black male identity was so pronounced that by the end of the 1800s etiquette manuals directed toward black men directed them to tone down their walks and clothing in order to better fit upper- and middle-class models of American masculinity. Despite this published advice a rich culture of black street style continued to develop during this period that was characterized by what the *New York Times* described as 'exaggerated styles and bright hues' (White and White 1998: 245). By 1931 black cultural centres such as Harlem were written up in the newspapers as centres of fashion leadership[3] and the style of African-American males began to affect dress styles of the fashion mainstream.

The zoot suit of the 1940s encapsulated the aesthetic preference for overstated and exaggerated style that characterized black male dress dating back to the slavery period. The entire look of a man wearing a zoot suit demanded attention. The jackets were cut long, the pants were dramatically baggy at the knee and pegged at the ankle, the hats and shoes were wide and flat, and the ties and collar extreme. It was the apparel donned by the most hip. Jazz musicians and young men with hot street style wore the zoot suit out to do their antics. The style was picked up by fashion-conscious youth as a symbol of rebellion in cities throughout the United States and was also worn in Paris (White and White 1998: 261). Kobena Mercer (1990) points out that by the 1940s the less extreme versions of the zoot suit style had entered the fashion mainstream. When viewed in retrospect, the zoot suit moved African-American male style into a position of fashion leadership and related black dress styles to popular music.

As black music continued to build a popular audience in the United States, black male style continued to influence overall American fashion trends. Ethnic dress of the 1960s and 1970s, disco fashions of the 1980s, and hip hop styles of the 1990s all emerged out of the interplay between music and fashion, all heavily influenced by African-American expressive culture. The aesthetic preference for strong bold presentation, carried over from the slavery period, is still a mainstay of contemporary black male hip hop fashions that rely heavily on over-sized baggy pants combined with regalia drawn from the world of sports such as starter jackets. Even more so than zoot suit fashions, hip hop influences the dress of broad sectors of American male and female youth, challenging the labelling of black culture as 'marginal' and granting black male style a formative role in American popular culture.

At the Beautillion Ball, stylistic excess and drama expressed through apparel choices are largely held in check by the prescribed dress codes followed by the participants. The organizers' clear intent is to impose a dress code that encourages the audience as well as the participants to interpret these young men as capable of infusion into the American mainstream. However, the decision to create a 'high style' formal event like the Gentlemen's Beautillion Ball to showcase exemplary young men from the community is in keeping with the reviewed historical emphasis on dramatic public shows of male accomplishment. The importance granted to styles of public presentation, and the pointed creation of a 'Salute to the Beaux' to afford each young man a time to 'strut his stuff' is in character with the black community's history of using smart suit styles and movement as a means of self-validation among men.

THE POLITICS OF THE HEAD: COIFFURE AND HAT STYLES OF BLACK MEN

The fusion of politics and hairstyles for black men dates back to the slavery period. While slaves' hair was sometimes shaved or cut as a form of punishment, generally styling the hair was a mode of self-expression allowed by the slavery system. Coiffures thus became a means of self-identification in the slave community. The West African tradition of devoting time to the styling of the hair among men thus continued in America, with evidence of distinct hairstyles captured in descriptions of runaway slaves published in newspapers of the period (White and White 1998: 41). Styles created by African-American slaves combined aspects of traditional West African coiffures with popular wig styles worn by white males during the period (White and White 1998: 51). The result was another example of African-American style emerging out of the creative ability to bring together African and Euro-American influences into a unique presentation. The showiness of terminating the head with a hat appealed to black men even during the slavery period as White and White (1998) cite evidence that men found ways of fashioning hats from scraps and hand-me-downs.

Following the more general trends of African-American male fashion history, the trend toward exaggerated coiffures and dramatic hat styles builds in the late nineteenth and early twentieth centuries and culminates in the 1940s zoot suit trend. The conk hairstyle that went with the zoot suit was as extreme as the clothes it topped. It was a modern dyed look; red artificial colouring defied the natural colour of black men's hair and announced modernity and cultural distinctness to a not-quite-ready American public. The style of the conk required a lengthy straightening process but Kobena Mercer is emphatic in arguing that the net result was far from a simple 'copying' of white men's coiffure, but rather a neo-African aesthetic expression demanding recognition and reaction:

> The conk involved a violent technology of straightening, but this was only the initial stage in a process of creolizing stylization. The various waves, curls and lengths introduced by practical styling served to differentiate the conk from the conventional white hair-styles of the day. Rather, the element of straightening suggested resemblance to white people's hair, but the nuances, inflections, and accentuations introduced by artificial means of stylization emphasized difference. In this way the political economy of the conk rested on its ambiguity, the way it 'played' with the given outline shapes of convention only to 'disturb' the norm and hence invite a 'double-take' demanding that you look twice. (1990: 259)

Topped with the overly wide zoot suit hat the 'double-take' effect was magnified. The zoot suit look was intended to stop and disturb the gaze of America, and its success was paid testimony by the public reaction to the style which was dramatic and sometimes violent.[4]

For the remainder of the twentieth century black men used their hats and hat styles to craft visually demanding images of themselves with references to modernity and to their West African roots. The range of elements are drawn from many cultures and recombined into a post-modern amalgamation of what it means to be an African-American male. Afros, cane-rows, dreadlocks, kente cloth hats, stocking caps, fedoras; all worn with a distinct style that draws attention and remarks.

I never observed hats being worn by the young men participating in the Beautillion Balls, but barbershops in Waterloo have opened to serve a young black male clientele who want patterns shaved into their hairstyles with a razor and electric clippers. These dramatic haircuts are often worn on the runway by young men who also have created distinct walking and movement styles that set them apart from the mainstream. A recent *New York Times* article described the status of Casper, an established barber serving a hip African-American clientele:

> His name is on the lips of the hip-hop set in Sunset Park. The teenagers in baggy pants and Michelin Man jackets up and down Fourth Avenue in Brooklyn know Pedro Quinones, though not as Pedro Quinones. They know him as Casper, the sultan of the shape-up, the master of the Number One Fade, the quick answer to the bad hair day. (Yardley 1999)

While the Waterloo black community is far from New York, young black men express linkages to hip urban style through barbers who carve the latest patterns into their hairstyles which they strut down the runway to an appreciative audience.

THE GENTLEMEN'S BEAUTILLION BALL: INTERPRETIVE ANALYSIS

On the surface the Gentlemen's Beautillion Ball appears to be a very simple ritual presentation of young black men reconstructed according to models of normative American success. The dictated dress code is uniform and conventional and the message to the young men that education is the key to success is a mainstream American myth. On a deeper level, however, the ritual

is more conflict laden and spirited. Yes, the young men dress in uniform and conventional male style linked in America to versions of institutionalized power, but within individual walks, gestures and hairstyles distinct expressions of African-American aesthetics of movement and art emerge.

Cornel West argues that black Americans have crafted strategies of survival and triumph from a selection of Euro-American and West African traditions. Validation and recognition, both key elements in this coming-of-age ritual for young black men, are highlighted by West in the following discussion of black Americans' struggle for identity:

> White supremacist assaults on Black intelligence, ability, beauty, and character required persistent Black efforts to hold self-doubt, self-contempt and even self-hatred at bay. Selective appropriation, incorporation and re-articulation of European ideologies, cultures and institutions alongside an African heritage—a heritage more or less confined to linguistic innovation in rhetorical practices, stylizations of the body in forms of occupying an alien social space (hair styles, ways of walking, standing, hand expressions, talking) and means of constituting and sustaining comradery and community (e.g. antiphonal, call-and-response styles, rhythmic repetition, risk-ridden syncopation in spectacular modes in musical and rhetorical expressions)—were some of the strategies employed. (1990: 27)

While the Beautillion Ball rises out of a formal dance tradition in Europe and the United States, as an institution it has been selected and reinterpreted by black Americans as a strategy for validating young black men as they enter into young adulthood.

The Beautillion Ball is an illustration of West's argument, as African-American heritage infuses the Beautillion with an energy emanating out of pride and connection to black history and culture. Body movements, gestures, playing with the expectations of the audience, call and response used within the Salute to the Beaux, are all important connections to West African aesthetics and culture that are important components of the Beautillion and Cotillion Balls. While audience members are clearly proud of the academic, community, and athletic records of the young men presented at the Beautillion, it is the gestures, the movements, the style of comradeship expressed during the Salute to the Beaux that draw the most spirited rounds of applause and visible delight. These communal expressions of shared African-American heritage and values validate not only the young men on stage but the community overall.

The models of ritual that I have used to frame my research stress the formative and communal aspects of performed ceremonies. Coming-of-age ceremonies therefore not only reflect cultural expectations for young men and women but help to formulate them. Key to the formative role of ritual in constructing gender is the expression of conflicts related to definitions of adult success. While certainly higher education and career-based success are stressed within the Beautillion Ball, there is also a counter-hegemonic model of masculinity that is expressed at the ball that validates young men based upon a different set of criteria. Being true to heritage, connected to the community, alive both in terms of spirituality and aesthetic consciousness are values expressed during the ritual that create a different model of masculinity with roots in African-American and West African culture.

Dress and presentation at the African-American balls I attended were both a neo-African aesthetic expression as well as a self-conscious effort toward reconstruction following in the footsteps of W.E.B. Du Bois. Clearly the organizers of the two balls deliberately established codes of dress and behaviour that created conventional images of men and women that exemplify attitudes and attributes that help to establish the potential and credibility of the young female and male participants. But at the same time, the young men and women bring an aesthetic and spiritual consciousness

into the event that is deeply rooted in their cultural heritage.

Clifford Geertz (1973) and Victor Turner (1988) both argue that ritual emerges in part as a result of cultural conflict. My research on African-American male and female coming-of-age balls revealed that versions of black style, as well as conscious efforts toward reconstruction combined within these rituals to help individuals and the community, struggle to express and resolve problems of growing up in the last decade of the twentieth century as young African-American men and women. The male and female coming-of-age balls that are sponsored by adults in the community are effective springboards for the young participants, launching them with confidence into positions within the world and within their communities.

NOTES

Reprinted with permission from Annette Lynch, "'It Was Style with a Capital "S"'. Versions of Being Male Presented at the Beautillion Ball," in *Dress, Gender and Cultural Change: Asian American and African American Rites of Passage* (Oxford and New York: Berg, 1999), 97–112.

1. Styles of walking described by Cooke included chicken walk, Slu Foot or 'down home' walk, soul walk, and pimp walk.
2. While Cooke was able to describe the basic walking styles of black women, their styles of movement were not given distinct names within the community and were not granted the same level of importance.
3. White and White (1998) quote the *New York Times,* 'It is said of Harlem that its fashion plates are several jumps ahead of the rest of the world' (1998: 245).
4. The zoot suit fashion caused riots in Los Angeles, Detroit, and Harlem in 1943 as groups of armed servicemen attacked men wearing zoot suits who were popularly interpreted as thumbing their nose at the war effort and patriotism as well as newly instituted rationing regulations (White and White 1998: 249).

34

NEW MEN AND NEW MARKETS

Frank Mort

The French sociologist Pierre Bourdieu, in his study of the academy and its intellectuals, has given a particular definition of cultural crisis.[1] Crisis moments, Bourdieu has observed, are essentially struggles over rival systems of classification. Positions are staked out, producing a number of clearly distinguishable camps and forcing participants to endow their arguments with a coherence which would not be required under more normal circumstances. Such moments are for Bourdieu not simply negative; they act as developers, stimulating knowledge and sites from which to speak. Bourdieu's paradigm has principally been used to analyze intellectual systems in the narrow sense. Yet his understanding could usefully be applied to the eruption of discourses about masculinity which occurred in Britain during the 1980s. Just in case anyone still doubts it, observed Judith Williamson, writing in the *New Statesman,* in the autumn of 1986, 'men are the most marketable category of the year'.[2] It was, she noted, all part of the mood of the moment. As a feminist film critic, Williamson was far from positive about the flurry of interest in this long-ignored subject. But her remarks were part of a growing crescendo of argument. In journalism and fashion, in commercial and manufacturing culture, as well as in the political and social arena, men were at the centre of a wide-ranging debate. The forms which discussions took were as varied as their conclusions. Amidst all the energy, one motif occurred repeatedly. This was the figure of the 'new man'. A hybrid character, his aetiology could not be attributed to one single source. He was rather the condensation of multiple concerns which were temporarily run together.

For the advertising and marketing industries, the appearance of such a personality was a symptom of growing commercial and cultural confusion. Journalist Phillip Hodson explained to the women's magazine *She* in July 1984 that this new form of masculinity was principally defined by self-doubt. Confronted by the loss of traditional gender certainties, many men were now being forced to question their social roles.[3] Such a sense of disorientation was having repercussions on traditionally stable consumer markets, especially among the young. 'So what on earth is the young British male?' queried an exasperated television production consultant, Steve Taylor, to the advertising world's in-house journal, *Campaign,* two years later.[4] 'Advanced' market researchers claimed to have solved the problem. Marketing consultants McCann Erickson's *Manstudy Report,* produced in 1984, hailed the new breed of man as the 'Avant Guardian'. Claiming statistical exactitude, their report insisted that the group covered precisely 13.5 per cent of all British males. With an 'optimistic outlook on life' and a strongly contemporary view of masculinity, these individuals were associated with premier consumer brands. But the report noted that they were also at the forefront of more serious discussions about the changing experience of gender.[5] Other commercial commentators offered different, but equally specific, accounts. The new man was linked to the more progressive and caring versions of fatherhood, portrayed in the marketing of stores such as Mothercare. In a different vein he was defined as a metropolitan phenomenon, supposedly visible in a number of London locations associated with consumer style. 'He's a good first-tier fashion person' enthused entrepreneur Bruce Isaacs, himself the owner of a successful West End restaurant, in 1987.[6] Attacking these commercial posturings, media consultant and man-about-town Peter York was much more critical. A highly contemporary personality, York reported in *The Times* the following year that the figure of the new man was nothing more than the advertising industry's dramatization of its own self-image. His ethics and morality were based only on a 'mean chic', which was driven by 'greed, competition and treachery'.[7]

The fashion industry believed that this confusion over representations of masculinity was entirely positive. For a sector in which diversity was its lifeblood, new personas were always to be welcomed. They were essentially a result of the growing proliferation of tastes and styles for men. The origins of the change were seen to lie in the current renaissance of British fashion, after the lean recession years of the late 1970s and early 1980s. 'Are You Gauguin, New Colonial, or Savile Row?' inquired *Men's Wear* journalist Thorn O'Dwyer archly, in his preview of the spring and summer menswear collections in *The Guardian* in 1987.[8] It mattered little which image his readers selected, the point was that a greater number of choices were now on offer. Such a celebration of individualism was often simply reduced to the level of fashion trivia. But at times the arguments strayed into more political territory. O'Dwyer proclaimed that men's fashion was 'coming out of the closets'.[9] Deliberately evoking the language of homosexual liberation, he implied that the appearance of the new man had much to do with the breaking down of sexual stereotypes, which was the

direct result of a decade of gay politics. Journalists Brian Kennedy and John Lyttle, assessing the significance of the phenomenon for urban life and leisure, in the London listings magazine, *City Limits,* in 1986, took up the same point. They argued that in Britain, as in North America, the new masculinity had its origins in the growing power of homosexual men, who had at last forced a grudging recognition from the gatekeepers of public culture.[10] This dissident reading was strenuously denied in more mainstream areas of popular taste, especially in the tabloid press. Forever on the look-out both to incite sex, and to police the perverse, *The Sun* produced its own interpretation of the new man, as part of a rhetoric of normative, but liberated, heterosexuality. From 1986, 'page seven guys', with unbuttoned flies and bared torsos, competed for attention with established female pin-ups: the famous 'page three girls'. The paper announced that the new visual erotica of men's bodies was available for the enjoyment of modern, fun-loving young women.[11]

The debate continued in a more serious vein within the arena of sexual politics. For progressive men, working in anti-sexist organisations and consciousness-raising groups, the growing concern over masculinity, however confused and chaotic, was to be supported. It was viewed as the culmination of a series of much broader initiatives, which were breaking open masculinity's best-kept secret; forcing men to look self-consciously at themselves and their identities, rather than as the concealed norm of power and privilege.[12] It revealed a point of vulnerability which was a potential source for change. For those men who also held some allegiance to more traditional forms of politics, especially to socialism, the implications went further still. In microcosm, the problem of men was bound up with the contemporary crisis in political culture itself. Inasmuch as formal politics was underpinned by a particular version of gendered privilege, the question of masculinity raised the long-repressed issues of subjectivity and language, and the ways in which such factors shaped political allegiances. A day conference in London, organised in the summer of 1987 under the auspices of the Communist Party journal *Marxism Today,* debated these and other themes. Yet the enthusiastic tone of the discussions was not shared by the majority of women. Feminist responses to the new men's politics were invariably more mixed. For those who rejected a biological or social essentialism about men, the process of shifting masculinity—crucially in relation to women—was seen to involve extensive and often painful change. It was, as Lynne Segal termed it in the title of her book on masculinity published in 1990, inevitably men in slow motion.[13] *The Guardian*'s feminist columnist, Polly Toynbee, doubted that the transformations which had taken place in men's experience were sufficient to merit the title of new man. Summing up the current debate in 1987, she remained wholly unconvinced:

> I have heard tell of the new man. For many years now there have been books and articles proclaiming his advent, even his arrival, I have met women who claim that their sons will be he, or that their daughters will marry him. I have met men who claim they are he. False prophets all, the new man is not here, and it does not seem likely that we shall see him in our lifetime.[14]

If the new scripts about masculinity had not changed the lives of the majority of men, as Toynbee argued, the new man was certainly not a mere chimera. In the 1980s the debate over men's changing roles was concretised in a wide variety of settings. But it was in one area in particular that the issue was given its most extended hearing. This was in the sphere of consumer culture. In all the exchanges, commercial debates over the identities and consumption patterns of younger men loomed large. Such discussions were urgent and energetic, and they competed for attention with the more sententious claims of sexual politics. For during the decade the dynamics of the marketplace

occupied a privileged place in shaping young men's wants and needs.

Commercial interest in young men was canvassed across many different sectors. But attention was most intensely focused around one specific commodity. This was the attempt to produce a general-interest, or 'lifestyle', magazine for men. The quest to crack this product became something of a cause célèbre, especially for the media industries. Frequently referred to as the 'holy grail' of publishing, the search for a successful formula was approached with all the vigour of a latter-day masculine crusade. The urgency which surrounded this project was an expression of large-scale ambitions, which extended well beyond the media. Successfully established, a men's magazine could provide the anchor point for a huge variety of goods and services. It could present the vision of masculine consumer society, in much the same way that the women's press had long done for female readers. The implications of this initiative were not lost on advertisers and marketers. As Zed Zawada, advertising director of East Midlands Allied Press Metro Group (EMAP) and an influential player in the debate, saw it in 1986:

> Publishers look at women's magazines, their circulation figures and bottom line and they think: if we put together a road test of a new Porsche with an in-depth interview with Giorgio Armani and some stuff about personal finance, then we'll hit some sort of composite male who has all these interests. If that were possible, it would be like finding the Holy Grail.[15]

Zawada's cynical analysis was both shrewd and practical. Focused on prestige consumption, it emphasized the need to assemble a type of synthetic male personality out of the flotsam and jetsam of contemporary commodities. This, he insisted, was the key to unlocking the men's market. Yet as he pointed out, competitors in the race needed to beware of growing uncertainty in the world of publishing.

Strictly speaking, the idea of a general-interest publication for men was not wholly new. The claims to innovation made in the mid-1980s need to be qualified in the light of much earlier post-war experiments. The most important development in this genre was *Man About Town*. Established in 1953 as a gentleman's tailoring magazine, it was restyled and renamed in 1960, on its acquisition by publishers Michael Heseltine and Clive Labovitch. *Man About Town,* later abbreviated to *About Town,* ran until 1968, with an ambitious mixture of photography and journalism. Paralleling the newspaper colour supplements of the period, the title blended fashion, politics and arts coverage, along with reports about international celebrities.[16] In the late 1960s the picture was further complicated by the brief appearance of three publications aimed explicitly at homosexual men: *Timm,* 1968, *Spartacus,* 1969 and *Jeremy,* 1969. Picturing the world from a gay point of view, the magazines worked with a similar focus on upmarket consumption.[17] Yet these precursors were rarely acknowledged by later editors. What was emphasized in the 1980s was the supposed originality of the men's magazine format.

Reviewing the publishing sector at the end of the 1980s for the advertising journal *Media Week,* Brian Braithwaite pronounced the decade as having been the most turbulent since 1945.[18] As publishing director of The National Magazine Company, he argued that the origins of this instability were both economic and cultural. The enforced introduction of new work disciplines and technologies, first seen at Rupert Murdoch's News International press at Wapping, had been coupled with significant shifts in retailing and distribution. The growth of supermarkets as major outlets for magazine titles, the rise of postal subscriptions, along with an upsurge in the number of free local papers, had radically reshaped the expectations of many consumers. But Braithwaite also drew the industry's attention to more specific influences. These were driven by the recomposition of key markets and their styles of journalism. Most especially,

it was among the publications for women and young people that change had been most hectic. Anxieties about falling sales and magazine closures had been offset by a series of spectacular breakthroughs. The successful launch of a number of women's weekly and monthly general-interest titles across the market range, coupled with the influx of foreign competitors (notably from Germany, France and Spain), had posed fresh questions about the future direction of consumer magazines. Editorial format and visual style, as well as journalistic content, were all under scrutiny. Shifts in women's publishing had been paralleled by transformations in the teenage market. A fresh generation of magazines, targeting girls and young women, were in the forefront of publishing change. What was significant about the newcomers in this area was that they had not emerged from the publishing leviathans, which had hitherto dominated the field, but from smaller regional and independent concerns. EMAP, which was based in Peterborough, scored a major victory for the independents with the launch of its pop music paper, *Smash Hits,* in 1978. It was followed by *Just Seventeen* in 1983, aimed more specifically at teenage girls. Both publications thumbed their noses at the staple format of a youth magazine. Their style of journalism and visual layout broadened the coverage of young women's lives, introducing some ironic distance on traditional cultures of femininity.[19] Taken together, these two publications, and their many imitators, functioned as a tangible symbol of a new type of journalism.

It was into this rapidly changing market that the publishing giant, the International Publishing Corporation (IPC), launched their magazine, *The Hit,* in September 1985. In-house advertising surrounding the new title, which was strategically placed in *Campaign,* rang the familiar tropes of radical innovation associated with any new product launch:

Never before has there been a magazine, a paper, or any other publication so specifically targeted at teenage 15–19 year old males. Never before has there been anything like the HIT. It's the only ... magazine to ZAP the core male youth market between the eyes.[20]

Beyond the advertising hype, the launch of the new magazine was an ambitious venture. Attracting substantial financial backing from IPC, which was keen to reassert its pre-eminence in the youth sector after the challenges from EMAP, the publishers assembled an experienced editorial team. This was headed by Phil McNeill—a journalist with a successful track record on the teenage music paper, *New Musical Express*. With an initial print run of 350,000 and an estimated settle-down target of half that figure, *The Hit* appeared to justify the £650,000 pre-launch advertising campaign, which was handled by the first-ranking Yellowhammer agency. Carrying a glossy, full-colour format, its journalism was wide-ranging. There were consumer items on fashion, sport and the latest media celebrities, social discussion of drug abuse, as well as more standard features on the music charts and pop bands. Prior to publication carefully prepared statements from the publishers pointed up the underlying strategy, for the benefit of manufacturers and advertisers. *The Hit* was aiming for a general-interest format. IPC's Holborn Publishing wing explained in the press release that the title was 'the result of a growing need among young men ... for a magazine to express their own tastes in the Eighties'.[21] As editor, McNeill looked towards the success stories in the young women's sector to justify his formula. *The Hit,* he claimed, sought to 'open up a new kind of market in the way that *Smash Hits* ... did for girls'.[22] Influential groupings within the advertising industry appeared to need little convincing. Prior to the launch, agency interest was running so high that IPC brought forward the publication date by a week. For Dave Porter, associate director of Yellowhammer, who worked closely on the plans, the new magazine proclaimed an individualistic

message. It shouted to young men: 'this is for you.'[23] Back at IPC, Jane Reid, the ex-editor of *Woman* and managing director of the Holborn Group, was convinced that the enthusiastic reception awarded to *The Hit* meant that a men's magazine was now imminent.[24]

But *The Hit* was a failure. The almost total collapse of the title, after only six issues, prompted some hard-hitting comment from publishers and advertisers alike. What went wrong? The basic snag, as Porter ruefully confessed, was that despite the enthusiasm of the experts, all too few 15- to 19-year-olds were tempted to buy the new publication.[25] The post-mortem on *The Hit*'s collapse was wide-ranging. In essence it reflected publishers' continuing confusion over the identities of their young male readers. According to IPC's audience research survey, the lifestyle coverage and layout of the magazine were correct. What surfaced, however, were reservations about the potential of a general-interest magazine to speak to young men. Mark Ellen, from EMAP, believed that, unlike girls of the same age, who identified strongly with a community of women, young men baulked at being addressed collectively as men. As Ellen expounded to *Campaign* a week after the title's closure, the difficulties were social and psychological. Young men 'might like BMX bikes, waterskiing and the Jesus and Mary Chain, but they don't like a magazine to suggest that other men within their age group feel the same way'.[26] In other words, addressing young men as men was seen to be a risky business, because it raised the troubled question of identity as gendered. Self-consciousness was perceived as permissible, even attractive, in young women, but weak and effeminate in men. Simon Marquis, media director at the advertising agency Fletcher Shelton Delaney, hinted that such problems appeared to be specific to British men, given the established male readership for consumer magazines in France, Italy and increasingly in the United States.[27] In Britain, the rules seemed to preclude any discussion of masculinity as a gendered community.

The demise of *The Hit* provided the ideal opportunity for a disgruntled professional coterie to break cover and attack the whole concept of a general-interest title for young men. Among this grouping were the editors and publishers of the well-established hobby press, with vested commercial interests at stake. Cars, bikes/music and pornography, they insisted, were far more effective ways of speaking to the youth market than some vague psychological notion of consumption. Mark Revelle, editor of *Bike* magazine, was particularly caustic. As he gloated in the wake of *The Hit*'s collapse: 'Modesty should prevent me (but it won't) from pointing out that one of my titles, *Bike* magazine, attracts 175,000 15–19 year old young male readers.'[28] The soft-porn publication *Mayfair* was even more triumphalist. Their editor claimed that the 'naturalness' of the male sexual urge would arouse young men far more effectively than any general consumer title: 'Boys will be boys … *Mayfair* delivers the young male market more efficiently than most other colour magazines. So if you've got toys for the boys. You'll sell them in *Mayfair*.'[29] Opponents of the lifestyle format were of course defending their own corner, which they felt might be threatened by a more all-inclusive newcomer. But professional objections were intertwined with more privately felt anxieties. Worries recurred about the ways in which the lifestyle format had the potential to disrupt conventional ideas about masculinity. As so often in these debates, professional and personal beliefs went hand in hand.

What does this vignette reveal about commercial attitudes to masculinity in the mid-1980s? Market failures often provide greater insights into business strategies than successful products. Despite the obvious difficulties, there was a strong alliance of publishers and advertisers who backed a lifestyle magazine for men. The search for a youthful male consumer was a quest for a more stable icon, in the context of increasingly capricious trading conditions. Such an undertaking was also bound up with the projection of new types of male identity. If this provoked opposition, it was because the area was recognised to be a disputed terrain, not simply in economic terms but in a cultural sense as well. Yet the closure of *The Hit* was by no means the end of the story. There were other players at large in the race to break open the men's market, who ultimately proved to be more successful in their quest. For these we move outside mainstream publishing and into a more cryptic and allegorical world.

NOTES

Reprinted with permission from Frank Mort, "New Men and New Markets," in *Cultures of Consumption: Masculinities and Social Space in Late Twentieth-Century Britain* (London: Routledge, 1996), 15–21.

1. P. Bourdieu (1988), *Homo Academicus,* trans. P. Collier, Cambridge: Polity Press, in association with Basil Blackwell: 174–81.

2. J. Williamson (1986), 'Male Order', *New Statesman,* 31 October, vol. 112, no. 2901: 25. See also Williamson's review (1986), 'Above the World', *New Statesman,* 10 October, vol. 112, no. 2898: 25.

3. P. Hodson (1984), 'New Man', *She,* July: 126.

4. S. Taylor (1986), 'Magazines for Men: On the Trail of the Typically British Male', *Campaign,* 29 August: 44. For similar arguments see R. Mayes (1985), 'Jumping on the Bands Wagon', *Media Week,* 6 September: 20–1.

5. McCann Erickson (1984), *Manstudy Report,* quoted in S. Marquis (1985), 'The Publishing Conundrum: How to Reach the "New Man"', *Campaign,* 26 July: 39.

6. B. Isaacs, quoted in C. Davis (1987), 'Brasserie Man—Open All Hours', *The Evening Standard,* 24 November: 33.

7. P. York, quoted in C. Bowen-Jones (1988), 'Adman Finds a New Woman', *The Times,* 16 March, p. 26.

8. T. O'Dwyer (1986), 'Are You Gauguin, New Colonial, or Savile Row?' *The Guardian,* 28 August: 11.

9. T. O'Dwyer (1984), 'Liberated Man Power Arrives', *Men's Wear,* 23 August: 8. For similar comments by O'Dwyer (1984), see: 'Public Image', *Men's Wear,* 5 July: 16; 'Style Counsel '85 ... New Blood', *Men's Wear,* 20 December: 17.

10. B. Kennedy and J. Lyttle (1986), 'Wolf in Chic Clothing', *City Limits,* 4–11 December: 14–17.

11. See for example: 'Girls! Is Your Guy a Page Seven Fella?', *The Sun,* 27 March 1987: 16–17; 'Sheer Joy with My Sexy Toyboy', *The Sun,* 15 February 1987: 9.

12. See for example: F. Mort (1986), 'Images Change: High Street Style and the New Man', *New Socialist,* November, no. 43: 6–8; A. Metcalf and M. Humphries, 'Introduction', in A. Metcalf and M. Humphries (eds) (1985), *The Sexuality of Men,* London: Pluto Press: 1–14; J. Rutherford, 'Who's That Man?' in R. Chapman and J. Rutherford (eds) (1988), *Male Order: Unwrapping Masculinity,* London: Lawrence & Wishart: 21–67; A. Jardine and P. Smith (eds) (1987), *Men in Feminism,* London: Methuen.

13. L. Segal (1990), *Slow Motion: Changing Masculinities, Changing Men,* London: Virago. For other sceptical commentaries see: R. Chapman, 'The Great Pretender: Variations on the New Man Theme', in Chapman and Rutherford (eds) (1987), *Male Order:* 225–48; S. Moore (1987), 'Target Man', *New Socialist,* January, no. 45: 4–5.

14. P. Toynbee (1987), 'The Incredible, Shrinking New Man', *The Guardian,* 6 April: 10.

15. Z. Zawada, quoted in Taylor, 'Magazines for Men': 41. For other similar comments see, among very many: S. Ludgate (1984), 'The Magazines for the Young Generation', *Campaign,* 16 March: 54–8; N. van Zanten (1984), 'In Search of Elusive Youth', *Campaign,* 16 March: 63–4; Marquis, 'The Publishing Conundrum': 37–41; S. Oriel (1988), 'The Ideal Homme Magazine', *Media Week,* 12 February: 43–5; S. Buckley (1988), 'How to Talk to More Men', *Media Week,* 12 February: 46.

16. For details of *Man About Town* and *About Town* see D. Cook (1993), 'From Pillar to "Post"', MA thesis submitted to the Royal College of Art, London (May).

17. For details of these magazines see P. Burton (1985), *Parallel Lives,* London: Gay Men's Press: 48–9.

18. B. Braithwaite (1989), 'The Eagle Has Landed', *Media Week,* 8 December: 28–9.

19. For analysis of *Smash Hits* and *Just Seventeen,* in the context of both shifts in magazine publishing and changes to the culture of young women in the 1980s, see: J. Winship (1987), 'A Girl Needs to Get Street-Wise: Magazines for the 1980s', *Feminist Review,* no. 21: 25–46, and *Inside Women's Magazines* (1987), London: Pandora: 148–62; A. McRobbie (1991), *Feminism and Youth Culture: From 'Jackie' to 'Just Seventeen',* Basingstoke: Macmillan: 135–88. The total circulation figures for teenage magazines in 1984 showed an 11 per cent increase on the previous year, at a time when magazine circulation as a whole dropped by 2 per cent. See: *Media Week,* 6 September 1985: 20; S. Nixon (1993), 'Looking for the Holy Grail: Publishing and Advertising Strategies for Contemporary Men's Magazines', *Cultural Studies,* vol. 7, no. 3: 467–92.

20. Advertisement for *The Hit, Campaign,* 6 September 1985: 26–7.

21. 'The Hit Hits the Stands', *Media Week,* 17 May 1985: 2.

22. P. McNeill, quoted in Mayes, 'Jumping on the Bands Wagon': 20.

23. D. Porter, quoted in A. Rawsthorn (1985), 'The Hit: Why It Failed so Miserably to Reach Its Male Target', *Campaign,* 15 November: 15.

24. J. Reid, quoted in S. d'Arcy (1985), 'Next for Men?' *Media Week,* 16 August: 10.

25. Porter, quoted in Rawsthorn, 'The Hit'. The magazine closed early in November 1985, after sales had dropped to 80,000.

26. M. Ellen, quoted in Rawsthorn, 'The Hit'.

27. Marquis, 'The Publishing Conundrum'. Italian and French men's magazine titles included *L'Uomo Vogue* and *L'Homme Vogue* respectively. The United States had seen a dramatic rise in men's magazines. *Esquire* was the most established title, with a circulation in 1986 of 700,000. *GQ,* or *Gentlemen's Quarterly,* was started as a trade magazine by *Esquire* in 1957, but underwent a transformation on its sale to Conde Nast in 1979. Circulation figures were 660,000 in

1986. Other titles with smaller circulations included M magazine and *MGF* (*Men's Guide to Fashion*). In the mid-1980s America's largest black-owned business, the Johnson's publishing company, launched *Ebony Man*. There was at this stage a second magazine aimed at black men entitled *MBM* (*Modern Black Men*). See

R. Bailey (1986), 'Men's Writes', *Media Week*, 2 May: 14–17.

28. M. Revelle (1985), Letters, 'The Specialist Press: An Ideal Youth Target', *Campaign*, 29 November: 28.

29. Advertisement for *Mayfair* magazine, *Campaign*, 15 February 1985: 32.

35

CONSUMING MASCULINITIES: STYLE, CONTENT AND MEN'S MAGAZINES

Tim Edwards

Men's magazines in the UK now constitute a growth market. But the so-called new style magazines for men are not new internationally and, in the UK, men's general interest magazines have an equally long history. It is, to put it simply, that they weren't *called* men's magazines and this is what constitutes the key difference: the self-conscious targeting of men as consumers of magazines designed to *interest* men if not necessarily to be *about* men. They were and, what is more, still are called car magazines, hi-fi magazines, sport magazines, and so on; in short, magazine journalism which quite clearly targets men's interests without targeting men themselves.

To expand upon some of these points in turn: firstly, in North America and some European countries, particularly France, men's style magazines have a long if far more limited history, similar to style magazines aimed at women. For example, *GQ* and *Esquire* in North America have existed since at least the Second World War and so, similarly, has *Vogue Hommes* in France. Secondly, there is an equally historic legacy of men's interest magazines as opposed to men's style magazines in the UK and yet over ten years ago you could not have purchased a single men's style magazine or even a men's general interest magazine. As I write in 1996, there are six monthly style titles with a total circulation of upwards of 500,000 and increasing monthly, plus several biannual fashion manuals, making the UK something of a world leader in

terms of men's style titles (Driscoll 1995). There is also a new series of style-influenced titles that concentrate on other issues such as health or sport in particular, yet persistently dip their toes into issues of men's style.

As a result, then, there are three sorts of men's magazines: the first is a list of fully style-conscious and self-conscious general interest magazines aimed directly and overtly at a male readership including *GQ, Esquire, Arena, For Him Magazine (FHM), Loaded* and *Maxim*; the second, a series of supposedly more specific periodicals with a more open readership that carry regular features concerning men's style and fashion including *Attitude, i-D, The Face, The Clothes Show Magazine, XL* and *Men's Health*; and the third, a gargantuan group of men's interest magazines which covertly target men as their primary readership including car, computing, photographic, sport and technical titles. Due to the concentration of this current text on men's fashion, the first and to some extent second groups are clearly of most relevance. However, I do not wish to exclude entirely consideration of other areas, particularly in terms of the contextual development of men's style magazines.

THE CONTEXTUAL DEVELOPMENT OF MEN'S STYLE MAGAZINES

The most interesting question concerning the so-called new crop of men's style magazines in the UK is, why now? When men are apparently more concerned with their economic survival than ever, why do they apparently respond so positively to such an initiative and why have marketers of such products thought it fit to take the risk? The answers to these questions are, I think, complex yet quite concretely located in the social, economic and political changes of the past ten to fifteen years. Firstly, economically, whilst many men have suffered financially it is also clear that others have advanced. In particular, young white, well-educated and middle-class men are still the primary employment group for professional and primary sector work. This connects up with a second, social and demographic factor that as more men now live alone or do not have children, some men have also seen increases in their personal incomes. Thirdly, and more politically, Thatcherism and Majorism in the UK have seen an equal encouragement of individualism and aspirationalism, in turn a key factor in men's style magazines and one which I wish to expand upon shortly. Fourthly, it is also argued that men are increasingly encouraged towards self-awareness via the impacts of women's magazines and gay movements which have equally challenged hegemonic notions of heterosexual masculinity. Yet lastly, and most significantly of all I think, it has become more socially acceptable for men to be consumers per se and, more importantly, to be consumers of their own masculinity or, in short, to look at themselves and other men as objects of desire to be bought and sold or imitated and copied. At least *some* male narcissism is now socially approved.

The difficulty concerns locating quite where this development has come from. It is easy to see feminism as the primary cause of male self-reflection, and yet I would question the logic of such a notion for there is often little evidence to suggest traditional heterosexual male practices have altered at all in relation to the home, workplace or sexual relationships. What has perhaps shifted is the perception rather than the practice of male sexuality itself as something more

artificial and floating, as opposed to natural and fixed.

The linking factor of significance here is the rise of a visible and partially more socially acceptable gay masculinity. Gay men, supposedly free from the hang-ups of heterosexual masculinity concerning the stereotypes of effeminacy associated with style-conscious consumption, have in many ways acted as a pilot consumer group for men in general. Gay men's relation to consumption does differ from heterosexual men's primarily on two counts: they tend to have fewer financial commitments and therefore often higher disposable incomes; and their consumption patterns are often used to reinforce their sexual orientation, whether through spending the pink pound or maintaining a distinctive lifestyle or identity, and Fashion is often quoted as an important example of this. It could, perhaps, also be argued that they have in turn become the bridge by which marketers have made inroads into mainstream heterosexual masculinity. This position is however easily overstated and leads to a series of negative and nonsensical stereotypes. But those affluent and high-spending gay men who *have* spent and consumed in a way of which marketers had previously merely dreamed, have also provided the template and take-off point for exploring consumer masculinity in general. As a result, gay sexuality remains a significant, if often unacknowledged, factor in the development of men's style magazines targeting men and masculinity.

An underlying factor of importance in all of this, though, is the development of style magazines themselves. These currently include such titles as *i-D, Details* and, most importantly, *The Face,* all of which developed in the early to mid-1980s to cater for the tastes of the young, affluent, style-conscious and the often city- as well as self-centred youth cultures, set around strong interests in music, dance and night life. Of particular concern here were the links with pop music, particularly the New Romanticism of groups such as Spandau Ballet and ABC as well as early Blitz nightclub culture; and the rise of lifestyle itself in concept and practice, a primary example in the UK coming in the form of Habitat. This high-style, mid-price household chain store turned coffee mugs and tea trays, let alone sofas and furnishings, into fashion accessories in the 1960s and all over again in the 1980s.

The development of style magazines for men has had two significant effects. It created a style cultural intelligentsia of experts disseminating their specialist know-how on matters of appearance, a point picked up on recently in Frank Mort's work (Mort 1996).[1] More significantly, though, it led to an immense emphasis upon consumption as a means to join the new style elite: wear the right suit, visit the right store, get seen in the right places in the right apparel (as whatever the 'wrong' apparel was or was not, it was always the cheaper option). What all this added up to was the primary (though still nearly always missed academically) role of men's style magazines in encouraging and perpetuating high spending. This, I would argue, is the foremost function of these magazines.

As a result of all of these elements, masculinity became a lifestyle commodity to be bought, sold, admired through retailers' windows and aspired to in style magazines, just like anything else. However, it is the question of a specific style and content of men's magazines to which I now turn in the next section.

THE STYLE AND CONTENT OF MEN'S MAGAZINES

The style and content of the new so-called men's magazines appears, initially, varied and free-floating, yet I wish to assert in this section that the style and content of these titles is in fact quite extraordinarily fixed, apart from superficial construction of what one could call product personality. The first point to make concerning this new crop of men's style and general interest titles is that they are all, without exception,

relatively expensive. Priced currently from £2 to £3 per issue, it is patently clear that we are not talking of competition with *Woman's Weekly!* The counterparts for women would more realistically include such titles as *Vogue* and *Vanity Fair,* if not *Tatler* and *Harpers & Queens.* As a consequence, despite any pretence to the contrary, all such titles clearly most directly appeal to affluent, professional or managerial men in socio-economic groups ABC and not to factory workers, mechanics or drop-outs. (The appeal of *Loaded* is more contradictory and a point I will explore shortly.) Market reports from two of the leaders, *GQ* and *Esquire,* also make it clear that this is quite overtly their target market.[2] The one exception to this rule is that students clearly make up a significant part of the readership (according to the same reports). The important point to make here, of course, is that students ultimately form the next generation of affluent professionals.

A second point to make is that, with the exception of *Attitude* as a more directly gay-oriented title, they all assert the heterosexuality of their readers often with a near-defensive vengeance. This is the most significant and contradictory point to make, for if affluent and professional gay men constitute a major target style-consuming group with money to spend and fewer hang-ups in doing so, then why do such titles tend to exclude and, on occasions, even directly offend their non-heterosexual readers? The answer would seem to be the high level of anxiety relating to the exclusion of heterosexual readers if homosexuality is too overtly or openly condoned. This does not explain, though, why such titles cannot apparently occupy a neutral or open territory of unspecified sexuality. The explanation, I suspect, lies in the felt necessity of off-setting the near-pornographic and homoerotic nature of much of the imagery used to advertise products or illustrate features on fashion and style, which varies from the phallic and sculpted to the soft-focused and artistic. In this sense these titles do covertly cater for their gay readers, although this also tends to fetishize and delegitimize homosexuality.

A third area of overlap concerns the overt legitimation of consumption itself as a socially acceptable leisure activity for men and as a symbolic part of a successful lifestyle. This is not only reflected in the high profile and level of advertising itself, it is also seen in the constant textual and visual attention paid to commodities and products as part of a material aspirationalism from clothes and accessories to cars and technology. A connected, and I think significant, factor is the implication that this then leads to the increasing construction of masculinity according to commodities. In other words, you are the man you are due to the cut of your suit, the cost of your hi-fi or the car you own. What this then leads to ultimately is masculinity as a matter of how one looks and not what one does.

This leads me on to the fourth and key point of aspirationalism. Even the style-defensive *Loaded* still espouses the pleasures of spending, the good life and looking sharp, whilst the others routinely define successful masculinity in terms of money equally conspicuously earned and spent. This is in many ways part of the overall 1980s trend towards lifestyle advertising along aspirational lines. As a result, these titles (quite didactically on occasions) inform their readers of the significance of fine tailoring, the glamour and sexiness of suits, ties and all the accessories, give instruction on casual correctness, and advise of the fundamental importance of personal appearance to success and even to personal security. This is not, I hasten to add, confined to suits, ties and accessories (although the never-ending concern with these items is a source of some fascination in itself), but spreads to cover toiletries, physique, cars, technology and even property. Most importantly, the stirring up of anxieties, all-consuming dreams, desires and allures is quite dazzling and only satisfied in equally endless spending.

Lastly, all these titles implicitly depend upon a city as opposed to a rural or even suburban mi-

lieu, both in terms of the products and services advertised only being accessible in big metropolitan cities and particularly London, and also in relation to the fast-lane lifestyles they promote. In sum, what these five points add up to, then, is a quite specific and often fixed targeting of single affluent, city-dwelling, high-earning and high-spending, primarily heterosexual men to the exclusion of all others: that is, all those who do not at least aspire to this way of living or its values. As a result, what advertisers in these titles tend to tap into is a semi-conscious daydreaming state where fantasies of self-image are of paramount importance (see Bowlby 1993; Campbell 1992; Radner 1995).

FROM NEW MAN TO NEW LAD: ANALYZING MEN'S MAGAZINES

New Lads are just as much a 'phony' marketing phenomenon as New Men.
Simpson 1996: 249

This section focuses on a content analysis of the so-called 'new' men's magazines as defined in the introduction to this chapter. In particular, I wish to refer to the content of four of the market leaders: *GQ, Esquire, Arena* and *For Him Magazine*. These are the most established and, as yet, biggest or most solid sellers in the market for men's style magazines. In addition, I also wish to consider the two newcomers, *Loaded* and *Maxim,* for which circulation figures are as yet unconfirmed.

GQ or *Gentlemen's Quarterly* is essentially the English version of its long-running North American counterpart, set up under the directorship of the American editorial entrepreneur Michael VerMeulen. *Arena* is the longest-running men's style magazine in the UK, started in 1986 under the editorship of Nik Logan, seeking product diversification following the international success of *The Face* magazine and similar in kind to *Details* in the USA. *Arena Homme Plus* is a biannual and additional fashion label bible based on *Vogue Hommes* in France, and was started successfully in 1994. *Esquire,* like *GQ,* was launched slightly later in the UK in 1991 as a counterpart to its highly successful equivalent in the USA. *For Him Magazine* is a corporate product of the magazine conglomerate EMAP in the UK and was launched initially under the simple title of *For Him* in 1985. *Loaded* was sprung in Spring 1994 and *Maxim,* the most recent of all the titles, had its premier edition in April 1995. Neither of these titles seems as yet to have an international parallel. *Attitude,* interestingly marketed as the magazine for real men, was launched in 1994 in the UK as a gay-oriented, if not gay-exclusive, style title (and as an alternative to the news-oriented *Gay Times*), similar in kind to *Genre* or *Out* in the USA.

The method of content analysis was very simple and intentionally quite unsophisticated, as it is the widest and most general features which are of interest here. Recent editions of all the titles were taken and analyzed according to the space they devoted to differing forms of content. Firstly, advertising content was distinguished from editorial features in the magazines. This is, in fact, not the hard and fast distinction it may seem, as many of the editorial features, particularly those in relation to fashion and lifestyle, have an implicit advertisement intention giving listings, stockists and prices for the items pictured and discussed. Secondly, categories were then created within these two groups according to easily recognized, overall definitions of the content involved. From this, ten central categories were devised to cover all of the features in the magazines, although not all the magazines ran features in all categories. The pages devoted to the categories were then totalled and converted into percentages of the entire magazine, including front covers. Circulation figures were derived from media information packs received from the magazines themselves upon request and compiled using ABC readership survey statistics. The results were then put into chart form as presented in table 35.1: A Content Analysis of Men's Magazines.

From this simplistic analysis, certain points are immediately apparent as important. The advertising content in all cases is significant and, at its highest, reflects the up-market, style-conscious and glossy emphasis of the titles concerned. *GQ, Arena* and *For Him Magazine,* as the most self-consciously style-centred of all the titles, have the highest figures here; and one may well expect the two lowest, *Loaded* and *Maxim,* to increase their advertising revenues as they increase their market significance. Within this and with the exception of *Loaded,* advertising for fashion, and its related accessories such as aftershaves and jewellery, wipes the floor with all other categories of advertising, taking up to a quarter of the entire content of the magazine. (*Loaded*'s low showing in this category is due to its advertising concentration upon the arts and, in particular, rock music, explained in terms of its ex-music-journalist editorship and editorial.)

In editorial, the fashion and lifestyle features category also tends to dwarf the others in most cases, again taking up to nearly a quarter of the entire text. It is also of significance here that the same three magazines which have the most advertising in this area, *GQ, Arena* and *FHM,* also have the three highest rates in the equivalent features category, creating a situation where nearly 50 per cent of these titles is concerned with fashion, lifestyle and accessories.

Certain titles display a particularly strong emphasis in specific categories. *Esquire,* for example, has the highest concentration of features on serious issues, reflecting its general interest rather than style-conscious focus; whilst *Loaded* and *Maxim* have a far higher joint emphasis on the arts and interviews than the others. This reflects their somewhat anti-style conscious opposition to the other four titles and is also part of a more working-class emphasis, in the loosest sense, as the arts mentioned are rock, pop music and cinema rather than classical music, opera and theatre. They are also, though, the

Table 35.1   A Content Analysis of Men's Magazines

	GQ	Esquire	Arena	FHM	Loaded	Maxim
Circulation	110/80	97/65	80/68	60/60	–	–
Editor	Michael VerMeulen	Rosie Boycott	Kathryn Flett	Mike Soutar	James Brown	Gill Hudson
Price	£2.40	£2.40	£2.40	£2.50	£2.00	£2.50
Advertising:	**34**	**24**	**35**	**33**	**25**	**19**
Fashion	25	15	23	23	11	8
Technology	4	5	4	5	1	6
Alc/Tobacco	3	2	6	4	2	3
Other	2	2	2	1	11	2
Features:	**66**	**76**	**65**	**67**	**75**	**81**
Listings	7	4	8	5	9	5
Lifestyle	24	20	21	21	13	13
Sport	5	2	7	2	7	5
Health/Fit	3	10	1	4	0	6
Sex/Women	1	0	6	5	10	15
General/Arts	5	15	10	12	15	20
Travel	4	5	0	0	2	3
Issues	5	11	2	2	0	6
Fiction	3	1	0	0	0	3
Interviews	9	8	13	11	19	3
Surveys	0	0	0	2	0	2
Total	**100**	**100**	**100**	**100**	**100**	**100**

Note: Results based on May 1995 editions.

Circulation figures for 1994/1991, in thousands.

All other figures given in percentages.

most grossly (hetero)sexist of the six, featuring the highest use of features on women and sex. *Maxim* in particular runs up to three times as many features here as the others. The other four in fact have a certain tendency to run one, near soft-core pornographic feature on sex or women which often seems set up in defensive opposition to the endlessly homoerotic displays of men's fashion, style and accessories. This is particularly the case with *GQ* and *FHM,* as *Arena* is rather more serious in its addressing of such issues and includes some minor attention to gay sexuality. Apart from interviews with a variety of famous faces, all other categories gain minor coverage, which makes the final point that, despite all pretences to the contrary, these are all in some way up-market titles strongly concerned with the self-conscious marketing and consumption of masculinity and narcissism employed in heavy uses of advertising and features on fashion, lifestyle and appearance. The peacock is indeed on parade, at least within the pages of these style titles. This also leads perhaps to the assumption that these titles perform an implicit function of reinforcing a style culture which does not in reality actually exist, adding some weight to similar discussion of women's magazines acting as escapist outlets (Craik 1994; Radner 1995; Winship, *Inside Women's Magazines,* 1987).

Within all of this though there are, as I have already mentioned, minor variations particularly in what one might call product personality. In particular, each of the titles concerned expresses a quite distinct set of characteristics or values which, most importantly, centres on a particular construction of masculinity or personality. For example, *GQ* nicknames itself as the magazine for men with an IQ and features extensive coverage of executive concerns from quality tailoring to property and corporate spending. More than anything else though, *GQ* represents the interests of the notorious yuppie, or the suit-wearing, swaggering, and narcissistic lover of money. Similarly, *Esquire,* whilst appealing to exactly the same socio-economic group, applies an anti-narcissistic, quintessentially English attention to detail and quality, eschewing issues of style in favour of general and often quite conservative interest. *Arena,* as an off-cut of *The Face,* sneers equally at such conservatism and asserts a counter-cultural art student's sense of elitist style that most men could not and, what is more, would not afford. It, was hardly surprising, then, that it was *Arena* that launched the biannual *Arena Homme Plus,* an unashamedly design-centred and haute-couture-focused fashion manual for the label-obsessed. In a sense, *FHM,* although usually the loss-leader of the four, is the most honest as a directly and self-consciously narcissistic style-centred glossy that takes little interest in worldly affairs, flogs free samples, and appeals to men who are still Brylcreem boys at heart. One would also say that there is something rather laddish about it were it not for *Loaded,* best described as a bargain bible for lager louts, being concerned with beer-swilling, shagging and looking sharp, or simply being objectionable, and often in that order. It is the most ambiguous of all the titles on offer, at once ironic and blindingly reactionary. In particular, it

is tempting to see *Loaded* as the sarcastic equivalent of the BBC TV programme *Men Behaving Badly* but whilst the latter is clearly intended to be funny, *Loaded* is all too easily taken seriously by those who don't know better which, incidentally, is the magazine's trademark.[3] *Maxim* is a less extreme variation on the same theme, with an unashamedly post-feminist or primordial viewpoint on sexual politics (depending on how you look at it), including a guide to getting a rich wife.

It would seem, then, that as the most recent additions to the list, *Loaded* and *Maxim* have equally set themselves up as the laddish and supposedly more down-to-earth opposition to the high-flown narcissism of some of the others, though this usually ends up in some kind of working-class machismo or undiluted misogyny. Interestingly, the success of *Loaded* has led other titles to drift increasingly towards using New Laddism, as opposed to narcissistic New Mannism, as a means of selling magazines. As a consequence, there is an increasing use of semi-naked women, frequently on the front cover, and many an article on stag-night antics. In particular, *GQ* and *Arena,* as previously the least gratuitously sexist of all the titles, now endlessly splash topless models amongst the advertising for designer suits; whilst *For Him Magazine,* desperately seeking increased circulation, sells free glimpses of the new Pirelli calendar and incorporates a separate letters page specifically for stories of lager-induced urinating accidents! As a result, the recent and reactionary drift of men's style magazines is increasingly giving cause for concern.[4]

In amongst all of this, there are in each case some genuine and serious attempts to inform and educate men, not only in relation to fashion and spending, but also in quite coherent and intelligent advice concerning health, money and sexual relationships. Whilst not progressive, then, even at their worst these titles do not misinform or actively promote violence and discrimination. The question of their exact intention, though, and in particular their relationship to men's fashion, is discussed in the next section.

INTERPRETATIONS AND INTENTIONS

Tim Edwards: What are the main aims, would you say, of most men's style magazines?

Michael VerMeulen: Entertain readers. Deliver readers to advertisers. In that respect, it's the same as any magazine. (Interview, January, 1995)

More academically, interpretations of men's style magazines, like many such developments of the 1980s, have tended to emerge around the theme of the New Man. The self-conscious style magazine for men was seen as the outcome of wider developments in sexual politics increasingly encouraging men to look at themselves and other men as men or, more simply, as the product of a redefinition of masculinity in terms of narcissism (Chapman and Rutherford 1988; Mort 1986, 1988, 1996; Nixon 1993a). Academic attention has tended to centre on the question of the interpretation of images of masculinity presented in these titles. In particular, much attention has focused on the late Ray Petri's work with *The Face* and other titles in constructing representations of heavy-lipped and pouting young men, often of mixed race, in particular. Such attention, whilst of significance of and to itself, has had the deleterious, if unintended, effect of reinforcing a frankly ridiculous notion that such representations—which are entirely unrepresentative of the overall presentation of masculinity in men's style magazines—constitute some kind of radical shift in the construction of masculinity; when the reality, as I have already asserted, was and still is far more conservative and linked to the fostering of an aspirational and narcissistic masculinity that makes money for the fashion and media industries alike.

In light of the prior commentary, then, it is perhaps more accurate to see men's style magazines primarily as vehicles for a new 'all-consuming' form of masculinity, encouraging men to spend time and money on developing consumer-oriented attitudes and practices from shopping to leisure activities and to enjoy their own masculinity: in short, a narcissistic and particularly introspective set of primarily auto-erotic pleasures. Men's style magazines have very little to do with sexual politics and a lot to do with new markets for the constant reconstruction of masculinity through consumption: buy this to be that; own a double-breasted suit, portable CD player or BMW and be a man! If men's style magazines respond to anything in sexual politics then it is the undermining of definitions of masculinity in terms of production or traditional work roles, and a deep-seated set of anxieties concerning the lack of future focus for young men, which has almost nothing to do with reactions to second-wave feminism and almost everything to do with the fear of unemployment. Reactions to second-wave feminism, whenever apparent, take one of two forms: disinterest or defensiveness. There is, therefore, little that is progressive here in terms of sexual politics, though a lot in terms of the shifting terrain and sands of masculinity.

The New Man has also received added nails in his coffin from the development of the New Lad, a counter-reaction if ever there was one (Margolis 1995). Where the New Man was caring and sharing, if overly concerned with the cut of his Calvin Kleins, the New Lad is selfish, loutish and inconsiderate to a point of infantile smelliness. He likes drinking, football and fucking and in that order of preference. Yet despite all the sneering at the perceived effeminacy of the New Man, the New Lad is oddly still all too self-conscious and quick to consider the cut of his jeans or the Lacoste label on his T-shirt: in short, he is that most ghastly of all configurations, defensively working class which also means defensively masculine. The link with style-conscious football is unsurprising here as football has historically always been a bastion of blow-drying, suit-swaggering, sharp-looking English laddism. In common, then, with other fads and fancies, he has his origins in other areas, namely pop music and the rise of fashionable football where loutishness has become elevated to an art form. For example, one only has to think of Eric Cantona who, successfully convicted of a violent offence, was *still* hailed as a hero; and Britpop, where the scruffy, badly behaved and derivative heroes of Blur, Oasis and Pulp are now being used to sell the latest designer labels. Herein, however, also lies the irony, for there is as much continuity as there is change in the development of New Laddism. If the New Man sold muscles and scent, Armani and Calvin Klein, then the New Lad sells T-shirts and trainers, Hugo by Hugo Boss and Prada. As a result, the styles may have altered, yet the drive to consume remains the same (Simpson 1996).

I raised the question of the exact intention of men's style magazines in several face-to-face interviews with some of their editors, which were conducted in early 1995. From these, a series of points emerged as particularly important. Firstly, developments in the economy and in social attitudes were cited as equally and mutually influential in the rise of interest in men's fashion, and the expansion of men's style magazines and retailing attendant with it—whether in relation to the fluidity of income or the social acceptance of design-consciousness. In particular, in relation to the rise of men's fashion in concept and practice, economic deregulation or democratization of income and the increased status of designer garments were seen as equally significant. Secondly, the centrality of a certain socio-economic group of high-earning and high-spending single men was seen as vital in fuelling these overall developments and, more specifically, the role of style-conscious and aspirational professionals was seen as particularly important. Thirdly, there was also an explicit assumption that this group is increasingly sophisticated and knowing in relation to its spending patterns and that this applies to issues of quality as well as style.

As a consequence, the didactic or educational as well as entertainment functions of men's style magazines were seen as equally important. For example, explaining the virtues of wool suits over polyester ones was cited as indicative of such didacticism rather than as a ploy for random unmitigated consumption and, as Nick Sullivan, fashion director at *Esquire,* pointed out to me: 'On one level it is about buying, but really it is to make sure the reader spends rightly, or makes the right choices. It's more about how to spend it and not to waste it.' This taps into the question, mentioned earlier, of the magazine's creation of a cultural elite. It also raises the issue of the role of men's style magazines in covertly perpetuating spending, often reinforcing the perception of fashion as confusing and complex and, therefore, the consumer as in need of guidance. The increased confusion concerning the casual–formal dividing line in particular was given as an example here, as suit jackets for instance were worn increasingly with jeans, and so on. Fourthly, these trends were also seen as the result of a generational change, as the fathers of the 1960s and 1970s were seen to pass on their sense of style to their sons. The difficulty here concerns accounting for the thousands of fathers and sons who were, and are, entirely disinterested in the issue and, in particular, the role of generational reaction and counter-reaction in creating differing trends in fashion. Finally, and perhaps most importantly, there was a strong, if implicit, sense of the expansion and untapped potential of the whole market for men's fashion, accessories, and perhaps for the consumption of masculinity itself, primarily due to marketers' increased recognition of men's, as opposed to women's, economic dominance and solvency.

CONCLUSIONS: CONSUMING MASCULINITIES

In conclusion, throughout this chapter I have stressed the importance of the development of a self-conscious and narcissistic masculinity actively promoted in the expansion of the so-called new men's magazines. I have also argued strongly that the rise of these magazines is most easily understood or accounted for in terms of a series of economic and demographic developments including the increasing significance of young, single men with high personal incomes; the impact of sexual political movements such as feminism and gay groups; and, in particular, the advance of an aspirational individualism in concept and practice, promoted politically through Conservative policy and ideology and acted out quite concretely at work as well as in the retail market.

Of critical importance in this, though, is the increasing acceptance of consumption itself as part of masculinity in identity and activity, as more and more men appear prepared to look into the mirror, purchase products for their skin or hair care, or wear a vast array of more fashion-conscious styles of clothes. This is, I think, not as new as it seems, as men in the 1960s and 1970s were concerned with their appearances, reacted against some forms of formalist conservatism in dress, and started to use products such as hairspray and deodorant in ways that only a decade earlier would have had their fathers quaking in their collars and ties. The net result of this is that the rise of a self-conscious or narcissistic New Man was not so much a passing fad as a continuation of a set of developments set in motion after the Second World War; and the advent of a series of up-market glossies designed to complement, cater to and more seriously exploit these developments is not so much a surprise as an expectation. In addition, there is much continuation of all of this in the current fad of the New Lad.

The question to answer, then, is not 'why did it all happen so suddenly?', rather 'why did it all take so long?' The answer would seem related to the very deep reservoirs of anxiety that still attend men's narcissism and sexuality, particularly in England, still a country where men put on a stiff upper lip more readily than a sharp suit or a self-conscious display of their own sexiness. And yet, despite all of this, it is still unequivocally the case that masculinity is increasingly sold, marketed and consumed as part of an overall series of social, economic and political processes that validate male narcissism. The peacock is not, perhaps, on parade yet, though he is certainly taking the first few steps upon the catwalk.

NOTES

Reprinted with permission from Tim Edwards, "Consuming Masculinities: Style, Content and Men's Magazines," in *Men in the Mirror: Men's Fashion, Masculinity and Consumer Society* (London: Cassell, 1997), 72–85.

1. It should be pointed out here that Frank Mort's application of the concept of a style elite is based on Bourdieu's analysis of the role of cultural intermediaries. The application is indeed an interesting one as the role of the more up-market style magazines for men in disseminating expertise, in particular, is of profound significance to their construction.

2. I refer here to the media information packs readily supplied by the magazines themselves and based, in turn, on ABC and NRS readership surveys.

3. The trademark slogan of *Loaded* is in fact 'The magazine for men who should know better'.

4. I am thinking here of Channel 4's *Without Walls* discussion of New Laddism shown in Spring 1996; and of Mark Simpson's recent work (Simpson 1996).

ANNOTATED GUIDE TO FURTHER READING

Edwards, Tim. *Cultures of Masculinity.* London: Routledge, 2006. *Cultures of Masculinity* presents a survey of the social, cultural, and theoretical issues that surround and inform our understanding of masculinity. The author examines fashion and men's style magazines as well as concerns and anxieties that surround masculinity in the contemporary world.

Featherstone, Mike. *Consumer Culture and Postmodernism.* London: Sage, 1991. Featherstone examines the idea of a postmodern society. He explores the roots of consumer culture, how it is defined and differentiated, and the extent to which it represents the arrival of a postmodern world. He examines the theories of consumption and postmodernism among contemporary social theorists and relates these to the actual nature of contemporary consumer culture.

Jobling, Paul. *Man Appeal: Advertising, Modernism and Menswear.* Oxford and New York: Berg, 2005. Covers a history of men's fashion advertising in the first half of the twentieth century. The author addresses key areas relating to professionalism, mass communication, marketing, and consumer psychology.

Martin, Richard, and Harold Koda, Harold. *Jocks and Nerds: Men's Style in the Twentieth Century.* New York: Rizzoli, 1989. Offers a visual history of the ways men have dressed in the twentieth century, tracing twelve social roles that have formed fashion and fashion leaders and profiling numerous trendsetters.

Nixon, Sean. "Have You Got the Look? Masculinities and Shopping Spectacles." In *Lifestyle Shopping: The Subject of Consumption,* ed. Rob Shields. London and New York: Routledge, 1992. The author looks at contemporary shopping spectacles and practices in terms of masculinity and the gaze. Design and fit-out of shopping spaces are also examined in the author's analysis of visual pleasure.

Osgerby, Bill. *Playboys in Paradise: Masculinity, Youth and Leisure-Style in Modern America.* Oxford and New York: Berg, 2001. This book charts middle-class America's move toward an ethos of conspicuous consumption and sexual license during the 1950s and 1960s. Focusing on two of the period's most visible icons—the swinging bachelor and the vibrant teenager—this book looks at the interconnected changes that took place for American youth culture and masculinity as consumption and leisure established themselves as the dominant features of middle-class life.

Polhemus, Ted. *Street Style: From Sidewalk to Catwalk.* London: Thames and Hudson, 1994. A guide to street fashion from 1940 to the present day. It documents the styles and their wearers on the street but also on the high-fashion catwalk.

Polhemus, Ted. *Style Surfing: What to Wear in the 3rd Millennium.* New York: Thames and Hudson, 1986. The author examines postmodern British fashion, showing how various ethnic, period, and street styles are being combined and transformed.

LIST OF FIGURES

LIST OF COLOR PLATES

NOTES ON CONTRIBUTORS

Holly Alford is an assistant professor in the Department of Fashion Design and Merchandising at Virginia Commonwealth University.

George A. Boeck Jr. completed his doctoral dissertation at the University of Pennsylvania. He is the author of *Texas Livestock Auctions: A Folklife Ethnography* (American Studies in Anthropology, 8).

Christopher Breward is deputy head of research, Victoria and Albert Museum, London. He is the author of *The Englishness of English Dress* (Berg, 2002), *The Culture of Fashion: A New History of Fashionable Dress* (1995), *Fashion's World Cities* (Berg, 2006), *Fashioning London: Clothing and the Modern Metropolis* (Berg, 2004), *Fashion and Modernity* (with Caroline Evans, 2005), *The London Look: Fashion from Street to Catwalk* (with Edwina Erhman and Caroline Evans, 2004), *Swinging Sixties* (with David Gilbert and Jenny Lister, 2006), and *Fashion* (Berg, 2003).

Stella Bruzzi is professor and head of the Department of Film and Television Studies, Warwick University, Coventry. She is the author of *Bringing Up Daddy: Fatherhood and Masculinity in Postwar Hollywood* (2005), *Fashion Cultures: Theories, Histories and Analysis* (coedited with Pamela Church Gibson, Routledge, 2000), and

Undressing Cinema: Clothing and Identity in the Movies (Routledge, 1997).

Barbara Burman teaches at Winchester School of Art, University of Southampton, where she was director of the Centre for the History of Textiles and Dress. Her research interests and publications focus on the cultural and social history of dress and textiles in the modern period. She has edited *The Culture of Sewing: Gender, Consumption and Home Dressmaking* (Berg. 1999) and *Material Strategies: Dress and Gender in Historical Perspective* (with Carole Turbin, Blackwell, 2003). Her latest project is *History of Pockets*.

Michael Carter is an honorary associate in the Department of Art History and Theory, University of Sydney. He is the author of *Putting a Face on Things: Studies in Imaginary Materials* (1997), *Fashion Classics from Carlyle to Barthes* (2003), and *The Language of Fashion* (2006).

Shaun Cole is a research fellow in the Centre for Fashion, the Body and Material Cultures, University of the Arts London. Cole's research focuses on men's fashion, particularly gay men's dress and subcultural style. His work has addressed the significance of dress in the formation of gay male sexual identity, the adaptation and adoption of subcultural dress, and the relationship between subcultural styles and mainstream fashion.

Becky Conekin is senior research fellow, principle lecturer in history and cultural studies, and the director of the MA in History and Culture of Fashion at the University of the Arts London.

Jennifer Craik is professor of communication and cultural studies, School of Creative Communication at the University of Canberra and adjunct professor of fashion and textiles at the Royal Melbourne Institute of Technology. Her publications include *Uniforms Exposed: From Conformity to Transgression* (Berg, 2005) and *The Face of Fashion: Cultural Studies in Fashion* (Routledge, 1994).

Tim Edwards is senior lecturer in sociology at Leicester University. His primary research interests include analyses of masculinity, sexualities, fashion and consumer culture, the interface between social and cultural theory, and social divisions. He is the author of *Cultures of Masculinity* (Routledge, 2006), *Contradictions of Consumption: Concepts, Practices and Politics in Consumer Society* (Open University Press, 2000), *Men in the Mirror: Men's Fashion, Masculinity and Consumer Society* (Cassell, 1997), and *Erotics and Politics: Gay Male Sexuality, Masculinity and Feminism* (Routledge, 1994).

Joanne Entwistle is reader in fashion at the London College of Fashion, University of the Arts, London, and codirector of the Research Centre for Fashion, the Body, and Material Cultures. She received her doctorate in sociology from Goldsmiths College, University of London, in 1997 and works in the areas of fashion, dress, the body, and gender. Her publications include *The Fashioned Body: Fashion, Dress and Modern Social Theory* (Polity Press, 2000), *Body Dressing* (co-edited with Elizabeth Wilson, Berg, 2001),

and *The Cultural Economy of Fashion* (Berg, forthcoming, 2009).

Mark Francis was the exhibition cocurator and author (with Dieter Koepplin) of *Andy Warhol Drawings: 1942–1987* (The Andy Warhol Museum, 1999) and the author (with Margery King) of *The Warhol Look: Glamour, Style, Fashion* (Bulfinch, 1997).

Marjorie Garber is William R. Kenan, Jr., Professor of English and American Literature and Language and chair of the Department of Visual and Environmental Studies and the director, Carpenter Center for the Visual Arts, Harvard University. Her publications include *Vested Interests: Cross-Dressing and Cultural Anxiety* (Routledge, 1992).

Beverly Gordon is professor in the Environment, Textiles and Design Department, School of Human Ecology, University of Wisconsin–Madison.

Elisabeth Hackspiel-Mikosch is an art historian focusing on the cultural history of textiles and clothing. She teaches textile engineering at the University of Applied Sciences Moenchengladbach in Germany.

Judith Halberstam is professor of English and gender studies at the University of Southern California. Halberstam works in the areas of popular, visual, and queer culture with an emphasis on subcultures. She is the author of *Skin Shows: Gothic Horror and the Technology of Monsters* (1995), *Female Masculinity* (1998), *In a Queer Time and Place: Transgender Bodies, Subcultural Lives* (2005), *The Drag King Book* (with Del LaGrace Volcano, 1999), and *Posthuman Bodies* (an anthology coedited with Ira Livingston, 1995).

John Harvey is lecturer in English and reader in literature and visual culture, Emmanuel College, Cambridge University. He is the author of *Men in Black* (Reaktion, 1995).

Dick Hebdige is professor of film and media studies and art studio and the director of the Interdisciplinary Humanities Center, University of California, Santa Barbara. His books include *Subculture: The Meaning of Style* (Methuen, 1979), *Cut 'n' Mix: Culture, Identity and Caribbean Music* (Methuen, 1987), and *Hiding in the Light: On Images and Things* (Routledge, Methuen, 1988).

Tony Jefferson is professor at the Research Institute for Law, Politics and Justice, Keele University. His publications include *Resistance through Rituals* (with Stuart Hall, Routledge, 1975, 2006) and *Policing the Crisis* (with Stuart Hall, 1978).

Vicki Karaminas is senior lecturer in fashion theory and design studies at the School of Design, University of Technology Sydney and the area chair for "Subcultural Style and Identity" for the Popular Culture Association of America. She is a critical theory and cultural studies scholar with a background in gender studies and visual culture. She is the editor of *Fashion in Fiction: Text and Clothing in Literature, Film, and Television* (with Peter McNeil and Catherine Cole, Berg, 2009).

Margery King is a curator who has organized numerous exhibitions, focusing on the work of Jean Cocteau, Ron Galella, Mariko Mori, and Yinka Shonibare, among others. She has written on artists from Andy Warhol to James VanDerZee. From 1991 through 2002, she was a curator at the Andy Warhol Museum, where she co-organized "The Warhol Look/Glamour Style Fashion." She curated Greer Lankton's 1996 exhibition at the Mattress Factory. She is the author (with Mark Francis) of *The Warhol Look: Glamour, Style, Fashion* (Bulfinch, 1997).

David Kuchta is adjunct professor of history at the University of New England, Biddeford. He is the author of *The Three-Piece Suit and Modern Masculinity* (University of California Press, 2002).

Clare Lomas is lecturer in cultural studies at the London College of Fashion, University of the Arts, London.

Annette Lynch, PhD, is a professor of textiles and apparel and women's studies at the University of Northern Iowa. Her research interests are focused in the area of cultural construction of gendered appearance through dress and performance. She has published two books with Berg Publishers: *Dress, Gender and Cultural Change* and *Changing Fashion: A Critical Introduction to Trend Analysis and Meaning* (with Mitchell D. Strauss).

Richard Martin was the curator of the Costume Institute of the Metropolitan Museum, a position he held for seven years until his death in 1999. He won numerous awards for his curatorial and written work and was especially noted, along with co-curator Harold Koda, for his innovative study of men's fashion. He held a doctorate in art history from Columbia University and was the author of numerous fashion publications, including *Fashion and Surrealism* (Rizzoli, 1987).

Noel McLaughlin is media lecturer and head of media theory and contextual studies for media production at Northumbria University, United Kingdom.

Peter McNeil is professor of design history at the University of Technology, Sydney, and foundation chair of fashion studies at Stockholm University. He is the editor of *Shoes: A History from Sandals to Sneakers* (with Giorgio Riello, Berg) and *Fashion: Critical and Primary Sources—Renaissance to the Present* (Berg, forthcoming).

Frank Mort is professor of cultural histories, Manchester University. He is the author of *Cultures of Consumption: Masculinities and Social Space in Late-Twentieth Century Britain* (Routledge, 1996, 2000).

William R. Scott is an assistant professor of history at the University of Delaware. He received his AB from Dartmouth College and his MA and PhD from the University of California, Berkeley. Scott's current research focuses on the rise of leisure wear and the transformation of men's fashions in the twentieth century.

Rob Shields is H.M. Tory Chair and professor of sociology in art/design, University of Alberta, Canada. His publications include *Lifestyle Shopping: The Subject of Consumption,* (editor, Routledge, 1993) and *Places on the Margin: Alternative Geographies of Modernity* (Routledge, 1991).

Mark Simpson is a British journalist, writer, and broadcaster specializing in pop culture, media, and masculinity. He is the author of *Saint Morrissey* (2004), *Sex Terror: Erotic Misadventures in Pop Culture* (2002), *The Queen Is Dead: A Story of Jarheads, Eggheads, Serial Killers and Bad Sex* (with Steven Zeeland, 2001), *Anti-Gay* (1996), *It's a Queer World: Deviant Adventures in Pop Culture* (1995), and *Male Impersonators* (1994).

Toby Slade completed his PhD at the University of Sydney in 2006, researching the modernity of Japanese clothing and the implications of this unique sartorial history for contemporary theories of fashion. In 2003 he won a two-year Japanese government scholarship to research clothing history in Japan at the University of Tsukuba. He is assistant professor at the University of Tokyo.

Laura Ugolini is reader in history and director of the Centre for the History of Retailing and Distribution, University of Wolverhampton. She is the editor (with John Benson) of *A Nation of Shopkeepers: Five Centuries of British Retailing* (IB Tauris, 2003), *Cultures of Selling: Perspectives on Consumption and Society since 1700* (Ashgate, 2006), and *Men and Menswear: Sartorial Consumption in Britain 1880–1939* (Ashgate, 2007).

Olga Vainshtein is senior researcher and professor at the Institute for Advanced Studies in the Humanities at the Russian State University for the Humanities. She is the author of *Dandy: Fashion, Literature, Life Style* (2006) and the editor of *Barbey D'Aurevilly: On Dandyism and George Brummell* (2000) and *Smells and Perfumes in the History of Culture* (Vol. 1–2, 2003). She is a member of the editorial boards of *Fashion Theory: The Journal of Dress, Body and Culture* and *Russian Fashion Theory.*

Michael Zakim lectures in the faculty of history, University of Tel Aviv. He is the author of *Ready-Made Democracy: A History of Men's Dress in the American Republic 1760–1860* (University of Chicago, 2003).

BIBLIOGRAPHY

A-1 Manufacturing Company. Advertisement. *California Men's Stylist* 4 (July 1945): 12.

Abelson, Elaine. *When Ladies Go A Thieving: Middle Class Shoplifters in the Victorian Department Store*. Oxford: Oxford University Press, 1989.

Abrams, M. *The Teenage Consumer*. London: London Press Exchange, 1959.

Adams, James Eli. *Dandies and Desert Saints: Styles of Victorian Masculinity*. New York: Cornell University Press, 1995.

Adburgham, Alison. *Shops and Shopping, 1800–1914: Where, and in What Manner, the Well-Dressed Englishwoman Bought Her Clothes*. London: George Allen and Unwin, 1964.

Adshead, S.A.M. *Material Culture in Europe and China, 1400–1800*. Basingstoke, UK: Macmillan, 1997.

Advertisement for *The Hit. Campaign,* September 6, 1985, 26–7.

Advertisement for *Mayfair* magazine. *Campaign,* February 15, 1985, 32.

Ainslie, James L. *The Doctrines of Ministerial Order in the Reformed Churches of the 16th and 17th Centuries*. Edinburgh, 1940.

Albion, Robert Greenhalgh, with Jennie Barnes Pope. *The Rise of New York Port, 1815–1860*. New York: Charles Scribner's Sons, 1939.

Alexander, David. *Retailing in England during the Industrial Revolution*. London: Athlone, 1970.

Alexander, Dick. "A Las Vegas Where There's No Better Fun." *San Francisco Examiner,* July 22, 1990.

Alexander, Hilary. "Fashion: Mr Jones Strikes Again." *Daily Telegraph,* May 10, 1999.

Alfred, Randy. "Will the Real Clone Please Stand Out?" *Advocate* 18 (March 1982).

Allen, Richard. *The Moving Pageant: A Literary Sourcebook on London Streetlife 1700–1914*. London: Routledge, 1998.

Allen, Robert J. *The Clubs of Augustan London*. Hamden, CT: Archon, 1967.

Altman, Dennis. *The Homosexualization of America: The Americanization of the Homosexual*. New York: St. Martin's, 1982.

Anderson, Fiona. "Fashioning the Gentleman: A Study of Henry Poole and Co., Savile Row Tailors, 1861–1900." *Fashion Theory* 4, no. 4 (November 2000): 405–26.

Anderson, Frances. "The Tale of the Flying Fish." *California Men's Stylist* 2 (January 1943): 48–51.

Anderson, Frank. "New Styles Are Set at Palm Springs." *California Men's Stylist* 1 (January 1942): 19.

Anderson, Perry. *Lineages of the Absolutist State*. London: Verso, 1974.

Andrassy, Hannah. "Smart but Casual: Masculinity and the Modernisation of Men's Fashion 1930–1950." Master's thesis, Victoria and Albert Museum/Royal College of Arts, 1995.

"Anheuser-Busch Publishes Brochure on Black Greeks." *Jet,* September 1985, 22.

Anonymous. *The Bottle and Friends [sic] Garland, containing Four Excellent New Songs … V. The Macaroni*. N.p., n.d. [c. 1765].

Anonymous. "Burtons' Future." *Men's Wear,* May 14, 1970, 8.

Anonymous. "Casual Wear." *Men's Wear,* April 12, 1958, 11.

Anonymous. "Casual Wear, Special 48 Page Feature." *Men's Wear,* April 19, 1958, xxiii.

Anonymous. "The Fifties: A Decade of Progress." *Men's Wear,* January 2, 1960, 15.

Anonymous. "The Tales: A Decade of Progress." *Men's Wear,* January 2, 1960, 15.

Anstey, Christopher. *An Election Ball.* 1776. Reprinted with introduction and notes by Gavin Turner. Bristol, UK: Broadcast Books, 1997.

Anstey, Christopher. *The New Bath Guide.* 1766. Reprinted with introduction and notes by Gavin Turner. Bristol, UK: Broadcast Books, 1994.

Appel, Timothy. "US Fraternities: Changing Image Brings on 'Rush.'" *Christian Science Monitor,* May 28, 1981, 13.

Appleby, J. O. *Economic Thought and Ideology in Seventeenth-Century England.* Princeton, NJ: Princeton University Press, 1978.

"Are Men Afraid of Being Too Beautiful? Slaves to Dress. Sex Differences in Modern Attire. 'Snobbery.' Women's Costumes Indicted by a Professor." *Herself in Australia's Affairs* 1, no. 12 (December 5, 1929): 10.

Ariès, Philippe, and Georges Duby, eds. *A History of Private Life.* Vols. 3–4. Cambridge, MA, and London: Belknap Press of Harvard University Press, 1990. Originally published in French, 1987.

Arthur, T. S. *The Seamstress: A Tale of the Times.* Philadelphia: R. G. Berford, 1843.

Arthur, T. S. "The Trials of a Needlewoman." *Godey's Lady's Book,* April 1854, 330.

Arthur Levy's Broadway Cash Tailoring Establishment. Advertisement. *New York Herald,* March 23, 1841.

Ash, Juliet. "The Tie: Presence and Absence." In *The Gendered Object,* ed. P. Kirkham. Manchester, UK: Manchester University Press.

Ashelford, Jane. *Dress in the Age of Elizabeth I.* London: Batsford, 1988.

The Athenian Oracle: Being an Entire Collection of the Valuable Questions and Answers in the Old Athenian Mercuries. London, 1703.

Ayling, Stanley. *Fox, The Life of Charles James Fox.* London: John Murray, 1991.

Bachelard, G. *Poetics of Space.* Boston: Beacon, 1961.

Badfads Museum. *Zoot Suit.* 2000. http://www.bad fads.com/pages/fashion/zootsuit.html (accessed March 12, 2003).

Bailey, P. "Ally Sloper's Half Holiday: Comic Art in the 1880s." *History Workshop Journal* 16 (1983): 4–31.

Bailey, Peter. "Champagne Charlie: Performance and Ideology in the Music Hall Swell Song." In *Music Hall: Performance and Style,* ed. J. S. Bratton. Milton Keynes, UK: Open University Press, 1986.

Bailey, R. "Men's Writes." *Media Week,* May 2, 1986, 14–17.

Bakhtin, M. "Author and Hero in Aesthetic Activity." In *Art and Answerability: Early Philosophical Essays by Mikhail Bakhtin,* trans. V. Liapunov and K. Brostrom. Austin: University of Texas Press, 1990.

Bakhtin, M. *The Dialogic Imagination.* Trans. C. Emerson and M. Holquist. Austin: University of Texas Press, 1981.

Bakhtin, M. *Problems of Dostoevsky's Poetics.* Trans. R. W. Rotsel. Ann Arbor, MI: Ardis, 1973.

Bakhtin, M. *Rabelais and His World.* Trans. Helene Iswolsky. Bloomington: Indiana University Press, 1984.

Baldwin, Billy, and Michael Gardine. *Billy Baldwin: An Autobiography.* Boston and Toronto: Little, Brown and Company, 1985.

Banks, Joseph. *Prosperity and Parenthood: A Study of Family Planning among the Victorian Middle Classes.* London: Routledge, 1954.

Barker-Benfield, G. J. *The Culture of Sensibility: Sex and Society in Eighteenth-Century Britain.* Chicago and London: University of Chicago Press, 1992.

Barnes, R. *Mods!* London: Eel Pie Publishing, 1979.

Barron, James. "Liberace, Flamboyant Pianist, Is Dead." *New York Times,* February 5, 1987.

Bartels, Robert. *The History of Marketing Thought.* 3rd ed. Columbus, OH: Publishing Horizons, 1988.

Barthes, R. *The Fashion System.* Trans. Matthew Ward and Richard Howard. New York: Hill and Wang, 1983. Reprint, Los Angeles: University of California Press, 1990.

Barthes, R. *Image, Music, Text.* Trans. S. Heath. London: Fontana, 1977.

Barthes, R. *The Language of Fashion.* Ed. Andy Stafford and Michael Carter. Trans. Andy Stafford. Oxford and New York: Berg, 2006.

Barthes, R. *Système de la mode.* Paris: Editions du Seuil, 1967.

Baudelaire, Charles. "Edgar Allan Poe." In *Charles Baudelaire, The Painter of Modern Life and Other Essays,* trans. Jonathan Mayne. New York: De Capo, 1986.

Baudelaire, Charles. *Les fleurs de mal,* presented by Jean-Paul Sartre. Paris: Flammarion, 1861.

Baudelaire, Charles. "The Painter of Modern Life." In *Baudelaire: Selected Writings on Art and Artists,* trans. P. E. Charvet. Cambridge: Cambridge University Press, 1972.

Bauman, Zygmund. *Hermeneutics and the Social Sciences.* London: Hutchinson, 1978.

Baumann, Richard. *Landknechte: Ihre Geschichte und Kultur vom späten Mittelalter bis zum Dreißigjährigen Krieg.* Munich, Germany: Beck, 1994.

Beagle, Peter. *American Denim: A New Folk Art.* Presented by Richard M. Owens and Tony Lane. New York: Harry N. Abrams, 1975.

"Beauty Pageant's 'Roger & Me' Lesson." Outtakes column, reprinted from the *Los Angeles Times. San Francisco Chronicle,* February 12, 1990.

Bechofer, Frank. *The Petit Bourgeoisie: Comparative Studies of the Uneasy Stratum.* London: Macmillan, 1981.

Becker, Bill. "California's Sartorial Outlook Is Making Inroads on 'Ivy' East." *New York Times,* February 9, 1964.

Beerbohm, Max. "Dandies and Dandies." In *The Incomparable Max Beerbohm.* London: Icon, 1964.

Benjamin, Walter. "The Work of Art in the Age of Mechanical Reproduction." In *Illuminations,* trans. Harry Zohn. New York: Schocken, 1969.

Bennetts, Leslie. "Ivy League Women Trace Social Barriers." *New York Times,* January 1984, national edition, 18.

Benson, John. *The Rise of Consumer Society in Britain 1880–1980.* London: Longman, 1994.

Benson, John, and Gareth Shaw, eds. *The Evolution of Retail Systems c. 1800–1914.* Leicester, UK: Leicester University Press, 1992.

Berendt, John. "Blue Jeans." *Esquire,* September 1986, 24–26.

Berger, J. *Ways of Seeing.* Harmondsworth, UK: Penguin, 1972.

Berger, P. "The Suit." In *Introducing Popular Culture,* ed. C. Mukerji and M. Schudson. Berkeley: University of California Press, 1990.

Berry, Christopher J. *The Idea of Luxury: A Conceptual and Historical Investigation.* Cambridge: Cambridge University Press, 1994.

Besant, Walter. *London North of the Thames.* London: Adam & Charles Black, 1911.

Besant, Walter. *The Survey of London: London City.* London: A. & C. Black, 1910.

Betjeman, J. *John Betjeman's Oxford.* 1938. Oxford: Oxford University Press, 1990.

Billig, M. *Banal Nationalism.* London: Sage, 1995.

Blachford, Gregg. "Male Dominance and the Gay World." In *The Making of the Modern Homosexual,* ed. Kenneth Plummer. Totowa, NJ: Barnes and Noble, 1981.

Blair, Claude. *European Armour: Circa 1066 to circa 1700.* London, 1958.

Blake, John. *The Money God: A Tale of the City.* London: Heinemann, 1904.

Blanc, Odile. "From Battlefield to Court: The Invention of Fashion in the Fourteenth Century." In *Encountering Medieval Textiles and Dress: Objects, Texts, Images,* ed. Désirée Koslin and Janet Snyder. New York: Palgrave Macmillan, 2002.

Blanchard, Tamsin. "The Fashion Victims of Football." *Independent,* May 16, 1998.

Blanchot, M. *De l'insolence considérée comme un des beaux-arts.* Paris: Gallimard, 1943.

Blaszczyk, Regina Lee. *American Consumer Society, 1865–2005.* Wheeling, IL: Harlan Davidson, 2008.

Blaszczyk, Regina Lee. *Imagining Consumers: Design and Innovation from Wedgwood to Corning.* Baltimore, MD: Johns Hopkins University Press, 2000.

Bleckwenn, Hans. *Altpreussische Offiziersporträts: Studien aus dem Nachlass.* Ed. Bernard Kroener and Joachim Niemeyer. Osnabrück, Germany: Biblio-Verlag, 2000.

Bockris, Victor. *The Life and Death of Andy Warhol.* New York: Bantam Books, 1989.

Bogatyrev, P. "Costume as Sign." In *Semiotics of Art,* ed. L. Matejka and I. R. Titunik. Cambridge, MA: MIT Press, 1976.

Bogatyrev, P. *The Function of Folk Costume in Moravian Slovakia.* Trans. R. G. Crum. The Hague, Netherlands: Mouton, 1971.

Bongco, M. *Reading Comics: Language, Culture and the Concept of the Superhero in Comic Books.* New York: Garland, 2000.

Boone, S. A. *Radiance from the Water: Ideals of Feminine Beauty in Mende Art.* New Haven, CT, and London: Yale University Press, 1986.

Bordo, S. *The Male Body: A New Look at Men in Public and in Private.* New York: Farrar, Straus and Giroux, 1999.

Borsodi, William. *Men's Wear Advertising.* New York: Advertisers' Cyclopedia, 1910.

Bostian, J. M. *Directions for Measuring and Drafting Garments.* Sunbury: J. M. Bostian, 1850.

Boston, L. *Men of Color: Fashion, History, Fundamentals*. New York: Artisan, 1998.

Botham, Noel, and Peter Donnelly. *Valentino: The Love God*. London: Everest, 1976.

Botsford, Jay Barrett. *English Society in the Eighteenth Century as Influenced from Oversea [sic]*. New York: Macmillan, 1924.

Botzas, S. "Biff! Bang! Pow! Captain America Enlists to Fight for Bush in Iraq." *Sunday Herald* (London), November 14, 2004.

Boucher, F. *20,000 Years of Fashion*. New York: Abrams, 1966.

Boucher, François. *A History of Costume in the West*. Trans. John Ross. 1966. New ed., London: Thames and Hudson, 1987.

Bourdieu, P. *La distinction: Critique sociale du jugement*. Paris: Minuit, 1979. Translation published under the title *Distinction: A Social Critique of the Judgement of Taste* (Cambridge, MA: Harvard University Press, 1984).

Bourdieu, P. *Homo Academicus*. Trans. P. Collier. Cambridge: Polity Press, in association with Basil Blackwell, 1988.

Bowen-Jones, C. "Adman Finds a New Woman." *The Times*, March 16, 1988, 26.

Bowlby, R. *Shopping with Freud*. London: Routledge, 1993.

Bradley, Dennis. *Vogue: A Catalogue for Pope and Bradley*. London, 1912.

Braggiotti, Mary. "California Clothes Bring Sunshine." *New York Post*, October 17, 1940.

Braithwaite, B. "The Eagle Has Landed." *Media Week*, December 8, 1989, 28–29.

Brändli, Sabina. *"Der herrlich biedere Mann": Vom Siegeszug des bürgerlichen Herrenanzugs im 19. Jahrhundert*. Zürich, Switzerland: Chronos, 1998.

Brändli, Sabina. "Von 'schneidigen Offizieren' und 'Militärcrinolinen': Aspekte symbolischer Männlichkeit am Beispiel preußischer und schweizerischer Uniformen des 19. Jahrhunderts." In *Militär und Gesellschaft im 19. und 20. Jahrhundert*, ed. Ute Frevert. Stuttgart: Klett-Cotta, 1997.

Breazeale, K. "In Spite of Women: *Esquire* Magazine and the Construction of the Male Consumer." *Signs* 20 (1994): 1–22. Reprinted in *The Gender and Consumer Culture Reader*, ed. Jennifer Scanlon. New York: New York University Press, 2000.

Bremmer, Jan, and Herman Roodenburg, eds. *A Cultural History of Gesture*. Ithaca, NY: Cornell University Press, 1991.

Breward, Christopher. *The Culture of Fashion: A New History of Fashionable Dress*. Manchester, UK, and New York: Manchester University Press, 1995.

Breward, Christopher. *Fashioning London: Clothing and the Modern Metropolis*. Oxford and New York: Berg, 2004.

Breward, Christopher. "Fashioning Masculinity: Men's Footwear and Modernity." In *Shoes: A History from Sandals to Sneakers*, ed. Giorgio Riello and Peter McNeil. Oxford and New York: Berg, 2006.

Breward, Christopher. *The Hidden Consumer: Masculinities, Fashion and City Life 1860–1914*. Manchester, UK, and New York: Manchester University Press, 1999.

Breward, Christopher. "Manliness and the Pleasures of Consumption: Masculinities, Fashion and London Life." PhD diss., Royal College of Art, London, 1998.

Brewer, J., R. Porter, S. Staves, and A. Bermingham, eds. *Consumption and the World of Goods*. London: Routledge, 1993.

Bristow, J. "Dowdies and Dandies—Oscar Wilde and the Refashioning of Society Comedy." *Modern Drama* 37, no. 1 (1994): 53–70.

Bristow, Joseph. "Being Gay: Politics, Identity, Pleasure." *New Formations* 9 (1989): 61–81.

Brod, Harry, ed. *The Making of Masculinities: The New Men's Studies*. Boston: Allen and Unwin, 1987.

Brod, Harry, and Michael Kaufman, eds. *Theorizing Masculinities*. Thousand Oaks, CA: Sage, 1994.

Brook, Timothy. *The Confusions of Pleasure: Commerce and Culture in Ming China*. Berkeley and Los Angeles: University of California Press, 1998.

Brooks, Andree. "Greek Row Glows Golden Again." *New York Times*, November 9, 1986, national edition.

Brooks, C. *The Jive Dictionary*. 2003a. http://www.cab calloway.ee/jive_dictionary.htm (accessed June 2, 2003).

Brooks, C. *Notes of Interest*. 2003b. http:/www.cab calloway.cc/notesofinterest.htm (accessed June 2, 2003).

Brooks, John. "Annals of Business: A Friendly Product." *New Yorker*, November 12, 1979, 58–80.

Brooks, Thomas. *London's Lamentations: Or, A Serious Discourse Concerning That Late Fiery Dispensation That Turned Our (Once Renowned) City into a Ruinous Heap.* London: John Hancock and Nathaniel Ponder, 1670.

Brooks Brothers Centenary, 1818–1918. New York: Brooks Brothers, 1918.

Brown, M. "A Teenage Trendsetter, Aged 36." *The Sunday Times* (London), May 8, 1983, 14.

Browne, Sir Thomas. *The Works of Sir Thomas Browne.* Ed. Charles Sayle. Edinburgh, 1912.

Browning, William C. "The Clothing and Furnishing Trade." In *One Hundred Years of American Commerce, 1795–1895,* ed. Chauncey M. Depew. New York: D. O. Haynes, 1895.

Bruzzi, S. "Mannish Girl: k. d. lang—from Cowpunk to Androgyny." In *Sexing the Groove: Popular Music and Gender,* ed. S. Whiteley. London: Routledge, 1997a.

Bruzzi, S. *Undressing Cinema: Clothing and Identity in the Movies.* London: Routledge, 1997b.

Bryce, Alexander. *Ideal Health or the Laws of Life and Health.* 1901. Reprint, Bristol and London, 1909.

Buck, Anne. *Dress in Eighteenth-Century England.* New York: Holmes and Meier, 1979.

Buckley, Peter. "To the Opera House: Culture and Society in New York City, 1820–1860." PhD diss., State University of New York at Stony Brook, 1984.

Buckley, S. "How to Talk to More Men." *Media Week,* February 12, 1988, 46.

Buffalo Bill's Wild West and Congress of Rough Riders of the World; Historical Sketches and Programme. Chicago: Cody and Salsbury, 1893.

Bukatman, S. "X-Bodies (the Torment of the Mutant Superhero)." In *Uncontrollable Bodies: Testimonies of Identity and Culture,* ed. R. Sappington and T. Stallings. Seattle, WA: Bay Press, 1994.

Bulwer-Lytton, Edward. *Pelham or the Adventures of a Gentleman.* Lincoln: University of Nebraska Press, 1972. New York: John Lovell, n.d.

Burke, Peter. *The Fortunes of the Courtier: The European Reception of Castiglione's Cortegiano.* Cambridge: Polity, 1995.

Burke, Peter. *Popular Culture in Early Modern Europe.* London: Temple Smith, 1978.

Burke, Thomas. *Nights in Town: A London Autobiography.* London: George Allen & Unwin, 1915.

Burke, Tom. "The New Homosexuality." *Esquire,* 1969, 72.

Burman, Barbara, and Melissa Leventon. "The Men's Dress Reform Party 1929–1937." *Costume* 21 (1987).

Burton, P. *Parallel Lives.* London: Gay Men's Press, 1985.

Butler, J. *Bodies That Matter.* London: Routledge, 1993.

Butler, J. *Gender Trouble: Feminism and the Subversion of Identity.* London and New York: Routledge, 1990.

Butler, J. "Preface to New Edition." In *Gender Trouble: Feminism and the Subversion of Identity.* London and New York: Routledge, 1999.

"'Buy New York Products' Drive Is Begun to Offset Diversion of the Apparel Trade." *New York Times,* April 6, 1939.

Bymers, Gwendolyn June. "A Study of Employment in Women's and Misses' Outerwear Manufacturing." PhD diss., University of California, Los Angeles, 1958.

Byngham, Dion. "Why Not Beauty for Men?" *New Health Journal* (1932): 21–22.

Byrde, Penelope. *The Male Image: Men's Fashion in Britain 1300–1970.* London: B. T. Batsford, 1979.

"California Fashion Scene, as Viewed by the Matilda Bergman Resident Buying Office of Los Angeles." Report, Special Collections Department, Gladys Marcus Library, Fashion Institute of Technology, New York, 1942.

"California Glamour Comes to Life at Roundup Show." *California Apparel News,* October 31, 1947.

"California 'Sells' for You." *California Men's Stylist* 3 (January 1944): 39.

California Shop Records, Archives Center, Smithsonian National Museum of American History, Washington, D.C.: box 1, series 3, acc. no. 572.

California Sportswear Company. Advertisement. *Men's Wear,* April 27, 1951, 91.

"California Styles." *Wall Street Journal,* August 27, 1945.

Campbell, C. "The Desire for the New—Its Nature and Location as Presented in Theories of Fashion and Modern Consumerism." In *Consuming Technologies: Media and Information in Domestic*

Spaces, ed. R. Silverstone and E. Hirsch. London: Routledge, 1992.

Campbell, C. "Understanding Traditional and Modern Patterns of Consumption in Eighteenth Century England: A Character Action Approach." In *Consumption and the World of Goods,* ed. J. Brewer and R. Porter. New York: Routledge, 1993.

Canady, Hortense. "Black Women Leaders: The Case of Delta Sigma Theta." *Urban League Review,* Summer 1985, 92–95.

"Canady's National Challenge: Sorority Plans to Aid Single Black Mothers." *Washington Post,* January 28, 1984.

Carey, John. *The Intellectuals and the Masses.* London: Faber, 1992.

Carlin, John. "The Iconography of Elvis," Idiolects, 14 (1984).

Carlyle, Thomas. *Critical and Miscellaneous Essays.* London, 1872. Reprint, London: Kessinger, 2003.

Carlyle, Thomas. *Past and Present.* London: Chapman & Hall, 1906.

Carlyle, Thomas. *Sartor Resartus.* Ed. K. McSweeney and Peter Sabor. Oxford: Oxford University Press, 1987.

Carlyle, Thomas. *Sartor Resartus. The Life and Opinions of Herr Teufelsdröckh in Three Books.* London: T. Nelson and Sons, n.d.

Carlyle, Thomas. "Signs of the Times." 1829. In *Carlyle, Critical and Miscellaneous Essays.* Vol. 1. Boston and New York: Colonial Press, n.d.

Carnes, Valerie. "Icons of Popular Fashion." In *Icons of America,* ed. Ray N. Browne and Marshall Fishwick. Bowling Green, OH: Bowling Green State University Popular Press, 1978.

Carpenter, Edward. "Simplification of Life." In *England's Ideal.* 1886. London: Allen & Unwin, 1919.

Carpenter, John T. "Twisted Poses: The Kabuku Aesthetic in Early Edo Genre Painting." In *Kazari: Decoration and Display in Japan 15th–19th Centuries,* ed. Nicole Coolidge Rousmaniere. London: The British Museum Press/The Japan Society, 2002.

Carter, M. "Superman's Costume." *Form/Work: An Interdisciplinary Journal of Design and the Built Environment, The Fashion Issue* 4 (March 2000): 26–41.

Castiglione, Baldassare. *The Book of the Courtier.* Trans. Sir Thomas Hoby. 1561. Ed. J. H. Whitfield. London, 1974.

Castiglione, Baldassare. *Etiquette for Renaissance Gentlemen.* Trans. George Bull. 1967. Abridged ed., London: Penguin, 1995.

Catalogue of the Collection of English, Scottish and Irish Proclamations in the University Library. London: University of London Press.

Catalogue of the Yasukuni Jinga Yushukan. Tokyo, 2003.

Cats' Corner. *The Zoot Suit.* 1997. http://www.catscorner.com/zoot.htm (accessed May 5, 2003).

Chabot, Gabriel Henry. *The Tailors' Compasses; or, An Abridged and Accurate Method of Measurement.* Baltimore, MD: J. Matchett, 1829.

Chamberlayne, Edward. *Anglia Notitia: Or the Present State of England.* 3rd ed., London: J. Playford, 1669; 6th ed., London: J. Playford, 1672; 8th ed., London: J. Playford, 1674.

Chambers, R., ed. *The Book of Days, A Miscellany of Popular Antiquities in Connection with the Calendar, Including Anecdote, Biography, and History, Curiosities of Literature and Oddities of Human Life and Character.* Vol. 2, July 7, 1864.

Chancellor, E. Beresford. *The XVIIIth Century in London: An Account of Its Social Life and Arts.* London: B. T. Batsford, n.d. [1920].

"The Changing Image of College Sororities." *New York Times,* January 23, 1984, national edition.

Chapman, R. "The Great Pretender: Variations on the New Man Theme." In *Male Order: Unwrapping Masculinity,* ed. R. Chapman and J. Rutherford. London: Lawrence and Wishart, 1988.

Chapman, Rowena, and Jonathon Rutherford, eds. *Male Order: Unwrapping Masculinity.* London: Lawrence and Wishart, 1988.

Chappel, Will. "There'll Come a Day." *California Men's Stylist* 3 (October 1944): 85.

Character of a Pilfering Tailor, or a True Anatomy of Monsieur Stitch, in All His Tricks and Qualities. London,1675.

Charles II. "His Majesty's most gracious Speech, together with the Lord Chancellor's, to the Two Houses of Parliament, at their Prorogation, on Monday the 19th of May, 1662." In *A Collection of Scarce and Valuable Tracts* (Somers Tracts), ed. Walter Scott. London: T. Cadell and W. Davies, 1812.

Chauncey, G. *Gay New York: Gender, Urban Culture and the Making of the Gay Male World 1890–1940.* London: Flamingo, 1994.

Chaussinand-Nogaret, Guy. *The French Nobility in the Eighteenth Century, from Feudalism to Enlightenment.* Trans. William Doyle. Cambridge: Cambridge University Press, 1985.

Chenoune, Farid. *A History of Men's Fashion.* Trans. from the French by Deke Dusinbere. Paris: Flammarion, 1993.

The Cherwell, 1930–1939.

Chrisman, Kimberly. "*L'émigration à la mode:* Clothing Worn and Produced by the French Émigré Community in England from the Revolution to the Restoration." Master's thesis, Courtauld Institute of Art, 1997.

Church Gibson, P. "Film Costume." In *The Oxford Guide to Film Studies,* ed. J. Hill and P. Church Gibson. Oxford: Oxford University Press, 1998.

Cicolini, Alice. *The New English Dandy.* London: Thames and Hudson, 2005.

The City of London Directory for 1900. London: W. H. & L. Collingridge, 1900.

Clarke, Benjamin. *Glimpses of Ancient Hackney & Stoke Newington.* London: London Borough of Hackney, 1986.

Cleaveland, A. M. *No Life for a Lady.* Boston: Houghton Mifflin, 1941.

Clemente, Deirdre. "Making the Princeton Man: Collegiate Clothing and Campus Culture, 1900–1920." In *The Places and Spaces of Fashion, 1800–2007,* ed. John Potvin. New York and Abingdon: Routledge, forthcoming.

"The Clothing Trade." *Hunt's Merchant's Magazine,* March 1864, 233.

"CMA Convention." *Men's Wear,* March 1950, 89–93.

Cohan, Steven. "So Functional for Its Purposes: Rock Hudson's Bachelor Apartment in *Pillow Talk.*" In *Stud: Architectures of Masculinity,* ed. Joel Sanders. Princeton, NJ: Princeton University Press, 1996.

Cohen, P. "Subcultural Conflict and Working Class Community." Working Papers in Cultural Studies 2. Birmingham, UK: University of Birmingham, CCCS, 1972.

Cohn, N. *Today There Are No Gentlemen: The Changes in Englishmen's Clothes since the War.* London: Weidenfeld and Nicolson, 1971.

Cole, D. H., and M. Cole. *Off with Her Head!* London: Collins, 1938.

Cole, Shaun. *'Don We Now Our Gay Apparel': Gay Men's Dress in the Twentieth Century.* Oxford and New York: Berg, 2000.

Coleridge, S. T. *The Portable Coleridge.* Ed. I. A. Richards. New York: Viking, 1950.

Collier, R. "'Nutty Professors', 'Men in Suits' and 'New Entrepreneurs': Corporeality, Subjectivity and Change in the Law School and Legal Practice." *Social and Legal Studies* 7, no. 1 (1998): 27–53.

Collins, Glenn. "Columbia Fraternities Revive a Rite of Spring." *New York Times,* April 10, 1981.

Collins, James H. "On the Map as a Garment Town." *Southern California Business* 10 (March 1931): 13.

Comer, James P. *Beyond Black and White.* New York: Quadrangle Books, 1972.

Commons, John R., ed. *A Documentary History of American Industrial Society.* Vol. 1–10. Cleveland, OH: Arthur H. Clark, 1910.

Conant, Jennet. "Sexy Does It." *Newsweek,* September 15, 1986, 64.

Connell, R. *Gender and Power: Society, the Person and Sexual Politics.* Cambridge: Polity, 1987.

Connell, Robert W. *Masculinities.* Cambridge: Polity; St. Leonards, Australia: Allen and Unwin, 1995.

Conspicuous Waist: Waistcoats and Waistcoat Designs 1700–1952. Edited by Everett P. Lesley Jr. and William Osmun. New York: Cooper Union Museum for the Arts of Decoration, 1952. An exhibition catalog.

Constantino, M. *Men's Fashion in the Twentieth Century: From Frock Coats to Intelligent Fibres.* London: B. T. Batsford, 1997.

Cook, D. "From Pillar to 'Post.'" Master's thesis, Royal College of Art, London, 1993.

Cook, Daniel Thomas. *The Commodification of Childhood: The Children's Clothing Industry and the Rise of the Child Consumer.* Durham, NC: Duke University Press, 2004.

Cooke, B. G. "Non-Verbal Communication among Afro-Americans: An Initial Classification." In *Rappin and Stylin Out: Communication in Urban Black America,* ed. T. Kochman. Urbana, Chicago, and London: University of Illinois Press, 1972.

Cosgrove, S. "The Zoot Suit and Style Warfare." *History Workshop Journal* 18 (Autumn 1984): 77–91.

Costumes de la Cour impériale de France. Neueste Hof- und Staatstrachten in Frankreich, vorgeschrieben vom Kaiser Napoleon I. Leipzig, Germany: Industrie Comptoir, ca. 1810.

Couts, Joseph. *A Practical Guide for the Tailor's Cutting-Room.* London: Blackie and Son, 1848.

Craig, Steve, ed. *Men, Masculinity and the Media.* Newbury Park, CA: Sage, 1992.

Craik, J. *The Face of Fashion: Cultural Studies in Fashion.* London and New York: Routledge, 1994.

Crary, J. *Techniques of the Observer: On Vision and Modernity in the Nineteenth Century.* Cambridge, MA, and London: MIT Press, 1996.

Cronin, A. *Comments in the Space and Consumption Seminar, Culture and Communication Programme.* Lancaster University, 1996.

Cross, F. L. *The Oxford Dictionary of the Christian Church.* Oxford, 1958.

Crossick, Geoffrey, and Heinz-Gerhard Haupt. *The Petit Bourgeoisie in Europe 1780–1914.* London: Routledge, 1995.

Csikszentmihalyi, Mihaly, and Eugene Rochberg-Halton. *The Meaning of Things: Domestic Symbols and the Self.* Cambridge: Cambridge University Press, 1981.

Cundall, James. *London: A Guide for the Visitor, Sportsman and Naturalist.* London: Greening & Co., 1902.

d'Allemagne, Henry René. *Les Accessoires du Costume et du Mobilier, depuis le treizieme jusqu'au milieu du dix-neuvième siècle.* 3 vols. Paris: Schemit, 1928.

Daniels, H. D. "Los Angeles Zoot Suit Race Riot, the Pachuco and Black Music Culture." *Journal of Negro History* 82, no. 2 (1997): 201–20.

d'Arcy, S. "Next for Men?" *Media Week,* August 16, 1985, 10.

[Darrell, William.] *A Gentleman Instructed in the Conduct of a Virtuous and Happy Life: Written for the Instruction of a Young Nobleman.* London: E. Evets, 1704.

Dataller, R. *A Pitman Looks at Oxford.* London: Dent, 1933.

David, Hugh. *On Queer Street: A Social History of British Homosexuality 1895–1995.* London: Harper Collins, 1997.

"David and Victoria: Their Complete Story." *OK!: The Premium Millennium Edition.* 1999.

"David and Victoria Beckham." *OK!* (March 21, 2000): 4–11.

"David and Victoria's Style Sensation." *OK!* (March 31, 2000).

Davidson, Alexander. *Blazers, Badges and Boaters: A Pictorial History of School Uniforms.* Horndean, Hants: Scope Books, 1990.

Davies, A. *Leisure, Gender and Poverty: Working-Class Culture in Salford and Manchester, 1900–1939.* Buckingham, UK: Open University Press, 1992.

Davies, Pete. *All Played Out: The Full Story of Italia 90.* London: Heinemann, 1990.

Davis, C. "Brasserie Man—Open All Hours." *The Evening Standard,* November 24, 1987, 33.

Davis, Clark. *Company Men: White-Collar Life and Corporate Cultures in Los Angeles, 1892–1941.* Baltimore, MD: Johns Hopkins University Press, 2000.

Davis, Dorothy. *A History of Shopping.* London: Routledge & Kegan Paul, 1966.

Davis, F. *Fashion, Culture, and Identity.* Chicago: University of Chicago Press, 1992.

Davis-Meyers, Mary L. "The Development of American Menswear Pattern Technology, 1822 to 1860." *Clothing and Textiles Research Journal* 10, no. 3 (Spring 1992): 12–20.

de Beer, Esmond S. "King Charles II's Own Fashion: An Episode in Anglo-French Relations 1666–1670." *Journal of the Warburg and Courtauld Institutes* 2 (1938–1939): 105–15.

de Brunel, Antoine. "Voyage d'Espagne." *Revue Hispanique* 30 (1914): 119–375.

DeCerteau, Michel. *The Practice of Everyday Life.* Berkeley: University of California Press, 1984.

de Grazia, V. "Introduction." In *The Sex of Things: Gender and Consumption in Historical Perspective,* ed. V. de Grazia and E. Furlough. Berkeley, Los Angeles, and London: University of California Press, 1996.

Deleuze, G., and F. Guattari. *Thousand Plateaux.* Paris: Minuit, 1976.

Deloria, Philip. *Playing Indian.* New Haven, CT: Yale University Press, 1998.

de Marly, Diana. *Fashion for Men: An Illustrated History.* London: B. T. Batsford, 1985.

de Marly, Diana. "King Charles II's Own Fashion: The Theatrical Origins of the English Vest." *Journal of the Warburg and Courtauld Institutes* 37 (1974): 378–81.

"Denim Rides Again." *Life,* September 1986, 76–78.

"Denims: Here's How to Buy the Best and Fade Them Fast." *Mademoiselle,* August 1981, 258.

Dennis, John. *An Essay upon Publick Spirit; Being A Satyr in Prose upon the Manners and Luxury of the Times, The Chief Source of our Present Parties and Divisions.* London: Bernard Lintott, 1711.

Denski, Stan, and David Sholle. "Metal Men and Glamour Boys." In *Men, Masculinity and Media,* ed. Steven Craig. Newbury Park, CA: Sage, 1992.

Deriège, F. *Physiologie du Lion.* Paris: Delahaye, 1841.

de Rocheford, Jorevin. "Description of England and Ireland, In the Seventeenth Century: By Jorevin." In *The Antiquarian Repertory: A Miscellaneous Assemblage of Topography, History, Biography, Customs, and Manners,* ed. Francis Grose. Vol. 4. London: Edward Jeffery, 1809.

Derry, John W. *Charles James Fox.* London: B. T. Batsford, 1972.

"Designing the Blues." *New York,* November 17, 1986, 78–79.

Diaman, Tony. "The Search of the Total Man." *Come Out* (1970).

Dibble, Jerry A. *The Drunken Pythia's Song: Thomas Carlyle's Sartor Resartus and the Style Problem in German Idealist Philosophy.* The Hague, Netherlands: Nijhoff, 1978.

"Dignitaries Welcome Visitors." *California Apparel News,* October 29, 1948.

Dines, Gail. "'I Buy It for the Articles': *Playboy* Magazine and the Sexualization of Consumption." In *Gender, Race and Class in Media: A Text-Reader,* ed. Gail Dines and Jean M. Humez. Thousand Oaks, CA, London, and New Delhi: Sage, 1995.

Dinges, Martin. "Soldatenkörper in der Frühen Neuzeit: Erfahrungen mit einem unzureichend geschützten, formierten und verletzten Körper in Selbstzeugnissen." In *Körper-Geschichten,* ed. Richard van Dülmen. Frankfurt/M.: Fischer-Taschenbuch-Verlag, 1996.

Dobbs, S. P. *The Clothing Workers of Great Britain.* London: Routledge, 1928.

Doggett's New York Business Directory for 1841–42. New York: John Doggett, 1841–1842.

Doggett's New York Business Directory for 1844–45. New York: John Doggett, 1844–1845.

Doherty, B. "Fashionable Ladies, Dada Dandies + Clothes and Avant-Garde Art." *Art Journal* 54, no. 1 (1995): 46–50.

"Do It Up Denim!" *Mademoiselle,* February 1978, 140–44.

Donald, Diana. *The Age of Caricature, Satirical Prints in the Reign of George III.* New Haven, CT, and London: Yale University Press, 1996.

Dougill, J. E. *Oxford in English Literature: The Making and Undoing of "The English Athens."* Ann Arbor: University of Michigan Press, 1998.

Downes, D. *The Delinquent Solution.* London: Routledge and Kegan Paul, 1966.

Drinkwater, John. *Mr. Charles, King of England.* London: Hudder and Stoughton, 1926.

Driscoll, M. "Non-Drip Gloss for Men." *Sunday Times,* April 9, 1995.

Driver, Felix, and David Gilbert. "Heart of Empire? Landscape, Space and Performance in Imperial London." *Society and Space* 16, no. 1 (1998).

Duberman, M., M. Vicinus, and G. Chauncey. *Hidden from History: Reclaiming the Gay and Lesbian Past.* London: Penguin, 1989.

Duke, Alastair, Gillian Lewis, and Andrew Pettegree, eds. *Calvinism in Europe, 1540–1610.* London, 1992.

Dunn, David. "What Does It Take to Turn You On?: Suede, Gender and Performativity." Paper presented at the School of Art, the University of Northumbria, May 1998.

Durflinger, S. M. *Disturbances of June 1944: Language Conflict a Problem of Civil-Military Relations or Youthful Over-Exuberance.* 1998. http://www.civilization.ca/cmc/index_e.aspx?DetailId=19972.

Dyer, Richard. *Stars.* London: BFI, 1979.

Dyer, Richard. *White.* London: Routledge, 1997.

Easthope, A. *What a Man's Gotta Do: The Masculine Myth in Popular Culture.* London and New York: Routledge, 1992.

Easton Ellis, B. *Glamorama.* New York: Pimlico, 1998.

Eaton Company, Ltd., Toronto. *The 1901 Edition of the T. Eaton Co., Ltd., Catalogues for Spring and Summer, Fall and Winter.* Toronto: Musson, 1970.

Echard, Laurence. *The History of England.* London: Jacob Tonson, 1707–1708.

Eco, Umberto, and Thomas A. Sebeok, eds. *C. Ginzburg, Morelli, Freud, and Sherlock Holmes: Clues and Scientific Method: The Sign of Three: Dupin, Holmes, Peirce.* Bloomington: Indiana University Press, 1984.

Edgerton, John. "Elvis Lives!" *The Progressive* 43, no. 3 (March 1979): 23.

Edney, James M., of New York, N.Y., letter book to Francis H. Cooke, of Augusta, Georgia, 1835–37, letter of February 13, 1836. Special Collections, Rutgers University, New Brunswick, New Jersey.

Edwards, T. *Men in the Mirror: Men's Fashion, Masculinity and Consumer Society.* London: Cassell, 1997.

Edwards, Tim. *Cultures of Masculinity.* London: Routledge, 2006.

Egan, Pierce. *Grose's Classical Dictionary of the Vulgar Tongue, Revised and Corrected, with the Addition of Numerous Slang Phrases, Collected from Tried Authorities.* 1785. Revised ed., London: for the Editor, 1823.

Egan, Pierce. *Life in London.* London: Sherwood, Neely & Jones, 1821.

Ehrenreich, Barbara. "Playboy Joins the Battle of the Sexes." In *The Hearts of Men: American Dreams and the Flight from Commitment.* New York: Anchor, Doubleday, 1983.

Eig, J. "Zoot Suit Fox Dead at Age 86." *Drum Beat* 63, no. 11 (1996): 16.

Elias, Stephen N. *Alexander T. Stewart: The Forgotten Merchant Prince.* Westport, CT: Praeger, 1992.

Eliot, T. S. "Shakespeare and the Stoicism of Seneca." In *Selected Essays,* 3rd ed. London, 1951.

Ellison, R. *The Invisible Man.* London: London Press, 1965.

Elms, Robert. "Saturday Best." *Arena,* June 1996, 142–44.

Elton, Lord. *Among Others.* London: Collins, 1938.

"Elvis Presley Imitations in Spirit and Flesh." *Rolling Stone,* March 23, 1978.

Engels, Friedrich. *The Condition of the Working Class in England in 1844.* London, 1892.

Entwistle, J. "The Aesthetic Economy: The Production of Value in the Field of Fashion Modeling." *Journal of Consumer Culture* 2 (2002): 317–39.

Entwistle, J. "Fashion and the Fleshy Body: Dress as Situated Practice." *Fashion Theory: Dress, Body and Culture* 3, no. 4 (2000a): 323–48.

Entwistle, J. *The Fashioned Body: Fashion, Dress and Modern Social Theory.* Cambridge and Malden, MA: Polity, 2000b.

Entwistle, J. "Fashioning the Career Woman: Power Dressing as a Strategy of Consumption." In *All the World and Her Husband: Women and Consumption in the Twentieth Century,* ed. M. Talbot and M. Andrews. London: Cassell, 2000c.

Entwistle, J. "Power Dressing and the Fashioning of the Career Woman." In *Buy This Book: Studies in Advertising and Consumption,* ed. M. Nava, I. MacRury, A. Blake, and B. Richards. London: Routledge, 1997.

Evelyn, John. *The Diary of John Evelyn.* Ed. Guy de la Bedoyere. London: Boydell Press, 2004.

Evelyn, John. *Tyrannus or the Mode: In a Discourse of Sumptuary Lawes.* London: G. Bedel and T. Collins, 1661.

Evelyn, John. *Tyrannus or the Mode,* ed. J. L. Nevinson. Oxford: Luttrell Society Reprints, 1951.

Ewen, Stuart. *Captains of Consciousness: Advertising and the Social Roots of the Consumer Culture.* New York: McGraw-Hill, 1976.

The Exclusives. London: Henry Colburn and Richard Bentley, 1830.

Exell, A. "Morris Motors in the 1930s." *History Workshop Journal* 6 (1978): 52–78.

"Extreme Styles Shown at Men's Wear Exhibit." *Rochester Democrat and Chronicle,* January 9, 1950.

"The Face." *The Face* 61 (May 1985): 110–12.

"Fact Sheet: Men's and Boys' Apparel Guilds in California." Los Angeles: Men's and Boys' Apparel Guilds in California, 1956.

Fairchild, Robert. "For the Modern Man." *Los Angeles Times,* July 20, 1935.

Farren, M. *The Black Leather Jacket.* New York: Abbeville Press, 1985.

"Fashion Is a Fairy." *Esquire,* April 1938, 35–36.

"Fashion Pioneer's Creditors Meet: £25,000 Liabilities." *Men's Wear,* February 6, 1969, 7–8.

Fasnacht, R. *A History of the City of Oxford.* Oxford: Basil Blackwell, 1954.

Fass, Paula S. *The Damned and the Beautiful: American Youth in the 1920s.* Oxford and New York: Oxford University Press, 1977.

Fawcett, Trevor. "Eighteenth-Century Shops and the Luxury Trade." *Bath History* 2 (1990): 49–75.

Featherstone, Mike. *Consumer Culture and Postmodernism.* London: Sage, 1991.

Feher, Michel, with Ramona Naddaff and Nadia Tazi, eds. *Fragments for a History of the Human Body.* Part 2. New York: Zone, 1989.

Fehr, Barbara. *Yankee Denim Dandies.* Blue Earth, MN: Piper Press, 1974.

Feldman, Egal. *Fit for Men.* Washington, DC: Public Affairs Press, 1961.

Feldman, Egal. "New York's Men's Clothing Trade, 1800 to 1861." PhD diss., University of Pennsylvania, 1959.

Fenin, G. N., and W. K. Everson. *The Western from Silents to Cinerama.* New York: Orion, 1962.

"50 Most Stylish Sportsmen of This Century." *Homme Plus* (Spring/Summer 1996): 89–99.

Fillin-Yeh, S. "Dandies, Marginality and Modernism, Georgia O'Keefe, Marcel Duchamp, and the Other Cross-Dressers." *Oxford Art Journal* 18, no. 2 (1995): 33–44.

Fillin-Yeh, S., ed. *Dandies: Fashion and Finesse in Art and Culture.* New York: New York University Press, 2001.

Finestone, Harold. "Cats, Kicks and Colour." In *The Other Side: Perspectives on Deviance,* ed. H. S Becker. New York: Free Press, 1964.

Finkelstein, J. *The Fashioned Self.* Cambridge: Polity, 1991.

Finlayson, Iain. *Denim.* Norwich, UK: Parke Sutton, 1990.

Fischer, D. H. *Albion's Seed.* New York, 1969.

Fischer, Hal. *Gay Semiotics.* San Francisco: NFS, 1977.

Fisher, Will. "The Renaissance Beard: Masculinity in Early Modern England." *Renaissance Quarterly* 54, no. 1 (Spring 2001): 155–87.

Fiske, J. "British Cultural Studies." In *Channels of Discourse, Reassembled,* ed. R. C. Allen. London and New York: Routledge, 1992.

Fitzmaurice. Advertisement. *New York Herald,* August 21, 1841.

Flexner, S. *Hear America Singing.* New York: Van Nostrand, Reinhold, 1976.

Flintrop, Kerstin. "Die Disziplinierung des männlichen Körpers—Uniformen im historischen Vergleich von Schnittführung und Verarbeitung." In *Nach Rang und Stand: Deutsche Ziviluniformen im 19. Jahrhundert* (Deutsches Textilmuseum Krefeld, March 24–June 23, 2002, curated by Elisabeth Hackspiel-Mikosch). Krefeld: Deutsches Textilmuseum Krefeld, 2002.

Flügel, J. C. *Men and Their Motives: Psycho-Analytical Studies, with Two Essays by Ingeborg Flügel.* London: Kegan Paul, Trench, Trubner & Co., 1934.

Flügel, J. C. *The Psychology of Clothes.* London: Hogarth, 1930; New York: International Universities Press, 1969.

"For a Mere $1,250, Sculptor Bob Edlund Will See to It That Your Jeans Never Wear Out." *People,* November 11, 1985, 79.

Ford, Richard. "Rules of the House." *Esquire,* June 1986, 231.

"Formation of Fraternities Is on the Increase at Yale." *New York Times,* May 12, 1985, national edition.

Fortrey, Samuel. *Englands Interest and Improvement. Consisting in the Increase of the Store, and Trade of this Kingdom.* London: Nathanael Brook, 1673.

Forty, Adrian. *Objects of Desire: Design and Society 1750–1980.* London: Thames & Hudson, 1986.

Foulkes, Nicholas. "Fit for a King." *Country Life,* October 5, 1995, 40–43.

Fowler, D. "Teenage Consumers? Young Wage-Earners and Leisure in Manchester, 1919–1939." In *Workers' Worlds: Cultures and Communities in Manchester and Salford, 1880–1939,* ed. A. Davies and S. Fielding. Manchester, UK: Manchester University Press, 1992.

Fox, George P. *Fashion: The Power That Influences the World.* 3rd ed. New York: Sheldon & Co., 1872.

Frank, Thomas. *The Conquest of Cool: Business Culture, Counterculture, and the Rise of Hip Consumerism.* Chicago: University of Chicago Press, 1997.

Frantz, J. B., and J. E. Choate Jr. *The American Cowboy: The Myth and the Reality.* Norman: University of Oklahoma, 1962.

"Fraternities and Sororities: A Dramatic Comeback on Campus." *Ebony,* December 1983, 93f.

Freedley, Edwin T. *Philadelphia and Its Manufactures.* Philadelphia: Edward Young, 1858.

Freedman, H. "Hello Girls." *Guardian,* March 5, 2002.

Freud, Sigmund, from "The 'Uncanny'" [Das Unheimliche] (1919). From Standard Edition, Vol. XVII, trans. James Strachey. London: Hogarth Press, 1955, pp. 217–256.

Frevert, Ute. "Männer in Uniform: Habitus und Signalzeichen im 19. und 20. Jahrhundert." In *Männlichkeit als Maskerade,* ed. Claudia Benthien. Cologne, Vienna, and Weimar: Böhlau, 2003.

Frevert, Ute, ed. *Militär und Gesellschaft im 19. und 20. Jahrhundert.* Stuttgart: Klett-Cotta, 1997.

Frevert, Ute. "Soldaten und Staatsbürger—Überlegungen zur historischen Konstruktion von Männlichkeit." In *Männergeschichte—Geschlechtergeschichte: Männlichkeit im Wandel der Moderne,* ed. Thomas Kühne. Frankfurt, 1996.

Frith, S. "Afterthoughts." In *On Record: Rock, Pop and the Written Word,* ed. S. Frith and A. Goodwin. London: Routledge, 1990.

Frith, S. "Confessions of a Rock Critic." In *Music for Pleasure: Essays in the Sociology of Pop.* New York: Routledge, 1988.

Frith, S. *Performing Rites: On the Value of Popular Music.* Oxford: Oxford University Press, 1996.

Frith, S. "The Suburban Sensibility in British Rock and Pop." In *Visions of Suburbia,* ed. Roger Silverstone. London and New York: Routledge, 1997.

Frith, S., and A. Goodwin, eds. *On Record: Rock, Pop and the Written Word.* London: Routledge, 1990.

Frith, S., and H. Home. *Art into Pop*. London: Methuen, 1987.

Frith, S., and A. McRobbie. "Rock and Sexuality." In *On Record: Rock, Pop and the Written Word*, ed. S. Frith and A. Goodwin. London: Routledge, 1990.

Fujitani, T. *Splendid Monarchy: Power and Pageantry in Modern Japan*. Berkeley: University of California Press, 1996.

Fulton, Tamara. "*Arena*'s Essential Guide to Style and Fashion." *Arena*, June 1996.

Fyvel, T. R. *The Insecure Offenders*. London: Chatto and Windus, 1963.

Galton, F. W. *Select Documents Illustrating the History of Trade Unionism*. Vol. 1, *The Tailoring Trade*. London: Longmans, Green, 1896.

Game, A. *Comments in the Space and Consumption Seminar, Culture and Communication Programme*. Lancaster University, 1996.

Garber, M. *Vested Interests: Cross Dressing and Cultural Anxiety*. New York: Routledge, 1992.

Garelick, Rhonda K. *Rising Star: Dandyism, Gender, and Performance in the Fin de Siècle*. Princeton, NJ: Princeton University Press, 1998.

Garland, Rodney. *The Heart of Exile*. Brighton, UK: Millivres, 1995.

Gatens, M. *Imaginary Bodies: Ethics, Power and Corporealities*. London: Routledge, 1996.

Gates, H. L. Jr. *Thirteen Ways of Looking at a Black Man*. New York: Random House, 1997.

"Gaudy Shirts, Slacks Shown for Men, Boys." *Detroit Times*, January 10, 1950.

Gaugele, Elke. "Uni-Formen des Begehrens, Fetischismus und die textile Konstruktion moderner Genderidentitäten." In *Civilian Uniforms as Symbolic Communication*, ed. Elisabeth Hackspiel-Mikosch and Stefan Haas. Stuttgart: Steiner-Verlag, 2006.

Geertz, Clifford. *The Interpretations of Culture*. New York: Basic Books, 1973.

Geist, William E. "About New York: Liberace Is Here, with His Glitter Undimmed." *New York Times*, April 3, 1985.

Gelder, K. *The Subcultural Studies Reader*. 2nd ed. London and New York: Routledge, 2005.

Gelder, Ken, and Sarah Thorton, eds. *The Subcultures Reader*. London and New York: Routledge, 1997.

The Gem, or Fashionable Business Directory. New York, 1844.

Genet, J. *The Blacks*. London: Faber, 1966.

The Gentlemen's Library, Containing Rules for Conduct in All Parts of Life, Written by a Gentleman. London: W. Mears and J. Brown, 1715.

George, Mary Dorothy. *Catalogue of Political and Personal Satires Preserved in the Department of Prints and Drawings in the British Museum*. Vol. V, *1771–1783*. London: Trustees of the British Museum, 1935.

George, Mary Dorothy. *England in Johnson's Day*. London: Methuen, 1928.

Gifford, George. *Before the Honorable Philip F. Thomas . . . in the Matter of the Application of Elias Howe, Jr., for an Extension of His Patent for Sewing Machines*. New York: W. W. Rose, 1860.

Gilbert, James. *Men in the Middle: Searching for Masculinity in the 1950s*. Chicago: University of Chicago Press, 2005.

Gill, Alison. "Limousines for the Feet: The Rhetoric of Trainers." In *Shoes: A History from Sandals to Sneakers*, ed. Giorgio Riello and Peter McNeil. Oxford and New York: Berg, 2006.

Gill, Eric. *Clothes*. London: Jonathan Cape, 1931.

Gill, J. *Queer Noises: Male and Female Homosexuality in Twentieth-Century Music*. London: Cassell, 1995.

Gill, R., K. Henwood, and C. McLean. "The Tyranny of the 'Six-Pack'? Understanding Men's Responses to Representations of the Male Body in Popular Culture." In *Culture in Psychology*, ed. C. Squire. London: Routledge, 2000.

Gilroy, P. *The Black Atlantic: Modernity and Double Consciousness*. London: Verso, 1993.

Ginsburg, Steve. "Despite a Feud, Marcianos Make Guesswork Pay." *Women's Wear Daily*, November 25, 1986, 4–5.

"Girls! Is Your Guy a Page Seven Fella?" *The Sun*, March 27, 1987, 16–17.

Glasser, R. *Gorbals Boy at Oxford*. London: Chatto & Windus, 1988.

Gluck, Carol. *Japan's Modern Myths: Ideology in the Late Meiji Period*. Princeton, NJ: Princeton University Press, 1985.

Gold, Herbert, et al. "The Beat Mystique." *Playboy* 5, no. 2 (February 1958): 20–26, 50, 74–75, 84–87.

"Gold and Bronze, Other Vivid Hues Will 'Color Men.'" *Fresno Bee*, May 21, 1948.

Goldman, Albert. *Elvis*. New York: McGraw-Hill, 1981.

Goodman, Charles S. *The Location of Fashion Industries with Special Reference to California Apparel*

Markets. Ann Arbor: University of Michigan Press, 1948.

Goodman, Paul. "Objective Values." In *The Dialectics of Liberation,* ed. C. Cooper. London: Penguin, 1968.

Goodman, Wendy. "Upscale Blues." *New York Times,* February 10, 1986, 48–51.

Goodwin, A. *Dancing in the Distraction Factory: Music Television and Popular Culture.* London: Routledge, 1993.

Gorrigan, P. 'Doing Nothing." In *Resistance through Rituals: Youth Subcultures in Post-War Britain,* ed. S. Hall and T. Jefferson. London: Hutchinson, 1976.

Gosling, R. *Sum Total.* London: Faber, 1962.

Graves, R., and A. Hodge. *The Long Weekend: A Social History of Great Britain 1918–1939.* 1940. London: Abacus, 1995.

Greek-Lettered Organizations with an African Heritage. St. Louis: Anheuser-Busch, n.d.

Greeley, Horace, and Michael Hudson, ed.*The Great Industries of the United States.* Hartford, CT: J. B. Burr & Hyde, 1872.

Green, Mary Anne Everett, ed. *Calendar of State Papers, Domestic Series, of the Reign of Charles II. 1666–1667.* 1666. London: Longman, Green, Longman, Roberts and Green, 1864.

Green, Robert L. "The Look of a Winner: Speed Week in Nassau Sets the Pace for Sports Car Fashions." *Playboy* 6, no. 4 (April 1959): 28–30, 89.

Green, Robert L. "Loose Living." *Playboy* 22, no. 8 (August 1975): 114–15.

Green, Robert L. "Loose Threads." *Playboy* 21, no. 5 (May 1974): 125–27.

Green, Robert L. "Meet Me at the Club: Right Raiment for Three Sporting Propositions." *Playboy* 7, no. 4 (April 1960): 37–38, 101.

Green, Robert L. "Wardrobe for a Jet Weekend: The Continent is Just Seven Hours from Broadway." *Playboy* 6, no. 5 (May 1959): 38–39.

Greenberg, Simon. "Three Lions, the Pitch and the Wardrobe." *Evening Standard* (London), June 8, 1998.

Greene, Asa. *A Glance at New York.* New York: A. Greene, 1837.

Greenfield, J., S. O'Connell, and C. Read. "Gender, Consumer Culture and the Middle-Class Male." In *Gender, Civic Culture and Consumerism: Middle-Class Identity in Britain, 1800–1940,* ed. A. Kidd and D. Nicholls. Manchester, UK: Manchester University Press, 1999.

Greenslade, William. "Fitness and the Fin-de-Siècle." In *Fin de Siècle/Fin du Globe: Fears and Fantasies of the Late Nineteenth-Century,* ed. John Stokes. London: Macmillan, 1992.

Grey, Ian. *Ivan the Terrible.* London, 1964.

Grey, Toby, and Kirsty Lang. "Model Footballers Kick into Fashion." *The Sunday Times,* May 31, 1998.

Grossberg, L. "The Media Economy of Rock Culture: Cinema, Post–Modernism and Authenticity." In *Sound and Vision: The Music Video Reader,* ed. S. Frith, A. Goodwin, and L. Grossberg. London: Routledge, 1993.

Grunwald, Fred. "California Futurization." *California Men's and Boys' Stylist,* November 1947.

Gunn, S. "The Public Sphere, Modernity and Consumption: New Perspectives on the History of the English Middle-Class." In *Gender, Civic Culture and Consumerism: Middle-Class Identity in Britain, 1800–1940,* ed. A. Kidd and D. Nicholls. Manchester, UK: Manchester University Press, 1999.

Guralnick, Peter. *The Rolling Stone Illustrated History of Rock and Roll.* Ed. Jim Miller. New York: Random House/Rolling Stone Press, 1980.

Gutsmuths, J. F. *Gymnastik für die Jugend.* Schnepfenthal, Germany: Buchhandel der Erziehungsanstalt, 1793.

Gutsmuths, J. F. *Turnbuch für die Söhne des Vaterlands.* Frankfurt/M.: Wilmans, 1817.

Haas, Stefan. "Der Körper der Beamten." In *Die Kultur der Verwaltung: Zur Umsetzung der preußischen Reformen 1808–1848.* Frankfurt/M.: Campus-Verlag, 2005.

Haas, Stefan. "Vom ständischen zum modernen Staat—Die politische und symbolische Bedeutung der zivilen Uniform." In *Nach Rang und Stand: Deutsche Ziviluniformen im 19. Jahrhundert* (Deutsches Textilmuseum Krefeld, March 24–June 23, 2002, curated by Elisabeth Hackspiel-Mikosch). Krefeld: Deutsches Textilmuseum Krefeld, 2002.

Hackney Borough Council. *Official Guide to the Metropolitan Borough of Hackney.* London: Hackney Borough Council, 1914.

Hackspiel-Mikosch, Elisabeth. "Beauty in Uniform: The Creation of Ideal Masculinity during the Nineteenth Century." In *On Men: Masculine Dress Code from the Ancient Greeks to Cowboys,* ed. Regine

Falkenberg, Adelheid Rasche, and Christine Waidenschlager. Proceedings of the ICOM Costume Committee, 57th annual general meeting in Berlin, June 13–17, 2005. Berlin: ICOM, 2005.

Hackspiel-Mikosch, Elisabeth. "Vorläufer der zivilen Uniformen im 18. Jahrhundert: Hofmonturen als Inszenierung fürstlicher Macht im höfischen Fest." In *Civilian Uniforms as Symbolic Communication,* ed. Elisabeth Hackspiel-Mikosch and Stefan Haas. Stuttgart: Steiner-Verlag, 2006.

Hagar, Sammy. *Raw Magazine,* no. 122 (April 1993): 48.

Hagemann, Karen. *"Männlicher Muth und Teutsche Ehre": Nation, Militär und Geschlecht zur Zeit der Anti-napoleonischen Kriege Preußens.* Paderborn, Germany: Schöningh, 1997.

Haiken, Elizabeth. *Venus Envy: A History of Cosmetic Surgery.* Baltimore, MD: Johns Hopkins University Press, 1999.

Hail-Carpenter Archives/Gay Men's Oral History Group. *Walking after Midnight: Gay Men's Life Stories.* 1989. London: Routledge, 1990.

Hain, M. *Das Lebensbild eines oberhessischen Trachtensdorfes von bäuerlicher Tracht und Gemeinschaft.* Jena, Germany: Eugen Diederichs, 1936.

Hajiimu, Nakaano. "Introduction to the Work of Kuki Shūzō." In *Iki no kōzō* (Reflections on Japanese Taste: The Structure of *Iki*), by Kuki Shūzō. Trans. John Clark. Sydney, Australia: Power Publications, 1997.

Halberstam, David. *The Fifties.* New York: Fawcett Columbine, 1993.

Halberstam, Judith. *Female Masculinity.* London: Duke University Press, 1998.

Hall, John Whitney. *Japan from Prehistory to Modern Times.* New York: Dell, 1970.

Hall, Marian, and Marjorie Carne. *California Fashion: From the Old West to New Hollywood.* New York: Abrams, 2002.

Hall, S., and T. Jefferson. *Resistance through Rituals: Youth Subcultures in Post-War Britain.* 1976. London: Hutchinson University Library, 1995. 2nd ed., London and New York: Routledge, 2006.

Hamilton, Ian. "Gazza Agonistes." *Granta* 45 (Autumn 1993).

Hämmerle, Christa. "Zur Relevanz des Connell'-schen Konzepts hegemonialer Männlichkeit für Militär und Männlichkeit/en in der Habsburgmonarchie 1868–1914/18." In *Männer—Macht—Körper:*

Hegemoniale Männlichkeiten vom Mittelalter bis heute, ed. Martin Dinges. Frankfurt/M.: Campus-Verlag, 2005.

Hammontree, Patsy Guy. *Elvis Presley, A Bio-Bibliography.* Westport, CT: Greenwood, 1985.

Hannerz, U. *Soulside: An Inquiry into Ghetto Culture and Community.* New York: Columbia, 1969.

Hansen, Miriam. "Pleasure, Ambivalence, Identification: Valentino and Female Spectatorship." *Cinema Journal* 25, no. 4 (Summer 1986): 25.

Harbinson, William Allen. *The Illustrated Elvis.* New York: Grosset & Dunlap, 1977.

Harlow, Eve. *The Jeans Scene.* New York: Drake, 1973.

Harries, Meirion. *Soldiers of the Sun: The Rise and Fall of the Imperial Japanese Army.* New York: Random House, 1991.

Hart, Avril. *Ties.* London: V&A Publications, 1998.

Harvey, John Hooper. *The Black Prince and His Age.* Totowa, NJ: Rowman and Littlefield, 1976.

Harvey, John. *Men in Black.* London: Reaktion, 1995.

Hatton, Lois P. "Palm Springs Show Inspires New Shop." *St. Paul Pioneer-Press,* December 4, 1948.

Hawkins, S. "The Pet Shop Boys: Musicology, Masculinity, Banality." In *Sexing the Groove: Popular Music and Gender,* ed. S. Whiteley. London: Routledge, 1997.

Hayes, C.J.H. *A Generation of Materialism, 1871–1900.* New York: Harper, 1941.

Hazlitt, W. *Brummelliana: The Complete Works in 22 Volumes.* Ed. P. Howe. Vol. 20. London: J. M. Dent, 1934.

Heath, Richard. "Studies in English Costume: A Charles the Second Military Coat." *The Magazine of Art* 11 (1888): 11–15.

Heath, S. *The Sexual Fix.* Basingstoke, UK: Macmillan, 1982.

Heath, Stephen. "Joan Riviere and the Masquerade." In *Formations of Fantasy,* ed. V. Burgin, J. Donald, and C. Kaplan. London: Methuen, 1986.

Hebdige, D. *Hiding in the Light: On Images and Things.* London: Routledge, 1988.

Hebdige, D. *Subculture: The Meaning of Style.* London: Routledge, 1979; London: Routledge, 1987.

Hechinger, Fred M. "The Fraternities Show Signs of New Strength." *New York Times,* May 21, 1985, national edition.

Hefner, Hugh M. "The Playboy Philosophy. Part Two: Playboy's Editor–Publisher Spells Out—for

Friends and Critics Alike—Our Guiding Principles and Editorial Credo." *Playboy* 10, no. 1 (January 1963): 41–52.

Hegel, G.W.F. *The Philosophy of History.* New York: Dover, 1956.

Henley, Clark. *Butch Manual: The Current Drag and How to Do It.* New York: Sea Horse Press, 1982.

Hentoff, Nat. *The Jazz Life.* New York: Panther, 1964.

Herford Percy, C. H., and Evelyn Simpson, eds. *Ben Jonson.* Oxford, 1941.

Herlihy, James Leo. *Midnight Cowboy.* London: Panther, 1970.

Higgs, D. *Queer Sites: Gay Urban History since 1600.* London: Routledge, 1999.

Hill, J. *British Cinema in the 1980s: Issues and Themes.* Oxford: Clarendon, 1999.

Himes, C. B. "Zoot Riots Are Race Riots." *Crisis* 50, no. 7 (1943).

Hinds, Allen B., ed. *Calendar of State Papers—Venetian.* Vol. 35 (1666–1668). London: HMSO, 1935.

Hiro, D. *Black British, White British.* London: Penguin, 1972.

"The Hit Hits the Stands." *Media Week,* May 17, 1985, 2.

Hoare, Philip. "I Love a Man in Uniform: The Dandy Esprit de Corps." *Fashion Theory, The Journal of Dress, Body and Culture* 9, no. 3 (September 2005): 263–82.

Hodson, P. "New Man." *She,* July 1984, 126.

Hollander, Anne. *Seeing through Clothes.* New York: Avon, 1980.

Hollander, Anne. *Sex and Suits.* New York: A. A. Knopf, 1994.

Hollander, Anne. *Sex and Suits: The Evolution of Modern Dress.* New York: Kodansha, 1995.

Holleran, A. "The Petrification of Clonestyle." *Christopher Street* 69 (1982).

Holloway, John. *The Victorian Sage.* New York: Norton, 1965.

Honeyman, K. "Following Suit: Men, Masculinity and Gendered Practices in the Clothing Trade in Leeds, England, 1890–1940." *Gender and History* 14, no. 3 (November 2002): 426–46.

Hood, Thomas. "Song of the Shirt." Published anonymously in *Punch* (1843).

Horan, J. D. *The Great American West: A Pictorial History from Coronado to the Last Frontier.* New York: Crown, 1959.

Hough, Emerson. *The Story of the Cowboy.* New York: Appleton, 1897.

Houlbrook, M. "'Lady Austin's Camp Boys': Constituting the Queer Subject in 1930s London." *Gender and History* 14, no. 1 (April 2002): 31–61.

Houlbrook, M. "The Private World of Public Urinals: London 1918–1957." *London Journal* 25, no. 1 (2000): 52–70.

Houlbrook, M. "'A Sun among Cities': Space, Identities and Queer Male Practices, London 1918–57." PhD diss., University of Essex, 2002.

Hower, Ralph. *History of Macy's of New York, 1858–1919.* Cambridge, MA: Harvard University Press, 1943.

Hueffer, Ford Madox. *The Soul of London: A Survey of a Modern City.* London: Alston Rivers, 1904.

"Huge Growth Forecast for Apparel Industry." *Los Angeles Times,* June 4, 1944.

Huizinga, Johan. *The Waning of the Middle Ages.* New York: Dover Reprint, 1998.

Hume, David. *The History of England from the Invasion of Julius Caesar to the Accession of Henry VII.* London, 1762.

Humphreys, Laud. "New Styles in Homosexual Manliness." *Transaction* 8 (1971): 38.

Humphries, Martin. "Gay Machismo." In *The Sexuality of Men,* ed. Andy Metcalf and Martin Humphreys. London: Pluto, 1985.

Humphries, S., and P. Gordon. *A Man's World: From Boyhood to Manhood, 1900–1960.* London: BBC Books, 1996.

Hyde, Jack. "California Dateline." *Men's Wear,* January 12, 1951, 168.

Hyde, Jack. "California Dateline." *Men's Wear,* March 20, 1953, 132–34.

Hyde, Jack. "Thorsen Heads Men's Wear Manufacturers of Los Angeles." *Daily News Record,* January 9, 1948.

"Institute Report: Denim Update." *Good Housekeeping,* September 1984, 124.

Ivins, Molly. "Presley Fans Mourn in Memphis . . ." *New York Times,* August 18, 1977.

Jackson-Stops, Gervase, ed. *The Treasure Houses of Britain, Five Hundred Years of Private Patronage and Art Collecting.* New Haven, CT, and London: National Gallery of Art, Washington, and Yale University Press, 1985.

Jacopetti, Alexandra. *Native Funk and Flash.* San Francisco: Scrimshaw, 1974.

Jahn, Friedrich Ludwig. *Die deutsche Turnkunst.* Eiselen: Self-published, 1816.

Jakobsen, Lyn. "Greek Affiliation and Attitude Change: Developmental Implications." *Journal of College Student Personnel* 27 (1986): 523–27.

Jansen, Marius B. *The Nineteenth Century.* Vol. 5 of *The Cambridge History of Japan,* general eds. John Whitney Hall, Marius B. Jansen, Madoka Kanai, and Denis Twitchett. Cambridge: Cambridge University Press, 1988–1999.

Jansen, Marius B. *China in the Tokugawa World.* Cambridge, MA: Harvard University Press, 1992.

Jansen, Marius B. *The Making of Modern Japan.* Cambridge, MA: Harvard University Press, 2000.

Jardine, A., and P. Smith, eds. *Men in Feminism.* London: Methuen, 1987.

Jennings, William. Advertisement. *New York Tribune,* October 3, 1845.

Jennings, William. Advertisement. *Sheldon & Co.'s Business or Advertising Directory, 1845.* New York: John E Trow, 1845.

Jentsch, Andrea. "Der uniformierte Mann im Spiegel der Karikatur." In *Nach Rang und Stand: Deutsche Ziviluniformen im 19. Jahrhundert* (Deutsches Textilmuseum Krefeld, March 24–June 23, 2002, curated by Elisabeth Hackspiel-Mikosch). Krefeld: Deutsches Textilmuseum Krefeld, 2002.

Jesse, W. *The Life of George Brummell, Esq., Commonly Called Beau Brummell.* 2 vols. London: Saunders and Otley, 1844.

Jobling, Paul. *Fashion Spreads: Word and Image in Fashion Photography since 1980.* Oxford and New York: Berg, 1999.

Jobling, Paul. *Man Appeal: Advertising, Modernism and Menswear.* Oxford and New York: Berg, 2005.

Jobling, Paul. "Statue Men: The Phallic Body, Identity and Ambiguity in Fashion Photography." In *Fashion Spreads: Word and Image in Fashion Photography since 1980.* London and New York: Berg, 1999.

John Johnson Collection of Printed Ephemera. Bodleian Library, Men's Clothing.

Johnson, Jann. *The Jeans Book.* New York: Ballantine, 1972.

Johnson, Paul. "'Art' and the Language of Progress in Early-Industrial Paterson: Sam Patch at Clinton Bridge." *American Quarterly* 40, no. 4 (December 1988): 433–49.

Jones, Ann Rosalind. and Peter Stallybrass. *Renaissance Clothing and the Materials of Memory.* Cambridge: Cambridge University Press, 2000.

Jones, Emrys. *The Origins of Shakespeare.* London, 1977.

Jones, Le-Roi. *Blues People.* New York: MacGibbon and Kee, 1975.

Jones, Mablen. *Getting It On: The Clothing of Rock 'n' Roll.* New York: Abbeville, 1987.

Jordan, Dr. A. C. Letter to the editor. *The Times,* June 12, 1929.

Jordan, Dr. A. C. Letter to *The Times,* July 15, 1929. Reprinted in *Sunlight,* September 1929, 30, 31.

Jordan, Dr. A. C. *Men's Wear Organiser,* August 1929, 70.

Jordan, Winthrop D. *White over Black.* Chapel Hill, NC, 1968.

Jordon, T. G. *Trails to Texas: Southern Roots of Western Cattle Ranching.* Lincoln: University of Nebraska, 1981.

Joseph, Nathan. *Uniforms and Nonuniforms: Communication through Clothing.* New York: Greenwood, 1986.

Jump, John, ed. *Casebook, Shakespeare: Hamlet.* London, 1968.

Kahn, Alice. "A Whole Lotta Elvis Going On." *San Francisco Chronicle,* June 11, 1990.

Kaiser, Susan B. *The Psychology of Clothing.* New York: Macmillan, 1985.

Kaplan, Caren, Norma Alarcon, and Minoo Moallem, eds. *Between Woman and Nation: Nationalisms, Transnational Feminisms, and the State.* Durham, NC: Duke University Press, 1999.

Kaplan, E. A. *Rocking Around the Clock: Music Television, Postmodernism and Consumer Culture.* New York and London: Methuen, 1987.

Kaplan, Fred. *Thomas Carlyle: A Biography.* New York: Cornell University Press, 1983.

Karaka, D. F. *The Pulse of Oxford.* London: Dent, 1933.

Kaufmann, Thomas da Costa. *Court, Cloister and City: The Art and Culture of Central Europe 1450–1800.* Chicago: University of Chicago Press, 1995.

Keenan, William. "Introduction: *Sartor Resartus* Restored: Dress Studies in Carlylean Perspective." In *Dressed to Impress: Looking the Part,* ed. W.J.F. Keenan. New York and Oxford: Berg, 2001.

Keller, Michael J., and Hart, Derrell. "The Effects of Sorority and Fraternity Rush on Students' Self

Images." *Journal of College Student Personnel* 23 (1982): 257–61.

Kelley, R.D.G. *Race Rebels: Culture, Politics and the Black Working Class.* New York: Free Press, 1994.

Kelly, Francis M. "A Comely Vest after the Persian Mode." *The Connoisseur* 88 (1931): 96.

Kelly, I. *Beau Brummell: The Ultimate Man of Style.* New York: Free Press, 2006.

Kelly's Hackney, Dalston, Old Ford & Bow Directory for 1890. London: Kelly & Co., 1890.

Kemper, R. H. *Costume.* New York: Newsweek, 1977.

Kennedy, B., and J. Lyttle. "Wolf in Chic Clothing." *City Limits,* December 4–11, 1986, 14–17.

Kennedy, Dominic. "Team in Red, White and Blue Wears Paul Smith." *The Times,* May 15, 1998.

Kerouac, Jack. "The Origins of the Beat Generation." *Playboy* 6, no. 6 (June 1959): 31–32, 42, 79.

Kessie, Jack J. "The Basic Wardrobe." *Playboy* 2, no. 9 (September 1955): 27–28, 34, 42.

Kessie, Jack J. "The Marks of the Well-Dressed Man: A Top-to-Bottom Take-Out on the Fine Points of Fashion." *Playboy* 4, no. 3 (March 1957): 47, 69–70.

Kessie, Jack J. "Summa Cum Style." *Playboy* 2, no. 10 (October 1955): 18–19, 52.

Kessie, Jack J. "The Well-Dressed Playboy: *Playboy's* Position on Proper Male Attire." *Playboy* 2, no. 2 (January 1955): 38–39.

Kessie, Jack J. "Well-Groomed Featherweights for Spring: They're Light on the Man and His Wallet." *Playboy* 2, no. 5 (May 1955): 27.

Kettel, Thomas P. "Clothing Trade." In *Eighty Years' Progress of the United States.* Hartford, CT: L. Stebbins, 1869.

Kidwell, Claudia B. *Cutting a Fashionable Fit: Dressmakers' Draftmaking Systems in the United States.* Washington, DC: Smithsonian Institution Press, 1979.

Kidwell, Claudia B., and Margaret C. Christman. *Suiting Everyone: The Democratization of Clothing in America.* Washington, DC: Smithsonian Institution Press, 1974.

Kidwell, Claudia B., and Valerie Steele. *Men and Women: Dressing the Part.* Washington, DC: Smithsonian Institution Press, 1989.

Kimmel, Michael, ed. *Men and Masculinities: A Social, Cultural and Historical Encyclopaedia.* Vol. 1. Santa Barbara, Denver, and Oxford: ABC-Clio, 2004.

"The King Is Dead, but Long Lives the King in a Showbiz Bonanza." *People,* October 10, 1977, 29.

Klein, A. M. *Little Big Men: Body Building Subculture and Gender Construction.* Albany: State University of New York Press, 1993.

Klein, Kerwin L. *Frontiers of Historical Imagination.* Berkeley: University of California Press, 1997.

King, Pat. "New Wave Networkers." *Black Enterprise,* December 1983, 89.

Kirk, Kris, and Ed Heath. *Men in Frocks.* London: Gay Men's Press, 1984.

Kleinberg, Seymour. "Where Have All the Sissies Gone?" *Christopher Street,* March 1978.

Koshetz, Herbert. "Laundry Offers New Way to Age Jeans." *New York Times,* August 7, 1973.

Koslin, Désirée, and Janet Snyder, eds. "Introduction." In *Encountering Medieval Textiles and Dress: Objects, Texts, Images.* New York: Palgrave Macmillan, 2002.

Krueger, Robert, ed. *The Poems of Sir John Davies.* Oxford, 1975.

Kuchta, David. "'Graceful, Virile, and Useful': The Origins of the Three-Piece Suit." *Dress* 17 (1990): 118–26.

Kuchta, David. "The Making of the Self-Made Man: Class, Clothing, and English Masculinity, 1688–1832." In *The Sex of Things,* ed. Victoria de Grazia. Berkeley: University of California Press, 2002.

Kuchta, David. *The Three-Piece Suit and Modern Masculinity: England, 1550–1850.* Berkeley: University of California Press, 2002.

Kühne, Thomas, ed. *Männergeschichte—Geschlechtergeschichte: Männlichkeit im Wandel der Moderne.* Frankfurt/M.: Campus-Verlag, 1996.

Kurbsky, Prince A.M. *History of Ivan the Terrible.* Ed. and trans. J.L.I. Fennell. Cambridge, 1965.

Kureishi, H., and J. Savage, eds. *The Faber Book of Pop.* London: Faber & Faber, 1995.

Kurzel-Runtscheiner, Monica. "Vom 'Mantelkleid' zu Staatsfrack und Waffenrock: Anfänge und Entwicklung der Ziviluniformen in Österreich." In *Civilian Uniforms as Symbolic Communication,* ed. Elisabeth Hackspiel-Mikosch and Stefan Haas. Stuttgart: Steiner-Verlag, 2006.

Lacan, Jacques. "The Signification of the Phallus." In *Ecrits: A Selection,* trans. Alan Sheridan. New York: W. W. Norton, 1977.

La Ferla, Ruth. "Singing the Blues." *New York Times Magazine,* July 13, 1986, sec. 6, 60.

Lajer-Burcharth, Ewa. *Necklines: The Art of Jacques-Louis David after the Terror*. New Haven, CT, and London: Yale University Press, 1999.

Lanfranchi, P., ed. *Il Calcio e Il Suo Popolo*. Naples, Rome, and Milan: Edizioni Scientifiche Italiane, 1992.

Lanfranchi, P. "Italy and the World Cup: The Impact of Football in Italy and the Example of Italia 90." In *Hosts and Champions: Soccer Cultures, National Identities and the USA World Cup,* ed. John Sugden and Alan Tomlinson. Aldershot, UK: Arena, 1994.

Lansdale, Phil. "An Unliterary Digest of Los Angeles Sportswear." *California Men's Stylist* 1 (January 1942): 45.

"L.A. Ranks 2nd in World as Apparel Industry Center." 1958. Clipping, folder: "Garment Industry—Los Angeles." Vertical File, Los Angeles Public Library, Los Angeles.

La Roche, Sophie V. *Sophie in London, 1786. Being the Diary of Sophie V. La Roche*. Trans. Clare Williams. London: Jonathan Cape, 1933.

Latham, Robert Gordon. *A Dictionary of the English Language* ... 2 vols. London, 1870.

Laver, James. *The Age of Optimism: Manners and Morals, 1848–1914*. London: Weidenfeld & Nicolson, 1966.

Laver, James. *British Military Uniforms*. London: Penguin, 1948.

Laver, James. *Costume Illustration: The Nineteenth Century*. London: Victoria & Albert Museum, 1947.

Laver, James. *Dandies*. London: Weidenfeld & Nicolson, 1968.

Lawrence, A. *Man in the Making*. London: Peter Robinson, 1912.

Lawrence, D. H. *Lady Chatterley's Lover*. 1928. London: Penguin, 1961.

Lawrence, D. H. *Twilight in Italy*. 1916. London: Penguin, 1960.

"Leadership of California Sportswear Stressed." *Los Angeles Times*, April 28, 1948.

Leavis, F. R. "Diabolic Intellect and the Noble Hero." In *The Common Pursuit*. Harmondsworth, UK, 1962.

Lee, Adrian. "Players Get the Blues over Hoddle's Beige." *The Times* (London), June 9, 1998.

Lefebvre, H. *The Production of Space*. Trans. Nicholson-Smith. Oxford: Basil Blackwell, 1991.

Leger, Mark. "The Drag Queen in the Age of Mechanical Reproduction." *Out/Look* 6 (Fall 1989): 29.

Lehmann, Ulrich. "Language of the PurSuit [sic]: Cary Grant's Clothes in Alfred Hitchcock's 'North by Northwest.'" *Fashion Theory* 4, no. 4 (December 2000): 467–86.

Lehmann, Ulrich. *Tigersprung: Fashion in Modernity*. Cambridge, MA: MIT Press, 2000.

Lemire, Beverly. *Fashion's Favourite: The Cotton Trade and the Consumer in Britain, 1660–1800*. Oxford: Oxford University Press, 1991.

Lemire, Beverly. "Redressing the History of the Clothing Trade in England: Ready-Made Clothing, Guilds, and Women Workers, 1650–1800." *Dress* 21 (1994): 62–64.

Lemoine-Luccioni, Eugénie. *La Robe*. Paris: Seuil, 1983.

Levine, Martin P. *Gay Macho: The Life and Death of the Homosexual Clone*. London and New York: New York University Press, 1998.

Levi-Strauss, C. *The Way of the Masks*. Seattle: University of Washington Press, 1988.

Levy, H. *The Shops of Britain: A Study of Retail Distribution*. London: Kegan Paul, 1948.

Lewis, Wilmarth S., ed. *The Yale Edition of Horace Walpole's Correspondence*. 48 vols. New Haven, CT, and London: Yale University Press, 1937–1983.

Liberace. *The Wonderful Private World of Liberace*. New York: Harper & Row, 1986.

Light, A. *Forever England: Femininity, Literature and Conservatism between the Wars*. London: Routledge, 1991.

Lilla, Joachim. "'Trost tanzwütiger Jungferlein?'—Streiflichter zu den Krefelder 'Tanzhusaren' und deren Wirkung in der Öffentlichkeit." In *Nach Rang und Stand: Deutsche Ziviluniformen im 19. Jahrhundert* (Deutsches Textilmuseum Krefeld, March 24–June 23, 2002, curated by Elisabeth Hackspiel-Mikosch). Krefeld: Deutsches Textilmuseum Krefeld, 2002.

Lindstrom, Diane. *Economic Development in the Philadelphia Region, 1810–1850*. New York: Columbia University Press, 1978.

Lipovetsky, G. *Empire of Fashion: Dressing Modern Democracy*. Princeton, NJ: Princeton University Press, 1994.

Lockwood, David. *The Blackcoated Worker: A Study in Class Consciousness*. Oxford: Clarendon, 1989.

Loeb, Lori. *Consuming Angels: Advertising and Victorian Women.* Oxford: Oxford University Press, 1994.

Longworth's American Almanac, New-York Register, and City Directory, 1805–19. New York: David Longworth, 1805–1819.

Loos, Adolf. "'Men's Fashion' and 'Men's Hats.'" 1898. Reprinted in *The Rise of Fashion: A Reader,* ed. Daniel Leonhard Purdy. Minneapolis: University of Minnesota, 2004.

Lord, M. G. "Frats and Sororities: The Greek Rites of Exclusion." *Nation,* July 4, 1987, 10f.

Lorenz, Maren. *Leibhaftige Vergangenheit: Einführung in die Körpergeschichte.* Tübingen: Ed. Diskord, 2000.

"Los Angeles' Little Cutters: Their Sportswear Always Had Honor in Its Own Country." *Fortune* 31 (May 1945): 134, 182.

"Los Angeles Retailers Pledge Bank of Windows for Roundup." *Boys' Outfitter,* September 1947.

Luciano, Lynne. *Looking Good: Male Body Image in Modern America.* New York: Hill and Wang, 2002.

Ludgate, S. "The Magazines for the Young Generation." *Campaign,* March 16, 1984, 54–58.

Lurie, Alison. *The Language of Clothes.* New York: Random House, 1981.

Lynch, A. Field Notes, Gentlemen's Beautillion Ball. 1996.

MacCabe, Colin. *Performance.* London: BFI, 1998.

Mackenzie, Norman A. *The Magic of Rudolph Valentino.* London: Research Publishing Co., 1974.

Madison, J. O. *Elements of Garment Cutting.* Hartford, CT: Case, Lockwood & Brainard, 1878.

Maffesoli, Michel. *The Time of the Tribes: The Decline of Individualism in Mass Society.* Trans. Don Smith. London: Sage, 1996.

"MAGIC Arranges for Visitors to Fly to Palm Springs Roundup." *Los Angeles Daily News Record,* December 23, 1949.

Mahan, Francis. *Mahan's Protractor and Proof Systems of Garment Cutting.* Spring and Summer Report for 1839, no. 8 (Philadelphia).

Maidment, B. "101 Things to Do with a Fantail Hat—Dustmen, Dirt, and Dandyism 1820–1860." Paper presented at the "Work and the Image" conference, University of Leeds, 1998.

Malossi, Giannino, ed. *Material Man: Masculinity, Sexuality, Style.* New York: Harry N. Abrams, 2000.

Mander, David, and Jenny Golden. *The London Borough of Hackney in Old Photographs 1890–1960.* Stroud, UK: Alan Sutton, 1991.

The Man of Manners: or, Plebeian Polished . . . London: J. Roberts, n.d.

"Manufacturers Plan Training Program." *California Apparel News,* November 28, 1947.

Marchand, Roland. *Advertising the American Dream: Making Way for Modernity, 1920–1940.* Berkeley: University of California Press, 1985.

Marcus, Steven. *Engels, Manchester and the Working Class.* New York: Random House, 1975.

"Margate Still Hesitates but Has Almost Come Round to the Side of Health and Sense." *New Health,* November 1932, 22–23.

Margolis, J. "Last Orders for the New Lad Fad." *Sunday Times,* Style Supplement, April 23, 1995, 4–5.

Marquis, S. "The Publishing Conundrum: How to Reach the 'New Man.'" *Campaign,* July 26, 1985, 37–41.

Marriott, Michel. "Pioneer's Crusade Goes On: Cofounder Sees Growth of Oldest Black Sorority." *Washington Post,* July 23, 1984.

Marshall, John. "Pansies, Perverts and Macho Men: Changing Conceptions of Male Homosexuality." In *The Making of the Modern Homosexual,* ed. Kenneth Plummer. London: Barnes and Noble, 1981.

Martin, Richard. "A Note: A Charismatic Art: The Balance of Ingratiation and Outrage in Contemporary Fashion." *Fashion Theory* 1, no. 1 (1997): 91–104.

Martin, Richard, and Harold Koda. *Jocks and Nerds: Men's Style in the Twentieth Century.* New York: Rizzoli, 1989.

Martin's tailoring shop. Advertisements. *New York Herald,* August 2, 1841, and May 22, 1842.

Marvell, Andrew. "The Kings Vowes." [1670s?] In *The Poems and Letters of Andrew Marvell,* ed. H. M. Margoliouth. Oxford: Clarendon, 1927.

Masterman, C.F.G. *The Condition of England.* London: Methuen, 1909.

Matsunosuke, Nishiyama. *Edo Culture: Daily Life and Diversions in Urban Japan, 1600–1868.* Trans. Gerald Groemer. Honolulu: University of Hawaii Press, 1997.

Maurice, Dick. *Las Vegas Sun,* March 1986.

May, Elaine Tyler. *Homeward Bound: American Families in the Cold War Era.* New York: Basic Books, 1988.

May, Kirse Granat. *Golden State, Golden Youth: The California Image in Popular Culture, 1955–1966.* Chapel Hill: University of North Carolina Press, 2002.

Mayer, Arno. *The Persistence of the Old Regime: Europe to the Great War.* London: Croom Helm, 1981.

Mayes, R. "Jumping on the Bands Wagon." *Media Week,* September 6, 1985, 20–21.

Mazon, Mauricio. *The Zoot-Suit Riots: The Psychology of Symbolic Annihilation.* Austin: University of Texas Press, 1984.

McBride, Dwight A. *Why I Hate Abercrombie and Fitch: Essays on Race and Sexuality.* New York: New York University Press, 2005.

McClellan, E. *Historic Dress in America, 1607–1800, [1800–1870].* Philadelphia, PA: George W. Jacobs, 1917.

McClintock, Anne, Aamir Mufti, and Ella Shohat, eds. *Dangerous Liaisons: Gender, Nation, and Postcolonial Perspectives.* Minneapolis: University of Minnesota Press, 1997.

McCord, Jacqueline. "Blue Jean Country." *New York Times Magazine,* April 29, 1979, 115.

McDonald, Gerald D., Michael Conway, and Mark Ricci, eds. *The Films of Charlie Chaplin.* Secaucus, NJ: Citadel Press, 1971.

McDonald, P. "Feeling and Fun: Romance, Dance and the Performing Male Body in the Take That Videos." In *Sexing the Groove: Popular Music and Gender,* ed. S. Whiteley. London: Routledge, 1997.

McDowell, Colin. *The Man of Fashion: Peacock Males and Perfect Gentlemen.* London: Thames and Hudson, 1997.

McKendrick, Neil, John Brewer, and J. H. Plumb. *The Birth of a Consumer Society: The Commercialization of Eighteenth-Century England.* Bloomington: Indiana University Press, 1982.

McManigal, J. W. *Farmtown: A Memoir of the 1930s.* Brattleboro, VT: Stephen Green, 1974.

McNeil, Peter. "Fashion Victims: Macaroni Dress at the ROM." *Rotunda, The Magazine of the Royal Ontario Museum* 32, no. 3 (2000a): 36–42.

McNeil, Peter. "Macaroni Masculinities." *Fashion Theory* 4, no. 4 (2000b): 373–404.

McNeil, Peter. "'That Doubtful Gender': Macaroni Dress and Male Sexualities." *Fashion Theory* 3, no. 4 (1999): 411–49.

McRobbie, A. *Feminism and Youth Culture: From "Jackie" to "Just Seventeen."* Basingstoke, UK: Macmillan, 1991.

McRobbie, A. *In the Culture Society: Art, Fashion and Popular Music.* London: Routledge, 1999.

McRobbie, A. "Second-Hand Dresses and the Role of the Ragmarket." In *Zoot Suits and Second-Hand Dresses: An Anthology of Fashion and Music,* ed. A. McRobbie. Basingstoke, UK: Macmillan, 1989.

McRobbie, A., ed. *Zoot Suits and Second-Hand Dresses: An Anthology of Fashion and Music.* London: Macmillan, 1989.

Medevoi, Leerom. "A Yippie-Panther Pipe Dream: Rethinking Sex, Race, and the Sexual Revolution." In *Swinging Single: Representing Sexuality in the 1960s,* ed. Hilary Radner and Moya Luckett. Minneapolis: University of Minnesota Press, 1999.

Meech-Pekarik, Julia. *The World of the Meiji Print.* New York and Tokyo: Weatherhill, 1986.

Meister, Henry. *Letters Written during a Residence in England.* London: T. N. Longman & O. Rees, 1799.

Melly, George. *Revolt into Style.* Harmondsworth: Penguin, 1970.

Melzer, Sara E., and Kathryn Norberg, eds. *From the Royal to the Republican Body: Incorporating the Political in Seventeenth-and Eighteenth-Century France.* Berkeley: University of California Press, 1998.

Mendes, V., and A. de la Haye. *20th Century Fashion.* London: Thames and Hudson, 1999.

"Men's and Boys' Market Began Century Ago." *California Apparel News,* January 13, 1950.

Men's Apparel Research Guild. "The California Market and Its Importance to Men's Wear Retailers." New York: Men's Apparel Research Guild, 1947.

Men's Dress Reform Party. Pamphlet for the Revel on June 24, 1931.

Men's Dress Reform Party. Pamphlet for the Dinner Debate on June 21, 1933.

Mercer, K. "Black Hair/Style Politics." *New Formations* 3 (Winter 1987): 33–54. Reprinted in *Out There: Marginalization and Contemporary Culture,* ed. R. Ferguson, M. Grever, T. T. Minh-ha, and C. West (New York: The New Museum of Contemporary Arts, 1990) and in *The Subcultural Studies Reader,* ed. K. Gelder. 2nd ed. (London and New York: Routledge, 2005).

Merleau-Ponty, M. *Le Visible et l'invisible.* Paris: Gallimard, 1964.

Merleau-Ponty, M. *Basic Writings,* ed. Thomas Baldwin. London: Routledge, 2004.

The Merry Andrew; or, Macaroni Jester. A Choice Collection of Funny Jokes, Merry Stories, Droll

Adventures, Frolicksome Tales, Witty Quibbles, Youthful Pranks... London: n.p., 1786.

Merta, Klaus-Peter. *Das Heerwesen in Brandenburg und Preussen von 1640–1805: Die Uniformierung.* 2nd ed. Berlin: Brandenburgisches Verlags-Haus, 2001.

Metcalf, A., and M. Humphries. "Introduction." In *The Sexuality of Men.* London: Pluto, 1985.

Meyer, C., and Clementina Black. *Makers of Our Clothes: A Case for Trade Boards.* London: Duckworth, 1909.

Meyer, Moe, ed. *The Politics and Poetics of Camp.* London and New York: Routledge, 1994.

Meyer, Richard. "Rock Hudson's Body." In *Inside/Out: Lesbian Theories, Gay Theories,* ed. Diana Fuss. New York: Routledge, 1991.

Meyers, Marvin. *The Jacksonian Persuasion: Politics and Belief.* New York: Vintage, 1957.

Middleton, R. *Studying Popular Music.* Milton Keynes, UK: Open University Press, 1990.

Miege, Guy. *The New State of England under their Majesties K. William and Q. Mary.* 3 vols. London: Jonathon Robinson, 1691.

Mignon, Patrick. "Fans and Heroes." In *France and the 1998 World Cup: The National Impact of a World Sporting Event,* ed. Hugh Dauncey and Geoff Hare. London and Portland, OR: Frank Cass, 1999.

Mikosch, Elisabeth. "Court Dress and Ceremony in the Age of the Baroque: The Royal/Imperial Wedding of 1719 in Dresden." PhD diss., New York University, 1999.

"Milady Had Nothing on the Gentlemen." *American-Statesmen,* November 2, 1947.

Miller, Angela. *The Empire of the Eye: Landscape Representation and American Cultural Politics, 1825–1875.* Ithaca, NY: Cornell University Press, 1993.

Miller, Russell. *Bunny: The Real Story of Playboy.* London: Michael Joseph, 1984.

Miller, Ruth. "Palm Springs Round Up." *Display World,* December 1948.

Mills, Jane. *Womanwords.* London: Virago, 1991.

Milward, John. *The Diary of John Milward,* ed. Carole Robbins. Cambridge: Cambridge University Press, 1938.

Mitchell, Leslie George. *Charles James Fox.* Oxford: Oxford University Press, 1992.

Mitton, Geraldine. *The Fascination of London: Hackney and Stoke Newington.* London: Adam & Charles Black, 1908.

Moers, E. *The Dandy: Brummell to Beerhohm.* London: Secker & Warburg; New York: Viking, 1960.

Monroy, Douglas. *Rebirth: Mexican Los Angeles from the Great Migration to the Great Depression.* Berkeley: University of California Press, 1999.

Moore, S. "Target Man." *New Socialist* 45 (January 1987): 4–5.

Morgan, Lady. *France in 1829–1830.* London: Saunders & Otley, 1831.

Morris, J. *Oxford.* 1965. Oxford: Oxford University Press, 1987.

Mort, F. "Boy's Own? Masculinity, Style and Popular Culture." *Male Order: Unwrapping Masculinity,* ed. R. Chapman and J. Rutherford. London: Lawrence and Wishart, 1988.

Mort, F. *Cultures of Consumption: Masculinities and Social Space in Late Twentieth-Century Britain.* London: Routledge, 1996.

Mort, F. "Images Change: High Street Style and the New Man." *New Socialist* 43 (November 1986): 6–8.

Mort, F. "Mapping Sexual London: The Wolfenden Committee on Homosexual Offences and Prostitution 1954–1957." *New Formations: Sexual Geographies, Journal of Culture/Theory/Politics* 37 (Spring 1999): 92–113.

Mort, F. "Sexuality—Regulation and Contestation in Gay Left Collective." In *Homosexuality: Power and Politics.* London: Alison and Busby, 1980.

Mort, F., and P. Thompson. "Retailing, Community Culture and Masculinity in 1950s Britain: The Case of Montague Burton, Tailor of Taste." *History Workshop Journal* 38 (1994): 106–27.

Morton, Linda. "American Pattern Drafting Systems for Men in the Nineteenth Century." Master's thesis, Colorado State University, 1981.

Mosse, George L. *The Image of Man: The Creation of Modern Masculinity.* New York: Oxford University Press, 1996.

Mouland, Bill. "The Men in Beige." *Daily Mail,* June 9, 1998.

"Mr Green's Catalogues Once Had the 007 Look." *Men's Wear,* March 21, 1964, 20

MTV Networks. *George Michael: Music, Money. Love, Faith.* 1998. DVD Archive.

Muggleton, David. *Inside Subculture: The Postmodern Meaning of Style.* Oxford and New York: Berg, 2004.

Muggleton, David, and Rupert Weinzierl. *The Post-Subcultures Reader*. Oxford and New York: Berg, 2004.

Mulvey, L. "Visual Pleasure and Narrative Cinema." *Screen* 16, no. 3 (1975): 6–18.

Murray, Jacqueline, and Konrad Eisenbichler, eds. *Desire and Discipline: Sex and Sexuality in the Premodern West*. Toronto: University of Toronto Press, 1996.

Musée de la Mode et du Costume. *Indispensables Accessoires XVIe–XXe siècle*. Paris: Musée de la Mode et du Costume, 1983. An exhibition catalog.

Myerly, Scott Hughes. *British Military Spectacle: From the Napoleonic Wars through the Crimea*. Cambridge, MA: Harvard University Press, 1996.

Nach Rang und Stand: Deutsche Ziviluniformen im 19. Jahrhundert (Deutsches Textilmuseum Krefeld, March 24–June 23, 2002, curated by Elisabeth Hackspiel-Mikosch). Krefeld: Deutsches Textilmuseum Krefeld, 2002. An exhibition catalog.

Nardi, P. *Gay Masculinities*. London: Sage, 2000.

Nava, Mica. "Modernity's Disavowal: Women, the City and the Department Store." In *Modern Times: Reflections on a Century of English Modernity*, ed. Mica Nava and Alan O'Shea. London: Routledge, 1996.

Nead, Lynda. "Mapping the Self: Gender, Space and Modernity in Mid-Victorian London." In *Reuniting the Self: Histories from the Renaissance to the Present*, ed. Roy Porter. London: Routledge, 1996.

"New Look for Thriving Greeks." *Time*, March 10, 1986, 77.

Newman, Dorman, and T. Cockrel. *The Ancient Trades Decayed, Repaired Again*. London, 1678.

Newton, Esther. *Mother Camp: Female Impersonators in America*. Englewood Cliffs, NJ: Prentice Hall, 1972.

Newton, Samuel. *The Diary of Samuel Newton Alderman of Cambridge*. 1662–1717. Reprint, Cambridge: Cambridge Antiquarian Society, 1890.

Newton, Stella Mary. *Health, Art and Reason*. London: John Murray, 1974.

Nixon, Alan, and Harry Harris. "Football: Fashion Victim." *Daily Mirror*, October 1, 1999.

Nixon, S. "Distinguishing Looks: Masculinities, the Visual and Men's Magazines." In *Pleasure Principles: Politics, Sexuality and Ethics*, ed. Victoria Harwood, Kay Parkinson, and David Oswell. London: Lawrence and Wishart, 1993a.

Nixon, S. *Hard Looks: Masculinities, Spectatorship and Contemporary Consumption*. London: UCL; New York: St. Martins, 1996.

Nixon, S. "Have You Got the Look? Masculinities and Shopping Spectacles." In *Lifestyle Shopping: The Subject of Consumption*, ed. Rob Shields. London and New York: Routledge, 1992.

Nixon, S. "Looking for the Holy Grail: Publishing and Advertising Strategies for Contemporary Men's Magazines." *Cultural Studies*, 7, no. 3 (1993b): 467–92.

Noble, Jeanne. "A Sense of Place." *Essence*, May 1985, 131f.

Nystrom, P. H. *Economics of Fashion*. New York: Ronald Press, 1928.

O'Connor, John J. "'Elvis' The Series: Poor Boy Makes Good." *New York Times*, February 6, 1990.

O'Dwyer, T. "Are You Gauguin, New Colonial, or Savile Row?" *The Guardian*, August 28, 1986, 11.

O'Dwyer, T. "Liberated Man Power Arrives." *Men's Wear*, August 23, 1984, 8.

O'Dwyer, T. "Public Image." *Men's Wear*, July 5, 1984, 16.

O'Dwyer, T. "Style Counsel '85 ... New Blood." *Men's Wear*, December 20, 1984, 17.

"Of Course ... When You Say CALIFORNIA You're Saying Maurice Holman." *Men's Wear*, April 24, 1953, 133.

Ogborn, Miles. *Spaces of Modernity: London Geographies, 1680–1780*. New York and London: Guilford Press, 1998.

Ohnuki-Tierney, Emiko. *Kamikaze, Cherry Blossoms, and Nationalisms: The Militarization of Aesthetics in Japanese History*. Chicago: University of Chicago Press, 2001.

O'Malley, John W. *The First Jesuits*. Cambridge, MA, 1993.

O'Neill, Alistair. "John Stephen: A Carnaby Street Presentation of Masculinity 1957–1975." *Fashion Theory* 4, no. 4 (December 2000): 487–506.

O'Neill, Alistair. *London: After a Fashion*. London: Reaktion, 2007.

Opfer, Kirstin. *The Mexican American Experience: The Zoot Suit Riots*, 1999. http://frankandkirstin.com/id29.html.

Ordonez, Margaret Thompson. "A Frontier Reflected in Costume: Tallahassee, Leon County, Florida, 1824–1861." PhD diss., Florida State University, 1978.

Orgel, Stephen. *Impersonations: The Performance of Gender in Shakespeare's England.* Cambridge: Cambridge University Press, 1996.

Oriel, S. "The Ideal Homme Magazine." *Media Week,* February 12, 1988, 43–45.

Ormond, Leonée A. *Alfred Tennyson: A Literary Life.* London, 1993.

Orwell, G. *The Road to Wigan Pier.* 1937. London: Heinemann Educational, 1965.

Osborne, Thomas. *Thomas Osborne, Earl of Danby and Duke of Leeds, 1632–1712.* Ed. Andrew Browning. Glasgow: Jackson, Son, 1944.

Osgerby, Bill. *Playboys in Paradise: Masculinity, Youth and Leisure-Style in Modern America.* Oxford and New York: Berg, 2001.

"Over 1,200 to Attend Palm Springs Roundup Starting Tomorrow." *Los Angeles Daily News Record,* October 23, 1947.

Pagán, Eduardo Obregón. *Murder at the Sleepy Lagoon: Zoot Suits, Race, and Riot in Wartime L.A.* Chapel Hill: University of North Carolina Press, 2003.

"Palm Springs . . . Countless Promotional Opportunities." *Men's and Boys' Stylist,* September 1948.

Paoletti, Jo Barraclough. "Ridicule and Role Models as Factors in American Men's Fashion Change, 1880–1910." *Costume* 19 (1985): 121–34.

Parker, Geoffrey. *Philip II.* London: Hutchinson, 1979.

Parker, T. *The Plough Boy.* UK: Arrow Books, 1969.

Paston, George. *Social Caricature in the Eighteenth Century.* London: Methuen and Co., 1905.

Peacham, Henry. *The Worth of a Penny, Or, A Caution to Keep Money.* London: William Lee, 1647.

Peacocks and Pinstripes: A Snapshot of Masculine Style. London: The Fashion and Textile Museum, 2008.

Pendergast, Tom. *Creating the Modern Man: American Magazines and Consumer Culture, 1900–1950.* Columbia: University of Missouri Press, 2000.

Pennaccia, Mario. *Il Calcio in Italia.* 2 vols. Torino: UTET, 2000.

Pepys, Samuel. *Diary.* New York: Cassell, 1966.

Perrot, Philippe. *Fashioning the Bourgeoisie: A History of Clothing in the Nineteenth Century.* Trans. Richard Bienvenu. Princeton, NJ: Princeton University Press, 1994.

Picano, Felice. *The Lure.* New York: Hard Candy, 1996.

Pierson, B. T. *Directory of Newark.* Newark, NJ: Price & Lee, 1846–1847.

Pierson, H. A. Advertisement. *Floridian,* October 25, 1834.

Pietsch, Johannes, and Karen Stolleis, with a contribution by Nadine Piechatschek (2008). *Kölner Patrizier- und Bürgerkleidung des 17. Jahrhunderts: Die Kostümsammlung Hüpsch im Hessischen Landesmuseum Darmstadt.* Abegg-Stiftung: Riggisberger Berichte, vol. 15. 2008.

"Pink Powder Puffs." *Chicago Sunday Tribune,* July 18, 1926.

Pintard, John. *Letters from John Pintard to His Daughter.* New York: New-York Historical Society, 1940.

"The Playboy Reader." *Playboy* 2 (September 1955): 36–37.

"Playboy's Penthouse Apartment." *Playboy* 3, no. 9 (September 1956): 54–60.

"Playboy's Penthouse Apartment, Part II." *Playboy* 3, no. 10 (October 1956): 65–70.

Plummer, K. *The Making of the Modern Homosexual.* 2nd ed. London: Hutchinson, 2000.

[Plunkett, C.]. Lord Dunsany [pseudonym]. *If I Were Dictator: The Pronouncements of the Grand Macaroni.* London: Methuen, 1934.

Poe, Edgar Allan. "The Business Man." In *Comedies and Satires,* 100–108. New York: Penguin, 1987.

Poe, Edgar Allen. "Some Words with a Mummy." *American Review,* April 1845.

Pointon, Marcia. *Hanging the Head: Portraiture and Social Formation in Eighteenth-Century England.* New Haven, CT, and London: Yale University Press, 1993.

Polhemus, Ted. *Fashion and Anti-Fashion: An Anthropology of Clothing and Adornment.* London: Hudson, 1978.

Polhemus, Ted. *Street Style: From Sidewalk to Catwalk.* London: Thames and Hudson, 1994.

Polhemus, Ted. *Style Surfing: What to Wear in the 3rd Millennium.* London: Thames and Hudson, 1986.

Pope, Jesse Eliphant. *The Clothing Industry in New York.* Columbia: University of Missouri Press, 1905.

Porter, C. "A Cut Above." *Guardian,* May 25, 2001.

"A Potpourri of Student Concerns: What They're Reading, Wearing, Joining, Applauding, Protesting." *Chronicle of Higher Education,* September 4, 1985, 30–32.

Priestley, J. B. *English Journey*. 1934. London: The Folio Society, 1997.

Pritchard, Rosalind. *London and Londoners: What to See: What to Do: When to Shop: And Practical Hints*. London: Scientific Press, 1898.

"Promoting California." *California Men's Stylist* 3 (January 1944): 43.

Prude, Jonathan. "To Look upon the 'Lower Sort': Runaway Ads and the Appearance of Unfree Laborers in America, 1750–1800." *Journal of American History* 78, no. 1 (June 1991): 124–59.

"P.S.R.U. [Palm Springs Round Up] Guest Register." *California Apparel News*, October 29, 1948.

Pugh, Edwin. *The City of the World: A Book about London and the Londoner*. London: Thomas Nelson, 1908.

Purcel, C. "Flying Colours." *Sydney Morning Herald*, Spectrum, Weekend Edition, January 15–16, 2005, 16.

Quicherat, J. *Histoire du Costume en France depuis les temps les plus reculés jusqu'à la fin du XVIIIe siècle*. Paris: Hachette, 1875.

Quinn, Carin C. "The Jeaning of America—and the World." *American Heritage*, April 1978, 14–21.

Quinn, Krystal. "Fraternity Protests Apartheid." *The Washington Post*, July 31, 1986.

Racinet, Auguste. *Le costume historique*. Paris: Firmin-Didot, 1888.

Radcliffe, Susan M., ed. *Sir Joshua's Nephew. Being Letters written, 1769–1778, by a Young Man to his Sisters*. London: John Murray, 1930.

Radner, H. *Shopping Around: Feminine Culture and the Pursuit of Pleasure*. London: Routledge, 1995.

Ramming, Jochen. "Motivation! Disziplin! Autorität! Zu den Lenkungswirkungen der bayerischen Beamtenuniformierung zwischen 1799 und 1848." In *Nach Rang und Stand: Deutsche Ziviluniformen im 19. Jahrhundert* (Deutsches Textilmuseum Krefeld, March 24–June 23, 2002, curated by Elisabeth Hackspiel-Mikosch). Krefeld: Deutsches Textilmuseum Krefeld, 2002.

Ratner, Elaine. "Levi's." *Dress* 1 (1975): 1–5.

Rawsthorn, A. "The Hit: Why It Failed So Miserably to Reach Its Male Target." *Campaign*, November 15, 1985, 15.

Read, B., and H. Bodman. *New Superlative System of Cutting*. London and New York, 1837.

Reade, Brian. *The Dominance of Spain, 1550–1660*. London, 1951.

Rechy, John. *City of Night*. New York: Grove, 1964; New York: Evergreen, 1984.

Rechy, John. *Numbers*. New York: Grove, 1984.

Redhead, Steve. *Football with Attitude*. Manchester, UK: Wordsmith, 1991.

Redhead, Steve, ed. *The Passion and the Fashion: Football Fandom in New Europe*. Aldershot, UK: Avebury, 1993.

Redhead, Steve. *Subculture to Clubcultures: An Introduction to Popular Cultural Studies*. Oxford: Blackwell, 1997.

Reed, Christopher. "Introduction." In *Not at Home: The Suppression of Domesticity in Modern Art and Architecture*, ed. Christopher Reed. London: Thames and Hudson, 1996.

Reilly, Maureen. *California Casual: Fashions, 1930s–1970s*. Atglen, PA: Schiffer, 2001.

Renbourn, E. T., and W. H. Rees. *Materials and Clothing in Health and Disease*. London: H. K. Lewis, 1972.

Revelle, M. Letters, "The Specialist Press: An Ideal Youth Target." *Campaign*, November 29, 1985, 28.

Reynolds, R. *Superheroes: A Modern Mythology*. London: B. T. Batsford, 1992.

Reynolds, Stanley. *Punch* (April 1983).

Reynolds, S., and J. Press. *The Sex Revolts: Gender, Rebellion and Rock and Roll*. London: Serpent's Tail, 1995.

Ribeiro, Aileen. *Dress and Morality*. New York: Holmes and Meier, 1986.

Richards, J. *The Age of the Dream Palace: Cinema and Society in Britain 1930–1939*. 1984. London: Routledge, 1989.

Ridge, William Pett. *I Like to Remember*. London: Hodder & Stoughton, 1925.

Riesman, David. *The Lonely Crowd: A Study of the Changing American Character*. Garden City, NY: Doubleday, 1953.

Ritchie, B. "Tête-à-tête with The Face." *The Sunday Times*, March 7, 1982, 54.

Riviere, Joan. "Womanliness as a Masquerade." In *Formations of Fantasy*, ed. Victor Burgin, James Donald, and Cora Kaplan. 1929. London: Methuen, 1986.

Roach, Mary Ellen, and Joanne B. Eicher. *The Visible Self: Perspectives on Dress*. Englewood Cliffs, NJ: Prentice-Hall, 1973.

Robinson, Revd Hastings, ed. *Zurich Letters: 2nd Series*. Cambridge: Cambridge University Press, 1845.

Roche, Daniel. *The Culture of Clothing: Dress and Fashion in the "Ancien régime."* Trans. Jean Birrell. Cambridge: Cambridge University Press, 1994.

Rock, P., and S. Cohen. "The Teddy Boy." In *The Age of Affluence, 1951–1964,* ed. V Bogdanor and R. Skidelsky. London: Macmillan, 1970.

Rojek, C. *Capitalism and Leisure Theory.* London: Tavistock, 1985.

Rose, William Watts, Jr. "Palm Springs: Highs in the Roundup." *Apparel Arts,* December 1949.

Rosenberg, Sharon, and Joan Wiener Bordow. *The Denim Book.* Englewood Cliffs, NJ: Prentice Hall, 1978.

Rosenberg, Sharon, and Joan Wiener. *The Illustrated Hassle-Free Make Your Own Clothes Book.* San Francisco: Straight Arrow Press, 1971.

Ross, Andrew. "Uses of Camp." In *No Respect: Intellectuals and Popular Culture.* New York: Routledge, 1989.

Ross, William P. M. *The Accountant's Own Book and Business Man's Manual.* Philadelphia: G. B. Zieber, 1848.

"Roundup Huge Success." *California Apparel News,* November 5, 1948.

Rousseau, Jean-Jacques. *Emile.* 1762. Trans. Barbara Foxley. London: J. M. Dent, 1993.

Rudofsky, Bernard. *Are Clothes Modern? An Essay on Contemporary Apparel.* Chicago: Paul Theobald, 1947. Reprinted as *The Unfashionable Human Body* (New York: Anchor Books, Doubleday, 1971), new edition with different plates from the 1947 text *Are Clothes Modern?*

Rule, Sheila. "The Men Who Would Be Elvis." *New York Times,* June 26, 1990.

Rupp, Becky. "In Praise of Bluejeans: The Denimization of America." *Blair Ketchum's Country Journal,* December 1985, 82–86.

Rushgrove, B. A. *The Birth of the Edwardians.* N.d. http://www.metronet.co.uk/marl/birth.htm(accessed June 2, 2003).

Russell, Douglas A. *Costume History and Style.* Englewood Cliffs, NJ: Prentice-Hall, 1983.

Rutherford, Blake. "Formal Forecast: The Return to Black." *Playboy* 5, no. 1 (January 1958): 60–62.

Rutherford, Blake. "Ivy Action: The Right Look for the Beach, Boating, Tennis and the Links." *Playboy* 4, no. 7 (July 1957): 20–22.

Rutherford, J. "Who's That Man?" In *Male Order: Unwrapping Masculinity,* ed. R. Chapman and J. Rutherford. London: Lawrence and Wishart, 1988.

Ruttenberg, E. M. "Palm Springs Preview." *Men's Wear,* September 24, 1948, 61–67.

Ryan, P. "Going to Business in London." In *Living London,* ed. George Sims. Vol. 1. London: Cassell, 1903.

Ryder Brothers. Advertisement. *New York Herald,* June 25, 1844.

Ryon, Art. "Plunging Neckline in Male Styles." *Los Angeles Times,* October 28, 1957.

Sabin, R., ed. *Punk Rock: So What? The Cultural Legacy of Punk.* London: Routledge, 1999.

Saleeby, C. W. *The Methods of Race Regeneration.* London: Cassell, 1911.

Saleeby, C. W. *Practical Dress Reform.* Report of the Committee on Designs of the Men's Dress Reform Party, 1929.

Sánchez, George. *Becoming Mexican American: Ethnicity, Culture and Identity in Chicano Los Angeles, 1900–1945.* New York: Oxford University Press, 1993.

Sancroft, William. *Lex Ignea: Or the School of Righteousness.* London: Timothy Garthwait. 1666.

Sand, Jordan. *House and Home in Modern Japan: Architecture, Domestic Space, and Bourgeois Culture 1880–1930.* Cambridge, MA: Harvard University Press, 2003.

Sandberg, M. *Living Pictures, Missing Persons: Mannequins, Museums and Modernity.* Princeton, NJ: Princeton University Press, 2003.

Sanders, Joel, ed. *Stud: Architectures of Masculinity.* New York: Princeton Architectural Press, 1996.

Sandford, Francis. *The Order and Ceremonies Used for, and at the Solemn Internment of the Most High, Mighty and Most Noble Prince George Duke of Albemarle.* London: Francis Sandford, 1670.

Sandilands, J. "Whatever Happened to the Teddy Boys?" *Daily Telegraph Magazine* 217 (November 29, 1968).

Sandys, W., ed. *Specimens of Macaronic Poetry.* London: Richard Beckley, 1831.

Sanford & Knowles. Advertisement. *Carroll's New York City Directory, 1859.* New York: Carroll, 1859.

Savage, J. *Time Travel: From the Sex Pistols to Nirvana: Pop, Media and Sexuality, 1977–96.* London: Chatto & Windus, 1996.

Savil, George, First Marquis of Halifax. *The Character of a Trimmer.* London: n.p., 1688.

Scagnetti, Jack. *The Intimate Life of Rudolph Valentino.* Middle Village, NY: Jonathan David, 1975.

Schama, Simon. *The Embarrassment of Riches.* London, 1987.

Schecter, Laurie. "Red-Hot Blues." *Rolling Stone,* May 8, 1986, 67–71.

Schehl, Carl. *Vom Rhein zur Moskwa, Erinnerungen des jüngsten niederrheinischen Veteranen der großen Armee.* 1812. Ed. Jürgen Olmes. Krefeld: Obermann, 1957.

Schmale, Wolfgang. *Geschichte der Männlichkeit in Europa (1450–2000).* Vienna: Böhlau, 2003.

Schrager, Rick H. "The Impact of Living Group Social Climate on Student Academic Performance." *Research in Higher Education* 25 (1986): 265–76.

Schwartz, Carol Halpert. "Retail Trade Development in New York State in the Nineteenth Century, with Special Reference to the Country Store." PhD diss., Columbia University, 1963.

Scott, Genio, and James Wilson. *A Treatise on Cutting Garments to Fit the Human Form … Accompanied by a Periodical Report of Fashions.* New York, 1841.

Scott, Vernon. "Elvis Ten Million Dollars Later." *McCall's,* February 1963, 124.

Scott and Perkins. *The Tailor's Master-Piece, Being the Tailor's Complete Guide, for Instruction in the Whole Art of Measuring and Cutting, According to the Variety of Fashion and Form, with Plates, Illustrative of the Same.* New York, 1837.

Searle, G. R. *Eugenics and Politics in Britain 1900–1914.* Leyden: Noordhoff International Publishing, 1976.

Sears, Roebuck and Company. *1908 Catalogue, no. 117: The Great Price Marker.* Chicago: Follett, 1969.

Segal, L. *Slow Motion: Changing Masculinities, Changing Men.* London: Virago, 1990.

Segal, Lynne. *Straight Sex: The Politics of Pleasure.* London: Virago, 1994.

Seidler, Franz. *Das Militär in der Karikatur: Kaiserliches Heer, Reichswehr, Wehrmacht, Bundeswehr, Nationale Volksarmee im Spiegel der Pressezeitung.* Munich: Bernard und Graefe, 1982.

Seltzer, Mark. *Bodies and Machines.* New York: Routledge, 1992.

Sennett, R. *The Fall of Public Man.* Cambridge: Cambridge University Press, 1977.

Sennett, Richard. *Flesh and Stone: The Body and the City in Western Civilization.* New York: Norton, 1996.

[Settle, Elkanah.] *Pastor Fido: Or, The Faithful Shepherd.* London: William Cademan, 1677.

Shakespeare, William. *Hamlet.* In *Works of William Shakespeare: Hamlet,* ed. Harold Jenkins. London: Arden, 1982.

Shakespeare, William. *The Merchant of Venice.* Ed. John Russell Brown. London, 1959.

Shakespeare, William. *Othello.* Ed. M. R. Ridley. London: Arden [sic], 1958.

Shakespeare, William. *Titus Andronicus.* Ed. J. C. Maxwell. London: New Arden, 1953.

Shammas, Carole. *The Pre-Industrial Consumer in England and America.* Oxford: Clarendon, 1990.

Shannon, Brent. *The Cut of His Coat: Men, Dress and Consumer Culture in Britain, 1860–1914.* Athens: Ohio University Press, 2006.

Shaw, Donald. *London in the Sixties by One of the Old Brigade.* London: Everett & Co., 1908.

Shea, Robert. "Yesterday's Leggings Are Today's Fashion Craze." *Today's Health,* March 1975, 29.

"Sheer Joy with My Sexy Toyboy." *The Sun,* February 15, 1987, 9.

Sheldon & Co.'s Business or Advertising Directory. New York: John E Trow & Co., 1845.

Shephard, John, of New York, N.Y. Merchant Tailoring Accounts, Ac. 861 and Ac. 1721. Special Collections, Rutgers University, New Brunswick, New Jersey.

"Sheriff of Los Angeles." *California Men's Stylist* 4 (January 1945): 46.

Shields, R. "Feel Good Here?" In *Critical Urban Perspectives,* ed. J. Caulfield and L. Peake. Toronto: University of Toronto Press, 1997.

Shields, R. *Places on the Margin.* London: Routledge, 1989.

Shumway, D. R. "Rock & Roll as a Cultural Practice." In *Present Tense: Rock 'n' Roll and Contemporary Culture,* ed. A. DeCurtis. Durham, NC, and London: Duke University Press, 1992.

Shūzō, Kuki. *Iki no kōzō* (Reflections on Japanese Taste: The Structure of *Iki*). Trans. John Clark. Sydney, Australia: Power Publications, 1997.

Siegfried, Susan L. *The Art of Louis-Leopold Boilly: Modern Life in Napoleonic France.* New Haven, CT: Yale University Press, 1995.

Sigsworth, E. M. *Montague Burton: The Tailor of Taste.* Manchester, UK: Manchester University Press, 1990.

Silverman, Kaja. "Fragments of a Fashionable Discourse." In *Studies in Entertainment: Critical*

Approaches to Mass Culture, ed. Tania Modleski. Bloomington: Indiana University Press, 1986.

Silverman, Kaja. *Male Subjectivity at the Margins.* London: Routledge, 1992.

Silverman, Kenneth. *Edgar A. Poe: Mournful and Never-Ending Remembrance.* New York: Harper Perennial, 1991.

Simons, Seward C. "Dressing Up Los Angeles." *Southern California Business* 7 (February 1928): 18.

Simons, Seward C. "The West's Greatest Garment Center." *Southern California Business* 4 (October 1925): 17.

Simpson, M. *It's a Queer World.* London: Vintage, 1996.

Simpson, Mark. *Male Impersonators: Men Performing Masculinity.* New York: Routledge, 1994.

Sims, George. "Off the Track in London: Around Hackney Wick." *The Strand Magazine,* September 1904, 40.

Sinclair, J. G. *Portrait of Oxford.* Sturry, UK: Veracity, 1931.

"A Six Dollar Stone Wash." *Newsweek,* September 22, 1986, 77.

Slutsker, Gary. "The Smoking Bun." *Forbes,* March 25, 1985, 210.

Smelik, A. "Gay and Lesbian Criticism." In *The Oxford Guide to Film Studies,* ed. J. Hill and P. Church Gibson. Oxford: Oxford University Press, 1998.

Smith, K. "A Superman for all Seasons." *T.V. Guide,* December 8, 2004.

Smith, Liz. "Gossip." *San Francisco Chronicle,* May 9, 1990.

Smith, Terry. *Making the Modern: Industry, Art and Design in America.* Chicago: Chicago University Press, 1993.

Sombart, W. "Economy and Fashion: A Theoretical Contribution on the Formation of Modern Consumer Demand." 1902. Reprinted in *The Rise of Fashion: A Reader,* ed. D. L. Purdy. Minneapolis and London: University of Minnesota Press, 2006.

Sontag, Susan. "Notes on Camp." In *Against Interpretation.* 1966. New York: Octagon, 1978.

"A Sorority Sets New Goals." *New York Times,* May 28, 1983, national edition.

Southworth, Eleanor Ewart. "Mirrors for a Growing Metropolis: Printed Views of Broadway, 1830–1850." Master's thesis, University of Delaware, 1985.

Spencer, Mimi. "How Can England Score in Beige?" *Evening Standard,* June 8, 1998.

Spooner, John D. "Bow Ties: Some Rules of Thumb for the Neck." *Atlantic Monthly,* November 1995, 46–49.

"Sportswear Concern Opens $2 Million Unit." *Los Angeles Times,* September 25, 1960.

"Sportswear: How California Captured the Sportswear Market." *California Stylist* 3 (February 1939): 5.

"Sportswear Round Up at Palm Springs." *California Men's Stylist* 1 (January 1942): 51.

Stafford, B. *Artful Science.* Cambridge, MA: MIT Press, 1994.

Stafford, B. *Body Criticism.* Cambridge, MA: MIT Press, 1993.

Staniland, Kay. "Clothing Provision and the Great Wardrobe in the Mid-Thirteenth Century." *Textile History* 22 (1991): 239–252.

Stanton, Donna C. *The Aristocrat as Art: A Study of the Honnête Homme and the Dandy in Seventeenth- and Nineteenth-Century French Literature.* New York: Columbia University Press, 1980.

Steele, R., ed. *Tudor and Stuart Royal Proclamations, 1485–1714.* Oxford: Oxford University Press, 1910.

Steele, Valerie. "The Social and Political Significance of Macaroni Fashion." *Costume* 19 (1985): 94–109.

Stemper, William H. (Rev.). "Fraternities, Where Men May Come to Terms with Other Men." Editorial, *New York Times,* June 16, 1985, national edition.

Stephens, Frederick George, and Edward Hawkins. *Catalogue of Prints and Drawings in the British Museum. Division I. Political and Personal Satires, 4, AD 1761—c. AD 1770.* London: Trustees of the British Museum, 1883.

Stern, J. David. "The King Is Back." *TV Guide* 38, no. 7 (February 1990): 6–7.

Stinemets, W. H. *A Complete and Permanent System of Cutting.* New York: Narine, 1844.

Stinemets. Advertisement. *New York Herald,* May 1, 1846.

Stirling, A.M.W. *Annals of a Yorkshire House from the Papers of a Macaroni & His Kindred.* 2 vols. London: John Lane, 1911.

Stokes, Charles, and Edward T. Taylor. *Charles Stokes & Co.'s Illustrated Almanac of Fashion.* Philadelphia, 1864.

Stone, George Winchester, Jr., and George M. Kahrl. *David Garrick, A Critical Biography.* Carbondale and Edwardsville: Southern Illinois University Press, 1979.

Stone, Lawrence. *The Crisis of the Aristocracy.* Oxford: Clarendon, 1965.

Strange, Carney. "Greek Affiliation and Goal of the Academy: A Commentary." *Journal of College Student Personnel* 27 (1986): 519–23.

Straw, W. "Popular Music and Postmodernism in the 1980s." In *Sound and Vision: The Music Video Reader,* ed. S. Frith, A. Goodwin, and L. Grossberg. London: Routledge, 1993.

Street, J. *Politics and Popular Culture.* Cambridge: Polity, 1997.

Strong, George Templeton. *The Diary of George Templeton Strong, Young Man in New York, 1835–1849,* ed. Allan Nevins. New York: Macmillan, 1952.

Strong, Roy. "Charles I's Clothes for the Years 1633 to 1635." *Costume* 14 (1980): 73–89.

"Styles for the City of Los Angeles." *Southern California Business* 5 (February 1926): 28.

Sullivan, Robert J. "Stitch in Time." *Wall Street Journal,* January 20, 1948.

"Sun and Swim Fashions." *Men's Wear,* January 9, 1953, 39.

Surman, P. *Pride of the Morning: An Oxford Childhood.* Stroud, UK: Alan Sutton, 1992.

Sutton, Anne F. "Order and Fashion in Clothes: The King, His Household and the City of London at the End of the Fifteenth Century." *Textile History* 22, no. 2 (1991): 253–76.

Swanson, D. J., ed. "Reporting on a Wartime Social Experience: Heroes, Hooligans, and the Zoot Suit Riots." Paper presented at the 41st Annual Conference of the Western Social Science Association, Fort Worth, Texas (April 23, 1999). Net Library.

Swienicki, Mark A. "Consuming Brotherhood: Men's Culture, Style and Recreation as Consumer Culture, 1880–1930." In *Consumer Society in American History: A Reader,* ed. Lawrence B. Glickman, 207–40. Ithaca, NY: Cornell University Press, 1999.

Tacitus. *The Agricola and the Germanica.* London: Penguin, 1975.

Tait, Hugh, ed. *The Art of the Jeweller.* London: British Museum, 1984.

Tantner, A. "Jazz Youth Subculture in Nazi Europe." *ISHA Journal: History of Daily Life* 2, no. 94 (1994): 2228, http://mailbox.univieac.at/anton. Tantner/publikationem/TantnerJazzYouthsubcultures_ISHAJournall994_2.pdf.

Taylor, Barbara. "'The Men Are as Bad as Their Masters …': Socialism, Feminism and Sexual Antagonism in the London Tailoring Trade in the 1830s." In *Sex and Class in Women's History,* ed. Judith L. Newton, Mary P. Ryan, and Judith R. Walkowitz. London: Routledge & Kegan Paul, 1983.

Taylor, Kerry. "Bunny Roger: The Wardrobe of a 20th Century Dandy." In *The Roger Collection.* London: Sotheby's, January 28–30, 1998.

Taylor, Kerry. "Inside the Windsor Style: The Wardrobe of the Duke of Windsor." In *Property from the Collection of The Duke and Duchess of Windsor.* New York: Sotheby's, September 11–19, 1997. Information volume.

Taylor, Lou. Review of "John Harvey, Men in Black, London, Reaktion Books, 1995." *Journal of Design History* 9, no. 4 (1996): 301–303.

Taylor, S. "Magazines for Men: On the Trail of the Typically British Male." *Campaign,* August 29, 1986, 44.

Temin, Peter. *The Jacksonian Economy.* New York: W. W. Norton, 1969.

Tennyson, G. B. *Sartor Called Resartus: The Genesis, Structure and Style of Thomas Carlyle's First Major Work.* Princeton, NJ: Princeton University Press, 1965.

Terry, Samuel. *How to Keep a Store.* New York: Fowler & Wells, 1891.

Tharpe, Jac L. *Elvis: Images and Fancies.* Jackson: University of Mississippi Press, 1979.

Theweleit, Klaus. *Male Fantasies.* Cambridge: Polity, 1987.

"They're Still Talking about Palm Springs!" *California Men's Stylist* 1 (April 1942): 29.

This Fabulous Century: Sixty Years of American Life. New York: Time-Life, 1969.

Thomas, Bob. *Liberace.* New York: St. Martin's Press, 1987.

Thomas, David, ed. *Theatre in Europe: A Documentary History. Restoration and Georgian England, 1660–1788.* Cambridge: Cambridge University Press, 1989.

Thompson, E. P. *Customs in Common.* London: Penguin, 1993.

Thompson, F.M.L., ed. *The Rise of Suburbia.* Leicester, UK: Leicester University Press, 1982.

Thompson, R. *African Art in Motion: Icon and Act.* Los Angeles, Berkeley, and London: University of California Press, 1974.

Thornton, S. *Club Cultures: Music, Media and Subcultural Capital.* Cambridge: Polity/Wesleyan University Press, 1995.

Thwaite, A., ed. *My Oxford.* 1976. London: Robson, 1986.

Tillyard, Stell. *Aristocrats: Caroline, Emily, Louisa, and Sarah Lennox 1740–1832.* New York: Farrar, Straus and Giroux, 1994.

Todhunter, Hazel. *Make It in Denim.* New York: Taplinger, 1977.

Tolson, A. "The Language of Fatalism." *Working Papers in Cultural Studies,* no. 9 (1977): 147–154. University of Birmingham.

Tomlins, Christopher L. *Law, Labor, and Ideology in the Early American Republic.* New York: Cambridge University Press, 1993.

Torbet, Laura. *Clothing Liberation: Or Out of the Closet and Into the Streets.* New York: Ballantine, 1973.

Tovares, J. (producer). *The Zoot Suit Riots* (documentary). 2001. http://www.pbs.org/wgbh/amex/zoot/eng_timeline/index.html (accessed May 14, 2003).

Toynbee, P. "The Incredible, Shrinking New Man." *The Guardian,* April 6, 1987, 10.

Toynbee, Paget, ed. *Satirical Poems Published Anonymously by William Mason with Notes by Horace Walpole, Now First Printed from His Manuscript.* Oxford: Clarendon, 1926.

Trautman, Patricia A. "Captain Edward Marrett, a Gentleman Tailor." PhD diss., University of Colorado, 1982.

Trevelyan, George Otto. *The Early History of Charles James Fox.* London: Longman, Green, and Co., 1880.

Tseëlon, E. "From Fashion to Masquerade: Towards an Ungendered Paradigm." In *Body Dressing,* ed. J. Entwhistle and E. Wilson. Oxford: Berg, 2001.

Tsukahira, Toshio George. *Feudal Control in Tokugawa Japan: The Sankin-kôtai System.* Cambridge, MA: Harvard University Press, 1966.

Turbin, Carole. "Collars and Consumers: Changing Images of American Manliness and Business." In *Beauty and Business: Commerce, Gender, and Culture in Modern America,* ed. Philip Scranton. New York: Routledge, 2001.

Turner, C. S. "The City at High Noon." In *Living London,* ed. G. Sims. Vol. 2. London: Cassell, 1903.

Turner, V. *Process, Performance and Pilgrimage.* New Delhi: Concept, 1979.

Turner, Victor. *The Anthropology of Performance.* New York: PAJ, 1988.

Ulrich, Bernd, Jakob Vogel, and Benjamin Ziemann, eds. *Untertan in Uniform: Militär und Militarismus im Kaiserreich 1871–1914.* Frankfurt/M.: Fischer-Taschenbuch-Verlag, 2001.

Universal Magazine of Knowledge and Pleasure, October 1772.

U.S. Census Office. *Manufactures of the United States in 1860.* Compiled from the Original Returns of the Eighth Census. Washington, DC: Government Printing Office, 1865.

U.S. Census Office. Seventh Census, Manufactures Schedule, raw data, New York County, New York, 1850.

U.S. Department of Commerce, Business and Defense Services Administration. *Leisure and Work Clothing.* Washington, DC: Government Printing Office, 1961.

Usher, John. *City of London Past and Present.* Oxford: Oxford Illustrated Press, 1976.

Uspensky, B. A. "Antipovedenie v kulture drevnej Rusi." In *Izbrannie trydi.* Moscow: Gnozis, 1994.

Vaidhanathan, Siva. "A Bombs, Bebop and C Rations: Jazz as Cultural Call to Arms against 1940's Anxieties." *Jazz and American Culture* (Fall 1997), online.

Vainshtein, Olga. *Dandy; moda, literatyra, stil zhizni.* Moscow: NLO, 2006.

Van DeBurg, W. L. *New Day in Babylon: The Black Power Movement and American Culture, 1965–1975.* Chicago and London: University of Chicago Press, 1992.

Vanderbilt, C. *Ranches and Ranch Life in America.* New York: Crown, 1968.

van Zanten, N. "In Search of Elusive Youth." *Campaign,* March 16, 1984, 63–64.

Varey, Simon. *Space and the Eighteenth-Century English Novel.* Cambridge: Cambridge University Press, 1990.

Varney, Carleton. *The Draper Touch: The High Life and High Style of Dorothy Draper.* New York: Prentice Hall, 1988.

The Vauxhall Affray: Or, the Macaroni Defeated (1773), quoted in *The Visibility of Visuality: Vision in Context,* by Peter de Bolla. Ed. T. Brennan and M. Jay. New York: Routledge, 1996.

Veblen, T. *The Theory of the Leisure Class.* 1899. New York: The Modern Library, 1939; New York: Dover, 1994.

Vickery, Amanda. *The Gentleman's Daughter: Women's Lives in Georgian England.* New Haven, CT, and London: Yale University Press, 1988.

Vigarello, Georges. *Concepts of Cleanliness: Changing Attitudes in France since the Middle Ages.* Trans. Jean Birrell. Cambridge: Cambridge University Press, 1988. Originally published in French as *Le Propre et le sale* (Paris: Editions du Seuil, 1985).

Vigarello, Georges. "The Upward Training of the Body from the Age of Chivalry to Courtly Civility." In *Fragments for a History of the Human Body,* ed. Michel Feher with Ramona Naddaff and Nadia Tazi, part 2, 148–199. New York: Zone, 1989.

Vincent, Sue. "To Fashion a Self: Dressing in Seventeenth-Century England." *Fashion Theory* 3, no. 2 (June 1999): 197–218.

von Rohr, Julius Bernhard. *Einleitung zur Ceremoniel-Wissenschaft der grossen Herren.* Ed. Monika Schlechte. 1733. Leipzig: Edition Leipzig, 1990.

Votolato, Gregory. *American Design in the Twentieth Century.* Manchester, UK, and New York: Manchester University Press, 1998.

Wafeer, Howard. "In Boots and Boutiques George Was Always the Best." *The Journal,* August 3, 1999.

Wagner, Peter, ed. *The Languages of Civil Society.* New York and Oxford: Berghahn Books, 2006.

Walden, G. *Who Is a Dandy?* London: Gibson Square Books, 2002.

Walker, Alexander. *Rudolph Valentino.* London: Elm Tree Books/Hamish Hamilton, 1976.

Walker, H. R. "The Outdoor Movement in England and Wales, 1900–1939." PhD diss., University of Sussex, 1987.

Walker, Isaac. *Dress: As It Has Been, Is, and Will Be.* New York: Isaac Walker, 1885.

Walker, Lynne. "Vistas of Pleasure: Women Consumers of Urban Space in the West End of London 1850–1900." In *Women in the Victorian Art World,* ed. C. Campbell Orr. Manchester, UK: Manchester University Press, 1995.

Walkerdine, Valerie. *Schoolgirl Fictions.* London and New York: Verso, 1990.

Walpole, B. C. *Recollections of the Life of the Late Right Honourable Charles James Fox; exhibiting a faithful account of the most remarkable events of his political career, and a delineation of his character as a statesman, senator, and man of fashion* . . . London: James Cundee, 1806.

Walters, B. "Take It like a Man." In *The Fab Book of Pop,* ed. H. Kureishi and J. Savage. London: Faber & Faber, 1993.

Ward, Samuel A., and Asahel F. Ward. *The Philadelphia Fashions and Tailors' Archetypes.* Philadelphia: n.p., 1849.

Ward, William. "Letter from Rome." *The Face,* May 1990, 50–51.

Warner Bros, USA. "Pressbook." *Barry Lyndon.* Warner Bros., 1976.

Warren, Carol. *Identity and Community in the Gay World.* New York: John Wiley and Sons, 1974.

Warwick, A. and Cavallaro, D. *Fashioning the Frame: Boundaries, Dress and the Body.* Oxford: Berg, 1998.

Washington, Joseph R., Jr. *Anti-Blackness in English Religion, 1500–1800.* New York, 1984.

Waugh, E. *Brideshead Revisited.* 1945. London: Penguin, 1980.

Waugh, Norah. *The Cut of Men's Clothes, 1600–1900.* London: Faber and Faber, 1964. Reprint, New York: Theatre Arts Books, 1987.

Weatherill, Lorna. *Consumer Behaviour and Material Culture in Britain 1660–1760.* 2nd ed. London and New York: Routledge, 1996.

Weatherill, Lorna. "Consumer Behaviour, Textiles and Dress in the Late Seventeenth and Early Eighteenth Centuries." *Textile History* 22, no. 2 (1991): 297–310.

Webb, Ben. "You'll Never Score in That Kit, Boys." *The Times,* June 6, 1998.

Weeks, J. *Sexuality and Its Discontents: Meanings, Myth and Modern Sexuality.* 1985. London: Routledge, 1999.

Weeks, J., and K. Porter. *Between the Acts: Lives of Homosexual Men 1885–1967.* 1991. London: Rivers Oram, 1998.

Wenzel, Siegfried. *Macaronic Sermons: Bilingualism and Preaching in Late-Medieval England.* Ann Arbor: University of Michigan Press, 1994.

West, C. "The New Cultural Politics of Difference." In *Out There: Marginalization and Contemporary Culture,* ed. R. Ferguson, M. Grever, T. T. Minh-ha, and C. West. New York: The New Museum of Contemporary Arts, 1990.

"West Germany: A Booming Market in Counterfeit Jeans." *Business Week,* August 8, 1977, 37–39.

"What with Repeal and All, the Shirtless Swimmers Are Going In for a 'Nude Deal' All Their Own." *Apparel Arts* 4 (1934): 71.

White, Charles. *The Life and Times of Little Richard.* New York: Pocket Books, 1984.

White, Cynthia L. *Women's Magazines 1693–1968.* London: Michael Joseph, 1970.

White, Jim. "FA Cup Final." *Guardian,* May 20, 2000, sport section, 1–2.

White, S., and G. White. *Stylin': African American Expressive Culture from Its Beginnings to the Zoot Suit.* Ithaca, NY: Cornell University Press, 1998.

Whiting, R. C. *The View from Cowley: The Impact of Industrialization upon Oxford, 1918–1939.* Oxford: Clarendon, 1983.

Whittock, Nathaniel. *The Complete Book of Trades.* London: John Bennett, 1837.

Whyte, William Hollingsworth. *The Organization Man.* New York: Simon & Shuster, 1956.

Wilder, David, and Arlyne E. Hoyt "Greek Affiliation and Attitude Change: A Reply to Jakobsen and Strange." *Journal of College Student Personnel* 27 (1986): 527–30.

Wilder, David H., Arlyne E. Hoyt, Beth Shuster Surbeck, Janet C. Wilder, and Patricia Imperatrice Carney. "Greek Affiliation and Attitude Change in College Students." *Journal of College Student Personnel* 27 (1986): 510–19.

Willett, C., and Phillis Cunnington. *Handbook of English Costume in the Eighteenth Century.* Boston: Plays Inc., 1972.

Williams, Edwin, ed. *Citizens' Advertising Directory.* New York: J. Disturnell, 1833.

Williams, John. "English Football Stadiums after Hillsborough." *The Stadium and the City,* ed. John Bale and Olof Moen. Stoke-on-Trent, UK: Keele University Press, 1995.

Williams, John, and Stephen Wagg, eds. *British Football and Social Change: Getting into Europe.* Leicester, UK: Leicester University Press, 1991.

Williams, Leonard. Letter to editor. *New Health,* August 1929.

Williams, Rosalind. *Dream Worlds: Mass Consumption in Late Nineteenth Century France.* Berkeley: University of California Press, 1982.

Williamson, J. "Above the World." *New Statesman* 112, no. 2898 (October 10, 1986): 25.

Williamson, J. "Male Order." *New Statesman* 112, no. 2901 (October 31, 1986): 25.

Willis, D. *Early Days in Oxford.* Oxford: Amate, 1987.

Willis, Nathaniel Parker. "Ephemera." In *Dashes at Life with a Free Pencil.* New York: J. S. Redfield, 1847.

Willis, Nathaniel Parker. "Walk in Broadway." *New Mirror,* October 21, 1843.

Wilson, A. Foreword. In *Speak My Name: Black Men on Masculinity and the American Dream,* ed. D. Belton. Boston: Beacon, 1995.

Wilson, E. *Adorned in Dreams, Fashion and Modernity.* London: Virago, 1985.

Wilson, Sloan. *What Shall We Wear to This Party?: The Man in the Gray Flannel Suit Twenty Years Before and After.* New York: Arbor, 1976.

Winckelmann, Johann Joachim. *Geschichte des klassischen Altertums.* Dresden, 1764. Reprint, Berlin: E-Book Edition, 2003. http://www.math.hu-berlin.de/~mrw/Geschichte_der_Kunst_des_Altertums.pdf.

Windsor, The Duchess of. *The Heart Has Its Reasons.* London: Readers' Book Club, 1958.

Winship, J. "A Girl Needs to Get Street-Wise: Magazines for the 1980s." *Feminist Review* 21 (1987a): 25–46. Also published in *Inside Women's Magazines* (London: Pandora, 1987).

Winship, J. *Inside Women's Magazines.* London: Pandora, 1987b.

Wise, N. *Suede: An Illustrated Biography.* London: Omnibus, 1998.

Wolf, T. *Radical Chic Mau-mauing the Flak Catchers.* New York: Farrar, Straus and Giroux, 1970.

Wolter, Gundula. *Die Verpackung des männlichen Geschlechts: Eine illustrierte Geschichte der Hose.* Berlin: Aufbau-Taschenbuch-Verlag, 2001.

Wood, Anthony. *The Life and Times of Anthony Wood, Antiquary, of Oxford, 1632–1695, Described by Himself.* Oxford: Clarendon, 1891–1900.

Wordsworth, W. *The Prelude.* Ed. E. Selincourt and H. Darbishire. Oxford: Oxford University Press, 1959.

Wright, B. W. *Comic Book Nation: The Transformation of Youth Culture in America.* Baltimore, MD: John Hopkins University Press, 2001.

Wylie, Philip. "The Abdicating Male." *Playboy* 4 (November 1956): 23–24.

Wyse, Francis. *America, Its Realities and Resources.* London: T. C. Newby, 1846.

Yardley, J. "Building Fame for $15 a Head: Young Barbers Cultivate Fierce Loyalty of Teen-Age Clients." *New York Times,* March 5, 1999.

Yarwood, D. *Fashion in the Western World.* London: BT Batsford, 1992.

Yarwood, Doreen. *English Costume.* London: Batsford, 1961.

Yee, C. *The Silent Traveler in Oxford.* London: Methuen, 1944.

York, P., and C. Jennings. *Peter York's Eighties.* London: BBC Books, 1995.

Young, Jock. *The Drug Takers.* London: Paladin, 1971.

"Youth Gangs Leading Cause of Delinquency." *Los Angeles Times,* June 2, 1943.

Zakim, Michael. *Ready-Made Democracy: A History of Men's Dress in the American Republic, 1760–1860.* Chicago: University of Chicago Press, 2003.

Zakim, Michael. "Sartorial Ideologies: From Homespun to Ready-Made." *American Historical Review* 16, no. 5 (2001): 1553–86.

Z: *Zoot Suit.* 1994. http:7www.edc.org (accessed March 18, 2003).

"Zoot-Suitors Learn Lesson in Fight with Servicemen." *Los Angeles Times,* June 9, 1943.

INDEX